BUDAPEST

Rick Steves & Cameron Hewitt

CONTENTS

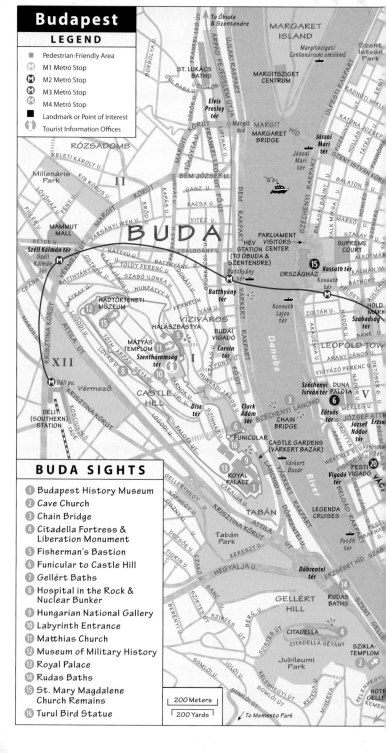

Budapest

LEGEND

- ■ Pedestrian-Friendly Area
- Ⓜ M1 Métró Stop
- Ⓜ M2 Métró Stop
- Ⓜ M3 Métró Stop
- Ⓜ M4 Métró Stop
- ■ Landmark or Point of Interest
- ⓘ Tourist Information Offices

BUDA SIGHTS

1. Budapest History Museum
2. Cave Church
3. Chain Bridge
4. Citadella Fortress & Liberation Monument
5. Fisherman's Bastion
6. Funicular to Castle Hill
7. Gellért Baths
8. Hospital in the Rock & Nuclear Bunker
9. Hungarian National Gallery
10. Labyrinth Entrance
11. Matthias Church
12. Museum of Military History
13. Royal Palace
14. Rudas Baths
15. St. Mary Magdalene Church Remains
16. Turul Bird Statue

200 Meters
200 Yards

To Memento Park

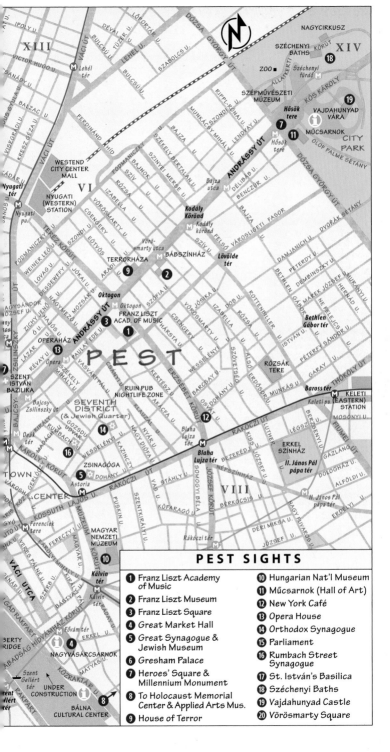

PEST SIGHTS

1. Franz Liszt Academy of Music
2. Franz Liszt Museum
3. Franz Liszt Square
4. Great Market Hall
5. Great Synagogue & Jewish Museum
6. Gresham Palace
7. Heroes' Square & Millennium Monument
8. To Holocaust Memorial Center & Applied Arts Mus.
9. House of Terror
10. Hungarian Nat'l Museum
11. Műcsarnok (Hall of Art)
12. New York Café
13. Opera House
14. Orthodox Synagogue
15. Parliament
16. Rumbach Street Synagogue
17. St. István's Basilica
18. Széchenyi Baths
19. Vajdahunyad Castle
20. Vörösmarty Square

Memento Park

Hungarian Parliament

Széchenyi Baths

Great Market Hall

Old Town Sopron

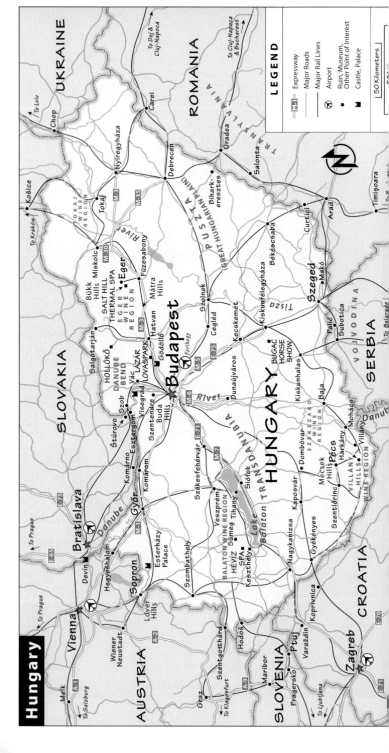

Rick Steves®

BUDAPEST

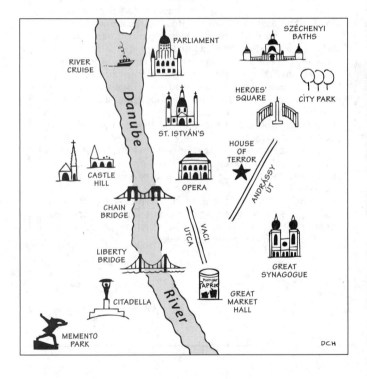

Welcome to Rick Steves' Europe

Travel is intensified living—maximum thrills per minute and one of the last great sources of legal adventure. Travel is freedom. It's recess, and we need it.

I discovered a passion for European travel as a teen and have been sharing it ever since—

through my tours, public television and radio shows, and travel guidebooks. Over the years, I've taught thousands of travelers how to best enjoy Europe's blockbuster sights—and experience "Back Door" discoveries that most tourists miss.

Written with my talented co-author, Cameron Hewitt, this book offers you a balanced mix of Budapest, from its grand parliament and opera house to its intentionally seedy "ruin pubs"—as well as the top small-town side trips in Hungary. It's selective: Rather than listing dozens of thermal baths, we recommend only the best ones. And it's in-depth: Our self-guided museum tours and city walks provide insight into Budapest's (and Hungary's) vibrant history and the living, breathing culture of today.

We advocate traveling simply and smartly. Take advantage of our money- and time-saving tips on sightseeing, transportation, and more. Try local, characteristic alternatives to expensive hotels and restaurants. In many ways, spending more money only builds a thicker wall between you and what you traveled so far to see.

We visit Hungary to experience it—to become temporary locals. Thoughtful travel engages us with the world, as we learn to appreciate other cultures and new ways to measure quality of life.

Judging by the positive feedback we receive from our readers, this book will help you enjoy a fun, affordable, and rewarding vacation—whether it's your first trip or your tenth.

Thanks and *jó utat*—Happy travels!

Rick Steves

INTRODUCTION

Budapest (locals say "BOO-daw-pesht") is a unique metropolis at the heart of a unique nation. Here you'll find experiences like nothing else in Europe: Feel your stress ebb away as you soak in hundred-degree water, surrounded by opulent Baroque domes... and by Speedo- and bikini-clad Hungarians. Ogle some of Europe's most richly decorated interiors, which echo a proud little nation's bygone glory days. Take in a first-rate performance at one of the world's top opera houses—at bargain prices. Ponder the region's bleak communist era as you stroll amid giant Soviet-style statues designed to evoke fear and obedience. Try to wrap your head around Hungary's colorful history...and your tongue around its notoriously difficult language. Dive into a bowl of goulash, the famous paprika-flavored peasant soup with a kick. Go for an after-dinner stroll along the Danube, immersed in a grand city that's bathed in floodlights.

The heart and soul of Central Europe, Budapest excites good travelers...and exasperates bad ones. I love this city for its flaws as much as for its persistent personality. As a tour guide, for years I've introduced travelers to Budapest: walked them step-by-step through the byzantine entry procedure at the thermal baths; handed them a glass of local wine with an unpronounceable name and an unforgettable flavor; and taught them to greet their new Hungarian friends with a robust, *"Jó napot kívánok!"* I've watched them struggle to understand—and gradually succumb to the charms of—this fascinating but beguiling place. And I've taken careful notes. This book represents the lessons I've learned, organized to help you experience Budapest with the wisdom of a return visitor.

Planning Your Trip

This section will help you get started planning your trip—with advice on trip costs, when to go, and what you should know before you take off.

TRIP COSTS

Traveling in Budapest (and throughout Hungary) is a great value. While Budapest feels modern and sophisticated, it remains among the more affordable European capitals.

Five components make up your trip costs: airfare to Europe, transportation in Europe, room and board, sightseeing and entertainment, and shopping and miscellany.

Airfare to Europe: A basic round-trip flight from the US to Budapest can cost, on average, about $1,000-2,000 total, depending on where you fly from and when (cheaper in winter). If Budapest is part of a longer trip, consider saving time and money in Europe by flying into one city and out of another; for instance, into Budapest and out of Prague. Overall, Kayak.com is the best place to start searching for flights on a combination of mainstream and budget carriers.

Transportation in Europe: For a typical one-week visit, figure about $100. That includes $18 for a week-long Budapest transit pass, $70 for side-trips to other Hungarian towns (e.g., about $30 round-trip to Eger and $40 round-trip to Pécs), plus an extra $12 for miscellaneous taxi rides. Add around $20 per person for each transfer between the airport and downtown Budapest (cheaper but slower if you take public transportation). If you rent a car for a few days of side-tripping, figure about $100 per day (cheaper per day for longer rentals). To connect farther-flung destinations, rail passes normally must be purchased outside Europe but aren't necessarily your best option—you may save money by simply buying tickets as you go. A short flight can be cheaper than the train (check www.skyscanner.com for intra-European flights). For more on public transportation and car rental, see "Transportation" in Practicalities.

Room and Board: You can thrive in Budapest on $100 a day per person for room and board. This allows $10 for lunch, $25 for dinner, and $65 for lodging (based on two people splitting the cost of a $130 double room that includes breakfast). Students and tightwads can enjoy Budapest for as little as $40 a day ($20 per hostel bed, $20 for meals and snacks). If you're traveling beyond Budapest, accommodations cost much less in smaller Hungarian towns and cities (a comfortable double typically costs no more than $90, bringing your budget down to $80 per day per person for two people traveling together).

Sightseeing and Entertainment: Figure about $10-20 per

major sight (House of Terror, touring the Parliament or Opera House), $3-6 for minor ones, and $15-25 for splurge experiences (soaking in a thermal bath, taking a nighttime boat cruise on the Danube, going to a tourist concert or opera). You can hire your own private guide for four hours for around $125—a great value when divided between two or more people. An overall average of $20-35 a day works for most people. Don't skimp here. After all, this category is the driving force behind your trip—you came to sightsee, enjoy, and experience Budapest.

Shopping and Miscellany: Figure $1-2 per postcard, coffee, beer, or ice-cream cone. Shopping can vary in cost from nearly nothing to a small fortune. Good budget travelers find that this category has little to do with assembling a trip full of lifelong memories.

SIGHTSEEING PRIORITIES
So much to see, so little time. How to choose? Depending on the length of your trip, assuming you're using public transportation, and taking geographic proximity into account, here are my recommended priorities:

3 days:	Budapest
5 days, add:	Eger and one more day in Budapest
7 days, add:	Pécs and another day in Budapest, or choose a day trip
10 days, add:	Bratislava, Sopron, and additional day trips
More days, add:	More time in Budapest and more day trips; also see "More Hungarian Destinations" on page 323.

This includes nearly everything on the map on page 8. If you don't have time to see it all, prioritize according to your interests. The "Budapest at a Glance" sidebar can help you decide where to go (page 40).

Note that Bratislava fits well on the way if you're going between Budapest and Vienna. For more tips, see "Planning Your Time" on page 21.

WHEN TO GO
The "tourist season" runs roughly from May through September. Book ahead for festivals and national holidays that occur throughout the year (for a list, see the appendix).

Summer (July and Aug) has its advantages: very long days, the busiest schedule of tourist fun and special festivals, and virtually no business travelers to compete with for hotel rooms. However, because Hungary has a nearly Mediterranean climate, summer temperatures can skyrocket to the 80s or 90s (choose a hotel with

🎧 Rick Steves Audio Europe

My Rick Steves Audio Europe app makes it easy to download audio content to enhance your trip. This includes my audio tours of many of Europe's top destinations, as well as a far-reaching library of insightful travel interviews from my public radio show with experts from Hungary and around the globe. The app and all of its content are entirely free. (And new content is added about twice a year.) You can download the app via Apple's App Store, Google Play, or Amazon's Appstore. For more info, see www.ricksteves.com/audioeurope.

air-conditioning). And many cultural events (such as the opera) are on summer vacation.

In spring and fall—May, June, September, and early October—travelers enjoy fewer tourist crowds and milder weather. This is my favorite time to visit Budapest. However, it's also prime convention time (especially September), when hotels tend to fill up and charge their top rates.

Winter travelers find concert season in full swing, with absolutely no tourist crowds, but some accommodations and sights are either closed or run on a limited schedule. Confirm your sightseeing plans locally, especially when traveling off-season. The weather can be cold and dreary, and night will draw the shades on your sightseeing before dinnertime. For weather specifics, see the climate chart in the appendix.

BEFORE YOU GO

You'll have a smoother trip if you tackle a few things ahead of time. For more information on these topics, see the Practicalities chapter (and www.ricksteves.com, which has helpful travel tips and talks).

Make sure your passport is valid. If it's due to expire within six months of your ticketed date of return, you need to renew it. Allow up to six weeks to renew or get a passport (www.travel.state.gov).

Arrange your transportation. Book your international flights. You won't want a car in congested Budapest, but if you'll be touring the countryside beyond, figure out your main form of transportation: You can buy train tickets as you go, get a rail pass, rent a car, or book a cheap flight. (You can wing it in Europe, but it may cost more.) Drivers: Consider bringing an International Driving Permit (sold at AAA offices in the US, www.aaa.com) along with your license.

Book rooms well in advance, especially if your trip falls during peak season or any major holidays or festivals.

Make reservations or buy tickets ahead for major sights. If you'd like to **tour the Hungarian Parliament,** consider reserving online several days ahead to ensure your choice of entrance time (see page 39).

Consider travel insurance. Compare the cost of the insurance to the cost of your potential loss. Check whether your existing insurance (health, homeowners, or renters) covers you and your possessions overseas.

Call your bank. Alert your bank that you'll be using your debit and credit cards in Europe. Ask about transaction fees, and get the PIN number for your credit card. You don't need to bring forints for your trip; you can withdraw forints from cash machines in Hungary.

Use your smartphone smartly. Sign up for an international service plan to reduce your costs, or rely on Wi-Fi in Europe instead. Download any apps you'll want on the road, such as maps, translation, transit schedules, and Rick Steves Audio Europe (see sidebar).

Pack light. You'll walk with your luggage more than you think. Bring a single carry-on bag and a daypack. Use the packing checklist in the appendix as a guide.

Travel Smart

If you have a positive attitude, equip yourself with good information (this book), and expect to travel smart, you will.

Read—and reread—this book. To have an "A" trip, be an "A" student. Note opening hours of sights, closed days, crowd-beating tips, and whether reservations are required or advisable. Check the latest at www.ricksteves.com/update.

Be your own tour guide. As you travel, get up-to-date info on sights, reserve tickets and tours, reconfirm hotels and travel arrangements, and check transit connections. Visit local tourist information offices (TIs). Upon arrival in a new town, lay the groundwork for a smooth departure; confirm the train, bus, or road you'll take when you leave.

Outsmart thieves. Pickpockets abound in crowded places where tourists congregate. Treat commotions as smokescreens for theft. Keep your cash, credit cards, and passport secure in a money belt tucked under your clothes; carry only a day's spending money in your front pocket. Don't set valuable items down on counters or café tabletops, where they can be quickly stolen or easily forgotten.

Minimize potential loss. Keep expensive gear to a minimum. Bring photocopies or take photos of important documents (passport and cards) to aid in replacement if they're lost or stolen. Back up photos and files frequently.

Beat the summer heat. If you wilt easily, choose a hotel with air-conditioning, start your day early, take a midday siesta at your hotel, and resume your sightseeing later. Churches offer a cool haven. Take frequent ice cream breaks.

Guard your time and energy. Taking a taxi can be a good value if it saves you a long wait for a cheap bus or an exhausting walk across town. To avoid long lines, follow my crowd-beating tips, such as making advance reservations, or sightseeing early or late.

Be flexible. Even if you have a well-planned itinerary, expect changes, strikes, closures, sore feet, bad weather, and so on. Your Plan B could turn out to be even better.

Learn the language. Most Hungarians—especially in the tourist trade and in cities—speak English, but if you learn some Hungarian, even just a few phrases, you'll get more smiles and make more friends. Practice the survival phrases near the end of this book, and even better, bring a phrase book.

Connect with the culture. Interacting with locals carbonates your experience. Enjoy the friendliness of the Hungarian people. Ask questions; most locals are happy to point you in their idea of the right direction. Set up your own quest for the best thermal bath, bowl of goulash, nostalgic Golden Age interior, or atmospheric café. When an opportunity pops up, make it a habit to say "yes."

Hungary...here you come!

HUNGARY

Magyarország

Hungary is an island of Asian-descended Magyars in a sea of Slavs. Even though the Hungarians have thoroughly integrated with their Slavic and German neighbors in the millennium-plus since they arrived, there's still something about the place that's distinctly Magyar (MUD-jar). Here in quirky, idiosyncratic Hungary, everything's a little different from the rest of Europe in terms of history, language, culture, customs, and cuisine—but it's hard to put your finger on exactly how.

Travelers to Hungary notice many endearing peculiarities. Hungarians list a person's family name first, and the given name is last—just as in many other Eastern cultures (think of Kim Jong-un). So the composer known as "Franz Liszt" in German is "Liszt Ferenc" in his homeland. Hungarians have a charming habit of using the English word "hello" for both "hi" and "bye," just like the Italians use "ciao." You might overhear a Hungarian end a telephone conversation with a cheery "Hello! Hello! Hello!" Hungarians even drove on the left side of the road until 1941.

Just a century ago, this country controlled half of one of Europe's grandest realms: the Austro-Hungarian Empire. Today, perhaps clinging to their former greatness, many Hungarians remain old-fashioned and nostalgic. With their dusty museums and bushy moustaches, they love to remember the good old days. Buildings all over the country are marked with plaques boasting *MŰEMLÉK* ("historical monument").

Thanks to this focus on tradition, the Hungarians you'll encounter are generally polite, formal, and professional. Hungarians have class. Everything here is done with a proud flourish. When a waiter comes to your table in a restaurant, he'll say, *"Tessék parancsolni"*—literally, "Please command, sir." The standard greeting, *"Jó napot kívánok,"* means, "I wish you a good

day." Women sometimes hear the even more formal greeting, *"Kezét csókolom"*—"I kiss your hand." And when your train or bus makes a stop, you won't be alerted by a mindless, blaring beep—but instead, by peppy music. (You'll be humming these contagious little ditties all day.)

Hungarians are also orderly and tidy...in their own sometimes unexpected ways. Yes, Hungary has its share of litter, graffiti, and crumbling buildings, but you'll find great reason within the chaos. The Hungarian railroad has a long list of discounted fares—for seniors, kids, dogs...and monkeys. (It could happen.) My favorite town name in Hungary: Hatvan. This means "Sixty" in Hungarian...and it's exactly 60 kilometers from Budapest. You can't argue with that logic.

This tradition of left-brained thinking hasn't produced many great Hungarian painters or poets who are known outside their homeland. But the Hungarians, renowned for their ingenuity, have made tremendous contributions to science, technology, business, and industry. Hungarians of note include Edward Teller (instrumental in creating the H-bomb), John von Neumann (a pioneer of computer science), András Gróf (who, as Andy Grove, emigrated to the US and became the CEO of Intel), George Soros (the billionaire investor famous—or notorious—for supporting left-wing causes), and László József Bíró (inventor of the ballpoint pen). A popular local joke claims that Hungarians are so clever that they can enter a revolving door behind you and exit in front of you.

Perhaps the most famous Hungarian "scientist" invented something you probably have in a box in your basement: Ernő

Hungary Almanac

Official Name: Magyarország (Hungary).

Population: Hungary's 10 million people are 85 percent ethnic Hungarians. One in 50 is Roma (Gypsy). About 40 percent of the populace is Catholic, and nearly 15 percent is Protestant. Of the world's approximately 12 million ethnic Hungarians, one in six lives outside Hungary (mostly in areas of Romania, Slovakia, Serbia, and Croatia that were once part of Hungary).

Latitude and Longitude: 47°N and 20°E; similar latitude to Seattle, Paris, and Vienna.

Area: 36,000 square miles, similar to Indiana or Maine.

Geography: Hungary sits in the Carpathian Basin, bound by the Carpathian Mountains (in the north) and the Dinaric Mountains (in the south). Though it's surrounded by mountains, Hungary itself is relatively flat, with some gently rolling hills. The Great Hungarian Plain—beginning on the east bank of the Danube in Budapest—stretches all the way to Asia. Hungary's two main rivers—the Danube and Tisza—run north-south through the country, neatly dividing it into three regions.

Biggest Cities: Budapest (the capital, nearly 2 million), Debrecen (in the east, 205,000), and Miskolc (in the north, 165,000).

Economy: The Gross Domestic Product is $290 billion, with a per capita GDP of nearly $30,000. Thanks to its progressive "goulash communism," Hungary had a head start on many other former Soviet Bloc countries and is now thriving, privatized...and largely foreign-owned. In the 1990s, many communist-era workers (especially women) lost their jobs. Today, the workforce is small (only 60 percent employment) but highly educated and skilled. Grains, metals, machinery, and automobiles are major exports, and about one-quarter of trade is with Germany.

Currency: 275 forints (Ft, or HUF) = about $1.

Government: The single-house National Assembly (199 seats) is the only ruling branch directly elected by popular vote. The legislators in turn select the figurehead president (currently János Áder) and the ruling prime minister (Viktor Orbán); both belong to the far right, nativist Fidesz party.

Flag: Three horizontal bands, top to bottom: red (representing strength), white (faithfulness), and green (hope). It often includes the Hungarian coat of arms: horizontal red-and-white stripes (on the left); the patriarchal, or double-barred, cross (on the right); and the Hungarian crown (on top).

The Average János: The typical Hungarian eats a pound of lard a week (they cook with it). The average family has three members and spends almost three-fourths of its income on housing. According to a condom-company survey, the average Hungarian has sex 131 times a year (behind only France and Greece), making them Europe's third-greatest liars.

Rubik, creator of the famous cube. Hungarians' enjoyment of a good mind-bending puzzle is also evident in their fascination with chess, which you'll see played in cafés, parks, and baths.

Like their Viennese neighbors, Hungarians know how to enjoy the good life. Favorite activities include splashing and soaking in their many thermal baths (see the Thermal Baths chapter). Taking the waters Hungarian-style deserves to be your top priority while you're here. Though public baths can sound intimidating, they're a delight. In this book I recommend my three favorite baths in Budapest, a fine bath in Eger, and a couple more just outside of Eger. For each, I've included instructions to help you enjoy the warm-water fun like a pro. (To allay your first fear: Yes, you can wear your swimsuit.)

Hungarians have also revived an elegant, Vienna-style café culture that was dismantled by the communists. Whiling away the afternoon at a genteel coffeehouse as you nurse a drink or a delicate dessert is a favorite pastime. (For the best options in Budapest, see "Budapest's Café Culture" on page 241.)

Classical music is revered in Hungary, perhaps as nowhere else outside Austria. Aside from scientists and businessmen, the best-known Hungarians are composers: Béla Bartók, Zoltán Kodály, and Franz Liszt. (For more on these figures, see "Hungarian Music" on page 264.)

While one in five Hungarians lives in Budapest, the country-side plays an important role in the country's economy—this has always been a highly agricultural region. The sprawling Great Hungarian Plain (Puszta) that makes up a vast swath of Hungary is the country's breadbasket. You'll pass through fields of wheat and corn, but the grains are secondary to Hungarians' (and tourists') true love: wine. Hungarian winemaking standards plummeted under the communists, but many vintner families have reclaimed their land, resumed their traditional methods, and are making wines worthy of pride once more. (For details, see "Hungarian Wines" on page 476.)

Somehow Hungary, at the crossroads of Europe, has managed to become cosmopolitan while remaining perfectly Hungarian. The Hungarians—like Hungary itself—are a cross-section of Central European cultures: Magyars, Germans, Czechs, Slovaks, Poles, Serbs, Jews, Ottomans, Romanians, Roma (Gypsies), and many others. Still, no matter how many generations removed they are from Magyar stock, there's something different about Hungarians. It's a unique European culture that's a pure joy to discover.

HUNGARIAN LANGUAGE

Even though Hungary is surrounded by Slavs, Hungarian is not at all related to Slavic languages (such as Polish, Czech, or Croatian).

In fact, Hungarian isn't related to *any* European language, except for very distant relatives Finnish and Estonian. It isn't even an Indo-European language—meaning that English is more closely related to Hindi, Russian, and French than it is to Hungarian.

Hungarian is agglutinative: To create meaning, you start with a root word and then tack on suffixes—sometimes resulting in a pileup of extra sounds. The emphasis always goes on the first syllable, and the following syllables are droned in a kind of a monotone—giving the language a distinctive cadence that Hungary's neighbors love to tease.

While the language can be overwhelming for tourists, one easy word is *"Szia"* (SEE-yaw), which means both hello and goodbye (like "ciao" or "aloha"). Sometimes Hungarians simply say the English word "hello" to mean either "hi" or "bye." Another handy word that Hungarians (and people throughout Central Europe) will understand is *Servus* (SEHR-voos, spelled *Szervusz* in Hungarian)—the old-fashioned greeting from the days of the Austro-Hungarian Empire. If you draw a blank on how to say hello, just offer a cheery, *"Servus!"*

Hungarian pronunciation is straightforward, once you remember a few key rules. The trickiest: *s* alone is pronounced "sh," while *sz* is pronounced "s." This explains why you'll hear in-the-know travelers pronouncing Budapest as "BOO-daw-pesht." You might catch the *busz* up to Castle Hill—pronounced "boose." And "Franz Liszt" is easier to pronounce than it looks: It sounds just like "list." To review:

s sounds like "sh" as in "shirt"

sz sounds like "s" as in "saint"

Hungarian has a set of unusual palatal sounds that don't quite have a counterpart in English. To make these sounds, gently press the thick part of your tongue to the roof of your mouth (instead of using the tip of your tongue behind your teeth, as we do in English):

gy sounds like "dg" as in "hedge"

ny sounds like "ny" as in "canyon" (not "nee")

ty sounds like "tch" as in "itch"

cs sounds like "ch" as in "church"

As for vowels: The letter *a* almost sounds like o (aw, as in "hot"); but with an accent *(á)*, it brightens up to the more standard "ah." Likewise, while *e* sounds like "eh," *é* sounds like "ay." An accent *(á, é, í, ó, ú)* indicates that you linger on that vowel, but not necessarily that you stress that syllable. Like German, Hungarian has umlauts *(ö, ü)*, meaning you purse your lips when you say that vowel: roughly, *ö* sounds like "ur" and *ü* sounds like "ew." A long umlaut *(ő, ű)* is the same sound, but you hold it a little longer. Words ending in *k* are often plural.

Here are a few other letters that sound different in Hungarian than in English:

c and **cz** both sound like "ts" as in "cats"

zs sounds like "zh" as in "leisure"

j and **ly** both sound like "y" as in "yellow"

OK, maybe it's not *so* simple. But you'll get the hang of it...and Hungarians will appreciate your efforts.

For a complete list of Hungarian survival phrases, see the appendix.

HUNGARY

BUDAPEST

ORIENTATION

Europe's most underrated big city, Budapest can be as challenging as it is enchanting. The sprawling Hungarian capital is a city of nuance and paradox—cosmopolitan, complicated, and tricky for the first-timer to get a handle on. Think of Budapest as that favorite Hungarian pastime, chess: It's simple to learn...but takes a lifetime to master. This chapter is your first lesson. Then it's your move.

BUDAPEST: A VERBAL MAP

Budapest is huge, with nearly two million people. Like Vienna, the city was built as the head of a much larger empire than it currently governs. But Budapest is surprisingly easy to manage once you get the lay of the land and learn the excellent public transportation network. Those who are comfortable with the Metró, trams, and buses have the city by the tail (see "Getting Around Budapest," later).

The city is split down the center by the Danube River. On the east side of the Danube is flat **Pest** (pronounced "pesht"), and on the west is hilly **Buda.** A third part of the city, **Óbuda,** sits to the north of Buda.

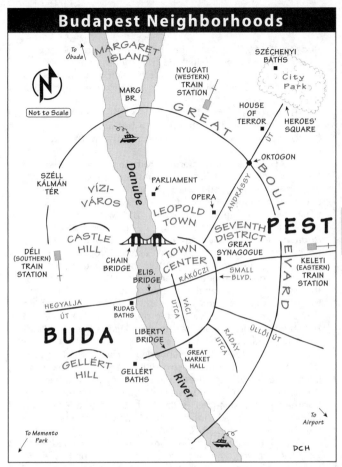

Budapest Neighborhoods

Buda and Pest are connected by a series of characteristic bridges. From north to south, there's the low-profile **Margaret Bridge** (Margit híd, crosses Margaret Island), the famous **Chain Bridge** (Széchenyi Lánchíd), the white and modern **Elisabeth Bridge** (Erzsébet híd), and the green **Liberty Bridge** (Szabadság híd). Four more bridges lie beyond the tourist zone: the Petőfi and Rákóczi bridges to the south, and Árpád and Megyeri bridges to the north.

Budapest uses a **district** system (like Paris and Vienna). There are 23 districts *(kerület)*, identified by Roman numerals. For example, Castle Hill is in district I, central Pest is district V, and City Park is in district XIV. Addresses often start with the district number (as a Roman numeral). Budapest's four-digit postal codes also give you a clue as to the district: The first digit (always 1) represents Budapest, then a two-digit number represents the district

ORIENTATION

Snapshot History of Budapest

Budapest is a rich cultural stew made up of Hungarians, Germans, Slavs, and Jews, with a dash of Turkish paprika, all simmered for centuries in a thermal bath. Each group has left its mark, but through it all, something has remained that is distinctly...Budapest.

Budapest sits on a thin layer of earth covering thermal springs. Those waters attracted the ancient Romans, who, 2,000 years ago, established Aquincum just north of today's city center.

In AD 896, a nomadic group from Central Asia called the Magyars took over the Carpathian Basin (roughly today's Hungary). After running roughshod over Europe, the Magyars—the ancestors of today's Hungarians—settled down, adopted Christianity, and became fully European. The twin towns of Buda and Pest emerged as the leading cities of Hungary. Gradually Buda and Pest became both a de facto capital and a melting pot for the peoples of Central and Eastern Europe.

In the 16th century, the Ottomans invaded. (Castle restorers have even found the remains of Ottoman camels in the area.) They occupied Budapest (and much of Hungary) for nearly a century and a half, introducing their way of life and practices—such as soaking in thermal baths. Finally, the Habsburg monarchs from neighboring Austria liberated Hungary—and kept it for themselves.

After many decades of Hungarian uprisings, the Compromise of 1867 created the Austro-Hungarian Empire; six years later, the cities of Buda, Pest, and Óbuda merged to become Budapest, which governed a sizeable chunk of Eastern Europe. For the next few decades, Budapest boomed, and Hungarian culture blossomed. A flurry of construction surrounded the year 1896—Hungary's 1,000th birthday.

But with World War I, Budapest's fortunes reversed: Hungary lost the war, and two-thirds of its land. Hungary again backed a loser in World War II; the ruins of Budapest were claimed by the Soviets, who introduced communism to the country. Although a bold uprising in 1956 was brutally put down, a milder "goulash communism" eventually emerged here. Budapest became a place where other Eastern Bloc residents could experiment with "Western evils," from Big Macs to Nikes.

By the end of communism in 1989, the city's rich architectural heritage was in shambles. Forever torn between a nostalgic instinct to cling to past glory days, and a modern drive to innovate, Budapest has reinvented its cityscape with a mix of old and new. The latest chapter in Budapest's history has been written by Prime Minister Viktor Orbán, who has overseen an unprecedented burst of urban renewal, but also a rise in authoritarianism and emotionally charged nationalism.

Budapest's uniquely epic story—still a work in progress—has shaped a glorious metropolis that fascinates both Hungarians and tourists alike. For a more complete recounting of the city's story, see the Hungary: Past & Present chapter.

(such as "05" for district V), then a final digit gives more specific information about the location.

As you navigate Budapest, remember these key Hungarian terms: *tér* (pronounced "tehr," square), *utca* (OOT-zaw, street), *út* (oot, boulevard), *körút* (KUR-root, ring road), *híd* (heed, bridge), and *város* (VAH-rohsh, town). To better match what you'll see locally, in this book I've mostly used these Hungarian terms (instead of the English equivalents).

BUDAPEST BY NEIGHBORHOOD

Let's take a tour through the places where you'll be spending your time, neighborhood by neighborhood. This section—like all of the sightseeing, sleeping, eating, and other advice in this book—is divided between Pest and Buda. (It might help to think of these as two separate cities, as they once were.)

Pest

Pest—the real-world commercial heart of the city—is where most tourists spend the majority of their time.

"Downtown" Pest (district V), just across the river from Castle Hill, is divided into two sections:

The more genteel northern half, called **Leopold Town** (Lipótváros, LEE-poht-vah-rohsh), surrounds the red-domed, riverside Parliament building. This is the governmental, business, and banking district, with fine monuments and grand buildings. Leopold Town is sleepy after hours.

The southern half, the grittier and more urban-feeling **Town Center** (Belváros, BEHL-vah-rohsh; literally "Inner Town"), is a thriving and touristy shopping, dining, and nightlife zone. The main pedestrian artery through the Town Center is the overrated Váci utca (VAHT-see OOT-zaw) shopping street, which runs parallel to the scenic Danube promenade one block inland. At the southern end of the Town Center is the Great Market Hall.

The Town Center is hemmed in by the first of Pest's four concentric **ring roads** *(körút)*. The innermost ring is the Kiskörút, or "Small Boulevard." The next ring, several blocks farther out, is the Nagykörút, or "Great Boulevard." These ring roads change names every few blocks, but they are always called *körút*. The Nagykörút is subdivided into sections named for Habsburg monarchs, such as Erzsébetkörút ("Elisabeth Boulevard"); each of these sections also defines a neighborhood, such as Erzsébetváros ("Elisabeth Town").

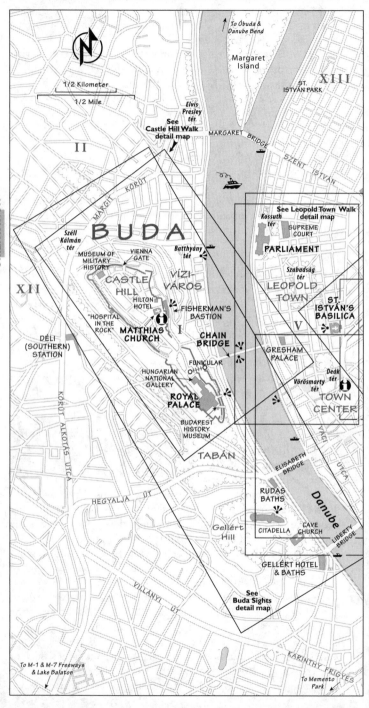

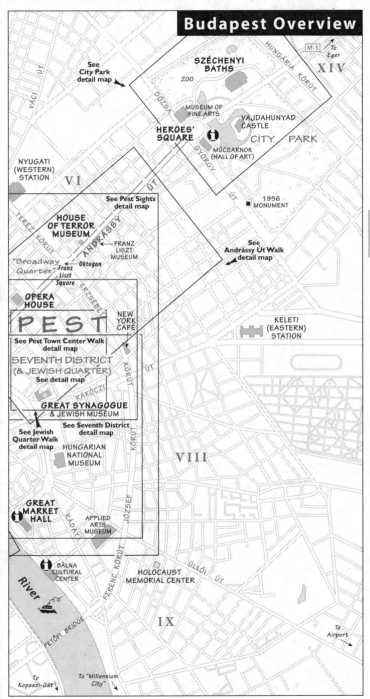

ORIENTATION

Budapest Overview

Beyond the Nagykörút are two more ring roads—the Hungária körút highway, and the M-0 expressway—that few tourists see.

Arterial **boulevards,** called *út,* stretch from central Pest into the suburbs like spokes on a wheel. The most interesting, **Andrássy út** (AWN-drah-shee oot), provides a useful spine for reaching some of Pest's best sights, restaurants, and accommodations. It begins at the Small Boulevard (near Deák tér) and extends past several key sights (including the Opera and the House of Terror museum) and dining zones (such as the "Broadway Quarter" and Franz Liszt Square) out to **City Park.** The park has its own collection of attractions, including the monumental Heroes' Square and Budapest's top experience: soaking in the Széchenyi Baths.

More key sights lie along the **Small Boulevard** ring road (connected by trams #47 and #49), including (from north to south) the Great Synagogue (marking the start of the **Seventh District,** which is home to both the Jewish Quarter and the bustling nightlife zone), the National Museum, and the Great Market Hall.

Several other points of interest are spread far and wide along the **Great Boulevard** ring road (circled by trams #4 and #6). From north to south, it passes Margaret Island (the city's playground, in the middle of the Danube); the Nyugati/Western train station; the Oktogon intersection, where it crosses Andrássy út; the opulent New York Café, with the Keleti/Eastern train station just up the street; and the intersection with Üllői út, near the Holocaust Memorial Center and the Applied Arts Museum.

Buda

The Buda side is dominated by two hills: **Castle Hill** (Várhegy, VAHR-hayj), topped by the green dome of the Royal Palace and the spiny Neo-Gothic spire of the Matthias Church; and to the south, the taller, wooded **Gellért Hill,** capped by a 150-year-old fortress and the Liberation Monument.

The historic **Castle District,** atop Castle Hill (in district I), is packed with tourists by day, and dead at night. The pleasant **Víziváros** (VEE-zee-vah-rohsh) residential neighborhood, or "Water Town," is squeezed between the castle and the river. The square called Batthyány tér, at the north end of Víziváros, is a hub for the neighborhood, with a handy Metró stop (M2/red line), tram stops, market hall, and eateries. Just north of Castle Hill (and Víziváros) is **Széll Kálmán tér,** another transit hub for Buda, with a Metró station (M2/red line), several tram stops, and the giant Mammut shopping mall.

Gellért Hill has three points of interest for visitors: the Gellért Baths (at the south end of the hill), the Rudas Baths (at the north end), and panoramic city views (from the top).

Central Buda is surrounded by a ring road, and the busy Hegyalja út rumbles through the middle of the tourists' Buda (between Castle and Gellért Hills). Behind Castle and Gellért Hills is a low-lying neighborhood of little interest to tourists (except for the Déli/Southern train station), and beyond that rise the **Buda Hills,** a scenic and upscale residential area.

Outer Budapest

The city doesn't end there. This book also includes tips for the Óbuda district north of central Buda; sights on the outskirts of town (but accessible on the suburban transit network), including Memento Park, Gödöllő Palace, and the small riverside town of Szentendre; and more.

PLANNING YOUR TIME

Budapest demands at least two full days—and that assumes you'll be selective and move fast. To slow down and really dig into the city, give it a third or fourth day. Adding more time allows for various day trips.

Budapest is quite decentralized: Strategize your sightseeing to minimize backtracking. Just about everything is walkable, but distances are far, and public transit saves valuable time.

Each of this book's self-guided walks acts as a sightseeing spine for a particular neighborhood or area: Pest's **Leopold Town, Town Center, Andrássy út, Heroes' Square and City Park,** and **Jewish Quarter,** and Buda's **Castle Hill.** Each walk offers an orientation overview, with several in-depth sightseeing options along the way. If you're ambitious, you can do several of these walks in a single day—but you'll have to skip some of the museums. To take your time and dip into each sight, spread the walks over several days.

When divvying your time between Buda and Pest, keep in mind that (aside from the Gellért and Rudas Baths) Buda's sightseeing is mostly concentrated on Castle Hill, and can easily be done in less than a day, while Pest deserves as much time as you're willing to give it. Save relatively laid-back Buda for when you need a break from the big city.

Below are some possible plans, depending on the length of your trip. Note that these very ambitious itineraries assume you want to sightsee at a speedy pace. In the **evening,** you have a wide range of options (detailed in the Entertainment in Budapest chapter): enjoying good restaurants, taking in an opera or concert, snuggling on a romantic floodlit river cruise, relaxing in a thermal bath,

Daily Reminder

Monday: Most of Budapest's museums are closed on Mondays. But you can still take advantage of plenty of other sights and activities: all three major baths, Memento Park, Great Synagogue and Jewish Quarter, Matthias Church on Castle Hill, St. István's Basilica, Parliament tour, Great Market Hall and Bálna Budapest, Opera House tour, City Park (and Zoo), Danube cruises, concerts, and bus, walking, and bike tours. Monday is also a great day to do the Leopold Town and Pest Town Center walks, since their major sights are virtually unaffected.

Tuesday: All major sights are open.

Wednesday: All major sights are open.

Thursday: Some shops are open later (until 20:00 or 21:00), as is the Műcsarnok (Hall of Art, until 20:00).

Friday: All major sights are open. The Orthodox Synagogue and Synagogue at Rumbach Street close early (usually around 13:30 or 16:00).

Saturday: The Great Synagogue, Orthodox Synagogue, and Synagogue at Rumbach Street are closed today. Most shops close early (usually 13:00 or 14:00), and the Great Market Hall closes at 15:00.

Sunday: The Great Market Hall, Zwack Museum, and Franz Liszt Museum are closed today, as are most shops, though large shopping malls remain open. Churches are closed in the morning (usually until about 13:00). The Szimpla ruin pub hosts a morning farmers market (9:00-14:00).

exploring the city's unique ruin pubs and other nightlife venues, or simply strolling the Danube embankments and bridges.

Budapest in Two Days

Day 1: Spend it in Pest. Start with the Leopold Town Walk, then the Pest Town Center Walk, ending at the Great Market Hall. Then circle around the Small Boulevard to Deák tér and consider the Andrássy út and Heroes' Square/City Park walks. Or, if you're exhausted already, just take the M1/yellow Metró line to Hősök tere, ogle the Heroes' Square statues and Vajdahunyad Castle, and reward yourself with a soak at Széchenyi Baths. Note that this schedule leaves virtually no time for entering museums, though you might be able to fit in one or two big sights; the most worthwhile are the Parliament (book tickets ahead online), the Opera House, and the House of Terror.

Day 2: In the morning, tackle any Pest sights you didn't have time for yesterday (or take the bus out to Memento Park). After lunch, ride bus #16 from Deák tér to Buda's Castle Hill and follow the Castle Hill Walk. Finally, head back to Pest for some final sightseeing and dinner.

Budapest in Three or More Days

Day 1: Get your bearings in Pest. Begin with the Leopold Town Walk (including a tour of the Parliament—book tickets ahead online), followed by the Andrássy út Walk (including touring the Opera House and the House of Terror). Then ride the Metró out to do the Heroes' Square and City Park Walk. End your day with a soak at the Széchenyi Baths.

Day 2: Delve deeper into Pest, starting with the Pest Town Center Walk. After visiting the Great Market Hall, you can cross the river to Buda for a soak at the Gellért or Rudas Baths, or circle around the Small Boulevard to see the National Museum and/or Great Synagogue and Jewish Quarter.

Day 3: Use the morning to see any remaining Pest sights, then ride from Deák tér out to Memento Park on the park's 11:00 direct bus. On returning, grab a quick lunch and take bus #16 from Deák tér to Castle Hill, where you'll do the Castle Hill Walk.

With More Time: If you have a fourth day, spread the Day 1 tours over more time, and circle back to any sights you've missed. If you've got five or more days, consider some of the tempting destinations below.

Beyond Budapest

Eger, at the heart of a popular wine region and packed with offbeat sights, is an easy day trip from Budapest (about 2 hours by train or bus each way). **Pécs,** with a gorgeously colorful streetscape and engaging sightseeing, is a bit farther away (3 hours by train), but arguably even more interesting. Roughly between Budapest and Vienna, the small town of **Sopron** (historic and charming) and the Slovak capital of **Bratislava** (big, bustling, and on the move) are both worthy stopovers. Each of these is covered in its own chapter. While any of these could be done as long day trips from Budapest, it's much more satisfying to spend the night (especially in Eger and Pécs).

The Day Trips from Budapest chapter covers excursions that are less appealing than the farther-flung towns mentioned above—but easier to do in a day from Budapest. The **Danube Bend** comprises three towns north of Budapest: the charming, Balkan-flavored artists' colony of **Szentendre;** the castle at **Visegrád;** and Hungary's most impressive church at **Esztergom.** (The Danube Bend is made-to-order by car on the way to Bratislava or Vienna.) To the east are **Gödöllő Palace** (dripping with Habsburg history, and an easy side-trip from Budapest), the **Lázár Lovaspark** traditional horse show (a must for horse lovers, or for anyone wanting a peek at a Hungarian farm), and the more distant village of **Hollókő,** an open-air folk museum come to life (by car, these two can be combined into a single rewarding day, and you'll be back in Budapest in time for dinner).

Overview

TOURIST INFORMATION

The city of Budapest runs several official TIs (tel. 1/438-8080, www.budapestinfo.hu). These are primarily interested in selling tickets for tour operators and concert companies that they partner with, but they do hand out good information and can answer some questions. The main branch is at **Deák tér,** a few steps from the M2 and M3 Metró station (daily 8:00-20:00, Sütő utca 2, near the McDonald's, district V). Other locations include **Heroes' Square** (in the ice rink building facing Vajdahunyad Castle, daily 9:00-19:00), in the middle of Castle Hill at **Szentháromság tér** (daily 10:00-18:00, Tárnok utca 15), in the **Bálna** building behind the Great Market Hall (daily 10:00-18:00), and in both terminals at the **airport** (daily until 22:00). Also look for TI "mobile info points" set up in highly trafficked areas (look for the teal-and-white umbrellas).

The helpfulness of Budapest's TIs can vary, but all sell the Budapest Card and offer free, useful publications, including the *Budapest Guide* booklet. Be aware that many for-profit agencies masquerade as "TIs" or "info points" (such as in the train stations); these are unofficial, but some can be helpful in a pinch.

Sightseeing Passes: The **Budapest Card** includes all public transportation, walking tours of Buda and Pest, admission to a handful of sights (including the National Museum, National Gallery, and Memento Park), access to a shuttle bus up to the castle area, and 10-50 percent discounts on many other major museums and attractions (€22/24 hours, €33/48 hours, €43/72 hours, www. budapest-card.com). If you take advantage of the included walking tours, the Budapest Card can be a good value for a very busy sightseer—do the arithmetic.

Absolute Tour Center: This office, conveniently located near Andrássy út (behind the Opera House at Lázár utca 16), can be helpful in answering questions. They also have bike rentals and secondhand books upstairs, and are the hub for walking, bike, and Segway tours—all described later, under "Tours in Budapest" (sporadic hours, usually open daily 9:00-20:00, Nov-March until 18:00, tel. 1/269-3843, mobile +3620-929-7506, www. absolutetours.com).

ARRIVAL IN BUDAPEST

For a comprehensive rundown on Budapest's train stations, bus stations, airport, driving tips, and boat connections, see the Budapest Connections chapter.

HELPFUL HINTS

Rip-Offs: Budapest is quite safe, especially for a city of its size. Occasionally tourists run into con artists or pickpockets; as in any big city, wear a money belt and secure your valuables in touristy places and on public transportation.

Restaurants on the Váci utca shopping street are notorious for overcharging tourists. Anywhere in Budapest, avoid restaurants that don't list prices on the menu. Check your bill carefully. Most restaurants add a 10-12 percent service charge; if you don't notice this, you might accidentally double-tip (for more on tipping, see page 458). Also, at Váci utca and at train stations, avoid using the rip-off currency exchange booths (such as Interchange or Checkpoint). You'll do much better simply getting cash from an ATM associated with a major bank (including OTP, MKB, K&H, and various big international banks).

Budapest's biggest crooks? Unscrupulous cabbies. For tips on outsmarting them, see "Getting Around Budapest—By Taxi," later. Bottom line: Locals *always* call for an official, regulated cab, rather than hail one on the street or at a taxi stand. Ask your hotel or restaurant to call one for you.

Medical Help: Near Buda's Széll Kálmán tér, **FirstMed Centers** is a private, pricey, English-speaking clinic (by appointment or urgent care, call first, Hattyú utca 14, 5th floor, district I, M2: Széll Kálmán tér, tel. 1/224-9090, www.firstmedcenters. com). Hospitals *(kórház)* are scattered around the city.

Calling Mobile Numbers: In Hungary, mobile numbers (generally beginning with +3620, +3630, +3631, or +3670) are uniquely confusing. In this book, I list these numbers as you'll dial them from any international line or any mobile phone (including a Hungarian one), starting with +36. However, if you are dialing these numbers from a fixed line within Hungary, you'll need to replace the "+36" with "06." So, to call a local guide with the number +3620-926-0557, you'd dial exactly that if calling from your American phone or from a Hungarian mobile phone. But if calling from your Budapest hotel room, dial 0620-926-0557. For more tips on calling, see page 480.

English Bookstore: There's a fine selection of new books, mostly in English, at **Bestsellers;** it's near St. István's Basilica (Mon-Fri 9:00-18:30, Sat 11:00-18:00, Sun 12:00-18:00, Október 6 utca 11—see map on page 234, tel. 1/312-1295).

Pharmacies: The helpful **BENU Gyógyszertár** pharmacy is dead-center in Pest, between Vörösmarty and Széchenyi squares. Because they cater to clientele from nearby international hotels, they have a useful directory that lists the Hungarian equivalent of US prescription medicines (Mon-Fri 8:00-20:00, closed Sat-Sun, Dorottya utca 13, district V, M1: Vörösmarty tér, for location see map on page 223, tel. 1/317-2374). Each district has one 24-hour pharmacy (these should be noted outside the entrance to any pharmacy).

Laundry: The self-service launderette chain **Bubbles** is open 24/7, unstaffed, automated, and takes credit cards. The most convenient location is near the Small Boulevard, at the inner edge of the Seventh District, at Paulay Ede 3, M1: Bajcsy-Zsilinszky út; check their website for others (www.bubbles.hu). Two additional, cheap self-service launderettes are also in the Seventh District: **Laundry Budapest** has lots of machines (daily 9:00-24:00, last wash at 22:00, Dohány utca 37, near M2: Blaha Lujza tér, tel. 1/781-0098, www.laundrybudapest.hu), and **Bazar Hostel** has a few (daily 24 hours, closer to the Great Synagogue, at Dohány utca 22). For locations, see the map on page 225.

For full service, **Broadway Hostel & Apartments** is just behind the Opera House (walk straight behind the Opera House and turn right on Ó utca, then look left for signs at #24—you'll go up the main stairs and turn left to find the laundry office in the arcade; if nobody is at the laundry office, ask at the apartment house reception nearby; district VI, M1: Opera, tel. +3670-771-9164). **Vajnóczki Tisztítószalon,** a block from the Oktogon, is a dry cleaner (next-day service, Mon-Fri 8:00-18:00, Sat until 13:00, closed Sun, Szófia utca 8, tel. 1/342-3796). For both locations, see the map on page 219.

Bike Rental: Budapest—with lots of traffic congestion—isn't the easiest place for cyclists. But as the city adds more bike lanes and traffic-free zones, those comfortable with urban cycling may be tempted. You can rent a bike at **Yellow Zebra** (3,500 Ft/all day, 4,500 Ft/24 hours; electric bikes-15,000 Ft/all day, 18,000 Ft/24 hours; see "Absolute Tour Center" listing, earlier under "Tourist Information").

Budapest also has a subsidized public bike network called **Bubi** (for "**Bu**dapest **Bi**kes"). Bike stations are scattered throughout the Town Center and adjoining areas; you can pick a bike up at any station and drop it off at any other. First, you buy a "ticket" at http://molbubi.bkk.hu or at a docking station (500 Ft/24 hours, 1,000 Ft/72 hours, 2,000 Ft/week, plus a 25,000-Ft deposit on your credit card for the duration

Tonight We're Gonna Party Like It's 1896

Visitors to Budapest need only remember one date: 1896. For the millennial celebration of their ancestors' arrival in Europe, Hungarians threw a blowout party. In the thousand years between 896 and 1896, the Magyars had gone from being a nomadic Central Asian tribe that terrorized the Continent to sharing the throne of one of the most successful empires Europe had ever seen.

On New Year's Day morning, 1896, church bells clanged through the streets of Buda and Pest. That June, the Habsburg royal couple Franz Josef and Sisi were among the 5.7 million people who came to enjoy the Hungarian National Exhibition at City Park. At Vérmező Park (behind Castle Hill), whole oxen were grilled on the spit to feed commoners.

Budapest used its millennial celebration as an excuse to build monuments and buildings appropriate for the co-capital of a huge empire, including these landmarks:

- **Heroes' Square** and **Millennium Monument**
- **Vajdahunyad Castle** (in City Park)
- **Parliament** building (96 meters tall, 96 front steps)
- **St. István's Basilica** (also 96 meters tall)
- M1/yellow Metró line, a.k.a. ***Földalatti*** ("Underground")
- **Great Market Hall** (and four other market halls)
- **Andrássy út** and most of the fine buildings lining it
- **Opera House**
- A complete rebuilding of **Matthias Church** (on Castle Hill)
- **Fisherman's Bastion** (by Matthias Church)
- Green **Liberty Bridge** (then called Franz Josef Bridge)

The key number in Hungary is 96—even the national anthem (when sung at the proper tempo) takes 96 seconds. But after all this fuss, it's too bad that the date was wrong: A commission—convened to establish the exact year of the Magyars' debut—determined it happened in 895. But city leaders knew they'd never make an 1895 deadline, and requested the finding be changed to 896.

of the ticket). Once you have a ticket, it's free to use a bike for 30 minutes or less, then costs 500 Ft for each additional 30 minutes. Ask at the TI if you need help figuring out the system.

Drivers: Friendly, English-speaking **Gábor Balázs** can drive you around the city or into the surrounding countryside

(5,000 Ft/hour, 3-hour minimum in city, 4-hour minimum in countryside—good for a Danube Bend excursion, mobile +3620-936-4317, bgabor.e@gmail.com). **Zsolt Gál** is also available for transfers, side-trips, and longer trips to Prague or Vienna, and specializes in helping people track down Jewish sites in the surrounding areas (mobile +3670-452-4900, forma111562@gmail.com). Note that these are drivers, not tour guides. For a licensed tour guide who also does countryside driving trips, see "Tours in Budapest," later.

Best Views: Budapest is a city of marvelous vistas. Some of the best are from the Citadella fortress (high on Gellért Hill), the promenade in front of the Royal Palace and the Fisherman's Bastion on top of Castle Hill, and the embankments or many bridges spanning the Danube (especially the Chain Bridge). Don't forget the view from the tour boats on the Danube—particularly lovely at night.

GETTING AROUND BUDAPEST

Budapest sprawls. Connecting your sightseeing just on foot is tedious and unnecessary. It's crucial to get comfortable with the well-coordinated public transportation system: Metró lines, trams, buses, trolley buses, and boats. Budapest's transit system website is www.bkk.hu.

Tickets

The same tickets work for the entire system. Buy them at kiosks, Metró ticket windows, or machines (with English instructions, credit cards accepted). As prices are affordable and it can be frustrating to find a ticket machine (especially when you see your tram or bus approaching), I generally invest in a multiday ticket to have the freedom of hopping on at will.

Your options are as follows:

• **Single ticket** (*vonaljegy,* for a ride of up to an hour on any means of transit; transfers allowed only within the Metró system)—350 Ft (or 450 Ft if bought from the driver)

• **Short single Metró ride** (*Metrószakaszjegy,* 3 stops or fewer on the Metró)—300 Ft

• **Transfer ticket** (*átszállójegy*—allowing up to 90 minutes, including one transfer between Metró and bus)—530 Ft

• **Pack of 10 single tickets** (*10 darabos gyűjtőjegy*), which can be shared—3,000 Ft (that's 300 Ft per ticket, saving you 50 Ft per

ORIENTATION

ticket; note that these must stay together as a single pack—they can't be sold separately)

• Unlimited multiday travel cards for Metró, bus, and tram, including a **24-hour travelcard** (*24 órás jegy,* 1,650 Ft/24 hours), **72-hour travelcard** (*72 órás jegy,* 4,150 Ft/72 hours), and **seven-day travelcard** (*hetijegy,* 4,950 Ft/7 days)

• **24-hour group travel card** (*csoportos 24 órás jegy,* 3,300 Ft), covering up to five adults—a great deal for groups of three to five people

• **Budapest Card,** which combines a multiday ticket with sightseeing discounts (see "Tourist Information," earlier)

Always validate single-ride tickets as you enter the bus, tram, or Metró station (stick it in the elbow-high box). On older buses and trams that have little red validation boxes, stick your ticket in the black slot, then pull the slot toward you to punch holes in your ticket. Multiday tickets need be validated only once. The stern-looking people with green armbands waiting as you enter or exit the Metró want to see your validated ticket. Cheaters are fined 8,000 Ft on the spot, and you'll be surprised how often you're checked. All public transit runs from 4:30 in the morning until 23:50; a few designated night buses and trams operate overnight.

New Transit Cards: Budapest plans to phase out paper tickets in favor of electronic pay-as-you-go cards (similar to London's Oyster card or New York's Metrocard). Ask around, or see www.bkk.hu for the latest.

Handy Terms: *Á ___ felé* means "in the direction of ___." *Megálló* means "stop" or "station," and *Végállomás* means "end of the line."

By Metró

Riding Budapest's efficient Metró, you really feel like you're down in the guts of the city. There are four working lines:

• **M1/yellow**—The first underground rail line on the Continent, this shallow line runs beneath Andrássy út from the center to City Park (see "Millennium Underground of 1896" on page 133).

• **M2/red**—Built during the communist days, it's 115 feet deep and designed to double as a bomb shelter. Going under the Danube to Buda, the M2 connects the Déli/Southern train station, Széll Kálmán tér (where you catch bus #16, #16A, or #116 to the top of Castle Hill), Batthyány tér (Víziváros

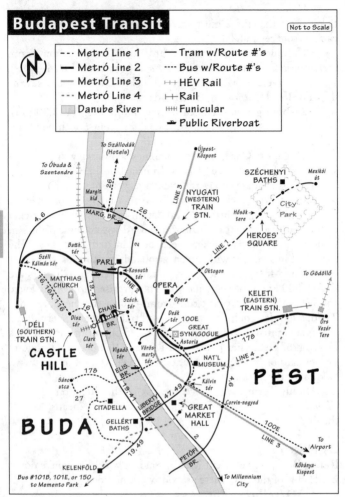

Budapest Transit

Not to Scale

--- Metró Line 1
— Metró Line 2
— Metró Line 3
--- Metró Line 4
Danube River
— Tram w/Route #'s
···· Bus w/Route #'s
+++ HÉV Rail
+ Rail
HHH Funicular
⇀ Public Riverboat

and the station where you catch the HÉV train to Óbuda or Szentendre), Kossuth tér (behind the Parliament), Astoria (near the Great Synagogue on the Small Boulevard), and the Keleti/Eastern train station (where it crosses the M4/green line).

• **M3/blue**—This line makes a broad, boomerang-shaped swoop north to south on the Pest side. Key stops include the Nyugati/Western train station, Ferenciek tere (in the heart of Pest's Town Center), Kálvin tér (near the Great Market Hall and many recommended hotels; this is also where it crosses the M4/green line), and Corvin-negyed (near the Holocaust Memorial Center).

• **M4/green**—This line runs from southern Buda to the Gellért Baths, under the Danube to Fővám tér (behind the Great Market Hall) and Kálvin tér (where it crosses the M3/blue line), then up to Rákóczi tér (on the Grand Boulevard) and the Keleti/Eastern train station (where it crosses the M2/red line). The M4 is the city's newest line (from 2014), and many of its stations boast boldly modern, waste-of-space concrete architecture that's eye-opening to simply stroll through; the one at Gellért tér has a thermal spring-fed waterfall coursing past the main staircase.

The three original lines—M1, M2, and M3—cross only once: at the **Deák tér** stop (often signed as *Deák Ferenc tér*) in the heart of Pest, near where Andrássy út begins.

Aside from the historic M1 line, most Metró stations are at intersections of ring roads and other major thoroughfares. You'll usually exit the Metró into a confusing underpass packed with kiosks, fast-food stands, and makeshift markets. Directional signs (listing which streets, addresses, and tram or bus stops are near each exit) help you find the right exit. Or do the prairie-dog routine: Surface to get your bearings, then head back underground to find the correct stairs up to your destination.

You'll ride very long, steep, fast-moving escalators to access most Metró stops (except on the shallow M1 line). Hang on tight, enjoy the gale as trains below shoot through the tunnels...and don't make yourself dizzy by trying to read the Burger King ads.

By HÉV

Budapest's suburban rail system, or HÉV (pronounced "hayv," stands for Helyiérdekű Vasút, "Railway of Local Interest"), branches off to the outskirts and beyond. Of the four lines, tourists are likely to use only two: the **Szentendre line** (H5/purple), which begins at Batthyány tér in Buda's Víziváros neighborhood (at the M2/red line stop of the same name) and heads through Óbuda to the charming Danube Bend town of Szentendre; and the **Gödöllő line** (H8/pink), which begins at Örs vezér tere (in outer Pest, at the end of the M2/red line) and heads to the town of Gödöllő, with its Habsburg palace. (Szentendre and Gödöllő are both described in the Day Trips from Budapest chapter.)

The HÉV is covered by standard transit tickets and passes for rides within the city of Budapest (such as to Óbuda). But if going beyond—such as to Szentendre or Gödöllő—you'll have to pay more. Tell the ticket-seller (or punch into the machine) where you're going, and you'll be issued the proper ticket. If you have a transit pass, you'll pay only the difference.

By Tram

Budapest's trams are handy and frequent, taking you virtually anywhere the Metró doesn't. Here are some trams you might use (note that all of these run in both directions):

Tram **#2:** Follows Pest's Danube embankment, parallel to Váci utca. From north to south, it begins at the Great Boulevard (Jászai Mari tér, near Margaret Bridge) and stops on either side of the Parliament (north side near the visitors center/Országház stop, as well as south side near the Kossuth tér Metró stop), Széchenyi István tér and the Chain Bridge, Vigadó tér, and the Great Market Hall (Fővám tér stop). From there, it continues southward past the Bálna cultural center to the Petőfi Bridge, then all the way to the "Millennium City" complex near Rákóczi Bridge (Millenniumi Kulturális Központ stop).

Trams **#19** and **#41:** Run along Buda's Danube embankment from Batthyány tér (with an M2/red Metró station, and HÉV trains to Óbuda and Szentendre). From Batthyány tér, these trams run (north to south) through Víziváros, with several helpful stops: Clark Ádám tér (the bottom of the Castle Hill funicular, near the stop for bus #16 up to Castle Hill), Várkert Bazár (Castle Park with escalators and elevators up to the Royal Palace); Rudas Gyógyfürdő (Rudas Baths); then around the base of Gellért Hill to Szent Gellért tér (Gellért Baths and M4/green Metró station).

Trams **#4** and **#6:** Zip around Pest's Great Boulevard ring road (Nagykörút), connecting Nyugati/Western train station and the Oktogon with the southern tip of Margaret Island and Buda's Széll Kálmán tér (with M2/red Metró station, and buses up to the castle). At night, this route is replaced by bus #6.

Trams **#47** and **#49:** Connect the Gellért Baths in Buda with Pest's Small Boulevard ring road (Kiskörút), with stops at the Great Market Hall (Fővám tér stop), the National Museum (Kálvin tér stop), the Great Synagogue (Astoria stop), and Deák tér (end of the line).

By Bus and Trolley Bus

I use the Metró and trams for most of my Budapest commuting. But some buses are useful for shortcuts within the city, or for reaching outlying sights. Note that the transit company draws a distinction between gas-powered "buses" and electric "trolley buses" (which are powered by overhead cables). Unless otherwise noted, you can assume the following are standard buses:

Buses **#16,** **#16A,** and **#116:** All head up to the top of Castle Hill (get off at Dísz tér, in the middle of the hill—the closest stop to the Royal Palace). You can catch any of these three at Széll Kálmán tér (M2/red Metró line). When coming from the other direction, bus #16 makes several handy stops in Pest (Deák tér, Széchenyi István tér), then crosses the Chain Bridge for more stops in Buda (including Clark Ádám tér, at Buda end of Chain Bridge on its way up to the castle).

Trolley buses **#70** and **#78:** These zip from near the Opera House (intersection of Andrássy út and Nagymező utca) to the Parliament (Kossuth tér).

Bus **#178:** Goes from Keleti/Eastern train station to central Pest (Astoria and Ferenciek tere Metró stops), then over the Elisabeth Bridge to Buda.

Bus **#26:** Begins at Nyugati/Western train station and heads around the Great Boulevard to Margaret Island, making several stops along the island.

Bus **#27:** Runs from either side of Gellért Hill to just below the Citadella fortress at the hill's peak (Búsuló Juhász stop).

Bus **#100E:** This handy, speedy express bus connects Liszt Ferenc Airport to Deák tér, with only two other stops en route (Astoria and Kálvin tér Metró stops).

Buses **#101B, #101E,** and **#150:** These run from Kelenföld (the end of the line for the M4/green Metró line, with some trains to Pécs) to Memento Park.

Buses **#54** and **#55:** These head from Boráros tér (at the Pest end of the Petőfi Bridge) to the Ecseri Flea Market (Naszód utca stop).

By Boat

Budapest's public transit authority operates a system of Danube riverboats (*hajójárat,* marked with a stylish *D* logo) that connect strategic locations throughout the city. The riverboat system has drawbacks: Frequency is sparse (weekdays only, 1-2/hour, may run on weekends in summer), and it's typically slower than hopping on the Metró or a tram. But it's also a romantic, cheap alternative to pricey riverboat cruises, and can be a handy way to connect some sightseeing points. A 750-Ft ticket covers any trip; it's also covered by a 24-hour, 72-hour, or seven-day travelcard (but not by the Budapest Card; if it's running on weekends, you have to buy a ticket regardless of your pass).

Lines #D11 and #D12 run in both directions through the city, including these stops within downtown Budapest: **Népfürdő utca (Árpád híd),** at the northern end of Margaret Island (the weekend boat also makes several additional stops on the island); **Jászai Mari tér,** at the Pest end of Margaret Bridge; **Batthyány tér,** on the Buda embankment in Víziváros; **Kossuth Lajos tér,** near the Parliament on the Pest side; **Várkert Bazár,** at the base of the grand entrance staircase to Buda Castle; **Petőfi tér,** on the Pest embankment next to the Legenda Cruises riverboats (dock 8); and **Szent Gellért tér,** at the Buda end of Liberty Bridge, next to the Gellért Baths. Some stops may be closed if the river level gets very low.

By Taxi

Budapest strictly regulates its official taxis, which must be painted yellow and have yellow license plates. These taxis are required to charge identical rates, regardless of company: a drop rate of 700 Ft, and then 300 Ft/kilometer, plus 75 Ft/minute for wait time. A 10 percent tip is expected. A typical ride within central Budapest shouldn't run more than 2,500 Ft.

If you take an unofficial taxi, there's a very high probability you'll get ripped off with much higher rates. Unfortunately, these cabbie crooks hang out at places frequented by tourists (such as at train stations). If you wave down a cab on the street, be sure it has a yellow license plate; otherwise, it's not official, and you might wind up paying double or triple. Better yet, do as the locals do and call a cab from a reputable company: **City Taxi** (tel. 1/211-1111), **Taxi 6x6** (tel. 1/266-6666), or **Főtaxi** (tel. 1/222-2222). Most dispatchers speak English, but if you're uncomfortable calling, you can ask your hotel or restaurant to call for you.

Uber currently does not operate in Hungary.

Tours in Budapest

BY FOOT
Local Guides

Budapest has an abundance of enthusiastic, hardworking young guides who speak perfect English and enjoy showing off their city.

A guide is particularly worthwhile if you have an appetite for Hungary's rich but complex history, or want to learn more about life under communism. While guides might be available last-minute, it's better to reserve in advance. **Péter Pölczman** is an exceptional guide who really puts you in touch with the Budapest you came to  see (€110/half-day, €190/full day, mobile +3620-926-0557, www.budapestyourself.com, peter.polczman@gmail.com). **Andrea Makkay** has professional polish and a smart understanding of what visitors really want to experience (€110/half-day, €190/full day, mobile +3620-962-9363, www.privateguidebudapest.com, andrea.makkay@gmail.com—arrange details by email; if Andrea is busy, she can send you with another guide). **George Farkas** is well-attuned to the stylish side of this fast-changing metropolis (€120/half-day, €240/full day, mobile +3670-335-8030, www.mybudapesttours.hu, georgefarkas@gmail.hu). And **Eszter Bokros** brings enthusiasm to sharing her city (€110/half-day, €190/full day, mobile +3670-625-6655, eszterbokros1@gmail.com).

Elemér Boreczky, a semi-retired university professor, leads walking tours with a soft-spoken, scholarly approach, emphasizing Budapest's rich tapestry of architecture as "frozen music." Elemér is ideal if you want a walking graduate-level seminar about the easy-to-miss nuances of this grand city (€30/hour, mobile +3630-491-1389, http://culturaltours.mlap.hu, boreczky.elemer@gmail.com).

Péter, Andrea, George, Eszter, and Elemér have all been indispensable help to me in writing and updating this book.

Walking Tours

Budapest's best-established walking-tour company is **Absolute Tours,** run by Oregonian Ben Frieday. Travelers with this book get a discount on almost all the tours they offer (15 percent if you book online—enter coupon code "RICK"—or 10 percent for tours booked in person). Their options include the 3.5-hour All in One walking tour, offering a good overview of Budapest; the Hammer & Sickle Tour, with visits to a mini museum of communist artifacts and sites related to the 1956 Uprising; two different food tours (one focusing on street food and craft beer, the other on traditional foods in the Great Market Hall and wine tasting); and Enchanted Budapest, an evening walk that includes a one-hour cruise on the Danube. For prices and schedules, see www.absolutetours.com or contact the office (tel. 1/269-3843, mobile +3620-929-7506).

You'll also see various companies advertising **"free" walking tours.** While there is no set fee to take these tours, guides are paid only if you tip (they're hoping for at least 2,000 Ft/person). They offer a basic 2.5-hour introduction to the city, as well as itineraries focusing on the communist era and the Jewish Quarter. Because they're working for tips, the guides are highly motivated to impress their customers. But because the "free" tag attracts very large groups, these tours tend to be less intimate than paid tours, and (especially the introductory tours) take a once-over-lightly "infotainment" approach. As this scene is continually evolving, look for local fliers to learn about the options and meeting points.

Food Tours

For ideas on food tours, cooking classes, and other culinary experiences, see "Food Experiences" on page 240.

BY BOAT
▲▲Danube Boat Tours

Cruising the Danube, while touristy, is a fun and convenient way to get a feel for the city's grand layout. The most established company, **Legenda Cruises,** is a class act that runs well-maintained, glassed-in panoramic boats day and night. All of their cruises include a free drink and romantic headphone commentary. By night, TV monitors show the interiors of the great buildings as you float by.

I've negotiated a special discount with Legenda for my readers—but you must book directly and ask for the Rick Steves price. By **day,** the 75-minute Duna Bella cruise costs 3,800 Ft for Rick Steves readers; if you want, you can hop off at Margaret Island to explore on your own, then return after 45 minutes on a later cruise (about hourly, in winter runs 1-2/day with no Margaret Island stop). By **night,** the one-hour "Danube Legend" cruise (with no Margaret Island visit) costs 4,800 Ft for Rick Steves readers (4/day, 2/day in winter). On weekends, it's smart to call ahead and reserve a spot for the evening cruises. Note: These special prices are for 2019, and may be slightly higher in 2020 and beyond.

The Legenda dock is in front of the Marriott on the Pest embankment (find pedestrian access under tram tracks at downriver end of Vigadó tér, district V, M1: Vörösmarty tér, tel. 1/317-2203, www.legenda.hu). Competing river-cruise companies are nearby, but given the quality and the discount, Legenda offers the best value.

ON WHEELS
Bike and Segway Tours

The best option for tours by bike and Segway (a stand-up electric scooter) is **Yellow Zebra,** a sister company of Absolute Tours (bike tours—9,000 Ft, 16,000 Ft by electronic bike, 4 hours, winter tours possible Fri-Sun if weather allows; Segway tours—21,000 Ft, 2.5 hours, begins with 30-minute training). My readers get a 15 percent discount when booking online (www.yellowzebratours.com, enter coupon code "RICK"), or 10 percent off if booking in person. These tours meet at the Absolute Tour Center behind the Opera House (see "Tourist Information," earlier).

ORIENTATION

Bus Tours

Various companies run hop-on, hop-off bus tours, which make 12 to 16 stops as they cruise around town on a two-hour loop with headphone commentary (generally around 8,000/24 hours). Most companies also offer a wide variety of other tours, including dinner boat cruises and trips to the Danube Bend. Pick up fliers about all these tours at the TI or in your hotel lobby.

RiverRide

This company offers a bus tour with a twist: Its amphibious bus can float on the Danube River, effectively making this a combination bus-and-boat tour. The live guide imparts dry English commentary as you roll (and float). While it's a fun gimmick, the entry ramp into the river (facing the north end of Margaret Island) is far from the most scenic stretch, and the river portion is slow-paced—showing you the same Margaret Island scenery twice, plus a circle in front of the Parliament. The Legenda Cruises boat tours, described earlier, give you more scenic bang for your buck (9,000 Ft, 2 hours, 3-4/day, departs from Széchenyi tér near Gresham Palace, tel. 1/332-2555, www.riverride.com).

PRIVATE TOURS INTO THE HUNGARIAN COUNTRYSIDE

The Hungarian countryside is well worth exploring. If you'd like a taste without driving yourself, hire **Ádám Kiss,** a licensed guide who lives in the folk-museum village of Hollókő (covered in the Day Trips from Budapest chapter). Ádám can pick you up in Budapest (at your hotel or the airport) and drive you to your choice of countryside destinations ($150 all day, plus travel costs; for example, for an all-day visit to Hollókő and Eger for two people, you'd pay about $300 total for round-trip transportation, guiding, admissions, and lunch). Ádám also enjoys helping people track down their roots in the Hungarian countryside. Contact him for pricing (mobile +3620-379-6132, adamtheguide@gmail.com).

SIGHTS IN BUDAPEST

The sights in this chapter are arranged by neighborhood for handy sightseeing. When you see a 📖 in a listing, it means the sight is covered in much more detail in one of my walks or self-guided tours. This is why Budapest's most important attractions get the least coverage in this chapter—we'll explore them later in the book.

Budapest boomed in the late 19th century, after it became the co-capital of the vast Austro-Hungarian Empire. Most of its finest buildings (and top sights) date from this age.

To appreciate an opulent interior—a Budapest experience worth ▲▲▲—prioritize touring either the Parliament or the Opera House, depending on your interests. The Opera tour is more crowd-pleasing, while the Parliament tour is grander and a bit drier (with a focus on history and parliamentary process). Seeing both is also a fine option. "Honorable mentions" go to the interiors of St. István's Basilica, the Great Synagogue, New York Café, and both the Széchenyi and the Gellért Baths. This diversity—government and the arts, Christian and Jewish, coffee drinkers and bathers—demonstrates how the shared prosperity of the late 19th century made it a Golden Age for a broad cross section of Budapest society.

The 21st century is also a boom time in Budapest. The city is busy creating an ambitious Museum Quarter in City Park. They're erecting new, purpose-built homes for the National Gallery; Museum of Ethnography; Museum of Science, Technology, and Transport; and new House of Hungarian Music. Progress is ongoing, with the various buildings slated to open gradually over the next few years. In the meantime, you'll likely see construction underway. For details, see www.ligetbudapest.org.

Remember, most sights in town offer a discount if you buy a Budapest Card (described on page 24).

Pest

Most of Pest's top sights cluster in five neighborhoods: **Leopold Town** and the **Town Center** (together forming the city's "downtown"); the **Jewish Quarter,** just outside the inner ring road; along the grand boulevard **Andrássy út;** and at that boulevard's end, near **Heroes' Square and City Park.** Each of these areas is covered by a separate self-guided walk chapter.

Several other excellent sights are not contained in these areas, and are covered in greater depth in this chapter: along the **Small Boulevard** (Kiskörút); along the **Great Boulevard** (Nagykörút); and along the boulevard called **Üllői út.**

LEOPOLD TOWN (LIPÓTVÁROS)

These sights are covered in detail in the 🕮 Leopold Town Walk chapter. If a sight is covered in the walk, I've listed only its essentials here. These are listed north to south.

▲▲Hungarian Parliament (Országház)

With an impressive facade and an even more extravagant interior, the oversized Hungarian Parliament dominates the Danube

riverbank. A hulking Neo-Gothic base topped by a soaring Neo-Renaissance dome, it's one of the city's top landmarks. Touring the building offers the chance to stroll through one of Budapest's best interiors. While the guides can be hit-or-miss, the dazzling building speaks for itself.

Cost and Hours: Buy in advance online—5,800 Ft, ticket includes tour; English tours run several times daily 8:00-18:00, Nov-March until 16:00 (these are last tour times). Check their website for specifics on the day you're visiting. On Mondays when parliament is in session (generally about two times per month Sept-May), there are no tours after 10:00.

Information: Tel. 1/441-4904, www.parlament.hu.

Advance Tickets Recommended: Tickets come with an appointed tour time and usually sell out. To ensure getting a space, book online several days in advance at www.jegymester.hu/parlament.

Budapest at a Glance

Pest

▲▲▲**Széchenyi Baths** Budapest's steamy soaking scene in City Park—the city's single best attraction. **Hours:** Daily 6:00-22:00. See page 52.

▲▲**Hungarian Parliament** Vast riverside government center with remarkable interior. **Hours:** English tours run daily 8:00-18:00; fewer on Mon and off-season. See page 39.

▲▲**Great Market Hall** Colorful Old World mall with produce, eateries, souvenirs, and great people-watching. **Hours:** Mon 6:00-17:00, Tue-Fri until 18:00, Sat until 15:00, closed Sun. See page 46.

▲▲**Great Synagogue** The world's second-largest, with fancy interior, good museum, and memorial garden. **Hours:** Sun-Thu 10:00-18:00 (May-Sept until 20:00), Fri 10:00-16:00; shorter hours off-season; always closed Sat and Jewish holidays. See page 48.

▲▲**Hungarian State Opera House** Neo-Renaissance splendor and affordable opera. **Hours:** Lobby/box office open Mon-Sat from 11:00 until show time—generally 19:00; Sun open 3 hours before performance—generally 16:00-19:00, or 10:00-13:00 if there's a matinee; English tours nearly daily at 14:00, 15:00, and 16:00. See page 49.

▲▲**House of Terror** Harrowing remembrance of Nazis and communist secret police in former headquarters/torture site. **Hours:** Tue-Sun 10:00-18:00, closed Mon. See page 50.

▲▲**Heroes' Square** Mammoth tribute to Hungary's historic figures, fronted by art museums. See page 51.

▲▲**City Park** Budapest's backyard, with Art Nouveau zoo, Transylvanian Vajdahunyad Castle replica, amusement park, and Széchenyi Baths. See page 51.

▲▲**Vajdahunyad Castle** Epcot-like replica of a Transylvanian castle and other historical buildings. See page 52.

▲▲**Holocaust Memorial Center** Excellent memorial and museum honoring Hungarian victims of the Holocaust. **Hours:** Tue-Sun 10:00-18:00, closed Mon. See page 53.

SIGHTS

▲**St. István's Basilica** Budapest's largest church, with a saint's withered fist and great city views. **Hours:** Mon-Sat 9:00-17:00, Sun from 13:00; panorama terrace daily 10:00-17:30, summer until 18:30, off-season until 16:30. See page 43.

▲**Hungarian National Museum** Expansive collection of fragments from Hungary's history. **Hours:** Tue-Sun 10:00-18:00, closed Mon. See page 47.

▲**Margaret Island** Budapest's traffic-free urban playground, with spas, ruins, gardens, a game farm, and fountains, set in the middle of the Danube. See page 58.

▲**Zwack Museum** Venerable Zwack family distillery and samples of Hungary's favorite liquor, Unicum. **Hours:** Mon-Sat 10:00-17:00, closed Sun. See page 56.

Buda
▲▲**Matthias Church** Landmark Neo-Gothic church with gilded history-book interior and revered 16th-century statue of Mary and Jesus. **Hours:** Mon-Sat 9:00-17:00, Sun from 13:00. See page 66.

▲▲**Gellért Baths** Touristy baths in historic Buda hotel. **Hours:** Daily 6:00-20:00. See page 70.

▲▲**Rudas Baths** Half-millennium-old Turkish dome over a series of hot-water pools. **Hours:** Daily 6:00-20:00. See page 70.

▲▲**Memento Park** Larger-than-life communist statues collected in one park, on the outskirts of town. **Hours:** Daily 10:00-sunset. See page 76.

▲**Hungarian National Gallery** Top works by Hungarian artists, housed in the Royal Palace. **Hours:** Tue-Sun 10:00-18:00, closed Mon. See page 60.

▲**Hospital in the Rock** Fascinating underground network of hospital and bomb-shelter corridors from World War II and the Cold War. **Hours:** Daily 10:00-20:00. See page 67.

▲**Buda Castle Park (Várkert Bázar) and Grand Staircase** Lovely Neo-Renaissance people zone from the Danube riverbank to the Royal Palace. See page 59.

SIGHTS

Select "Parliament Visit," then a date and time of an English tour, and print out your e-ticket (you'll have to create an account and pay a 250-Ft online booking fee). At your appointed time, head to the Parliament visitors center—a modern, underground space at the northern end of the long Parliament building (look for the statue of a lion on a pillar). If you can't print your ticket, arrive early and go to the information desk—not the ticket desk, which can have long lines—to ask them to print it for you.

If you didn't prebook a ticket, go to the visitors center ticket desk, which sells only same-day tickets, if any are left (6,000 Ft). Morning and late-afternoon tours are the most likely to have space—but no guarantees.

Getting There: Ride tram #2 to the Országház stop, which is next to the visitors center entrance (Kossuth tér 1, district V). You can also ride the M2/red Metró line to Kossuth tér, then walk to the other end of the Parliament building to find the visitors center.

Visiting the Parliament: The visitors center has WCs, a café, a gift shop, and the Museum of the History of the Hungarian National Assembly. With your ticket in hand, be at the airport-type security checkpoint inside the visitors center at least five minutes before your tour departure time.

On the 45-minute tour, your guide will explain the history and symbolism of the building's intricate decorations and offer a lesson in the Hungarian parliamentary system. You'll see dozens of bushy-mustachioed statues illustrating the occupations of workaday Hungarians through history, and find out why a really good speech was nicknamed a "Havana" by cigar-aficionado parliamentarians.

To begin the tour, you'll climb a 133-step staircase (with an elevator for those who need it) to see the building's monumental entryway and 96-step grand staircase—slathered in gold foil and frescoes, and bathed in shimmering stained-glass light. Then you'll gape up under the ornate gilded dome for a peek at the heavily guarded Hungarian crown (described on page 94), which is overlooked by statues of 16 great Hungarian monarchs, from St. István to Habsburg Empress Maria Theresa. Finally, you'll walk through a cushy lounge—across one of Europe's largest carpets—to see the legislative chamber.

Kossuth (Lajos) Tér

The giant square surrounding the Parliament is peppered with monuments honoring great Hungarian statesmen (Lajos Kossuth, Ferenc Rákóczi), artists (Attila József), and anonymous victims of past regimes (underfoot is a memorial to the 1956 Uprising, during which protesters were gunned down on this very square).

Pest 43

▲Szabadság Tér ("Liberty Square")
One of Budapest's most genteel squares, this space is marked by a controversial monument to the Soviet soldiers who liberated Hun-gary at the end of World War II, and ringed by both fancy old apartment blocks and important buildings (such as the former Hungarian State Television headquarters, the US Embassy, and the National Bank of Hungary). A fine café, fun-filled playgrounds, statues of prominent Americans (Ronald Reagan and Harry Hill Bandholtz), and yet another provocative monument (to the Hungarian victims of the Nazis) round out the square's landmarks. More architectural gems—including the Art Nouveau Bedő-Ház and the Postal Savings Bank in the Hungarian national style—are just a block away.

▲St. István's Basilica (Szent István Bazilika)
Budapest's biggest church is one of its top landmarks. The grand interior celebrates St. István, Hungary's first Christian king. You can see his withered, black-ened, millennium-old fist in a gilded reliquary. Or you can zip up on an eleva-tor (or climb up stairs part-way) to a panorama terrace with views over the roof-tops of Pest. The skippable treasury has ecclesiastical items, historical exhibits, and artwork.

Cost and Hours: Interior—free but 200-Ft donation strongly suggested, open to tourists Mon-Sat 9:00-17:00, Sun from 13:00, open slightly later for worshippers; panorama terrace—600 Ft, daily 10:00-17:30, summer until 18:30, off-season until 16:30; treasury-400 Ft, same hours as terrace; music concerts Mon, Tue, and Thu—see page 263; Szent István tér, district V, M1: Bajcsy-Zsilinszky út or M3: Arany János utca.

▲Chain Bridge (Széchenyi Lánchíd)
The city's most beloved bridge stretches from Pest's Széchenyi tér to Buda's Clark Ádám tér (named for the bridge's designer). The gift of Count István Széchenyi to the Hungarian people, the Chain Bridge was the first permanent link between the two towns that would soon merge to become Budapest.

SIGHTS

SIGHTS

To Parliament Visitors Center
SUPREME COURT
PARLIAMENT ❶
ALKOTMÁNY
KÁLMÁN IMRE
WEINER LEÓ
LOYAG
DESSEWFFY
JÓKAI
NAGYMEZŐ
Kossuth tér
Kossuth Lajos tér
GARIBALDI
KENT VÉCSEY
KOZMA FER.
AKADÉMIA
ZOLTÁN
STEINDL IMRE
SZÉCHENYI
VÉCSEY
PERCZEL M.
NAGY SÁNDOR
HOLD STREET MKT.
VADÁSZ
HÁJÓS
ZICHY JENŐ
ZRÍNYI
BAJCSY-ZSILINSZKY
"Broadway Quarter"
OPERA HOUSE
US EMBASSY
Szabadság tér
FMR. STATE TV HQ
KISS ERNŐ
POSTAL SAVINGS BANK
NATIONAL BANK
BANK
Arany János utca
LÁZÁR
RÉVAY
KÁLDY GYULA
GÖZSDU UDVAR
ANDRÁSSY
Tram #2
SZÉCHENYI RAKPART
ACADEMY OF SCIENCE
VIGYÁZÓ FER.
NÁDOR
ARANY JÁNOS
FORMER CENTRAL EURO. UNIV.
SAS
HERCEGPRÍMÁS
ST. ISTVÁN'S BASILICA
ZRÍNYI
Széchenyi István tér
DUNA PALOTA
GRESHAM PALACE
MÉRLEG
OKTÓBER 6
Bajcsy-Zsilinszky út
GÖZSDU UDVAR
CHAIN BRIDGE
Eötvös tér
JÓZSEF ATTILA ÚT
DOROTTYA
BÉCSI
ASBÓTH
MADÁCH
VÁRKERT
LÁNCHÍD
Tram #2
BELGRÁD RAKPART
APÁCZAI
WEKERLE S.M.
József Nádor tér
Erzsébet tér
Deák Ferenc tér
Deák tér ❸
RUMBACH STREET SYNAGOGUE
KÁROLY-KÖRÚT
GERBEAUD
Vörösmarty tér ❷
Vörösmarty tér
HARMINCAD
FERENC
Deák Ferenc
FEHÉRHAJÓ
BÁRCZY ISTVÁN
GERLÓCZY
SEMMELWEIS
Danube
PESTI VIGADÓ
Vigadó tér
TÜRR I.
CSERE
ARANY
RÉGIPOSTA
SALAMU
PETŐFI SÁNDOR
VÁROSHÁZ
CITY HALL
Kamermayer tér
COUNTY HALL
VÁRMEGYE
VÁRKERT BAZÁR GARDENS
Castle Hill
MAHART BOAT DOCK
RAKPART
LEGENDA BOAT DOCK
Petőfi tér
VÁCI
PETŐFI
VÁCI
JÁNOS
TOWN CENTER PARISH CHURCH
Ferenciek tere
KOS. LAJOS ÚT
KÁROLYI MIHÁLY
FERENCZY
DÖBRENTEI RAKPART
Márcíus 15 tér
PIARISTA
SZABAD SAJTÓ ÚT
BELGRÁD RAKPART
DUNA
CURIA
IRÁNYI
REÁLTANODA
HADNAGY
Petőfi tér
CENTER
ELTE LAW FACULTY
Döbrentei tér
ELISABETH BRIDGE SZABAD SAJTÓ ÚT
IRÁNYI
NYÁRI UTCA
SÖRHÁZ
MOLNÁR
HAVAS
SZARKA
F. GYÖRGY
SERBIAN CHURCH
RUDAS BATHS
Tram #2
SZT. GELLÉRT RAKPART
River
SZERB
SÓ
POST
Fővám tér
VÁMHÁZ
ÖRÖM
BÉRC
BUDA
Gellért Hill
CITADELLA
CITADELLA
SÉTÁNY
KŐSÁNY
SZIRTES
Jubileumi Park
CAVE CHURCH
LIBERTY BRIDGE
GREAT MARKET HALL
UNIV. OF ECONOMICS

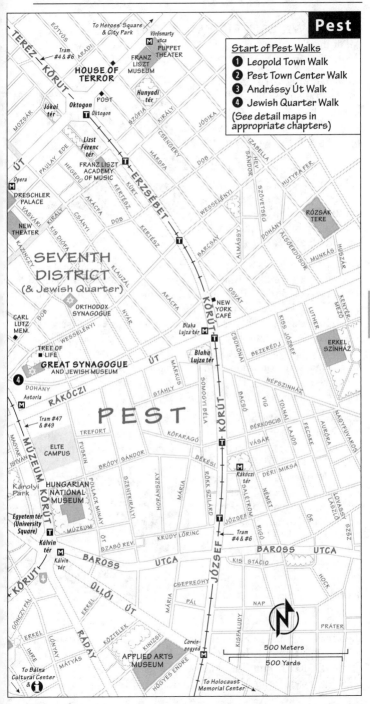

Pest

To Heroes' Square & City Park

Start of Pest Walks

1. Leopold Town Walk
2. Pest Town Center Walk
3. Andrássy Út Walk
4. Jewish Quarter Walk

(See detail maps in appropriate chapters)

EÖTVÖS
TERÉZ KÖRÚT
ARADI
Tram #4 & #6
Vörösmarty utca
M
PUPPET THEATER
HOUSE OF TERROR
FRANZ LISZT MUSEUM
Hunyadi tér
Jókai tér
POST
Oktogon
Oktogon
MOZSÁR
SZÓFIA
KIRÁLY
JÓSIKA
CSENGERY
HARSFA
DOB
IZABELLA
HÉV SÁNDOR
SZÖVETSÉG
MUTYRA FER.

ÚT
Lizst Ferenc tér
FRANZ LISZT ACADEMY OF MUSIC
Opera
DRESCHLER PALACE
NEW THEATER
PAULAY EDE
HEGEDŰ
VASVÁRI
KIRÁLY
KIS DIÓFA
CSÁNYI
AKÁCFA
DOB
KÜKT.
KERTÉSZ
ERZSÉBET
BARCSAI
ALMÁSSY
ALSÓERDŐSOR
DOHÁNY
RÓZSÁK TERE
MUNKÁS
HUBZÁR
KENYÉR-MEZŐ

KAZINCZY
KIRÁLY
KIS DIÓFA
DOB
NYÁR
KLAUZÁL
AKÁCFA
WESSELÉNYI
KÖRÚT
OSVÁT
KISS JÓZSEF
NÉPSZINHÁZ
LUTHER
ERKEL SZÍNHÁZ

SEVENTH DISTRICT
(& Jewish Quarter)

ORTHODOX SYNAGOGUE
CARL LUTZ MEM.
WESSELÉNYI
TREE OF LIFE
GREAT SYNAGOGUE AND JEWISH MUSEUM
DOHÁNY
Astoria
M
RÁKÓCZI

NEW YORK CAFÉ
Blaha Lujza tér
M
Blaha Lujza tér
CSOKONAI
BEZERÉDJ
VIG
TÓNNAI LAJOS
FECSKE
AURÓRA
NAGYFUVAROS

PEST

Tram #47 & #49
MAGYAR
ISTVÁN
MÚZEUM KÖRÚT
ELTE CAMPUS
TREFORT
PUSKIN
BRÓDY SÁNDOR
HORÁNSZKY
SZENTKIRÁLYI
MÁRIA
KŐFARAGÓ
STÁHLY
SOMOGYI BÉLA
BÉKÉSI
RÖKK SZILÁRD
KÖRÚT
BÉRKOCSIS
VÁSÁR
DÉRI MIKSA
NÉMET
LÓVASSY LÁSZLÓ
SZÉSZ

Károlyi Park
HUNGARIAN NATIONAL MUSEUM
POLLACK MIHÁY
Egyetem tér (University Square)
T
MÚZEUM
ÓT
SZABÓ REV.
KRÚDY LŐRINC
JÓZSEF
RÁKÓCZI tér
M
BACSÓ TÉR
RIGÓ
ÖR
Tram #4 & #6

Kálvin tér
M
Kálvin tér
BAROSS
UTCA
KIS STÁCIO
BAROSS UTCA
HOCK

KÖRÚT
ÜLLŐI ÚT
RÁDAY
ERKEL
KÖZTELEK
KINIZSI
CSEPREGHY
PÁL
MÁRIA
NAP
KISFALUDY
PRÁTER

GÖNCZEY PÁL
ERKEL
IMRE
LÓNYAY
MÁTYÁS
APPLIED ARTS MUSEUM
HŐGYES ENDRE
Corvin-negyed
M

To Bálna Cultural Center &
To Holocaust Memorial Center

N
500 Meters
500 Yards

SIGHTS

PEST TOWN CENTER (BELVÁROS)

All of these sights are covered in detail in the ▢ Pest Town Center Walk chapter.

▲Vörösmarty Tér

The central square of the Town Center, dominated by the venerable Gerbeaud coffee shop and a giant statue of the revered Romantic poet Mihály Vörösmarty, is the hub of Pest sightseeing. Within a few steps of here are the main walking street, Váci utca, the delightful Danube promenade, the "Fashion Street" of Deák utca, and much more.

Váci Utca

In Budapest's Golden Age, Váci Street was where well-heeled urbanites would shop, then show off for one another. During the Cold War, it was the first place in the Eastern Bloc where you could buy a Big Mac or Adidas sneakers. And today, it's an overrated, overpriced tourist trap disguised as a pretty street. I'll admit that I have a bad attitude about Váci utca. It's because more visitors get fleeced by overpriced shops and subpar restaurants here than anywhere else in town. Walk Váci utca to satisfy your curiosity, but then venture off it to discover the real Budapest.

▲▲Great Market Hall (Nagyvásárcsarnok)

"Great" indeed is this gigantic marketplace on three levels: produce, meats, and other foods on the ground floor; souvenirs upstairs; and

fish and pickles in the cellar. The Great Market Hall still keeps local shoppers happy, even as it has evolved into one of the city's top tourist attractions. Goose liver, embroidered tablecloths, golden Tokaji Aszú wine, pickled peppers, communist-kitsch T-shirts, savory *lángos* pastries, patriotic green-white-and-red flags, and paprika of every degree of spiciness...if it's Hungarian, you'll find it here. Come to shop for souvenirs, to buy a picnic, or just to rattle around inside this vast, picturesque, Industrial Age hall (Mon 6:00-17:00, Tue-Fri until 18:00, Sat until 15:00, closed Sun, Fővám körút 1, district IX, M4: Fővám tér or M3: Kálvin tér).

Bálna Budapest
This shopping mall and cultural center stands along the riverbank behind the Great Market Hall. Completed in 2013, the complex was created by bridging a pair of circa-1881 brick warehouses with a swooping glass canopy that earns its name, "The Whale" *(bálna)*. The architecture is striking (especially from the river), and the space inside is sleek and modern, but the building lacks a clear purpose: It's a mix of shops, offices, eateries, and conference rooms. If you'd like to take a peek, it's just a three-minute stroll beyond the back door of the Great Market Hall. Inside you'll also find a branch of the TI—open until 18:00 (Sun-Thu 10:00-20:00, Fri-Sat until 22:00, www.balnabudapest.hu).

ALONG THE SMALL BOULEVARD (KISKÖRÚT)
This museum is along the Small Boulevard, between the Liberty Bridge/Great Market Hall and Deák tér.

▲Hungarian National Museum (Magyar Nemzeti Múzeum)
One of Budapest's biggest museums features all manner of Hungarian historic bric-a-brac, from the Paleolithic age to a more recent in-

festation of dinosaurs (the communists). Artifacts are explained by good, if dry, English descriptions. The museum adds substance to your understanding of Hungary's story—but it helps to have a pretty firm foundation first (read this book's Hungary: Past & Present chapter). And the impressive Neoclassical building itself is historic: The 1848 Revolution against Habsburg rule was proclaimed from the front steps.

Cost and Hours: 1,600 Ft—but can change depending on temporary exhibits; Tue-Sun 10:00-18:00, closed Mon; audioguide available, near Great Market Hall at Múzeum körút 14, district VIII, M3: Kálvin tér, tel. 1/327-7773, www.hnm.hu.

Visiting the Museum: The first floor (one flight down from the entry) focuses on the Carpathian Basin in the pre-Magyar days, with ancient items and Roman remains. The basement features a lapidarium, with medieval tombstones and more Roman ruins.

Upstairs, the 20-room permanent exhibit provides a historic overview of the country. The first part begins with the Christianization of the Magyars in AD 1000 and continues through the Habsburgs' liberation of Buda from the Ottomans in 1686. You'll see a reconstructed 15th-century room, delicately inlaid wood choir stalls from the early 16th century, the Renaissance tomb of a Transylvanian duke, and exhibits on the "Wars of Expulsion" to kick out the Ottomans.

Part two picks things up in 1700 and brings the story up to the present day. Here you'll see artifacts from the wars of independence against the Habsburgs (18th-century regimental flags and weapons), a painting of István Széchenyi laying the cornerstone of the Chain Bridge, and (in room 16) nostalgic advertising from Hungary's early-20th-century glory days. Room 18 shows newsreel footage of the dark interwar period, after Hungary lost two-thirds of its territory in the Treaty of Trianon. In room 19, you'll see posters trumpeting the desire to reclaim Transylvania ("Erdély"), which was a key rallying point in allying Hungary with Hitler. And finally, in room 20 are items from the communist period—including both pro- and (illegal) anti-Party propaganda. The exhibit ends with video footage of the 1989 end of communism—demonstrations, monumental parliament votes, and a final farewell to the last Soviet troops leaving Hungarian soil.

SIGHTS

JEWISH QUARTER (ZSIDÓNEGYED)

The Great Synagogue and other sights in this area are described in greater detail in the □ Great Synagogue & Jewish Quarter Tour chapter.

▲▲Great Synagogue (Nagy Zsinagóga)

The world's second biggest synagogue sits tucked behind a workaday building on the Small Boulevard. Dating from the mid-19th century—a time when Budapest's Jews were eager to feel integrated with the larger community—this synagogue, with two symmetrical towers and a longitudinal floor plan, feels more like a Christian house of worship than a Jewish one. The gorgeously restored, intricately decorated interior is one of Budapest's finest. Attached to the synagogue is the small but well-presented Hungarian Jewish Museum, and behind it is an evocative memorial garden with the powerful *Tree of Life* monument to Hungarian victims of the Holocaust, as well as a symbolic grave for Swedish diplomat Raoul Wallenberg, who worked  to save the lives of Hungarian Jews during World War II.

Cost and Hours: 4,500 Ft for Great Synagogue, museum, and garden, includes free tour; Sun-Thu 10:00-18:00 (May-Sept until 20:00), Fri 10:00-16:00; Nov-Feb Sun-Thu 10:00-16:00, Fri until

14:00; closed Sat year-round and Jewish holidays; Dohány utca 2, district VII, near M2: Astoria or the Astoria stop on trams #47 and #49, tel. 1/343-0420, www.dohany-zsinagoga.hu.

Orthodox Synagogue

This colorfully decorated space is just two blocks behind the Great Synagogue.

Cost and Hours: 1,000 Ft; Sun-Thu 10:00-17:30, Fri until 16:00; Oct-April Sun-Thu 10:00-16:00, Fri until 13:30; closed Sat year-round; enter down little alley, Kazinczy utca 27, district VII, M2: Astoria.

Synagogue at Rumbach Street

This fine house of worship, designed by Otto Wagner and with a Moorish-style interior, should now be reopen after an extensive renovation.

Cost and Hours: If open, likely Sun-Thu 10:00-18:00, Fri until 16:00—earlier off-season, closed Sat. From the *Tree of Life* monument, it's two blocks down Rumbach utca toward Andrássy út (district VII, M2: Astoria).

ANDRÁSSY ÚT

All of these sights are covered in detail in the 🕮 Andrássy Út Walk chapter or the 🕮 House of Terror Tour chapter.

▲▲Hungarian State Opera House (Magyar Állami Operaház)

This is one of Europe's finest opera houses. Built in the late 19th century by patriotic Hungarians striving to thrust their capital onto the European stage, it also boasts one of Budapest's very best interiors—re-opening in late 2019 after an extensive restoration.

You can drop in whenever the box office is open to ogle the ostentatious **lobby** (Mon-Sat from 11:00 until show time—generally 19:00, or until 17:00 if there's no performance; Sun open three hours before the performance—generally 16:00-19:00, or 10:00-13:00 if there's a matinee; Andrássy út 22, district VI, M1: Opera).

The 45-minute **tours** of the Opera House are a must for music lovers, and enjoyable for anyone, though the quality of the guides varies: Most spout plenty of fun, if silly, legends, but others can be quite dry. You'll see the main entryway, the snooty lounge area, some of the cozy but plush boxes, and the lavish auditorium. You'll find out why clandestine lovers would meet in the cigar lounge, how the Opera House is designed to keep the big spenders away from the rabble in the nosebleed seats, and how to tell the difference between real marble and fake marble (3,000 Ft; English tours nearly daily at 14:00, 15:00, and 16:00; buy tickets at desk inside the lobby; it's smart to arrive about 30 minutes early—or drop by earlier in the day—to ensure getting a spot on the tour; mobile +3630-279-5677). For a small extra charge, you can also watch a five-minute performance of two arias after the tour...or you can hear the music just fine for free from the lobby.

▲▲House of Terror (Terror Háza)

The building at Andrássy út 60 was home to the vilest parts of two destructive regimes: first the Arrow Cross (the Gestapo-like enforcers of Nazi-occupied Hungary), then the ÁVO and ÁVH secret police (the insidious KGB-type wing of the Soviet satellite government). Now re-envisioned as the "House of Terror," this building uses highly conceptual, bombastic exhibits to document (if not proselytize about) the ugliest moments in

Hungary's difficult 20th century. Enlightening and well-presented, it rivals Memento Park as Budapest's best attraction about the communist age.

Cost and Hours: 3,000 Ft, Tue-Sun 10:00-18:00, closed Mon, audioguide-1,500 Ft, Andrássy út 60, district VI, M1: Vörösmarty utca—*not* the Vörösmarty tér stop, tel. 1/374-2600, www.terrorhaza.hu.

📖 See the House of Terror Tour chapter.

Franz Liszt Museum

In this surprisingly modest apartment where the composer once resided, you'll find a humble but appealing collection of artifacts. A pilgrimage site for Liszt fans, it's housed in the former Academy of Music, which also hosts Saturday-morning concerts (see the Entertainment in Budapest chapter).

Cost and Hours: 2,000 Ft; Mon-Fri 10:00-18:00, Sat 9:00-17:00, closed Sun; dry English audioguide with a few snippets of music-700 Ft, otherwise scarce English information—borrow the information sheet as you enter; Vörösmarty utca 35, district VI, M1: Vörösmarty utca—*not* Vörösmarty tér stop, tel. 1/322-9804, www.lisztmuseum.hu.

HEROES' SQUARE AND CITY PARK

All of these sights are covered in detail in the 🕮 Heroes' Square & City Park Walk chapter (including a statue-by-statue description of Heroes' Square). The Széchenyi Baths are described in the 🕮 Thermal Baths chapter. To reach this area, take the M1/yellow Metró line to Hősök tere (district XIV).

▲▲Heroes' Square (Hősök Tere)

Built in 1896 to celebrate the 1,000th anniversary of the Magyars' arrival in Hungary, this vast square culminates at a bold Millen-

nium Monument. Standing stoically in its colonnades are 14 Hungarian leaders who represent the whole span of this nation's colorful and illustrious history. In front, at the base of a high pillar, are the seven original Magyar chieftains, the Hungarian War Memorial, and young

Hungarian skateboarders of the 21st century. It's an ideal place to appreciate Budapest's greatness and to learn a little about its story. The square is also flanked by the two museums described below.

Museum of Fine Arts (Szépművészeti Múzeum)

This collection of Habsburg art—mostly Germanic, Dutch, Belgian, and Spanish, rather than Hungarian—is Budapest's best chance to appreciate some European masters.

Cost and Hours: 1,400 Ft, may be more for special exhibits; Tue-Sun 10:00-18:00, closed Mon, last entry one hour before closing; WC and coat check downstairs, Dózsa György út 41, tel. 1/469-7100, www.szepmuveszeti.hu.

Műcsarnok ("Hall of Art")

Facing the Museum of Fine Arts from across Heroes' Square, the Műcsarnok shows temporary exhibits by contemporary artists—of interest only to art lovers. The price varies depending on the exhibits and on which parts you tour.

Cost and Hours: Price depends on current exhibits; Tue-Sun 10:00-18:00 except Thu 12:00-20:00, closed Mon; Dózsa György út 37, tel. 1/460-7000, www.mucsarnok.hu.

▲▲City Park (Városliget)

This particularly enjoyable corner of Budapest, which sprawls behind Heroes' Square, is endlessly entertaining. Explore the fantasy castle of Vajdahunyad (described below). Visit the animals and ogle the playful Art Nouveau buildings inside the city's zoo, or enjoy a circus under the big top (all described in the Budapest with Children chapter). Go for a stroll, rent a rowboat, eat some cotton candy, or challenge a local Bobby Fischer to a game of chess. Or, best of all, take a dip in Budapest's ultimate thermal spa, the Széchenyi Baths. This is a fine place to just be on vacation. Be aware that parts of the park may be torn up, as the city is rejuvenating the area as a new Museum Quarter.

▲▲Vajdahunyad Castle (Vajdahunyad Vára)

The people of Budapest couldn't bear to tear down this elaborate pavilion after their millennial celebration ended a century ago, and

Vajdahunyad Castle has since become a fixture of City Park. Divided into four parts—representing four typical, traditional schools of Hungarian architecture—this "little Epcot" is free and always open to explore. It's dominated by a fanciful replica of a Renaissance-era Transylvanian castle. Deeper in the complex, a curlicue-covered Baroque mansion houses (unexpectedly) the **Museum of Hungarian Agriculture,** with a grand interior (Magyar Mezőgazdasági Múzeum, www.mezogazdasagimuzeum.hu).

▲▲▲Széchenyi Baths (Széchenyi Fürdő)

Visiting the Széchenyi Baths is my favorite activity in Budapest. It's the ideal way to reward yourself for the hard work of sightsee-

ing while enjoying a culturally enlightening experience. Soak in hundred-degree water, surrounded by portly Hungarians squeezed into tiny swimsuits, while jets and cascades pound away your tension. Go for a vigorous swim in the lap pool, giggle and bump your way around the whirlpool, submerge yourself to the nostrils in water green with minerals, feel the bubbles from an underwater jet gradually caress their way up your leg, or challenge the locals to a game of Speedo-clad chess. And it's all surrounded by an opulent yellow palace with shiny copper domes. The bright blue-and-white of the sky, the yellow of the buildings, the pale pink of the skin, the turquoise of the water...Budapest simply doesn't get any better.

Cost and Hours: 5,500 Ft for locker (in gender-segregated locker room), 500 Ft more for personal changing cabin, cheaper after 19:00, 200 Ft more on weekends; admission includes outdoor swimming pool area, indoor thermal baths, and sauna; open daily 6:00-22:00, may be open later on summer weekends, last entry one hour before closing, Állatkerti körút 11, district XIV, M1: Széchenyi fürdő, tel. 1/363-3210, www.szechenyibath.hu.

ON THE GREAT BOULEVARD (NAGYKÖRÚT)
▲New York Café

My vote for the most over-the-top extravagant cof-feehouse in Budapest, if not Europe, this restored space ranks up there with the city's most impressive old interiors. There's often a line of tourists at the door waiting for a table (where they'll pay royally to sit and nurse a coffee),

but you can take a quick peek from inside the door for free (daily 9:00-24:00, Erzsébet körút 9, district VII, M2: Blaha Lujza tér, tel. 1/886-6167). For more details, see the Eating in Budapest chapter.

SOUTH OF DOWNTOWN PEST

These two areas (Üllői út and Millennium City Center) are a short commute to the south from the center of Pest (10-15 minutes by tram or Metró). Both offer a peek at some worthwhile, workaday areas where relatively few tourists venture.

Museums near Üllői Út

These two museums are near the city center, on the boulevard called Üllői út. You could stroll there in about 10 minutes from the Small Boulevard ring road (walking the length of the Ráday utca café street gets you very close), or hop on the M3/blue Metró line to Corvin-negyed (just one stop beyond Kálvin tér).

▲▲Holocaust Memorial Center (Holokauszt Emlékközpont)

This sight honors the nearly 600,000 Hungarian victims of the Nazis...one out of every 10 Holocaust victims. The impressive modern complex (with a beautifully restored 1920s synagogue as its centerpiece) is a museum of the Hungarian Holocaust, a monu-ment to its victims, a space for temporary exhibits, and a research and documentation center of Nazi atrocities. Interesting to any-body, but essential to those interested in the Holocaust, this is Budapest's best sight about that dark time—and one of Europe's best, as well. For background, see page 173.

Cost and Hours: 1,400 Ft; Tue-Sun 10:00-18:00, closed Mon, last entry one hour before closing; Páva utca 39, district IX, M3: Corvin-negyed, tel. 1/455-3333, www.hdke.hu.

Getting There: From the Corvin-negyed Metró stop, use the exit marked *Holokauszt Emlékközpont* and take the left fork at the exit. Walk straight ahead two long blocks, then turn right down Páva utca.

Visiting the Center: You'll pass through a security checkpoint to reach the courtyard. Once inside, a black marble wall is etched with the names of victims. Head downstairs to buy your ticket.

The excellent permanent exhibit, called "From Deprivation of Rights to Genocide," traces (in English) the gradual process of disenfranchisement, marginalization, exploitation, dehumanization, and eventually extermination that befell Hungary's Jews as World War II wore on. From the entrance, a long hallway with the sound of shuffling feet replicates the forced march of prisoners. The one-way route through darkened halls uses high-tech exhibits, including interactive touch screens and movies, to tell the story. By demonstrating that pervasive anti-Semitism existed here long before World War II, the pointed commentary casts doubt on the widely held belief that Hungary initially allied itself with the Nazis partly to protect its Jews. Occasionally the exhibit zooms in to tell the story of an individual or a single family, following their personal story through those horrific years. One powerful room is devoted to the notorious Auschwitz-Birkenau concentration camp, where some 430,000 Hungarian Jews were sent—most to be executed immediately upon arrival. The main exhibit ends with a thoughtful consideration of "Liberation and Calling to Account," analyzing the wrenching question of how a society responds to and recovers from such a tragedy.

The finale is the interior of the **synagogue,** now a touching memorial filled with glass seats, each one etched with the image of a Jewish worshipper who once filled it. Up above, on the mezzanine level, you'll find temporary exhibits and an information center that helps teary-eyed descendants of Hungarian Jews track down the fate of their relatives.

Applied Arts Museum (Iparművészeti Múzeum)

This museum—closed for renovation, likely at least through 2020—fills a remarkable late-19th-century building. The fanciful green-roofed castle that seems out of place in an otherwise dreary urban area was designed by Ödön Lechner (who also did the Postal Savings Bank that's described in the Leopold Town Walk). The interior is equally striking: Because historians of the  day speculated about possible ties between the Magyars and India, Lechner decorated it with Mughal motifs (from the Indian dynasty best known for the Taj Mahal). Strolling through the forest of dripping-with-white-stucco arches and columns, you might just forget to pay attention to the exhibits...which would be a shame. The small but excellent permanent collection displays furniture, clothes, ceramics, and other everyday items, with an emphasis on curvy Art Nouveau (all described in English). If you're visiting the nearby Holocaust Memorial Center, consider at least dropping by here for a look at the building.

Cost and Hours: Ticket price varies with exhibits; typically Tue-Sun 10:00-18:00, closed Mon—but confirm it's open before making the trip; Üllői út 33, district IX, M3: Corvin-negyed, tel. 1/456-5100, www.imm.hu.

Getting There: From the Corvin-negyed Metró stop, follow signs to *Iparművészeti Múzeum* and bear right up the stairs.

Millennium City Center

Along the Danube riverbank at the Rákóczi Bridge, you'll find a cutting-edge cultural complex with some of Budapest's top modern venues for music and theater. While there's not much "sightseeing" here (aside from a contemporary art gallery and the quirky distillery museum), it's enjoyable to wander the riverside park amid the impressive buildings. A row of glass office blocks effectively seals off the inviting park from the busy highway, creating a pleasant place to simply stroll. (Don't confuse this with the similarly named Millenáris Park, at the northern edge of Buda.)

Getting There: Though it looks far on the map, this area is easy to reach: From anywhere along the Pest embankment, hop on tram #2 and ride it south about 10-15 minutes to the Millenniumi Kulturális Központ stop.

Nearby: Across the bridge and just downstream is the entertaining **Kopaszi-Gát,** a dike lined with parks, cafés, and playgrounds, and a great place to stroll with Hungarian families on a sunny day.

National Theater (Nemzeti Színház)

This facility anchors the complex with an elaborate industrial-Organic facade, studded with statues honoring the Hungarian theatrical tradition. The surrounding park is a lively people zone laden with whimsical art—Hungarian theater greats in stone, a vast terrace shaped like a ship's prow, a toppled colonnade, and a stone archway that evokes an opening theater curtain. Twist up to the top of the adjacent, yellow-brick ziggurat tower for views over the complex.

Palace of Arts (Művészetek Palotája)

With a sterner facade, this gigantic facility—"Müpa" for short—houses the 1,700-seat Béla Bartók National Concert Hall and the 460-seat Festival Theater (free to enter the building, open daily 10:00-20:00 or until end of last performance, www.mupa.hu). The complex is also home to the Ludwig Museum, Budapest's premier collection of contemporary art, with mostly changing exhibits of today's biggest names (price varies depending on exhibits, Tue-Sun 10:00-18:00, temporary exhibits may stay open until 20:00, closed Mon, Komor Marcell utca 1, tel. 1/555-3444, www.ludwigmuseum.hu).

▲Zwack Museum

This museum and visitors center is housed in a corner of the sprawling distillery complex that produces Unicum, the abundantly flavored liquor that's Hungary's favorite spirit (described on page 476). The Zwack family is a Hungarian institution, like the Anheuser-Busch clan in the US. The museum offers a doting look at the Zwacks and their company, which has been headquartered right here since 1892 (with a 45-year break during commu-

nism). The Zwacks' story is a fascinating case study in how communism affected longstanding industry—privatization, exile, and triumphant return. And, while the Zwacks' museum feels a bit like a shrine to their own ingenuity, it's worthwhile for Unicum fans, or for anyone who enjoys learning how booze gets made. Hungary's entire production of Unicum—three million liters annually—still takes place right here.

Cost and Hours: 2,200 Ft, Mon-Sat 10:00-17:00, tours in English at 14:00 and likely at other times—call ahead to check, closed Sun, Soroksári út 26, enter around the corner on Dandár utca, tel. 1/476-2383, www.unicum.hu.

Getting There: It's near the Haller utca stop on tram #2 (the stop just before Millennium Park); from the tram stop, walk back a block and head up Dandár utca.

Background: Unicum has a history as complicated as its flavor. Invented by a Doctor Zwack in the late 18th century, the drink impressed Habsburg Emperor Josef II, who supposedly declared: *"Das ist ein Unikum!"* ("This is something special!"). The Zwack company went on to thrive during Budapest's late-19th-century Golden Age (when Unicum was the subject of many whimsical Guinness-type ads). After all of Budapest's bridges spanning the Danube were destroyed in World War II, a temporary barge bridge was built from Unicum barrels. But when the communists took over in the postwar era, the Zwacks fled to America—taking along their secret recipe for Unicum. The communists continued to market the drink with their own formula, which left Hungarians with a bad taste in their mouths...in every sense. In a landmark case, the Zwacks sued the communists for infringing on their copyright, and won. In 1991, Péter Zwack—who had been living in exile in Italy—triumphantly returned to Hungary and resurrected the original family recipe. More recently, to entice younger palates, they've added some smoother variations: Unicum Next (citrus) and Unicum Szilva (plum). But whatever the flavor, Unicum remains a proud national symbol.

Visiting the Museum: Your visit has three parts: a 20-minute film in English (mostly about the family); a fine little museum upstairs (glass display cases jammed with old ads, documents, and—up in the gallery—thousands of tiny bottles); and—the highlight—a guided tour of the refurbished original distillery building and the cellars where the spirit is aged. On this fascinating tour, you'll be able to touch and smell several of the more than 40 herbs used to make Unicum and learn about how it's made (components are distilled in two separate batches, then mixed and aged for six months). Then you'll head down into the cellars where 500 gigantic, 10,000-liter oak casks offer the perfect atmosphere for sampling two types of Unicum straight from the barrel.

The Danube (Duna)

The mighty river coursing through the heart of the city defines Budapest. Make time for a stroll along the delightful riverfront embankments of both Buda and Pest. For many visitors, a highlight is taking a touristy but beautiful boat cruise up and down the Danube—especially at night (see "Tours in Budapest, By Boat" on page 36). Or visit the river's best island...

▲Margaret Island (Margitsziget)

In the Middle Ages, this island in the Danube (just north of the Parliament) was known as the "Isle of Hares." In the 13th century, a desperate King Béla IV swore that if God were to deliver Hungary from the invading Tatars, he would dedicate his youngest daughter Margaret to the Church. When the Tatars left, Margaret was shipped to a nunnery here. Margaret embraced her new life as a castaway nun, and later refused her father's efforts to force her into a politically expedient marriage with a Bohemian king. As a reward for her faith, she became St. Margaret of Hungary.

Margaret Island remained largely undeveloped until the 19th century, when a Habsburg aristocrat built a hunting palace here. It gradually evolved into a lively garden district, connected to Buda and Pest by a paddleboat steamer—and then, in 1901, by the Margaret Bridge.

Today, while the island officially has no permanent residents, urbanites flock here to relax in a huge, leafy park in the midst of the busy city...yet so far away. No cars are allowed on the island—just public buses. The island rivals City Park as the best spot in town for strolling, jogging, biking, and people-watching. Margaret Island is also home to some of Budapest's many baths, one of which (Palatinus Strandfürdő) is like a mini water park. Rounding out the island's attractions are an iconic old water tower, the remains of Margaret's convent, a rose garden, a game farm, and a "musical fountain" that performs to the strains of Hungarian folk tunes.

Perhaps the best way to enjoy Margaret Island is to rent some wheels. **Bringóhintó** ("Bike Castle"), with branches at both ends of the island, rents all manner of wheeled entertainment (tel. 1/329-2073, www.bringohinto.hu). Their main office is a few steps from the bus stop called "Szállodák (Hotels)." Pick up a bicycle or a fun bike cart—a four-wheeled carriage with two sets of pedals, a steering wheel, handbrake, and canopy. Because they have two

locations, you can take bus #26 to the northern end of the island, rent a bike and pay the deposit, bike one-way to the southern tip of the island, and return your bike there to reclaim your deposit. Follow this route (using the helpful map posted inside the bike cart): water tower, monastery ruins, rose garden, past the game farm, and along the east side of the island to the dancing fountain. With more time, go along the main road or the west side of the island to check out the baths.

Getting There: Bus #26 begins at Nyugati/Western train station, crosses the Margaret Bridge, then drives up through the middle of the island—allowing visitors to easily get from one end to the other (3-6/hour). **Trams** #4 and #6, which circulate around the Great Boulevard, cross the Margaret Bridge and stop at the southern tip of the island, a short walk from some of the attractions. You can also reach the island by **public riverboat**—weekday boats reach the two ends of the island, and weekend ones make several stops along the way. It's also a long but scenic **walk** between Margaret Island and other points in the city.

Buda

Nearly all of Buda's top sights are concentrated on or near its two riverside hills: Castle Hill and Gellért Hill.

CASTLE HILL (VÁRHEGY)
Most of these sights are covered in detail in the 🕮 Castle Hill Walk chapter.

Between the Danube and the Royal Palace
▲Castle Park (Várkert Bazár)
The city has recently refurbished the long-decrepit gateway, gallery, garden, and staircase that stretches from the riverbank up to the Royal Palace. Originally designed by Miklós Ybl (of Opera House fame) in the 1870s, this Neo-Renaissance people zone evokes a more genteel time.

Cost and Hours: Garden free to enter and open daily 6:00-24:00; exhibits have their own costs and hours (www.varkertbazar.hu). It's along the Buda embankment, at Ybl Miklós tér (tram #19 or #41 to Várkert Bazár stop).

Visiting the Park: Walk through the ornate archway (up and around the fountain) and climb the stairs to a cozy plateau with lush, flowery parklands ringed by monumental buildings. Originally, this "Castle Garden Bazaar" was mostly a shopping zone, as its name implies. Its colonnade is flanked by two restored buildings—the Guards' Palace and the Southern Palace—that now host temporary exhibits, mostly geared toward Hungarians (look for posters or check in at the ticket office to see what's on).

The park also offers a handy and free way to **ascend Castle Hill:** Ride up the covered escalator on the right. From the top, you can either hook left to walk the rest of the way up; or continue straight ahead to the rust-colored canopy, where an elevator zips you right up to the view terrace in front of the Royal Palace.

Royal Palace and Nearby
Royal Palace (Királyi Palota)

While imposing and grand-seeming from afar, the palace perched atop Castle Hill is essentially a shoddily rebuilt shell. But the terrace out front offers glorious Pest panoramas, there are signs of life in some of its nooks and crannies (such as a playful fountain depicting King Matthias' hunting party), and the complex houses two museums, described below.

▲Hungarian National Gallery (Magyar Nemzeti Galéria)

Hungarians are the first to admit that they're not known for their artists. But this collection of Hungarian art—with an emphasis on the 19th and 20th centuries, and an excellent collection of medieval altars, with fine English descriptions throughout—offers even non-art lovers a telling glimpse into the Magyar psyche. For art lovers or those captivated by Hungarian culture, it's worth ▲▲. The National Gallery is eventually slated to be relocated to a new, purpose-built museum in City Park.

Cost and Hours: 1,800 Ft, Tue-Sun 10:00-18:00, closed Mon, audioguide-800 Ft, required bag check for large bags, café, in the Royal Palace—enter from terrace by Eugene of Savoy statue, district I, mobile +3620-439-7325, www.mng.hu.

⊘ Self-Guided Tour: This once-over-lightly tour touches on

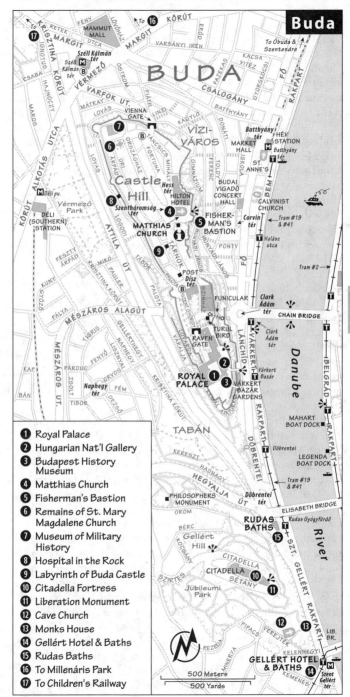

Buda

1. Royal Palace
2. Hungarian Nat'l Gallery
3. Budapest History Museum
4. Matthias Church
5. Fisherman's Bastion
6. Remains of St. Mary Magdalene Church
7. Museum of Military History
8. Hospital in the Rock
9. Labyrinth of Buda Castle
10. Citadella Fortress
11. Liberation Monument
12. Cave Church
13. Monks House
14. Gellért Hotel & Baths
15. Rudas Baths
16. To Millenáris Park
17. To Children's Railway

500 Meters
500 Yards

the most insightful pieces in this sprawling museum. As the collection is often rearranged, expect changes.

From the atrium, head up two flights on the grand staircase. On the first floor, go through the second door on the right and walk through a room of gloomy paintings (which we'll return to in a moment). Enter the hallway and turn right, then take an immediate left to reach the excellent collection of **15th-century winged altars.** Take a moment to appreciate the beautifully carved statues of saints wearing gilded robes. The ornately decorated hinged wings could be opened or closed to acknowledge special occasions and holidays. Most of these come from "Upper Hungary," or today's Slovakia—which is more heavily wooded than modern (Lower) Hungary, making woodcarving a popular way to worship there. These date from a time when Hungary was at its peak—before the Ottomans and Habsburgs ruined the fun.

Backtrack to the room of **gloomy paintings** from the 1850s and 1860s. We've just gone from one of Hungary's highest points to one of its lowest. In the two decades between the failed 1848 Revolution and the Compromise of 1867, the Hungarians were colossally depressed—and these paintings show it. Take a moment to psychoanalyze this moment in Hungarian history, perusing the paintings in these two rooms.

Begin in the farther room, closer to the atrium. On the left wall is a painting of a corpse covered by a blood-stained sheet—Viktor Madarász's grim *The Bewailing of László Hunyadi,* which commemorates the death of the beloved Hungarian heir-apparent. (The Hungarians couldn't explicitly condemn their Habsburg oppressors, but invoking this dark event from the Middle Ages had much the same effect.) Another popular theme of this era was the Ottoman invasion of Hungary—another stand-in for unwanted Habsburg rule. In this room, two different paintings illustrate the tale of Mihály Dobozi, a Hungarian nobleman who famously stabbed his wife (at her insistence) to prevent her from being raped. In the canvas just to the right, she bares her breast, waiting to be slain; across the room is a different version, in which Dobozi stabs her while on horseback, fleeing from the invaders. While Hungarian culture tends to be less than upbeat, this period took things to a new low.

Flanking the door into the next room are two paintings that are as optimistic as the Hungarians could muster. In both cases, people prepare to fight off their enemies: On the left, Imre Thököly takes leave of his father (likely for the last time) as he prepares to take to the battlefield against the Habsburgs; on the right, the women of the town of Eger stand strong against an Ottoman siege (for the full story, see page 337).

More angst awaits in the next room. On the right wall, the corpse of King Louis II is discovered on the battlefield after the Battle of Mohács; to the right, the hero of the Battle of Belgrade gestures to his compatriots before falling to a valiant death. But on the facing wall, more positive themes come up: Matthias Corvinus is returning from a hunting expedition to his family's Transylvanian palace. (A fanciful replica of this palace is in Budapest's City Park today.) Two sculptures of the "Good King Matthias" are also displayed in this room. During dark times, Hungarians looked back to this powerful Renaissance king.

Finally, the large canvas dominating the room represents a turning point: St. István (or Vajk, his heathen name) is being baptized and accepting European Christianity in the year 1000. Not surprisingly, this was painted at the time of the Compromise of 1867, when Hungary was ceded authority within the Catholic Habsburg Empire. Again, the painter uses a historical story as a tip of the hat to contemporary events.

The rest of the collection is spread through several rooms on this floor. Exit into the atrium, turn left, and go in the glass doors on your left (at the top of the stairs). This section—eloquently described in English—traces the evolution of Hungarian painting through the 19th century, as a national style emerged. You'll see influences from Italy (Romanticism and Neoclassicism), Biedermeier, the Enlightenment (landscapes), as well as a romantic affinity for the East—as this was a time when Hungarians began to feel a connection with their Central Asian roots. Local artists wove all of this into their own Hungarian tapestry.

The long room at the far end of this wing explains how, with the flurry of ornate construction around the year 1896, there were a lot of new, grandiose buildings to decorate with bombastic paintings and ceiling frescoes.

Continuing straight ahead from this room, you'll be drawn to the lovely scene of people enjoying a day in the park—this is *Picnic in May* by Pál Szinyei-Merse. While the scene is innocent today, men and women socializing freely was scandalous at the time (1873). Note

the stark contrast with the gloomy canvases across the atrium: By this time, the Great Compromise had taken root, and Hungarians had much more to be optimistic about. This was the age of the Romantics: bucolic landscapes, portraits, literary themes, the exotic, and the erotic. Also in this section are examples of Naturalism—slices of life, in the country and the city, depicting lifestyles both rich and poor. As Hungary approached the turn of the 20th century, they embraced the "Heroism of Modern Life."

After circling through these rooms, you'll wind up on the other side of the atrium. Exiting this section, do a U-turn (to the left) to enter the next section, with more scenes from everyday life and meditations on humanity's relationship with nature. In the hall at the end, go right to enter the next section—called "Mihály Munkácsy and the Realism of the End of the Century." Mihály Munkácsy (1844-1900) lived in France alongside the big-name Impressionists and Post-Impressionists. Many of these paintings are gritty slices-of-life, showing the hardships of the poor; notice the sloppier, more Impressionistic brushstrokes. For example, in the second room, on the right, see the hazy, almost Turner-esque *Dusty Road II*.

In the third room, take a break from Munkácsy with works by László Paál (1846-1879), who primarily painted murky nature scenes—sun-dappled paths through the forest, pondering the connection between humanity and nature. In the fourth room, on the left, Munkácsy captures the intensity of English poet John Milton dictating *Paradise Lost* to his daughters. (The wealthy and popular Munkácsy was also frequently hired to paint portraits.)

The next room features **Géza Mészöly** (1844-1887), Munkácsy's contemporary, who painted scenes of country life around Lake Balaton, as well as those showing the poverty of peasant life.

Backtrack to the atrium, then climb up one more flight of stairs. Straight ahead from the landing are three works by **Tivadar Csontváry Kosztka,** the "Hungarian Van Gogh" (for more on Csontváry, see page 367). Here are a few of this well-traveled painter's destinations: the giant canvas in the center depicts the theater at Taormina, Sicily; on the left are the waterfalls of Schaffhausen, Germany; and

on the right is a cedar tree in Lebanon. Colorful, allegorical, and expressionistic, Csontváry is one of the most in-demand and expensive of Hungarian artists. If you enjoy Csontváry's works and are headed to his hometown of Pécs, don't miss his museum there (see that chapter).

Up one more flight, the National Gallery shows off Hungarian painting between 1896 and World War II. Here you can see how Impressionistic trends found expression in Hungary. The exhibit continues across the atrium, displaying Károly Ferenczy's sunny, open-air scenes with messy brushstrokes. And up one more floor is art from after 1945.

Budapest History Museum (Budapesti Történeti Múzeum)

This good but stodgy museum celebrates the earlier grandeur of Castle Hill. It's particularly strong in early history (prehistoric, ancient, medieval; for modern history, the National Museum is better).

Cost and Hours: 2,000 Ft; Tue-Sun 10:00-18:00, Nov-Feb until 16:00, closed Mon year-round; audioguide-1,200 Ft, some good English descriptions posted; district I, tel. 1/487-8800, www.btm.hu.

Visiting the Museum: On the ground floor (back-right corner, in a darkened room), stroll through the collection of 14th-century sculpture fragments. Many have strong Magyar features—notice that they look Central Asian (similar to Mongolians). In a small room at the end of this wing is a tapestry mixing the coats of arms of the Magyar Árpád dynasty (red-and-white stripes) with the French Anjou dynasty (fleur-de-lis)—the first two royal houses of Hungary—which was found balled up in a wad of mud.

One floor up, the good exhibit called "Light and Shadow" traces a thousand years of the city's history, with concise English descriptions. The top floor has artifacts of Budapest's prehistoric residents. The cellar illustrates just how much this hill has changed over the centuries—and how dull today's version is by comparison. You'll wander through a maze of old palace parts, including the remains of an original Gothic chapel, a knights' hall, and marble remnants (reliefs and fountains) of Matthias Corvinus' lavish Renaissance palace.

Matthias Church and Nearby
▲▲Matthias Church (Mátyás-Templom)

Arguably Budapest's finest church inside and out, this historic house of worship—with a frilly Neo-Gothic spire and gilded Hun-

garian historical motifs slathered on every interior wall—is
Castle Hill's best sight. From
the humble Loreto Chapel (with
a tranquil statue of the Virgin
that helped defeat the Ottomans), to altars devoted to top
Hungarian kings, to a replica
of the crown of Hungary, every
inch of the church oozes history.

Cost and Hours: 1,800 Ft; Mon-Sat 9:00-17:00 (may close Sat afternoons in summer for weddings), Sun from 13:00; Szentháromság tér 2, district I, tel. 1/488-7716, www.matyas-templom.hu.

Church Tower: For an extra 1,800 Ft, you can take a 30-minute tour up the 197 steps to the top of the church tower (departs at the top of each hour, daily 10:00-17:00). You'll see a few architectural exhibits partway up, and fine views from the top.

For a self-guided tour of the Matthias Church, see the 🕮 Castle Hill Walk chapter.

Fisherman's Bastion (Halászbástya)

Seven pointy domes and a double-decker rampart run along the cliff in front of Matthias Church. Evoking the original seven Mag-

yar tribes, and built for the millennial celebration of their arrival, the Fisherman's Bastion is one of Budapest's top landmarks. This
fanciful structure adorns Castle Hill like a
decorative frieze or wedding-cake flowers.
While some suckers pay for the views from
here, you can enjoy virtually the same view
through the windows next to the bastion
café for free.

Cost and Hours: 1,000 Ft, buy ticket
at ticket office along the park wall across the
square from Matthias Church, daily 9:00-
20:00; after closing time and off-season, no
tickets are sold, but bastion is open and free
to enter; Szentháromság tér 5, district I.

North Castle Hill
Remains of St. Mary Magdalene Church

Standing like a lonely afterthought at the northern tip of Castle Hill, St. Mary Magdalene was the crosstown rival of the Matthias Church. After the hill was recaptured from the Ottomans, only one church was needed, so St. Mary sat in ruins. But ultimately, they rebuilt the church tower—which today evokes the rich but now-missing cultural tapestry that was once draped over this hill. The ruins are free and always viewable, but you can pay 1,500 Ft to hike the 172 steps up to the top of the tower (daily 10:00-dusk).

Museum of Military History (Hadtörténeti Múzeum)

This museum—of interest mostly to military and history buffs—explains various Hungarian military actions over time in painstaking detail. Watch uniforms and weaponry evolve from the time of Árpád to today—with enough old artifacts to keep an army-surplus store in stock for a decade. The museum's highlight is a permanent exhibit about World War I—a major benchmark in Hungarian history.

Cost and Hours: 1,500 Ft, Tue-Sun 10:00-17:00, closed Mon, Tóth Árpád sétány 40, district I, tel. 1/325-1600.

Under Castle Hill

The hill is honeycombed with caves and passages, which are accessible to tourists in two different locations: The better option (Hospital in the Rock) comes with a fascinating tour illustrating how the caves were in active use during World War II and the Cold War; the Labyrinth offers a quicker visit with only a lightweight, quasi-historical exhibit.

▲Hospital in the Rock and Nuclear Bunker (Sziklakórház és Atombunker)

Bring your Castle Hill visit into modern times with this engaging tour. Sprawling beneath Castle Hill is a 25,000-square-foot labyrinthine network of hospital and fallout-shelter corridors built during the mid-20th century. (Hidden access points are scattered throughout the tourist zone, above ground.) While pricey, this visit is a must for doctors, nurses, and World War II buffs. I enjoy this as a lively interactive experience to balance out an otherwise sedate Castle Hill visit.

Cost and Hours: 4,000 Ft for required one-hour tour, 10 percent discount if you have a Matthias Church ticket (but not vice-versa), daily 10:00-20:00, English tours run 1-2/hour, last tour departs at 19:00, gift shop like an army-surplus store, Lovas utca 4C, district I, mobile +3670-701-0101, www.sziklakorhaz.eu.

Getting There: To find the hospital, stand with your back to

Matthias Church and the Fisherman's Bastion. Walk straight past the plague column and down the little street (Szentháromság utca), then go down the covered steps at the wall (or ride the elevator). At the bottom, turn right on Lovas utca, and walk 50 yards to the well-marked bunker entrance.

Background: At the outbreak of World War II, in 1939, the Hungarian government began building a secret emergency surgical hospital here in the heart of Budapest. When the war finally reached Hungary, in 1945, the hospital was in heavy use. While designed for 200 patients, eventually it held more than 600 at a time. Later, the forgotten hospital was used for two months to care for those injured in the 1956 Uprising. Then, as nuclear paranoia grew intense in the late 1950s and early 1960s, it was expanded to include a giant bomb shelter and potential post-nuclear-holocaust hospital.

Visiting the Hospital and Bunker: First you'll watch a 10-minute movie (with English subtitles) about the history of the place. Then, on the tour, your guide leads you through the tunnels to see room after room of perfectly preserved WWII and 1960s-era medical supplies and equipment, most still in working order. More than 200 wax figures engagingly bring the various hospital rooms to life: giant sick ward, operating room, and so on. On your way to the fallout shelter, you'll pass the decontamination showers, and see primitive radiation detectors and communist propaganda directing comrades on how to save themselves in case of capitalist bombs or gas attacks. In the bunker, you'll also tour the various mechanical rooms that provided water and ventilation to this sprawling underground city, and you'll learn about the atom bomb explosions in Hiroshima and Nagasaki.

Labyrinth of Buda Castle (Budavári Labirintus)

Armchair spelunkers can explore these dank and hazy caverns, with some wax figures in period costume, sparse historical information in English, a few actual stone artifacts, and a hokey Dracula exhibit (based on likely true notions that the "real" Dracula, the Transylvanian Prince Vlad Țepeș, was briefly imprisoned under Buda Castle). As this is indeed a labyrinth, expect to get lost—but don't worry; you'll find your way out eventually. After 18:00, they turn the lights out and give everyone gas lanterns. This tourist trap pales in comparison with the other underground option, the Hospital in the Rock and Nuclear Bunker (see above).

Cost and Hours: 2,500 Ft, daily 10:00-19:30, last entry at 19:00, entrance between Royal Palace and Matthias Church at Úri utca 9, district I, tel. 1/212-0207, www.labirintus.com/hu.

GELLÉRT HILL (GELLÉRTHEGY) AND NEARBY

Gellért Hill rises from the Danube just downriver from the castle. When King István converted Hungary to Christianity in the year 1000, he brought in Bishop Gellért, a monk from Venice, to tutor his son. But some rebellious Magyars put the bishop in a barrel, drove long nails in from the outside, and rolled him down this hill... tenderizing him to death. Gellért became the patron saint of Budapest and gave his name to the hill that killed him. Today the hill is a fine place to commune with nature on a hike or jog, followed by a restorative splash in its namesake baths. The following sights are listed roughly from north to south.

Monument Hike

The north slope of Gellért Hill (facing Castle Hill) is good for a low-impact hike. You'll see many monuments, most notably the big memorial to Bishop Gellért himself (you can't miss him, standing in a grand colonnade, as you cross the Elisabeth Bridge on Hegyalja út). A bit farther up, seek out a newer monument to the world's great philosophers—Eastern, Western, and in between—from Gandhi to Plato to Jesus. Nearby is a scenic overlook with a king and a queen holding hands on either side of the Danube.

Citadella

This strategic, hill-capping fortress was built by the Habsburgs after the 1848 Revolution to keep an eye on their Hungarian subjects. There's not much to do up here (no museum or exhibits), but it's a good destination for an uphill hike, and provides the best panoramic view over all of Budapest.

The hill is crowned by the **Liberation Monument,** featuring a woman holding aloft a palm branch. Locals call it "the lady with the big fish" or "the great bottle opener." A heroic Soviet soldier, who once inspired the workers with a huge red star from the base of the monument, is now in Memento Park (see Memento Park listing, later).

Getting There: It's a steep hike up from the river to the Citadella. Bus #27 cuts some time off the trip, taking you up to the Búsuló Juhász stop (from which it's still an uphill hike to the fortress). You can catch bus #27 from either side of Gellért Hill. From the southern edge of the hill, catch this bus at the Móricz Zsigmond körtér stop (easy to reach: ride trams #19 or #41 south from anywhere along Buda's Danube embankment, or trams #47 or #49

SIGHTS

from Pest's Small Boulevard ring road; you can also catch any of these trams at Gellért tér, in front of the Gellért Hotel). Alternatively, on the northern edge of the hill, catch bus #27 along the busy highway (Hegyalja út) that bisects Buda, at the intersection with Sánc utca (from central Pest, you can get to this stop on bus #178 from Astoria or Ferenciek tere).

Cave Church (Sziklatemplom)

Hidden in the hillside on the south end of the hill (across the street from Gellért Hotel) is Budapest's atmospheric cave church—burrowed right into the rock face. The communists bricked up this church when they came to power, but today it's open for visitors (600 Ft, unpredictable hours, closed to sightseers during frequent services). Find the **monks house**—the little structure at the foot of the hill (with the pointy turret), where the monks who care for this church reside.

▲▲Gellért Baths

Located at the famous and once-exclusive Gellért Hotel, right at the Buda end of the Liberty Bridge, this elegant bath complex has long been the city's top choice for a swanky, hedonistic soak. It's also awash in tourists, and the Széchenyi Baths beat it out for pure fun...but the Gellért Baths' mysterious thermal spa rooms and its giddy outdoor wave pool make it an enticing option.

Cost and Hours: 5,900 Ft for a locker, 400 Ft more for a personal changing cabin, 200 Ft extra on weekends; open daily 6:00-20:00, last entry one hour before closing; Kelenhegyi út 4, district XI, M4: Gellért tér, tel. 1/466-6166, ext. 165, www.gellertbath.com.

See the 📖 Thermal Baths chapter.

▲▲Rudas Baths

Along the Danube toward Castle Hill from Gellért Baths, Rudas (ROO-dawsh) offers Budapest's most old-fashioned, Turkish-style bathing experience. The historic main pool of the thermal bath section sits under a 500-year-old Ottoman dome. Bathers move from pool to pool to tweak their body temperature. On weekdays, it's a nude, gender-segregated experience, while on weekends, it becomes more accessible (and mixed), when men and women put on swimsuits and mingle beneath that historic dome. Rudas also has a ho-hum swimming pool, and a state-of-the-art "wellness" section, with a variety of modern massage pools, a "sauna world," and an inviting hot tub/sun deck on the roof with a stunning Budapest panorama (these areas are mixed-gender every day).

Cost and Hours: Thermal baths—3,700 Ft on weekdays (4,300 Ft on weekends, discounted on weekday mornings); wellness center (saunas/pool)—3,500 Ft on weekdays (4,800 Ft on weekends); combo-ticket includes entire complex—5,200 Ft (6,500 Ft on weekends). Thermal baths open daily 6:00-20:00, wellness section daily 8:00-22:00, last entry one hour before closing; open for nighttime bathing with nightclub ambience Fri-Sat 22:00-late (5,100 Ft); wellness and swimming pool areas mixed-gender and clothed at all times; thermal baths men-only Mon and Wed-Fri, women-only Tue, mixed Sat-Sun and during nighttime bathing; Döbrentei tér 9, district I, tel. 1/375-8373, www.rudasbaths.com.

See the ▢ Thermal Baths chapter.

THE REST OF BUDA

There's not much of interest to tourists in Buda beyond Castle and Gellért Hills.

The **Víziváros** area, or "Water Town," is squeezed between Castle Hill and the Danube. While it's a useful home base for sleeping and eating (see those chapters for details), and home to the Budai Vigadó concert venue (see the Entertainment in Budapest chapter), there's little in the way of sightseeing. The riverfront Batthyány tér area, at the northern edge of Víziváros, is a hub both

for transportation (M2/red Metró line, HÉV suburban railway to Óbuda and Szentendre, and embankment trams) and for shopping and dining.

To the north of Castle Hill is **Széll Kálmán tér,** a transportation hub (for the M2/red Metró line, several trams, and buses #16, #16A, and #116 to Castle Hill) and shopping center (featuring the giant Mammut supermall). This unpretentious zone, while light on sightseeing, offers a chance to commune with workaday Budapest. Its one attraction is **Millenáris Park,** an inviting play zone for adults and kids that combines grassy fields and modern buildings. Though not worth going out of your way for, this park might be worth a stroll if the weather's nice and you're exploring the neighborhood (a long block behind Mammut mall).

Rózsadomb ("Rose Hill"), rising just north of Széll Kálmán tér, was so named for the rose garden planted on its slopes by a Turkish official 400 years ago. Today it's an upscale residential zone.

To the south, the district called the **Tabán**—roughly between Castle Hill and Gellért Hill—was once a colorful, ramshackle neighborhood of sailor pubs and brothels. After being virtually wiped out in World War II, now it's home to parks and a dull residential district.

Beyond riverfront Buda, the terrain becomes hilly. This area—the **Buda Hills**—is a pleasant getaway for a hike or stroll through wooded terrain that's still close to the city. One enjoyable way to explore these hills is by hopping a ride on the Children's Railway (see the Budapest with Children chapter). This area also has a chairlift that zips people up to high-altitude, distant views over the city (Zugligeti Libegő, operated by city transit company).

Two other major attractions—the part of town called **Óbuda** ("Old Buda") and **Memento Park**—are on the Buda side of the river but away from the center and are described in the following sections.

Outer Budapest

The following sights, while technically within Budapest, take a little more time to reach. For information on several sights just outside the city limits—the village of **Szentendre,** the Royal Palace at **Gödöllő,** and the engaging horse shows at **Lázár Lovaspark**—as well as some places farther afield (the royal castles at Visegrád, the great church at Esztergom, and the folk village of Hollókő), see the Day Trips from Budapest chapter.

ÓBUDA

Budapest was originally three cities: Buda, Pest, and Óbuda. Óbuda ("Old Buda") is the oldest of the three—the first known residents of the region (Celts) settled here, and today it's still littered with ruins from the following occupants (Romans). Despite all the history, this district (north of Buda) ranks relatively low on the list of Budapest's sightseeing priorities: Aside from a charming small-town ambience on its main square, it offers a pair of good museums on two important 20th-century Hungarian artists, and—a short train ride away—some Roman ruins.

Getting There: To reach the first three sights listed here, go to Batthyány tér in Buda (M2/red Metró line) and catch the HÉV suburban train (H5/purple line) north to the Szentlélek tér stop. The Vasarely Museum is 50 yards from the station (exit straight ahead, away from the river; it's on the right, behind the bus stops). The town square is 100 yards beyond that (bear right around the corner), and 100 yards later (turn left at the ladies with the umbrellas), you'll find the Imre Varga Collection. Aquincum is three stops farther north on the HÉV line. The trip to Óbuda is covered by a standard Metró ticket or travelcard, but going beyond this area on the same line—to Szentendre—requires paying a supplement.

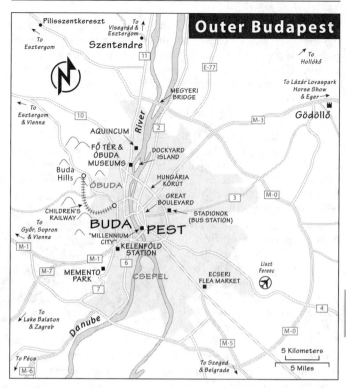

Outer Budapest

Pilisszentkereszt
To Esztergom
To Visegrád & Esztergom
Szentendre
11
To Hollókő
E-77
MEGYERI BRIDGE
To Lázár Lovaspark Horse Show & Eger
10
M-3
Gödöllő
To Esztergom & Vienna
AQUINCUM
River
2
DOCKYARD ISLAND
Buda Hills
FŐ TÉR & ÓBUDA MUSEUMS
ÓBUDA
HUNGÁRIA KÖRÚT
3
M-0
CHILDREN'S RAILWAY
GREAT BOULEVARD
To Győr, Sopron & Vienna
M-1
BUDA • PEST
STADIONOK (BUS STATION)
"MILLENNIUM CITY"
KELENFÖLD STATION
M-7
M-1
6
Liszt Ferenc
MEMENTO PARK
CSEPEL
ECSERI FLEA MARKET
4
7
To Lake Balaton & Zagreb
Danube
M-0
To Pécs
M-6
M-5
To Szeged & Belgrade
5 Kilometers
5 Miles

SIGHTS

▲Vasarely Museum

This museum features two floors of eye-popping, colorful paintings by Victor Vasarely (1906-1997), the founder of Op Art. If you're not going to Vasarely's hometown of Pécs, which has an even better museum of his works (see that chapter), this place gives you a good taste.

Cost and Hours: 1,000 Ft, Tue-Sun 10:00-17:45, closed Mon, Szentlélek tér 6, district III, tel. 1/388-7551, www.vasarely.hu.

Visiting the Museum: The exhibition—displayed in a large, white hall with each piece labeled in English—follows Vasarely's artistic evolution from his youth as a graphic designer to the playful optical illusions he was most famous for. Most of these trademark works (as well as temporary exhibits of other artists) are upstairs. Sit on a comfy bench and stare into Vasarely's mind-bending world.

Let yourself get a little woozy. Think of how this style combines right-brained abstraction with an almost rigidly left-brained, geometrical approach. It makes my brain hurt (or maybe it's just all the wavy lines). Vasarely and the movement he pioneered helped to inspire the trippy styles of the 1960s. If the art gets you pondering Rubik's Cube, it will come as no surprise that Ernő Rubik was a professor of mathematics here in Budapest.

Óbuda Main Square (Fő Tér)

If you keep going past the Vasarely Museum and turn right, you enter Óbuda's cute Main Square. The big, yellow building was the Óbuda Town Hall when this was its own city. Today it's still the office of the district mayor. While still well within the city limits of Budapest, this charming square feels like its own small town.

On the small, adjacent square to the right of the Town Hall is a whimsical, much-photographed statue of **women with umbrellas.** Replicas of this sculpture, by local artist Imre Varga, decorate the gardens of wealthy summer homes on Lake Balaton. Varga created many of Budapest's distinctive monuments, including the *Tree of Life* behind the Great Synagogue and a major work that's on display at Memento Park. His museum is just down the street (turn left at the umbrella ladies).

▲Imre Varga Collection (Varga Imre Gyűjtemény)

Imre Varga, who worked from the 1950s through the 2000s, is one of Hungary's most esteemed artists and its single best sculptor. This humble museum—crammed with his works (originals, as well as smaller replicas of Varga statues you'll see all over Hungary), and with a fine sculpture garden out back—offers a good introduction to the man's substantial talent. Made mostly of steel, his pieces can appear rough and tangled at times, but are always evocative and lifelike. Unfortunately, English information is virtually nonexistent here.

Cost and Hours: 800 Ft; Tue-Sun 10:00-18:00, Nov-March until 16:00, closed Mon year-round; Laktanya utca 7, district III, Szentlélek tér HÉV station, tel. 1/250-0274, www.budapestgaleria. hu.

Visiting the Museum: The first room holds a replica of a sculpture of St. István approaching the Virgin Mary, the original of which is in the Vatican. The next room has several small-scale copies of famous Varga works from around the country, including some you might recognize from Budapest (such as the *Tree of Life* from behind the Great Synagogue).

Pause at the statue with the headless, saluting soldier wearing medals. Through the communist times, there were three types of artists: banned, tolerated, and supported. Varga was tolerated, and works like this subtly commented on life under communism. In fact, the medallions nailed to the figure's chest were Varga's own, from his WWII military service. Anyone with such medallions was persecuted by communists in the 1950s...so Varga disposed of his this way.

Nearby is the exit to the garden out back, with a smattering of life-size portraits. Three prostitutes lean against a wall, illustrating the passing of time. And St. Elisabeth sits on her horse, having been sent to Thuringia to meet her husband (who stands next to her). The rest of the museum is predominantly filled with portraits (mostly busts) of various important Hungarians—look for Liszt, Kódaly, and Imre Nagy. You'll see variations on certain themes that intrigued Varga,

including mythical figures (Sisyphus, Orpheus, Prometheus) and a stretching ballerina.

Aquincum Museum

Long before Magyars laid eyes on the Danube, Óbuda was the Roman city of Aquincum. Here you can explore the remains of the 2,000-year-old Roman town and amphitheater. The museum is proud of its centerpiece, a water organ.

Cost and Hours: 1,600 Ft; grounds open Tue-Sun 9:00-18:00, Nov-March until 16:00, exhibitions open at 10:00, closed Mon year-round, outdoor site closed in bad weather; Szentendrei út 139, district III, HÉV north to Aquincum stop, tel. 1/250-1650, www.aquincum.hu.

Getting There: From the HÉV stop, cross the busy road and turn to the right. Go through the railway underpass, and you'll see the ruins ahead on the left as you emerge.

SIGHTS

▲▲MEMENTO PARK (A.K.A. STATUE PARK)

Little remains of the communist era in Budapest. To sample those drab and surreal times, head to this motley collection of statues, which seem to be preaching their Marxist ideology to each other in an open field on the outskirts of town. You'll see the great figures of the Soviet Bloc—both international (Lenin, Marx, and Engels) and Hungarian (local bigwig Béla Kun)—as well as gigantic, stoic figures representing Soviet ideals. This stiff dose of Socialist Realist art, while time-consuming to reach, is rewarding for those curious for a taste of history that most Hungarians would rather forget.

Cost and Hours: 1,500 Ft, daily 10:00-sunset, six miles southwest of city center at the corner of Balatoni út and Szabadka út, district XXII; take direct bus from Deák tér in downtown Pest, or ride Metró then bus (for details, see page 207); tel. 1/424-7500, www.mementopark.hu.

See the 📖 Memento Park Tour chapter.

THERMAL BATHS

Fürdő

Splashing and relaxing in Budapest's thermal baths is the city's top attraction. Though it might sound daunting, bathing with the Magyars is far more accessible than you'd think. The thermal baths I've described in this chapter are basically like your hometown swimming pool—except the water is a hundred degrees, there are plenty of jets and bubbles to massage away your stress, and you're surrounded by potbellied, scantily clad Hungarians. (For those seeking a more traditional, in-the-nude experience, Rudas Baths has that as well.)

All this fun goes way back. Hungary's Carpathian Basin is essentially a thin crust covering a vast reservoir of hot water. The

word "Pest" comes from a Slavic word for "oven." The Romans named their settlement near present-day Budapest Aquincum— "abundant waters"—and took advantage of those waters by building many baths. Centuries later, the occupying Ottomans revived the custom. And today, thermal baths are as Hungarian as can be.

Locals brag that if you poke a hole in the ground anywhere in Hungary, you'll find a hot-water spring. Judging from Budapest, they could be right: The city has 123 natural springs and some two dozen thermal baths *(fürdő)*. The baths, which are all operated by the same government agency, are actually a part of the health-care system. Doctors prescribe treatments that include massage, soaking in baths of various heat and mineral compositions, and swimming laps. For these patients, a visit to the bath is subsidized.

But increasingly, there's a new angle on Hungary's hot water:

entertainment. Adventure water parks are springing up all over the country, and even the staid old baths have been renovated, adding enjoyable jets and currents. Overcome your jitters, follow my instructions, and dive in...or miss out on *the* quintessential Budapest experience.

Baths Orientation

Some tourists may feel trepidation at the thought of bathing alongside locals. Relax! My readers overwhelmingly report that

the thermal baths were their top Hungarian experience. If you go into it with an easygoing attitude, I promise you'll have a blast. The system has been modernized, and most bath attendants speak enough English to help you find your way.

Dress Code: While Budapest has several mostly nude, gender-segregated Turkish baths, my favorites—Széchenyi and Gellért—are less intimidating: Men and women are usually together, and you can keep your swimsuit on the entire time. (At the more traditional, gender-segregated baths—like the thermal section of Rudas on certain days—locals may be nude or wearing a *kötény*—a loose-fitting loincloth.)

What to Bring: If you have them, bring a swimsuit, towel, flip-flops, bottle of water, soap and shampoo, comb or brush, swim cap if you want to do laps, plastic bag for your wet swimsuit, and maybe sunscreen and leisure reading. Hotels sometimes frown on guests taking their room towels to the baths; try asking nicely if they have some loaner towels just for this purpose. A swim cap is required in lap pools; you can rent or buy a flimsy one there, but if you know you'll be swimming laps, see if you can grab a shower cap from your hotel.

Rental Towels and Swimsuits: At Budapest's baths, you can usually rent a towel or swimsuit (for men, Speedos are always available, trunks sometimes). These are generally available at a separate desk inside the complex. Rent your towel before you change, as you'll need cash (generally about 1,000 Ft rental fee, 2,000-Ft deposit per item). At the end, you'll return your towel to get your deposit back; you may also be asked for your paper receipt, so don't lose it.

Entry Procedure: The baths may seem initially confusing, with long price lists and sometimes gruff staff. But the entry procedure is easier than it might seem. Credit cards are accepted (but you'll need cash to rent towels). Don't bother with the "prepaid" tickets for the baths that are advertised in hotel lobbies around town; it's the same price to buy your tickets directly, and there's rarely a line.

All of Budapest's baths use the same easy system: When you pay, you'll be given a waterproof wristband. Put it on and keep it on. Touch it to the panel on the turnstile to enter, then again to be assigned a changing cabin, then again to unlock your cabin. At most baths (except Rudas), the door of your cabin should lock automatically when you close it (but test it to be sure). If you paid for a locker, just choose any empty one and touch it with your wristband in order to lock it; from then on, it can only be locked and unlocked with the same wristband. You can use your wristband to reopen your cabin or locker as often as you like. If you forget the number of your cabin or locker, just touch your wristband to the panel, and it'll remind you.

If you get turned around, bath attendants are standing by to point you in the right direction. Most speak a little English, and all have mastered the sign language needed to direct confused tourists. It's OK to be a novice...don't be afraid to act like one.

Lockers and Cabins: The main choice when buying your ticket is locker or cabin. The locker price is slightly cheaper and gives you access to a gender-segregated, gymnasium-type locker room (which often has communal cabins where modest bathers can change). A cabin is all yours, offering more privacy for changing. I've found both cabins and lockers to be safe, but storing valuables here is at your own risk (if you're nervous, you can pay a few hundred forints to rent a safe).

Main Pools: Each bath complex has multiple pools, used for different purposes. Big pools with cooler water are for serious swimming, while the smaller, hotter thermal baths (*gyógyfürdő*, or simply *gőz*) are for relax-

ing, enjoying the jets and current pools, and playing chess. The water bubbles up from hot springs at 77° Celsius (170° Fahrenheit), then is mixed with cooler water to achieve the desired temperatures. Most pools are marked with the water temperature in Celsius (cooler pools are about 30°C/86°F; warmer pools are closer to 36°C/97°F or 38°C/100°F, about like the hot tub back home; and the hottest are 42°C/108°F...yowtch!). Locals hit the cooler pools first, then work their way up to the top temps.

Other Bath Features: Most thermal baths also have a dry

sauna, a wet steam room, a cold plunge pool (for a pleasurable jolt when you're feeling over-heated), and sunbathing areas (which may be gender segre-gated and clothing optional). Some baths have fun flourishes: bubbles, whirlpools, massage jets, waterfalls, wave pools, and so on. Be aware that the various water features sometimes take turns running. If a particularly fun feature of the pool doesn't seem to be working, just give it a few minutes.

Sanitary Concerns: While the lap pools are chlorinated, most of the thermal baths are only lightly chlorinated or not at all. Un-like swimming pools in the US—where the water is recycled back into the pool—water here is slowly drained out and replaced with fresh water from the hot springs. Locals figure this continuous natural flushing makes chemicals unnecessary. Still, germophobes may not be entirely comfortable at the baths; either convince your-self to go with the flow, or skip the trip.

Massages: Don't expect a relaxing, pampering experience; the baths are operated by the Hungarian government as a wing of their national health system, so these are more medicinal. There are two basic choices. A **"relax massage"** or **"aroma massage"** is a restful rubdown, typically using oil (often scented). This is what's sometimes called a Swedish-style massage. The other option is a **"scrub massage"** or **"skin-firming massage."** Similar to a Turkish-style massage, this is (for some) less restful, as it's intended to exfoliate your skin and involves some very hard scrubbing. In the lobby of each bath, you'll find a long menu of massage options. It's affordable—figure around 6,000 Ft (basic 20-minute massage) to around 12,000 Ft (45 minutes); more elaborate "VIP" treatments cost more. Pay and arrange a time when you're buying your ticket. On busy days (especially Mon, Fri, and Sat), you may have to wait an hour or two; at other times, you may be able to get your massage immediately (or whenever you want).

Yet another choice is a **Thai massage;** you'll see this advertised at some baths, sometimes in a separate section (since it's operated by a private agency). You'll lie on a mat close to the floor as the masseuse uses her feet, knees, and elbows to administer a full-body, stretching-and-cracking massage. Sometimes the Thai massage service also provides a more restful, scented-oils massage as well.

Leaving the Bath: After you've returned your towel (and reclaimed your deposit) and changed back to street clothes, ask whether there's a centrifuge *(centrifuga)* where you can give your

THERMAL BATHS

Useful Bath Words	
English	**Hungarian**
Bath	Fürdő (FEWR-dur)
Men	Férfi (FAYR-fee)
Women	Női (NUR-ee)
Changing cabin	Kabin (KAW-been)
Locker	Szekrény (SEHK-rayn)
Ticket office	Pénztár (PAYNZ-tar)
Thermal bath	Gyógyfürdő (JOHDGE-fewr-dur) or Gőz (gurz)

soggy swimsuit a spin. (Most baths have one, but they're often hidden away in the locker room.) After a minute or so, it's merely damp rather than dripping. When you exit, drop your wristband into a slot as you go through the turnstile.

The Baths

Of Budapest's two-dozen thermal baths, the three listed here are the best known, most representative, and most convenient for first-timers: The Széchenyi Baths are more casual and popular with locals; the Gellért Baths are touristy, famous, and genteel; and the Rudas Baths offer an appealing combination of a modern "wellness" section and a historic, 500-year-old, Turkish-feeling thermal section. To me, Széchenyi is second to none, but some travelers prefer the Gellért or Rudas experience. As they're all quite different, doing more than one is an excellent option. For more information on all of Budapest's baths, see www.spasbudapest.com.

SZÉCHENYI BATHS (SZÉCHENYI FÜRDŐ)

The big, yellow, copper-domed building in the middle of City Park, Széchenyi (SAY-chayn-yee) is the best of Budapest's many bath experiences and worth ▲▲▲. Although it's increasingly discovered by tourists, you'll still see plenty of Hungarians here. Magyars of all shapes and sizes stuff themselves into tiny swimsuits and strut their stuff. Bankers and homemakers float blissfully in the warm water. In-

THERMAL BATHS

tellectuals and roly-poly elder statesmen stand in chest-high water around chessboards and ponder their next moves. This is Budapest at its best.

Cost: 5,500 Ft for locker (in gender-segregated locker room), 500 Ft more for personal changing cabin, cheaper if you arrive after 19:00, 200 Ft more on weekends. Regardless of which entrance or ticket you use, the price includes both the outdoor swimming pool area and the indoor thermal bath and sauna.

Hours: Daily 6:00-22:00, last entry one hour before closing. On some summer weekends, the baths may be open later (see "Night Bathing," below).

Location and Entrances: In City Park at Állatkerti körút 11, district XIV, M1: Széchenyi fürdő (tel. 1/363-3210, www. szechenyibath.hu). The huge bath complex has three entrances. The

"**thermal bath entrance**" is the grand main entry, facing south (roughly toward Vajdahunyad Castle). I prefer the "**swimming pool entrance**," facing the zoo on the other side of the complex—it's more user-friendly and has shorter lines. A third, smaller "**medical entrance**" is between the other two (and near the Metró station). If there's a long line at one of the entrances, check the others.

Massage: In the lobby, an English menu lists a wide array of massages and other treatments. You can set up an appointment and pay at the office near the towel-rental desk (expect a 30-minute wait for your appointment when it's busy). Remember that these massages are more medicinal than hedonistic. But inside the complex are some more luxurious (and more expensive) options: a Thai massage parlor at the upper level of the complex (above the swimming pool entrance—just follow the signs) and a separate "information" desk just inside the swimming pool entrance where you can book a "VIP" massage, which comes with access to an adjoining palm house.

Night Bathing: The baths are a joy in the evening, when both the price and the crowds are reduced. In cool weather, even rain or snow, the pools maintain their hot temperatures—making this a delightful after-hours activity. Busy sightseers can be extremely efficient by closing down the museums, then heading to the baths.

Additionally, Széchenyi is open late into the night on weekends for a "sparty" event, where the bath complex basically becomes one big hot-water dance club (around 16,000 Ft, tickets sell out so

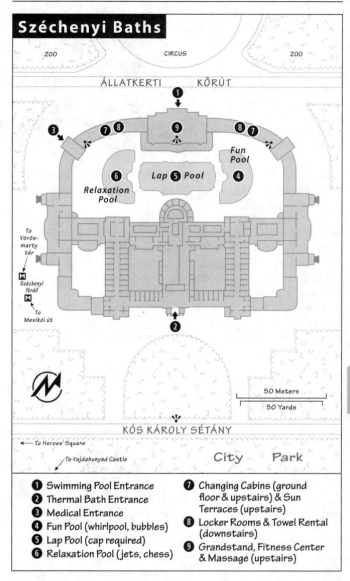

Széchenyi Baths

ZOO   CIRCUS   ZOO

ÁLLATKERTI   KÖRÚT

Fun Pool

Lap **5** Pool

Relaxation Pool

To Vörös-marty tér

Ⓜ Széchenyi fürdő Ⓜ

To Mexikói út

50 Meters

50 Yards

KÓS KÁROLY SÉTÁNY

To Heroes' Square

To Vajdahunyad Castle

City Park

1 Swimming Pool Entrance
2 Thermal Bath Entrance
3 Medical Entrance
4 Fun Pool (whirlpool, bubbles)
5 Lap Pool (cap required)
6 Relaxation Pool (jets, chess)

7 Changing Cabins (ground floor & upstairs) & Sun Terraces (upstairs)
8 Locker Rooms & Towel Rental (downstairs)
9 Grandstand, Fitness Center & Massage (upstairs)

THERMAL BATHS

book online in advance, mid-Feb–early Dec Sat 22:30–late, www.szechenyispabaths.com/sparties).

Entering the Baths: These instructions assume that you're using the swimming pool entrance. First, in the grand lobby, pay the cashier, then touch your wristband to the turnstile and enter. Pause to get oriented: Straight ahead is a row of private changing cabins. If you go **up the stairs,** you'll find more changing cabins, the Thai massage area, gender-segregated "solarium" sun terraces, a well-equipped fitness center, and a grandstand overlooking the main pool. It's worth heading upstairs just to snap some photos of the outdoor complex before you change. If you go **down the stairs,** you'll find the counter where you can rent a towel or

swimsuit. From here, a long hallway lined with hairdryers and mirrors leads to locker rooms at each end (remember, men are *férfi* and women are *női*).

When ready, report to the area that you paid for: If you paid for a **cabin,** head to the cabins on the main floor, look for an electronic panel on the wall, and hold your wristband against this panel for a few seconds—you'll automatically be assigned a number for a cabin. If you paid for a **locker,** you can head down to the locker room and choose one, then use your wristband to lock it.

Now that you've changed into your swimsuit and stored your belongings, let's have some fun.

Taking the Waters: The bath complex has two parts, outside and inside.

For most visitors, the best part is the swimming pool area **outside.** Orient yourself to the three pools (facing the main, domed building): The pool to the left is for **fun** (cooler water— 30°C/86°F, warmer in winter, lots of jets and bubbles, lively and often crowded, includes circular current pool). The pool on the right is for **relaxation** (warmer water—38°C/100°F, mellow atmosphere, a few massage jets,

chess). The **main (lap) pool** in the center is all business (cooler water—28°C/82°F in summer, 26°C/79°F in winter, people doing laps, swim cap required). You get extra credit for joining the gang in a chess match. Stairs to saunas (with cold plunge pools, cold showers, and even an ice maker) are below the doors to the indoor thermal bath complex.

If you're feeling waterlogged and need a break, it's fun simply to explore the sprawling complex. It's a bit of a maze...just poke around (but keep in mind that several areas—such as the locker rooms in the basement, and the solarium sun terraces up top—are clothing optional; again, men are *férfi* and women are *női*).

Inside the main building is the thermal bath section, a series of indoor pools; each of these is designed for a specific medical treatment. You'll notice each pool is labeled with the temperature (ranging from 28°C/82°F to 36°C/97°F to 38°C/100°F; you'll also find steam rooms with an 18°C/64°F cold plunge pool nearby). The pools also have varying types and amounts of healthy minerals—some of which can make the water quite green and/or stinky. Hungarians who use Széchenyi Baths medicinally are prescribed a specific regimen for moving from pool to pool. But if all of this smelly water is lost on you (as it is on many foreigners), it's totally fine to focus on the fun outdoor pools. (I've had many great visits to Széchenyi Baths without ever going inside.)

Leaving the Bath: When finished, continue your sightseeing... soggy but relaxed. If you're heading to the **Metró,** the station is very close but easy to miss: It's basically a pair of nondescript stairwells with yellow railings in the middle of the park, roughly toward Heroes' Square from the thermal bath entrance (look for the low-profile, yellow *Földalatti* sign; to head for downtown, take the stairwell marked *a Vörösmarty tér felé*).

GELLÉRT BATHS (GELLÉRT FÜRDŐ)
The ▲▲ baths at Gellért (GEH-layrt) Hotel cost a bit more than the Széchenyi Baths, and you won't run into as many locals; this

is definitely a more upscale, tourist-oriented scene. Gellért's indoor thermal pools are Budapest's most atmospheric—with exquisite porcelain details and an air of mystery. Its outdoor zone—mostly for sunbathing—is less interesting than Széchenyi, with one exception: It has a deliriously enjoyable wave pool that'll toss you around like a queasy surfer (summer only).

Cost: 5,900 Ft for a locker, 400 Ft more for a personal changing cabin; 200 Ft extra on weekends.

Hours: Daily 6:00-20:00, last entry one hour before closing.

Location: It's on the Buda side of the green Liberty Bridge (M4: Szent Gellért tér; or take trams #47 and #49 from Deák tér in Pest, or trams #19 and #41 along the Buda embankment from Víziváros below the castle, Gellért tér stop). The entrance to the baths is under the stone dome opposite the bridge, around the right side of the hotel (Kelenhegyi út 4, district XI, tel. 1/466-6166 ext. 165, www.gellertbath.com).

Entering the Baths: The grand entry hall is fully open to visitors, so feel free to poke around to get the lay of the land before buying your ticket (good views from the gallery up above). The entrance doors are flanked by ticket windows; just past those, on the right, is an information desk with English-speaking staff.

Choose your ticket—locker or cabin—and consider the dizzying array of **massages** and other treatment options (sort through your options and arrange a time when you buy your ticket). Upstairs, you can also book a Thai massage.

After buying your ticket, put on your wristband, and glide through the swanky lobby. You'll use the swimming pool entrance,

on your right, under the grand dome. Go down the stairs, pass through a long corridor (with underwater windows into the main swimming pool), then climb up the stairs to the cabin areas and locker rooms (men/*férfi* on the left side of the complex, and women/*női* on the right). Use your wristband to find and lock your cabin (or choose your own locker), as explained earlier. If you want to rent a towel or swimsuit, look for the desk near the entrance to the changing-cabin area.

Taking the Waters: Once you've changed, you can spend your time either indoors or out. From the locker room, look for signs *to the effervescent bath-pool* (for the indoor section) or *to the swimming-pool with artificial waves* (for the outdoor section).

Inside, the central, genteel-feeling hall is home to a cool-water swimming pool (swim cap required—you can buy a cheap one) and a crowded hot-water pool (36°C/97°F). This is used for swimming laps and for periodic water-exercise classes. On sunny days, they crank open the retractable roof; for nice views down onto the pool, find the stairs up near the locker

THERMAL BATHS

rooms. Back toward the main hall are doors to the thermal baths (easy to miss—walk to the far end of the pool and look for signs). These were once segregated into men's and women's sections, but they're now both open to everybody. These grand old halls are probably the most atmospheric part of the bath—slathered with colorful porcelain decorations. The former men's section is both hotter and more beautifully decorated than the women's section. (Hmmm...) I'd focus on the former men's section, which has big pools at either end: 36°C (97°F) and 38°C (100°F). Notice that these temperatures perfectly flank the normal temperature of the human body, allowing you to toggle your temp at will. At the far end of the bath are a steam room (45-50°C/113-122°F) and a cold plunge pool (18°C/64°F). Back out near the changing cabins is a dry sauna (a.k.a. "dry sweating rooms," 50-70°C/122-158°F). If you paid for a massage, report to the massage room in this section at your appointed time—or just show up and see if they can take you.

Outside, you'll find several sunbathing areas and a warm thermal pool, along with an atmospheric woody sauna and a big

barrel-shaped plunge pool with cold water (all hiding up the stairs on the right). But the main attraction is the big, unheated wave pool in the center (generally closed Oct-April, weather dependent). Not for the squeamish, this pool thrashes fun-loving swimmers around like driftwood. The swells in the deeper area are fun and easy to float on, but the crashing waves at the shallow end are vigorous, if not dangerous. If there are no waves, just wait around for a while (you'll hear a garbled message on the loudspeaker five minutes before the tide comes in).

RUDAS BATHS (RUDAS FÜRDŐ)

To get to the Turkish roots of Budapest's obsession with thermal baths, head for Rudas (ROO-dawsh). Worth ▲▲, it's the most

historic, local, and potentially intimidating of the three baths I list—but it may also be the most rewarding, as it offers the most variety.

Rudas has two main sections: the dark, historic, mysterious-feeling Turkish-style thermal bath zone; and the modern, fun wellness/"sauna world"/swimming pool section. Visiting both sections provides a nice contrast (and a well-rounded bath experience) and is worth paying extra for. However, on certain days the thermal section may be open only to men or only to women, which may make the decision for you.

Overview: Rudas' **thermal section** feels more like the classic Turkish baths of yore—with an octagonal central pool under a 500-year-old dome first built by the Ottoman Turks. These baths are not about splashy fun—there are no jets, bubbles, or whirlpools. Instead, Rudas is about history and about serious temperature modulation—stepping your body temperature up and down between very hot and very cold. The thermal section is for men only on Mon and Wed-Fri, women only on Tue, and all visitors on Sat-Sun, when men and women mingle in swimsuits under the fine old dome. On Fri-Sat nights, it becomes a modern nightclub until the wee hours.

The **wellness area**—with a handful of relaxing jet pools—is the modern, accessible yin to the thermal baths' antique yang. Both men and women (in swimsuits) have access to the wellness area every day. The main reason to visit this section is the rooftop terrace, where you can sunbathe or soak while looking out over sweeping views of the Budapest skyline. Imagine: You're up to your earlobes in hot water, looking out over commuters slogging across the city's clogged bridges...and feeling pretty happy to be on vacation. The wellness area is also attached to a "sauna world" (with a half-dozen different wet or dry hot rooms) and a swimming pool—far less elegant than Gellért's and intended only for those who want to swim laps.

Cost: **"All-in" ticket** includes the entire complex—5,200 Ft weekdays, 6,500 Ft weekends; **thermal baths** only—3,700 Ft weekdays, discounted Mon-Fri 9:00-12:00, 4,300 Ft weekends; **wellness/saunas/pool** only—3,500 Ft weekdays, 4,800 Ft weekends.

Hours: Thermal bath open daily 6:00-20:00, wellness section daily 8:00-22:00, last entry one hour before closing. While the wellness area is mixed gender every day, the thermal baths are open only to men Mon and Wed-Fri, only to women Tue, and to both men and women Sat-Sun. The night bathing (described later) is also mixed gender.

Location: It's in a low-profile building at the foot of Gellért Hill, just south of the white Elisabeth Bridge (Döbrentei tér 9, district I, tel. 1/375-8373, www.rudasbaths.com). Trams #19 and #41, which run along the Buda embankment, stop right out front (Rudas Gyógyfürdő stop). Those trams also work from Szent Gellért tér, as do trams #56 and #56A or bus #7. From Pest, you can ride bus #7 from Astoria or Ferenciek tere to the Rudas Gyógyfürdő stop.

Night Bathing: The baths are open—to both men and women, in swimsuits—with a dance hall ambience Fri-Sat 22:00-late (5,100 Ft).

Entering the Baths: At the ticket desk, buy your ticket, and if you want, book a massage—either a relaxing "aroma relax massage" or a rougher, exfoliating "water massage with soap" in a noisy, busy room. If you want to rent a towel or a swimsuit, you'll do so inside (find the desk in your changing area before you change, as you'll need cash).

Head inside. If you're doing the thermal bath only, you'll enter on the main floor into a corridor of wood changing cabins; press your wristband to the panel to be assigned a cabin. If you bought a wellness or "all-in" ticket, you'll go upstairs to a modern locker room, with men and women mixed (but with private cabins to change in). Choose any locker, and use your wristband to lock it.

Dress Code: In the wellness, sauna, and swimming pool areas, you'll wear your swimsuit everywhere. For the thermal bath area, if you're here on a mixed day, the dress code is swimsuits. On other days, bathers wear a flimsy loincloth called a *kötény* (issued as you enter). If you're a self-conscious, gawky tourist (it happens to the best of us), you can wear your swimsuit...although you might get some funny looks.

Taking the Waters: This complex has two completely different areas with completely different protocols: the thermal bath section and the wellness/sauna world/swimming pool section. With the "all-in" ticket, you can float freely between them (using your wristband to enter the turnstiles separating them).

Thermal Bath: Rudas' thermal bath transports you half a millennium back in time. The central chamber, under an original 35-foot-high Turkish dome supported by eight pillars, is the historic core of the baths. This area is all about modulating your body temperature—pushing your body to its limit with heat, then dousing off quickly with a bucket of cold water, then heating up again, and so on. Pools of different temperatures are designed to let you do this as gradually or quickly as you like.

The main, octagonal pool in the center is surrounded by four smaller pools, each labeled with its temperature: 28°C (82°F), 30°C (86°F), 33°C (91°F), and 42°C (108°F). Conveniently, the largest, central pool—at 36°C (97°F)—is not too hot, not too cold...juuuust right.

Along one wall are entrances to the wet sauna (*nedves gőzkamra*, to the left), with 50°C (122°F) scented steam; and the dry sauna (*hőlégkamra*, to the right), with three progressively hotter rooms ranging from 45°C (113° F) to 72°C (161°F). Near the entrance

THERMAL BATHS

to each one is a shower or—if you don't want to beat around the bush—a bucket of frigid water (if you're overheated, pull the rope for immediate relief...and a jolt).

Surrounding this central chamber are hallways with other areas: resting rooms, tanning beds (*szolarium*, costs extra), massage rooms, a cold plunge pool, and a scale to see how much sweat you've lost.

Float on your back for a while in the main octagonal pool, pondering the faintly glittering translucent tiles embedded in the dome. You'll notice that the voices echoing around that dome are mostly Hungarian—there are very few tourists here.

To move between the thermal bath and wellness sections, you'll cross through the lobby, past a snack bar, and use your wristband to go through the turnstile.

Wellness/Sauna/Pool: First you'll walk along the swimming pool (for laps, swim cap required)—either at pool level or upstairs along an outdoor sun terrace. Once you're in the far building, upstairs is the sauna world, where you can move between a variety of steam rooms and dry saunas—Finnish sauna, aroma sauna, even a salt sauna.

At the far end is the wellness area. The first room, with a huge window looking out over the busy embankment road, has three pools of different temperatures (32°C/90°F, 36°C/97°F, and a sweltering 42°C/108°F), all with powerful massage jets. In the cold plunge pool (12-14°C/54-57°F), notice the ice maker that continually drops in a cube or two, every few seconds. Thirsty? Get a drink at the stately ram's-head tiled fountains that line the walls.

But the real highlight of the wellness area is upstairs: At the end of the room, find the staircase and head on up, passing the restaurant on your way to the rooftop terrace. While other Budapest baths envelop you in opulent architecture, this is the only one that envelops you in Budapest itself. Whether soaking in rays on the sun deck or taking a dip in the 36°C/97°F thermal pool, you're surrounded by the bustle of the city. Scanning the horizon, you'll see a workaday burg going about its business...oblivious to the swimsuit-clad barnacle clinging to the base of Gellért Hill. Your solitude is broken only by the periodic rumble of trams trundling past on the road below you.

Leaving the Bath: After changing, return your rental towel and swimsuit to the attendant and get your receipt; present this at the front desk (along with your original towel receipt) to get your deposit back. Then drop your wristband through the little slot at the turnstile, head out the door, and stumble along the Danube...as relaxed as you'll ever be.

Aaaaahhh.

LEOPOLD TOWN WALK

Lipótváros, from the Parliament to the Chain Bridge

The Parliament building, which dominates Pest's skyline, is the centerpiece of a banking and business district that bustles by day but is relatively quiet at night and on weekends. Called Lipótváros ("Leopold Town"), this area is one of Budapest's most genteel quarters and features some of the best of the city's many monuments. This walk also takes in several of Budapest's most grandiose landmarks: the Parliament, St. István's Basilica, the Gresham Palace, and the Chain Bridge.

Note: If you're planning to tour the Parliament interior, book a ticket online several days in advance (or buy them, if they're still available, at the ticket office before you begin this walk; for details on buying tickets, see page 39). Do the first part of this walk while waiting for your Parliament tour to begin.

Orientation

Length of This Walk: Allow 1.5 hours, not including time to enter the sights.

Getting There: We'll begin on Kossuth tér, behind the Parliament. You can take the M2/red line to the Kossuth tér stop; or, from southern Pest (such as the Great Market Hall—at the end of the Pest Town Center Walk; or Vigadó tér near Vörösmarty tér), take tram #2 along the Danube embankment, and hop off at the looming Parliament building (Kossuth tér stop; if you need to get Parliament tickets first, stay on one more stop to Országház, which is next to the visitors center/ticket office). From near the Opera House, hop on trolley bus #70 or #78.

Parliament: Buy in advance online—5,800 Ft, ticket includes tour; English tours run several times each day (8:00-18:00,

Nov-March until 16:00, these are last tour times); Kossuth tér 1.

St. István's Basilica: Interior—free, but 200-Ft donation strongly suggested, open to tourists Mon-Sat 9:00-17:00, Sun from 13:00, open later for worshippers; panorama terrace—600 Ft, daily 10:00-17:30, summer until 18:30, off-season until 16:30; treasury—400 Ft, same hours as terrace; Szent István tér, district V.

Starring: Grand buildings, fine facades, contemporary politics, and monuments, monuments, monuments.

The Walk Begins

• *Start in the vast plaza on the east side of the gigantic, can't-miss-it, red-domed Parliament building (that is, on the opposite side from the riverbank). Position yourself near the bottom of the very tall, pointy flagpole, near the stiff guards. Follow their gaze to the...*

Hungarian Parliament (Országház)

The Parliament was built from 1885 to 1902 to celebrate the Hungarian millennium year of 1896 (see sidebar on page 27).

Its elegant, frilly spires and riverside location were inspired by its counterpart in London (where the architect studied). When completed, the Parliament was a striking and cutting-edge example of the mix-and-match Historicist style of the day. Like the Hungarian people, this building is at once grandly ambitious and a somewhat motley hodgepodge of various

influences—a Neo-Gothic palace topped with a Neo-Renaissance dome, which once had a huge, red communist star on top of the tallest spire. Fittingly, it's the city's top icon. The best views of the Parliament are from across the Danube—especially in the late-afternoon sunlight.

The enormous building—with literally miles of stairs—was appropriate for a time when Budapest ruled much of Eastern Europe. The Parliament was built in an exuberant age, when Hungary was junior partner

LEOPOLD TOWN WALK

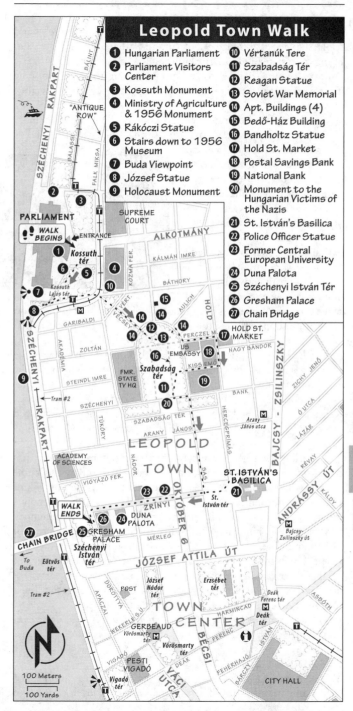

Leopold Town Walk

1. Hungarian Parliament
2. Parliament Visitors Center
3. Kossuth Monument
4. Ministry of Agriculture & 1956 Monument
5. Rákóczi Statue
6. Stairs down to 1956 Museum
7. Buda Viewpoint
8. József Statue
9. Holocaust Monument
10. Vértanúk Tere
11. Szabadság Tér
12. Reagan Statue
13. Soviet War Memorial
14. Apt. Buildings (4)
15. Bedő-Ház Building
16. Bandholtz Statue
17. Hold St. Market
18. Postal Savings Bank
19. National Bank
20. Monument to the Hungarian Victims of the Nazis
21. St. István's Basilica
22. Police Officer Statue
23. Former Central European University
24. Duna Palota
25. Széchenyi István Tér
26. Gresham Palace
27. Chain Bridge

in the Dual Monarchy—the "Austro-Hungarian Empire"—and triple the size it is today. Look at the Parliament with an 1896 Hungarian state of mind. The building is a celebration of Hungary, built with Hungarian hands and of Hungarian materials. But now it feels just plain too big—the legislature only occupies an eighth of the space.

The interior—decorated with 84 pounds of gold—is even more glorious than the facade. Apart from all that opulence, it also holds the **Hungarian crown** (you can  see it if you tour the interior; it's directly under the dome—surrounded, as if at a tribal summit, by over a thousand years' worth of Hungary's great kings). This quintessential symbol of Hungarian sovereignty is supposedly the original one that Pope Sylvester II sent to crown István on Christmas Day in the year 1000.

Since then, the crown has been hidden, stolen, lost, and found again and again...supposedly bending the cross on top in the process. That original, simple crown has been encrusted with jewels and (as a gift from a Byzantine emperor) adorned with a circlet. This makes the crown look like a hybrid of East and West—perhaps appropriately, as for much of history Budapest was seen as the gateway to the Orient. In modern times, the crown actually spent time in Fort Knox, Kentucky, where the US government kept it safe between the end of World War II and 1978, when Jimmy Carter returned it to Hungary. (For details on touring the Parliament, see page 39.)

During the 20th century, this building saw monarchists, nationalists, democrats, fascists, and communists. Today, the Hungarian parliament is controlled by the Fidesz party, led by Viktor Orbán. In addition to introducing you to old buildings and monuments, this walk will familiarize you with some of the contemporary politics in Hungary—including the controversial reforms of Orbán and Fidesz. A highly nationalistic, right-wing party, which swept to power after Hungarians grew weary of the bumblings of the poorly organized, shortsighted left-wing opposition party, Fidesz has exerted its influence over every walk of Hungarian life... beginning with the look of this building and square.

• *The vast square behind the Parliament is studded with attractions. Stay where you are for a quick...*

Kossuth Tér Spin-Tour

This square is sprinkled with interesting monuments and packed with Hungarian history. But it's gone through a lot of changes in the last few years, at the hands of architects and urban planners working under the steady guidance of Fidesz. The first big change was the square itself, which used to be a more higgledy-piggledy mix of ragged asphalt, parks, monuments, and trees. But Fidesz wanted the mighty Parliament building to stand bold and unobstructed. Several older monuments (including, ironically, an "eternal" flame honoring victims of the communists) were swept away. Trees were cut down overnight, before would-be protesters could make a peep. And today the square has a scrubbed-clean look that some critics consider fascist.

Check out the **flags** that are being flown from the Parliament building. In addition to the Hungarian flag (red, white, and green stripes), you may also see the flag of Transylvania (blue flag with a yellow stripe, and a star and crescent moon in the corner). Like many Hungarians, the leaders of Fidesz cling to the memory of a much larger, pre-WWI Hungary, which included Transylvania. Although the treaty ceding Transylvania to Romania was signed a century ago, Fidesz stubbornly flies this flag to bolster their suggestion that Romania grant Transylvania its independence (an idea that almost nobody takes seriously). Meanwhile, Fidesz has refused to fly the European Union's flag (a circle of yellow stars on a blue background).

Look to the right end of the Parliament. Poking up is a **pillar** topped by a lion being strangled and bitten by a giant snake—a proud, noble nation laid low by an insidious enemy. This pillar marks the entrance to the Parliament visitors center; if you want to check on the availability of tours today, now's a good time.

Looking a bit to the right, at the end of the park you'll see another stony tribute, this one to the square's namesake, **Lajos Kossuth,** who led the 1848 Revolution against the Habsburgs. Kossuth is flanked by his fellow revolutionaries, whose names you'll recognize from streets and squares around town: Deák, Széchenyi, Batthyány, and so on. And yet, they're all look-

ing downward, with a gloomy cast...perhaps anticipating that their revolution will end in failure. For more on Kossuth, see page 167.

The street that leaves this square behind Kossuth's left shoulder is Falk Miksa utca, Budapest's **"antique row"**—a great place to browse for nostalgic souvenirs (see page 257).

Panning right from the Kossuth statue, across the tram tracks you'll see a stately palace. The design was the first runner-up for the

1956

The year 1956 is etched into the Hungarian psyche. In that year, the people of Budapest staged the first major uprising against the communist regime. It also marked the first time that the Soviets implicitly acknowledged, in brutally putting down the uprising, that the people of Eastern Europe were not "communist by choice."

The seeds of revolution were sown with the death of a tyrant: Josef Stalin passed away on March 5, 1953. Suddenly the choke hold that Moscow had on its satellite states loosened. During this time of "de-Stalinization," Hungarian premier Imre Nagy presided over two years of mild reform, before his political opponents (and Moscow) became nervous and demoted him. (You can read more about Nagy later in this chapter.)

In 1955, Austria declared its neutrality in the Cold War. This thrust Hungary to the front line of the Iron Curtain and raised the stakes both for Hungarians who wanted freedom and for Soviets who wanted to preserve their buffer zone. When Stalin's successor, Nikita Khrushchev, condemned Stalin's crimes in a "secret speech" to communist leaders in February of 1956, it emboldened the Soviet Bloc's dissidents. A workers' strike in Poznań, Poland, in October inspired Hungarians to follow their example.

On October 23, 1956, the Hungarian uprising began. A student union group gathered in Budapest at 15:00 to articulate a list of 16 demands against the communist regime. Then they marched toward Parliament, their numbers gradually swelling. One protester defiantly cut the Soviet-style insignia out of the center of the Hungarian flag, which would become the uprising's symbol.

By nightfall, some 200,000 protesters filled Kossuth tér behind Parliament, calling for Imre Nagy, the one communist leader they believed could bring change. Nagy finally appeared around 21:00. Ever the pragmatic politician, he implored patience. Following the speech, a large band of protesters took matters into their own hands, marched to City Park, and tore down the hated Stalin statue that stood there (see page 215).

Another group went to the National Radio building to read their demands on the air. The ÁVH (communist police) refused to let them do it and eventually opened fire on the protesters. The peaceful protests evolved into an armed insurrection, as frightened civilians gathered weapons and supplies.

Overnight, Moscow decided to intervene. Budapesters awoke on October 24 to find Red Army troops occupying their city. That morning, Imre Nagy—who had just been promoted again to prime minister—promised reforms and tried to keep a lid on the simmering discontent.

The next day, October 25, a huge crowd gathered on Kossuth tér behind the Parliament to hear from Nagy. In the hubbub, shots rang out as Hungarian and Soviet soldiers opened fire on the (mostly unarmed) crowd. Of the victims, 72 deaths are known by name, but likely hundreds more were injured or perished.

The Hungarians fought back with an improvised guerilla resistance. They made use of any guns they could get their hands on, as well as Molotov cocktails, to strike against the Soviet occupiers. Many adolescents (the celebrated "Pest Youth") participated. The fighting tore apart the city, and some of the fallen were buried in impromptu graves in city parks.

Political infighting in Moscow paralyzed the Soviet response, and an uneasy cease-fire fell over Budapest. For 10 tense days, it appeared that the Soviets might allow Nagy to push through some reforms. Nagy, a firmly entrenched communist, had always envisioned a less repressive regime...but within limits. While he was at first reluctant to take on the mantle of the uprising's leadership, he gradually began to echo what he was hearing on the streets. He called for free elections, the abolishment of the ÁVH, the withdrawal of Soviet troops, and Hungary's secession from the Warsaw Pact.

But when the uprisers attacked and killed ÁVH officers and communist leaders in Budapest, it bolstered the case of the Moscow hardliners. On November 4, the Red Army launched a brutal counterattack in Budapest that left the rebels reeling. At 5:20 that morning, Imre Nagy's voice came over the radio to beg the world for assistance. Later that morning, he sought asylum at the Yugoslav Embassy across the street from City Park. He was never seen alive in public again.

János Kádár—an ally of Nagy's who was palatable to the uprisers, yet firmly loyal to Moscow—was installed as prime minister. The fighting dragged on for about another week, but the uprising was eventually crushed. By the end, 2,500 Hungarians and more than 700 Soviets were dead, and 20,000 Hungarians were injured. Communist authorities arrested more than 15,000 people, of whom at least 200 were executed (including Imre Nagy). Anyone who had participated in the uprising was blacklisted; fearing this and other forms of retribution, some 200,000 Hungarians fled to the West.

Though the 1956 Uprising met a tragic end, within a few years Kádár did succeed in softening the regime, and the milder, so-called "goulash communism" emerged. And today, even though the communists are long gone, the legacy of 1956 pervades the Hungarian consciousness. Some Budapest buildings are still pockmarked with bullet holes from '56, and many Hungarians who fled the country in that year still have not returned. October 23 remains Hungary's most cherished holiday.

Parliament building, so they built it here, to house the **Supreme Court.**

To the right, the **Ministry of Agriculture** was the second runner-up for the Parliament. Today it features a very low-profile,

but poignant, monument to the victims of the 1956 Uprising against Soviet rule: At the right end of the protruding arcade, notice that the walls are pock-marked with little metal dollops (you may have to walk closer to see these clearly). Two days into the uprising, on October 25, the ÁVH (communist police) and Soviet troops on the rooftop above opened fire on demonstrators gathered in this square—massacring many and leaving no doubt that Moscow would not tolerate dissent. In the monument, each of the little metal knobs represents a bullet.

In the foreground, between you and the two big palaces, is a long, rectangular **reflecting pond**—a memorial to the people killed by government troops when they revolted here in 1956.

Spin farther to the right, where a dramatic equestrian statue of **Ferenc Rákóczi** stands in the park. Rákóczi valiantly—but un-successfully—led the Hungarians in their War of Independence (1703-1711) against the Habsburgs. (For more on this leader, see page 166.) Although they lived more than a century apart, Rákóczi and Kossuth—who now face each other across this square—were aligned in their rebellion against the Habsburgs.

Complete your 360 and face the Parliament again. Every so often, costumed soldiers ap-pear on the front steps for a brief **"changing of the guard"** cer-emony set to recorded music... another patriotic custom, com-pliments of Fidesz.

Now walk toward the far-left side of the Parliament (toward the river). Just before reach-ing the corner of the building, find the underground memorial marked *1956* (free, daily 10:00-18:00). Head down the stairs to find a poignant memorial to the **1956 Uprising** that began on this very square. Follow the red line on the floor—first right, and then left. You'll see photos of the events, good English descriptions, and video interviews of eyewitnesses to the massacre on this square on October 25, 1956 (as well as other government mass shootings around Hungary that fall). At the end of the hall is a memorial tomb to those killed by Hungarian secret police, and the symbol of the uprising: a tattered Hungarian flag with a hole cut out of the center.

• *Now we'll head to a nice riverfront viewpoint—and, of course, more monuments. Circle around the left side of the giant Parliament building, passing another statue on a pillar (Gyula Andrássy, described in the sidebar on page 134). Belly up to the banister overlooking a spectacular...*

View of Buda

Slowly scan the skyline to get oriented to the older, hillier half of Buda-Pest. Far to the left, Gellért Hill is topped by the Soviet-era Liberation Monument. Castle Hill is dominated by the sprawling Royal Palace (with its green dome). Across the river from you, the pointy hilltop spires mark the Matthias Church and the fanciful Fisherman's Bastion; below that is the riverbank neighborhood called Víziváros. Just to the right, the two onion-domed churches bookend Batthyány tér, a local transportation hub. And far to the right, in the middle of the Danube, sits the tree-filled city park of Margaret Island, connected to both Pest and Buda by Margaret Bridge.

From this vantage point, you can gain a little insight into the turbulent political times in Hungary. As prime minister, Viktor Orbán has long had an office filling an entire floor at this end of the massive Parliament building. But in 2019, he plans to move from the traditional spot symbolizing representative democracy to a more royal setting: at the top of the castle, across the river in Buda (it's the big white structure on the horizon, just to the right of the Royal Palace). This doesn't sit well among democracy-loving Hungarians, who view this as their leader literally putting himself above his subjects.

• *Now walk along the banister to the left until you come upon a statue of a young man, lost deep in thought, gazing into the Danube.*

Attila József (1905-1937)

This beloved modern poet lived a tumultuous, productive, and short life before he killed himself by jumping in front of a train at age 32. József's poems of life, love, and death—mostly written in the 1920s and 1930s—are considered the high point of Hungarian literature. His birthday (April 11) is celebrated as National Hungarian Poetry Day.

Here József reenacts a

City of Monuments

There's a reason why Budapest is so monument-crazy. In 1897, German emperor Wilhelm II came to visit his ally and rival, Habsburg emperor Franz Josef, here in Budapest. Wilhelm commented on how few monuments graced the city streets, prompting a jealous Franz Josef to bankroll the immediate creation of 10 new statues around town. The Budapesters' enjoyment of a good monument continues today. Here are some noteworthy ones you'll find scattered around the city:

Attila József: The statue of this brooding, tragic young poet gazes into the Danube from the riverbank by the Parliament (see page 99).

Imre Nagy: The anticommunist leader's statue was removed from the Parliament area in 2018, but may be relocated to Jászai Mari tér near Margaret Bridge (see page 102).

Empty Shoes: Lining the Danube riverbank between the Parliament and the Chain Bridge, this poignant memorial honors the Jews who stood there before being executed by the Nazis (see page 101).

Anonymous: The first scribe to chronicle the history of the Hungarian people strikes a mysterious pose in City Park's Vajdahunyad Castle (see page 170).

George Washington: America's first president is just hanging out, minding his own business, deep in City Park near Vajdahunyad Castle (see page 169).

1956: This gigantic rusted-metal hull in City Park honors the way Hungarians came together to attempt to throw off Soviet rule (see page 96).

Heroes' Square: The vast square showcases 21 Hungarian leaders (and one angel) standing sternly as a Who's Who of Hungarian history (see page 158).

Memento Park: This park's collection of surviving communist-era statues and monuments evokes the Red old days (see page 207).

Ronald Reagan and the **Monument to the Hungarian Victims of the Nazis:** These are two highly controversial recent additions to Szabadság tér by the nationalistic Fidesz government (see page 106).

Peter Falk and His Dog: You'll find this statue at the far end of the street called Falk Miksa utca (running north from Parliament)—named for a relative of the *Columbo* actor.

LEOPOLD TOWN WALK

scene from one of his best poems, "At the Danube." It's a hot day—his jacket lies in a heap next to him, his shirtsleeves are rolled up, and he cradles his hat loosely in his left hand. "As I sat on the bank of the Danube, I watched a watermelon float by," he begins. "As if flowing out of my heart, murky, wise, and great was the Danube." In the poem, József uses the Danube as a metaphor for life—for the way it has interconnected cities and also times—as he reflects that his ancestors likely pondered the Danube from this same spot. Looking into his profound eyes, you sense the depth of this artist's tortured inner life.

• *Stand along the railing in front of József, just above the busy road. If you visually trace the Pest riverbank to the left about 100 yards, just before the tree-filled, riverfront park, you can barely see several low-profile dots lining the embankment. This is a...*

Holocaust Monument

Consisting of 50 pairs of bronze shoes, this monument commemo-rates the Jews who were killed when the Nazis' puppet govern-

ment, the Arrow Cross, came to power in Hungary in 1944. While many Jews were sent to concentration camps, the Arrow Cross massacred some of them right here, shooting them and letting their bodies fall into the Danube.

• *If you'd like a closer look at the shoes, use the crosswalk (50 yards to your right) to cross the busy embankment road and follow the water-line. I'll wait right here.*

When you're ready to move on, turn your back to the Danube and walk directly inland, following the tram tracks past an entrance to the Metró. From the back corner of Kossuth tér, veer right, to a little tree-filled park...

Vértanúk Tere and the Missing Imre Nagy Monument

This small square was once the site of a stirring monument to the 1956 hero Imre Nagy, who stood on a bridge facing the Parliament (see photo). Hungarians loved the symbolism: Nagy was literally keeping a watchful eye on the govern-ment. Unfortunately, late one night a few days after Christmas of 2018, Fidesz authorities removed the statue with little warning and no fanfare. While Nagy has

Imre Nagy (1896-1958)

The Hungarian politician Imre Nagy (IHM-reh nodge), now thought of as an anticommunist hero, was actually a lifelong communist. In the 1930s, he allegedly worked for the Soviet secret police. In the late 1940s, he quickly moved up the hierarchy of Hungary's communist government, becoming prime minister during a period of reform in 1953. But when his proposed changes alarmed Moscow, Nagy was quickly demoted.

When the 1956 Uprising broke out, Nagy was drafted (reluctantly, some say) to become the head of the movement to soften the severity of the communist regime. Because he was an insider, it briefly seemed that Nagy might hold the key to finding a middle path between the suffocating totalitarian model of Moscow and the freedom of the West. Some suspect that Nagy himself didn't fully grasp the dramatic sea change represented by the uprising. When he appeared at the Parliament building on the night of October 23 to speak to the reform-craving crowds for the first time, he began by addressing his compatriots—as communist politicians always did—with, "Dear comrades..." When the audience booed, he amended it: "Dear friends..." The crowd went wild.

But the optimism was short-lived. The Soviets violently put down the uprising, arrested and sham-tried Nagy, executed him, and buried him disgracefully, face-down in an unmarked grave. The regime forced Hungary to forget about Nagy.

Later, when communism was in its death throes in 1989, the Hungarian people rediscovered Nagy as a hero. His body was located, exhumed, and given a ceremonial funeral at Heroes' Square. (It was also something of a coming-out party for Viktor Orbán—today the prime minister—who, as a twentysomething rebel, delivered an impassioned speech at the ceremony.) This event is considered a pivotal benchmark in that year of tremendous change. By the year's end, the Berlin Wall would fall, and the Czechs and Slovaks would stage their Velvet Revolution. But Nagy's reburial was the first in that series of toppling dominoes.

The next chapter in Nagy's legacy has been written by Fidesz, who have recently reversed the rehabilitation of Nagy's image. Because Nagy's ties to communism place him firmly on the left, Fidesz views him as an ideological enemy. (Critics note the hypocrisy of Orbán, who made his name lauding Nagy, now sweeping him into the dustbin of history.) The 2018 removal of the Nagy statue facing the Parliament is just the latest in a long, sad history of this great reformer being exploited as a political pawn. Hungarian patriots wonder: Will Nagy ever be allowed to rest?

long been lionized as a Hungarian patriot, Viktor Orbán and Fidesz grew uncomfortable about the role he played within the communist system (see the sidebar). The removal of the statue is seen by historians as Fidesz taking yet one more step away from grappling with a nuanced, complicated past in a meaningful way, and instead marching in lockstep toward a whitewashed, authoritarian future. You may see a different statue in this space instead: Fidesz plans to reinstate a dull (and less open-to-interpretation) monument that previously stood on Vértanúk tere, honoring the "victims of communism" from 1918 to 1919. (If you'd like to pay your respects to Nagy, his statue may eventually be reinstated on Jászai Mari tér, near Margaret Bridge.)

• *Go up the short, diagonal street beyond Vértanúk tere, called Vécsey utca. After just one block, you emerge into...*

Szabadság Tér (Liberty Square)

"Liberty Square"—one of Budapest's most inviting public spaces—was so named when a Habsburg barracks here was torn down after the Hungarians gained some autonomy in the late 19th century.

• *The first person you'll see as you enter the square, striding confidently away from the Parliament, is an actor-turned-politician you may recognize...*

Ronald Reagan is respected in Hungary for his role as a Cold Warrior. But don't take this monument as a sign that he's universally adored by Hungarians. In truth, this statue, the result of a political stunt, was erected in 2011 to deflect attention from a brewing scandal: When Fidesz took power in 2010, they quickly began rolling back previous democratic reforms and imposing alarming constraints on the media. Many international observers—including the US government—spoke out against what they considered an infringement on freedom of the press. In an effort to appease American concerns, Prime Minister Viktor Orbán erected this statue on one of his capital's main squares—and then, perhaps not quite grasping the subtleties of American politics, invited Secretary of State Hillary Clinton to the unveiling. While Reagan played a role in ending the Cold War, many Hungarian patriots are offended that this monument overshadows the contributions and sacrifices of so many other important figures, including Imre Nagy. Either way, it's fun to watch the steady stream of passersby (both Hungarians and tourists) do a double-take, chuckle, then snap a photo with The Gipper.

• Walk around the stout obelisk to the center of the square. Stand facing the obelisk.

This is the **Soviet War Memorial,** commemorating "Liberation Day": April 4, 1945, when the Soviets officially forced the Nazis out of Hungary. As a very rare reminder of the Soviet days—you almost never see hammers-and-sickles in the streets of Hungary anymore—it has often been defaced. Some Budapesters feel that the memorial should be removed. Ponder for a moment this complex issue: Soviet troops did liberate Hungary from the Nazis. Does their leaders' later oppression of the Hungarians make these soldiers' sacrifice less worthy of being honored? One way or another, there's a certain irony now that Ronald Reagan stands just a few yards from the Soviet War Memorial—perhaps a fittingly schizophrenic metaphor for this city's complex history and allegiances.

Ringing the top of Szabadság tér (behind the memorial) are **four ornate apartment buildings,** typical of high-class townhouses from Budapest's Golden Age in the late 1800s. While each one is strikingly different from the next, they are all typical of Historicism—the mix-and-match aesthetic that was popular at the time. Like residential buildings throughout Pest, the ground floor has particularly high ceilings. But the second and third floors were more desirable—up away from the rabble of street

life, but with relatively few stairs (in a time before elevators were common). Notice that in each of these buildings, those are the only floors with balconies.

Here's an optional detour for architecture buffs: If you go up the middle street between these buildings (Honvéd utca, straight ahead from the middle of Szabadság tér), a few doors down on the right you'll find one of Budapest's finest Art Nouveau buildings, **Bedő-Ház.** The curvy green facade is a textbook example of the Hungarian Secession style (1903). Inside is a little café surrounded by Art Nouveau bric-a-brac and the small House of Secession museum (2,000 Ft, Mon-Sat 10:00-17:00, closed Sun, Honvéd utca 3, tel. 1/269-4622). The exhibit fills three floors like a musty home-decor and furniture store, circa 1900, with almost no explanation—just a jumbled collection of elegantly delicate Art Nouveau furniture, dishes, and other decorative arts.

• *Back in the middle of Szabadság tér, turn with your back to the Soviet memorial, and look down to the far end of the square.*

The genteel open-air **café** in the middle of the park is an inviting place for a coffee break.

On the left side of the square, behind car-bomb barriers and a heavily fortified fence, the yellow corner building is the **US embassy.** This is where Cardinal József Mindszenty holed up for 15 years during the Cold War to evade arrest by the communist authorities (see page 320). A hundred yards down the left side of the square (and worth a detour for military buffs) stands a statue of **Harry Hill Bandholtz,** a US officer from World War I who prevented treasured Hungarian art from being taken by Romania. This statue stood inside the US embassy for 40 chilly years (1949-1989), but now it's back out in the open.

• *We're headed down Perczel Mór utca, the street next to the US embassy—but you'll have to detour a bit to the left (and tiptoe around some barricades) to get there. Follow the oversized fortifications one block along Perczel Mór utca, and you'll run right into...*

Hold Utca

Look for the big *Belvárosi Piac* sign over the door, and step inside. **Hold Street Market Hall** was built around the same time as the Great Market Hall, but on a smaller scale (Mon 6:30-17:00, Tue-Fri until 18:00, Sat until 16:00, closed Sun). Until recently, it was just another neighborhood market hall. But now it has been converted into a foodie paradise—with a world of enticing, creative food stalls upstairs. Or you can gather a picnic here to eat at nearby Szabadság tér. If you're ready for lunch, this is a great choice. (For details, see the Eating in Budapest chapter.)

Exit the market building where you entered and turn left onto Hold utca. As you walk down this street, keep your eyes high on the green-and-yellow roofline of the building on the right. This **Postal Savings Bank,** designed by Ödön Lechner in the late 19th century, combines traditional folk motifs with cutting-edge Art Nouveau in an attempt to forge a new, distinctly

LEOPOLD TOWN WALK

Hungarian national style. A key element of this emerging style was the use of colorful mosaic tiles to decorate the roof (see page 374). The beehives along the rooftop are an appropriate symbol for a bank—where people store money as bees store honey. When asked why he lavished such attention on the rooftop, which few people can see, Lechner said, "To please the birds." The next building is the grand **National Bank of Hungary,** with entertaining reliefs tracing the history of money.

• *Return to Liberty Square by taking the street between these two banks, Kiss Ernő utca. Again you'll be following an almost comically heavy-duty fence for the US embassy. Emerging back into the square, turn left, then angle past the playground to reach yet another controversial monument. It's at the end of the square, near the fountain.*

Monument to the Hungarian Victims of the Nazis

This recent addition to the square—another heavy-handed Fidesz production—commemorates the German invasion of Hungary on March 19, 1944. Standing in the middle of a broken colonnade, an immaculate angel holds an orb with a double cross (part of the crown jewels and a symbol of Hungarian sovereignty). Overhead, a mechanical-looking black eagle (symbolizing Germany) screeches in, its talons poised to strike. In case the symbolism isn't clear enough, the eagle wears a hit-you-over-the-head armband that says *1944*.

Although offensive enough for its lack of artistry, this monument was instantly controversial for the way it whitewashes Hungarian history. Viewing this, you might imagine that Hungary was a peaceful land that was un-wittingly caught up in the Nazi war machine. In fact, the Hungarian government was an ally of Nazi Germany for more than three years before this invasion. While many Hungarians today emphasize that Jews here were not executed before the Germans arrived, tens of thousands of Jews did die from forced labor or by being exported to Nazi-controlled lands. And there's no question that, after the invasion, many Hungarians enthusiastically collaborated with their new Nazi overlords.

Mindful of the old adage about people who forget their own history, locals have created a **makeshift counter-memorial** to the victims of the World War II-era Hungarians (not just Germans) in front of this official monument. (If this informal memorial—a gathering of faded photographs and handwritten signs—is nowhere to be seen, it's a safe guess that Fidesz is cracking down on free speech.)

On a lighter note, the **fountain** that faces the monument is particularly entertaining. Sensors can tell when you're about to walk through the wall of water...and the curtain of water automatically parts just long enough for you to pass. Go ahead...play Moses.

• *Turning your back to the monument, go left, then take the first right (before the big, blocky bank building), and head down Sas utca for two blocks. Sas utca and neighboring streets are home to several good and trendy restaurants (including the recommended Café Kör and Borkonyha). Consider window shopping here and reserving a place for dinner tonight.*

You'll emerge into a broad plaza in front of Budapest's biggest Catholic church...

St. István's Basilica (Szent István Bazilika)

Though it looks grand and old, this church only dates back about 130 years—like so many Budapest landmarks, it was built around the millennial celebrations of 1896. Designed by three architects over more than 50 years, St. István's is particularly eclectic. Each architect had a favorite style: Neoclassical, Neo-Renaissance, and Neo-Baroque. Construction was delayed for a while when the giant dome collapsed midway through.

Head up the grand stairs to get oriented. To the right is the ticket desk, the elevator to the treasury, and the entrance to the church. To the left is the elevator to the panoramic tower.

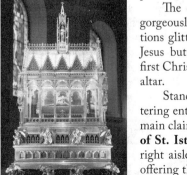

The church's **interior** is dimly lit but gorgeously restored; all the gilded decorations glitter in the low light. You'll see not Jesus but St. István (Stephen), Hungary's first Christian king, glowing above the high altar.

Stand in the back and enjoy the glittering entirety of the interior. The church's main claim to fame is the **"holy right hand" of St. István,** which you'll find along the right aisle, in front of a painting of István offering the Hungarian crown to the Virgin Mary. The sacred fist—a somewhat grotesque, 1,000-year-old withered stump—is inside a jeweled box. Pop in a 200-Ft coin for two minutes of light.

On your way out, in the exit foyer (back-left corner), you'll find a small exhibit about the building's history.

There are two other attractions at St. István's, each covered by a separate ticket. The **panoramic tower** offers views over Budapest's rooftops that are pretty distant (and disappointing without a good zoom lens), but it does provide a good sense of the sprawl of the city. You have various options: You can walk up the entire way (302 steps); or you can take an elevator to midlevel (with WCs), where you can follow signs to another elevator (plus 42 steps) or climb 137 steps to the top. To the right as you face the church, an elevator zips up to the skippable church **treasury,** a small collection of vestments, ecclesiastical gear, a model of the building, exhibits about its construction, a porcelain replica of the Hungarian crown, and a fine Murillo *Holy Family*—all well described in English.

The church also hosts regular **organ concerts** (advertised near the entry).

• *The square in front of the church is called...*

St. István Tér

This grand plaza is a classic example of how Budapest has spiffed up its once-gloomy downtown. A decade ago, this space was an ugly parking lot. Then, a few years back, a German engineering firm created an experimental, cutting-edge parking garage beneath this square. Instead of finding a parking space, drivers simply leave their car on a pallet and walk up to the square—while the car-loaded pallet is moved with a series of giant elevators and conveyor belts to a parking space. This futuristic system is all going on underfoot. Meanwhile, over the past few years, the streets around this once-sleepy plaza have been transformed into one of Budapest's trendiest nightlife zones, with lots of bars, restaurants, and cafés catering to local yuppies.

• *From here, you have two options. If you'd like to skip ahead to my* ***Andrássy Út Walk****, you're very close: Walk around the right side of the basilica, turn right on busy Bajcsy-Zsilinszky út, and you're one block from the start of Andrássy út (across the street, on your left).*

Or you can complete this walk to Vörösmarty tér, where you can begin the ***Pest Town Center Walk****. For this option, walk straight ahead from St. István's main staircase down...*

Zrínyi Utca

Traffic-free Zrínyi utca is a fine people zone and a handy way to connect St. István's to the river.

At the start of Zrínyi utca, on the right-hand corner (in front of the pizza shop), look for the **red fire hydrant** with a blue attachment on one end. This contraption—called *ivócsap* ("drinking tap"), the winner of a citywide design competition—allows passersby to use the hydrant as a drinking fountain. It's a typically clever Hungarian solution.

At the next corner (on the right), look for the bushy-mustachioed **police officer** statue, evoking the grand old days of the Austro-Hungarian Empire (just before World War I).

There's no particular story for this character: He's just for fun. In keeping with their rich tradition of monuments, the local district sponsors a contest each year to come up with the best statues. If you're ready for a snack, turn right and head a half-block up the street to find a place that makes and sells strudel *(rétes)*.

Farther down this block, on the right-hand corner, is the former headquarters of **Central European University**—yet another casualty of the Fidesz regime. Offering graduate study for Americans and students from all over Central and Eastern Europe, CEU is predominantly funded by George Soros, a Hungarian who escaped communism by emigrating to the US, then became a billionaire through shrewd investments. Today Soros' politics (and his generous support of left-wing causes) make him a favorite target of authoritarians like Viktor Orbán and Fidesz. In late 2018, CEU relocated to Vienna, after the Fidesz-controlled government refused to allow it to operate legally within Hungary. International observers consider this the first instance of a major university being forced out of a European Union country.

Continue down Zrínyi utca. After crossing Nádor utca, on the left you'll see **Duna Palota** ("Danube Palace")—a former casino, and today a venue and ticket office for Hungária Koncert's popular tourist shows. If you're up for a crowd-pleasing show of either classical or folk music, drop in here to check your options (see the Entertainment in Budapest chapter).

Zrínyi utca dead-ends at the big traffic circle called **Széchenyi István tér.** For decades, this was called Roosevelt tér, in honor of the American statesman who helped defeat the Nazis in World War II. But in 2010, Fidesz went on a (say it with me, now: *controversial*) renaming binge around the city and decided to christen this square for the Hungarian statesman whose statue stands on the right: István Széchenyi, the early-19th-century nobleman who, among other deeds, built the Chain Bridge and founded the Hungarian Academy of Sciences (both of which face this square). On the left is the statesman Ferenc Deák, who fought for Hungarian autonomy using peaceful means.

• *Turn left and walk a half-block to the entrance (on the left) of the...*

Gresham Palace

The Gresham Palace was Budapest's first building in the popular Historicist style—but it also incorporates elements of Art Nouveau. Budapest boomed at a time when architectural eclecticism—mashing together bits and pieces of different styles—was in vogue. But because much of the city's construction was compressed into a short window of time, even these disparate styles enjoy an unusual harmony.

Damaged in World War II, the building was an eyesore for decades. (Reportedly, an aging local actress refused to move out, so developers had to wait for her to, ahem, vacate before they could reclaim the building.) In 1999, the Gresham Palace was meticulously restored to its former glory and converted to a luxury hotel. Even if you can't afford to stay here (see the Sleeping in Budapest chapter), saunter into the lobby and absorb the gorgeous details. For example, not only did they have to re-create the unique decorative tiles, they also had to rebuild the original machines that made the tiles.

• *Be sure to get a good look at the Gresham Palace's fine facade—consider circling around the park and looking back. This also puts you right next to the bridge that grandly spans the Danube from here.*

Chain Bridge (Széchenyi Lánchíd)

One of the world's great bridges connects Pest's Széchenyi tér and Buda's Clark Ádám tér. This historic, iconic bridge, guarded by lions (symbolizing power), is Budapest's most enjoyable and convenient bridge to cross on foot.

Until the mid-19th century, only pontoon barges spanned the Danube between Buda and Pest. In the winter, the pontoons had to be pulled in, leaving locals to rely on ferries (in good weather) or a frozen river. People often walked across the frozen Danube, only to get stuck on the other side during a thaw, with nothing to do but wait for another cold snap.

Count István Széchenyi was stranded for a week trying to get to his father's funeral. After missing it, Széchenyi commissioned Budapest's first permanent bridge—which was also a major symbolic step toward another of Széchenyi's pet causes, the unification of Buda and Pest. The Chain Bridge was built by Scotsman Adam Clark between 1842 and 1849, and it immediately became an important symbol of Budapest. The biggest and longest span of its day, the Chain Bridge was a model for famous suspension bridges that followed, including the Golden Gate in San Francisco and the Verrazano-Narrows in New York.

Széchenyi—a man of the Enlightenment—charged both commoners and nobles a toll for crossing his bridge, making it an emblem of equality in those tense times. Like all of the city's bridges, the Chain Bridge was destroyed by the Nazis at the end of World War II, but it was quickly rebuilt.

• *Our walk is over. From Széchenyi tér, you can catch bus #16 from in front of the Hungarian Academy of Sciences (at the right end of the square) to Castle Hill, or simply walk across the Chain Bridge for great views.*

If you'd like to wind up in the heart of Pest, Vörösmarty tér (and the start of my **Pest Town Center Walk**—*see next chapter) is just two long blocks away: Turn left out of the Gresham Palace, and walk straight on Dorottya utca.*

PEST TOWN CENTER WALK

Belváros, from Vörösmarty Tér to the Great Market Hall

Pest's Belváros ("Inner Town") is its gritty urban heart—simultaneously its most beautiful and ugliest district. You'll see fancy facades, some of Pest's best views from the Danube embankment, richly decorated old coffeehouses that offer a whiff of the city's Golden Age, parks tucked like inviting oases between densely populated streets, recently pedestrianized streets that ooze urbane sophistication, and a cavernous, colorful market hall filled with Hungarian goodies. But you'll also experience crowds, grime, and pungent smells like nowhere else in Budapest. Atmospherically shot through with the crumbling elegance of former greatness, Budapest is a place where creaky old buildings and sleek modern ones feel equally at home. Remember: This is a city in transition. Enjoy the rough edges while you can. They're being sanded off at a remarkable pace—and soon, tourists like you will be nostalgic for the "authentic" old days.

Even if this whole walk doesn't appeal to you, don't miss the spectacular Great Market Hall, described at the end of this walk.

Orientation

Length of This Walk: Allow 1.5 hours.

Getting There: Take the M1/yellow Metró line to the Vörösmarty tér stop.

Károlyi Park: Free, open daily 8:00-dusk.

Great Market Hall: Free, Mon 6:00-17:00, Tue-Fri until 18:00, Sat until 15:00, closed Sun, Fővám körút 1.

Starring: The urban core of Budapest, a gorgeous riverfront promenade, several of the city's top cafés, and a grand finale at the Great Market Hall.

The Walk Begins

• *Start on the central square of the Town Center, Vörösmarty tér (at the M1 Metró stop of the same name). Face the giant, seated statue in the middle of the square.*

Vörösmarty Tér

As we begin exploring the central part of Pest, consider its humble history. In the mid-1600s, Pest was under Ottoman occupation and nearly deserted. By the 1710s, the Habsburgs had forced out the Ottomans, but this area remained a rough-and-tumble, often-flooded quarter just outside the Pest city walls. Peasants came here to enjoy bearbaiting (watching brutal, staged fights between bloodhounds and bears). The rebuilding of Pest was gradual; most of the buildings you'll see on this walk are no older than 200 years. That's why Budapest doesn't really have a charming "old town" center, like Prague or Warsaw.

Today this square—a hub of activity in the Town Center—is named for the 19th-century Romantic poet **Mihály Vörösmarty**

(1800-1855), whose statue dominates the little park in the square's center. Writing during the time of reforms in the early 19th century, Vörösmarty was a Romantic whose poetry still stirs the souls of patriotic Hungarians—he's like Shelley and Keats rolled into one. One of his most famous works is a patriotic song whose popularity rivals the national anthem's: "Be faithful to your country, all Hungarians." At Vörösmarty's feet, as if hearing those inspiring words chiseled into the stone, figures representing the Hungarian people rise up together. During Vörösmarty's age, the peasant Magyar tongue was, for the very first time, considered worthy of literature. The people began to think of themselves not merely as "subjects of the Habsburg Empire"...but as Hungarians.

• *Survey the square with a spin tour. First, facing the statue of Vörösmarty, turn 90 degrees to the left.*

At the north end of the square is the landmark **Gerbeaud café** and pastry shop. Between the world wars, the well-to-do ladies

To Parliament

ACADEMY OF SCI.

LEOPOLD

FORMER CENTRAL EUROPEAN UNIVERSITY

ST. ISTVÁN'S BASILICA

RÉVAY

ÚT

To Heroes' Square & City Park

ANDRÁSSY

SZÉKELY

KÁLDY

GYULA

VIGYÁZÓ FER.

NÁDOR

ZRINYI

OKTÓBER 6

SAS

ZSILINSZKY

BAJCSY-ZSILINSZKY

Széchenyi István tér

DUNA PALOTA

TOWN

Bajcsy-Zsilinszky út

GOZSDU UDVAR

HOLLÓ

GRESHAM PALACE

CHAIN BRIDGE

MÉRLEG

JÓZSEF ATTILA ÚT

RUMBACH STREET SYNAGOGUE

To Buda & Castle Hill

Eötvös tér

BELGRÁD

DOROTTYA

APÁCZAI

WEKERLE U.

POST

József Nádor tér

BÉCSI

Erzsébet tér

HARMINCAD

AKVÁRIUM KLUB

ANKERHÁZ

Deák Ferenc tér

Deák tér

KÁROLY

KÖRÚT

ABBÓTH

RUMBACH SEBESTYÉN

Tram #2

GERBEAUD CAFÉ

WALK BEGINS

Vörösmarty tér

Vörösmarty tér

PESTI VIGADÓ

Vigadó tér

MAHART BOAT DOCK

LEGENDA BOAT DOCK

FEHÉRHAJÓ

BÁRCZY ISTVÁN

VÁROSHÁZ

CITY HALL

Kamermayer tér

FORMER PILVAX CAFÉ

COUNTY HALL

VÁRMEGYE

SEMMELWEIS

KOSSUTH LAJOS UTCA

SZÉP

HISTORIC MCDONALD'S

JUGENDSTIL BLDG. (#18)

SORRARAS HISTORICISM BLDG. (#15)

TOWN

Ferenciek tere

FRANCISCAN CHURCH

REÁLTANODA

FERENCZY

Károlyi Park

Danube

Petőfi tér

Petőfi tér

PIARISTA UTCA

KIGYÓ

PIARISTA KÖZ

KLOTILD PALACES

KÁROLYI MIHÁLY

Egyetem tér

Tram #19 & #41

SZABAD SAJTÓ ÚT

Március 15 tér

CENTER

Döbrentei tér

ELISABETH BRIDGE

IRÁNYI

VÁCI UTCA

VERES PÁLNÉ

PAPNÖV.

ELTE LAW FACULTY

KIR. PÁL

Tram #2

BELGRÁD RAKPART

NYÁRI

SŐRHÁZ

SERBIAN CHURCH

SZERB

F. GYÖRGY

SZT. GELLÉRT RAKPART

River

MOLNÁR

HAVAS

SZARKA BÁGYA

POST

FŐVÁM TÉR

VÁMHÁZ

KÖRÚT

PIPA

Gellért Hill

CITADELLA

CITADELLA

SÉTÁNY

BUDA

WALK ENDS

GREAT MARKET HALL

UNIV. OF ECONOMICS

SÓHÁZ

CAVE CHURCH

VEREJTÉK

LIBERTY BRIDGE

N

200 Meters

200 Yards

KELENHEGYI

KEMENES

GELLÉRT HOTEL & BATHS

Szent Gellért tér

Szent Gellért tér

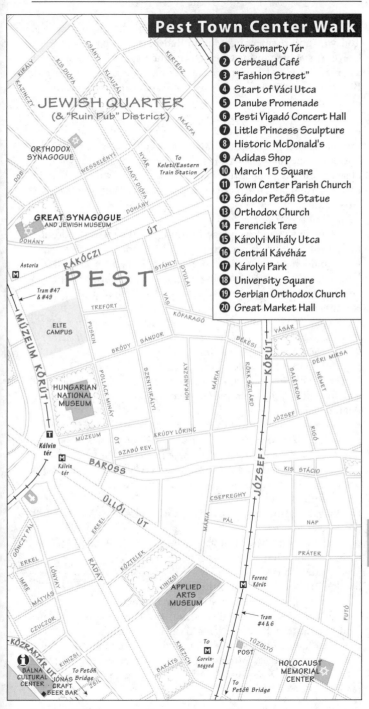

Pest Town Center Walk

1. Vörösmarty Tér
2. Gerbeaud Café
3. "Fashion Street"
4. Start of Váci Utca
5. Danube Promenade
6. Pesti Vigadó Concert Hall
7. Little Princess Sculpture
8. Historic McDonald's
9. Adidas Shop
10. March 15 Square
11. Town Center Parish Church
12. Sándor Petőfi Statue
13. Orthodox Church
14. Ferenciek Tere
15. Károlyi Mihály Utca
16. Centrál Kávéház
17. Károlyi Park
18. University Square
19. Serbian Orthodox Church
20. Great Market Hall

of Budapest would meet here after shopping their way up Váci utca. Today it's still *the* meeting point in Budapest...for tourists, at least. Consider stepping inside to appreciate the elegant old decor, or for a cup of coffee and a slice of cake (but meals here are overpriced). Better yet, hold off for now—even more appealing cafés await later on in this walk.

The yellow **M1 Metró stop** between Vörösmarty and Gerbeaud is the entrance to the shallow *Földalatti*, or "underground"—the first subway on the Continent (built for the Hungarian millennial celebration in 1896). Today, it still carries passengers to Andrássy út sights, running under that boulevard all the way to City Park (it basically runs beneath the feet of people following my Andrássy Út Walk).

• *Turn another 90 degrees to the left.*

This super-modern **glass building** is the newest addition to Vörösmarty tér. If you think its appearance is jarring, then you should have seen the communist-style eyesore it replaced. Downstairs is upscale shopping; higher up are offices; at the top are luxury apartments; and the vast glass atrium is simply an extravagant waste of space.

• *Turn another 90 degrees to the left, and walk to the beginning of the Váci utca pedestrian street. Look up the street that's to your left (with the yellow, pointy-topped building at the end).*

This traffic-free street (Deák utca)—also known as **"Fashion Street,"** with top-end shops—is the easiest and most pleasant way to walk to Deák tér and, beyond it, through Erzsébet tér to Andrássy út.

• *Extending straight ahead from Vörösmarty tér is a broad, bustling, pedestrianized shopping street. For now, look—but do not walk—down this street; we'll stroll a different stretch of it later on this walk.*

Dating from 1810-1850, **Váci utca** (VAHT-see OOT-zaw) is one of the oldest streets of Pest. *Váci utca* means "street to Vác"—a town 25 miles to the north. This has long been the street where the elite of Pest would go shopping, then strut their stuff for their neighbors on an evening promenade. Today, the tourists do the strutting here—and the

Hungarians go to American-style shopping malls.

This boulevard—Budapest's tourism artery—was a dreamland for Eastern Bloc residents back in the 1980s. It was here that they fantasized about what it might be like to be free, while drooling over Nikes, Adidas, and Big Macs before any of these "Western evils" were introduced elsewhere in the Warsaw Pact region.

Ironically, this street—once prized by Hungarians and other Eastern Europeans because it felt so Western—is what many Western tourists today mistakenly think is the "real Budapest." Visitors mesmerized by this stretch of souvenir stands, tourist-gouging eateries, and upscale boutiques are likely to miss some more interesting and authentic areas just a block or two away.

Don't fall for this trap. You can have a fun and fulfilling trip to this city without ever setting foot on Váci utca. In fact, this walk is designed to give you only the briefest taste of this famous street's tackiness. (If you're dying to saunter down Váci utca, this walk concludes at its far end—it takes about 20 minutes to walk back to its start.) Instead, we'll zigzag through the heart of Pest's Town Center for a look at the *real* "real Budapest."

• *Head for the river: Take the street that runs along the left side of the big glass building at the bottom of Vörösmarty tér. Cross the street and continue all the way to the railing and tram tracks. Swing about 30 yards to the right along the tracks, pausing by the statue of the girl with the dog. You're on the most colorful stretch of the...*

Danube Promenade (Dunakorzó)

Some of the best views in Budapest are from this walkway facing Castle Hill—especially this stretch, between the white Elisabeth Bridge (left) and the iconic Chain Bridge (right). This is a favorite place to promenade *(korzó)*, strolling aimlessly and greeting friends. Imagine the days before World War II, when—instead of midcentury monstrosities Marriott and InterConti-

nental—this strip was lined with elegant grand hotels: Hungaria, Bristol, Carlton. Pause to appreciate how recent EU subsidies have made this fine, people-friendly riverfront possible.

Take in the views of Buda, across the river (left to right): Gellért Hill, topped with its distinctive Liberation Monument; the green-domed Royal Palace, capping Castle Hill; and, farther along the hilltop, the colorful tile roof and spiny spire of the Matthias

Church, surrounded by the cone-shaped decorations of the Fisherman's Bastion.

Behind you (fronting the little park) is a big concert hall, which dominates this part of the promenade. This is the Neo-Romantic-style **Pesti Vigadó**—built in the 1880s and recently restored. Charmingly, the word *vigadó*— used to describe a concert hall— literally means "joyous place." In front, the playful statue of **the girl with her dog** captures the fun-loving spirit along this drag.

At the gap in the railing, notice the platform to catch **tram #2,** which goes frequently in each direction along the promenade—a handy way to connect riverside sights in Pest. It's also incredibly scenic—I consider this Europe's most beautiful tram ride. Take it once between the Great Market Hall (to the left) and the Parliament (to the right) just for fun. (This walk ends a few steps from one of its stops.)

• *About 30 more yards toward the Chain Bridge, find the little statue wearing a jester's hat. She's playing on the railing, with the castle behind her.*

The *Little Princess* is one of Budapest's symbols and a favorite photo-op for tourists. While many of the city's monuments have interesting backstories, more recent statues (like this one) are simply whimsical and fun.

• *Now walk along the promenade to the left (toward the white bridge). Directly in front of the corner Starbucks in the Marriott Hotel, watch for the easy-to-miss stairs leading down under the tram tracks, to a crosswalk that leads safely across the busy road to the riverbank. From the top of these stairs, look along the river.*

Lining the **embankment** are several long boats: Some are excursion boats for sightseeing trips up and down the Danube (especially pleasant at night), while others are overpriced (but scenic) restaurants. Kiosks along here dispense info and sell tickets for the various boat companies—look for Legenda Cruises (their dock is just downstream from here—go down the stairs, cross the road, then walk 100 yards left; for details, see the Orientation to Budapest chapter).

• *For now, continue walking downstream (left) along the promenade, passing in front of the blocky, dirty-white Marriott. When you reach the end of the Marriott complex, at the little parking lot, turn inland (left), cross the street, and walk up the street called Régi Posta utca (next to the colorfully graffitied building). Head for the Golden Arches. You deserve a break today.*

Historic McDonald's

The fancy McDonald's (on the left) was a landmark in Eastern Europe—the first McDonald's behind the Iron Curtain. Budapest has always been a little more rebellious, independent, and cosmopolitan than other Eastern European cities, whose citizens flocked here during the communist era. Váci utca (which we'll see next) was a showcase street during those grim times, making

this a strategic location for Ronald McDonald and Co. Since you had to wait in a long line—stretching around the block—to get a burger, it wasn't "fast food"...but at least it was "West food." Váci utca also had a "dollar store," where you could buy hard-to-find imported and luxury items as long as you had Western currency. During the Cold War, Budapest was sort of the "Sin City" of the Eastern Bloc. (What happened in Budapest, stayed in Budapest. Unless the secret police were watching...which they always were... uh-oh.)

• *After the McDonald's, Régi Posta utca crosses...*

Váci Utca

We'll follow this crowded drag for two blocks to the right. As we stroll, be sure to look up. Along this street and throughout Pest, spectacular facades begin on the second floor, above a plain entryway (in the 1970s, the communist government made ground-floor shop windows uniformly dull). Locals like to say these buildings are "wearing socks." Pan up above the knees to see

some of Pest's best architecture. These were the townhouses of the aristocracy, whose mansions dotted the countryside. You might notice that some of the facades are plain. Many of these used to be more ornate, like their neighbors, but were destroyed by WWII bombs and rebuilt in the stripped-down style of the austere years that followed.

As you head to the right down Váci utca, notice two buildings in particular. The second building on the right, at #15 (marked *Sörforrás*), features beautiful carved wood on the bottom and tile-and-stone decorations on the top. Combining everything that was typically thought of as "beautiful" in the late 19th century, this building exemplifies Historicism. Across the street and down one door (at #18), we see another architect's response to that facade: *Jugendstil* (Vienna's answer to Art Nouveau). Based in a movement called "The Secession" for the way it broke away from the frilly architectural excesses of the age, it proudly wears its more subdued boxy corners and graph-paper-like horizontal stripes. This building almost seems to be having a conversation with the one across the street: "Dude, tone it down. Be cool."

A few doors down (past the modern Mercure Hotel), on the left at #24, is any old **Adidas shop**...except, like the "any old McDonalds" we just saw, this was the *first* Adidas shop behind the Iron Curtain. And, like the McDonald's, back then you'd have to stand in an hours-long line just to get in the door.

Continue strolling down the street. Here and elsewhere along Váci utca, you'll see restaurants touting Hungarian fare. Avoid these places. Any restaurant along this street is guaranteed to be at least half as good and twice as expensive as other eateries nearby. (For better options—some just a few steps from Váci utca—see the Eating in Budapest chapter.)

• *After about two blocks, stop and look up to appreciate the facades. Then turn right down the street called Piarista utca. You'll emerge into a charming square called...*

March 15 Square (Március 15. Tér)

This fine riverfront square—facing the graceful modern lines of the Elisabeth Bridge and Gellért Hill—sits upon some serious his-tory. This was the site of **Con-tra-Aquincum,** a third-century fortress built across *(contra)* the Danube from Aquincum, the main Roman settlement just a few miles up the river, in today's Óbuda (described in the Sights in Budapest chapter). Contra-Aquincum fortified the narrow-est Danube crossing, where the

river is constricted at the base of Gellért Hill. Like so many others who have viewed Budapest as a boundary between West and East, the Romans considered the Danube the natural border of their empire—and fortresses like Contra-Aquincum helped keep the barbarian hordes at bay. For decades, the partially excavated ruins of Contra-Aquincum made this square an ugly jumble of fences and scaffolding, and it gained a reputation as one of downtown Budapest's most dangerous corners. But now it has been gorgeously restored as a fine park, and those ancient ruins are neatly displayed under glass.

The inland part of the square is enlivened by entertaining, kid-friendly fountains and a sprawling outdoor café, called, simply, **Kiosk.** While this walk passes a few genteel, old-fashioned coffeehouses, these days young urbanites flock to places like this instead. Just order at the bar, then take the scenic seat of your choice.

The twin spires belong to the **Town Center Parish Church** (Belvárosi Plébániatemplom). The oldest building in Pest, this church was founded in 1046 and has lived through many iterations: Romanesque basilica, Gothic hall church, Ottoman mosque. Today, the Gothic foundations are topped with frilly, Baroque, onion-domed steeples. When Franz Josef and Sisi, the Habsburg monarchs, were crowned as the Hungarian king and queen in 1867, they did it right here on this square (for more on the couple and their coronation, see page 292).

Closer to the river (to the right as you face it), you can see a jazzy statue of Hungary's national poet, **Sándor Petőfi**—sort of the Hungarian Lord Byron. On the morning of March 15, 1848, a collection of local intellectuals and artists—who came to be known as the "Pest Youth"—gathered at the Pilvax Café (just three blocks up from here, at the corner of Pilvax köz and Városház utca; it's now an Irish pub) to listen to their friend Sándor Petőfi read a new poem. Petőfi's call to arms so inspired the group that they decided to revolt against their Habsburg oppressors...right away. Later that day, Petőfi read his poem again on the steps of the National Museum, rebels broke a beloved patriot out of jail at the castle, the group printed up their list of 12 demands...and the 1848 Revolution had begun. The revolution was ultimately crushed—and Petőfi was killed fighting at the front line—but Hungarians still feel pride about their valiant defeat. (While powerful nations have the luxury of celebrating great military victories, underdogs like the Hungarians cherish their Alamos.) March 15—the namesake of this square—remains one of Hungary's national holidays.

The **Orthodox Church** facing Petőfi has noticeably mismatched steeples. The right one was blown off during World War II and never replaced.

• *Head to the right of the building at the top of March 15 Square, finding the grandly arcaded passage called Piarista köz, between the café and the church. You'll pass a shop selling* kürtőskalács, *Hungary's heavenly chimney-cake rotisserie pastries.*

Continue across Váci utca, and proceed straight ahead one more block up Kígyó utca. Emerging into a busy urban zone, survey...

Ferenciek Tere

"Franciscan Square"—so named for the church across the highway—is the perfect place to view Pest as a city in transition: a mix

of old, sooty, "diamond in the rough" architecture and gleaming, newly scrubbed facades. The boulevard was developed (like so much of Budapest) in the late 19th century, to connect the Keleti/Eastern train station (to the left, not visible from here) with the Elisabeth Bridge (to the right). Looking toward the Elisabeth Bridge, you'll see that the busy highway is flanked by twin apartment blocks called the Klotild Palaces. Recently both of these have been purchased by investors and turned into new hotels. On your left, a stunning shopping passage called Párisi udvar may be nearing completion. It sat neglected, in all its faded glory, for decades until it was renovated into a high-end hotel. If it's open, peek inside.

Imagine this area before 20th-century construction routed a major thoroughfare through it, when people could stroll freely amid these elaborate facades. Some city planners have proposed covering the highway to re-create those romantic glory days...but for now, breathe in the real Budapest.

• *Walk along the busy road until you reach the pedestrian underpass that's across from the church. Take it under the boulevard (or use the crosswalk over the street), and you'll emerge at the start of...*

Károlyi Mihály Utca

As you walk up the street, appreciate the pretty corner spires on the buildings. The yellow one marks the university library.

At the end of the block, cross Irányi utca, and you'll be face-to-face with the entrance to the recommended **Centrál Kávéház** (on the right-hand corner)—another of Budapest's classic cafés (see the Eating in Budapest chapter). Step inside to be transported to another time. If you haven't taken a coffee break yet, now's a good time.

Continue straight along Károlyi Mihály utca. Just past Centrál Kávéház, on the left (at #12), is the recently restored Neo-Renaissance **Ybl Palace,** designed by and named for the prominent architect Miklós Ybl (who also did the Opera House). You can usually pop inside the palace (now just filled with offices) and step into its fine inner courtyard to see the impressive remodel job.

• *Continue along Károlyi Mihály utca to the end of the block, then take the first left up Ferenczy István utca. After the long building, dip through the green fence on the right, into...*

Károlyi Park (Károlyi Kert)

This delightful, flower-filled oasis offers the perfect break from loud and gritty urban Pest. Once the private garden of the aristo-

cratic Károlyi family from eastern Hungary (whose mansion it's situated behind), it's now a public park beloved by people who live, work, and go to school in this neighborhood. The park is filled with tulips in the spring, potted palm trees in the summer, and vivid colors in the fall. On a sunny summer day, locals

escape here to read books, gossip with neighbors, or simply lie in the sun. Many schools are nearby. Teenagers hang out here after school, while younger kids enjoy the playground. (If you need a potty break after all that coffee, a WC is in the green pavilion in the far-right corner.)

• *Exit the park straight ahead from where you entered, and turn right down Henszlmann utca. At the end of the street, you'll come to a church with onion-dome steeples. The big plaza in front of it is...*

University Square (Egyetem Tér)

This square is one of Budapest's most recent to enjoy a makeover. An initiative called the "Heart of the City" is directing EU and

Hungarian funds at renovating city-center streets and squares like this one (as well as Károlyi Mihály utca, which we were walking down earlier). Traffic is carefully regulated. Notice the automatic bollard that goes up and down to let in

approved vehicles: buses, taxis, and local residents only. The modern lampposts and barriers are an interesting (and controversial) choice in this nostalgic city, where the priority is usually on re-creating the city exactly as it was a century ago. The idea in this case is to keep the original buildings but surround them with a modern streetscape.

The colonnaded building on the left is the law school for ELTE University (Hungary's biggest, with 30,000 students and colleges all over the city). As in much of the former Soviet Bloc—and western Europe, for that matter—the university system in Hungary is still heavily subsidized by the government. It's affordable to study here...*if* you can get in (competition is fierce).

• *Facing the university building, turn left, then take the first right down Szerb utca. After one long block, on the right, in the park behind the yellow fence, is a...*

Serbian Orthodox Church

This used to be a strongly Serbian neighborhood—there's still some Cyrillic writing on some of the buildings nearby. The church is rarely open, but if it is, step inside to be transported to the far-eastern reaches of Europe...heavy with incense and packed with icons.

The Serbs are just one of many foreign groups that have coexisted here. Traditionally, Hungary's territory included most of Slovakia and large parts of Romania, Croatia, and Serbia—and people from all of those places (along with Austrians, Jews, and Roma) flocked to Buda and Pest. And yet, most of the residents of this cosmopolitan city still speak Hungarian. Throughout centuries of foreign invasions and visitors, new arrivals have undergone a slow-but-sure process of "Magyarization"—"becoming" Hungarian (often against their will). This has made Budapest one of the greatest "melting pot" cities in Europe, if not the world.

• *Continue down Szerb utca, until it runs into Váci utca. Turn left, and set your sights on the colorful tiled roofs two blocks directly ahead. Across the street is the...*

Great Market Hall (Nagyvásárcsarnok)

This market hall (along with four others) was built—like so much of Budapest—around the millennial celebration year of 1896. Appreciate the colorful Zsolnay tiles lining the roof—frostproof and harder than stone, these

were an integral part of the Hungarian national style that emerged in the late 19th century.

To the right, the green **Liberty Bridge**—formerly named for Habsburg emperor Franz Josef—spans the Danube to the Gellért Baths, in the shadow of Gellért Hill. And to the left, the Small Boulevard (here named Vámház körút) curls around toward Deák tér, passing Kálvin tér, the National Museum, and the Great Synagogue along the way.

Step inside the market and get your bearings: The cavernous interior features three levels. The ground floor has produce stands,

bakeries, butcher stalls, heaps of paprika, goose liver, and salamis. Upstairs are stand-up eateries and souvenirs. And in the basement are a supermarket, a fish market, and piles of pickles. For more on the food and drinks described here, see the "Eating" section of the Practicalities chapter.

Main Floor

Before exploring, take this guided stroll along the market's "main drag" (straight ahead from the entry). Notice the floor slopes slightly downhill to the left. Locals say that the vendors along the right wall are (appropriately enough) higher-end, with more specialty items, while the ones along the left wall are cheaper. Just inside the door, to the right as you enter, notice the small electronic scale—so shoppers can double-check to be sure the merchants didn't cheat them.

In the first "block" of stalls, the corner showcase on the left explains how this stall has been in the same family since 1924, and includes photos of three generations.

Farther along in the first block (also on the left), notice the signs high up advertising three favorite Hungarian drinks: **Unicum** is the secret-recipe herbal liqueur beloved by Hungarians and undrinkable to everyone else. ***Pálinka*** is the local version of

schnapps, available in a wide variety of fruit flavors. And **Tokaji Aszú,** colored (and priced) like gold, is called "the wine of kings, and the king of wines." It's made with "noble rot" grapes, giving it a high sugar content.

In the second block, meat is on the right, and produce is on the left. At the end of this section on the left, you have a good opportunity to sample homemade **strudels** *(rétesek)* of various flavors.

In the third block, you'll see **paprika** on both sides. Additional (and less touristy) stalls are down the little alley on the left.

As you browse, remember that there are two types of paprika: sweet *(édes,* used for flavor) and hot *(csípős,* used sparingly to add some kick). While you're at it, pick up some spicy pastes (which hold their flavor better than the fast-degrading powders): the spicy *Erős Pista,* the sweet *Édes Anna,* the soup-enhancing *Gulyáskrém,* and the intensely spicy condiment called, simply, "Red Gold" *(Piros Arany).* Note that all of these are a bit cheaper if you buy them just off the market's main drag—and cheaper still at a supermarket.

Along the main drag—just after the stairs on the right, hung high amid the paprika (at the Kmetty & Kmetty stall)—is a photo

of **Margaret Thatcher** visiting this market in 1989. She expected atrocious conditions compared with English markets but was pleasantly surprised to find this place up to snuff. This was, after all, "goulash communism" (Hungary's pragmatic mix, which allowed a little private enterprise to keep people going). On the steps of this building, she delivered a historic speech about open society, heralding the impending arrival of the market economy.

At the fourth block, on the right, the corner showcase features another favorite Hungarian food: **goose liver** *(libamáj)*—not to be confused with the cheaper and less typical duck liver *(kacsamáj).* Goose liver comes in various forms: most traditional is packaged whole *(naturel* or *blokk),* others are pâté *(parfé* or *püré).* Hungary is, after France, the world's second-biggest producer of foie gras.

In the fifth block, on the left, look for another local favorite: Hungarian *szalámi* (Pick, a brand from the town of Szeged, is considered the best).

Reaching the sixth block, above the corner showcase on the right, you'll see a poster showing two types of uniquely Hungarian **livestock.** *Mangalica* is a hairy pig (with a thick, curly coat resembling a sheep's fleece) that almost went extinct but became popular again after butchers discovered it makes great ham—and has a lower fat content than other types of pork (look for this on local menus). *Szürkemarha* are gray longhorn cattle.

• *Head up the escalator at the back of the market (on the left).*

Upstairs

Along the upstairs back wall are historic photos of the market hall (and pay WCs).

This is a convenient place to look for souvenirs—with a great selection of both traditional (embroidery) and not-so-traditional (commie-kitsch T-shirts). While there are no real bargains here, the prices are a bit better than out along Váci utca. For tips, see the Shopping in Budapest chapter.

The left wall (as you face the front) is lined with fun, cheap, stand-up, Hungarian-style fast-food joints and six-stool pubs. However, 90 percent of the clientele is tourists—so the prices are high, and I don't recommend this area for a meal. (Meanwhile, the Hold Street Market on Hold utca—described on my Leopold Town Walk and in the Eating in Budapest chapter—is a similar scene but a far better option, since most patrons are local office workers. If you want a market-hall meal, go there instead.)

Walk along here to get a glimpse of traditional foods. You'll see many stands selling the deep-fried snack called *lángos* (LAHN-gohsh)—similar to elephant ears, but savory rather than sweet. The most typical version is *sajtos tejfölös*—with sour cream and cheese. You can also add garlic *(fokhagyma)*. A basic *lángos* like this will run you about 1,000 Ft. But beware the greedy vendors that offer to pile the toppings so high that you can't even see the *lángos* anymore... they charge per topping, and a deluxe can run upwards of 3,000 Ft. At the far end of the upper gallery, the **Fakanál Étterem** cafeteria above the main entrance is handy but pricey.

• *For a less glamorous look at the market, head down the escalators near the front of the market (below the restaurant) to the...*

Basement

The market basement has, in addition to a modern supermarket, a strip called "Hungarikum Utca," with informative display cases explaining local specialties.

Soon you reach some fragrant **pickle stands.** Stop at one and take a look. Hungarians pickle just about everything:

PEST TOWN CENTER

peppers and cukes, of course, but also cauliflower, cabbage, beets, tomatoes, garlic, and so on. They use particularly strong vinegar, which has a powerful flavor but keeps things very crispy. Until recently—before importing fruits and vegetables became more common—most "salads" out of season were pickled items like these. Vendors are usually happy to give you a sample; consider picking up a colorful jar of mixed pickled veggies for your picnic.

Next up, you'll reach the fresh **fish** area. And in this landlocked country that means tanks of still-swimming carp, catfish, and perch. While Budapesters have an appreciation for seafood, freshwater fish is a more local choice.

• *When your exploration is finished...so is this walk. Exit the hall the way you came in. Near the Great Market Hall, you have several sightseeing options. If you'd like to stroll back to Vörösmarty tér—this time along the touristy and commercial Váci utca—you can walk straight ahead from the market. The green Liberty Bridge next to the market leads straight to Gellért Hotel, with its famous hot-springs bath, at the foot of Gellért Hill (see the Thermal Baths chapter; **trams #47** and **#49** zip you there in one stop).*

*Convenient trams connect this area to the rest of Budapest: **Tram #2** runs from under the Liberty Bridge along the Danube directly back to Vigadó tér (at the promenade by Vörösmarty tér), the Chain Bridge, and the Parliament (where my* □ *Leopold Town Walk begins). **Trams #47** and **#49** (catch them directly in front of the market) zip to the right around the Small Boulevard to the National Museum (described in Sights in Budapest) and, beyond that, the Great Synagogue (for my* □ *Great Synagogue & Jewish Quarter Tour) and Deák tér (the starting point of my* □ *Andrássy Út Walk)—or you can simply walk around the Small Boulevard to reach these sights in about 15 minutes.*

PEST TOWN CENTER

ANDRÁSSY ÚT WALK

From Déak Tér to Heroes' Square

Connecting downtown Pest to City Park, Andrássy út is Budapest's main boulevard, lined with plane trees, shops, theaters, cafés, and locals living very well. Budapesters like to think of Andrássy út as the Champs-Elysées and Broadway rolled into one. While that's a stretch, it is a good place to stroll, get a feel for today's urban Pest, and visit a few top attractions (most notably the Opera House and the House of Terror) on the way to Heroes' Square and City Park.

Orientation

Length of This Walk: Allow an hour, not including time to enter the sights.

Overview: Andrássy út is divided roughly into thirds. The most interesting first section (from Deák tér to the Oktogon) is the focus of this walk. The middle section (between the Oktogon and Kodály körönd) features one major sight, the House of Terror. The final third (Kodály körönd to Heroes' Square), while pleasant and comparatively low-key, offers fewer sightseeing opportunities.

Shortcut: The M1/yellow Metró line runs every couple of minutes just under the street—so it's easy to skip several blocks ahead, or to backtrack (stops marked by yellow signs).

Getting There: The walk begins at Deák tér—easy to reach from anywhere in the city, as it's on three Metró lines. If you're coming from Vörösmarty tér in central Pest, simply hop the M1/yellow Metró line one stop, or walk five minutes up Deák utca. If you want to skip to the start of Andrássy út itself, you can ride the M1 to the Bajcsy-Zsilinszky út stop and start this walk at the "Millennium Underground of 1896" section.

Opera House: Lobby free to enter Mon-Sat 11:00 until 17:00 or

19:00 depending on if there's a performance; Sun open three hours before the performance—generally 16:00-19:00, or 10:00-13:00 if there's a matinee; 45-minute tours—3,000 Ft, small extra charge for five-minute miniconcert following the tour, in English nearly daily at 14:00, 15:00, and 16:00—buy tickets at desk in lobby (arrive about 30 minutes early—or drop by earlier in the day to secure a spot on the tour); Andrássy út 22.

House of Terror: 3,000 Ft, Tue-Sun 10:00-18:00, closed Mon, Andrássy út 60.

Franz Liszt Museum: 2,000 Ft; Mon-Fri 10:00-18:00, Sat 9:00-17:00, closed Sun; performances in concert hall Sat at 11:00 for 2,000 Ft; Vörösmarty utca 35.

Starring: Budapest's most elegant drag, with fine architecture, upscale shopping, great restaurants, and top-notch sightseeing—from opulent (Opera House) to sobering (House of Terror).

The Walk Begins

• *Begin in the middle of the paved square (near the M2/M3 Metró entrance) called...*

Deák Tér

This square is named for **Ferenc Deák** (1803-1876), a statesman who pushed for persistent international pressure on the Habsburgs to improve Hungary's status after his rabble-rousing compatriots failed in the 1848 Revolution. (The peace-loving Deák was sort of a Hungarian Jimmy Carter.) It worked. With the Compromise of 1867, Hungary was granted an impressive measure of autonomy in the empire.

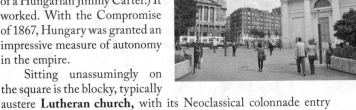

Sitting unassumingly on the square is the blocky, typically austere **Lutheran church,** with its Neoclassical colonnade entry and shallow dome. Looming over the square across the street is the landmark, but sadly neglected, yellow office block called the **Ankerház.** Like the square it dominates, this building isn't as important as it might seem.

On the upper part of the square (up the stairs) is an angular memorial to **Gábor Sztehlo,** a Lutheran pastor who rescued approximately 2,000 local Jews from the Arrow Cross regime during the Holocaust. Hungarian officials understandably love to celebrate

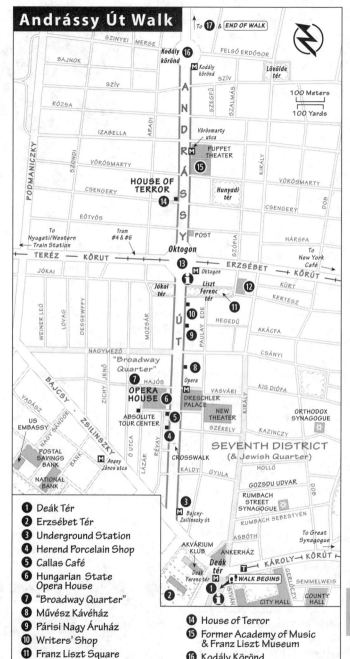

Andrássy Út Walk

To ⑰ & END OF WALK

SZINYEI MERSE
FELSŐ ERDŐSOR

BAJNOK

Kodály körönd ⑯

SZÍV

SZÍV

Lövölde tér

Kodály körönd

SZEGFŰ

SZALMÁS

RÓZSA

SZÍY

ARADI

IZABELLA

ANDRÁSSY

VÖRÖSMARTY

SZONDI

Vörösmarty utca

PUPPET THEATER ⑮

KIRÁLY

VÖRÖSMARTY

CSENGERY

HOUSE OF TERROR ⑭

Hunyadi tér

DOB

CSENGERY

EÖTVÖS

POST

HÁRSFA

To Nyugati/Western Train Station

Tram #4 & #6

SZÓFIA

To New York Café

TERÉZ KÖRÚT

Oktogon ⑬

ERZSÉBET KÖRÚT

JÓKAI

Oktogon

KÜRT

WEINER LEÓ

LOVAG

DESSEWFFY

MOZSÁR

Jókai tér

Liszt Ferenc tér ⑫

KERTÉSZ

ÚT

⑩ ⑪

PAULAY EDE

HEGEDŰ

AKÁCFA

⑨

NAGYMEZŐ

CSÁNYI

BAJCSY - ZSILINSZKY

ZICHY JENŐ

"Broadway Quarter"

⑦ HAJÓS

⑧

KIS DIÓFA

OPERA HOUSE ⑥

Opera

VASVÁRI

KIRÁLY

ORTHODOX SYNAGOGUE

VADÁSZ

NAGY SÁNDOR

DRESCHLER PALACE

US EMBASSY

ABSOLUTE TOUR CENTER

⑤

NEW THEATER

KAZINCZY

POSTAL SAVINGS BANK

Ó UTCA

LÁZÁR

RÉVAY

④

SZÉKELY

SEVENTH DISTRICT (& Jewish Quarter)

BANK

Arany János utca

CROSSWALK

KÁLDY

GYULA

HOLLÓ

NATIONAL BANK

③

GOZSDU UDVAR

RUMBACH STREET SYNAGOGUE

DOB

Bajcsy-Zsilinszky út

RUMBACH SEBESTYÉN

To Great Synagogue

ASBÓTH

AKVÁRIUM KLUB

ANKERHÁZ

Deák tér

KÁROLY KÖRÚT

SEMMELWEIS

Deák Ferenc tér

WALK BEGINS

GERLÓCZY

CITY HALL

COUNTY HALL

100 Meters
100 Yards

① Deák Tér
② Erzsébet Tér
③ Underground Station
④ Herend Porcelain Shop
⑤ Callas Café
⑥ Hungarian State Opera House
⑦ "Broadway Quarter"
⑧ Művész Kávéház
⑨ Párisi Nagy Áruház
⑩ Writers' Shop
⑪ Franz Liszt Square
⑫ Franz Liszt Acad. of Music
⑬ Oktogon

⑭ House of Terror
⑮ Former Academy of Music & Franz Liszt Museum
⑯ Kodály Körönd
⑰ To Diplomatic Quarter, Heroes' Square & City Park

ANDRÁSSY ÚT

these (relatively rare) "righteous Gentiles" who came to the rescue of the Jews.

• *From Deák tér, cross Harmincad street—the one with all the taxis and bus stops (including #16 to the Castle Hill, and the bus to Memento Park)—and head for...*

Erzsébet Tér

This pretty, leafy park was Pest's main market square. It's named for one of Deák's contemporaries: Elisabeth, the wife of the Habsburg emperor Franz Josef. While Deák pressed Franz Josef with diplomacy, Empress Elisabeth (a.k.a. Sisi) pressured him at home...Hungarian autonomy was one of her pet issues (for more on this "royal and imperial" couple, see page 292). You'll likely see—towering over the park—the **Budapest Eye** Ferris wheel, which is erected here most summers, offering a pricey view over the city (2,700 Ft, daily until late, usually closed off-season).

The park was long marred by the presence of a gloomy, polluting, communist-era international bus station. But now it has been reclaimed as a welcoming public zone, and the bus station has been converted into a lively food court called **Design Terminal** (marked by the Fröccsterasz outdoor bar/café).

Notice there are two parts to Erzsébet tér: the more traditional park behind the former bus station (with the Budapest Eye); and a sleek, modern new area in front of it.

A few years ago, the government planned to build a new national theater in the area to the right of the Design Terminal, and they even began to dig the foundation. But when the parliament switched hands, construction was aborted—leaving a giant hole that locals called "The National Ditch." Eventually they came up with a creative use for the space: an underground parking garage and a unique café/nightclub.

Walk across the grass, closer to the low wall at the end of the park near the busy street, and see how a long series of terraces filled with café tables leads down into the **Akvárium** nightclub. On balmy summer nights, outdoor performances take place here, and this whole area is filled with young locals. Walk a little farther through the park, to the left, to reach the artificial pond that covers part of the ditch. Look closely: Especially at night, you can see through

the glass floor of the very shallow pond and spot people walking around in the underground nightclub. (For more, see the Entertainment in Budapest chapter.)

• *At the far corner of Erzsébet tér (beyond the pool and the rack of loaner Bubi bikes), cross the busy Small Boulevard (here called Bajcsy-Zsilinszky út) to the beginning of Andrássy út. For now, stay on the right side of the boulevard.*

You'll pass a heavenly-smelling stand selling a delicious Hungarian treat, **kürtőskalács**—*a "chimney cake" that's slow-cooked on a rotisserie, then rolled in cinnamon, coconut, or other toppings. Be sure to get one that's hot and fresh.*

A few steps farther along, look for the yellow railings on either side of the street with the low-profile Földalatti *sign. This marks the Bajcsy-Zsilinszky út Metró stop. Go down the steps and back more than 100 years (if they ask you for your Metró ticket, just take a peek, then head back up).*

Millennium Underground of 1896

Built to get the masses conveniently out to Heroes' Square for the millennium festivities, this fun and extremely handy little Metró line follows Andrássy út from Vörösmarty tér (Pest's main square) to City Park. It was originally dubbed the "Franz Josef Underground Line"—in honor of the then-emperor—but later simply became known as the Underground *(Földalatti).* Just 20 steps below street level, it's so shallow that you must follow the signs on the street (listing end points—*Mexikói út felé* takes you toward City Park) to gauge the right direction, because there's no underpass for switching platforms. The first underground on the Continent (London's is older), it originally had horse-drawn cars. Trains depart every couple of minutes. Though recently renovated, the M1 line retains its 1896 atmosphere, with fun black-and-white photos of the age.

• *From the top of the stairs here, notice the great view across the street to St. István's Basilica. Now continue...*

Gyula Andrássy (1823-1890)

A key player in the 1848 Revolution, Count Gyula (Julius) Andrássy went on to help forge (along with Ferenc Deák) the Dual Monarchy of the Austro-Hungarian Empire. As Budapest boomed, Andrássy also served as an urban planner who championed the idea of building a grand boulevard from downtown to City Park. Andrássy was also the Hungarian prime minister and Austro-Hungarian foreign minister (1871-1879). Eventually he was forced to step down after his unpopular campaign to appropriate Bosnia-Herzegovina (and consequently boost the Slav population of the empire, which destabilized its delicate ethnic balance). But to most Hungarians, Andrássy is best known for his alleged relationship with Empress Sisi, who adored all things Hungarian (see page 292). Her third daughter—who some believed to be the count's—was known as the Little Hungarian Princess.

Strolling up Andrássy Út

This grand boulevard—140 feet wide and nearly two miles long—was begun in 1871, when city bigwigs decided that on-the-rise Budapest needed an answer to Paris' Champs-Elysées. But instead of leading to an Arc de Triomphe, Andrássy út culminates at the similarly triumphal Heroes' Square. The boulevard also provided a convenient link between the dense urban center of Pest and the green expanse of City Park, allowing city-dwellers to zip out for a break from the bustle without plodding along congested narrow streets. The boulevard was officially inaugurated with much fanfare in 1885. Because most of the buildings were built within about 15 years, Andrássy út enjoys a pleasant architectural harmony. Historicism—a creative merging of various complementary styles—was all the rage at the time. Look up as you stroll to see the heroic statuary adorning the tops of buildings.

Since being built, this boulevard has constantly changed names with the tenor of the times. Originally called Radial Boulevard (Sugárút), it was later christened for Count Andrássy, who had strongly promoted its construction. When the Soviets moved in, they renamed it Sztálin út; after the 1956 Uprising, it was briefly called Hungarian Youth Boulevard, before they redubbed it People's Republic Boulevard. And finally, with the fall of communism, it regained its historical name: Andrássy út.

Running parallel to Andrássy út, two blocks to the right, is **Király utca,** which is lined with home-improvement shops (a hot commodity in this swiftly gentrifying city, where so many people are fixing up flats). This area, known as the Seventh District, is generally more seedy than most parts of central Pest. But it also includes the Jewish Quarter and is the epicenter of the city's distinctive ruin-pub nightlife scene (described in the Entertainment in Budapest chapter).

• *At your first opportunity—about a block and a half up from the underground station—cross to the left side of Andrássy út to find the next few attractions. As you cross, look to the far end of the street, where you can already faintly see the column that marks Heroes' Square.*

Once across the street, peek into the window of the **Miniversum**—a model railroad that curls its way through miniature buildings from Budapest and around Hungary. While you could pay to enter, you can see most of it by peeking through the window.

This first stretch of Andrássy út is a cancan of big-money stores featuring international brands, such as Gucci and Louis Vuitton. But there are still some local shops—on the left, at #16, is a **Herend** shop, selling very expensive pieces of Hungary's top porcelain (see the Shopping in Budapest chapter).

Upscale as it has become, Andrássy út remains an artery for the city, often clogged with traffic...except during "critical mass," when 80,000 bikers take back the street twice a year (though these days it's occurring more and more often—generally on weekends). During these times, the street is closed to traffic for a full day

and given over to cyclists, in-line skaters, skateboarders, and pedestrians...a tempting taste of what could be.

On the left side of the street, on the corner at #20, look for the recommended **Callas café,** with elegant *Jugendstil* decor (for details, see the Eating in Budapest chapter).

• *On the left, just after Callas, is the can't-miss-it...*

Hungarian State Opera House (Magyar Állami Operaház)

The Neo-Renaissance home of the Hungarian State Opera features performances (almost daily except during outdoor music season, late June-early Sept) and delightful tours. The building dates from the 1890s, not long after Budapest had become co-capital of the Habsburg Empire. The

Hungarians wanted to put their city on the map as a legitimate European capital, and that meant they needed an opera house. Emperor Franz Josef provided half the funds...on the condition that it be smaller than the opera house in his hometown of Vienna. And so, Miklós Ybl designed a building that would exceed Vienna's famous Staatsoper in opulence, if not in size. (Franz Josef was reportedly displeased.) It was built using almost entirely Hungarian materials. After being damaged in World War II, it was painstakingly restored in the early 1980s. Today, with lavish marble-and-gold-leaf decor, a gorgeous gilded interior slathered with paintings of Greek myths, and high-quality performances at bargain prices, this is one of Europe's finest opera houses.

The Opera is scheduled to reopen in late 2019 following a lengthy renovation. Once it reopens, you can slip in the front door when the box office is open and check out the sumptuous entryway. For the full story (and to get into the remarkable auditorium), take one of the guided tours in English (see page 49). To see the Opera House in action, take in an excellent (and refreshingly affordable) performance—for specifics, see the Entertainment in Budapest chapter.

• *The Opera House marks the beginning of an emerging dining-and-nightlife zone dubbed the "Broadway Quarter." Cross to the right side of Andrássy út for the next few sights.*

"Broadway Quarter"

Across the street from the Opera House, and echoing its shape (although in a different style), is the **Dreschler Palace.** It was co-designed by Ödön Lechner, a leading architect whose works also include the Postal Savings Bank (described in the Leopold Town Walk chapter). In this building's late-19th-century heyday, one of Budapest's top cafés filled its gallery. More recently, it housed the Ballet Institute. And not long ago, the beautiful but ne-

glected building was purchased by a luxury hotel chain (you may see it under construction). Tucked behind it is the **New Theater** (Új Színház, with a fine *Jugendstil* facade), one of many popular venues around here for Hungarian-language plays (Paulay Ede utca 35, tel. 1/269-6021, www.ujszinhaz.hu).

A few steps up Andrássy út on the right (at #29) is another fine historic café, **Művész Kávéház.** Located near seven theaters, it is called "Artist Coffeehouse" because it is a favorite after-rehearsal haunt of actors and musicians—so it's your best chance to rub elbows with actual drama queens and divas.

The next major cross street, **Nagymező utca,** features a chic cluster of restaurants, bars, and theaters (especially on the left side of Andrássy). This is an enjoyable place to stroll on a summer evening. While you might be tempted to attend a show along Budapest's answer to Broadway, note that most of the plays and musicals here are in Hungarian only. So unless you want to hear "Music of the Night" sung in Hungarian (as it was meant to be), keep looking.

Continue straight across Nagymező utca, staying on the right side of Andrássy út. A half-block down on the right (at #39) is a grand old early 20th-century building marked **Párisi Nagy Áruház** (Paris Department Store). One of the city's first department stores, this was a popular shopping stop for years, even through communism. It has since been renovated, but has repeatedly changed hands in recent years. Inside and upstairs is a gorgeous old frescoed ballroom, called Lotz Hall, that's home to the Café Párisi, a coffeehouse in a grand setting. If you need a coffee break, this is a fine place to do it.

If you're here in summer, look immediately to the right of the Párisi Nagy Áruház to see the elevator that runs up to **360 Bar,** Budapest's best rooftop cocktail bar—with great views over the city's landmarks and rooftops (described in the Entertainment in Budapest chapter). Ride up, if only to see firsthand the trendy phenomenon of the rooftop cocktail bar. (And if the young clientele causes you to wonder, yes, the drinking age here is 18.)

At the end of the block on the right (at #45) is a historic bookstore: the **Writers' shop** (Írók Boltja). During Budapest's late-19th-century glory days, its café was the haunt of many of the great artistic minds that populated the city, including architect Ödön Lechner and poet Attila József.

• *Just after the bookshop is a popular outdoor dining area.*

Franz Liszt Square (Liszt Ferenc Tér)

This leafy square is surrounded by hip, expensive cafés and restaurants. (The best is the recommended restaurant **Menza.**)

Strangely, neither the statue on this square nor the one facing it, across Andrássy út, is of Franz Liszt. But deeper in the park, you'll find a modern statue of Liszt energetically playing an imaginary piano. And at the far end of the square, fronting a gorgeous piazza, is the **Franz**

Liszt Academy of Music, founded by and named for this half-Hungarian, half-Austrian composer who had a Hungarian name and passport. Liszt loved his family's Magyar heritage (though he didn't speak Hungarian) and spent his last six years in Budapest. His Academy of Music has been stunningly restored inside and out—step into the magnificent lobby. This space, though smaller, gives the Opera House a run for its money...and speaking of money, the concerts here are even cheaper than at the already reasonably priced Opera (for details on performances, and for more on Liszt, see the Entertainment in Budapest chapter).

• *One block up from Franz Liszt Square is the gigantic crossroads known as the...*

Oktogon

This vast intersection with its corners snipped off—where Andrássy út meets the Great Boulevard ring road (Nagykörút)—was called

Mussolini tér during World War II, then November 7 tér in honor of the Bolshevik Revolution. Today kids have nicknamed it American tér for the fast-food joints littering the square and streets nearby.

From here, if you have time to delve into workaday Bu-
dapest, hop on tram #4 or #6, which trundle in both directions around the ring road. If you have time for a short detour to the most opulent coffee break of your life, head for the recommended **New York Café** (described in the Eating in Budapest chapter). Just get on a tram to the right (tram #6 toward Móricz Zsigmond körtér or tram #4 toward Fehérvári út), and get off at the Wesselényi utca stop.

• *There's one more major sight between here and Heroes' Square. Walk two more blocks up Andrássy út to reach the...*

House of Terror (Terror Háza)

The building at Andrássy út 60 (on the left) has been painted a

lifeless blue-gray, and the word "TERROR" is carved into the overhanging eaves. This is the place where two evil regimes tortured their Hungarian sub-jects. Now a modern museum documenting the terror of Hun-gary's "double occupation"—first at the hands of the Nazis, then the Soviets—this is essential sightseeing for those intrigued by Budapest's dark 20th century, and interesting to anyone. For a self-guided tour of the museum, see the 📖 House of Terror Tour chapter.

In the tree-lined sidewalk strip in front of the House of Terror, notice two other symbolic landmarks of that dark time: a chunk of the **Berlin Wall,** and an actual **iron curtain** of heavy, rusted chains.

• *Two significant buildings stand across the boulevard from the House of Terror (on the right side of Andrássy út, just behind the Metró stop).*

Former Academy of Music (Franz Liszt Museum) and Puppet Theater

The yellow-brick building on the corner of Vörösmarty utca (at Andrássy #67) is the **former Academy of Music**—founded by Franz Liszt and later moved to the building we just saw on his square.

Upstairs is the small but endearing **Franz Liszt Museum,** in the old flat where the composer spent much of his time for the last six years of his life. This dusty collection might interest classical music buffs but will probably underwhelm most others. After putting on shoe covers, you glide through three rooms filled with period furniture and pianos (including ones custom-made for Liszt, and—on the lower shelf of a glass case—a "composing desk" with a small three-octave keyboard built by famous piano maker Ludwig Bösendorfer). Liszt's bedroom (to the right as you enter) contains his actual bed and a little personal altar where he knelt to pray. Look for the lithographs of Liszt sitting in this very room. The cupboard contains personal belongings, including a plate that belonged to writer (and Liszt friend) George Sand, and locks of the composer's hair that were saved by his fans. In his heyday, Liszt was adored as much as the biggest-name rock stars are today.

On Saturday mornings, **performances** take place in the building's small concert hall (for specifics, see the Entertainment in Budapest chapter).

The next building is the **Puppet Theater** (Bábszínház), a venue for top-notch puppet shows (for details, see the Budapest with Children chapter).

• *While you can hoof it from here to Heroes' Square (visible in the distance, about a 15-minute walk), there's less to see along the rest of Andrássy út. If you prefer, hop on the Metró here (from right in front of the Puppet Theater) and ride it three stops to Hősök tere.*

Or, if you continue walking up Andrássy út, after four blocks you'll reach the grand intersection called...

Kodály Körönd

This circular crossroads—which seems to echo the octagonal one we passed through earlier—is named for another great Hungarian composer, Zoltán Kodály (who lived in a mansion here, at #1, now a museum; for more on Kodály, see page 265). During the Nazi occupation, it had the jarring name Hitler tér.

Standing in the four wedge-shaped parks—overshadowed by the stately mansions surrounding them—are statues of four Hungarian heroes who fought against Ottoman invaders. Think of these as rejects from the Millennium Monument at Heroes' Square just up the boulevard. In fact, two of the original statues from Kodály körönd were eventually "promoted" to the colonnade there, and their spots here were taken by two different heroes.

• *After Kodály körönd, Andrássy út enters its final third, the...*

Diplomatic Quarter

Continuing up the street, notice that the buildings lining Andrássy út shrink and pull back from the busy boulevard, huddling behind trees. Instead of boasting bulky four- and five-story apartment blocks, it turns into a sleepy, leafy residential zone. These villas were formerly occupied by aristocrats, diplomats, and wealthy Jews. Today this is where many foreign states maintain their embassies. If you'd like to skip the final stretch, you can hop on the Metró at Kodály körönd. Or, to complete your stroll, keep going.

• *Andrássy út terminates at Heroes' Square.* 📖 *See the **Heroes' Square & City Park Walk** chapter.*

HOUSE OF TERROR TOUR

Terror Háza

Along one of the prettiest stretches of urban Budapest, in the house at 60 Andrássy Boulevard, some of the most horrific acts in Hungarian history took place. The former headquarters of two of the country's darkest regimes—the Arrow Cross (Nazi-occupied Hungary's version of the Gestapo) and the ÁVO/ÁVH (communist Hungary's secret police)—is now, fittingly, an excellent museum that recounts those times of terror. The high-tech, conceptual, and sometimes over-the-top exhibits attempt to document the atrocities endured by Hungary during the 20th century. This is a powerful experience, particularly for elderly Hungarians who knew both victims and perpetrators and have personal memories of the terrors that came with Hungary's "double occupation."

Note: There is some talk of updating this museum in the near future. And, given the ruling Fidesz party's penchant for re-envisioning history, it's possible some of these exhibits could change.

Orientation

Cost: 3,000 Ft.

Hours: Tue-Sun 10:00-18:00, closed Mon.

Information: Tel. 1/374-2600, www.terrorhaza.hu.

Getting There: It's located at Andrássy út 60, district VI, near the Vörösmarty utca stop of the M1/yellow Metró line. Note that this is Vörösmarty utca, not Vörösmarty tér (which is a different stop). Outside, an overhang casts the shadow outline of the word "TERROR" onto the building.

Visitor Information: A silver plaque in each room provides the basics (in English), and each room is stocked with free English fliers providing more in-depth information (very similar to what's covered by the audioguide).

Tours: The 1,500-Ft English audioguide is good but plodding and almost too thorough, and can be difficult to hear over the din of Hungarian soundtracks in each room.

Length of This Tour: 1-1.5 hours.

Services: Café, good bookshop, and WCs.

Starring: Fascism, communism, and the resilient Hungarian spirit.

BACKGROUND

In the lead-up to World War II, Hungary initially allied with Hitler—both to retain a degree of self-determination and to try to regain its huge territorial losses after World War I's devastating Treaty of Trianon (see page 442). As the rest of Europe fell into war, Hungary tiptoed between supporting the Nazis and, wherever possible, charting its own course. The Hungarians found themselves in the unenviable position of providing a buffer between Nazi Germany to the west and the Soviet Union to the east. They did just enough to stay in the Nazis' good graces (the Hungarian Second Army invaded the Soviet Union in 1941), while attempting to maintain what autonomy they could.

Hitler finally got fed up with Hungary's less-than-wholehearted support, and in March of 1944, the Nazi-affiliated Arrow Cross Party was forcibly installed as Hungary's new government. The Arrow Cross immediately set to work exterminating Budapest's Jews (most of whom had survived until then, although they had suffered under the earlier regime's anti-Semitic laws). The Nazi surrogates deported nearly 440,000 Jewish people to Auschwitz, murdered  thousands more on the streets of Budapest, and executed hundreds in the basement of this building. (For more on this ugly time, see page 173.)

The Red Army entered Hungary from the USSR in late August of 1944. After a hard-fought battle (and a devastating siege), they took Budapest on February 13, 1945, and forced the last Nazi soldier out of Hungary on April 4. Although the USSR characterized this as the "liberation" of Hungary, it soon became clear that the Hungarians had merely gone from the Nazi frying pan into the Soviet fire. Here in Budapest, the new communist leaders took over the same building as headquarters for their secret police (the ÁVO, later renamed ÁVH). To keep dissent to a minimum, the secret police terrorized, tried, deported, or executed anyone suspected of being an enemy of the state.

As you tour the exhibits, remember that as similar as their methods might seem, the Nazis and the communists represented opposite extremes of the political spectrum. Hungarians, like so many others in the 20th century, got caught in the crossfire. And the museum has not been without controversy: While it does address the Nazis and the Arrow Cross, it dispenses with those things fairly quickly, focusing more heavily on the communist regime. Given the political forces in Hungary that would like to whitewash the country's questionable role in World War II, this could be taken as an intentional omission.

The Tour Begins

• *Buy your ticket (and rent an audioguide, if you wish) and head into the museum.*

Atrium

The atrium features a Soviet T-54 tank, symbolizing the looming threat of violence that helped keep both regimes in power. Tanks like this one rolled into Hungary to crush the 1956 Uprising. Behind the tank, stretching to the ceiling, is a vast wall covered with 3,200 portraits of people who were murdered by the Nazis or the communists in this very building.

• *The one-way exhibit begins two floors up, then spirals down to the cellar—just follow signs for* Kiállítás/Exhibition. *To begin, you can either take the elevator (to floor 2), or walk up the red stairwell nearby, decorated with old Socialist Realist sculptures from the communist days (including, near the base of the stairs, two subjects you won't find at Memento Park: Josef Stalin and Mátyás Rákosi, the most severe communist leader of Hungary).*

Once upstairs, the first room gives an overview of the...

Double Occupation (Kettős Megszállás)

The video by the entrance sets the stage for Hungary's 20th century: its territorial losses after World War I; its alliance with, then invasion by, the Nazis; and its "liberation," then occupation, by the USSR (described earlier, under "Background").

The TV screens on the partition in the middle of the room

show grainy footage of both sides of the "double occupation": the Nazis on the black side and the Soviets (appropriately) on the red side. Do a slow counterclockwise loop, starting with the black (Nazi) side. See Hitler speaking and saluting in occupied Hungary, and Nazis goose-stepping down Andrássy út. The giant, ironic quote reads, "Last night I dreamed that the Nazis were gone...and nobody else came."

But come they did. The giant picture of the destroyed Chain Bridge (on the far wall) shows the passing of the torch between the two regimes and is a chilling reminder that these two equally brutal groups, which employed similar means of terror, were sworn enemies: As the Soviets' Red Army approached from the east to liberate Hungary, the Nazis made a last stand in Budapest (Hitler, who considered the Danube a natural border, ordered them never to retreat). The Nazis destroyed all of the bridges across the Danube (some without warning, while they were filled with civilians), then holed up on Castle Hill. The Soviets laid siege for 100 days, gradually devastating the city.

Circling around to the red (Soviet) side, you see Budapest in the aftermath of World War II and the early days of Soviet rule. The telephones on the wall play Hungarian sound clips from the time.

• *Go through the **Passage of Hungarian Nazis**, decorated with the words of a proclamation by Arrow Cross leader Ferenc Szálasi. Continue into the room of...*

Hungarian Nazis (Nyilas Terem)

The table is set with Arrow Cross china, bearing a V-for-victory emblem with a laurel wreath. At the head of the table stands an Arrow Cross uniform. Examine the armband: The red and white stripes are an old Hungarian royal pattern, dating from the days of St. István, and the insignia combines arrows, a cross, and an "H" for Hungary. On the loudspeaker, Arrow Cross leader Ferenc Szálasi preaches about reclaiming a "Greater Hungary" and about fighting against the Jews and the insidious influence of their Bolshevism. On the far wall, the footage of the frozen river shows where many of those Jews ended up: unceremoniously shot into the icy Danube. Listen for the sickening, periodic splash... splash...splash...

• *As you leave the room, the exhibit subtly (perhaps too subtly) turns the page from the Nazi period to the communist one.*

Gulag

After the Red Army drove the Nazis out of Hungary, they quickly set to work punishing people who had backed their enemies. A quote from Stalin in 1943 at the far end of the room reads, "Hungry must be punished" (for its alliance with the Nazis). Being sent to a gulag was one particularly hard fate.

The word "gulag" refers to a network of secret Soviet prison camps, mostly in Siberia. These were hard-labor camps where potential and actual dissidents were sent in order to punish them, remove their dangerous influence from society, and make an example of those who would dare to defy the regime. The Soviets euphemistically told them they were going away for "a little work" *(malenki robot)*. It was an understatement.

On the carpet, a giant map of the USSR shows the locations of some of these camps, where an estimated 600,000 to 700,000 Hungarian civilians and prisoners of war were sent...about half of whom never returned. And that only represents a tiny fraction of the millions of people from throughout Europe and the USSR thought to have perished in the gulag system. The lighted cones locate specific camps, with artifacts from those places. Video screens show grainy footage of transfer trains clattering through an icy countryside, gruesome scenes from the camps, and prisoner testimony. (For more on the atrocious conditions in the gulag, see the sidebar, later.)

People of Germanic heritage living in Hungary were targeted for deportation, but—due to a strict Moscow-imposed quota system—nobody was immune. Among the gulag victims was the Swedish diplomat Raoul Wallenberg, who had rescued many Hungarian Jews from the Nazis (see page 180).

Those who survived their experience with "corrective forced labor" were often not allowed to return to their families, and if they did, were sworn to secrecy...never allowed to tell of the horrors of the gulag until after 1989. The last Hungarian gulag prisoner, András Toma, finally returned from Siberia in 2000, having been interned in a mental hospital for decades after the gulags were dissolved—two years in a gulag followed by 53 years in an asylum. The doctors, unfamiliar with his tongue-twisting Hungarian language, assumed he was simply mad.

Changing Clothes (Átöltözés)

This locker room—with rotating figures dressed alternately in

Arrow Cross and communist uniforms—satirizes the readiness of many Hungarians to align themselves with whomever was in power. The sped-up video shows turncoat guards changing their uniforms. While it seems absurd that someone's allegiance could shift so quickly, many of these people were told that they'd be executed if they did not switch...or they could "change clothes," admit their mistake in joining the Arrow Cross, and pledge allegiance to the new communist regime. For most, it was an easy choice. Many people (including Cardinal József Mindszenty) were imprisoned by both regimes—and it's entirely plausible that they saw the same guards dressed in both uniforms.

The Fifties ('50-es Évek)

Of course, the transition was not always so straightforward. The insinuation of the communist regime into the fabric of Hungary was a gradual process. From the Red Army's "liberation" in 1945 until 1948, a power struggle raged between democratic factions and the Soviet-backed communist puppet leaders. The voting booths at the beginning of this room symbolize that, at first, the Soviets fostered an illusion of choice for the Hungarian people. Elections were held throughout the Soviet satellite states in the mid-1940s, with the assumption that the communist Hungarian Workers' Party would sweep into power. But in the 1945 parliamentary elections, the communists won only 17 percent of the vote. After this, the Soviets gradually eliminated opposition leaders by uncovering "plots," then executing the alleged perpetrators. In the following two elections, they also stacked the deck by allowing workers to vote as often as they liked—often five or six times apiece (using the blue ballot cards you'll see in the voting booths). Even so, in the 1947 election, the communists still had to disqualify 700,000 opposition votes in order to win.

Once in power, the Hungarian Workers' Party ruled with an iron fist and did away with the charade of elections entirely. Hungary became a "People's Republic" and was reorganized on the Soviet system. Private property was nationalized, the economy became fully socialistic, and the country fell into poverty.

Not that you'd know any of this from the sanitized, state-sponsored images of the time. In the voting booths, screens show a loop of communist propaganda from the 1950s. Lining the walls are glossy communist-era paintings, celebrating the peasants of the "people's revolution" (farmers, soldiers, and sailors looking boldly to the future), idyllic scenes of communities coming together,

and romanticized depictions of communist leaders (Lenin as the brave sailor; Mátyás Rákosi—the portly, bald communist leader of Hungary—as the kindly grandfather, gladly receiving flowers from a sweet young girl). Imagine the societal schizophrenia bred by the communists' good-cop, bad-cop methods: pretending to be a bunch of nice guys while at the same time terrorizing the people.

The distorted stage separates these two methods of people-control. The stretched-out images of Lenin, Rákosi, and Stalin imply the falsehood of everything we've just seen; backstage is the dark underbelly of the regime— the constant surveillance that bred paranoia among the people. The cases at the end display documentation for show trials. We'll learn more about these means of terror as we progress.

Soviet "Advisors" (Szovjet Tanácsadók)

These "advisors" were more like supervisors. On the wall plaque is a list of the Soviet ambassadors to Hungary, who wielded terrific influence over the communist leaders here. Yuri Andropov,

the ambassador during the 1956 Uprising, helped set up the ÁVH secret police and later became the Soviet premier. So shocked was Andropov at how quickly the uprising had escalated, that he later advocated for cracking down violently at the first signs of unrest in the empire (think of the Soviet tanks rolling into Czechoslovakia during the 1968 Prague Spring).

The desk displays items from the ambassador's office, and the video screens show footage of the ambassador garnering goodwill by visiting families, factories, and so on. A portrait of Stalin slyly surveys the scene.

Resistance (Ellenállás)

This room—empty aside from three very different kitchen tables—symbolizes the way that resistance to the regime emerged in every walk of life. Each table and chair represents a different social class: countryside peasant, middle-class urbanite, and bourgeoisie. On each table is a propaganda message that was printed by that dissident (and now used as evidence in their interrogation). Notice that, like the furniture, these messages evolve in sophistication from table to table.

• *Go down the stairs, and enter the room about...*

Resettlement and Deportation (Kitelepítés)

The creation of small nations from sprawling empires at the end of World War I had also created large minority groups, which could upset the delicate ethnic balance of a new country. Having learned this lesson, the Soviets strove to create homogeneous states without minorities. Ethnic cleansing on a staggering scale—or, in the more pleasant parlance of the time, "mutual population exchange"—took place throughout Central and Eastern Europe in the years following World War II (for example, three million ethnic Germans were forced out of Czechoslovakia). In Hungary, 230,000 Germans were uprooted and deported. Meanwhile, Hungarians who had become ethnically "stranded" in other nations after the Treaty of Trianon were sent to Hungary (100,000 from Slovakia, 140,000 from Romania, and 70,000 from Yugoslavia). Most have still not returned to their ancestral homes.

Notice the doorbell on the plaque at the room's entrance. Press the white button to hear the jarring sound that hundreds of thousands of people heard in the middle of the night, when authorities showed up at their doorstep to tell them they had to pack up and move. These people were forced to sign an "official agreement of repatriation" (see the deportation paperwork on the wall), and then were taken away by the ÁVO. They were strictly limited in the number of belongings they could bring; the rest was left behind, carefully inventoried, and folded into the wealth of the upwardly mobile communist bureaucrats—represented by the fancy black sedan with plush hammer-and-sickle upholstery draped in black in the middle of the room.

In the hallway at the end of this section, peer into the haunting **torture cell.** Inside you'll see original items used to beat and torture prisoners.

Victims and Victimizers

The foot soldiers of the secret police were civilians—workaday people who informed on their friends and neighbors in vast numbers. Anything could be cause for suspicion, even not clapping quite hard enough at a Hungarian Workers' Party rally. The regime routinely turned family members against one another. They were just as likely to compel you to implicate your father or brother as your neighbor or co-worker. Pavlik Morozov, a Soviet boy, was the literal poster child for this, after he informed on his father. It was common to be both an informant and informed upon by someone else.

Imagine walking down the street in 1950s Budapest. Like many, you are basically apolitical—you don't care who's in charge, as long as you can raise your family in peace and prosperity. One day on your way to work, a black van pulls up next to you, and in a blur, you're pulled inside. An intimidating agent asks you to report on your friends' water-cooler conversations—particularly any statements against the regime, no matter how casual. When you hesitate, the agent says, "Your son András is so very bright. It would be a shame if he could not attend university." Or maybe, "You appear to have a promising career in engineering ahead of you. And yet, it is so difficult to find employment in your chosen field. Well, there's always ditch digging."

The decision about whether to collaborate with the secret police suddenly becomes muddled. (Which would you choose? Are you *sure?*) Some people refused and endured years or decades of misery. Others capitulated, enjoyed relatively fulfilling lives, but regretted selling out their friends and even their families. In post-communist Hungary, both groups wonder if they made the right choice.

Surrender of Property and Land (Beszolgáltatás)

With the descent of the communist cloak, people were forced to surrender their belongings to the government. Land was redistributed. Even those who came out ahead in this transaction— formerly landless peasants—found that it was a raw deal, as they were now expected to meet often-impossible production quotas. The Soviet authorities terrorized the peasant class in order to pry as many people as possible away from their old-fashioned farming lifestyles (not to mention deeply held Hungarian traditions), and embrace the industrialization of the new regime. Some 72,000 wealthy peasants called *kulaks*, who did not want to turn over their belongings, ended up on a list to be deported; all told, some 300,000 people were ultimately ejected. (Eventually the regime sidestepped the peasant-farmer "middleman" completely, as farms were simply collectivized and run as giant units.)

Of the produce grown in Hungary, a significant amount was sent to other parts of the Soviet Bloc, leading to rampant shortages. The Hungarian people had to survive on increasingly sparse rations. Enter the labyrinth of pork-fat bricks, which remind old-timers of the harsh conditions of the 1950s. These one-kilo bricks of lard were actually a staple in the local diet: So often, dinner was simply lard on bread. Look for the ration coupons, which people had to present before being allowed to buy even these measly staples. The pig hiding out in the maze is another symbol of these tough times. Traditionally, peasants would slaughter a pig in order to sustain themselves through the winter. But the communist authorities could

seize that pig for their own uses, leaving the farmers to rely on the (unreliable) government to provide for their families. To avoid this, many farmers would slaughter their pigs illegally in the cellar, instead of out in the open.

ÁVO

The communist secret police (State Security Department, or ÁVO, later called the State Security Authority, or ÁVH) began as a means to identify and try war criminals. But the organization quickly mutated into an apparatus for intimidating the common people of Hungary—equivalent to the KGB in the Soviet Union. Before they were finished, the ÁVO/ÁVH imprisoned, abused, or murdered one person from every third Hungarian family. On the wall are pictures of secret police leaders and a Rákosi quote: "The ÁVH is the fist of the Party." This organization infiltrated every walk of Hungarian life. Factory workers and farmers, writers and singers, engineers and doctors, teenagers and senior citizens, even party leaders and ÁVO/ÁVH officers were vulnerable. Their power came from enlisting untold numbers of civilians as informants.

Gábor Péter's Office

Gábor Péter was the first director of the ÁVO/ÁVH. Like many former communist leaders, Péter wound up a prisoner himself (notice the prison motif lurking around the edges of the room). It became an almost expected part of the life cycle of a communist bigwig to eventually be fingered as an enemy...the more power you gained, the better an example you became. (In Péter's case, it didn't help that he was Jewish—anti-Semitism didn't leave Hungary with the Arrow Cross.) It was abundantly clear that nobody was safe. Péter went to his grave in 1993 without remorse for his participation in the Soviet regime.

"Justice" (Igazságszolgálatás)

This room explores "show trials"—high-profile, loudly publicized, and completely choreographed trials of people who had supposedly subverted the regime.

The burden of proof was on the accused, not on the accuser, and coerced confessions were fair game. From 1945 until the 1956 Uprising, more than 71,000 Hungarians were accused of political crimes, and 485 were executed.

The TV screen shows various show trials, including the one for Imre Nagy (leader of the 1956 Uprising—see page 96) and his associates. Nagy was found guilty and executed in 1958.

In some cases—as in Nagy's—the defendants had defied the regime. But in many cases, the accused were innocent. (The authorities simply wanted to make an example of someone—guilt or innocence was irrelevant.) For example, if there was a meat shortage, they'd arrest and try slaughterhouse workers, ferreting out the ones who "didn't do their best." They might even execute the foreman. Not only did this intimidate all the others to work harder, it also kept people who had gained some small measure of power in check.

Behind the stage you'll see the names of the trial judges, and photos of some of them. Looking at these people, consider that it was not unusual for judges who had conducted show trials to later go on trial themselves.

Propaganda

Next you'll encounter another more upbeat method for controlling the people: bright, cheery communist propaganda. The motivational film (on the right) extols the value of productivity. Below is the chalkboard where workers

would keep track of the "work competition" *(munkaverseny híradó)* by noting the best workers and how far above the average productivity they achieved.

The next room shows how advertising became more colorful in the 1970s and 1980s. (Because there was no real competition

in the marketplace, glossy posters were relatively rare.) Look at a few of the posters: Several tout Bambi Narancs, the first Hungarian soft drink (from a time when Coke and Pepsi were pipe dreams). The poster about the Amerikai Bogár warns of the threat of the "American Beetle" (from Kolorádó), which threatened Hungarian crops. When the communists collectivized traditional family farm plots, they removed the trees and hedgerows that separated them—thereby removing birds that had kept pest populations in check. When a potato beetle epidemic hit, rather than acknowledging their own fault, the communists blamed an American conspiracy.

"Hungarian Silver" (Magyar Ezüst)

This was a nickname for aluminum, which was produced in large quantities from local bauxite (the pile of rocks in the middle of the room). The walls are lined with items made of this communist equivalent of "silver," lampooning the lowbrow aesthetic of that era.

Religion (Felekezetek)

In 1949, nearly 7 out of every 10 Hungarians identified themselves as Catholics. Over the next four decades, that number declined precipitously. The communist regime infiltrated church leadership, and bishops, priests, monks, and nuns filled Hungarian prisons. Many people worshipped in private (hence the glowing cross hidden under the floorboards). Those who were publicly faithful were discriminated against, closely supervised by the secret police, and often arrested. As things mellowed in the 1960s and 1970s, it was easier to be openly religious, but people of faith were still considered an "enemy of the class" and risked being blacklisted (they might have difficulty finding a job, or their children could be denied an education). Hungarians had to choose between church and

HOUSE OF TERROR

Gulag and Work Camps

The stories that later emerged from the Soviet gulag system (and Hungary's work camps) are unthinkable. Prisoners lived in makeshift barracks with wide gaps between the boards that allowed winter winds to howl through. They were forced to do

backbreaking manual labor (such as quarrying stone) and were punished when they failed to meet their impossible quotas. Nutrition was laughable—prisoners quickly became walking skeletons. While the gulags were not formally "death camps," many prisoners died of exposure, overwork, accidents, punishment, and disease. Two unlucky prisoners, who had served time both at the Nazi-run Dachau concentration camp and at the communist Recsk work camp in Hungary, reported that conditions had been better at Dachau.

Keep in mind that—quite appallingly—many innocent people were sent to work camps. One prisoner was accidentally arrested because his name was similar to a suspect's. But by the time the mistake was sorted out, it was too late to let him go. Another prisoner was recruited by the secret police to make a list of dissidents. Instead he made a list of the people he disliked the most, then signed his own name at the bottom. Later, a black van pulled up on the street and he was thrown in the back—face-to-face with all the people he'd accused.

And yet, for some prisoners, their time in a work camp was strangely enjoyable. Dissidents were surrounded by fellow intellectuals and could engage in enlightening conversation all day while they worked. Think of the Greek myth of Sisyphus, who's condemned to spend eternity rolling a stone up a hill again and again...and so, lacking other options, Sisyphus chooses to be happy. (One good book about the work camp experience, by George Faludy, has the insightful title *My Happy Days in Hell*.)

Though one outspoken university professor was not imprisoned, he could only find work as a ditch digger. But he came to appreciate the job because he could converse and debate with other ousted professors who dug ditches alongside him.

Hungary's work camps were closed soon after Stalin's death in 1953. The regime denied their existence, and the topic was taboo through the 1980s. Only since 1989 have the victims' families been allowed to mourn publicly.

success. The loudspeakers at the end of the room, which belched communist propaganda, stand at odds with the vestments.

The next hallway contains a tribute to **Cardinal József Mindszenty,** who was arrested and beaten by the communists and later sought refuge in the US embassy for 15 years (see the sidebar on page 320).

• *Now head down to the basement in a creepy...*

Elevator

The elevator gradually lowers into the cellar. As it descends, you'll watch a three-minute video of a guard explaining the grotesque execution process.

• *When the door opens, you're in the...*

Prison Cellar (Pincebörtön)

It's chilling to think of this space's history: In the early 1950s, it was the scene of torture; in 1956, it became a clubhouse of sorts for the local communist youth. It has been reconstructed and now looks as it might have circa 1955.

Wander through **former cells** used for different purposes. On the right side of the hall are a "wet cell" (where the prisoner was forced to sit in water) and a cramped "foxhole cell" (where the prisoner was forced to crouch). On the left side of the corridor are a "standing cell" (where the prisoner was forced to stand 24 hours a day) and a padded cell. On both sides, you'll also see standard cells with photos of the men who once filled them.

In the large room after the cells, you'll see a stool with a lamp; nearby are the **torture** devices: hot pads and electrical appliances. The bucket and hose were used to revive torture victims who had blacked out. Interrogations would normally happen at night, after food, water, and sleep had been withheld from the prisoner for days. Communist interrogators employed techniques still beloved by some torture connoisseurs today, such as "stress positions"... though waterboarding was still just a glimmer in some young sadist's eye. Simple beatings, however, were commonplace.

After the torture room, a small room on the right contains

a **gallows** that was used for executions (described earlier on your journey, in the elevator video).

As you think of the people who were imprisoned and murdered here, feel the vibration of traffic on Andrássy út just outside—these victims were so close to the "normal" world, yet so far away.

Internment (Internálás)

While the most notorious gulag network was in Siberia, a similar system also emerged in the Soviet satellites, such as Hungary, which had its own network of work camps (including a secret one at a quarry overlooking the village of Recsk, not far from Eger—symbolized by the pile of rocks in the center of the room). In just three years (1945-1948), more than 40,000 people were sent to such camps, and the practice continued until 1953 (see sidebar, earlier). A subtitled video shows a wealthy woman talking about her own experience being sent to one such camp to "learn how to work."

1956 Uprising ('56 Forradalom)

This room commemorates the 1956 Uprising (see page 96). The Hungarian flag with a hole cut out of the middle (a hastily removed Soviet emblem) and the slogan *Ruszkik Haza!* ("Russkies go home!") are important symbols of that time. The clothes and bicycle recall the "Pest Youth," teenagers and preteens who played a major role in the uprising. The Molotov cocktail—a bottle of flammable liquid with a cloth wick—was a weapon of choice for the uprisers. Screens show the events of '56.

In the next room **(Megtorlás)** stand six symbolic gallows—actually used for executions (though not in this building). Children's voices quietly read aloud the names of some of those killed in the aftermath of 1956. Some 230 were formally executed, while another 15,000 were indicted. (On the gallows, see the legal paperwork for execution.)

Emigration (Kivándorlás)

More than 200,000 Hungarians simply fled the country after the uprising. A wall of postcards commemorates these emigrants, who flocked to every corner of the Western world. Once they reached Austrian refugee camps, these desperate Hungarians could choose where to go—the US offered to fly them anywhere in America to get them started. A video screen shows people leaving Hungary and arriving at their destination, with the help of the United States. Only 11,000 of them would eventually return to their homeland.

Hall of Tears (Könnyek Terme)

This somber memorial commemorates all the victims of the communists from 1945 to 1967 (when the final prisoners were released from this building).

Room of Farewell (Búcsú Terme)

This room shows several color video clips that provide a (relatively) happy ending: the festive and exhilarating days in 1991 when the Soviets departed, making way for freedom; the reburial of the Hungarian hero, Imre Nagy, at Heroes' Square; and the dedication of this museum. In the film that shows the Soviets' goodbye, watch for the poignant moment when the final Russian officer crosses the bridge on foot, with a half-hearted salute and a look of relief.

Victimizers (Tettesek)

The chilling finale: walls of photographs of the "victimizers"—members and supporters of the Arrow Cross and ÁVO, many of whom are still living and who were never brought to justice. The Hungarians have a long way to go to reconcile everything they lived through in the 20th  century. For many of them, this museum is an important first step.

Outside the Museum

Leaving the House of Terror, take another look at the building—part of an elegant neighborhood, and yet, its basement windows have hidden such horror. Mug shots of victims line the wall. Across the sidewalk, two small monuments—an actual slice of the Berlin Wall and a literal "iron curtain"—remind all who pass of a terrible chapter in the history of Europe that ended only a generation ago.

HEROES' SQUARE & CITY PARK WALK

Hősök Tere és Városliget

The grand finale of Andrássy út, at the edge of the city center, is also one of Budapest's most entertaining quarters. Here you'll find the grand Heroes' Square, dripping with history (both monumental and recent); the vast tree-filled expanse of City Park, dressed up with fanciful buildings that include an Art Nouveau zoo and a replica of a Transylvanian castle; and, tucked in the middle of it all, Budapest's finest thermal spa and single best experience, the Széchenyi Baths. Over time, the vision is to relocate many of Budapest's leading museums to this park—creating a kind of museum quarter. If the sightseeing grind gets you down, take a mini vacation from your busy vacation and relax the way Budapesters do: Escape to City Park.

Orientation

Construction Alert: You may find large parts of City Park torn up as Budapest implements an ambitious rejuvenation project. Old museums are being restored, new ones are being built, and landscaping is being refreshed. Work is scheduled to be complete by the early 2020s; in the meantime, expect some disarray in and around the park. For the latest, see www. ligetbudapest.org.

Length of This Walk: One hour, not including museum visits or the baths.

What to Bring: If taking a dip in the Széchenyi Baths, bring your swimsuit and a towel (or rent these items there). You may also want to bring flip-flops, sunscreen, and soap and shampoo.

Getting There: If you walk the full length of Andrássy út (see the Andrássy Út Walk chapter), you'll run right into Heroes' Square. But most visitors hightail it out here on the M1/

yellow Metró line, and hop off at the Hősök tere stop. You'll exit the Metró in the middle of busy Andrássy út. Cross the street three times (making three-quarters of a circle) to work your way to the middle of Heroes' Square, with a great view of the Millennium Monument. (If you're heading directly for the baths, you could ride the M1 line one stop farther, to the Széchenyi fürdő stop.)

Museum of Fine Arts: 1,400 Ft, may be more for special exhibits; Tue-Sun 10:00-18:00, closed Mon, last entry one hour before closing; Dózsa György út 41.

Műcsarnok ("Hall of Art"): Price depends on current exhibits; Tue-Sun 10:00-18:00 except Thu 12:00-20:00, closed Mon; Dózsa György út 37.

Széchenyi Baths: 5,200 Ft for locker, 500 Ft more for personal changing cabin, 200 Ft more on weekends, cheaper after 19:00; open daily 6:00-22:00, may be open later on summer weekends, last entry one hour before closing; Állatkerti körút 11, district XIV.

Starring: A lineup of looming Hungarian greats, a faux-Transylvanian castle, Budapest's best baths, and the city's most enticing green patch.

The Walk Begins

• *Stand in the middle of...*

HEROES' SQUARE (HŐSÖK TERE)

Like much of Budapest, this Who's Who of Hungarian history at the end of Andrássy út was commissioned to celebrate the country's 1,000th birthday in 1896 (see page 27). Ironically, it wasn't finished until 1929—well after Hungary had lost World War I (and two-thirds of its historical territory) and was facing its darkest hour. Today, more than just the hottest place in town for skateboarding, this is the site of several museums and the gateway to City Park.

• *The giant colonnades and tall column that dominate the square make up the...*

Millennium Monument

Step right up to meet the world's most historic Hungarians (who look to me like their language sounds). Take a moment to explore

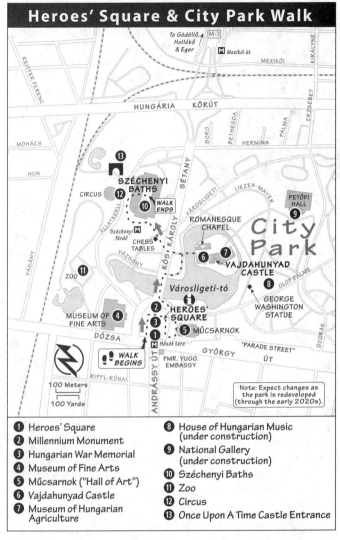

Heroes' Square & City Park Walk

HEROES' SQUARE & CITY PARK

1. Heroes' Square
2. Millennium Monument
3. Hungarian War Memorial
4. Museum of Fine Arts
5. Műcsarnok ("Hall of Art")
6. Vajdahunyad Castle
7. Museum of Hungarian Agriculture
8. House of Hungarian Music (under construction)
9. National Gallery (under construction)
10. Széchenyi Baths
11. Zoo
12. Circus
13. Once Upon A Time Castle Entrance

this monument, which offers a step-by-step lesson in the story of the Hungarians. (Or, to skip the history lesson, you can move ahead to the "Museum of Fine Arts" stop.)

Central Column: The Magyars

The granddaddy of all Magyars, **Árpád** stands proudly at the bottom of the pillar, peering down Andrássy út. He's surrounded by six other chieftains; altogether, seven Magyar tribes first arrived in the Carpathian Basin (today's Hungary) in the year 896. Remember that these ancestors of today's Hungarians were from

Central Asia and barely resembled the romanticized, more European-looking figures you see here. (Only one detail of these statues is authentically Magyar: the bushy mustaches.) Magyar horsemen were known and feared for their speed: They rode sleek Mongolian horses (rather than the powerful beasts shown here), and their use of stirrups—revolutionary in Europe at the time—allowed them to ride fast and turn on a dime in order to quickly overrun their battlefield opponents. Bows and spears were their weapons of choice; they'd have had little interest in the chain mail, heavy clubs, and battle axes that Romantic sculptors gave them. They used these skills to run roughshod over the Continent, laying waste to much of Europe.

The 118-foot-tall pillar supports the archangel **Gabriel** as he offers the crown to Árpád's great-great-grandson, István (as we'll learn, he accepted it and Christianized the Magyars—which enabled Hungary to survive as a nation rather than be plowed under by history and forgotten, as so many other such tribes were in the rough-and-tumble ethnographic jungle of Europe).

In front of the pillar is the **Hungarian War Memorial** (fenced in to keep skateboarders from enjoying its perfect slope).

The **sculptures** on the top corners of the two colonnades represent, in order from left to right: Work and Welfare, War, Peace, and the Importance of Packing Light.

Each statue in the two colonnades represents a great Hungarian leader, with a relief below showing a defining moment in his life. Likewise, each one represents a trait or trend in the colorful story of this dynamic people. The figures on the left date from the 10th to the 14th centuries, and are mostly kings of an independent Hungary; those on the right (dating from the 15th century onward) are mostly aristocrats and nobles rather than sovereigns—as during these centuries, Hungary was generally ruled by outsiders. (For details, see the Hungary: Past & Present chapter.)

• *Behind the pillar, look to the...*

First (Left) Colonnade

The first colonnade features rulers from the early glory days of Hungary.

St. István (c. 967-1038)

After decades of terrorizing Europe, the Magyars were finally defeated at the Battle of Augsburg in 955. Géza, Grand Prince of the Hungarians, realized that unless they could learn to get along with their neighbors, the Magyars' military would only garner them short-term prosperity. Géza baptized his son, Vajk, gave him the Christian name István (Stephen), and married him off to a Bavarian princess. On Christmas Day in the year 1000, commissioners of the pope (pictured in the relief below) brought to István the same crown that still sits under the Parliament dome. To historians, this event marks the beginning of the Christian—and therefore European—chapter of Magyar history. (For more on István, see page 203.)

St. László I (c. 1040-1095)

Known as Ladislas in English, László was a powerful knight/king who carried the Christian torch first taken up by his cousin István. Joining the drive of his fellow European Christian leaders, he led troops into battle to expand his territory into today's Croatia. Don't let the dainty chain-mail skirt fool you... that axe ain't for chopping wood. In the relief below, see László swing the axe against a pagan soldier who had taken Christian women hostage. László won a chunk of Croatia, then lost it... but was sainted anyway (hence the halo). László's story is the first of many we'll hear about territorial expansion and loss—a crucial issue to Hungarian leaders across the centuries (and even today).

Kálmán (c. 1070-1116)

Kálmán (Coloman) traded his uncle László's bloody axe for a stack of books. Known as "the Book Lover," Kálmán was enlightened before his time, acclaimed as being the most educated king of his era.

HEROES' SQUARE & CITY PARK

He was the first European ruler to prohibit the trial or burning of women as witches (on the relief, see him intervening to save the cowering woman in the bottom-right corner). He was also the king who retook Croatia yet again, bringing it into the Hungarian sphere of influence through the early 20th century. Kálmán reminds us that Hungarians take pride in being highly intellectual, as demonstrated by the many scientists, economists, and other great minds they've produced. (As you walk through City Park in a few minutes, keep an eye out for chess players.)

András II (c. 1177-1235)

András (Andrew) II is associated with the golden charter he holds in his hand (with the golden medallion dangling from it)—the Golden Bull of 1222. This decree granted some measure of power to the nobility, releasing the king's stranglehold and acknowledging that his power was not absolute. This was the trend across Europe at the time (the Magna Carta, a similarly important document, was signed in 1215 by England's King John). András demonstrates the importance Hungarians place on self-determination: Like many small Central European nations, Hungary has often been dominated by a foreign power...but has always shown an uncrushable willingness to fight back. (We'll meet some modern-day Hungarian freedom fighters shortly.) It's no surprise that so many place names in Hungary include the word Szabadság ("Liberty"). The relief shows that Hungarians are willing to fight for this ideal for others, as well: András is called "The Jerosolimitan" for his success in the Fifth Crusade, in which his army liberated Jerusalem. Here he is depicted alongside the pope kissing the rescued "true cross."

Despite his achievements, András is far less remembered today than his daughter **Elisabeth** (1207-1231, not depicted here), who was sent away to Germany for a politically expedient marriage. She is the subject of an often-told legend: The pious, kindly Elisabeth was known to sneak scraps of food out of the house to give to poor people on the street. One evening, her cruel confessor saw her leaving the house and stopped her. Seeing her full apron (which was loaded with bread for the poor), he demanded to know what she was carrying. "Roses," she replied. "Show me," he growled. Elisabeth opened her apron, the bread was gone, and rose petals miraculously cascaded out onto the floor. In her short life, Elisabeth went on to found hospitals and carry out other charitable acts, and she (unlike her father) became a saint. Elisabeth remains a popular symbol of charity not only in Hungary, but also in Germany. (It's easy to confuse St. Elisabeth with the equally adored Empress Elisabeth, a.k.a. Sisi, the Habsburg monarch.)

Béla IV (1206-1270)

Having governed over one of the most challenging periods of Hungarian history, the defiant-looking Béla—St. Elisabeth's brother—is celebrated as the "Second Founder of the Country" (after István). Béla led Hungary when the Tatars swept in from Central Asia, devastating Buda, most of Hungary, and a vast swath of Central and Eastern Europe. Because his predecessors had squandered away Hungary's holdings, Béla found himself defenseless against the onslaught. In the relief, we see Béla surveying the destruction left by the Tatars. Béla made a deal with God to send his daughter Margaret to a nunnery (on the island that would someday bear her name—see page 58) in exchange for sparing Hungary from complete destruction. After the Tatars left, he rebuilt his ruined nation. It was Béla who moved Buda to its strategic location atop Castle Hill and built a wall around it, to be better prepared for any future invasion. This was the first of many times that Budapest (and Hungary) was devastated by invaders;

later came the Ottomans, the Nazis, and the Soviets. But each time, like Béla, the resilient Hungarian people rolled up their sleeves to rebuild.

Károly Róbert (1288-1342)

Everyone we've met so far was a member of the Árpád dynasty—descendants of the tough guys at the base of the big column. But when that line died out in 1301, the Hungarian throne was left vacant. The Hungarian nobility turned to "Charles Robert," a Naples-born prince from the French Anjou (or Angevin) dynasty who had married into

Hungarian royalty. (His shield combines the red-and-white stripes of Hungary with the fleur-de-lis of France.) The Hungarians were slow to accept Robert—he had to be crowned four different times to convince everybody, and he was actually banned from Buda. (He built his own palace, which still stands, at Visegrád up the Danube—see page 315.) Eventually he managed to win them over and stabilize the country, even capturing new lands for Hungary (see the relief). Károly Róbert represents the many Hungarian people who are not fully, or even partially, Magyar. Today's Hungarians are a cultural cocktail of the various peoples—German, Slavic, Jewish, Roma, and many others—that have lived here and been "Magyarized" to adopt Hungarian language, culture, and names.

Nagy Lajos (1326-1382)

"Louis the Great" built on his father Károly Róbert's successes and presided over the high-water mark of Hungarian history. He expanded Hungarian territory to its historical maximum—including parts of today's Dalmatia (Croatia), Bulgaria, and Bosnia-Herzegovina—and even attempted to retake his father's native Naples (pictured in the relief). Hungarians still look back with great pride on these days more than six centuries ago, when they were a vast and mighty kingdom.

• *Now turn your attention to the...*

Second (Right) Colonnade

The gap between the colonnades coincides with some dark times for the Hungarians. The invading **Ottomans** swept up the Balkan Peninsula from today's Turkey, creeping deeper and deeper into Hungarian territory...eventually even taking over Buda and Pest

for a century and a half. Hungarian nobility retreated to the farthest corners of their lands, today's Slovakia and Transylvania, and soldiered on.

Salvation came in the form of the **Habsburgs,** rulers of a fast-expanding Austrian Empire, who presented Hungary with a classic "good news, bad news" scenario: They forced out the Ottomans, then claimed Hungary as part of their realm. While the Habsburgs eventually granted the Hungarians some leadership in the empire, the Habsburg era was a time of frustration and rebellion. In fact, at the time of this monument's construction—when Budapest was controlled from Vienna—Habsburg rulers stood in the last five slots of the right-hand colonnade. (The statue of Empress Maria Theresa now stands in the lobby of the Museum of Fine Arts, across the street.) But after the monument was damaged in World War II, locals seized on the opportunity to replace the Habsburgs with Hungarians...who were famous for fighting against the former occupants of those slots. The lineup begins with...

János Hunyadi (c. 1387-1456)

A military hero who achieved rare success fighting the Ottomans, Hunyadi won the fiercest-fought skirmish of the era, the Battle of

Belgrade (Nándorfehérvár in Hungarian). The relief depicts a particularly violent encounter in that battle. (The guy holding the cross is János Kapisztran, a.k.a. St. John Capistrano, an Italian friar and Hunyadi's right-hand man.) This victory halted the Ottomans' advance into Hungary for decades. Owing largely to his military prowess, Hunyadi was extremely popular among the people and became wealthier than even the king. He led Hungary for a time as regent, when the preschool-age king was too young to rule. After he died of the plague, Hunyadi's reputation allowed his son Mátyás to step up as ruler....

Mátyás Corvinus (1443-1490)

Perhaps the most beloved of all Hungarian rulers, Mátyás (Matthias) Corvinus was a Renaissance king who revolutionized the monarchy. He was a clever military tactician and a champion of

the downtrodden, known among commoners as "the people's king." The long hair and laurel wreath (instead of a crown) attest to his knowledge and enlightenment. And most importantly, he was the first (and last) Hungarian-blooded king from the death of the Árpád dynasty in 1301 until today. Building on his father's military success against the Ottomans, Matthias achieved a diplomatic peace with them—allowing him to actually expand his territory while other kings of this era were losing it. (He even had time for some vanity building projects—the relief shows him appreciating a model of his namesake church, which still stands atop Castle Hill.) Matthias' death represented the death of Hungarian sovereignty. After him, Hungary was quickly swallowed up by the Ottomans, then the Habsburgs. For more on King Matthias, see page 197.

Appropriately, Matthias is the final head of state at Heroes' Square. Reflecting the sea change after his death, the rest of the heroes here are freedom-fighters who rallied against Habsburg influence.

István Bocskai (1557-1606), Gábor Bethlen (1580-1629), and Imre Thököly (1657-1705)

After Matthias, the Ottomans took over most of Hungary. Transylvania, the eastern fringe of the realm, was fragmented and in

a state of ever-fluctuating semi-independence—sometimes under the firm control of sovereign princes, at other times controlled by the Ottomans. The three Hungarian dukes depicted here helped to unify their people through this difficult spell (see the reliefs): Bocskai and Thököly found rare success on the battlefield against the Habsburgs, while Bethlen made peace with the Czechs and united with them to fight against the Habsburgs.

The next two statues are of Ferenc Rákóczi and Lajos Kossuth, arguably the greatest Hungarian heroes of the Habsburg era and the namesakes of streets and squares throughout the country.

Ferenc Rákóczi II (1676-1735)

Although he was a wealthy aristocrat educated in Vienna, Rákóczi (Thököly's stepson) resented Habsburg rule over Hungary. When his countrymen mobilized into a ragtag peasant army to stage a

War of Independence (1703-1711), Rákóczi reluctantly took charge. (The relief depicts an unpleasant moment in Rákóczi's life, when he realizes just how miserable his army will be.) Allied with the French (who were trying to wrest power from the Habsburgs' western territory, Spain), Rákóczi mounted an attack that caught the Habsburgs off guard. Moving west from his home region of Transylvania, Rákóczi succeeded in reclaiming Hungary all the way to the Danube. But the tide turned when, during a pivotal battle, Rákóczi fell from his horse and was presumed dead by his army. His officers retreated and appealed to the Habsburgs for mercy, effectively ending the revolution. Rákóczi left Hungary in disgrace and rattled around Europe—to like-minded Habsburg enemies Poland, France, and the Ottoman Empire—in a desperate attempt to gain diplomatic support for a free Hungary. He died in exile in a small Turkish town, but his persistence still inspires Hungarians today.

Lajos Kossuth (1802-1894)

Kossuth was a nobleman and parliamentarian known for his rebellious spirit. When the winds of change swept across Europe in 1848, the Hungarians began to murmur once again about more independence from the Habsburgs—and Kossuth emerged as the movement's leader (in the relief, he's calling his countrymen to arms). After a bitterly fought revolution, Habsburg Emperor Franz Josef enlisted the help of the Russian czar to put down the Hungarian uprising, shattering Kossuth's dream. (For more on the 1848 Revolution, see the Hungary: Past & Present chapter.) Kossuth went into exile and traveled the world, tirelessly lobbying foreign governments to support Hungary's bid for independence. He even made his pitch to the US Congress...and today, a bust of Kossuth is one of only three sculptures depicting non-Americans in the US Capitol. After Kossuth died in exile in 1894, his body was returned to Budapest for an elaborate three-day funeral. The Habsburg Emperor Franz Josef—who knew how to hold a grudge—refused to declare the former revolutionary's death a national holiday, so Catholic church bells did not toll...but Protestant ones did.

The less-than-cheerful ending to this survey of Hungarian history is fitting. Hungarians tend to have a pessimistic view of their past...not to mention their present and future. In the Hungarian psyche, life is a constant struggle, and you get points just for playing your heart out, even if you don't win.

• *Two museums flank Heroes' Square. As you face the Millennium Monument, to your left is the...*

Museum of Fine Arts (Szépművészeti Múzeum)

The Museum of Fine Arts—a collection of mostly European art—is the underachieving cousin of the famous Kunsthistorisches Museum in Vienna. It's strong in art from areas in the Habsburgs' cultural orbit: Germanic countries (Dürer, Cranach), the Low Countries (Brueghel, Hals, Steen, Van Dyck), France (Boudin, Gaugin, Rodin), Italy (Raphael, Giotto, Titian, Canaletto), and especially Spain (Murillo, Zubarán, Velázquez, El Greco, Goya). The collection belonged to the noble Eszter-

házy family, and was later bought and expanded by the Hungarian government. While I prefer seeing Hungarian art when in Hungary (for that, visit the National Gallery on Castle Hill), this is the best place in town for Old Masters.

• *Across Heroes' Square (to the right as you face the Millennium Monument) is the...*

Műcsarnok ("Hall of Art")

Used for cutting-edge contemporary art exhibits, the Műcsarnok (comparable to a German Kunsthalle) has five or six temporary

exhibits each year. While art lovers enjoy this place, it's more difficult to appreciate than some other Budapest museums.

The Műcsarnok was also the site of a major event in recent history. On June 16, 1989, several anticommunist heroes who had been executed by the regime were finally given a proper funeral on the steps of this building. The Műcsarnok was draped in black-and-white banners, and in front were four actual coffins (including one with the recently exhumed remains of reformist hero Imre Nagy—see page 102), and a fifth, empty coffin to honor others who were lost. One of the most memorable speakers from that occasion was a 25-year-old, shaggy-haired burgeoning politician named Viktor Orbán—who now leads the right-of-center Fidesz Party that's attempting to reshape modern Hungary. The last place Imre Nagy was seen alive in public was at the Yugoslav Embassy, which was in the building across the busy ring road from Heroes' Square (on the left-hand corner).

• *Let's head for the park. The safest way to reach City Park is to begin in front of the Műcsarnok, then use the crosswalk to circle around across the street from the Millennium Monument to reach the bridge directly behind it. (There's no crosswalk from the monument to the bridge.)*

Begin walking over the bridge into...

CITY PARK (VÁROSLIGET)

Budapest's not-so-central "Central Park" was the private hunting ground of wealthy aristocrats until the mid-19th century, when it

was opened to the public. Soon after, it became the site of the overblown 1896 Millennium Exhibition, celebrating Hungary's 1,000th birthday. It's still packed with huge party decorations from that bash: a zoo with quirky Art Nouveau buildings, a circus, a replica of a Transylvanian castle, a massive bath/swimming complex, and walking paths. City Park is also filled with unwinding locals, with paddleboat rentals in summer and an ice-skating rink in winter.

Orient yourself from the bridge: The huge Vajdahunyad Castle is across the bridge and on your right. Straight into the park and on the left are the big copper domes of the fun, relaxing Széchenyi Baths. And the zoo is on the left, beyond the lake.

Remember: City authorities are boldly remaking City Park, including new landscaping and new buildings to house several museums. If your progress through the park is impeded by construction, be sure to come back in a few years for the payoff.

• *Cross the bridge, take the immediate right turn, and follow the path to the entrance of...*

Vajdahunyad Castle (Vajdahunyad Vára)

Many of the buildings for Hungary's Millennial National Exhibition were erected with temporary materials, to be torn down at the

end of the festival—as was the case for most world fairs at the time. But locals so loved Vajdahunyad Castle that it was rebuilt in brick and stone. The complex actually has four parts, each representing a high point in Hungarian architectural style: Ro-

manesque chapel, Gothic gate, Renaissance castle, and Baroque palace (free and always open to walk around the grounds).

From this direction, the **Renaissance castle** dominates the view. It's a replica of a famous castle in Transylvania that once belonged to the Hunyadi family (János and Mátyás Corvinus—both of whom we met back on Heroes' Square). Notice its distinctive trapezoidal tower—typical of castles in Transylvania.

Cross over the bridge and through the Gothic gateway. Once inside the complex, on the left is a replica of a 13th-century Romanesque Benedictine chapel. Consecrated as an actual church, this is Budapest's most popular spot for weddings on summer weekends.

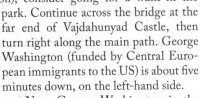

Farther ahead on the right is a big Baroque mansion housing the **Museum of Hungarian Agriculture** (Magyar Mezőgazdasági Múzeum). It brags that it's Europe's biggest agriculture museum, but most visitors find the lavish interior more interesting than the exhibits.

Facing the museum entry is a monument to **Anonymous**—specifically, the Anonymous from the court of King Béla IV who penned the first Hungarian history in the Middle Ages.

For an optional detour to yet another monument (of György —er, George—Washington), consider going for a walk in the

park. Continue across the bridge at the far end of Vajdahunyad Castle, then turn right along the main path. George Washington (funded by Central European immigrants to the US) is about five minutes down, on the left-hand side.

Near George Washington is the building site for the new **House of Hungarian Music**, designed by acclaimed Japanese architect Sou Fujimoto. When open, it will feature an interactive, hands-on exhibit about the world of music.

Deeper in the park is the site of the impressive, sprawling new home for the **National Gallery.** Designed by the Tokyo-based SANAA architecture firm, this will house the collection of Hungarian art that currently fills the Royal Palace on Castle Hill.

• *Time for some fun. Head back out to the busy main road, and cross it. Under the trees, you'll pass some red outdoor tables where you'll likely see elderly locals playing chess. Beyond the tables and a bit to the right, the pretty gardens and copper dome mark the famous...*

Széchenyi Baths (Széchenyi Fürdő)

Budapest's best thermal spa—and (for me) its single best ex-

perience, period—the
Széchenyi Baths offer a
refreshing and culturally
enlightening Hungarian
experience. Reward your-
self with a soak. For all the
details, see the 📖 Thermal
Baths chapter.

• *The best entrance to the
baths is around the back side.
That's also where you'll find...*

Attractions Behind Széchenyi Baths

Lining the street behind the baths are kid-friendly attractions.
From the steps of the swimming pool entrance, look through the
fence across the street to see the **zoo**'s colorful
Art Nouveau elephant house (see photo), slathered with Zsolnay tiles outside and mosaics inside. To the right is Budapest's 120-year-old **circus** (marked Nagycirkusz), then the **Once Upon
a Time Castle** amusement park. For more details on these attractions, see the Budapest with
Children chapter.

• *Our walk is over. Your options are endless. Soak in
the bath, visit the zoo, rent a rowboat, buy some cotton candy...enjoy City Park any way you like.*

When you're ready to head home, the M1/yel-
low Metró line (with effortless connections to the
House of Terror, Opera, the Metró hub of Deák tér,
or Vörösmarty tér in downtown Pest) has two handy stops here: The entrance to the Széchenyi fürdő stop is at the southwest corner of the yellow
bath complex (easy to miss—to the left and a bit around the side as you
face the main entry, just a stairway in the middle of the park); and the
Hősök tere stop is back across the street from Heroes' Square, where we
began this walk.

GREAT SYNAGOGUE & JEWISH QUARTER TOUR

Zsinagóga / Zsidónegyed

With an elegant history cut brutally short by the Holocaust, Pest's Jewish Quarter is gradually restoring its sights and embracing its long-dormant heritage. Today's Jewish Quarter contains several synagogues, Jewish-themed restaurants, and other remnants of a once-thriving Jewish community. And since the turn of the millennium, this neighborhood has also emerged as Budapest's most lively nightlife zone—known as the Seventh District. Each year, there seem to be more and more distinctive "ruin pubs," art galleries, fashion boutiques, hot restaurants, and all the trappings of hipster culture. This means that two very different cultures coexist in these streets: traditional Jewish heritage and cutting-edge, hard-partying trendiness. Somehow, it works.

The area's main attraction is the spectacular Great Synagogue, which I cover in Part 1 of this tour. Some might find it worthwhile to also explore the nearby sights and monuments, including two other synagogues, which I've linked with a short walk in Part 2.

Orientation

Length of This Tour: One hour for the synagogue and its garden, plus one more hour for the rest of the walk.

Dress Code: To visit the interiors of the Great Synagogue and the Orthodox Synagogue, men will need to cover their heads, and women, their shoulders (loaner yarmulkes and scarves are available at the door). Inside the Great Synagogue, short shorts and tank tops are prohibited, but they hand out loaner cover-ups.

Getting There: The Great Synagogue is at Dohány utca 2, district VII. From M2: Astoria (or the Astoria stop on trams #47 and #49), it's a five-minute walk—but it can be hard to find since the synagogue hides behind a line of modern buildings. Just follow the Small Boulevard (here called Károly körút) and keep an eye to the right.

Tour Guide: A member of the local Jewish community who also lived in Israel, **Juli Lengyel** offers insightful tours of the Jewish Quarter (€37/hour, mobile +3620-976-6786, jumi@t-online.hu).

Great Synagogue, Hungarian Jewish Museum, and Memorial Garden: 4,500 Ft, includes free 45-minute tour—note English tour times on the sign outside; Sun-Thu 10:00-18:00 (May-Sept until 20:00), Fri 10:00-16:00; Nov-Feb Sun-Thu 10:00-16:00, Fri until 14:00; closed Sat year-round and Jewish holidays.

Orthodox Synagogue: 1,000 Ft; Sun-Thu 10:00-17:30, Fri until 16:00; Oct-April Sun-Thu 10:00-16:00, Fri until 13:30, closed Sat year-round.

Synagogue at Rumbach Street: Should be open again by the time you visit; likely hours—Sun-Thu 10:00-18:00, Fri until 16:00—earlier off-season, closed Sat.

Genealogy Research: If you'd like help tracking down family roots, the **Hungarian Jewish Archives and Family Research Center** charges a small fee to use its archives with some help from staff. Bring your family name, ancestors' birth and death dates (if possible), and any other data you have (Mon-Thu 10:00-17:00, Fri until 15:00, closed Sat-Sun, closes one hour earlier Nov-Feb; in the Goldmark Hall Jewish cultural center just behind the Great Synagogue—entrance at Síp utca 12; it's best to contact them in advance to let them know you're coming—tel. 1/413-5547, www.milev.hu and click on "Family Research," milev6@gmail.com).

Eating: This area has more than its share of excellent restaurants, including some of the city's trendiest. You'll find everything from traditional Jewish (even kosher) fare to food trucks to high-end splurges. For ideas, see page 230 of the Eating in Budapest chapter.

Starring: Budapest's rich tapestry of Jewish history, including Europe's largest and most beautiful synagogue.

BACKGROUND

As the former co-capital of an empire that included millions of Jews, Budapest always had a high concentration of Jewish residents. Before World War II, five percent of Hungary's population and 25 percent of Budapest's were Jewish (and the city was nicknamed "Judapest").

In the 1780s, the progressive Habsburg emperor Josef II extended new rights to the Jews of his empire, allowing them

to live and do business in the city of Pest. Because they were still not allowed to purchase property within the city, many settled in the area just outside the city wall (today marked by the Small Boulevard ring road), in what would become the Jewish Quarter. At the same time, many Jews (like other minorities) went through a process of "Magyarization"—taking on Hungarian language and culture, and even adopting Hungarian spellings of their names. And many Jews were eager to win the acceptance of their Catholic neighbors—which might explain why the Great Synagogue, built in the mid-19th century, feels more like a Christian house of worship than a Jewish one.

The anti-Semitism that infected Europe around the turn of the 20th century also tainted Budapest. In fact, Hungary—and not Germany—was the first European country to enforce "Jewish laws," in the early 20th century. A long tradition of resentment toward Jews had been amplified by a more recent perception of the Jewish connection to Bolshevism. Furious and humiliated after losing two-thirds of their territory in the Treaty of Trianon that ended World War I, the Hungarians sought a handy scapegoat— and Jews filled that role.

When Hitler was on the rise in Germany, Hungary allied with him, allowing local politicians some degree of self-determination. The Hungarians sometimes interned or deported their Jewish citizenry, but refused to execute them—even as the Nazis began to institute their "Final Solution" of Jewish genocide in the lands they controlled. On the other hand, Nazi-allied Hungary was hardly blameless. Military service was compulsory, but Jews weren't allowed in the armed forces—so instead, many joined forced-labor brigades; tens of thousands died from the horrific conditions.

Hitler grew impatient and invaded Hungary in March of 1944, installing the Arrow Cross regime. Within two months of the Nazi takeover, trains began carrying Hungarian Jews to Auschwitz; by the middle of July, about 430,000 had already been deported. The remaining Budapest Jews were forced to live in a small, walled ghetto surrounding the Great Synagogue, and allowed no contact with the outside world. (For more on the Arrow Cross, see the House of Terror Tour chapter.)

As the end of the war neared, Hungarian Nazi collaborators resorted to desperate measures, such as lining up Jews along the Danube and shooting them into the river (now commemorated by a monument near the Parliament—see page 101). To save bullets,

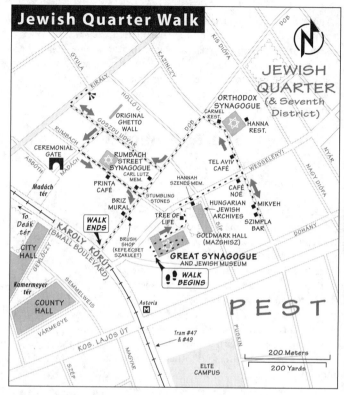

Jewish Quarter Walk

JEWISH QUARTER (& Seventh District)

ORTHODOX SYNAGOGUE
CARMEL REST.
HANNA REST.
ORIGINAL GHETTO WALL
CEREMONIAL GATE
RUMBACH STREET SYNAGOGUE
CARL LUTZ MEM.
TEL AVIV CAFÉ
PRINTA CAFÉ
HANNAH SZENES MEM.
CAFÉ NOÉ
BRIZ MURAL
STUMBLING STONES
HUNGARIAN JEWISH ARCHIVES
MIKVEH
WALK ENDS
TREE OF LIFE
SZIMPLA BAR
Madách tér
To Deák tér
KÁROLY KÖRÚT (SMALL BOULEVARD)
BRUSH SHOP (KEFE.ECSET SZAKÜLET)
GOLDMARK HALL (MAZSHISZ)
GREAT SYNAGOGUE AND JEWISH MUSEUM
CITY HALL
WALK BEGINS
Kámermeyer tér
COUNTY HALL
Astoria
PEST
Tram #47 & #49
ELTE CAMPUS

200 Meters
200 Yards

they'd sometimes tie several victims together, shoot one of them, and throw him into the freezing Danube—dragging the others in with him.

Hungary lost nearly 600,000 Jews to the Holocaust, and during the atheistic, anti-Semitic communist era, the most devout Jewish survivors left the country to resettle in Israel, North America, or other parts of Europe. Many who remained shied away from their Jewish identity, often becoming fully assimilated with Hungarian culture (a common occurrence throughout Hungary's melting-pot history). But since the thawing of communism, many of these Jewish Hungarians are taking a renewed interest in their heritage. Today, there are an estimated 100,000 people of Jewish descent in the Budapest area—which represents the largest Jewish population of any city in Central Europe.

After the Holocaust, the Great Synagogue sat neglected for 40 years. But in 1990, it was painstakingly rebuilt, largely with financial support from the Hungarian-American cosmetics magnate Estée Lauder. Theodor Herzl, a pioneer of Zionism, was born in a house next door to the Great Synagogue (now gone).

Other people of Hungarian-Jewish descent include big names from every walk of life: Harry Houdini (born Erich Weisz), Elie Wiesel, Joseph Pulitzer, Tony Curtis (and his daughter Jamie Lee), George Cukor, Goldie Hawn, George Soros, Peter Lorre, and Eva and Zsa Zsa Gabor. A visit to the Great Synagogue and surrounding Jewish Quarter offers insight into this vital facet of Hungarian history and contemporary life.

The Tour Begins

PART 1: GREAT SYNAGOGUE TOUR
• *Stand in front of the...*

Great Synagogue (Nagy Zsinagóga)

Also called the Dohány Street Synagogue, Budapest's gorgeous synagogue is the biggest in Europe and the second biggest in the world (after the Temple Emanu-El of New York). A visit here has three parts: touring its ornately decorated interior; exploring the attached museum, which offers a concise lesson in the Jewish faith; and lingering in the evocative memorial garden, with its weeping-willow *Tree of Life* sculpture and other poignant monuments.

• *Buy your ticket at the desk to the left of the main entrance gate. Admission includes a guided tour—ask about the next departure. Or simply tour the complex on your own, using the information here.*

After buying your ticket, head through the airport-type security checkpoint and turn right. Plant yourself in front of the...

Synagogue Facade

The synagogue's striking exterior captures the rich history of the building and the people it represents: The synagogue was built in 1859 just outside what was then the city limits. Although Budapest's Jews held fast to their own faith, they also wished to demonstrate their worth and how well-integrated they were with the greater community. Building this new synagogue was partially an attempt to impress the city's Gentile majority.

Budapest's Jewish leaders commissioned the Austrian (and

non-Jewish) architect Ludwig Förster to create a synagogue in Budapest that would top the Stadttempel recently built in Vienna (also designed by a Gentile). Because Förster didn't fully understand what synagogue architecture was supposed to look like, this design is his own, fanciful invention—loosely based on biblical descriptions of the Temple of Solomon in Jerusalem. This explains the two tall towers, which are not typical of traditional synagogues. The Moorish-flavored architecture is a sign of the Historicism of the time, which borrowed eclectic elements from past styles. Specifically, it evokes the Sephardic Jewish culture that flourished in Iberia; many Hungarian Jews are descended from that group, who fled here after being expelled from Spain in 1492. To some, the towers evoke Moorish minarets. Others note how these towers—along with the rosette (rose window)—helped the synagogue resemble Christian churches of the time. In fact, when it was built, the synagogue was dubbed by one cynic as "the most beautiful Catholic synagogue in the world."

• *Now step inside.*

Synagogue Interior

Notice that the synagogue interior feels like a church with the symbols switched—with a basilica floor plan, three naves, two pulpits, and even a pipe organ. The organ—which Franz Liszt played for the building's inauguration—is a clue that this synagogue belonged to the most progressive of the three branches of Judaism here at the time. (Orthodox Jews would never be permitted to do the "work" of playing an organ on the Sabbath.) Of the various synagogues in this district, this one belonged to the Neolog Jewish congregation (close to Conservative Judaism in the US).

In the ark, at the front of the main aisle, 25 surviving Torah scrolls are kept. Catholic priests hid these scrolls during World War

II (burying them temporarily in a cemetery). Though it was damaged in the war, the synagogue itself avoided being completely destroyed because the occupying Nazis protected it for their own uses: They put radio antennas in the two towers, stabled horses in the nave, and (according to some reports) might have even had a Gestapo base in the balcony above the main entrance.

The two biggest chandeliers are typical neither of synagogues nor of churches; they were likely inspired by concert halls of the day. During the war, the chandeliers were melted down and used to make bullets, but have since been recast. The pews are original, as are the kneelers—another borrowed Christian feature not typically used in Jewish worship.

The two-tiered balconies on the sides of the nave were originally for women, who worshipped separately from the men. (These galleries are accessed by separate staircases, from outside.) Today, men and women can sing together in the choir, but they still sit apart: men in the two inner rows, and women in the two outer rows. The service, attended by several hundred local Jews each Sabbath (and a couple thousand on high holidays), is still said in Hebrew. However, due to security concerns, people who are not members of the local congregation are generally not invited to attend.

• *When you're finished inside, exit through the main doors, turn right, and go to the opposite end of the front courtyard. Enter the building, then head upstairs (by stairs or elevator) to the...*

Hungarian Jewish Museum (Magyar Zsidó Múzeum)

This small but informative museum illuminates the Jewish faith, displaying a wide range of artifacts and succinct but engaging English explanations. The collection is always somewhat in flux, but typically you'll see objects representing the stages of Jewish life: a day, a week, a year, a lifetime. Everyday items reveal how Judaism was interwoven with all aspects of life. It also explains the major holidays of the Jewish calendar—from Rosh Hashanah and Yom Kippur to Purim and Hanukkah. One of the museum's prized pieces—typically displayed on the top floor—is a third-century tombstone from the Roman province of Pannonia (today's Hungary), roughly etched with a menorah.

• *Exiting back into the front courtyard, go down the passageway between the synagogue and the museum (straight ahead from the security checkpoint).*

Tree of Life and Memorial Garden

As you walk alongside the Great Synagogue, notice the small **garden** on your left. During the Soviet siege that ended the Nazi occupation of Budapest in the winter of 1944-1945, many Jews in the ghetto here died of exposure, starvation, and disease. Soon after the Soviets liberated the city, an estimated 2,281 Jews were buried here—considered Hungary's largest mass grave from the Holocaust. The trees and headstones (donated by survivors) were added later. The pillars you'll pass have historical photos of the synagogue and Jewish Quarter.

At the far end of the cemetery, look for the small, angular **sculpture** on the pedestal by renowned artist Imre Varga (for more on Varga, see page 74). This represents a forced march—with clearly defined figures at the front, melting into a blocky mass at the

back. When the Nazi-puppet Arrow Cross regime took over Hungary, they wanted to quickly transport as many Jews as possible to death camps. The trains couldn't take the Jews away fast enough, so the Arrow Cross made them march hundreds of miles to their final destination. Among the victims was a poet named Miklós Radnóti, who was compelled to fight with the Hungarian Army, and then forced to march back to Hungary after a defeat. He died and was buried along the way. A year and a half later, his body was exhumed. In his pocket was a notebook with poignant handwritten poems about his experience. In one, Radnóti daydreams about a life to which (he seems to suspect) he would never return:

If only once again I heard the quiet hum
Of bees on the veranda, the jar of orchard plums
Cooling with late summer, the gardens half asleep,
Voluptuous fruit lolling on branches dipping deep,
And she before the hedgerow stood with sun-bleached hair,
The lazy morning scrawling vague shadows on the air...
Why not? The moon is full, her circle is complete.
Don't leave me, friend, shout out, and see! I'm on my feet!

The building just past the garden is the **Heroes' Temple,** completed in 1931 in Art Deco style to honor Hungarian Jews who had fought in World War I.

In the garden behind the synagogue is the *Tree of Life,* also created by Imre Varga. This weeping willow, cast in steel, was erected in 1990, soon after the fall of communism made it possible to acknowledge the Holocaust. The willow makes an upside-down menorah, and each of the 4,000 metal leaves is etched with the name of a Holocaust victim. New leaves are added

all the time, donated by families of the victims. Notice that at the end of each branch is a Roman numeral, to assist people in finding their relatives' names. The large black-marble gateway represents a temple; the Hebrew inscription reads, "Is there a bigger pain than mine?" The plaques embedded in the base of the sculpture bear messages (many in English) from donors.

In the center of the garden is a symbolic grave for the many

diplomats from other nations who saved Hungarian Jews. The most famous of these—and the biggest name on the monument—is **Raoul Wallenberg** (1912-1947). An improbable hero, this ne'er-do-well Swedish playboy from a prominent family was sent as a diplomat to Hungary because nobody else wanted the post. He was empowered by the Swedish government to do whatever he could—bribe, threaten, lie, or blackmail—to save as many Jews as possible from the Nazis. He surpassed everyone's low expectations by dedicating (and ultimately sacrificing) his life to the cause.

By giving Swedish passports to Jews and admitting them to safe houses, he succeeded in rescuing tens of thousands of people from certain death. Shortly after the Soviets arrived, Wallenberg was arrested, accused of being a US spy, sent to a gulag...and never seen alive again. (Later, Russian authorities acknowledged he was

executed in 1947, in Moscow's Lubyanka prison.)

The grave is also etched with the names of other "Righteous Among the Nations" who went above and beyond to save Jews. According to the Talmud, "Whoever saves one life, saves the world entire." The small stones placed on graves are typical of Jewish cemeteries: Each stone is a sign of remembrance. Surrounding the grave are four rose-colored pillars with the names of other non-Jews who saved individuals or families. The list is still growing, with periodic new additions. In the big stained-glass window that stands near the grave, the fire symbolizes the Holocaust (the Hebrew word is *Shoah*, literally, "catastrophe"), and the curling snake represents fascism.

Along the back wall behind the stained glass, find the little **alcoves** labeled for individual victims, with lights that go on after dark. The alcoves—like other memorials in this garden—are filled with small stones.

To the right of the alcoves stands a small (relocated) stretch of the **wall** that enclosed the ghetto. (You can get a peek at a small stretch of the original wall later on this walk.)

• *The exit of the Great Synagogue complex is through the fence, near the* Tree of Life. *You'll exit onto Wesselényi utca. From here, you can turn left and walk a block to the busy square in front of the synagogue, at the Small Boulevard, with ample connections around the city.*

However, if you'd like to learn more about this neighborhood's Jewish story, continue on to Part 2.

PART 2: JEWISH QUARTER WALK

While this area was shrouded in soot and gloom during the communist period, today Budapest's Jewish Quarter is coming back to life. You'll find monuments and artifacts of Jewish history in these streets—but you sometimes have to hunt for them a bit. This walk also takes you through an area with some of the city's trendiest eateries and liveliest nightlife ("ruin pubs" and other venues), which also sprouted here after communism.

• *Exiting the Great Synagogue grounds by the* Tree of Life, *turn right up...*

Wesselényi Utca

The large building on your right—which faces the memorial garden—is **Goldmark Hall,** a cultural center for the Association of Jewish Communities in Hungary (MAZSHISZ). It presents occasional concerts of traditional Jewish music (look for signs) and houses the **Hungarian Jewish Archives and Family Research Center,** which invites people with Hungarian Jewish ancestry to use their archives for a small fee.

At the first corner—just outside the garden's gate—you may see a makeshift memorial honoring **Hannah Szenes** (1921-1944), a Hungarian-born poet and soldier who migrated to what was then British Palestine and lived on a kibbutz, working toward building an Israeli state. During World War II, she enlisted with the RAF and parachuted into Yugoslavia with a mission to free Hungarian Jews bound for Auschwitz. She was captured at the Hungarian border, tortured, and executed. This memorial was part of the controversial "Shoah Cellar"—a private, for-profit exhibit that many members of the local Jewish community considered exploitative. Under heavy pressure, the exhibit closed its doors. The experience stoked an important conversation about who "owns" the Jewish story of Budapest, and serves as a reminder that the 21st-century Jewish Hungarian identity is still evolving.

Head up Wesselényi street, noticing the eclectic **architecture** around you. After a devastating flood in 1838, this neighborhood was rebuilt—starting with the Great Synagogue (1859), followed by the townhouses around it. Most of what you see here dates from the late 19th or early 20th centuries. Some are nicely renovated; others are still soot-covered. And mixed in are some much newer buildings (like the glassy office tower at the next corner, on the left). These replaced houses that were destroyed in WWII bombings, or those that fell into severe disrepair with depopulation following the Holocaust. It's only been after the fall of communism that this neighborhood has seen more investment, starting with the work of the "ruin pub" entrepreneurs (we'll see an example of this soon).

At the end of the second block on Wesselényi street, on the right at #13, step into **Café Noé** ("Noah"). This is a good spot to try the traditional Hungarian Jewish cake called *flódni*—a dense, flavorful layer cake with poppy seeds, walnuts, and apples (this version adds plum jam). This shop is owned by a rabbi's daughter, and the Judaica shop next door is owned by her mother.

• *Just beyond the café, you reach the cross-street called...*

Kazinczy Utca: "Ruin Pub Row"

This street is the main artery of Budapest's "ruin pub" nightlife zone, the Seventh District. Even if it's daytime, turn right on Kazinczy and walk a few doors down to the building that looks like it's seen much better days (on the right, at #14). This is **Szimpla,** the original (and still the best) of the city's ruin pubs—convivial, youthful bars with ramshackle furniture sprawling through should-be-condemned buildings and courtyards. The juxtaposition of sober Jewish sites with trendy nightspots may seem jarring. But it's not a coincidence: The Holocaust left this area largely vacant, and it remained a slum during communist times. It's only in the last two decades that its central location and low rents have attracted creative young bar owners and restaurateurs. Some members of the local community are displeased with the rowdy late-night scene that has erupted here—you'll notice "Please be quiet" signs by many doors. And some local, Jewish-owned shops have closed due to increased rents. But other locals see the benefits of the increased awareness and gentrification for this until now overlooked part of the city.

And yet, even tucked amid the ruin pubs, ramen bars, and taco stands, you'll find faint echoes of this quarter's Jewish heritage. Next door to Szimpla, between the ruin pub and the vacant lot with food trucks, notice the austere, boxy, two-story building (at #16). This is a **mikveh**—a traditional Jewish ritual bath, used by Orthodox Jews to bathe before the Sabbath and other holy days. The door on the left is for men; the one on the right is for women (but the complex is not open to the public).

Turn around and head back the way you came, continuing straight along Kazinczy street across Wesselényi street. This stretch of Kazinczy is lined with a mix of modern, international eateries and traditional Jewish ones. The street has a variety of **kosher eateries:** Tel Aviv Café, on the left (at #28), sells kosher dairy products, while Carmel, farther along (just past the synagogue, on the right at #31) sells kosher meat. Tucked back in the synagogue courtyard is yet another kosher restaurant, Hanna.

• *In the middle of this scene—on the right, where Kazinczy utca curves—you'll see the...*

Orthodox Synagogue

Built in the Vienna-inspired Secession style in 1912, this temple stood damaged and deserted for decades after World War II until being renovated in 2006.

Today it invites visitors to see its colorful, sumptuously decorated interior. While grandly opulent, this place is more typical of synagogue architecture than the Great Synagogue.

Inside, the green pillars at the front flanking the ark evoke the Torah scrolls, and the red columns (with Zsolnay tile decorations) echo the Temple of Solomon. The seat on the left was filled by the synagogue's first rabbi, Koppel Reich (1838-1929), who was a pillar of the community: He advised Habsburg Emperor Franz Josef and was a member of the Hungarian Parliament. Out of deference to him, nobody has sat in this seat since his death. The temple is still used by a small but dedicated local Orthodox congregation of about 50 people.

• *From the Orthodox Synagogue, continue along Kazinczy utca. At the end of the block, turn left onto Dob utca. After about a block and a half on your right, at #16, is the easy-to-miss entrance to...*

Gozsdu Udvar

This long series of courtyards burrows through the middle of a city block, between Dob utca 16 and Király utca 13. When this neighborhood hosted a fast-growing Jewish population and space was at a premium, courtyards like this one were filled with community life: restaurants, shops, and other businesses. (Gozsdu Udvar—the best surviving example of this—was built by and named for a prominent 19th-century

Jewish attorney from Transylvania, today part of Romania, who established a foundation to fund Transylvanians who wanted to study here.)

After decades of neglect, this passage was spruced up and opened to the public. This genteel space—which evokes the Golden Age of Jewish life in Budapest—is once again filled with cafés and bars, and after hours it's a bustling nightlife hub.

Head down Gozsdu Udvar, perhaps window-shopping for a meal or drink to enjoy later. You'll go about two-thirds of the way down the passage; at the place where the corridor opens up, you'll turn left to reach our next stop.

But before you do, consider this...

Optional Detour to the Ghetto Wall: Almost nothing survives of the wall that surrounded the Budapest ghetto during Nazi occupation. But a five-minute walk takes you to a place where you can get a (distant) peek, from across a courtyard.

To find it, carry straight on through Gozsdu Udvar to the far end. Emerging at Király utca, turn right and continue a few doors up the street. Pause at the main door for #15, on the right (likely under a wooden scaffolding, and marked with a plaque). Peek through the hole in the door and you'll see—at the far end of the courtyard—a rough stone wall that was rebuilt here, using the original stones. When the Nazis invaded Hungary, they forced all Budapest Jews to live in a small area near the Great Synagogue, enclosed it with this wall (in November of 1944), and prohibited them from interacting with the rest of the city. The wall was erected within interior courtyards like this one—rather than along public streets—to disguise it as much as possible from non-Jewish residents.

• *Back inside Gozsdu Udvar, find the intersection with Madách Imre út—an alley that cuts through the middle of the passage. Look for the tall skyscraper with a semicircular roofline looming just overhead. Turn toward that skyscraper, then past it. In a short block, you'll pass the funky café/ruin pub/art gallery Telep (on your right) before reaching the intersection with the street called...*

Rumbach Utca

Look straight ahead, at the giant brick **arch** spanning the narrow street. This gateway was designed in the 1930s to be the entrance of an elaborate thoroughfare connecting the Small and Great Boulevards. The great road was never built, but the zone on either side of the gateway has evolved into an inviting plaza where locals enjoy lounging and relaxing on sunny days (the Deák tér stop for trams #47 and #49 is just on the other side). This arch also marks the site of the long-gone Orczy-Ház, one of the first Jewish apartment buildings erected after Jews were allowed to settle within the city in the 1780s. This was something of a cradle of Jewish culture, growing over time into a sprawling complex with more than 140 apartments, merchants, cellar warehouses, kosher eateries, a ritual bath, and a synagogue.

Turn left and walk along Rumbach street. Up ahead on the right, painted on the side of a building jutting into the street, is a nostalgic **Sisi mural** celebrating empress Elisabeth, who strove for greater autonomy for Hungarians within the sprawling Austro-Hungarian empire (see page 292). While this neighborhood is known as the Jewish Quarter and the Seventh District, it's also part of the Erzsébetváros—"Elisabeth Town"—which stretches all the way to City Park.

Across the street from the Sisi mural (on the left) is the **Syna-gogue at Rumbach Street.** This synagogue's colorful Moorish-style interior survives from the Golden Age of Jewish culture in Budapest. The late-19th-century building was designed by the great Viennese architect Otto Wagner. It was abandoned for years, but today it's wrapping up a lengthy, desperately needed renovation—and if it's open, it's well worth a look. You'll wander through the relatively small but very tall space, appreciating its lavish decorations.

Just after the synagogue (and past the Sisi mural), on the right, step into **Printa Café** (closed Sun, Rumbach 10, www.printa.hu). This inviting design shop/silkscreen studio/art gallery/coffeehouse offers a perfect glimpse at the hipster culture that's taking over this area of Budapest—designer fair-trade coffee, local artists exhibiting their works, and a wide array of "trashion" accessories made from reused materials (stylish bags made from old leather jackets, belts made from discarded shirts, and so on).

Like all things in this neighborhood, this building also holds an important place in Jewish history: It was the location of the main communal kitchen during the time when Budapest's Jews were crammed into a ghetto. And this street was also a collection point for local Jews in 1941. Under autonomous Hungarian rule, years before the Nazis invaded, Jews without citizenship were gathered on Rumbach Street in order to be deported to Ukraine. Once there, an estimated 20,000 were massacred by SS troops—the Holocaust's first mass killing of victims numbering in the five digits. While today's ruling Fidesz government—so enamored of Hungary's great past—would rather brush aside details about

Hungarian participation in the Holocaust, members of the local Jewish community feel it's important to tell these stories.

Peeking through the gate just past Printa Café (on the right), you can see another **chain of courtyards** similar to Gozsdu Udvar—this one closed to the public and not yet renovated.

Across the street and a couple of doors down (at #7), pause and look at the pavement below. Embedded in the concrete are a pair of low-profile, bronze **stumbling stones,** which identify Jews who lived at this address before they were murdered in the Holocaust. This type of memorial began in Germany (you'll find them all over Berlin) and is a more recent arrival to Budapest. Keep an eye out for small-but-poignant memorials, particularly in this district—they help humanize the difficult-to-fathom toll of the Holocaust.

• *Continue to the end of the block, at the intersection with...*

Dob Utca

First, turn left up Dob street, passing through a narrow park. At the end of the park, about 10 feet overhead on the wall, notice the **monument to Carl Lutz** (1895-1975).

This is one of several monuments in this area honoring international diplomats who—like Raoul Wallenberg (described earlier)—risked their lives to save Hungarian Jews. Born in Switzerland and educated in the US, Carl Lutz became a Swiss vice-consul to Hungary during World War II. After the Nazis invaded and began sending Hungarian Jews to death camps, Lutz set up safe houses around the city (which he formally registered as "Swiss soil") and issued permission for tens of thousands of Jews to emigrate. In the monument, the figure on the side of the building (representing Lutz) extends a lifeline to the vulnerable figure lying on the ground below him. Lutz is credited, ultimately, with saving 62,000 Jewish lives. (This monument also marks the edge of the WWII-era ghetto.)

Now do an about-face, and head back down Dob street the way you came. Crossing Rumbach street, continue another half-block. On the left side of Dob, at #3, the low-profile *Javítás* and *Készítés* signs mark **Kefe Ecset Szakulet,** one of the few tradition-al, Jewish-owned shops that still survive in this rapidly gentrifying neighborhood. This shop, owned by the Markovics family since just after World War I (and operated by the founder's granddaughter), sells brushes and brooms, some made right here. Inside, notice the little kitchen on the right; traditionally, shopkeepers would also live on the premises. Consider buying something here just to support the family business—it's an endearing, authentic slice of life that's at risk of fading away (closed Sat-Sun).

Leaving the shop, continue down Dob street a few more steps, then look back, up, and across the street at a colorful **mural of Ángel Sanz Briz** (1910-1980), a Spanish diplomat who helped save 5,200 Jews from the Nazis by issuing them Spanish passports, even purchasing houses where they could live until it was safe for them to escape. Spaniards call him the "Angel of Budapest"—but fortunately, Budapest had many such angels in its darkest hour. The colorful mural, created by a renowned Spanish street artist, feels like a celebration of life.

As does all of the Jewish Quarter these days. Things are changing, but mostly for the better. And even as some aspects of this area's Jewish heritage are being gentrified away, others are stronger than they have been in generations. A walk through Budapest's Jewish Quarter is an inspiring peek into this proud, once endangered, now rebounding facet of Hungarian life.

• *Our walk is finished. If you continue to the end of Dob street—just a few steps past the mural—you'll pop out at the Small Boulevard (Károly körút). The Great Synagogue, where we started our walk, is just to the left. From here, trams #47 and #49 circle the Small Boulevard; you can ride either one to the left, to the National Museum, Great Market Hall, and Gellért Baths. To the right, a five-minute walk takes you to Deák tér, which is the terminus for those trams, a handy Metró hub (where lines M1, M2, and M3 intersect), and the starting point for the* 📖 *Andrassy Út Walk.*

CASTLE HILL WALK

Várhegy

Once the seat of Hungarian royalty, and now the city's highest-profile tourist zone, Castle Hill is a historic spit of land looming above the Buda bank of the Danube. Scenic from afar, but (frankly) a bit soulless from up close, it's best seen quickly. The major landmarks are the huge, green-domed Royal Palace—otherwise known as Buda Castle—at the south end of the hill (housing a pair of museums) and the frilly-spired Matthias Church near the north end (with the hill's best interior). In between are tourist-filled pedestrian streets and historic buildings rebuilt after a WWII bombing. This walk gives you the lay of the land and links up the hill's most worthwhile attractions and museums, including the Matthias Church, the Fisherman's Bastion, the Hungarian National Gallery, and the WWII-era Hospital in the Rock. You'll also appreciate the bird's-eye views across the Danube to Pest.

Orientation

Length of This Walk: Allow about two hours, including a brief visit to Matthias Church; you'll need more time to enter additional sights (especially the Hungarian National Gallery, the Hospital in the Rock, or the Matthias Church tower).

When to Visit: Castle Hill is jammed with tour groups in the morning, but it's much less crowded in the afternoon. Since restaurants up here are touristy and a bad value, Castle Hill is an ideal after-lunch activity.

Getting There: The Metró and trams won't take you to the top of Castle Hill, but you have several other good options.

For a free and scenic approach, you can **walk** up through the castle gardens called Várkert Bazár (trams #19 and #41 stop right in front). From the monumental gateway facing the

Danube embankment, head up the stairs into the park, then look right for the covered escalator. From its top, you can either turn left to hike the rest of the way up (on the switchback path), or you can carry on straight ahead to find an elevator (under a rust-colored canopy) that zips you right up to the view terrace in front of the Royal Palace (floor 2). From here, you can begin the walk at ❷, the viewpoint in front of the palace, then see the Turul bird statue and funicular station on your way back across the hill later. This is a good option if there's a line for the funicular.

From Pest, it's usually fastest to hop on **bus #16,** with stops near the Deák tér Metró hub (on Harmincad utca alongside Erzsébet tér; use exit "E" from the station underpass) and at Széchenyi tér, at the Pest end of the Chain Bridge. (You can also catch it at Clark Ádám tér at the Buda end of the Chain Bridge—across the street from the lower funicular station, and much cheaper than the funicular.) Or you can go via Széll Kálmán tér (on the M2/red Metró line, or by taking tram #4 or #6 around Pest's Great Boulevard); from here, bus #16, as well as buses **#16A** and **#116,** head up to the castle. All of these buses stop at Dísz tér, at the crest of the hill, about halfway along its length (most people on the bus will be getting off there, too). From Dísz tér, cross the street and walk five minutes along the row of flagpoles toward the green dome, then bear left to find the big Turul bird statue at the start of this walk.

The **funicular** (*sikló,* SHEE-kloh), which lifts visitors from the Chain Bridge to the top of Castle Hill, is a Budapest landmark that was built in 1870 to provide transportation to Castle Hill workers (1,200 Ft one-way, 1,800 Ft round-trip, not covered by transit pass, daily 7:30-22:00, departs every 5-10 minutes, closed  for maintenance every other Mon). It leaves you right at the Turul bird statue, where this walk begins. (If there's a long line at the lower funicular station, just hop on bus #16 across the roundabout—described above.)

Finally, you'll see an oversized golf cart labeled **"official Budapest castle bus."** This runs every 15 minutes from points at the base of the castle (including near the bottom station of the funicular, and in front of the Várkert Bazár) up to essentially the same stops the public bus uses at the top of the castle. While handy, this is a pricey little tourist trip (2,100 Ft round-trip, runs daily 9:00-17:00) compared to simply taking a public bus; the only reason I'd take this is if I had a Budapest Card, which covers it.

To **leave the hilltop,** most visitors find it easiest just to walk down after their visit (see the end of this tour). But if you'll be taking the public bus down, it's smart to buy tickets for the return trip before you ascend Castle Hill—the only place to buy them up top is at the post office near Dísz tér (Mon-Fri 8:00-16:00, closed Sat-Sun).

Changing of the Guard: On the hour, uniformed soldiers do a changing-of-the-guard ceremony at Sándor Palace (the president's residence, near the top of the funicular), with a more elaborate show at 12:00. While not worth planning your day around (it's just a few guys in modern military uniforms slinging rifles), it's fun to watch if you happen to be nearby.

Hungarian National Gallery: 1,800 Ft, Tue-Sun 10:00-18:00, closed Mon, Szent György tér 2.

Budapest History Museum: 2,000 Ft; Tue-Sun 10:00-18:00, Nov-Feb until 16:00, closed Mon year-round; Szent György tér 2.

Golden Eagle Pharmacy Museum: 800 Ft, Tue-Sun 10:30-18:00, Nov-mid-March until 16:00, closed Mon year-round, Tárnok utca 18, http://budacastlebudapest.com.

Matthias Church: Church—1,800 Ft, Mon-Sat 9:00-17:00 (may close Sat afternoons in summer for weddings), Sun from 13:00, Szentháromság tér 2; tower—1,800 Ft for 30-minute tour, departs at the top of each hour daily 10:00-17:00.

Fisherman's Bastion: 1,000 Ft, daily 9:00-20:00; after closing time and off-season, no tickets are sold but bastion is open and free to enter; Szentháromság tér 5.

Eateries: In the Eating in Budapest chapter, I've suggested a few lunch options up here—but for more choices, head just downhill to Batthyány tér.

Starring: Budapest's most historic quarter, with a palace (and a top collection of Hungarian art), a gorgeous church interior, sweeping vistas over city rooftops, and layers of history.

BACKGROUND

This hilltop has a history as complex and layered as Hungary's. In the 13th century, Tatars swept through Eastern Europe, destroying much of Hungary (including then-capital Esztergom). King Béla IV, who was forced to rebuild his kingdom, relocated the capital to Buda—a more protected location—and fortified the town.

By the early 15th century, Castle Hill had one of Europe's biggest palaces. Mátyás (Matthias) Corvinus, the Renaissance king, made it even more extravagant, putting Buda—and Hungary—on the map. But just a few decades later, the invading Ottomans occupied Buda and turned the palace into a military garrison. When the Habsburgs laid siege to the hill for 77 days in 1686, gunpowder stored in the cellar exploded, destroying the palace. The Habsburgs (with a motley, pan-European army that included few Hungarians) took the hill, but Buda was deserted and in ruins.

The town was resettled by Austrians, who built a new Baroque palace, hoping that the Habsburg monarch would move in—but none ever did. The useless palace again became a garrison and was damaged yet again during the 1848 Revolution.

As World War II drew to a close, Budapest became the front line between the Nazis and the approaching Soviets. The labyrinth of natural caves under the hill was adapted for use as a secret military hospital (the tourable Hospital in the Rock). The Nazis, who believed the Danube to be a natural border for their empire, destroyed bridges across the river and staged a desperate "last stand" on Castle Hill. The Red Army laid siege to the hill for 100 days. They eventually succeeded in taking Budapest...but the city—and the hill—was devastated once again. Since then, the Royal Palace and hilltop town have been rebuilt once more, with a mix-and-match style that attempts, with only some success, to evoke the site's grand legacy. And today, Hungary's strong-arm leader, Viktor Orbán, is making parts of the castle his own—he has moved into a new palace here, and is rebuilding or taking over several other sections of the complex.

The Walk Begins

• *Orient yourself from the top of the funicular, enjoying the views over the Danube. (We'll get a full visual tour from a better viewpoint later.) At the top of the nearby staircase, notice the giant bird that looks like a vulture. This is the...*

❶ Turul Bird

This mythical bird of Magyar folktales supposedly led the Hungarian migrations from the steppes of Central Asia in the ninth

CASTLE HILL

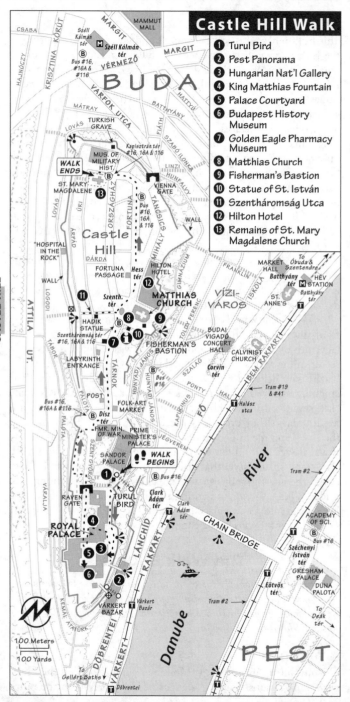

Castle Hill Walk

1. Turul Bird
2. Pest Panorama
3. Hungarian Nat'l Gallery
4. King Matthias Fountain
5. Palace Courtyard
6. Budapest History Museum
7. Golden Eagle Pharmacy Museum
8. Matthias Church
9. Fisherman's Bastion
10. Statue of St. István
11. Szentháromság Utca
12. Hilton Hotel
13. Remains of St. Mary Magdalene Church

century. He dropped his sword in the Carpathian Basin, indicating that this was to be the permanent home of the Magyar people. While the Hungarians have long since integrated into Europe, the Turul remains a symbol of Magyar pride. During a surge of nationalism in the 1920s, a movement named after this bird helped revive traditional Hungarian culture. And today, the bird is invoked by right-wing nationalist politicians—something of a dog whistle for rallying their base (similar to how the Confederate flag might be used in certain circles in the United States).

• *We'll return this way later. But for now, go through the monumental gateway by the Turul and climb down the stairs, then walk along the broad terrace in front of the...*

Royal Palace (Királyi Palota)

The imposing palace on Castle Hill barely hints at the colorful story of this hill since the day that the legendary Turul dropped his sword.

It was once the top Renaissance palace in Europe... but that was several centuries and several versions ago. The current palace— a historically inaccurate, post-WWII reconstruction—is a loose rebuilding of previous versions. It's big but soulless. The most prominent feature of today's palace—the green dome—didn't even exist in earlier versions. Fortunately, the palace does house some worthwhile museums (described later), and boasts the fine terrace you're strolling on, with some of Budapest's best views.

Walk all the way down the terrace to the big equestrian statue in front of the dome. This depicts **Eugene of Savoy,** a general who had great success fighting the Hungarians' hated enemies, the Ottomans. Eugene was a fascinating character: He was extremely short in stature, had a huge nose and buck teeth, and was gay (and involved with the brother of Louis XIV)—*and* his mother was caught up in an embarrassing scandal. For these reasons, he was deemed not fit for a leadership position in the French military—so he offered his

CASTLE HILL

services to the Habsburgs instead, beginning an illustrious career. First he helped break the Turkish Siege of Vienna in 1683, then he led the successful Siege of Belgrade in 1717; together, these victories marked the beginning of the end of the Ottoman advance into Europe. Eugene—who fought under three successive Habsburg emperors—was hugely popular across a Europe that was terrified of the always-looming Ottoman threat. He was the Patton or Eisenhower of his day—a great war hero admired and appreciated by all. This explains why a Frenchman gets a place of honor in front of Hungary's Royal Palace.

• *With the palace at your back, notice the long, skinny promontory sticking out from Castle Hill (on your right). Walk out to the tip of that promontory to enjoy Castle Hill's best...*

❼ Pest Panorama

From here, you can see how topographically different the two halves of Budapest really are. The hill you're on is considered one of the last foothills of the Alps, which ripple from here all the way to France. But immediately across the Danube, everything is oh so flat. Here begins the so-called Great Hungarian Plain, which comprises much of the country—a vast expanse that stretches all the way to Asia. For this reason, Budapest has historically been thought of as being on the bubble between West and East. From the ancient Romans—who considered the river the line between the civilized Roman world and a vast realm beyond that they called "the land of the Hun"—to Adolf Hitler, many past rulers have viewed the Danube through Budapest as a natural border for Europe.

Scan Pest on the horizon, from left to right. Tree-filled Margaret Island, a popular recreation spot, sits in the middle of the Danube. Following the Pest riverbank, you can't miss the spiny Parliament, with its giant red dome. Straight ahead, you enjoy views of the Chain Bridge, with Gresham Palace and the 1896-era St. István's Basilica lined up just beyond it. (The Parliament and St. István's are both exactly 96 meters tall, in honor of the auspicious millennial celebration in 1896.)

The Chain Bridge cuts downtown Pest in two: The left half, or "Leopold Town," is administrative, with government ministries, embassies, banks, and so on; the right half is the commercial and touristic center of Pest, with the best riverside promenade. (Each of these is covered by a different self-guided walk in this book.) To the right is the white Elisabeth Bridge, named for the Austrian empress ("Sisi") who so loved her Hungarian subjects. Downriver (to the right) is the green Liberty Bridge, formerly named for Elisabeth's hubby Franz Josef. (If you squint, you might be able to see the Turul birds that top the pillars of this bridge.) And the tall hill to the right, named for the martyred St. Gellért (who patiently attempted to convert the rowdy Magyars after their king adopted Christianity), is topped by the Soviet-era Liberation Monument. At your feet, to the right, sprawl the inviting gardens of the Várkert Bazár terrace (accessible by the nearby elevator and described on page 59).

• *Head back to the statue on the terrace. Facing Eugene's rear end is the main entrance to the...*

❸ Hungarian National Gallery (Magyar Nemzeti Galéria)

While not quite a must-see, this museum is the best place in Hungary to appreciate the works of homegrown artists, and to get a

peek into the often-morose Hungarian worldview. The collection—which is eventually scheduled to move to a new home in City Park—includes a remarkable group of 15th-century, wood-carved altars from Slovakia (then "Upper Hungary"); piles of gloomy canvases dating from the dark days after the failed 1848 Revolution; several works by two great Hungarian Realist painters, Mihály Munkácsy and László Paál; and paintings by the troubled, enigmatic, and recently in-vogue Post-Impressionist Tivadar Csontváry Kosztka. The collection's highlights can be viewed quickly. For a self-guided tour of the top pieces, see page 60.

• *Head back out to the Eugene statue and face the palace. Go through the passage to the right of the National Gallery entrance (next to the café). You'll emerge into a courtyard decorated with the...*

❹ King Matthias Fountain

This fountain depicts King Matthias enjoying one of his favorite pastimes, hunting. (Notice the distinctive, floppy-eared Hungarian hound dog, or Vizsla.) At the bottom of the fountain, the guy on the left is Matthias' scribe, while the woman on the right is Ilonka ("The

Beautiful"). While Matthias was on an incognito hunting trip, he wooed Ilonka, who fell desperately in love with him—oblivious to the fact he was the king. When he left suddenly to return to Buda, Ilonka tracked him down and realized who he was. Understanding that his rank meant they could never be together, Ilonka committed suicide. This is typical of many Hungarian legends, which tend to be melancholic and end badly.

• *On that cheerful note, go around the right side of the fountain and through the passage, into the...*

❺ Palace Courtyard

This space, while impressive, somehow feels like an empty husk...a too-big office building. The entrance to the Budapest History Museum (described next) is at the far end of the courtyard. But first, duck through the door and down the hallway on your right as you go through the passage (free entry). The hall is lined with exhibits from the museum, giving you a free glimpse (and English descriptions) of the evolution of this site over the centuries, including stone fragments, paintings, drawings, and photo-

graphs of the palace in different eras. If you like what you see here, consider visiting the museum; if not, skip ahead.

Windows on the right offer a view of newly rebuilt parts of the palace complex, which were destroyed in World War II. The building with the ornate copper roof, lower on the hill, was the pavilion of the **Riding School** (Budapest's answer to Vienna's famous Spanish Riding School). Uphill from that is the main building of the **Hungarian Royal Guard.**

❻ Budapest History Museum (Budapesti Történeti Múzeum)

This earnest but dusty collection strains to bring the history of this city to life. If Budapest really intrigues you, this is a fine place to explore its history. Otherwise, skip it. The dimly lit fragments of 14th-century sculptures, depicting early Magyars, allow you to see how Asian those original Hungarians truly looked. The "Light and Shadow" exhibit deliberately but effectively traces the union between Buda and Pest. Rounding out the collection are exhibits on prehistoric residents and a sprawling cellar that unveils fragments from the oh-so-many buildings that have perched on this hill over the centuries. For a rundown of its collection, see page 65.

Mátyás (Matthias) Corvinus: The Last Hungarian King

The Árpád dynasty—descendants of the original Magyar tribes—died out in 1301. For more than 600 years, Hungary would be ruled by elected foreign rulers...with one exception.

In the mid-15th century, the Hungarian military general János Hunyadi enjoyed great success on the battlefield against the Ottomans (including a pivotal victory in 1456's Battle of Belgrade). Meanwhile, Hungary's imported kings kept dying unexpectedly. Finally, the Hungarian nobility took a chance on a Hungarian-born ruler and offered the throne to Hunyadi's son, Mátyás (or Matthias in English). According to legend, they sent a raven with a ring in its mouth to notify Matthias, who was away in Prague. He returned to Buda, and took the raven both as his symbol and as his royal nickname: Corvinus (Latin for "raven").

Matthias Corvinus (r. 1458-1490) became the first Hungarian-descended king in more than 150 years. Progressive and well educated in the Humanist tradition, Matthias Corvinus was the quintessential Renaissance king. A lover of the Italian Renaissance, he patronized the arts and built palaces legendary for their beauty. As a benefactor of the poor, he dressed as a commoner and ventured into the streets to see firsthand how the nobles of his realm treated his people.

A strong, savvy leader, Matthias created Central Europe's first standing army—30,000 mercenaries known as the Black Army. No longer reliant on the nobility for military support, Good King Matthias was able to drain power from the nobles—earning him the nickname the "people's king."

Matthias was also a shrewd military tactician. Realizing that skirmishing with the Ottomans would squander his resources, he made peace with the sultan to stabilize Hungary's southern border. Then he swept north, invading Moravia, Bohemia, and even Austria. By 1485, Matthias moved into his new palace in Vienna, and Hungary was enjoying a Golden Age.

But just five years later, Matthias died mysteriously at the age of 47, and his empire disintegrated. Before long the Ottomans flooded back into Hungary, and the country entered a dark period. It is said that when Matthias died, justice died with him. To this day, Hungarians rank him the greatest of all kings, and they sing of his siege of Vienna in their national anthem. They're proud that for a few decades they had a truly Hungarian king—and a great one at that.

CASTLE HILL

Walk to Matthias Church

Leaving the palace courtyard, walk straight up the slight incline (with the rebuilt Hungarian Royal Guard building on your left). Then you'll pass under a gate with a raven holding a ring in its mouth (a symbol of King Matthias). As you continue along the line of flagpoles, the big white building on your right (near the funicular station) is the **Sándor Palace,** the Hungarian president's office. This is where you

can see the relatively low-key changing of the guard each hour on the hour, with a special show at noon.

After Sándor Palace is the yellow former **Court Theater** (Várszínház), which has seen many great performances over the centuries—including a visit from Beethoven in 1800. A few years back, Prime Minister Viktor Orbán (not known for humble gestures) grew jealous of the president's swanky digs, kicked out the dancers, and renovated this building as the prime minister's residence. Orbán's critics see this as a troubling gesture: The Parliament was intentionally built along the river to remind leaders of the common people. Orbán's move up to the castle smacks of putting himself above his subjects. (For much more on Orbán's shenanigans, see the Leopold Town Walk chapter.)

In the field in the middle of this terrace, you'll notice the **ruins** of a medieval monastery and church. Along the left side (past the flagpoles) is the ongoing excavation of the medieval Jewish quarter—more reminders that most of what you see on today's Castle Hill has been destroyed and rebuilt many times over.

Notice the bridge on the left, crossing over some of those ruins, as well as a trench around the castle wall. Go over that bridge to a viewpoint for a look at the **Buda Hills**—the "Beverly Hills" of Hungary, draped with orchards, vineyards, and the homes of the wealthiest Budapesters.

Walk along this outer terrace, enjoying the views, then hook right to reach the **former Ministry of War.** Until 2013, this was still a bombed-out shell, with war damage from both World War II and the brutal Soviet response to the 1956 Uprising. You could still see faint bullet holes and shrapnel marks—intentionally left here as a memorial. But Orbán—as a part of his broader theme of whitewashing Hungarian history—decided he didn't want to see those ugly scars from his new home nearby, so he had them repaired.

Cross the street in front of the former Ministry of War to reach **Dísz tér** (Parade Square). Here you'll see convenient bus stops for connecting to other parts of Budapest (bus #16, #16A, or #116 to

Széll Kálmán tér; or—departing from the stop directly in front of the post office on the left—bus #16 to the Pest side of the Chain Bridge; bus tickets sold at post office Mon-Fri 8:00-16:00, closed Sat-Sun). On the right, behind the low wall, is a courtyard with an open-air Hungarian **folk-art market.** While it's fun to browse, prices here are high (haggle away). The Great Market Hall has a better selection and generally lower prices (described at the end of the Pest Town Center Walk chapter).

Continue straight uphill on **Tárnok utca,** bearing right at the park; soon after, on the left, is the recommended Vár Bistro (a handy if uninspired lunch cafeteria). This area often disappoints visitors. After being destroyed by Ottomans, it was rebuilt in sensible Baroque, lacking the romantic time-capsule charm of a medieval old town. But if you poke your head into some courtyards, you'll almost always see some original Gothic arches and other medieval features.

As you continue along, ponder the fact that miles of **caves** were burrowed under Castle Hill—carved out by water, expanded by the Ottomans, and used by locals during the siege of Buda at the end of World War II. If you'd like to spelunk under Castle Hill, there are two different sightseeing options: To learn about how the caves were used during the 20th century, it's worth going on the lengthy Hospital in the Rock tour. For just a quick look, you can check out the touristy Labyrinth of Buda Castle cave, with a sparse, hokey historical exhibit (both options are described starting on page 68).

As you approach the church tower, on your left at #18 is the low-profile entrance to the ❼ **Golden Eagle Pharmacy Museum** (dark-orange building, look for *Arany Sas Patika* sign). Consider dipping into this modest three-room collection of historic pharmaceutical bric-a-brac, including a cute old pharmacy counter and an alchemist's lab.

On the left, the **Prima grocery store** sells reasonably priced cold drinks, and has a coffee shop upstairs. A good spot for dessert is just up the little lane in front of the grocery store, under the passage: **Rétesbár,** selling strudel *(rétes)* with various fillings (daily 8:00-20:00, Balta köz).

The white, circular building in the park across from the grocery store is a TI that can answer questions and has a handy pictorial map of the castle area (daily 10:00-18:00).

Just beyond the grocery store, a warty plague column from 1713 marks **Szentháromság tér** (Holy Trinity Square), the main square of old Buda.

• *Dominating the square is the...*

❽ Matthias Church (Mátyás-Templom)

Budapest's best church has been destroyed and rebuilt several times in the 800 years since it was founded by King Béla IV. Today's

version—renovated at great expense in the late 19th century and restored after World War II—is an ornately decorated lesson in Hungarian history. The church's unofficial namesake isn't a saint, so it can't be formally named for him. Its official name is the Church of Our Lady or the Coronation Church, but everyone calls it the Matthias Church, for Matthias Corvinus, the popular Renaissance king who got married here—twice.

❍ Self-Guided Tour: Examine the **exterior.** While the nucleus of the church is Gothic, most of what you see outside—including the frilly, flamboyant steeple—was added for the 1896 millennial celebrations. At the top of the stone corner tower facing the river, notice the raven—the ever-present symbol of King Matthias Corvinus.

Buy your ticket across the square from the church's side door, at the ticket windows embedded in the wall. Then enter the church. The good English descriptions post-

ed throughout will supplement this tour.

The sumptuous **interior** is wallpapered with gilded pages from a Hungarian history textbook. Different eras are represented by symbolic motifs. Entering the side door, turn left and go to the back end of the church. The wall on the left represents the Renaissance, with a giant coat of arms of beloved King Matthias Corvinus. (The tough guys in armor on either side are members of his mercenary Black Army, the source of his power.) Notice another raven, with a ring in its beak.

Work your way clockwise around the church. The first chapel (in the back corner, to the left as you face the closed main doors)—the **Loreto Chapel**—holds the church's prize possession: a 1515 statue of Mary and Jesus. Anticipating Ottoman plundering, locals walled over its niche. The occupying Ottomans used the church as their primary mosque—oblivious to the precious statue hidden behind the plaster. Then, a century and a half later, during the siege of Buda in 1686, gunpowder stored in the castle up the street detonated, and the wall crumbled. Mary's

triumphant face showed through, terrifying the Ottomans. Supposedly this was the only part of town taken from the Ottomans without a fight.

Facing the doors, look about four paces to the right. At about eye-level, at the top of the stout pillar, a **carved capital** shows two men gesturing excitedly at a book. Dating from 1260, these carvings are some of the earliest surviving features in this church, which has changed much over the centuries.

As you look down the **nave,** notice the banners. They've hung here since the Mass that celebrated Habsburg monarch Franz Josef's coronation at this church on June 8, 1867. In a sly political compromise to curry favor in the Hungarian part of his territory, Franz Josef was "emperor" *(Kaiser)* of Austria, but only "king" *(König)* of Hungary. (If you see the old German phrase "K+K"—still used today as a boast of royal quality— it refers to this *"König und Kaiser"* arrangement.) So, after F. J. was crowned emperor in Vienna, he came down the Danube and said to the Hungarians, "King me."

Continue circling around the church. Along the left aisle (toward the main altar from the gift shop) is the **altar of St. Imre,** the son of the great King (and later Saint) István—who is standing to the left of him. This heir to the Hungarian throne was mysteriously killed by a boar while hunting when he was only 19 years old. Though Imre didn't live long enough to do anything important, he rode his father's coattails to sainthood. Lacking a direct heir, István dedicated his country to Mary—which is why she's wearing a crown in this altar, and at this church's main one (which we'll see soon).

The next chapel is the **tomb of Béla III,** utterly insignificant except that this is one of only two tombs of Hungarian kings that still exist in the country. The rest—including all of the biggies— were defiled by the Ottomans.

Now stand at the modern altar in the middle of the church, and look down the nave to the **main altar.** Mary floats above it all, and hovering over her is a full-scale replica of the Hungarian crown, which was blessed by Pope John Paul II. More than a millennium after István, Mary still officially wears this nation's crown.

Left of the altar is the **László Chapel,** venerating a great Christian knight who fought pagans in the 11th century.

Climb the circular staircase (in the front-left corner) up to the **gallery.** Walk along the royal oratory to a small mezzanine that overlooks the altar area—giving you a better look at the altar's details. Then head back along the gallery. In the room with a small organ is a modest exhibit about Sisi—Empress Elisabeth—who has an almost cult following among Hungarians. From here, huff up even more steps to a few more modest exhibits, including a replica of the Hungarian crown, orb, and scepter.

Back down at ground level, you exit the church under a replica of a fine Gothic **tympanum.** The weathered original is on display below, offering an unusual close-up look. The carved scene celebrates the centrality of the book in spreading the word of God.

• *You can also choose to head up to the...*

Church Tower: Covered on a separate ticket, the tower offers fine views over both sides of the Danube (and the colorfully tiled rooftop of the church itself). At the top of the hour, your guide will lead you up the 197 tight, twisty stone steps. A third of the way up, you'll pause to catch your breath and see a few copper architectural elements from the church and letters found in a time capsule from the 19th century. You'll pause again in the

belfry before popping out at the panorama terrace. Snap a few photos, then head back down the way you came. The whole experience takes about 30 minutes; the views are nice, but similar to what you can see for free from the terrace of our next stop, the Fisherman's Bastion.

• *Back outside, at the end of the square next to the Matthias Church, is the...*

❾ Fisherman's Bastion (Halászbástya)

This Neo-Romanesque fantasy rampart offers beautiful views over the Danube to Pest. In the Middle Ages, the fish market was just below here (in today's Víziváros, or "Water Town"), so this part of the rampart actually was guarded by fishermen. The current structure, however, is completely artificial—yet another example of Budapest sprucing itself up for 1896. Its seven pointy towers represent the seven Magyar tribes. The cone-headed arcades are reminiscent of tents the nomadic Magyars called home before they moved west

to Europe. The fanciful bastion was designed both to be seen from across the river to remind people of their rich heritage and as a romantic playground from which to enjoy some of the best views in town.

Paying the fee to climb up the bastion makes no sense—several parts of the terrace are free and just as good (peek through the windows to the left of the main area). Here and elsewhere along the bastion are several cafés that offer a nice, scenic break.

There's a pay WC to the right of the bastion. Also note that the grand staircase leading down from the bastion offers a handy shortcut to the Víziváros neighborhood and Batthyány tér (for affordable restaurants there, see page 239).

• *Between the bastion and the church stands a...*

❿ Statue of St. István

Hungary's first Christian king tamed the nomadic, pagan Magyars and established strict laws and the concept of private property. In

the late 900s, Géza, Grand Prince of the Hungarians, lost a major battle against the forces of Christian Europe—and realized that he must raise his son Vajk (c. 967-1038) as a Catholic and convert his people, or they would be forcefully driven out of Europe. Vajk took the Christian name István (EESHT-vahn, "Stephen") and was baptized in the year 1000. The reliefs on this statue show the commissioners of the pope crowning St. István, bringing Hungary into the fold of Christendom. This pragmatic move put Hungary on the map as a fully European kingdom, forging alliances that would endure for centuries. Without this pivotal event, Hungarians believe that the Magyar nation would have been lost. A passionate evangelist—more for the survival of his Magyar nation than for the salvation of his people—István beheaded those who wouldn't convert. To make his point perfectly clear, he quartered his reluctant uncle and sent him on four separate, simultaneous tours of the country to show Hungarians that Christianity was a smart choice. Gruesome as he was, István was sainted within 30 years of his death.

• *Directly across from Matthias Church is a charming little street called...*

⓫ Szentháromság Utca

Halfway down this street on the right, look for the venerable, recommended **Ruszwurm** café—the oldest in Budapest (see listing on page 243). At the end of the street is an equestrian statue of the war hero **András Hadik.** If you examine the horse closely, you'll see that his, ahem, undercarriage has been polished to a high shine. Local students rub these for good luck before a big exam. (I guess you could say students really have a ball preparing for tests.)

Continue out to the terrace and appreciate more views of the Buda Hills. If you go down the stairs or elevator here, then turn right up the street, you'll reach the entrance of the World War II-era **Hospital in the Rock,** where you can take an excellent tour to learn about the Nazi and Cold War era of Castle Hill (described on page 67).

• *Retrace your steps back to Matthias Church. Some visitors will have had their fill of Castle Hill; if so, you can make a graceful exit down the big staircase below the Fisherman's Bastion. You'll wind up in Víziváros, on the embankment. Or, from across the square facing the church, you can catch bus #16 to Deák tér and the center of Pest.*

If you wish, you can extend your walk to the northern part of Castle Hill, which is much quieter, less touristy, and (frankly) a bit less interesting. Start at the plague column, and go up the street next to the modern building.

⓬ Hilton Hotel

Built in 1976, the Hilton was the first plush Western hotel in town. Before 1989, it was a gleaming center of capitalism, offering a cushy refuge for Western travelers and a stark contrast to what was, at the time, a very gloomy city. To minimize the controversy of building upon so much history, architects thoughtfully incorporated the medieval ruins into their modern design.

Halfway down the hotel's facade (after the first set of doors, at the base of the tower), you'll see fragments of a 13th-century wall, with a **monument to King Matthias Corvinus.**

After the wall, continue along the second half of the Hilton Hotel facade. Turn right into the gift-shop entry, and then go right again inside the second glass door. Continuing straight ahead, you'll pop out at the lobby café-bar. Look out the back windows to see fragments of the **13th-century Dominican**

church incorporated into the structure of the hotel. If you stood here eight centuries ago, you'd be looking straight down the church's nave. You can even see tomb markers in the floor.

Back out on the street, cross the little park, turn right down Fortuna utca, and walk toward the mosaic roof (passing the recommended 21 Magyar Vendéglő on your right—a good place for an upscale meal). Reaching the end of the street, look right to see the low-profile **Vienna Gate.** If you go through it and walk for about 10 days, you'll get to Vienna. Just inside the Vienna Gate, notice the bus stop—handy for leaving Castle Hill when you're finished.

• *Now turn left and walk along the hulking, mosaic-roofed National Archive building (with your back to the Danube) until you reach the...*

⓭ Remains of St. Mary Magdalene Church

This was once known as the Kapisztrán Templom, named after a hero of the Battle of Belgrade in 1456, an early success in the struggle to keep the Ottomans out of Europe. (King Matthias' father,

János Hunyadi, led the Hungarians in that battle.) The pope was so tickled by the victory that he decreed that all church bells should toll at noon in memory of the battle—and, technically, they still do. (Californians might recognize Kapisztrán's Spanish name: San Juan Capistrano.) This church was destroyed by bombs in World War II, though no worse than Matthias Church. But, since this part of town was depopulated after the war, there was no longer a need for a second church. The remains of the church were torn down, the steeple was rebuilt as a memorial, and a carillon was added—so that every day at noon, the bells can still toll...and be enjoyed by the monument of János Kapisztrán, just across the square. You can pay 1,500 Ft to climbs its 172 steps for the view (daily 10:00-dusk)—but the views from the Matthias Church tower are far better.

• *Our walk is finished, but there are a few more options nearby. You can walk out to the terrace just beyond the big building for another look at the Buda Hills. From here, just to the right (near the flagpole), is the entrance to the* **Museum of Military History,** *with a mountain of army-surplus artifacts from Hungary's gloriously unsuccessful military past (see the listing in the Sights in Budapest chapter). If you continue around the terrace past the museum, at the northern point of Castle Hill you'll find an old* **Turkish grave** *(see photo on next page), honoring a pasha who once ruled here during Ottoman times.*

If you're ready to leave Castle Hill, you can backtrack to the Fisher-

man's Bastion and walk down the grand staircase there (into the Víziváros neighborhood). Or, from the square just inside Vienna Gate, you can catch bus #16, #16A, or #116 to Széll Kálmán tér—or head out through the gate and follow the road downhill. You'll run into bustling Széll Kálmán tér, which has a handy Metró stop (M2/red line) and the huge, modern Mammut shopping complex.

MEMENTO PARK TOUR

a.k.a. Statue Park (Szoborpark)

When regimes fall, so do their monuments...literally. Just think of all the statues of Stalin and Lenin that crashed to the ground in late 1989, when people throughout Eastern Europe couldn't wait to get rid of those reminders of their oppressors. But some clever entrepreneur hoarded Budapest's, collecting them in a park in the countryside just southwest of the city—where tourists flock to get a taste of the communist era. Though it can be time-consuming to visit, this collection is worth ▲▲▲ for those fascinated by Hungary's commie past.

Orientation

Cost: 1,500 Ft.

Hours: Daily 10:00-sunset.

Information: Tel. 1/424-7500, www.mementopark.hu.

Getting There: It's in the countryside six miles southwest of the city center, at the corner of Balatoni út and Szabadka út, in district XXII.

    The park runs a convenient **direct bus** from Deák tér in downtown Budapest (where three Metró lines converge; bus stop is near the Ritz-Carlton, facing the leafy Erzsébet tér). The trip takes 2.5 hours total, including a 1.5-hour visit to the park (4,900-Ft ticket includes round-trip and park entry, 20 percent discount if you book online at park website, runs daily at 11:00).

    The **public transport** option requires a transfer: Ride the Metró's M4/green line to its end at Kelenföld. Follow signs to *Őrmező* and *Péterhegyi út* (exit B). Emerging in this bus-stop zone, consult the electronic board for the next departure time; a map directs you to your stop. You want bus #101B or

#101E, which zip to Memento Park in about 10 minutes (every 10-20 minutes, Mon-Fri only). Bus #150 takes longer (about 20 minutes), but it's the only option on weekends (2-4/hour, runs daily). If you're taking bus #150, you can download a free "bonus tour" from the park website, which explains some of the landmarks you'll pass en route. On any bus, be sure the driver knows where you want to get off.

Hiring a **taxi** for the round-trip, including about an hour of waiting time at the park, should cost around 20,000 Ft (ask your hotel to call one for you, and confirm the price before you set out).

Visitor Information: The 1,500-Ft English guidebook, *In the Shadow of Stalin's Boots,* is very informative.

Tours: English tours depart from the entrance and last 50 minutes (1,200 Ft, 20 percent discount if you book online; April-Oct daily at 11:45—shortly after direct bus arrives from Deák tér, additional tours in high season).

Starring: Marx, Engels, Lenin, stiff soldiers, passionate patriots... and other ghosts of Hungary's communist past.

BACKGROUND

Under the communists, creativity was discouraged. The primary purpose of art was to further the goals of the state, with creative expression only an afterthought. Promoting **Socialist Realist** art served to encourage complicity with the brave new world the communists were forging. It was also a break with the "decadent" bourgeois art that came before it (Impressionism, Post-Impressionism, and other modern -isms). From 1949 until 1956,

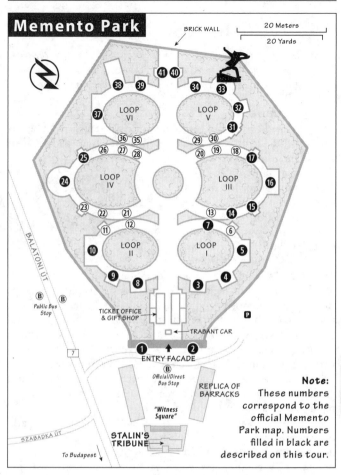

Memento Park

BRICK WALL

20 Meters
20 Yards

LOOP VI
LOOP V
LOOP IV
LOOP III
LOOP II
LOOP I

BALATONI ÚT

Public Bus Stop

TICKET OFFICE & GIFT SHOP

TRABANT CAR

ENTRY FACADE

Official/Direct Bus Stop

REPLICA OF BARRACKS

"Witness Square"

STALIN'S TRIBUNE

SZABADKA ÚT

To Budapest

Note: These numbers correspond to the official Memento Park map. Numbers filled in black are described on this tour.

MEMENTO PARK

Socialist Realism was legally enforced as the sole artistic style of the Soviet Bloc.

As propaganda was an essential weapon in the Soviet arsenal, the regime made ample use of Socialist Realist art. Aside from a few important figureheads, individuals didn't matter. Everyone was a cog in the machine—strong, stoic, and doing their jobs well and proudly for the good of the people. Individual characteristics and distinguishing features were unimportant; people were represented as automatons serving their nation. Artistic merit was virtually ignored. Most figures are trapped in stiff, unnatural poses that ignore the 3,000 years of artistic evolution since the Egyptians. Sculptures and buildings alike from this era were designed to evoke feelings of power and permanence.

The Tour Begins

• *The numbers in the following tour match the statue labels in the park, the official park map, and the map in this chapter.*

As you approach the park, you encounter the imposing red-brick...

Entry Facade

You're greeted by three of the Communist All-Stars: ❶ **Vladimir Lenin,** a leader of Russia's Bolshevik Revolution; and ❷ **Karl Marx** and **Friedrich Engels,**
the German philosophers whose *Communist Manifesto* first articulated the principles behind communism in 1848. (These three figures weren't offensive enough to be destroyed, but very few statues survive anywhere of

the biggest "star" of all, the hated Josef Stalin.)

Like the rest of the park, the gate's design is highly conceptual: It looks impressive and monumental...but, like the rotted-out pomp of communism, there's nothing behind it. It's a glossy stage-set with no substance. If you try to go through the main, central part of the gate, you'll run into an always-locked door. Instead, as with the communist system, you have to find another way around (in this case, the side gate to the left). Etched in the door is Hungarian poet Gyula Illyés' "One Sentence About Tyranny," a poem published after the 1956 Uprising.

Inside the gate, buy your ticket and head into the park. Survey the layout and note that the main road takes you confidently toward...a dead end (the brick wall). Once again, as with life under the communists, you'll have to deviate from this main axis to actually accomplish anything. Even so, notice that the six walkways branching off the main road all loop you right back to where you started—representing the endless futility of communism. The loops are thematically tied together in pairs: Roughly, the first figure-eight focuses on Hungarian-Soviet friendship; the second figure-eight celebrates the heroes of communism; and the third figure-eight shows off the idealized concepts of communism. The statues are also organized very loosely chronologically; those near the entrance are generally older than the ones farther into the park.

• *Now we'll zigzag back and forth through each of the six loops. Begin with the loop to the right as you enter the park.*

Liberation Monuments (Loop I)

All of these statues celebrate the Soviet Army's triumphant rescue of Hungary from the Nazis in 1945.

Dominating this loop is a ❸ **giant soldier** holding the Soviet flag. This statue once stood at the base of the Liberation Monument that still overlooks the Danube from Gellért Hill. Typical of Socialist Realist art, the soldier has a clenched fist (symbolizing strength) and a face that is inspired by his egalitarian ideology. After the fall of communism, some critics wanted the entire monument torn down. As a compromise, they removed the overt communist themes (the red star and this soldier), covered what remained with a sheet for a while to exorcise the communist mojo, then unveiled it.

To the left of this soldier, see the ❹ **two comrades** stiffly shaking hands: the Hungarian worker thrilled to meet the Soviet soldier—protector of the proletariat.

Beyond them is a ❺ **long wall,** with a triumphant worker breaking through the left end—too busy doing his job to be very excited. Just another brick in the wall. (The three big blocks protruding from the wall were for hanging commemorative wreaths.)

The big ❼ **panel** came from an apartment building in a conservative Buda Hills neighborhood. Each neighborhood had a similar monument to the liberation. The nail holes once held letters that proclaimed in Hungarian and Russian: "Everlasting praise for the freedom of the Soviet Union, for its independence, and for its fallen heroes in the battle to liberate Hungary."

• *Cross "main street" to a group of statues commemorating the key communist holiday of...*

April 4, 1945 (Loop II)

On this date, the Soviets forced the final Nazi soldier out of Hungary. The tall panel nearest the entrance shows a Hungarian woman and a Soviet woman setting free the ❽ **doves of peace.** According to the inscription, "Our freedom and peace is founded upon the enduring Hungarian-Soviet friendship." (With friends like these...)

The ❾ **woman holding the palm leaf** is reminiscent of the Liberation Monument back on the Danube—which, after all, celebrates the same glorious day. Check out the size of that palm leaf: Seems like she's overcompensating...

At the back of the loop, the ❿ **Hungarian worker and Soviet soldier** (who appear to be doing calisthenics) are absurdly rigid even though they're trying to be dynamic. (Even the statues couldn't muster genuine enthusiasm for communist ideals.)

• *Cross over and head up to the next loop to pay homage to...*

Heroes of the Workers' Movement (Loop III)

Look for the ⓮ bust of the Bulgarian communist leader **Georgi Dimitrov** (ruled 1946-1949)—one of communist Hungary's many Soviet Bloc comrades. During the 1956 Uprising, protesters put a noose around this bust's neck and hung it from a tree. Next is a ⓯ full-size statue of Dimitrov, a gift from "the working people of Sofia." (Talk about a white elephant.)

At the back of this loop are ⓰ three blocky portraits. The middle figure is the granddaddy of Hungarian communism: **Béla Kun** (1886-1938) fought for the Austro-Hungarian Empire in World War I. He was captured by the Russian Army, taken to a prisoner-of-war camp inside Russia, and became mysteriously smitten with communism. After prov-

ing himself too far left even for Lenin, Kun returned to Hungary in 1918 and formed a Hungarian Communist Party at a time when communism was most definitely not in vogue. We'll see more of Kun later in the park.

To the left is one of the park's best-loved, most-photographed, and most artistic statues: ⓱ **Vladimir Lenin,** in his famous "hailing a cab" pose. It once stood at the entrance to the giant industrial complex in Budapest's Csepel district.

MEMENTO PARK

• *Cross over—passing the giant red star made of flowers (resembling one that was once planted in the middle of the roundabout at the Buda end of the Chain Bridge)—to meet...*

More Communist Heroes (Loop IV)

This group—which includes a ㉕ statue of an interior minister made a foot shorter at the bottom when the Iron Curtain fell—is

dominated by a ㉔ dramatic, unusually emotive sculpture by a genuine artist, **Imre Varga** (described on page 74). Designed to commemorate the 100th anniversary of Béla Kun's birth, this clever statue accomplishes seemingly con-

tradictory feats. On the one hand, it reinforces the communist message: Under the able leadership of Béla Kun (safely overlooking the fray from above), the crusty, bourgeois old regime of the Habsburg Empire (on the left, with the umbrellas and fancy clothes) was converted into the workers' fighting force of the Red Army (on the right, with the bayonets). And yet, those silvery civilians in back seem more appealing than the lunging soldiers in front. And notice the lamppost next to Kun: In Hungarian literature, a lamppost is a metaphor for the gallows. This reminds viewers that Kun—in spite of his groundbreaking and heroic work for the communist movement in Hungary—was ultimately executed by communists in the Soviet Union during Stalin's purges of the late 1930s.

• *Zig and head up again, for a lesson in...*

Communist Concepts (Loop V)

Look for a rusty pair of ㉛ **workers' hands** holding a sphere (which was once adorned with a red star). This represented the hard-won ideals of communism, carefully protected by the hands—but also held out for others to appreciate.

The ㉜ **monument to Hungarian soldiers** (who look like saluting Rockettes) honors those who fought against the fascist Francisco Franco in the Spanish Civil War.

MEMENTO PARK

Dominating this group is a ❸ **communist worker** charging into the future, clutching the Soviet flag. Budapesters of the time had a different interpretation: a thermal bath attendant running after a customer who'd forgotten his towel. This is a favorite spot for goofy posed photos.

To the left is a monument to the communist version of the Boy Scouts: the elementary-school-age ❸ **Little Drummers** and the older **Pioneers.** While these organizations existed before the communists, they were slowly infiltrated and turned into propaganda machines by the regime. These kids—with their jaunty red and blue neckerchiefs—were sent to camp to be properly raised as good little communists; today, many of them have forgotten the brainwashing but still have fond memories of the socializing.

• *Now zag once more to learn about...*

More Communist Concepts (Loop VI)

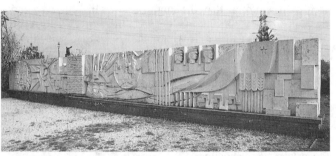

The ❸ long, **white wall** at the back of this section tells quite a story (from left to right): The bullet holes lead up to a jumbled, frightful clutter (reminiscent of Pablo Picasso's *Guernica*) representing World War II. Then comes the bright light of the Soviet system, and by the end everyone's properly regimented—striking *Charlie's Angels* poses—and looking boldly to the future (and enjoying a bountiful crop, to boot). The names in the center represent "heroes" who stayed true to the ideology, party, and nation and died in "defense of proletarian power" in 1956. Some became household names to older locals, who show their age by still referring to places using their communist titles (from 1956 until 1990, many Budapest streets were named in honor of these "heroes").

Next is a ❸ **fallen hero** with arm outstretched, about to

collapse to the ground—mortally wounded, yet victorious. This monument to "the Martyrs of the Counter-Revolution" also commemorates those who died attempting to put down the 1956 Uprising.

Finally you'll see a ❸❾ **plundered monument.** Missing its figures and red star, it was destroyed in 1989 by jubilant Hungarians celebrating their freedom.

• *Now continue down the main drag to, um, a....*

Dead End

The main path dead-ends at the wall, symbolizing life's frustrations under communism. Here stand statues of two Soviet officers who negotiated with the Nazis to end the WWII siege of Budapest.

❹❶ **Captain Miklós Steinmetz** (on the right) was killed by a Nazi land mine, while ❹❶ **Ilja Ostapenko** (on the left) was shot under mysterious circumstances as he returned from the successful summit. Both became heroes for the communist cause. Were they killed by wayward Nazi soldiers, as the Soviets explained—or by their own Red Army, to create a pair of convenient martyrs? These two statues once flanked the road out of Budapest toward the popular resort area at Lake Balaton. Locals eager to get out of town would hitchhike "at Ostapenko."

When you return to the entry gate, peruse the fun parade of communist kitsch at the **gift shop.** The stirring music may just move you to pick up the CD of *Communism's Greatest Hits,* and maybe a model of a Trabant (the classic two-stroke commie-mobile). A real **Trabant** is often parked just inside the gate.

• *Now head out across the parking lot to find...*

Stalin's Tribune

This section of the complex is a re-creation of the giant grandstand that once stood along "Parade Street" (the boulevard next to City Park). Hungarian and Soviet leaders stood here, at the feet of a giant Stalin statue, to survey military and civilian processions. But during the 1956 Uprising, protesters cut Stalin off at the knees... leaving only the boots. (The entire tribune was later dismantled, and Stalin disappeared without a trace.) If you circle around behind the tribune, you'll find stairs up top for a view over the park.

• *Flanking the lot in front of the tribune are replicas of...*

Barracks

These are reminiscent of the ramshackle barracks where political prisoners lived in communist-era work camps (sometimes called gulags, described on page 153). These hold special exhibits, often including a good explanation of "Stalin's Boots" (with a plaster replica, and photos of the original tribune) and the events of 1956. Sit down for the creepy film, *The Life of an Agent*—a loop of four training films (10-15 minutes each) that were actually used to teach novice spies about secret-police methods and policies.

• *Our tour is over. Now, inspired by the bold propaganda of your Hungarian comrades, march proudly into the dawn of a new day.*

SLEEPING IN BUDAPEST

I've focused my recommendations on safe, handy, and colorful neighborhoods in Pest and Buda. I recommend the best values in each, from cheap dorm beds to deluxe €600 doubles with all the comforts.

In Budapest, most hotels quote rates in euros (for the convenience of international guests), and I've ranked them the same way. (Outside of the capital, hotels more often quote rates in forints.) However, most places prefer to be paid in forints. If paying with credit card and given a choice of currencies, choose forints to avoid excessive conversion fees. The majority of hotels don't include the 4 percent tourist tax in their rates.

Before choosing a hotel, consider the pros and cons of the neighborhood. Most travelers find staying in Pest more convenient than sleeping in Buda. Most sights worth seeing are in Pest, which also has a much higher concentration of Metró and tram stops, making it a snap to get around. Pest feels more lively and local than stodgy, touristy Buda, but it's also much more urban. If you don't enjoy big cities, sleep in Buda instead.

For some travelers, short-term, Airbnb-type rentals can be a good alternative; search for places in my recommended hotel neighborhoods. For proximity to sights and restaurants, aim for something within Pest's Great Boulevard (though staying outside of that zone is cheaper). Within this core, the Seventh District/Jewish Quarter has great restaurants and nightlife, but can be very noisy. Leopold Town—between the Parliament and Chain Bridge—is quiet and central, but with fewer restaurants. The Town Center (Belváros) is convenient, but areas near the Váci utca walking street feel more touristy and can suffer from some noise. Andrássy út (and neighboring streets)—particularly the near side of the Oktogon—is a fine and fun zone, but be aware that apartments facing the boulevard can come with street noise. For a more sedate, less urban environment, look on the Buda side; around the base of Castle Hill (Víziváros, facing the river, is convenient and scenic).

I rank accommodations from **$** budget to **$$$$** splurge. To get the best deal, contact my family-run accommodations directly by phone or email. When you book direct, the owner avoids a roughly 20 percent commission and may be able to offer you a discount. Book your accommodations well in advance if you'll be traveling during peak season or if your trip coincides with a major holiday or festival (see the appendix). For more information on rates and deals, making reservations, finding a short-term rental, and more, see the "Sleeping" section in the Practicalities chapter.

PEST

I've arranged my listings by neighborhood, clustered around the most important sightseeing sectors.

Near Andrássy Út

Andrássy Boulevard is handy, local-feeling, and endlessly entertaining. With its ample restaurants, upscale-residential vibe, and easy connection to downtown (via the M1/yellow line), it's the neighborhood where I prefer to sleep. The first three places listed are comparably priced, professional, and ideally located, close to the Opera House.

$$$ K+K Hotel Opera, wonderfully situated beside the Opera House, has 200 classy rooms and helpful, professional service. The rates are variable, but you can often land a great value (air-con, elevator, pay parking garage, Révay utca 24, district VI, M1: Opera, tel. 1/269-0222, www.kkhotels.com, reservations. opera@kkhotels.com).

$$$ Hotel Moments has 99 Art Deco rooms, a pristine atrium with iron railings, professional service, and a good location at the downtown end of Andrássy út, making this a fine choice at the higher end of this price range. Because it's surrounded by busy streets, light sleepers may be bothered by passing traffic (air-con, elevator, free coffee bar, Andrássy út 8, district VI, M1: Bajcsy-Zsilinszky út, tel. 1/611-7000, www.hotelmomentsbudapest.hu, reservation@hotelmoments.hu).

$$$ Casati Budapest Hotel is a solid value, and conveniently located a block off Andrássy út (across the boulevard from the Opera House, then down a side street). This classy, Swiss-run hotel has 25 rooms in four different styles, ranging from "classic" to "cool" (all the same price—review your options online and choose

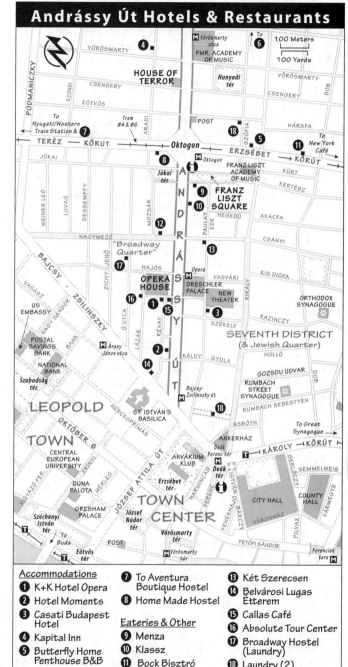

Andrássy Út Hotels & Restaurants

Accommodations
1. K+K Hotel Opera
2. Hotel Moments
3. Casati Budapest Hotel
4. Kapital Inn
5. Butterfly Home Penthouse B&B
6. To Budapest B&B
7. To Aventura Boutique Hostel
8. Home Made Hostel

Eateries & Other
9. Menza
10. Klassz
11. Bock Bisztró
12. Pesti Disznó
13. Két Szerecsen
14. Belvárosi Lugas Étterem
15. Callas Café
16. Absolute Tour Center
17. Broadway Hostel (Laundry)
18. Laundry (2)

your favorite). Many rooms surround a peaceful courtyard—in this potentially noisy neighborhood, it's worth requesting one of these (air-con, elevator, free sauna and fitness room, Paulay Ede utca 31, district VI, M1: Opera, tel. 1/343-1198, www.casatibudapesthotel. hu, info@casatibudapesthotel.com).

$$ Kapital Inn is an upscale boutique B&B tucked behind the House of Terror. Its six rooms are perfectly stylish—there's not a pillow out of place. Albert, who lived in Boston, gives his B&B a sense of real hospitality. You'll enjoy the public spaces, from the restful, momentum-killing terrace to the giant kitchen, where Albert serves breakfast at a huge shared counter (cheaper room with shared bath, air-con, free communal minibar, pay laundry service, up several flights of stairs with no elevator, Aradi utca 30, district VI, M1: Vörösmarty utca, mobile +3630-915-2029, www. kapitalinn.com, kapitalinn@kapitalinn.com).

$$ Butterfly Home Penthouse B&B—run with care by András (OHN-drash) and Timea—has three rooms near the Oktogon (air-con, elevator, Teréz körút 1, 4th floor, suite #2, buzzer #44, district VI, M1: Oktogon, mobile +3630-964-7287, www.butterflyhome.hu, info@butterflyhome.hu). They also run **$ Budapest Bed and Breakfast,** with five cheaper, simple yet well-equipped rooms farther from the center—in the quiet diplomatic quarter halfway between the Oktogon and City Park (air-con, a long block off Andrássy út at Benczúr utca 3, district VI, M1: Kodály körönd, mobile +3630-964-7287, info@butterflyhome.hu). And they rent rooms in the Town Center, near the Great Market Hall (see Butterfly Home Danube B&B, later).

In the Seventh District/Jewish Quarter: A short walk from Andrássy út, **$$ ROOMbach Hotel Budapest Center**—tucked down a gloomy but central street facing the Rumbach Street Synagogue—has 99 sleek, basic, smallish rooms with a stylish industrial-mod design. It feels modern and solid, and the triple-glazed windows do their best to keep out the ruin-pub noise (air-con, elevator, pay parking, Rumbach Sebestyén utca 14, tel. 1/413-0253, www.roombach.com, hotel@roombach.com).

Pest Town Center (Belváros), near Váci Utca

Most hotels on the very central and convenient Váci utca come with overly inflated prices. But these less-expensive options—just a block or two off Váci utca—offer some of the best values in Budapest.

$$$ Hotel Rum is a sleek retreat overlooking the rejuvenated University Square, in the heart of Pest's Town Center. Its 38 industrial-mod rooms come with concrete floors, subway tile, and ample style, and the top-floor bar has great views (air-con, elevator, Királyi Pál utca 4, district V, M3/M4: Kálvin tér, tel. 1/424-9060, www.hotelrumbudapest.com, hello@hotelrumbudapest.com).

$$ Gerlóczy Café & Rooms, which also serves good coffee and meals in its recommended café, is the best spot in central Budapest for affordable elegance. The 19 rooms, set around a classy old spiral-staircase atrium with a stained-glass ceiling, are thoughtfully and stylishly appointed. This gem is an exceptional value (breakfast extra, air-con, elevator, some street noise, just off Városház utca at Gerlóczy utca 1, district V, M3: Ferenciek tere or M2: Astoria or M1/M2/M3: Deák tér, tel. 1/501-4000, www.gerloczy.hu, info@gerloczy.hu).

$$ Butterfly Home Danube B&B, run by András (from the Butterfly Home Penthouse B&B, listed earlier), has eight rooms and Danube views (air-con, elevator, Fővám tér 2-3, 2nd floor, suite #2, district V, M4: Fővám tér, mobile +3630-964-7287, www.butterflyhome.hu, info@butterflyhome.hu).

$ Katona Apartments, with five simple units just around the corner from busy Ferenciek tere, is conscientiously run by János and Virág. It's a family-friendly budget option in the very center of the city, facing a drab—but appealingly quiet—central courtyard (no breakfast but kitchenette, air-con, elevator, Petőfi Sándor utca 6, mobile +3670-221-1797, www.katonaapartments.hu, info@katonaapartments.hu).

Near the National Museum

These places are within a couple of blocks of the National Museum, just across the Small Boulevard from the Town Center, near M3/M4: Kálvin tér (district VIII).

$$ Brody House, a hipster hangout with sprawling public spaces, began as an art gallery that provided a place for its guests to crash, and has evolved into a comfortable, full-service B&B. With a trendy, scuffed, ruin-pub vibe, it's classy yet ramshackle. It fills three spacious floors of a townhouse with eight rooms and three apartments that all ooze a funky, idiosyncratic style. Each room is named for an artist who once used it as a studio (breakfast extra, air-con in most rooms, two stories up with no elevator, Bródy Sándor utca 10, tel. 1/266-1211, www.brody.land/brody-house, bookings@brody.land).

$ Budapest Rooms is a great budget option, where the Boda family rents five simple but surprisingly stylish, nicely appointed rooms in a dull residential zone (family room, one room has private bathroom across the hall, Szentkirályi 15, tel. 1/630-4743, mobile +3620-569-9513, www.budapestrooms.eu, info@budapestrooms.eu).

Leopold Town, near the Chain Bridge

The Four Seasons is the city's most prestigious address; the Starlight is a nicely located business-class option that is worth booking if you

SLEEPING

To Parliament

ACADEMY OF SCI.

LEOPOLD

Széchenyi István tér

VIGYÁZÓ FER.

NÁDOR

ZRÍNYI

DUNA PALOTA

GRESHAM PALACE

MÉRLEG

CHAIN BRIDGE

To Buda & Castle Hill

Eötvös tér

Tram #2

BELGRÁD

RAKPART

APÁCZAI

FORMER CENTRAL EUROPEAN UNIVERSITY

OKTÓBER 6

SAS

ST. ISTVÁN'S BASILICA

BAJCSY - ZSILINSZKY

REVAY

ÚT

ANDRÁSSY

KÁLDY

SZÉKELY

GYULA

To Heroes' Square & City Park

Bajcsy-Zsilinszky út

HOLLÓ

GOZSDU UDVAR

JÓZSEF ATTILA ÚT

BÉCSI

TOWN

Erzsébet tér

HARMINCAD

AKVÁRIUM KLUB

Deák Ferenc tér

9 ANKERHÁZ

ASBÓTH

RUMBACH STREET SYNAGOGUE

RUMBACH SEBESTYÉN

11 POST

József Nádor tér

WEKERLE S.U.

GERBEAUD CAFÉ

Vörösmarty tér

VIGADÓ

DEÁK

Deák tér

FERENC

KÁROLY - KÖRÚT

GERLÓCZY

FEHÉRHAJÓ - ISTVÁN

BÁRCZY

VÁROSHÁZ

CITY HALL

SEMMELWEIS

Kamermayer tér **2**

County Hall

Vigadó tér

Vigadó

MAHART BOAT DOCK

LEGENDA BOAT DOCK

Danube

TÜRR I.

ARANY

RÉGIPOSTA

JÁNOS

PETŐFI

CSERE

VIGADÓ

PESTI VIGADÓ

HISTORIC MCDONALD'S

VÁCI UTCA

PETŐFI SÁNDOR

JUGENDSTIL BLDG. (#18)

FORMER PILVAX CAFÉ

PILVAX

VARMEGYE

KOSSUTH LAJOS UTCA

SZÉP

County Hall

"SORRARAS" HISTORICISM BLDG. (#15)

Petőfi tér

PIARISTA UTCA

KÍGYÓ

TOWN

4

Ferenciek tere

Franciscan Church

RÉÁLTANODA

FERENCZY

Petőfi tér

PIARISTA KÖZ

KLOTILD PALACES

Károlyi Park

SZABAD SAJTÓ ÚT

Tram #19 & #41

ELISABETH BRIDGE

IRÁNYI

Március 15 tér

IRÁNYI

CENTER

10

KÁROLYI MIHÁLY

PAPNÖV.

Egyetem tér

9

Károlyi Park

ELTE LAW FACULTY

1

F. GYÖRGY

KIR. PÁL

7

Döbrentei tér

RUDAS BATHS

Gellért Hill

CITADELLA

CITADELLA

SÉTÁNY

BUDA

CAVE CHURCH

VEREJTÉK

River

SZT. GELLÉRT RAKPART

Tram #2

BELGRÁD

RAKPART

VÁCI UTCA

NYÁRI

SÖRHÁZ

PÁL

VERES PÁLNÉ

Serbian Church

SZERB

MOLNÁR

HAVAS

SZARKA BÁSTYA

SÓ

3 POST

Fővám tér

VÁMHÁZ

KÖRÚT

8

GREAT MARKET HALL

UNIV. OF ECONOMICS

PIPA

SÓHÁZ

LIBERTY BRIDGE

N

200 Meters

200 Yards

KELENHEGYI

GELLÉRT HOTEL & BATHS

Szent Gellért tér

KEMENES

Szent Gellért tér

Pest Town Center Hotels & Restaurants

Accommodations
1. Hotel Rum
2. Gerlóczy Café & Rooms
3. Butterfly Home Danube B&B
4. Katona Apartments
5. Brody House
6. Budapest Rooms

Eateries & Other
7. Borssó Bistro
8. Great Market Hall
9. Hummus Bar (2)
10. Centrál Kávéház
11. Pharmacy

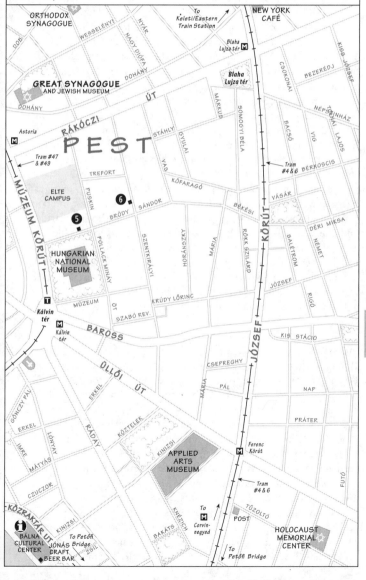

can get a discounted rate. Both are a short stroll from the delightful St. István tér/Zrínyi utca restaurant zone. For locations of these places, see the map on page 234.

$$$$ Four Seasons Gresham Palace is unquestionably Budapest's top hotel. Stay here only if money is truly no object. You'll sleep in what is arguably Budapest's finest Art Nouveau building. Damaged in World War II, the Gresham Palace sat in disrepair for decades. Today it sparkles from head to toe, and every detail in its lavish public spaces and 179 rooms is perfectly in place. Even if you're not sleeping here, dip into the lobby to soak in the elegance (air-con, elevator, top-floor spa, Széchenyi tér 5, district V, between M1: Vörösmarty tér and M2: Kossuth tér, tel. 1/268-6000, www.fourseasons.com/budapest, budapest.reservations@fourseasons.com). For more on the building's history, see page 110.

$$ Starlight Suiten has 54 spacious, good-value suites—each with a living room, bedroom, and kitchenette—on a sleepy, sterile street directly behind the Gresham Palace (air-con, elevator, free fitness room and sauna, Mérleg utca 6, district V, M1: Vörösmarty tér, tel. 1/484-3700, www.starlighthotels.com, reservation.starlight@cpihotels.com).

Apartments near Leopold Town: $ GuestBed Budapest has a few apartments scattered around town (two in a mellow residential zone north of Leopold Town, near the Margaret Bridge and the Great Boulevard, and another near the Opera House—all well-described on their website). The apartments all come with full kitchens, and you'll enjoy the welcoming and conscientious owners, János and Jószef (Katona József utca 39, district XIII, tram #4/#6: Jászai Mari tér, mobile +3670-258-5194, www.guestbudapestapartment.com, budapestrentapartment@gmail.com).

Hostels

Budapest has seemingly dozens of apartments that have been taken over by young entrepreneurs, offering basic, rough-around-the-edges hostel charm. You'll buzz in at the door and climb up a creaky, dank, and smelly staircase to a funky little enclave of fellow backpackers. Most of these places have just three rooms (one double and two small dorms). As each fills a niche (party, artsy, communist-themed, etc.), it's hard to recommend just one—read reviews on a hostel site (such as www.hostelworld.com) and find one that suits your philosophy. For hostel locations, see the "Andrássy Út Hotels & Restaurants" map, earlier.

¢ Aventura Boutique Hostel is a low-key, colorful, and stylish place in a dreary urban neighborhood near the Nyugati/Western train station. Well-run by friendly Ágnes, it's both homey and tastefully mod, with imaginatively decorated rooms (across the

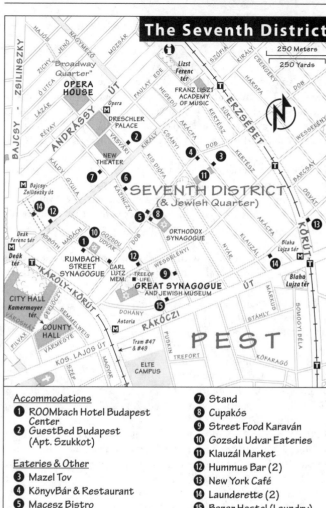

The Seventh District

250 Meters
250 Yards

SEVENTH DISTRICT
(& Jewish Quarter)

PEST

Accommodations
1 ROOMbach Hotel Budapest Center
2 GuestBed Budapest (Apt. Szukkot)

Eateries & Other
3 Mazel Tov
4 KönyvBár & Restaurant
5 Macesz Bistro
6 Kőleves

7 Stand
8 Cupakós
9 Street Food Karaván
10 Gozsdu Udvar Eateries
11 Klauzál Market
12 Hummus Bar (2)
13 New York Café
14 Launderette (2)
15 Bazar Hostel (Laundry)

busy Great Boulevard ring road and a very long block from Nyugati train station at 12 Visegrádi utca, district XIII, M3: Nyugati pu., tel. 1/239-0782, www.aventurahostel.com, info@aventurahostel. com). They also rent several apartments—two nearby, the other near St. István's Basilica.

¢ **Home Made Hostel** is a fun-and-funky slumbermill artfully littered with secondhand furniture. With 20 beds in four rooms located near the Oktogon, it's managed and decorated with a sense of humor (Teréz körút 22, district VI, M1: Oktogon, tel. 1/302-2103, www.homemadehostel.com, info@homemadehostel.com).

BUDA
Víziváros

The Víziváros neighborhood—or "Water Town"—is the lively part of Buda squeezed between Castle Hill and the Danube, where fishermen and tanners used to live. Víziváros is the most pleasant and central area to stay on the Buda side of the Danube, with fine views across the river toward the Parliament building and bustling Pest. It's expensive and a little less convenient than Pest, but feels less urban.

The following hotels are in district I, between the Chain Bridge and Buda's busy Margit körút ring road. Trams #19 and #41 zip along the embankment in either direction. Batthyány tér, a few minutes' walk away, is a handy center with lots of restaurants, a Metró stop (M2/red line), and the HÉV train to Óbuda and Szentendre.

$$$ Hotel Victoria, with 27 stylish, spotless, business-class rooms—each with a grand river view and attention to detail—is a class act. This tall, narrow place (three rooms on each of nine floors) is run with pride and attention to detail by on-the-ball manager Zoltán and his friendly staff (air-con, elevator, free sauna, free afternoon tea for guests 16:00-17:00, reserve ahead for pay parking garage, Bem rakpart 11, tel. 1/457-

8080, www.victoria.hu, victoria@victoria.hu). The painstakingly restored 19th-century Hubay Palace behind the hotel (entrance next to reception) is used for concerts and other events. It feels like a museum, with inlaid floors, stained-glass windows, and stuccoed walls and ceilings.

$$$ At Art'otel, every detail—from the breakfast dishes to the carpets to the good-luck blackbird perched in each room—was designed by American artist Donald Sultan. This stylish hotel has 165 rooms spread between two attached buildings: the new section fronting the Danube and, just behind it, a restored older house with views of the castle (breakfast extra, air-con, elevator, free sauna and mini exercise room, Bem rakpart 16, tel. 1/487-9487, www.artotels.com, budapest@artotels.com).

$ Bellevue B&B hides in a quiet residential area on the Víziváros hillside, just below the Fisherman's Bastion staircase. This gem is owned by retired economists Judit (YOO-deet) and Lajos (LIE-yosh) Szuhay, who lived in Canada for four years; most days, you'll meet their right-hand man, Bálint. The break-

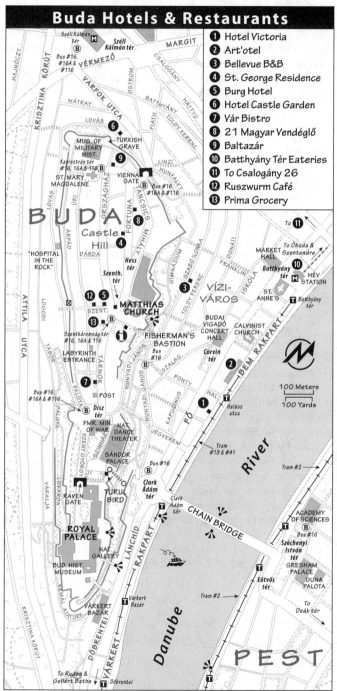

Buda Hotels & Restaurants

1. Hotel Victoria
2. Art'otel
3. Bellevue B&B
4. St. George Residence
5. Burg Hotel
6. Hotel Castle Garden
7. Vár Bistro
8. 21 Magyar Vendéglő
9. Baltazár
10. Batthyány Tér Eateries
11. To Csalogány 26
12. Ruszwurm Café
13. Prima Grocery

SLEEPING

fast room and some of the six straightforward, comfortable rooms have views across the Danube to the Parliament and Pest. Judit, Lajos, and Bálint love to chat, and pride themselves on offering genuine hospitality and a warm welcome—let them know what time you're arriving (cash only, air-con; M2: Batthyány tér plus a 10-minute uphill walk, or bus #16 from Deák, Széchenyi, or Clark Ádám squares to Dónati utca plus a 2-minute walk uphill, then downhill—they'll email you detailed directions; Szabó Ilonka utca 15/B, mobile +3630-964-7287, www.bellevuebudapest.com, judit@bellevuebudapest.com).

Castle Hill

Romantics may enjoy calling Castle Hill home (district I). These places couldn't be closer to the Castle Hill sights, but they're in a tourist zone—dead at night, and less convenient to Pest than other listings.

$$ St. George Residence, just a couple of short blocks from Matthias Church, is historical and classy. They rent 24 elegant rooms—each one different, all with kitchenettes—around a restful garden courtyard (air-con, Fortuna utca 4, tel. 1/393-5700, www.stgeorgehotel.hu, info@stgeorgehotel.hu).

$$ Burg Hotel, with 26 rooms on Holy Trinity Square (Szentháromság tér), is efficient: concrete, spacious, and comfy, if a bit worn, with a professional staff. If you simply *must* stay in a modern hotel across the street from Matthias Church, this is it (RS%, request view room for no extra charge, family rooms, air-con, no elevator, top-floor rooms are extremely long, Szentháromság tér 7, tel. 1/212-0269, www.burghotelbudapest.hu, info@burghotelbudapest.hu).

$$ Hotel Castle Garden rents 39 businesslike rooms above an Italian restaurant in a tranquil, parklike neighborhood just outside the castle's Vienna Gate (north end). As it's roughly on the way between the castle and Széll Kálmán tér, it's relatively handy, though still less convenient than the Víziváros listings (air-con, elevator, pay parking garage, Lovas út 41, M2: Széll Kálmán tér; exit the castle through the Vienna Gate and turn left along the wall, or hike up from Széll Kálmán tér and turn right along the castle wall; tel. 1/224-7420, www.castlegarden.hu, hotel@castlegarden.hu).

EATING IN BUDAPEST

Budapest may be one of Europe's most underrated culinary destinations. Hungarian cuisine is excellent—rich, spicy, smooth, and delicious. And Budapest specializes in trendy restaurants that mix Hungarian flavors with international flair, making the food here even more interesting and fun to sample. Best of all, the prices are reasonable, especially if you venture off the main tourist trail.

Thanks to Budapest's fast-evolving culinary scene, there's no shortage of places to dine. It pays to research what's brand-new and hot; I've focused my listings on places that have been around long enough to be reliable.

International restaurants provide a break from Hungarian fare (in the unlikely event you need one). Budapest has abundant vegetarian, Italian, Indian, Chinese, and other non-Hungarian eateries; I've listed a few favorites. Once you leave the capital, these options are sparse, and the food gets even heartier and cheaper.

EATING TIPS

I rank eateries from **$** budget to **$$$$** splurge. For even more advice on eating in Budapest, including details on ordering, dining, and tipping in restaurants, the types of eateries you'll encounter, and Hungarian cuisine and beverages (including a summary of top Hungarian wines), see the "Eating" section of the Practicalities chapter.

Tipping: Most restaurants in Budapest automatically add a service charge to the bill (look for "service," "tip," *felszolgálási díj*, or *szervízdíj*); if it's been included, an additional tip is not necessary. Otherwise, round up about 10 percent.

Dining Hours: Most Hungarians dine between 19:00 and 21:00, peaking around 20:00; trendy zones such as St. István Square and Franz Liszt Square, which attract an after-work crowd, are lively earlier in the evening.

Lunch Specials: Many Budapest restaurants—even some high-end places—offer affordable lunch specials, called *napimenü*, on weekdays. As these are designed for local office workers on their lunch breaks rather than for tourists, they're often not advertised in English—but if you see the magic word *napimenü*, ask about it.

PEST

I've listed these options by neighborhood, emphasizing the areas with the best and most interesting options, for easy reference with your sightseeing.

Seventh District (Ruin-Pub Zone and Jewish Quarter)

Along with the rise of "ruin pubs" (see the Entertainment in Budapest chapter), the Seventh District has seen the arrival of a world of great restaurants. While a few of these feature Jewish food (in a nod to this area's Jewish heritage), others are more eclectic, catering to a younger clientele. For locations, see "The Seventh District" map on page 225.

$$$ Mazel Tov, one of Budapest's trendiest eateries (reserve ahead), fills a dilapidated old building at the edge of the ruin-

pub zone. Stepping across the tattered threshold, you emerge into a vine-strewn, bare-brick courtyard where twinkling lights are strung over the hardworking open kitchen. With a wink to this district's Jewish origins, they serve creative cocktails and Israeli/Middle Eastern dishes like kebabs, shawarma, falafel, tabbouleh, and *shakshuka* (tomato-poached eggs). The joyful atmosphere captures Budapest's thriving foodie energy (Mon-Fri 12:00-late, Sat-Sun 10:00-even later, food until 23:00, Akácfa utca 47, district VII, between M1: Opera and M2: Blaha Lujza tér, mobile +3670-626-4280, www.mazeltov.hu).

$$$ KönyvBár & Restaurant, just around the corner from Mazel Tov, is refined, mellow, and creative. The small dining room feels like a sleek, minimalist library, and the menu has a fun literary theme (*könyv* means "book"). As it's small and all indoors, it can be warm. Bibliophiles should reserve ahead for an appealing dining experience (Mon-Sat 12:00-24:00, closed Sun, Dob utca 45, district VII, between M1: Opera and M2: Blaha Lujza tér, mobile +3620-922-7027, www.konyvbar.hu).

$$$ **Macesz Bistro** is a grandma's-dining-room-cozy corner restaurant serving traditional Jewish recipes with modern ingredients and technique. They also offer a seasonal menu of modern Israeli food—hummus, tabbouleh, and so on—making it easier for everyone to find something they'll like (daily 12:00-16:00 & 18:00-23:00, Dob utca 26, district VII, M1: Opera, tel. 1/787-6164).

$$ **Kőleves** ("Stone Soup"), filling an old kosher sausage factory, feels upscale and put-together without being stuffy. The eclectic, international menu includes several Jewish dishes. This is steps away from Macesz Bistro (see above), and worth trying if that place is full (daily 8:00-24:00, Kazinczy utca 41, district VII, M1: Opera, mobile +3620-213-5999). Their adjacent garden courtyard (one of several ruin pubs on this street) serves cheap pub grub.

$$$$ **Stand,** operated by celebrity chefs Szabina Szulló and Tamás Széll (who run the high-end lunch eatery in the Hold Street Market—described later), is the refined choice in this neighborhood. Open since 2018, it's making a play to become one of Budapest's top restaurants, with a fixed-price menu of well-executed modern Hungarian and international dishes and impeccable service in a clean, contemporary setting with an open kitchen (Mon 18:30-21:00, Tue-Sat 12:00-13:00 & 18:30-21:00, closed Sun, these are last seating times for dinner, Székely Mihály ucta 2, mobile +3630-785-9139, www.standrestaurant.hu).

$$ **Cupakós** has won awards for its street food inspired menu of hearty dishes. Its motto is "Meat, meat, meat." (Vegetarians—skip it.) With a casual, industrial-mod interior of concrete and subway tile, it's a filling and affordable choice in this increasingly upscale dining area (daily 11:30-24:00, Dob 31, mobile +3670-908-4404).

Food Trucks: Just a couple of doors down from Szimpla (the oldest and best of the ruin pubs—see page 268), the $ **Street Food Karaván** fills a gravel lot with an array of creative food trucks and picnic tables. Options include burgers, burritos, sausages, paneer "burgers," soup in a bread bowl, pan-Asian dishes, and for dessert, *kürtőskalács*—delicious chimney cake (daily 11:30-late, Kazinczy utca 18, district VII, M1: Opera).

Gozsdu Udvar: This passage—which laces together a series of courtyards as it runs under apartment blocks through the busy Seventh District—is jammed with bars and restaurants, and fun for a drink, snack, meal, or just people-watching. It's a thriving and youthful mix that sprawls for blocks, with options including fish

EATING

(Stég), craft beers (Léhütö), all-day breakfast joints, homemade pasta bars, Italian, karaoke rooms for rent...and even Hungarian cuisine.

Market Hall with Cheap Eats: At the northern edge of the ruin-pub zone is the **$ Klauzál Market,** a neighborhood market hall built in 1897. With soaring steel girders over pristinely restored food stalls and a handy Spar supermarket, it's a fine place to browse for a picnic or grab some street food (most vendors open until about 17:00; supermarket open Mon-Sat 6:30-21:00, Sun 7:00-18:00; Klauzál tér 6, runs through the block between Klauzál utca and Akácfa utca, district VII, between M1: Opera and M2: Blaha Lujza tér).

Near Andrássy Út

For locations, see the "Andrássy Út Hotels & Restaurants" map on page 219. Note that the Seventh District eateries (in the previous section) are also nearby.

$$$ Menza (the old communist word for "School Cafeteria"), the only restaurant seriously worth considering on touristy Franz Liszt Square, wins the "Best Design" award. Recycling 1970s-era furniture and an orange-brown-gray color scheme, it's a postmodern parody of an old communist café—half kitschy-retro, half contemporary-stylish. With tasty and well-priced updated Hungarian and international cuisine, embroidered leather-bound menus, brisk but efficient service, and indoor or outdoor seating, it's a memorable spot (daily 11:00-23:00, halfway up Andrássy út at Liszt Ferenc tér 2, district VII, M1: Oktogon, tel. 1/413-1482, www.menza.co.hu).

$$$ Klassz, right on Andrássy út, is a bistro with a similarly postmodern "eclectic-mod" aesthetic, both in its decor and its food. They serve a short menu of reasonably priced, if hit-or-miss, international/nouvelle cuisine with Hungarian flair (daily 11:30-22:30, Andrássy út 41, district VI, between M1: Opera and M1: Oktogon, no reservations possible).

$$$$ Bock Bisztró, run by a prominent vintner from Villány, offers traditional Hungarian staples presented with modern flourish—almost "deconstructed," but still recognizable. It has a wine-bar ambience, with cork-filled tables. Pricey and well-regarded, with a list of 250 wines (including dozens by the glass), it's a good opportunity to sample food and wine from around the country. The service can be stuffy, but the food lives up to its reputation. Reservations are essential (daily 12:00-16:00 & 18:00-24:00, in the Corinthia Grand Royal Hotel, a couple of blocks west of the Oktogon on the Great Boulevard, Erzsébet körút 43, district VII, M1: Oktogon, right by Király utca stop on trams #4 and #6, tel. 1/321-0340, www.bockbisztropest.hu).

$$$ Pesti Disznó ("Pest Pig"), set right in the "Broadway Quarter" along the liveliest stretch of theaters in town, celebrates the prized Hungarian hairy pig called *mangalica*. The menu ranges from well-executed classics to international fare to creative fusion dishes—like a *mangalica* burger. While the interior, with tall tables surrounding the open kitchen, is fine, I'd rather sit out under the red-and-white striped awnings facing the bright lights of Budapest's theater scene (daily 11:00-24:00, Nagymező 19, district VI, M1: Oktogon, tel. 1/951-4061, www.pestidiszno.hu).

$$$ Két Szerecsen ("Two Saracens"), named for a historic coffee shop at this location that a trader filled with exotic goods, stays true to that eclectic spirit by featuring a wide variety of international cuisines—from Mediterranean to Asian. It has good indoor and outdoor seating, relatively small portions, and a menu that offers something for everyone (daily 9:00-24:00, a block off Andrássy út at Nagymező utca 14, district VI, M1: Opera, tel. 1/343-1984).

Near St. István's Basilica

The streets in front of St. István's Basilica are jammed with upscale, dressy, yuppie-oriented eateries (district V, M1: Bajcsy-Zsilinszky út). Several options line Zrínyi utca (which stretches straight down to the Danube from the basilica's front door) and its cross streets. The following choices are worth seeking out. For locations, see the "Leopold Town Restaurants & Hotels" map.

$$$ Café Kör ("Circle") is a reliable mainstay in this otherwise fast-evolving zone. This stylish but unsnooty eatery serves up mostly Hungarian and some international fare in a tasteful, tight, one-room interior and at a few sidewalk tables. It prides itself on being friendly and providing a good value. Because it's beloved by Budapest foodies, reservations are smart and essential on weekends (Mon-Sat 10:00-22:00, closed Sun, small portions available, good salads, daily specials, cash only, Sas utca 17, tel. 1/311-0053).

$$$$ Borkonyha ("Winekitchen"), with a Michelin star, serves up top-quality modern Hungarian cuisine ("Hungarian dishes—but less paprika, less fat"). And, as the name implies, they're evangelical about high-quality Hungarian wines—with about 45 types sold by the glass. The menu—especially the adventurous chalkboard specials—ventures into "nose-to-tail" cooking, using ingredients you won't find everywhere. The decor is sophisticated black, white, and gold—a dressy place where wine snobs feel at home—and they also have sidewalk seating out front. Reservations are essential (Mon-Sat 12:00-16:00 & 18:00-24:00, closed Sun, Sas utca 3, tel. 1/266-0835, www.borkonyha.hu).

$$$$ Mák Bistro is pricey but unpretentious, with a loyal following (reservations are smart). It feels like a well-kept secret,

EATING

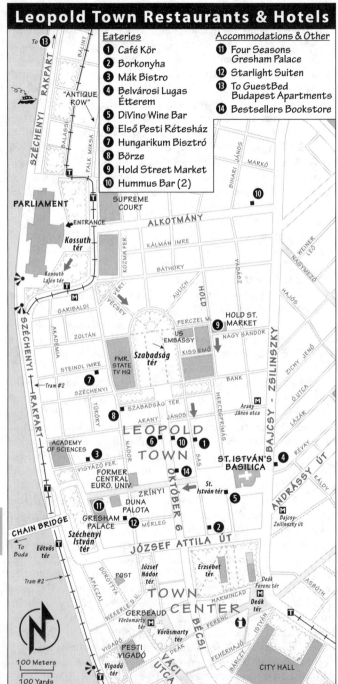

Leopold Town Restaurants & Hotels

Eateries
1. Café Kör
2. Borkonyha
3. Mák Bistro
4. Belvárosi Lugas Étterem
5. DiVino Wine Bar
6. Első Pesti Rétesház
7. Hungarikum Bisztró
8. Börze
9. Hold Street Market
10. Hummus Bar (2)

Accommodations & Other
11. Four Seasons Gresham Palace
12. Starlight Suiten
13. To GuestBed Budapest Apartments
14. Bestsellers Bookstore

tucked down a forgotten side street parallel to the bustling Zrínyi utca pedestrian drag. Inside, it has a lively brasserie ambience under white-painted brick vaults. The short, carefully selected seasonal menu is based on what's fresh. The good-value lunch specials are an affordable way to sample the fine cuisine (Tue-Sat 12:00-15:00 & 18:00-23:00, closed Sun-Mon, Vigyázó Ferenc 4, mobile +3630-723-9383, www.mak.hu).

$$ Belvárosi Lugas Étterem is your cheap-and-charming, no-frills option for straightforward, traditional Hungarian food. *Lugas* is a Hungarian word for a welcoming garden strewn with grape vines, and the cozy dining room—with a dozen tables under overhanging vines—captures that spirit. Or sit at one of their sidewalk tables outside on busy Bajcsy-Zsilinszky út, directly behind and across the street from the basilica (daily 12:00-23:30, Bajcsy-Zsilinszky út 15, district VI, tel. 1/302-5393).

Hungarian Wines: For a wine-focused adventure, **$$ DiVino Wine Bar** serves 130 types of exclusively Hungarian wines, listed by region on the chalkboard—all available by the glass or bottle. The well-versed staff can help introduce you to Hungary's underrated wines—just tell them what you like and let them guide you. While DiVino doesn't do flights or tastings per se, couples are encouraged to share glasses (many less than 1,000 Ft) to try several varieties. The interior has a hip atmosphere, and there's also inviting seating out on the square, facing the basilica (daily 16:00-24:00, St. István tér 3, mobile +3670-935-3980).

Homemade Strudel: See how strudel *(rétes)* is made at **Első Pesti Rétesház,** a folkloric favorite among fans of this treat. Step inside to watch them roll out the long, paper-thin sheets of dough, then wrap them around a variety of fillings. Get a piece to go at the takeaway counter, or sit and enjoy your *rétes* with a cup of coffee (daily 9:00-23:00, also has a full food menu of traditional Hungarian dishes, Október 6 utca 22, tel. 1/428-0134).

Near Liberty Square and the Parliament

These restaurants near Liberty Square can be found on the "Leopold Town Restaurants & Hotels" map.

$$ Hungarikum Bisztró, tucked in an unassuming neighborhood between big government ministries, is my pick for authentic, traditional Hungarian cuisine. Rather than gouging tourists, the youthful owners consider themselves ambassadors for the dishes their grandma raised them on. The mellow, unpretentious interior—with warm service and red-and-white-checked tablecloths—complements the strictly old-fashioned cuisine. Reservations are required here—be sure to book ahead (daily 11:30-14:30 & 18:00-22:00, Steindl Imre utca 13, district V, M2: Kossuth Lajos tér, tel. 1/797-7177, www.hungarikumbisztro.hu).

$$$ Börze, tucked just off Liberty Square, is a classic "locals-only" Budapest eatery. While it sits just a couple of blocks from the tourist zone, its clientele is mostly office workers enjoying Hungarian/international dishes in an attractive, bright, brass-and-subway-tile brasserie environment. They also feature affordable weekday lunch specials (daily 7:30-24:00, Nádor utca 23, tel. 1/426-5460, www.borzeetterem.hu).

Hold Street Market (Belvárósi Piac)

The Great Market Hall was one of several neighborhood markets—with similar Industrial Age decor—built around 1896. And while that most famous example is exclusively for tourists, the market hall on Hold Street, a short walk from the Parliament and one block off Liberty Square, is what you wish the Great Market Hall could be: a truly local, affordable-yet-high-end food hall catering to neighborhood shoppers and office workers seeking an efficient, affordable, but above all *good* lunch. Eating here, you'll be surrounded by Budapesters (and by a handful of savvy foodie travelers who've done their homework). There are few more satisfying places in the city to go looking for lunch (Mon 6:30-17:00, Tue-Fri until 18:00, Sat until 16:00, closed Sun). The ground floor has mostly market vendors—meat, veggies, spices, and so on—while cheap, efficient eateries ring the upstairs. Anchoring the whole space—in the middle of the main floor—is Stand 25.

$$$$ Stand 25 is *the* choice for a quality lunch in central Budapest. Celebrity chefs Szabina Szulló and Tamás Széll created this outpost to show off their mastery of Hungarian and international fare—a delightful fusion that combines the best of both, to wonderful effect. While it's mostly a lunch spot (choose two or three courses), they're also open for dinner on weekends. Reservations—for lunch or dinner—are recommended (Mon 8:00-17:00, Tue-Thu until 18:00, Fri-Sat until 22:00, closed Sun, three-quarters of the way down the market hall's main floor on the right, mobile +3630-961-3262).

$-$$ Upstairs Food Stalls: Find a wonderful variety of food stalls upstairs. You'll see a basic, grubby cafeteria; a branch of a local sausage chain; a stand selling Thai-style *khao man gai* (poached chicken in garlicky sauce); and lots more. Here are a few to check out before deciding: **Buja Disznó(k)** serves up wooden platters with massive schnit-

zels. **Lakatos Műhely** is the place for gourmet sausage. **Moszkva-tér**—named for the since-rechristened "Moscow Square"—serves

Russian food. **Kandalló Market** does gourmet burgers. And perhaps best of all for those who want to stay traditional, **A Séf Utcaja** dishes up hearty Hungarian classics, but with modern presentation.

Pest's Town Center (Belváros), near Váci Utca

When you ask natives about good places to eat on Váci utca, they just roll their eyes. Budapesters understand that only rich tourists who don't know better would throw their money away on the relatively bad food and service along this high-profile pedestrian drag. But wander a few blocks off the tourist route, and you'll discover a few alternatives with fair prices and better food. For locations, see the "Pest Town Center Hotels & Restaurants" map on page 223.

$$$ **Gerlóczy Café,** tucked on a peaceful little square next to the giant City Hall, features attentive service and a concise, tasty

menu of French, Hungarian, and international cuisine. The clientele is a mix of tourists and upscale-urban Budapesters, including local politicians and actors from nearby theaters. With a take-your-time ambience that's almost Parisian—and with live piano music on weekends after 19:00—this is a classy, particularly inviting spot (good breakfasts, weekday lunch specials, good-value fixed-price dinners, daily 8:00-23:00, 2 blocks from Váci utca, just off Városház utca at Gerlóczy utca 1, district V, M3: Ferenciek tere, tel. 1/501-4000).

$$$$ **Borssó Bistro,** near University Square (Egyetem tér), is a trendy splurge offering small portions of delicately assembled modern French cuisine with a bit of Hungarian flair. The cozy two-story interior's ambience, like the cuisine, is an elegant yet accessible blend of old and new. They also have outdoor tables and occasional live music. Reservations are important (Tue-Sun 12:00-23:00, Mon from 18:00, Király Pál utca 14, district V, M3/M4: Kálvin tér, tel. 1/789-0975, www.borsso.hu).

EATING

Great Market Hall: At the far south end of Váci utca, you can eat a quick lunch on the upper floor of the Great Market Hall (Nagyvásárcsarnok). Unfortunately, eateries here cater almost entirely to tourists; for a truly authentic market hall meal, try the far better choices at the Hold Street Market (described earlier). But if you're nearby and hungry, here are some options inside the Great Market Hall: **$$ Fakanál Étterem**—the glassed-in, sit-down cafeteria above the main entrance—is touristy, but offers good seating (Mon-Fri 10:00-17:00, Sat until 14:00, closed Sun; live music most days 12:00-15:00). The **$ sloppy, stand-up stalls** along the right side of the building are cheaper, but quality can vary. A favorite is the heavy fry bread called *lángos* (like a savory elephant ear). Get the basic one—slathered with sour cream, cheese, and (if you dare) garlic—for about 1,000 Ft; order carefully, or they could add piles of toppings to triple or quadruple your bill. Another fun option is to use the market to assemble a **picnic,** visiting the produce and butcher stands that line the main floor; get whatever else you need at the Aldi supermarket in the basement (market hall open Mon 6:00-17:00, Tue-Fri until 18:00, Sat until 15:00, closed Sun; supermarket open longer hours, Fővám körút 1, district IX, M4: Fővám tér).

BUDA

Eateries on Castle Hill are generally overpriced and touristy—as with Váci utca, locals never eat here. The Víziváros ("Water Town") neighborhood, between the castle and the river, is a bit better. Even if you sleep in Buda, try to dine in Pest—that's where you'll find the city's best restaurants. All of the restaurants listed here (except Szent Jupát) are in district I. For locations, see the "Buda Hotels & Restaurants" map on page 227.

Castle Hill

For a quick bite, visit the handy, affordable **Prima grocery store** (Mon-Sat 7:00-20:00, Sun 9:00-18:00, on Tárnok utca near Szentháromság tér).

For coffee and cakes, try the historic **Ruszwurm** (described later, under "Budapest's Café Culture"). If you'd rather have a meal—and don't want to head down to Víziváros—try the following choices:

$ Vár Bistro is a convenient, affordable cafeteria that makes for an easy and quick way to grab a meal between sightseeing. The food is uninspired but filling, and it has delightful (if crowded) outdoor seating overlooking a pretty park. They also have a counter in front with basic sandwiches and cakes (daily 8:00-20:00, Dísz tér 8, mobile +3630-237-0039).

$$$ 21 Magyar Vendéglő ("21 Hungarian Kitchen") features traditional Hungarian fare that's updated for the 21st century (hence the name). While the mod interior is pleasant, it's also fun to sit out on pretty Fortuna utca (near the north end of the hill). Most restaurants on Castle Hill are overpriced, and this is no exception—but the quality is good. This is a rare castle-zone eatery that really takes pride in its food rather than being a crank-'em-out tourism machine (daily 11:00-24:00, Fortuna utca 21, tel. 1/202-2113).

$$$ Baltazár, near the ruins of St. Mary Magdalene Church (a few short blocks from the main sights), is trying to inject some youthful liveliness into the staid, sleepy north end of Castle Hill. It's a fun choice, with bright, brash decor, pleasant outdoor seating, and a wood-fired charcoal grill that churns out smoky dishes (daily 7:30-24:00, Országház utca 31, tel. 1/300-7050). In the summer, you may see their inviting beer garden just up the street, under the church tower.

Batthyány Tér and Nearby

This bustling square—the transportation hub for Víziváros (on the M2 line)—is overlooked by a modernized, late-19th-century market hall (today housing a big Spar supermarket and various shops). Several worthwhile, affordable eateries—nothing fancy, just practical—cluster around this square. Survey your options before settling in.

$ Nagyi Palacsintázója ("Granny's Pancakes")—just to the right of the market hall entrance—serves up cheap sweet and savory crêpes *(palacsinta)* to a local crowd (open daily 24 hours, individual crêpes are small—order a combo for a filling meal, ask for English menu, Batthyány tér 5).

As you face the market hall, go up the street that runs along its left side (Markovits Iván utca) to reach more good eateries: At the end of the block on the right is **$ Édeni Végan,** a self-service, point-and-shoot vegetarian cafeteria (daily 8:00-20:00, tel. 1/375-7575). And tucked behind the market hall is **$ Bratwursthäusle/Kolbászda,** a fun little beer hall/beer garden with Bavarian specialties and blue-and-white checkerboard decor to match. Sit outside, or in the woody interior (daily 11:00-23:00, Gyorskocsi utca 6, tel. 1/225-3674).

Fine Dining near Batthyány Tér: The stylish, splurgy **$$$$ Csalogány 26** is a few short blocks from Batthyány tér in an otherwise dull urban neighborhood. Its modern international cuisine, served in a classy contemporary dining room, has earned its raves as one of the best eateries in this part of town—reserve ahead (Tue-Sat 12:00-15:00 & 19:00-22:00, closed Sun-Mon, Csalogány utca 26, tel. 1/201-7892, www.csalogany26.hu).

SNACKS AND LIGHT MEALS

When you're in the mood for something halfway between a restaurant and a picnic meal, look for takeout food stands, bakeries (with sandwiches to go), grocers willing to make you a sandwich, and simple eateries for fast and easy sit-down restaurant food.

Lángos is a popular snack—a savory deep-fried flatbread (similar to an elephant ear or Native American fry bread). Sold at stands on the street and upstairs in the Great Market Hall (see earlier), the most typical versions are spread with cheese and sour cream, and sometimes topped with garlic.

$ Hummus Bar, while not authentically Hungarian, is a popular expat-run chain that offers cheap Middle Eastern vegetarian meals (tasty falafel, sandwiches, and combination plates, eat in or to go) to grateful backpackers and young locals. They have multiple locations, including in the Town Center on University Square (Egyetem tér, at Kecskeméti utca 1, district V, M3/M4: Kálvin tér); in Leopold Town (Alkotmány utca 20, district V, M2: Kossuth tér); between Liberty Square and St. István Square (Október 6 utca 19); and two in the Seventh District (one at Király 8, and the other at the corner of Síp and Wesselényi). All are open roughly the same hours (Mon-Fri 10:00-22:00, Sat-Sun from 12:00).

Kürtőskalács is the best sweet street food in Budapest. This "chimney cake" pastry is twisted around a spindle, rolled in sugar,

and then slowly baked on a rotisserie until it's coated in a sweet, caramelized crust. They roll it in toppings (cinnamon, coconut, chocolate) and hand it over hot. Watch for vendors at the start of Andrássy út, in front of the Nyugati/Western train station, along Váci utca near March 15 Square, in the Seventh District's food-truck zone, and elsewhere around town.

FOOD EXPERIENCES

Some of these companies—with an international customer base—list prices in euros, while others list them in dollars.

Cooking Classes

Chefparade's cooking classes offer a fun way to delve into Hungarian cuisine. In a casual setting, a local chef walks you through preparing a traditional Hungarian menu (€75-85/person, 3-hour class; "premium package" for €45 extra gets you an apron, cookbook, bottle of wine, and taxi transfer to the class; add a tour of the Great Market Hall to shop for ingredients for €25; various locations, including Páva utca 13 in Pest, district IX, M3: Corvin-negyed; Sas utca 21 in Pest, district V, M1: Bajcsy-Zsilinszky út or M3: Arany János utca; or Bécsi út 27 in Buda, district II, HÉV suburban train from Batthyány tér to Szépvölgyi út stop; mobile +3620-316-1876, www.cookingbudapest.com).

Food Tours

Taste Hungary, run by American Carolyn and her Hungarian husband Gábor, offers a busy program of English-language food tours and tastings (RS%—15 percent off when you book direct, use code: RICK, www.tastehungary.com). Guided walks (generally about four hours and $100) have you eating your way through various Budapest neighborhoods for lunch or dinner, going Jewish, sampling ruin pubs, or venturing into the countryside. They also offer two wine tastings daily, with the expertise of their sommelier, at their Tasting Table location ($39, Bródy Sándor utca 9 near Astoria Metró, mobile +3630-690-4913).

Eating in a Local Home

Eat & Meet puts you in touch with locals, who invite travelers for a meal in their home (€35/person). In the summer, they sometimes move the feast outdoors. The program's coordinator, tour guide Suzie Goldbach, also leads culinary tours around town and wine tours in the countryside. For details, see www.eatmeet-hungary.com (mobile +3630-517-5180, info@eatmeet-hungary.com).

Budapest's Café Culture

In the late 19th century, a vibrant café culture boomed here in Budapest, just as it did in Vienna and Paris. The *kávéház* ("coffeehouse") was a local institution. By 1900, Budapest had more than 600 cafés. In this crowded and fast-growing cityscape, a neighborhood café allowed urbanites to escape their tiny flats (or get a jolt of caffeine to power them through a 12-hour work-

day). Local people, many of whom had moved to the city from the countryside, didn't want to pay to heat their homes during the day. So instead, for the price of a cup of coffee, they could come to a café to enjoy warmth, companionship, and loaner newspapers.

Realizing that these neighborhood living rooms were breeding grounds for dissidents, the communists closed the cafés or converted them into *eszpresszós* (with uncomfortable stools instead of easy chairs) or *bisztrós* (stand-up fast-food joints with no chairs at all). But after 1989, nostalgia brought back the *kávéház* culture—both as a place to get coffee and food, and as a social institution. While some serve only coffee and cakes, most serve light meals, and some offer full meals (as noted below).

While meals at some of these grand cafés are pricey, a budget alternative is to nurse an afternoon coffee and cake in opulent surroundings. Hungary has a proud tradition of cakes and pastries, which make liberal use of sweet cheese curds *(turós)* and poppy seeds *(mákszem)*. Here are a few Hungarian favorites to look for: The classic *Dobos torta* is a sponge-cake-and-buttercream concoction with alternating layers of chocolate and vanilla, all topped with caramelized sugar. *Rákóczi turós* is a dense cake of sweet cheese curds with jam on top. *Somlói galuska* is three delectable balls of moist sponge cake—often in different flavors (walnut, chocolate, etc.)—soaked in rum, mixed with whipped cream, and drizzled with chocolate. *Krémes* is custard sandwiched between delicate wafers. And *flódni*, which originated in the Jewish community, is earthy and filling, with layers of apple, walnuts, and poppy seeds.

On the Great Boulevard

$$$$ New York Café makes the others listed here look like Star-bucks. Originally built in 1894 by a big American insurance com-

pany (who believed that having the most extravagant café imag-inable for their clients would in-spire confidence), this fanciful, over-the-top explosion of Neo-Baroque and Neo-Renaissance epitomizes the "mix and match, but plenty of everything" His-toricist style of the day. In the early 20th century, artists, writ-ers, and musicians came here to sip overpriced coffee and bask in opulence. In the early 21st century, it's overrun by gawking, selfie-taking tourists...but still visually magnificent. There's often a line behind a fancy cord waiting for a table. While non-customers aren't allowed in, you're welcome to steal a peek from this entrance area. The food is drastically overpriced—but consider investing in a cof-fee and cake, just for the experience. Be sure to read the fun his-tory in the menu (daily 8:00-24:00, inside the Boscolo Hotel at Erzsébet körút 9, district VII, tel. 1/886-6167). Take the M2/red Metró line to Blaha Lujza tér, and exit toward *Erzsébet körút* and walk a block. You can also take tram #4 or #6 from the Oktogon (at Andrássy út) around the Great Boulevard to the Wesselényi utca stop. For location, see the map on page 225.

Two Blocks Up from Váci Utca

For the locations of these places, see the map on page 223.

$$$ Gerlóczy Café, listed as a restaurant in Pest's Town Center, earlier, nicely recaptures Budapest's early-1900s ambience, with loaner newspapers on racks and a management that encourages loitering.

$$$ Centrál Kávéház is another venerable favorite. While I'd skip the food, it has an enjoyable and atmospheric two-story interior and is great for a drink (daily 8:00-23:00, Károlyi Mihály utca 9, district V, M3: Ferenciek tere, tel. 1/266-2110).

On Andrássy Út, near the Opera House

$$$$ Callas features ideal outdoor seating facing the Opera House, and one of the finest Art Nouveau interiors in town, with gorgeous Jugendstil chandeliers. While their full meals are pricey, this is a wonderful spot in a prime Andrássy út location for a coffee break, a tasty dessert, or breakfast (Mon-Sat 10:00-24:00, Sun until 20:00, Andrássy út 20—see the map on page 219, district VI, M1: Opera, tel. 1/354-0954).

In Buda, atop Castle Hill

$$ Ruszwurm lays claim to being Budapest's oldest café (since 1827). Tiny but classy, with old-style Biedermeier furnishings and fine sidewalk seating, it upholds its venerable reputation with pride. Its dead-central location—a block in front of Matthias Church in the heart of the castle district—means that it has become a popular tourist spot (though it remains dear to locals' hearts). Look for gussied-up locals chatting here after the Sunday morning Mass at the church (daily 10:00-19:00, Szentháromság utca 7—see the map on page 227.

EATING

BUDAPEST WITH CHILDREN

Despite its reputation as a big, gloomy metropolis, Budapest is surprisingly kid-friendly. Many of the city's best experiences—such as splashing around in a warm-water whirlpool at Széchenyi Baths, or ogling giant monuments from the communist days at Memento Park—bring out the kid in any traveler.

Trip Tips

PLAN AHEAD
Involve your kids in trip planning. Have them read about the places that you may include in your itinerary (even the hotels you're considering), and let them help with your decisions.

Where to Stay
- Choose hotels in a kid-friendly area near a park. Hotels near Andrássy út are a short Metró ride from City Park. And the delightful Károly Park, in the heart of Pest's Town Center, is ideal for kids.
- Apartment rentals offer kitchens and more space, making them a good choice for families—particularly for those staying more than a couple of nights.

What to Bring
- If traveling with infants, plan on bringing a light stroller for neighborhood walks and a child backpack for bus and Metró rides.
- For a touch of home at the hotel, bring some favorite movies.
- Bring swimsuits, water shoes, goggles, and other swim gear to enjoy Hungary's wonderful thermal baths and water parks.

EATING

Try these tips to keep your kids content throughout the day.

What to Eat

- Hungarian food is generally flavorful, filling, and easy to enjoy. But a few common ingredients (such as liver and spicy paprika) may gross out finicky eaters.
- Try local treats—like Túró Rudi, a light candy bar of semisweet cheese curds dipped in chocolate...as tasty as it is fun to say (TOO-roh ROO-dee).
- While the official drinking age in Hungary is 18, younger teenagers are sometimes offered wine or beer in restaurants, especially when accompanied by a parent. It's best to decide on a family policy beforehand.

Where (and When) to Eat

- Picnic lunches and dinners work well. Supermarkets and grocery stores abound in the city center, and assembling a picnic at one of the city's many turn-of-the-century market halls (especially the Great Market Hall or the Hold Street Market) is a fun cultural experience.
- Choose easy eateries. All of the places listed under "Snacks and Light Meals" on page 239—including cafeterias, hummus bars, and *kürtőskalács* stands—are quick and easy, and kids can see what they're getting before they order.
- If you're browsing the Great Market Hall, the food stands upstairs are another easy choice; even better options are at the Hold Street Market.
- Eating al fresco is great with kids; try places on squares where kids can run free while you dine. Skip fancy or famous places, which are too formal for kids to really enjoy.
- Eat dinner relatively early (around 18:00) to miss the romantic crowd.

DISCOUNTS

- While I haven't listed kids' prices in this book beyond this chapter, most sights charge much less for children than for adults—always ask.
- Budapest's hotels often give price breaks for kids.
- If you're taking the train outside of the city, ask about family or child discounts.

SIGHTSEEING

The key to a successful Budapest family vacation is to slow down and incorporate your child's interests into each day's plans.

Planning Your Time

- Let your kids make some decisions, such as choosing lunch spots or deciding which stores or museums to visit.
- Follow this book's crowd-beating tips to a T to avoid long waits in line.
- Don't overdo it. Tackle one or two key sights each day, mix in a healthy dose of pure fun at a park or thermal bath, and take extended breaks as needed.

Successful Sightseeing

- Deputize your child to lead you on my self-guided walks and museum tours. Turn your kid into your personal tour guide and navigator of the Metró system. (They'll enjoy the little ditties that play at each stop.) Challenge them to master the complicated Hungarian pronunciation.
- Get kids engaged in age-appropriate museum fun. Younger kids might enjoy a scavenger hunt approach: Buy postcards of sights in the museum gift shop (or give them this book with its photos) and let them find the art.
- Museum audioguides help older children and teens get the most out of a sight.
- Public WCs can be hard to find. Try shopping malls, museums, cafés, and restaurants (particularly fast-food places).

Making or Finding Quality Souvenirs

- Buy your kids a trip journal and encourage them to write down their observations, thoughts, and best memories. This journal could end up being their favorite souvenir.
- For a group project, keep a family journal. Pack a small diary and a glue stick. While relaxing over an ice cream, take turns writing or drawing about the day's events and include mementos such as ticket stubs from museums and postcards.
- Teens might love shopping (or even window-shopping). See the Shopping in Budapest chapter for fun areas.

MONEY AND SAFETY

Before your trip gets underway, talk to your kids about safety and money.

- If you allow kids to explore a museum or neighborhood on their own, be sure to establish a clear meeting time and place.
- Give your child a money belt and an expanded allowance; you

are on vacation, after all. Let your children budget their funds by comparing and contrasting the dollar and forint.

- Have a "what if" procedure in case something goes wrong. Give each child a business card from your hotel, along with your contact information and taxi fare, to use if you get separated.

STAYING CONNECTED

- If your kids have mobile phones, show them how to make calls in Hungary (see "Staying Connected" in the Practicalities chapter).
- Most parents find it worth the peace of mind to buy supplemental messaging and data plans for the whole family. Adults can stay connected to teenagers while allowing them maximum independence, and teens can keep in touch with friends at home—and Europeans they meet—via apps such as WhatsApp, Snapchat, Google Talk, FaceTime, or Skype.
- Hotel guest computers and Wi-Fi hotspots are a godsend. Readily available Wi-Fi (at hotels, some cafés, and all Starbucks and McDonald's) makes bringing a mobile device worthwhile.

Top Kids' Sights and Activities

THERMAL BATHS

The top attraction for kids is the same as it is for adults: thermal baths (□ see the Thermal Baths chapter). **Széchenyi Baths**—with colorful outdoor pools and mostly mixed-gender areas—are fun for families (though children under 14 are not allowed in the indoor thermal pools). **Gellért Baths'** outdoor area and fun wave pool offer the best thermal bath thrills for kids in Budapest. The **Rudas Baths'** "wellness" area can be fun for kids, but note the thermal section is only for ages 15 and up. At baths, children over two years old pay full price.

For a more kid-oriented water park, you have two good options: **Aquaworld** is about nine miles north of downtown, but still in the city limits (www.aqua-world.hu); **Aquaréna** is about 20 miles northeast of Budapest, in the countryside near Gödöllő Palace and the Lázár Lovaspark horse show (on the way to Eger, in the village of Mogyoród, open summer only, www.aquarena.hu).

There are also fun-for-kids thermal baths in and near **Eger** (see page 344).

PLAYGROUNDS

Local parents filled me in on their favorite playgrounds. Many of these are in parks also described in more detail in this book, and are fun for moms and dads, too.

Károly Park: This hidden park, tucked in the very heart of Pest's Town Center, is a relaxing place for both kids and parents to hang out. It has generous benches, public WCs, and a fun playground area. (This park is described on page 123 of the Pest Town Center Walk).

Szabadság Tér: A pair of inviting playgrounds flank the bottom (south) end of this square, which is ringed with some of Budapest's grandest buildings. Nearby is a fun, interactive fountain, where kids step on panels to make the fountains start and stop. The café in the middle of the park is perfect for parents to sit out in the sun and sip a coffee. And the excellent Hold Street Market—with lots of tempting food stands—is just a block away. (This square is described in detail on page 103.)

Híld Tér: Tucked in the very heart of downtown Pest, kitty-corner from Elisabeth Square, this small, leafy square has a handy playground that's popular with local kids and their parents.

Olimpia Park: Just north of the Parliament on the Danube embankment, this sprawling green space has playsets, jungle gyms, and sports fields.

City Park: Enjoyable playgrounds are scattered throughout this park, as well as other attractions listed below.

Millenáris Park: This highly conceptual park is tucked behind the Mammut shopping center (near M2: Széll Kálmán tér). In addition to a fun playground, entertaining exhibits called "House of the Future" and "Palace of Miracles" might appeal to older kids.

PARKS

On a sunny day, there's no better place to have fun than in City Park or on Margaret Island.

City Park

The fun, dynamic statues at Heroes' Square help bring Hungarian history to life. The fairy-tale Vajdahunyad Castle also captures young imaginations. You can rent bikes or bike carts, and the big artificial pond near Vajdahunyad Castle usually offers paddleboats in summer and ice skating in the winter. If the weather's good, just spread out a picnic blanket and enjoy the park like a local. The park is in the middle of an ambitious, multiyear renovation project, which should result in even better facilities for kids (but in the meantime, it may be a bit torn up). With a little more energy, tackle one of the following attractions. (For more on this area, see the 📖 Heroes' Square & City Park Walk.)

Budapest Zoo and Botanical Garden (Fővárosi Állat- és Növénykert): Budapest has an entertaining big-city zoo complex,

with a "safari park," butterfly house, petting zoo, and more. It also has redeeming sightseeing value: Many of its structures are playful bits of turn-of-the-20th-century Art Nouveau. (Look for the white-and-turquoise towers of the beautiful Art Nouveau elephant house.) Sometimes on summer weekends, kids can feed the animals (2,000 Ft for kids 2-14, 3,000 Ft for adults, 8,400 Ft for family ticket covering two adults and two kids; Mon-Thu 9:00-18:00, Fri-Sun until 19:00, shorter hours in off-season, last entry one hour before closing; Állatkerti körút 6-12, district XIV, M1: Hősök tere, tel. 1/364-0109, www.zoobudapest.com).

Once Upon a Time Castle (Holnemvolt Vár): Near the zoo, this area has several entertaining attractions. The main one is a four-story indoor playground, inspired by Hungarian folk tales. There's also a petting zoo, crafts workshops, and more (combo-ticket with zoo or available separately, www.holnemvoltvar.hu).

Circus (Nagycirkusz): This old-fashioned big-top act includes clowns, gymnasts, and animals. In operation since 1891, the circus moved into its current City Park home—nestled next to the zoo, facing the swimming pool entrance for Széchenyi Baths—in 1970 (1,500-3,100 Ft for kids, 1,500-4,500 Ft for adults, show schedule varies but typically 2-3 shows per day on weekends, M1: Széchenyi fürdő, tel. 1/343-8300, www.fnc.hu).

Margaret Island

This delightful island in the Danube is filled with diversions, including baths/swimming pools, a small petting zoo, great bike trails, and fun bike-cart rentals. For details, see page 58.

Kopaszi-Gát

This long, skinny, inviting park—stretching out into the Danube at the southern edge of the city, near Rákóczi Bridge—is a popular place for local families to hang out, stroll, and play.

Gellért Hill

Kids with hill-climbing stamina might enjoy the trails that twist up this peak overlooking the Danube to great views.

PLAYHOUSES AND ADVENTURE PARK

Budapest has several playhouses (*játszóház*) for young kids—basically big, colorful, indoor jungle gyms with lots of hands-on activities. While most of the clientele are Hungarian tots, others are welcome, and it could be a good opportunity for your child to make a Magyar buddy. One example is the **Millipop Játszóház** on the Buda side, in the Millenáris Park near the Mammut shopping mall (3,000 Ft, daily 10:00-20:00, Kis Rókus utca 16-20, M2: Széll Kálmán tér, www.millipopjatszo.hu).

For something even more exciting—especially for bigger kids—the outdoor **Római Kalandpark** (Adventure Park) has high-ropes courses, a giant sandbox, and laser tag (at the north end of Óbuda, past Aquincum and on the way to Szentendre at Szentendrei út 189, take the Szentendre/H5/purple HÉV line from Batthyány tér to the Rómaifürdő stop, www.romaikalandpark.hu).

CHILDREN'S RAILWAY (GYERMEKVASÚT)

This unusual attraction in the Buda Hills is a holdover from the communist days, when kids were primed from an early age to eagerly work for the betterment of their society. While the commies are long gone, their railway's kid-friendly message of "work is fun!" is full steam ahead—and the line is still manned entirely by children (aside from driving the engines, of course). Children get a kick out of seeing fellow kids selling tickets, acting as conductor, and so on.

The only drawback is that it's on the outskirts of town and requires a few transit changes, but if you and your kids have a spirit of adventure, it's a fun ride through the Buda Hills (see map on page 73). The easiest trip is this: From Buda's Széll Kálmán tér (on the M2/red Metró line), hop on tram #59 or #61 and ride to Városmajor (or simply walk 10 minutes along the busy road called Szilágyi Erzsébet fasor away from the Danube). Here you can switch to the rack railway (*fogaskerekű vasút*), which climbs up in about 15 minutes to the end of the line at Széchenyihegy. From this stop, it's a short walk to the starting station of the Children's Railway line, which putters seven miles in about 40 minutes through the hills (part of a national park) to the other end at Hűvösvölgy. Near this station is a stop for tram #61 back to Széll Kálmán tér.

Cost and Hours: Public transit covered by regular transit tickets; Children's Railway tickets: 400 Ft one-way for kids 6-18, free for kids 5 and under, 800 Ft for adults; 4,000 Ft for "family day ticket"; train runs about hourly, sometimes 2/hour on summer weekends; daily 9:00-19:00, until 17:00 and closed Mon in off-season; old-fashioned steam engine runs occasionally for an extra charge, confirm schedules on website: www.gyermekvasut.hu.

OTHER ACTIVITIES

The **Lázár Lovaspark horse show**—near Gödöllő Palace, about 33 miles northeast of downtown—is entertaining for the entire family, and gives your kids the chance to explore a real, working, traditional Hungarian farm, complete with all of the unique livestock this country is known for (wooly pigs, giant longhorn cattle, twisty-antlered goats, dreadlocked dogs, and so on). The public-transit option for getting here is a hassle; consider making it easier with taxi rides to and from the Gödöllő train station, or hire a driver for the entire day. Notice that this is also close to **Gödöllő Palace** (with some upper-crust history that could bore some kids—but the Empress Sisi stories may fascinate others) and to the **Aquaréna** waterpark mentioned earlier; these could be combined into a very busy, but fun, day out from the big city. The horse show and palace are explained in the Day Trips from Budapest chapter.

Memento Park, with its gigantic statues, captures kids' imaginations—and offers a good springboard for a lesson about the communist days. (Teenagers might enjoy learning more at the **House of Terror**—though that engaging exhibit is too powerful for most young children.) See the individual tour chapters for details.

The **Puppet Theater** (Bábszínház) offers frequent morning and afternoon performances, in three different venues. The playful "children" shows feature light Hungarian folk tales, while the "youth/adult" shows can include weightier opera performances and avant-garde modern puppetry (1,000-3,600 Ft depending on show and time; typically closed in summer). Performances are generally not in English or subtitled, but the puppets still entertain (across from the House of Terror at Andrássy út 69, district VI, M1: Vörösmarty utca—see map on page 260 for location, tel. 1/342-2702, www.budapestbabszinhaz.hu).

Kids might also enjoy the touristy, crowd-pleasing

Hungarian folk music and dancing shows presented by **Hungária Koncert** (see the Entertainment in Budapest chapter).

The **Labyrinth of Buda Castle,** while a bit too hokey for serious adults, might entertain children with the opportunity to explore the caves beneath Castle Hill. It's especially enjoyable (and a bit spooky) after 18:00, when it's lit only by lanterns. For details, see page 68.

SHOPPING IN BUDAPEST

While it's not quite a shopper's mecca, Budapest does offer some enjoyable opportunities to hunt for that perfect Hungarian souvenir.

For a look at local life and a chance to buy some mementos, Budapest's single best shopping venue is the **Great Market Hall** (described in detail on page 46). In addition to all the colorful produce downstairs, the upstairs gallery is full of fiercely competitive souvenir vendors. There's also a **folk-art market on Castle Hill** (near the bus stop at Dísz tér), but it's generally more touristy and a little more expensive. And, while **Váci utca** has been Budapest's main shopping thoroughfare for generations, today it features the city's highest prices and worst values.

For something a bit less touristy, drop by the **Bálna ("Whale") Cultural Center,** which sits along the Danube just behind the Great Market Hall (described on page 47). You'll see some souvenir stands similar to what's upstairs in the Great Market Hall, as well as a few one-off designers. While it may be potluck for shoppers, it's worth exploring—and the architecture is interesting.

As a big, cosmopolitan capital, Budapest has its share of international fashion boutiques. Most of these are along or near **Deák utca** (called "Fashion Street," connecting Vörösmarty tér and Deák tér), or along the first stretch of **Andrássy út.** A few more big-ticket shops are along and near **Váci utca,** with an intriguing cluster along the cross-street **Irányi utca** (just south of Ferenciek tere, near the river in the Town Center). A block over, at Nyáry

Pál utca 7, **Eventuell Gallery** displays and sells the works of local designers (www.eventuell.hu).

To see how Hungarian urbanites renovate their flats, don't miss the home-improvement shops that line **Király utca,** which runs parallel to Andrássy út (two short blocks south). For a taste of the good old days—which somehow just feels right, here in nostalgic Budapest—wander up the city's **"antique row,"** Falk Miksa utca, just north of the Parliament (described later).

Budapesters do most of their shopping in big, American-style **shopping malls**—three of which (WestEnd City Center, Mammut, and Arena Plaza) are downtown and described later.

Budapest has an excellent **English bookstore.** For details, see page 25.

Hours: Smaller shops tend to be open Monday through Friday from 10:00 to 18:00 (sometimes later—until 20:00 or 21:00—on Thursday), Saturday from 10:00 to 13:00 or 14:00, and are closed Sunday. Big malls have longer hours.

Bargaining: At touristy markets (but not established shops), haggling is common for pricier items (more than about 4,000 Ft)—but you'll likely get the merchant to come down only about 10 percent (maybe down to 20 percent for multiple items). If you pay with a credit card, you're less likely to snare a discount.

VAT Refunds and Customs Regulations: For tips on getting a VAT (Value-Added Tax) refund, and getting your purchases through customs, see the "Money" section of the Practicalities chapter.

SOUVENIR IDEAS

The most popular souvenir is that quintessential Hungarian spice, **paprika.** Sold in metal cans, linen bags, or porcelain vases—and often accompanied by a tiny wooden scoop—it's a nice way to spice up your cooking with memories of your trip. (But remember that only sealed containers will make it through customs on your way back home.) For more, see "Paprika Primer" on page 474.

If you want a top-notch Hungarian **cookbook,** *Culinaria Hungary* beautifully describes and illustrates Hungary's culinary tradition. Another excellent cookbook is ChefParade's *Hungarian Classics,* which is well-illustrated with lots of photos and makes traditional recipes accessible to the modern chef. Both of these are also available on Amazon.com.

Special drinks are a fun souvenir, though they're tricky

to bring home (you'll have to wrap them very carefully and put them in your checked luggage). Good choices include the unique Hungarian spirit **Unicum** or a bottle of Hungarian **wine** (such as the famous Tokaji Aszú). For more on these drinks, see page 475.

Another popular item is a hand-embroidered **linen tablecloth.** The colors are often red and green—the national colors of Hungary—but white-on-white designs are also available (and classy). If the thread is thick and the stitching is very even, it was probably done by machine, and obviously is less valuable.

Other handicrafts to look for include **chess sets** (most from Transylvania) and **nesting dolls.** While these dolls have more to do with Russia than with Hungary, you'll see just about every modern combination available: from classic peasant-girl *matryoshkas,* to Russian heads of state, to infamous terrorists, to American presidents. Tacky...but fun.

Fans of **communist kitsch** can look for ironic T-shirts that poke fun at that bygone era. But remember that the best selection is at the Memento Park gift shop, which also sells communist memorabilia and CDs of commie anthems (see page 215).

For a wearable souvenir, **Tisza shoes** (Tisza Cipő) are retro and newly hip. The company dates from communist times, but went bust when Western brands became widely available. Recently, the brand was rescued by an investor with a renewed dedication to quality. They make both athletic and work shoes, as well as bags, shirts, and accessories. While you'll find Tisza products sold around the country, their flagship store is along the Small Boulevard near the Great Synagogue (at Károly körút 1, www.tiszacipo.hu).

HIPSTER DESIGN AND VINTAGE

Budapest is becoming a hipster mecca, and that means fun and idiosyncratic design, home decor, and vintage shops are popping up all around town. The fast-evolving scene makes it tricky to recommend a specific shop, but many intriguing boutiques have emerged in the **Seventh District/"Ruin Pub" zone.** Scout the possibilities on Király (with an emphasis on home decor), Dob, Rumbach, Dohány, Wesselényi, Kazinczy, and neighboring streets. **Printa,** the print shop described on page 185, is one reliable place to get a taste of the neighborhood's vendors. **Szimpla**—the original ruin pub—hosts a colorful farmers market each Sunday (9:00-14:00, Kazinczy utca 14, www.szimpla.hu).

Very nearby—just across Andrássy út from the Seventh District—you'll also find a smattering of intriguing shops along **Hajós utca,** behind the Opera House.

Check to see if you're in town for the **Wamp Design Fair.** One or two Sundays each month, dozens of local artists and designers gather to show off their products (free entry, 11:00-19:00, schedule at www.wamp.hu). In summer, this takes place in the city-center Elisabeth Square, while off-season it moves to an indoor venue at Millenáris Park (on the Buda side, near M2: Széll Kálmán tér).

PORCELAIN

Hungary has two major porcelain manufacturers. While very pricey, their works might interest collectors.

Herend, arguably the best (and most expensive) of all, produces tableware with intricately detailed color patterns on a white base. They've created porcelain for Queen Victoria, Emperor Maximilian of Mexico, and other historic heads of state. Herend, produced in a town of the same name near Lake Balaton, is also exported (including to the US). In Budapest, the main shop—with the best selection—is in central Pest, just off Vörösmarty tér (go around the right side of Gerbeaud café, József Nádor tér 11, www.herend.com). There are also locations at Castle Hill (in front of the Matthias Church, Szentháromság utca 5), in the

Hotel Klotild Palota on Ferenciek tere (Váci utca 34), and on Andrássy út (at #16).

Zsolnay also produces tableware, but it's better known for its decorative architectural tiles, which adorn the facades and roofs of many major Budapest buildings. You can buy Zsolnay pieces at several shops in Budapest (see www.zsolnay.hu). For more about Zsolnay, see the sidebar on page 374 in the chapter on the city of Pécs, where the porcelain originates.

For **antique porcelain,** check the several shops along Pest's "antique row" (described below). However, don't buy porcelain (or any glass) at the Great Market Hall, as it will include a significant markup.

SHOPPING

MODERN SHOPPING MALLS

Budapest has a range of modern, American-style shopping malls in the city center (most shops generally open Mon-Sat 10:00-21:00, Sun until 18:00). The biggest and most convenient options include **WestEnd City Center,** next door to Nyugati/Western train station (Váci út 1, district VI, M3: Nyugati pu., tel. 1/374-6573, www.westend.hu); **Mammut** ("Mammoth"), two separate malls a few steps from Buda's Széll Kálmán tér (Lövőház utca 2, district II, M2: Széll Kálmán tér, tel. 1/345-8020, www.mammut.hu); and **Arena Plaza,** near Keleti/Eastern train station (Kerepesi út 9, district XIV, M2: Keleti pu., tel. 1/880-7000, www.arenaplaza.hu).

PEST'S "ANTIQUE ROW": FALK MIKSA UTCA

Get into the nostalgic spirit of Budapest with a stroll down Falk Miksa utca, which extends from Kossuth tér (behind the Parliament) four blocks north to the Great Boulevard (near the end point of tram #2; also at Jászaí Mari tér stop for trams #4 and #6 around the Great Boulevard). Browse your way up and down this drag, with several hole-in-the-wall shops selling furniture, porcelain, and other antiques (most shops generally open Mon-Fri 10:00-18:00, Sat until 13:00 or 14:00, closed Sun). Look for signs that say *antik* or *antikvitás.* (The hulking building on the east side of the street is the Defense Ministry—sort of the "Hungarian Pentagon.") At the far end of Falk Miksa utca are a pair of particularly interesting shops, both facing the Great Boulevard. On the left is **BÁV,** the state-run antique shop. On the right, look for **Kieselbach Galéria,** which specializes in top-notch modern and contemporary works by Hungarian artists.

FLEA MARKET (BOLHAPIAC)

The gigantic **Ecseri Flea Market** (sometimes called "Tangó"), on the outskirts of town, is an authentic, down-and-dirty scene where the fringes of society meet to swap goods (free entry, Mon-Fri 8:00-16:00, Sat 6:00-15:00, Sun 8:00-13:00, best on Sat-Sun, mostly under cover, entrance at Nagykörösi út 156, district XIX). The public transit connection is tricky (from Boráros tér, at the Pest end of the Petőfi Bridge, catch bus #54 or #55 and ride it for about 25 minutes, get off at the Naszód utca stop, and take the pedestrian walkway over the busy road); it's easier to take a taxi. This is prime pickpocket territory—keep an eye on your valuables.

ENTERTAINMENT IN BUDAPEST

Budapest, the cultural capital of Hungary (and much of Central Europe), is endlessly entertaining. Whether it's opera, folk music and dancing, a twilight stroll or boat trip, raving into the wee hours at a thermal spa, or holing up in one of the city's uniquely ramshackle ruin pubs, Budapest offers something for everybody. The scene here has grabbed international attention: Szimpla, the first and greatest of Budapest's ruin pubs, frequently shows up on lists of "best bars in the world."

The following **helpful websites** offer current advice on cultural events and nightlife in Budapest: www.wherebudapest.hu (general), www.funzine.hu (general, with a younger bent), www.servus.hu (culture, also available in print), www.est.hu (general), www.muzsikalendarium.hu (classical music), www.welovebudapest.com (general), and www.xpatloop.com. At many places you can buy **tickets** directly, or for many Budapest events, tickets are available at www.jegymester.hu and www.kulturinfo.hu.

What's on can vary by **season.** Some of the best nightclubs and bars are partly or entirely outdoors, so they're far more enjoyable in the summer. Meanwhile, the Hungarian State Opera, Puppet Theater, and other indoor cultural events tend to take a summer break from late June into early September (though that's prime time for outdoor music and Hungária Koncert's touristy shows).

For a list of some local **festivals,** which often include excellent live music, see "Holidays & Festivals" in the appendix.

Budapest's Music Scene

Budapest is a great place to catch a good—and inexpensive—musical performance. In fact, music lovers from Vienna often make the three-hour trip here just to take in a fine opera in a luxurious setting at a bargain price. Options range from a performance at one of the world's great opera houses to light, touristy Hungarian folk concerts. The tourist concerts are the simplest option—you'll see fliers everywhere—but if you appreciate great music, do some homework to find real quality. See the resources listed earlier, including the good classical music schedules at www.muzsikalendarium.hu.

Locals dress up for the more "serious" concerts and opera, but many tourists wear casual clothes—as long as you don't show up in shorts, sneakers, or flip-flops, you'll be fine.

A NIGHT AT THE OPERA

Take in an opera by one of the best companies in Europe, in one of Europe's loveliest opera houses, for bargain prices. The Hungarian

State Opera performs almost nightly (except late June through early September), both at the main **Opera House** (Andrássy út 22, district VI, M1: Opera, see page 135) and in the **Erkel Színház theater** (not nearly as impressive—described under "Other Venues," later). If you want classical opulence, choose a performance in the Opera House, which is scheduled to reopen in time for the 2019-2020 season. Most performances are in the original language with Hungarian and English supertitles.

Ticket prices range from 1,500 to 20,000 Ft, but the best music deal in Europe may be the 600-Ft, obstructed-view tickets (easy to get, as they rarely run out—even when other tickets are sold out). If you buy one of these $2 opera tickets, you can choose whether to sit and see nothing, or stand and crane your neck to see about half the stage. Either way, you'll hear every note along with the big spenders.

To get tickets, book online (www.opera.hu or www.jegy.hu), print your ticket, and waltz right in. Or you can book by phone with a credit card (tel. 1/353-0170, phone answered daily 10:00-20:00), then pick up your ticket at the Opera House before the performance. Maybe best of all, just drop by in person and see what's available during your visit. There are often a few tickets for sale at the door, even if it's supposedly "sold out" (box office open Mon-Sat from 11:00 until show time—generally 19:00, or until 17:00 if there's no performance; Sun open three hours before the performance—generally 16:00-19:00, or 10:00-13:00 if there's a matinee). If you're desperate to attend a specific performance and it

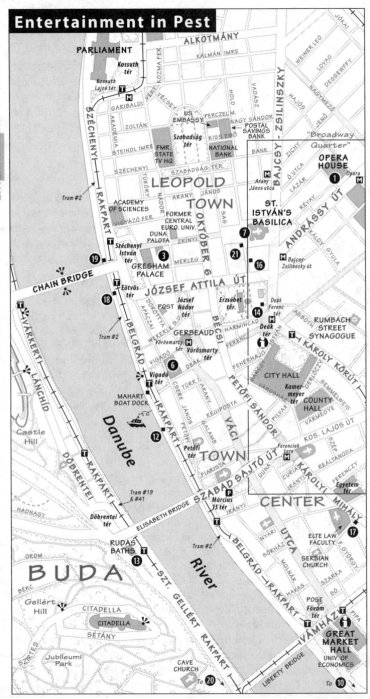

Entertainment in Pest

ENTERTAINMENT (side margin)

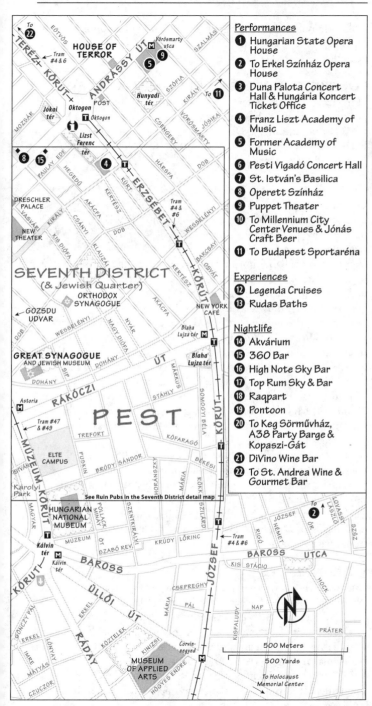

ENTERTAINMENT

Performances

1. Hungarian State Opera House
2. To Erkel Színház Opera House
3. Duna Palota Concert Hall & Hungária Koncert Ticket Office
4. Franz Liszt Academy of Music
5. Former Academy of Music
6. Pesti Vigadó Concert Hall
7. St. István's Basilica
8. Operett Színház
9. Puppet Theater
10. To Millennium City Center Venues & Jónás Craft Beer
11. To Budapest Sportaréna

Experiences

12. Legenda Cruises
13. Rudas Baths

Nightlife

14. Akvárium
15. 360 Bar
16. High Note Sky Bar
17. Top Rum Sky & Bar
18. Raqpart
19. Pontoon
20. To Keg Sörművház, A38 Party Barge & Kopaszi-Gát
21. DiVino Wine Bar
22. To St. Andrea Wine & Gourmet Bar

looks sold out online, don't give up: Try calling or stopping by the Opera House, or ask your hotelier. There's almost always a way to get a ticket.

TOURIST CONCERTS BY HUNGÁRIA KONCERT

Hungária Koncert offers a wide range of made-for-tourists performances of traditional music. Most of these take place in the **Duna Palota** ("Danube Palace")—formerly the Budapest Ritz, three long blocks north of Vörösmarty tér in Pest (behind Széchenyi tér and the Gresham Palace at Zrínyi utca 5, district V, M1: Vörösmarty tér). A few performances may take place at the gorgeous **Pesti**

Vigadó concert hall, right along the river in central Pest (see "Other Venues," later), or at the **Budai Vigadó** concert hall, on the Buda embankment near Batthyány tér.

While highbrow classical music buffs will want a more serious concert, these shows are crowd-pleasers. The most popular options are **Hungarian Folklore** music-and-dance shows by various interchangeable troupes (7,200-10,900 Ft, May-Oct Sun-Fri at 20:00, once weekly through much of the winter, at Duna Palota or Budai Vigadó) and the **Budapest Gala Concert,** mixing classical "greatest hits" with some folkloric music, ballet, and opera (10,200-12,600 Ft, May-Oct Sat at 20:00, usually at Duna Palota but occasionally at Pesti Vigadó). Or you can take in an **organ concert** at St. István's Basilica (see "Other Venues," later).

For any performance, book direct (RS%—10 percent off when you book direct in person, by phone, or by email; on their website, you can book the "student rate"; discount may not be honored if you buy your tickets through your hotel). The main office is in the Duna Palota at Zrínyi utca 5 (daily 9:00-22:00, winter until 20:00, tel. 1/317-2754 or 1/317-1377, www.budapestxplore.com, frontoffice@hungariagroup.com).

OTHER VENUES

Budapest has many other grand spaces for enjoying a performance. Notice that *Színház* ("scene house") means "Theater."

The **Franz Liszt Academy of Music** (Liszt Ferenc Zeneművészeti Egyetem, a.k.a. Zeneakadémia), on Franz Liszt Square, hosts high-quality professional concerts every night, and occasional free concerts by its students. Restored to its stunning late-19th-century splendor, this venue rivals even the Opera House for opulence; if you can't take in an opera while you're in Buda-

pest, this is a suitable substitute—and can be much more affordable. There are various halls in this building, but the main attraction is the Grand Hall (Nagyterem)—if attending a concert, make sure it's there (1,200-14,900-Ft tickets in Grand Hall depending on performance—many have tickets averaging 3,000-5,000 Ft, can be much less expensive in other venues, fewer performances when school's out July-Aug, box office open daily 10:00-18:00—or until the first intermission if there's an evening show, Liszt Ferenc tér 8, just off of Andrássy út, district VI, M1: Oktogon, tel. 1/321-0690, www.zeneakademia.hu). They also do one-hour guided tours of the theater in English, daily at 13:30 (3,500 Ft, includes brief concert by a student).

The **former Academy of Music** (Régi Zeneakadémia)—just up Andrássy út near the House of Terror—houses the Franz Liszt Museum and hosts performances on Saturday mornings at 11:00 (2,000 Ft, Vörösmarty utca 35, tel. 1/322-9804, www.lfze.hu).

The **Pesti Vigadó** ("Pest Concert Hall"), gorgeously restored and sitting proudly on the Pest embankment, is another fine place for a concert in elegant surroundings (mostly classical, 4,000-5,500 Ft tickets, Vigadó tér 1, district V, M1: Vörösmarty tér, tel. 1/266-6177, www.vigado.hu).

The city's two finest churches—both with sumptuous interiors—host tourist-oriented concerts. As these are operated by different companies, you'll have to do a little homework to understand all of your options. Most of the shows in **St. István's Basilica** are organ concerts, including one by Hungária Koncert that usually mixes Bach and Mozart with Liszt or Bartók (Thu at 20:00 May-Dec; 6,000-9,200 Ft—see listing earlier for ticket and Rick Steves discount information). Other organ concerts are on Mondays (17:00 year-round or at 19:00 in Oct, 3,500 Ft) and Friday nights (20:00 April-Dec, 4,500-7,000 Ft; see www.organconcert.hu). There's also a classical ensemble Tuesdays at 20:00 (7,000-12,500 Ft, www.concertsinbudapest.com). Up on Castle Hill, **Matthias Church** hosts a variety of touristy shows, from organ recitals to string orchestras (www.matyas-templom.hu).

The **National Dance Theater** (Nemzeti Táncszínház) puts on performances ranging from ballet to folk to contemporary at various venues around town, including the Palace of Arts (at the Millennium City Center—see later), the MOM Cultural Center (near the Great Synagogue, at Csörsz utca 18), and the Royal

Hungarian Music

As a leading city of the music-loving Habsburg Empire, where so many great composers thrived, Budapest has seen a steady parade of great musical talent waltz through its streets. And, for such a small country, Hungary boasts an exceptional musical tradition. The local music is typified by a unique mingling of powdered-wig classical influences and down-home campfire hoedowns. Even the great classical Hungarian composers freely admitted to drawing inspiration from their humble Magyar heritage.

Hungary's traditional music—like its language, cuisine, and everything else—still shows the influence of its Central Asian roots. Almost hauntingly discordant to foreign ears, it makes ample use of stringed instruments, especially violins and the cimbalom (*czembalom,* similar to a hammered dulcimer). These soulful melodies seem to pluck the strings of the Hungarian soul; more than once I've seen Hungarians (especially after sipping some local wine) spontaneously break into a traditional *csárdás* or *verbunkos* dance, with the womenfolk periodically punctuating the proceedings with an excited little yelp. Popular tunes include the lively "Az a Szép" ("He is Handsome") and the downbeat "Virágom, Virágom" ("My Flower, My Flower").

Another Asian-descended group, the Roma (called Gypsies in the past), have also had a strong influence on Hungarian music. Because of the similarities in these two peoples' music, and the convergence of their cultures in the Hungarian (and Transylvanian) countryside, "Hungarian folk" music and "Gypsy" music are virtually indistinguishable to the casual listener. For example, Roma composer Grigoraș Dinicu's "The Lark"—a high-speed violin piece that replicates a bird's chirp—is a favorite show-off song for Hungarian violin virtuosos. The rollicking high spirits that accompany a lively music session are described with the Roma term *mulatság*.

The "big three" Hungarian composers all borrowed tunes from their Magyar ancestors:

Franz Liszt (pronounced "list," 1811-1886) was raised speaking German, but had a Hungarian surname and ancestry, and loved what he considered his homeland of Hungary. This master composer, conductor, pedagogue, and (above all) pianist was prodigiously talented and traveled far and wide to share his skill ("Liszt played here" signs are plastered on buildings all over Hungary). He died never having mastered the Magyar tongue, but his countrymen embrace him anyway. Liszt composed what's probably the definitive piece of Magyar music, Hungarian Rhapsody No. 2 in D Minor. His former Budapest apartment now hosts a modest museum to the composer (see page 139).

Béla Bartók (BAR-tohk, 1881-1945), from Transylvania, was as much an ethnomusicologist as a composer. He collected and catalogued folk songs from the distant corners of the Hungarian realm and beyond. In addition to composing the well-known choral work *Cantata Profana* and the symphonic *Concerto for Orchestra,* he also penned the opera *Bluebeard's Castle.* His erotic ballet, *The Miraculous Mandarin,* caused a scandal at its 1926 debut; after that he wrote only concert pieces. Bartók is particularly well-known to Americans because he fled to New York City during World War II. He never again set foot in Hungary, dying of leukemia before the war ended.

Zoltán Kodály (KOH-dye, 1882-1967) was also an ethnomusicologist, who strove to analyze folk music on a scientific basis. Like Bartók, he harvested many songs in the fertile soil of rustic Transylvania. But unlike Bartók, Kodály focused on understanding and forging a uniquely Hungarian folk sound. Kodály was also a composer, but he's best known today as the namesake of the solfège sight-singing method called the "Kodály Method"—the principle behind "do, re, mi..."

Other (non-Hungarian) composers were also inspired by Magyar music. For example, Johannes Brahms (1833-1897), from Germany, composed a series of Hungarian Folk Dances (the most famous is No. 5/Allegro, which the Hungarians have adopted as an anthem).

Traditional Hungarian music was discouraged by the communists because it stoked Magyar patriotism, but it was kept alive by the underground *tánchéz* ("dance house") movement. Today, traditional music is enjoying a renaissance—popular not only with visitors (touristy Budapest restaurants often have live "Gypsy music"), but also among locals. Muzsikás is a well-respected band that performs classic folk music with a very old-fashioned sound (www.muzsikas.hu), while the Roma bands Ando Drom and Besh o droM each have a following of their own.

Garden Pavilion in the Várkert Bázár complex, along the Buda riverbank just below the Royal Palace (tel. 1/201-4407, www. dancetheatre.hu).

As noted earlier, the modern **Erkel Színház** is the State Opera's "second venue" (near the Keleti/Eastern train station at Köztársaság tér 30, district VIII, M2: Keleti pu., tel. 1/333-0540, www.opera.hu).

In the heart of the "Broadway Quarter," the **Operett Színház** specializes in operettas and modern musical theater performances, usually in Hungarian (just off Andrássy út at Nagymező utca 17, district VI, M1: Opera, tel. 1/312-4866, www.operettszinhaz.hu).

For something a bit more playful, consider the **Puppet Theater** (Bábszínház; across from the House of Terror), which offers puppet performances that please young and old alike (see page 251).

The **Millennium City Center** complex, sitting on the Pest riverbank near the Rákóczi Bridge south of downtown (district IX), is a state-of-the-art facility with multiple venues. The **Palace of Arts** (Művészetek Palotája) features art installations as well as musical performances in two venues: the 1,700-seat Béla Bartók National Concert Hall and the 460-seat Festival Theater (tel. 1/555-3001, www.mupa.hu). The **National Theater** (Nemzeti Színház) presents mostly Hungarian-language drama and lectures (tel. 1/476-6868, www.nemzetiszinhaz.hu). For more information on this complex, including how to ride the tram there from downtown, see page 55.

Major rock acts perform at the **Budapest Sportaréna** (a.k.a. Papp László Sportaréna; southeast of City Park at intersection of Hungária körút and Kerepesi út, district XIV, M2: Stadionok, www.budapestarena.hu).

Nightlife in Budapest

Budapest is a youthful and lively city, with no shortage of after-hours fun. I've listed these options roughly in increasing order of edginess, from "asleep by 10:00 (p.m.)" to "asleep by 10:00 (a.m.)."

LOW-IMPACT NIGHTLIFE

This beautiful city is gorgeously lit after dark. Strolling along either the Buda or the Pest **promenade** along the Danube rewards you with wonderful views. To nurse a twilight drink here, see the "Danube Riverbank Bars at the Chain Bridge," later.

NIGHTTIME DANUBE CRUISE

For a different angle on Budapest, consider joining one of these fun, romantic, crowd-pleasing boat trips. **Legenda**'s cruises include two drinks and evocative commentary about the floodlit buildings you pass (for details, see page 36).

BATHING AFTER DARK

If you need some rejuvenation after a busy day of sightseeing, soak and splash at **Széchenyi Baths** (open until 22:00, last entry 21:00). And on weekends, both Széchenyi and the historic, Turkish-style **Rudas Baths** become nightclubs until the wee hours (for specific schedules, see the Thermal Baths chapter).

YUPPIE DRINKING ZONES

The plaza in front of **St. István's Basilica** is Budapest's most fashionable locale for a glass of wine. Of the many upscale restaurants and bars in this area, DiVino—a bar with contemporary decor and a wide range of Hungarian wines by the glass—is a good choice (see page 235).

Franz Liszt Square (Liszt Ferenc tér), a leafy and inviting zone just off Andrássy út, is lined with mostly tourist-oriented bars. The pedestrianized **Ráday utca,** near Kálvin tér just north of the Great Market Hall, has a similar scene.

For something a bit more genteel—evocative of this city's late-19th-century Golden Age—locals pass their evenings sipping wine or nibbling dessert at a **café** (see "Budapest's Café Culture" in the Eating in Budapest chapter).

IN THE "NATIONAL DITCH"

Akvárium, below street level at the central square in Pest, fills what would have been the foundation for the never-completed new National Theater, at Erzsébet tér (next to Deák tér, where three Metró lines converge). It's a café by day and a music club by night, when the sprawling subterranean space (which is faintly visible below the surface of the park's shallow pond) hosts an eclectic range of concerts—from DJs and rock bands to folklore shows and electronica. In the summer, people fill the tables on the terraces that lead down into the club, and hang out on the lawn nearby—creating a fun and engaging scene (Erzsébet tér, district V, M1/M2/M3: Deák tér, mobile +3630-860-3368, www.akvariumklub.hu). For more on the history of this odd site—nicknamed the "National Ditch"—see page 132.

RUIN PUBS

Budapest is becoming known worldwide as a nightlife destination. And that's thanks largely to the ruin-pub phenomenon. These lively

pubs are filled with ramshackle secondhand furniture, a bohemian-junkyard vibe—and plenty of drinkers (both locals and tourists) having the time of their lives. Think of it as pretending you're a squatter for a few hours, before returning to the comfort of your hotel.

Each ruin pub *(romkocsma)* is different—from mellow hangouts to hopping dance clubs—so survey several to find your favorite. Most of the clientele are in their 20s or 30s, but hip oldsters feel perfectly welcome. While some ruin pubs are edgy and high-energy, others are more fit for a hammock. To seek out your ideal ruin pub, know the terminology. A ruin pub may bill itself as a *mulató* (club, usually higher-energy) or a *kávézó* (coffeehouse, usually mellower). In good weather, the best part of a ruin pub is outdoors. Many have a *kert* ("garden"), filling deteriorating buildings' courtyards with strings of lights, hammocks, mismatched chandeliers, parachute-quilt awnings, lush houseplants, and artful graffiti. Others have a *tető* ("rooftop"), where you can get some fresh air and—often—views over the floodlit city. In winter or bad weather, find one with a cozy interior. The bigger ruin pubs often have a burly bouncer stationed outside—but curious travelers are more than welcome. For more info, including additional listings, see www.ruinpubs.com.

Ruin-Pub Crawl in the Seventh District

Budapest's Seventh District—the historic Jewish Quarter, behind the Great Synagogue—has emerged as Budapest's prime nightlife zone for both locals and visitors. The neighborhood teems with clubs, bars, and creative little hole-in-the-wall eateries. Why are so many of these funky bars concentrated in the Jewish Quarter? Because it's conveniently central, yet remained largely deserted and dilapidated after the communists took over—keeping rents very low and fostering just the right rickety-chic vibe for ruin pub purveyors.

This little pub crawl connects my four favorite ruin pubs, all within a few short blocks on Kazinczy street: Szimpla, Kőleves, Ellátó, and Mika. I'd head for a nice dinner in the Seventh District (see recommendations in the Eating in Budapest chapter), then check out this scene to see what appeals. If you only have time and interest for one, head straight to the first and best, Szimpla. With

Ruin Pubs in the Seventh District

- ❶ Szimpla Kert
- ❷ Street Food Karaván
- ❸ El Rapido
- ❹ Ramenka
- ❺ Kőleves
- ❻ Ellátó Kert
- ❼ Mika Kert
- ❽ Négyszáz
- ❾ Csendes
- ❿ Farm, BlindBar & Most Bistro
- ⓫ Telep
- ⓬ Anker't

a little more time and a spirit of adventure, check out the others as well.

This area can be very lively any night of the week (especially in good weather), but it's best Thursday through Saturday. During the peak of summer (July-Aug), most Budapesters are out of town on holiday, making this scene a bit more touristy.

The first stop, Szimpla, is situated in the middle of this district, a couple of blocks behind the Great Synagogue, between the busy streets Wesselényi and Dohány. Just look for the street with a hubbub of nightlife and cheap eateries.

Szimpla Kert ("Simple Garden") sprawls through an old

building that ought to be condemned, and spills out into an equally shoddy courtyard. Surrounding the garden is a warren of tiny rooms—each one different. It's on the route of the tourist pub-crawls, so it's gotten pretty touristy. Still, it's an amazing scene. There's live music in a soundproof concert room, and a selection of decent food upstairs (Szimpla Kitchen has the most serious menu). For a more sophisticated corner, drop by the Saloon (air-conditioned, upstairs above the front door); there's a craft beer bar and Fussball room next to the Saloon. As you enter, pick up the Szimpla map/program to get a sense of its community mission (Mon-Fri 12:00-late, Sat-Sun

9:00-late, Kazinczy utca 14, www.szimpla.hu). This space hosts Hungarian Folk Dances on Monday evenings, and a farmers' market on Sunday mornings (9:00-14:00).

Note: The building that Szimpla occupies has reportedly been sold to an investor. It's possible that it may relocate—but as the neighborhood's big trendsetter, there's very little chance it'd go away entirely. If it's not here, ask around or check their website.

Szimpla anchors a street of imitators and hangers-on, though none of them qualify as "ruin pubs." However, this is a good place to find street food. Next door to Szimpla is the handy **Street Food Karaván** food truck pod (see page 231); nearby you'll find tacos (El Rapido, at #11), ramen noodles (Ramenka, at #9), and lots more.

Let's continue with the crawl: With Szimpla at your back, turn left and walk along Kazinczy utca. You'll cross Wesselényi utca, then pass the Orthodox Synagogue (on your right). Crossing Dob street, partway down the next block on your right (on #41) is the garden *(kert)* for **Kőleves** ("Stone Soup"). The ruin pub garden has lazy hammocks and a nice, mellow vibe; it feels a bit more mature, without the stag-party chaos of some. They have basic food in the garden, and the attached restaurant has good sit-down meals (see page 231).

Continue along Kazinczy utca. A bit farther, on the left at #48, is **Ellátó Kert** ("Supplier")—a mostly outdoor ruin pub with mismatched furniture under tents, and with Latino flair and food. Since it's hidden farther down the alley, it gets fewer tourist drop-ins, and feels more purely local.

Nearly across the street (at #47) is another good ruin pub garden, **Mika Kert,** with more of a beer-garden feel.

From here, nightlife sprawls in all directions. While not quite "ruin pubs," if you're enjoying yourself, follow this little extension to some additional memorable spots: Carry on along Kazinczy. A few steps past Mika Kert, on the left, make your way down the

Escape Room Games

If you enjoy haunted houses at Halloween, you'll love a popular Budapest pastime: escape room games. Taking root in the fertile soil of the ruin-pub scene, dozens of local tour operators set up this fun (for some) and terrifying (for others) experience: Your small group is locked in a room in a spooky, derelict building. To escape, you must solve a series of clues and puzzles (in English) within the allotted time. Various hazards and hurdles pop up as you go, and you'll need to work together to achieve the goal. The escape room game concept—popular for team-building outings, but accessible to curious tourists—has taken off in a big way, and Hungary has exported the games to other cities in Europe and beyond. Companies come and go, but well-established options include www.claustrophilia.hu, www.trap.hu, www.exitpointgames.hu, and www.parapark.hu. As the lineup is constantly changing and each outfit has its own personality, read some online reviews to find the one that suits your interests. Then book ahead, have fun...and good luck.

unnamed alley (marked by Pirítós), and plunge into the cacophony of a bewildering variety of outdoor bars, cafés, and nightspots. The best of these is probably **Négyszáz** ("400"), flanking the alley (officially at Kazinczy 52).

Continuing straight ahead to the end of the lane, you enter right into the middle of the long series of courtyards called **Gozsdu Udvar.** Stretching in both directions, Gozsdu Udvar is jammed with lively bars, cafés, and restaurants. Exploring here is a fun way to finish your ruin-pub evening (for details, see page 183).

Note that several additional ruin pubs (and similar nightspots) are close by (5-10 minutes walking). Peruse the list below and go explore.

More Ruin Pubs and Similar Nightspots Nearby

Csendes ("Silent"), with two adjacent branches, is a mellower, more grown-up-feeling (but still artistically ramshackle) ruin pub tucked behind Károlyi Park, right in the core of the Town Center. The junk-cluttered main "art bar" is at Ferenczy István utca 7 (closed Sun). The Csendes Társ ("Silent Partner") wine bar—a bit more upmarket and snooty—has delightful outdoor tables across the street at the gate to the park, and is typically open only in good weather (daily 10:00-late; Magyar utca 16).

Farm, behind the Opera House, feels like a cross between a garden sale and an upscale, minimalist ruin pub. This farm-to-table "gastro bar" serves a creative menu of cocktails (focusing on fresh herbs and fruits) and small plates of locally sourced snacks—such as cheeses and salamis (Mon-Sat 18:00-24:00, closed Sun, Ó utca 14, mobile +3630-622-7500). In back is the **BlindBar,** where you can dine entirely in the dark to enhance your senses of taste and smell, served by night-vision-goggle-wearing waiters (www.blindbar.hu). And just up the street, filling a vacant lot, is the **Most Bistro**—less ruin-pubby, but a nice outdoor alternative.

Telep ("Site") is a tumble-down secondhand bar incongruously located in a residential and office-block neighborhood just around the corner from the heart of the ruin-pub scene (steps from Gozsdu Udvar). There's an art gallery upstairs, and often live music (Madách Imre utca 8, just off Rumbach utca, http://telepgaleria.tumblr.com).

Anker't, a young, brash, and slightly snooty offshoot of a popular nightclub (Anker), has a minimalist charm. It's conveniently located a short block off Andrássy út—look for the |A| sign (across the street from the Opera House at Paulay Ede utca 33).

SUMMER TERRACES (TETŐ)

In addition to *kert* ("garden"), a key term for enjoying Budapest in the summer is *tető* ("roof"). Rooftop terraces offer laid-back

scenery high above the congested city. Most roof terraces are open only in the summer (typically May-Sept), in good weather, and start serving drinks and light food around midafternoon. Several offer live music. While this is an emerging scene, here are a few places worth checking out.

360 Bar is my favorite, with a handy location right along Andrássy út and a fun menu of refreshing, summery craft cocktails and tasty bites. An elevator zips you up to the seventh floor and a world of chill Hungarian hipsters enjoying a unique view on their capital. Order at the bar and find the table, bench, or beanbag chair of your choice. Reservations are possible only through Facebook (daily 14:00-late, find door just to the right of the old Párisi Nagy Áruház, Andrássy út 39, M1: Opera, www.360bar.hu).

High Note Sky Bar (atop the posh, gaudy Aria Hotel) has vivid yellow sofas and point-blank views of St. István's. Don't miss the glassed-in passage that leads to spiral stairs up to the two towers—both of which offer even higher, better, unobstructed views (daily 12:00-24:00, Hercegprímás utca 5, district V, www.ariahotelbudapest.com).

Top Rum Sky & Bar, above the recommended Rum Hotel in Pest's Town Center, overlooks University Square. This one is mostly enclosed (though the roof can roll back), and comes with a younger but still upscale atmosphere, including furry chairs (Királyi Pál utca 4, district V, M3/M4: Kálvin tér, www.hotelrumbudapest.com).

DANUBE RIVERBANK BARS AT THE CHAIN BRIDGE

Two bars with very different characters flank the Chain Bridge on the Pest side, offering views of the landmark bridge and the castle. This is a fine spot at twilight—when the castle is floodlit, the bridge's lights twinkle on, and the sky is a hazy purple.

The more upscale-feeling option is **Raqpart,** with a modern vibe (in front of the Hotel InterContinental on Jane Haining rakpart, mobile +3630-464-0646, www.raqpart.hu). On the same side of the Danube just north of the bridge, **Pontoon** feels more rustic and downscale...almost like a ruin pub, with cheap plastic furniture spilling out under the trees onto the embankment. On a nice, warm evening, Pontoon is particularly tempting because you can take your drink out by the river, with an A-plus view of the Chain Bridge and the Royal Palace on Castle Hill beyond; settle in for sunset and the onset of twilight (daily 12:00-late, closed off-season, Antall József rakpart 1).

LOCAL CRAFT BEER AND HUNGARIAN WINE

If you want to sample a local beverage, choose your poison—beer or wine?

Craft Beer: Budapest has an increasing number of pubs specializing in both Hungarian and international microbrews. If you're a beer pilgrim, consider one of these places. **Keg Sörművház,** a long block up from the Gellért Baths (and Szent Gellért tér tram and Metró stop), is a nondescript cellar with 32 craft beers on tap, flashing on the electronic menu board (daily 11:30-23:00, Orlay utca 1). **Jonás,** at the far end of the "Whale" building (Bálna)—get it?—is another good option for trying craft beers on tap. It's less about the beer and more about the setting—with lots of outdoor tables arrayed along the Danube (street food kiosks, daily 11:00-late, Fővám tér 11).

Wine: If you prefer grapes to hops, there are several great spots to sample Hungarian wine. For perhaps the best option—with a wide range of choices available by the glass, and lively outdoor seating on the lovely Szent István tér—check out **DiVino Wine Bar** (see listing in the Eating in Budapest chapter). For top-end wines by one particularly renowned vintner, check out the **St. Andrea Wine & Gourmet Bar,** near the Nyugati/Western train station (closed Sun, Bajcsy-Zsilinszky út 78, district V, M3: Nyugati pályaudvar).

NIGHTCLUBS AND OUTDOOR VENUES

Budapest has a thriving nightlife scene for twentysomethings. In general, places are hopping Wednesday through Saturday nights—and pretty dead Sunday through Tuesday. In the summer, many Budapesters head to nearby Lake Balaton (which has its own share of nightspots) for the weekend—leaving Budapest's clubs mostly for tourists. To mingle with Hungarians, Thursday nights are best. Many of the places I mention here are outdoor and summer-only—look for the words *kert* (garden), *terasz* (terrace), *udvar* (courtyard), or "beach." Off-season (Oct-April) or in questionable weather, skip the trip. Note that some clubs charge a cover (usually for men only). While this scene is constantly changing, the places listed here are well-established. But before venturing to any specific place, ask around for the latest advice (youth hostels and backpackers are a great source of tips). Look around town (including at some TIs and hotels) for the free weeklies *Budapest Funzine* (www.funzine.hu) and *Pesti Est* (www.est.hu).

Warning: Gentlemen, be highly suspicious if a gorgeous local woman fawns all over you. (Sorry, you're not *that* handsome, even here in upside-down Hungary.) She's a *konzumlány* ("consumption girl"), and the foreplay going on here will climax in your grand rip-off: You'll wind up at her "favorite bar," with astronomical prices enforced by a burly bouncer who knows where the nearest ATM is. And many of the city's strip clubs are expert at semilegally extorting enormous sums of cash from out-of-towners. Even if you're accustomed to visiting strip clubs back home, it's best to steer clear here. (If you're looking for advice on which specific strip clubs are better than others...you bought the wrong book, buddy.)

"Dockyard Island" (Hajógyári Sziget)

One of the most happening zones—especially in the summer—is the island in the Danube just north of Margaret Island (near Óbuda, a.k.a. Óbudai Island, district III). An ever-changing lineup of several clubs keeps this island throbbing. This is a thriving and sprawling scene, with imported beaches, rental boats, and a meat-market vibe. (It's also known for its drug scene and can be seedy—be cautious exploring after dark.) You can take the HÉV suburban railway from Batthyány tér and get off at the Filatorigát stop, then walk across the bridge to the island—or just take a taxi from downtown. This island is also the site of Budapest's biggest bash, the **Sziget Festival,** which attracts huge-name, midlevel, and small-name acts for a week each August (www.sziget.hu). This "Hungarian Coachella," typically attended by nearly 400,000 people, is one of Europe's top parties.

South of Downtown Budapest, Along the River

Near Petőfi Bridge: More summer-only options cluster just south of downtown, next to the Petőfi Bridge (near Boráros tér, district IX, take tram #2 south from Pest Town Center, or tram #4 or #6 around the Great Boulevard). Floating in the river on the Pest side is the party barge/live music venue called **A38** (known for its big-name local acts, www.a38.hu).

Near Rákóczi Bridge: Just a bit farther south, on the west side of the Rákóczi Bridge, stretches a long, skinny dike called **Kopaszi-Gát.** Its recently spiffed-up boardwalk is lined with a family-friendly scene of parks, playgrounds, cafés, restaurants, and terraces—worth exploring on a warm summer evening.

BUDAPEST CONNECTIONS

Budapest is the transportation hub for all of Hungary; from here, train lines and expressways fan out like spokes on a wheel. This chapter covers arrivals and departures by train, bus, plane, and car. For details on taking the riverboat to Danube Bend towns (Szentendre, Visegrád, and Esztergom), see page 307.

By Train

Budapest has three major train stations (*pályaudvar*, abbreviated *pu.*): Keleti ("Eastern") station, Nyugati ("Western") station, and Déli ("Southern") station; a fourth, suburban station—Kelenföld—is a common transfer point for destinations to the south (including Pécs). A century ago, the name of the station indicated which part of Europe it served. But these days, there's no correlation: Trains going to the east might leave from the "western" station, and vice versa. Before departing from Budapest, it's essential to confirm which station your train leaves from.

The Keleti/Eastern and Nyugati/Western train stations, in Pest, are both cavernous, slightly run-down, late-19th-century masterpieces. The Déli/Southern train station—behind Castle Hill in Buda—mingles its dinginess with modern, concrete flair. All three stations are seedy and overdue for renovation. But once you get your bearings, they're easy to navigate. At all stations, access to the tracks is monitored: You might have to show your ticket to reach the platforms (though this is loosely enforced).

Getting into Town: The taxi stands in front of each train station are notorious for ripping off tourists; it's better to stick to public transit. But if you must take a taxi, it's far more reliable to phone for one (call 211-1111 or 266-6666, and tell the English-speaking dispatcher where you are). For tips on this—and on using the Metró system to connect into downtown Budapest—see "Getting Around Budapest" on page 28.

Buying Train Tickets: For domestic tickets, it's easiest to book **online** on the Hungarian Railways website: www.mavcsoport.hu. While low-tech, the site is in English and accepts American credit cards. You can send an e-ticket to your phone (you may have to create a login to do this); then on the train, just flash your e-ticket to the conductor, who may ask to see your ID.

International connections must be issued on **paper tickets,** which means you'll have to go to a train station. Do as the locals do and use the ubiquitous MÁV ticket machines in the station. They have English instructions and take American credit cards. If you can't get one to work, look for a staffed ticket desk—marked *pénztár* or *jegypénztár*. Sometimes international tickets are sold only at a special window (marked *nemzetközi*).

Other key words: *Vágány* is track, *induló vonatok* is departures, and *érkező vonatok* is arrivals.

KELETI/EASTERN STATION

Keleti train station (Keleti pu.) is just south of City Park, east of central Pest. The station faces a newly renovated plaza called Baross tér, with stops for two different Metró lines (M2/red and M4/green).

On arrival, go to the front of long tracks 6-9 to reach the exits and services. Several travel agencies masquerading as TIs cluster near the head of the tracks. A handy OTP **ATM** is just to the left of the main door (other ATMs inside the station have rip-off rates—but two more legitimate ATMs are inside banks that face the square out front). Train ticket machines are also just inside the main door. There's no official TI at the station, but the railroad runs a customer service office with train advice and basic city info (near the front of track 9, in the left corner, near the ATM).

Along **track 6,** from back to front, you'll see a side door (leading to a beautifully restored arrivals hall and an exit to a taxi stand), Interchange exchange booth (with bad rates—use the OTP ATM instead), international ticket windows *(nemzetközi jegypénztár),* grubby gyro stands, and the classy Baross Restaurant (described later). Pay WCs are down the hall past the gyro places. Across the main hall, more services run along **track 9,** including domestic ("inland") ticket windows and lockers. The big staircase at the head

CONNECTIONS

of the tracks leads down to more domestic ticket windows, WCs, telephones, and more lockers.

If you have time (or forints) to kill while waiting for your train, the **Arena Plaza** shopping mall is roughly across the street from the station.

To take the **Metró** into town, head down the main stairs where the tracks dead-end, pass through a ticket area, and then (on your right) a handy public transit ticket and information office. Just beyond that, the underpass opens up: Turn left to reach the M2/red Metró line, or right to reach the M4/green Metró line. **Taxis** wait alongside the station (through the exit by track 6).

Eating at Keleti Station: At the head of track 6, **$$ Baross Restaurant** captures some of the turn-of-the-20th-century gentility that this grand station once enjoyed. A time warp with dingy woodwork, chandeliers, and fake marble, it serves up tired Hungarian classics worth considering if you want a meal while waiting for your train (daily 8:00-20:00).

NYUGATI/WESTERN STATION

Nyugati train station (Nyugati pu.) is the most central of Budapest's stations, facing the Great Boulevard on the northeast edge of downtown Pest.

Most trains use the shorter **tracks 1-9,** which are set back from the main entrance. From the head of these tracks, use the stairs or escalator just inside the doors to reach an underpass and the Metró (M3/blue line). Or exit straight ahead into a parking lot with buses, taxis,

and—around to the right—the WestEnd City Center shopping mall. (The useful trams around the Great Boulevard are outside the main door, at the head of the longer tracks 10-13.)

The longer **tracks 10-13** extend all the way to the main entrance. Ticket machines line the tracks; ticket windows are through an easy-to-miss door by platform 13 (marked *jegypénztár* and *információ*). This area is being renovated, so you may have to hunt around for international ticket windows *(nemzetközi jegypénztár)* and for lockers. An **ATM** is just inside the main door, on the right (use the one marked with the OTP logo).

From the head of tracks 10-13, exit straight ahead out the **main entrance** and you'll be on Teréz körút, the very busy Great Boulevard ring road. In front of the building is the stop for the handy trams #4 and #6 (which zip around the Great Boulevard); to the right are stairs leading to an underpass (use it to avoid crossing this busy intersection, or to reach the Metró's M3/blue line); and to the left is the classiest Art Nouveau McDonald's on the planet, filling the station's former waiting room. (Seriously. Take a look inside.)

Trains to the **airport** generally depart from the longer tracks on the far side (tracks 14 and higher).

DÉLI/SOUTHERN STATION
In the late 19th century, local newlyweds caught the train at Déli train station (Déli pu.) for their honeymoon in Venice. Renovated by the heavy-handed communists, today the station—tucked behind Castle Hill on the Buda side—is dreary. From the tracks, go straight ahead into the vast main hall, with well-marked domestic and international ticket windows at opposite ends. A left-luggage desk is outside beyond track 1. Downstairs, you'll find several shops and eateries, and access to the very convenient M2/red Metró line, which takes you to several key points in town: Batthyány tér (on the Buda embankment, at the north end of the Víziváros neighborhood), Deák tér (the heart of Pest, with connections to two other Metró lines), and Keleti train station (where you can transfer to the M4/green Metró line).

TRAIN CONNECTIONS
There's no telling which station any given train will use, especially since it can change from year to year—always confirm the station your train leaves from. For schedules, check www.bahn.com or www.mavcsoport.hu.

To Destinations in Hungary: Eger (every 2 hours direct, 2 hours, more with transfer in Füzesabony, usually from Keleti/Eastern station), **Pécs** (every 2 hours direct, 3 hours; a few more connections possible with transfer at suburban Kelenföld station), **Sopron** (every 2 hours direct, 2.5 hours, more with transfer at Kelenföld), **Visegrád** (trains arrive at Nagymaros-Visegrád station, across the river—take shuttle boat to Visegrád; 1-2/hour, 45 minutes, from Nyugati/Western station), **Esztergom** (hourly, 1 hour, usually from Nyugati/Western station; but Esztergom's train station is far from the basilica, making the bus—described later—a better option), **Kecskemét** (hourly, 1.5 hours), **Szeged** (hourly, 2.5 hours). Note that Nagymaros (the station for Visegrád) and Esztergom are on opposite sides of the river—and on different train lines. To reach **Szentendre** and **Gödöllő,** take the suburban HÉV line (see "By HÉV," later).

To International Destinations: Bratislava (*Pozsony* in Hungarian, every 2 hours direct, 2.5 hours; more with changes), **Vienna** (*Bécs* in Hungarian, every 2 hours direct on express Railjet, 2.5 hours; more with changes), **Prague** (5/day direct, 6.5 hours;

plus 1 night train/day, 9.5 hours), **Kraków** (1/day, 9 hours, change in Bohumin, longer connections with more changes; 1 direct night train/day, 11 hours), **Zagreb** (2/day direct, 5.5 hours), **Ljubljana** (1/day direct, 8.5 hours; additional options with changes, 9 hours; plus 1 direct night train/day, 10 hours), **Cluj-Napoca** (hub for Transylvania in Romania, 2/day direct, 7.5 hours), **Munich** (every 2 hours direct on express RailJet, 7 hours; 1 direct night train/day, 9.5 hours). Or, for many of these destinations, consider taking a long-distance bus (described later).

By HÉV: Budapest has its own suburban rail network, called HÉV. For tourists, this is mostly useful for reaching **Szentendre** (from M2: Batthyány tér) and **Gödöllő** (from M2: Örs vezér tere). For more on the HÉV system, see page 31.

By Bus

Buses can be relatively inexpensive, but are typically slower and less convenient than trains. You can search bus schedules at the (Hungarian-only) website www.menetrendek.hu. Budapest lacks a single, consolidated bus station; instead, buses fan out from several points around town, each one next to—and named for—a Metró stop. (While these aren't all "bus stations" in the strict sense, they are handy transit hubs.) A few are particularly useful for tourists:

From the **Újpest-Városkapu** bus station (on the M3/blue line), buses depart about hourly to trace the Danube Bend around to **Szentendre** (30 minutes), **Visegrád** (75 minutes), and **Esztergom** (2 hours).

The **Stadionok** bus station (on the M2/red line) serves **Eger** (2/hour, about 2 hours), **Hollókő** (1-2/day, 2 hours), and **Lázár Lovaspark** (sporadic departures, ride about 50 minutes to Domonyvölgy stop).

The **Árpád híd** bus station (on the M3/blue line) has buses taking the faster overland route to **Esztergom** (1-2/hour, 1.5 hours).

The **Népliget** bus station (on the M3/blue line) is mostly used by international buses (including to **Bratislava:** 2/day, 3 hours), as well as buses to **Pécs** (about every 2 hours direct, 4 hours). Trains are faster to these destinations.

Long-Distance Buses: For international journeys, consider FlixBus, which offers affordable, frequent express connections from Budapest to **Bratislava** (2.5 hours), **Vienna** (3 hours), **Kraków** (7 hours), **Prague** (7 hours; this same bus sometimes continues to **Dresden** and **Berlin**), **Zagreb** (4.5 hours), **Ljubljana** (6.5 hours), **Cluj-Napoca** (hub for Transylvania in Romania, 8 hours), and more (www.flixbus.com).

By Plane

BUDAPEST LISZT FERENC AIRPORT

Budapest's airport is 10 miles southeast of the center (code: BUD, tel. 1/296-7000, www.bud.hu). Many Hungarians still call the airport by its former name, "Ferihegy." The airport's lone passenger terminal is called "Terminal 2" ("Terminal 1" closed years ago). The terminal has two adjacent parts, which you can walk between in just a few minutes: the smaller Terminal 2A is for flights from EU/Schengen countries (no passport control required), while Terminal 2B is for flights from other countries. Both sections have ATMs and TI desks (open daily 8:00-23:00 in 2A, and daily 10:00-22:00 in 2B). Car rental desks are in the arrivals area for 2B.

Getting Between the Airport and Downtown Budapest: Public bus #100E is the most cost-effective option, conveniently connecting the airport to downtown before making just three stops near key Metró stations: Astoria, Kálvin tér, and Deák tér. You can buy the 900-Ft ticket at the machine before you board, or—with exact change only—from the driver (2/hour, 40-60 minutes depending on traffic).

The fastest door-to-door option is to take a **taxi.** Főtaxi has a monopoly at the taxi stand out front; figure about 7,500 Ft to downtown, depending on traffic.

The **airport shuttle** minibus is a decent value for solo travelers, but two people will pay just a few dollars more to share a taxi (4,900 Ft/1 person, 6,000 Ft/2 people; minibus ride to any hotel in the city center takes about 30-60 minutes depending on hotel location, plus waiting time; tel. 1/550-0000, www.minibud.hu; if arranging a minibus transfer *to* the airport, call at least 24 hours in advance). Because they prefer to take several people at once, you may have to wait awhile at the airport for a quorum to show up.

By Car

Avoid driving in Budapest if you can—roads are narrow, and fellow drivers, bikes, and pedestrians make the roads feel like an obstacle course. Especially during rush hour (7:00-9:00 and 16:00-18:00), congestion is maddening, and since there's no complete expressway bypass, much of the traffic going through the city has to go *through* the city. Don't drive down roads marked with a red circle, or in lanes marked for buses; these can be monitored by automatic traffic cameras, and you could be mailed a ticket.

There are three concentric ring roads, all of them slow: the Small Boulevard (Kiskörút), Great Boulevard (Nagykörút), and outermost Hungária körút, from which highways and expressways spin off to other destinations. Farther out, the M-0 expressway

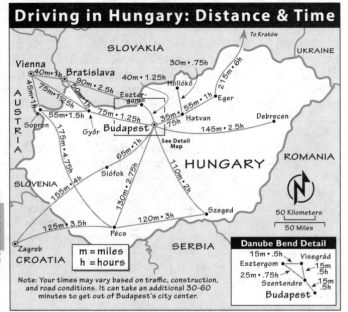

Driving in Hungary: Distance & Time

makes a not-quite-complete circle around the city center, helping to divert some traffic.

Parking: While in Budapest, unless you're heading to an out-of-town sight (such as Memento Park), park the car at or near your hotel and take public transportation. Public street parking costs 175-525 Ft per hour (pay in advance at machine and put ticket on dashboard). Within the Great Boulevard, it's generally free to park from 20:00 until 8:00 the next morning (farther out, it's free after 18:00). But in some heavily touristed areas, you may have to pay around the clock. Always check signs carefully, and confirm with a local (such as your hotelier) that you've parked appropriately. Also, be sure to park within the lines—otherwise, your car is likely to get "booted" (I've seen more than one confused tourist puzzling over the giant red brace on his wheel). A guarded parking lot is safer, but more expensive (figure 3,000-4,000 Ft/day, ask your hotel or look for the blue *P*s on maps). As rental-car theft can be a problem, ask at your hotel for advice.

ROUTE TIPS FOR DRIVERS
To Eger and Other Points East: Head out of the city center on Andrássy út, circling behind Heroes' Square to access Kós Károly sétány through the middle of City Park. You'll pass Széchenyi Baths on the left, then (exiting the park) go over the Hungária körút ring road, before getting on M-3. This expressway zips you

conveniently to Eger (exit #114 for Füzesabony; go north on road 33, then follow road 3, then road 25 into Eger). Between Budapest and Eger, M-3 also passes Gödöllő (with its Royal Palace; also exit here for the Lázár Lovaspark horse show) and Hatvan (where you can exit for Hollókő).

To Bratislava, Vienna, and Other Points West: From central Pest, head over the Danube on the white, modern Elisabeth Bridge (Erzsébet híd). Once in Buda, the road becomes Hegyalja út; simply follow *Bécs-Wien* signs to get on M-1.

To the Danube Bend: For tips on driving around the Danube Bend (Szentendre, Visegrád, and Esztergom), see page 322.

CONNECTIONS

BEYOND
BUDAPEST

DAY TRIPS FROM BUDAPEST

*Gödöllő Palace • Lázár Lovaspark
• Hollókő • Szentendre • Visegrád
• Esztergom • More Hungarian
Destinations*

The most rewarding destinations outside Budapest are Eger, Pécs, Sopron, and Bratislava (Slovakia). But each of those (covered in their own chapters) is more than two hours away; for a shorter visit, the region immediately surrounding Budapest offers some enticing options for a break from the big city.

I've arranged these in geographical clusters, east and west of the capital. To the east, just outside Budapest, Gödöllő Palace is the best spot in Hungary to commune with its past Habsburg monarchs, the larger-than-life Franz Josef and Sisi. Nearby, Lázár Lovaspark is the handiest opportunity to take in a traditional Hungarian cowboy show. The tiny village of Hollókő, tucked in the hills northeast of Budapest, combines a living community with an open-air folk museum.

North of Budapest, three river towns along the Danube Bend offer an easy escape: the charming village of Szentendre is an art colony with a colorful history to match; the castles of Visegrád boast a sweeping history and equally grand views over the Bend; and Esztergom is home to Hungary's top church.

At the end of this chapter, I've briefly outlined two areas that—while a bit too far for a day trip—are worth knowing about for those who want to extend their Hungarian explorations: the Great Hungarian Plain (including the city of Szeged) and Lake Balaton.

PLANNING YOUR TIME

Of this chapter's main attractions, Gödöllő Palace and Szentendre are the easiest to reach from Budapest (each one is a quick ride away on the suburban train, or HÉV). These sights can be done in just a few hours each. Lázár Lovaspark is an easy taxi ride from Gödöllő. The other sights (Hollókő, Visegrád, and Esztergom) are

Day Trips from Budapest

SLO-VAKIA

HUNGARY

To Bratislava

See The Danube Bend Map

Nagymaros-Visegrád Station

Rétság

To Hollókő · Salgótarján

Pásztó

21

Štúrovo · 11 · Esztergom

Visegrád

Vác

Zagyvaszántó

·Dorog

To Vienna

Pilisszent-kereszt

Szentendre

River

E-77

Hatvan

LÁZÁR LOVASPARK ■ · M-3 · To Eger

·Bag

Pomáz

10

To Győr, Sopron & Vienna

M-1

ÓBUDA

AQUARÉNA

Gödöllő

3

Rail

HÉV

BUDA PEST

MEMENTO PARK

Ferihegy

M-0

N

To Lake Balaton & Zagreb

M-7

Danube

To Pécs / M-6

M-5

4

To Szeged & Belgrade

10 Kilometers

10 Miles

DAY TRIPS

farther afield and less rewarding; do these only if you have a special interest, or if you have a car and they're on the way to your next stop.

For efficient sightseeing, cluster your visits to these sights strategically. If you have a car, some combination of Gödöllő Palace, Lázár Lovaspark, and Hollókő can be done in a day (round-trip from Budapest, or en route between Budapest and Eger; for details, see page 282). The Danube Bend sights (Szentendre, Visegrád, and Esztergom) also go well together if you have a car, and line up conveniently between Budapest and Bratislava or Vienna.

East of Budapest

These three attractions—Gödöllő Palace, Lázár Lovaspark horse show, and the folk village of Hollókő—line up east of Budapest. Each one is a detour from the M-3 expressway that heads northeast; consider stopping at one or more of these on your way to Eger, or seeing two or three as a side trip from Budapest. Gödöllő Palace is also easy to reach by train from Budapest.

Budapest Day Trips at a Glance

If you only have a day or two to venture outside of Budapest, this overview might help you decide where to go. I've listed these sights roughly in order of worthiness.

▲▲▲**Eger** This appealing midsized town, packed with gorgeous Baroque architecture, has one of Hungary's most historic castles, some quirky museums, excellent local wines, and relaxing thermal baths (including two in the nearby countryside). Eger is the best look at workaday Hungary outside Budapest. Allow a full day or overnight. See the Eger chapter.

▲▲**Pécs** A medium-sized city in southern Hungary, Pécs features a rich history (typified by the unique mosque-turned-church on its main square), surprisingly top-notch museums, and beautiful buildings slathered with colorful local Zsolnay tiles. Allow a full day or overnight. See the Pécs chapter.

▲▲**Bratislava, Slovakia** The Slovak capital—conveniently situated between Budapest and Vienna—is worth a look for its increasingly rejuvenated Old Town and taste of Slovak culture. Allow a half-day to a full day (most convenient on the way to Vienna). See the Bratislava chapter.

▲▲**Gödöllő Palace** This summer palace of the Habsburg monarchs is the best place in Hungary to get to know the "royal and imperial" couple, Franz Josef and Sisi (open daily). It's easy to see in a half-day from Budapest (or, by car, combine with Lázár Lovaspark or Hollókő for a full day). See page 290.

▲▲**Esztergom Basilica** Hungary's biggest and most important church, packed with history, looms above the Danube (open daily). Allow a full day combined with other Danube Bend sights (Szentendre and possibly Visegrád). See page 318.

▲**Szentendre** This colorful, Balkan-feeling artist colony is the easiest (and most touristy) small town to visit from Budapest. Allow a half-day from Budapest, or combine with a full-day trip around the Danube Bend. See page 308.

▲**Lázár Lovaspark** This entertaining demonstration of traditional Hungarian equestrian arts includes some thrilling horseback tricks, and a chance to meet local livestock (shows generally daily in summer, but confirm times before making the trip). Allow about two hours for the complete visit, ideally combined with nearby Gödöllő Palace. See page 297.

▲**Sopron** A small-town alternative that's also between Budapest and Vienna, Sopron has a charmingly well-preserved Old Town peppered with dusty museums and historic buildings. Allow a

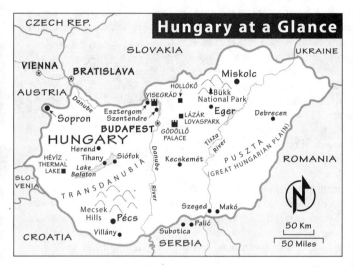

half-day to a full day (most convenient on the way to Vienna). See the Sopron chapter.

▲**Hollókő** This intriguing village-meets-open-air folk museum hides in the middle of nowhere an hour and a half northeast of Budapest. Visit only if you have a car and are interested in the culture and architecture of the Hungarian countryside. Allow a full day (by car, it can be combined with Gödöllő Palace and/ or Lázár Lovaspark for a full-day side trip, or visited en route between Budapest and Eger). Best on summer weekends, it's sleepy Mondays and off-season. See page 300.

Visegrád The least engaging of the Danube Bend sights, Visegrád offers a small riverside palace museum and a hilltop castle with fine views over the Bend. Visit only if it's on the way during your Danube Bend day. See page 315.

Great Hungarian Plain Hungary's "Big Sky Country" boasts cowboy shows, the bustling cultural capital of Szeged, colorful Kecskemet, the wild Organic architecture of Makó, and an easy side trip to Subotica, Serbia. This area is worth considering if you have ample time (or a special interest) and want to see more of Hungary. See page 323.

Lake Balaton The freshwater "Hungarian Riviera" has lots of beach resorts, the historic hill-capping town of Tihany, the unique thermal lake of Hévíz, and the Herend porcelain factory. Consider stopping off here on your way between Budapest and regions to the southwest. See page 327.

Gödöllő Palace

Holding court in an unassuming town on the outskirts of Budapest, Gödöllő Royal Palace (Gödöllői Királyi Kastély; pronounced roughly "GER-der-ler") is Hun-

gary's largest Baroque palace and most interesting royal interior to tour. The pink-and-white, U-shaped complex is haunted by Habsburg ghosts: Once the residence of Habsburg Emperor Franz Josef and his wife, Empress Elisabeth—better known as Sisi—Gödöllő has recently been restored to its *"K und K"* (royal and imperial) splendor. Compared to other Habsburg properties, Gödöllő is compact, well-presented, and pleasantly uncrowded. If you want a Habsburg fix and aren't going to Vienna—or if you're a Habsburg completist—Gödöllő is worth ▲▲, and well worth a half-day visit from Budapest.

GETTING THERE

Gödöllő Palace is an easy side trip from Budapest, by HÉV suburban train or by car. By **public transit,** take the M2/red Metró line to the end of the line at Örs vezér tere, then go under the street to the HÉV suburban train (H8/pink line) and hop a train marked for Gödöllő (2/hour). Once in Gödöllő, get off at the Szabadság tér station (about an hour total from central Budapest). The palace is across the street, kitty-corner from the station. **Drivers** will find the palace 17 miles east of Budapest, just off the M-3 expressway (well-signed, on the way to Eger and other points east). You'll find pay-and-display parking directly in front of the palace.

PLANNING YOUR TIME

By public transportation, figure an hour each way from central Budapest, plus another hour or so to tour the palace. You'll need additional time to visit the other sights at the palace (such as the Baroque theater or WWII-era bunker).

ORIENTATION TO GÖDÖLLŐ PALACE

Cost and Hours: 2,600 Ft for permanent exhibit (main palace apartments); Mon-Thu 9:00-17:00, Fri-Sun 10:00-18:00, last entry one hour before closing; Nov-March open only by guided tour at :30 past each hour Mon-Fri 10:30-14:30 (palace closes at 16:00), Sat-Sun 10:00-17:00. For the cost and hours of the other palace attractions, see later.

Information: Tel. 28/410-124, www.kiralyikastely.hu.

Audioguide: You can rent an 800-Ft audioguide for the permanent exhibit, but this chapter's self-guided tour covers the basics, and enough English descriptions are posted throughout to bring meaning to each of the rooms and exhibits.

Services: The palace houses a café that Sisi would appreciate. There's also baggage storage (no bags are allowed within the tourable parts of the palace).

Starring: That quintessential royal and imperial couple, Franz Josef and Sisi.

BACKGROUND

The palace was built in the 1740s by Count Antal Grassalkovich, a Hungarian aristocrat who was loyal to Habsburg Empress Maria Theresa (at a time when most Hungarians were chafing under Habsburg rule). When the Compromise of 1867 made Habsburg rulers Franz Josef and Sisi "king and queen of Hungary" (see sidebar), the couple needed a summer home where they could relax in their Hungarian realm—and Gödöllő Palace was it. Sisi adored Hungary (in many ways preferring it to Vienna) and spent much of her time here; Franz Josef especially enjoyed hunting in the surrounding woods. The family spent many Christmases at Gödöllő. More than 900 servants worked hard to make this a pleasant second home for just one family.

After the fall of the monarchy, Gödöllő Palace became a residence of Admiral Miklós Horthy, who led Hungary between the World Wars. The palace fell into disrepair during the communist period (when the Soviets gutted it of period furniture and used it as military barracks, then as a nursing home). But it was recently rehabilitated to Habsburg specifications and opened to the public. Two wings of the palace are still in ruins, and renovations are ongoing.

❷ SELF-GUIDED TOUR

The most interesting part of the palace is its permanent exhibit, which fills several wings: the Grassalkovich wing, Franz Josef wing, Sisi wing, and Gisella wing, which you'll visit in that order. Pleasant gardens stretch behind the palace. Various other parts of the palace—such as a Baroque theater, the stables, and Admiral Horthy's bunker—are also tourable, but not really geared toward English speakers. See the details for these after the self-guided tour.

• *After buying your ticket, head upstairs and go left, following the marked tourist route. To help you find your way, the numbers noted below correspond to the audioguide numbers you'll see posted in each room.*

DAY TRIPS

Franz Josef (1830-1916) and Sisi (1837-1898): Emperor and Empress of Austria, King and Queen of Hungary

In a unique power-sharing compromise, the emperor and empress of the Austrian realm were only the "king" and "queen" of Hungary. (This was known as *"K und K"* in German, for *König und Kaiser,* king and emperor...same guy.) From the beginning of this "K+K" arrangement in 1867, the "royal and imperial" couple was Franz Josef and Sisi.

Franz Josef I—who ruled for 68 years (1848-1916)—was the embodiment of the Habsburg Empire as it finished its six-century-long ride. Born in 1830, Franz Josef had a stern upbringing that instilled in him a powerful sense of duty and—like so many men of power—a love of all things military.

His uncle, Ferdinand I, suffered from profound epilepsy, which prevented him from effectively ruling. As the revolutions of 1848 (including Hungary's) were rattling royal families throughout Europe, the Habsburgs forced Ferdinand to abdicate, and put 18-year-old Franz Josef on the throne. Ironically, as one of his first acts as emperor, Franz Josef—whose wife would later become closely identified with Hungarian independence—marched into Budapest to put down the 1848 Revolution. He spent the beginning of his long reign understandably paranoid, as social discontent continued to simmer.

Franz Josef was very conservative. But worse, he wrongly believed that he was a talented military tactician, and led Austria into catastrophic battles. Wearing his uniform to the end, he couldn't see what a dinosaur his monarchy was becoming, and never thought it strange that the majority of his subjects didn't even speak German. Like Queen Victoria, his contemporary, Franz Josef was the embodiment of his empire—old-fashioned but sacrosanct. His passion for low-grade paperwork earned him the nickname "Joe Bureaucrat." Mired in these petty details, he missed the big picture. In 1914, he helped start a Great War that ultimately ended the age of the divine monarchs.

Franz Josef and Grassalkovich Wings

You'll begin in the **small dining room** (#4)—where the table is set with exquisite Herend porcelain made specifically for this palace—then see the **butler's pantry** (#5), displaying more porcelain. The actual kitchens were in another building, across the park, because Sisi didn't care for the smell of cooking food.

Head down the long hallway, bypassing the small side-rooms

Empress **Elisabeth**—Franz Josef's mysterious, narcissistic wife—has been compared to Princess Diana because of her beauty, bittersweet life, and tragic death.

Sisi, as she's lovingly called, was mostly silent. Her main goals in life seem to have been preserving her reputation as a precious empress, maintaining her Barbie-doll figure, and tending to her

fairy-tale, ankle-length hair. In the 1860s, she was considered one of the most beautiful women in the world. But, age took its toll. After turning 30, she allowed no more portraits to be painted of her and was generally seen in public with a fan covering her face (and bad teeth).

Sisi was adored by Franz Josef, whom she respected. Although Franz Josef was supposed to marry her sister Helene (in an arranged marriage), he fell in love with Sisi instead. It was one of the Habsburgs' few marriages for love. Still,

Sisi never felt fully accepted by her mother-in-law...which made the Hungarians—who also felt misunderstood and not taken seriously by the Habsburgs—appreciate her even more.

Sisi's personal mission and political cause was promoting Hungary's bid for autonomy within the empire. While she was married to Emperor Franz Josef, she spent seven years in Budapest and at Gödöllő, enjoying horseback riding, the local cuisine...and the company of the dashing Count Gyula Andrássy. (For more on the count, see page 134.) Hungarians, who call Sisi their "guardian angel," partly credit her for the Compromise of 1867, which elevated their status within the Habsburg Empire.

Sisi's personal tragedy was the death of her son Rudolf, the crown prince, in an apparent suicide. Disliking Vienna and the confines of the court, Sisi traveled more and more frequently. As years passed, the restless Sisi and her hardworking husband became estranged. In 1898, while visiting Geneva, Switzerland, she was murdered by an Italian anarchist.

A final note: While for simplicity in this book I've referred to these figures as history knows them—"Emperor Franz Josef" and "Empress Sisi"—Hungarians might bristle at these imperial titles. After all, they (and *only* they) called the couple "King Franz Josef" and "Queen Sisi."

DAY TRIPS

for now. At the end of the hall, do a quick clockwise loop through the adjoining **Grassalkovich wing,** named for the aristocratic family that built the original palace. (When this family died out in 1841, the palace went to the Habsburgs.) If this obscure blue blood doesn't thrill you, take the opportunity to simply appreciate the opulent apartments. From Room #7 (displaying a countess' robin's-egg-blue gown), you'll hook to the right, through a small armory collection, to reach the oratory (#10/#11), which peeks down into the chapel. This room allowed the royal couple to attend Mass without mingling with the rabble. Notice the chapel's perfect Baroque symmetry: two matching pulpits, two matching chandeliers, and so on. Continue your loop, watching on the right for the hidden indoor toilet, and then—built into the door frame—the secret entrance to passages where servants scurried around inside the walls like mice, serving their masters unseen and unheard. (Notice that the stoves have no doors—they were fed from behind, inside the walls.)

Circling the rest of the way around to the blue gown, turn left, then head back down the long hallway. Turn left near the end of the hall into the **Franz Josef wing,** starting in the Adjunct General's Quarters (#15). In the next room—the **coronation chamber** (#16)—we finally catch up with the Habsburgs. Look for the giant painting of Franz Josef being crowned king of Hungary at Matthias Church, on top of Buda's Castle Hill, in 1867. (On the right side, hat in hand, is Count Andrássy. He gestures with the air of a circus ringmaster—which makes sense, as he was a kind of MC of both this coronation and the Hungarian government in general. Andrássy is the namesake of Pest's main drag...and was the reputed lover of Franz Josef's wife, Sisi.) Across the room is a painting of another Franz Josef coronation, this time at today's March 15 Square in Pest. Back then, Buda and Pest were separate cities—so two coronations were required.

In the **study of Franz Josef** (#17), on the right wall, we see a portrait of the emperor, with his trademark bushy 'stache and 'burns. The painting of the small boy (to the left) depicts Franz Josef's great-great-nephew Otto von Habsburg, the Man Who Would Be Emperor, if the empire still existed. Otto (1912-2011) was an early proponent of the creation of the European Union. (The EU's vision for a benevolent, multiethnic state bears striking

similarities to the Habsburg Empire of Franz Josef's time.) Otto celebrated his 90th birthday (in 2002) here at Gödöllő Palace. The bust depicts Otto's father—Austrian Emperor Charles I, a.k.a. Hungarian King Károly IV. He was the last Habsburg emperor, ruling from the death of Franz Josef in 1916 to the end of World War I (and the end of that great dynasty) in 1918. Sisi looks on from across the room.

The **reception room of Franz Josef** (#18) displays a map of the Habsburg Empire at its peak, flanked by etchings featuring 12 of the many different nationalities it ruled. The big painting on the right wall shows the Hungarian Millennium celebrations of 1896 at the Royal Palace at Buda Castle. Also in this room, near the smoking area, notice the very colorful reconstructed stove.

The lavishly chandeliered **grand ballroom** (#19) still hosts concerts. Above the main door, notice the screened-in loft where musicians could play—heard, but not seen. This placement freed up floor space for dancing in this smaller-than-average ballroom.
• *At the far end of the grand ballroom, you enter the...*

Sisi Wing

This wing—where the red color scheme gives way to violet—is dedicated to the enigmatic figure that most people call "Empress Elisabeth," but whom Hungarians call "our Queen Elisabeth." Sisi adored her Hungarian subjects, and the feeling was mutual. At certain times in her life, Sisi spent more time here at Gödöllő Palace than in Vienna. While the Sisi fixation is hardly unusual at Habsburg sights, notice that the exhibits here are particularly doting...and always drive home Sisi's Hungarian affinities.

In the **reception room** (#20), along with the first of many Sisi portraits, you'll see the portrait of Count Gyula Andrássy. Sisi's enthusiasm for all things Hungarian reportedly extended to this dashing aristocrat, who enjoyed riding horses with Sisi...and allegedly sired her third daughter, Marie Valerie—nicknamed the "Little Hungarian Princess."

In Sisi's **study** (#21), see the engagement portraits of the fresh-faced Franz Josef (age 23) and Sisi (age 16). Although they supposedly married for love, Sisi is said to have later regretted joining the imperial family. The book by beloved Hungarian poet Sándor Petőfi, from Sisi's bedside, is a reminder that Sisi could read and enjoy the difficult Magyar tongue. (It's also a reminder of Sisi's courageous empathy for the Hungarian cause, as Petőfi was killed—effectively by Sisi's husband—in the Revolution of 1848.)

You'll then pass through Sisi's **dressing room** (#23, with small family portraits) and **bedroom** (#24, with faux marble decor). Habsburg Empress Maria Theresa spent two nights here in 1751, a century before it became Sisi's bedroom. Next up are three more rooms with exhibits on Sisi. In the second room, look for the letter in Hungarian, written in Sisi's own hand (marked as item #17 in the display case) and an invitation to her wedding (set with the fancy lace collar). The third room, with a bust of Sisi, is filled with images of edifices throughout Hungary that are dedicated to this beloved Hungarian queen (such as Budapest's Elisabeth Bridge).
• *Now proceed into the...*

Gisella Wing

Explore these six rooms, which are filled with an exhibit that brings the palace's history up to the 21st century. In the first room, you'll see a huge painting of Sisi mourning Ferenc Deák, the statesman who made great diplomatic strides advocating for Hungarian interests within the Habsburg realm. There's also a more-intimate-than-usual portrait of Franz Josef, with the faint echoes of a real personality.

Also in this wing are interactive children's exhibits. The blue room introduces you to Sisi's children, including Gisella (the wing's namesake), Rudolf (whose suicide caused his cousin Franz Ferdinand to become the Habsburg heir apparent), and Marie Valerie (the so-called "Little Hungarian Princess").

Finishing your tour, you'll learn how, in the post-Habsburg era, this building became a summer home for Admiral Miklós Horthy, and later a military base and nursing home, with photographs showing the buildings during each of those periods. The final room displays impressive before-and-after photos illustrating how this derelict complex was only recently restored to its past (and current) glory. You'll exit into a gallery with (surprise, surprise) even more Habsburg portraits.

• *The permanent collection is enough for most visitors. But there are also several intriguing...*

OTHER SIGHTS AT GÖDÖLLŐ PALACE

These extra activities add different dimensions to your experience here. Unfortunately, they're primarily geared toward Hungarian visitors—most require joining a guided tour, which rarely run in English. You can call to ask if an English tour is scheduled; also, some palace guides speak English, and may be willing to tell you a few details after their Hungarian spiel.

Baroque Theater

This reconstructed, fully functional, 120-seat theater can be visited only with a 30-minute guided tour. You'll go backstage to get a good look at the hand-painted scenery, and below the stage to see the pulleys that move that scenery on and offstage. While it's fascinating to theater buffs, the facility feels new rather than old (it's computer-operated), diminishing the "Baroque" historical charm.

Cost and Hours: 1,600 Ft, or 1,200 Ft with palace ticket, English tour may be possible 1-2/day on weekends but unlikely on weekdays, otherwise join Hungarian tour and use English handout.

DAY TRIPS

Stables, Riding Hall, and 3-D Movie

One ticket covers a 40-minute tour of these three sights. The equestrian sights may interest horse lovers, and the movie is interesting to anyone.

The beautifully restored **stables** lead to the high-ceilinged, chandeliered **riding hall** that can still seat 400 people for special events. Upstairs is a small, good **museum** (in English) on Hungary's proud equestrian tradition, with high-tech displays and lots of old uniforms, saddles, and other equipment.

The 10-minute **3-D movie** does a good job of illustrating the history of the royal palace, including virtual re-creations of past versions of the building and its gardens, and dramatic re-enactments of Franz Josef and Sisi's favorite pastimes here. While normally shown in Hungarian, you can try requesting a showing of the English version.

Cost and Hours: 1,400 Ft, or 1,000 Ft with palace ticket, tours at :30 past each hour Thu-Sun 10:30-16:30, no tours Mon-Wed, generally in Hungarian with English handout.

▲WWII-Era Bunker Tour

Gödöllő was a summer residence of Miklós Horthy, the sea admiral who ruled this landlocked country between the World Wars (during Hungary's "kingdom without a king" period). It was Horthy who chose to ally Hungary with Nazi Germany, and it was Horthy who frequently defied Hitler's will—knowing he was risking invasion. Near the end of his reign, Horthy had a stout bunker built underneath the palace. On the 30-minute required tour, you'll see the two oddly charming, wood-paneled rooms where Horthy and his family would have holed up. (The hominess was designed to make the space more tolerable for Horthy's deeply claustrophobic wife.) The bunker wasn't even finished until after the Nazis took over, and the communist government stored gasoline here for decades—you can still smell the fumes.

Cost and Hours: 900 Ft, or 750 Ft with palace ticket, tours daily year-round at 10:30 and 14:00, generally in Hungarian with an English handout.

DAY TRIPS

Lázár Lovaspark Horse Show

Hungary has a rich equestrian tradition dating back to the time when those first Magyars rode across the Asian steppes to Central Europe. And, like the American West, Hungary's rugged Great Plain was settled by brave cowboys (here called *csikós*). As in the US, a world of vivid folklore surrounds these rough-and-tumble cattle wranglers, who are romantically thought of as camping out under the stars and slow-simmering a rich paprika broth in a cop-

per kettle over an open fire (the origin of *gulyás leves*, "shepherd's soup"—a.k.a. goulash). Today, several places around Hungary offer the chance to see a working farm with Hungary's many unique livestock, and take in a thrilling presentation that telescopes a millennium of show-off equestrian talent into one big extravaganza. While authentic, these traditions are kept alive mostly for curious tourists—so Hungarian horse shows can feel a little hokey. But if you surrender yourself to the remarkable equestrian skill, and the connection riders have with their magnificent animals, it's a hoot.

Most horse shows are performed in places where real-life Hungarian cowboys roamed: on the Great Hungarian Plain (see "More Hungarian Destinations," later in this chapter). But a much closer alternative is the family-run Lázár Lovaspark, worth ▲. This working farm is picturesquely set at the base of gently rolling hills. The Lázár brothers have won 21 world championships in carriage riding, and *lovas* is a term meaning, roughly, "equestrian arts." Lázár Lovaspark is in the village of Domonyvölgy, in Budapest's northeastern suburbs—27 miles from the capital, and just 9 miles from Gödöllő, making it easy to combine with the royal palace or Hollókő folk village for a busy but fun day out.

GETTING THERE

It's workable by **public transportation,** but taxis are helpful to connect the dots. From the train station in Gödöllő (connected by frequent trains to downtown Budapest—see the "Getting There" section for Gödöllő, earlier in this chapter), you can take a taxi to Lázár Lovaspark (figure about 2,000 Ft one-way, 15 minutes). You can also reach Lázár Lovaspark directly by public bus from Budapest (runs sporadically Mon-Fri, fewer Sat-Sun): From the Stadionok bus station (on the M2/red Metró line), ride the bus about 50 minutes, get off at the Domonyvölgy stop (with a small wooden bus shelter), and walk about a half-mile to the park (from the bus stop, cross the street to the other bus stop, and walk down the road—Fenyő utca).

Drivers can exit the M-3 expressway east of Budapest for *Gödöllő*, then follow signs for *Domonyvölgy*. (It's at Fenyő utca 47 in Domonyvölgy.) Consider hiring a driver for a day trip to both Gödöllő and Lázár Lovaspark, or stop off on the drive from Budapest to Eger.

ORIENTATION TO LÁZÁR LOVASPARK

Cost: 5,000 Ft, includes welcome snack and schnapps, horse show, brief tour, and carriage ride—about 90 minutes in total.

Hours: Shows generally take place April-Oct daily at 12:00 and 15:00 (additional performances are possible). However, the schedule can vary, so it's essential to call ahead to confirm the time and to let them know you're coming. Off-season, shows are often held for private groups (others are welcome to join), but the schedule is less predictable—again, call ahead.

Information: Tel. 28/576-510, mobile +3630-871-3424, www. lazarteam.hu, lazarteam@lazarteam.hu.

Eating: A filling traditional Hungarian lunch is available at the park for 5,800 Ft extra per person, but you have to request it in advance.

VISITING LÁZÁR LOVASPARK

Your visit to the park has several parts.

Museum, Stables, and Barnyard Tour: A 20-minute tour takes you to a small "hall of champions" museum celebrating the Lázár clan's illustrious history, and the stables where the horses live (each stall marked with its occupant's prestigious bloodlines). Then you'll visit the barnyard, with the fascinating opportunity to meet several only-in-Hungary animals: the woolly pig, *mangalica;* the giant gray longhorn cattle, *szürkemarha;* and the corkscrew-antlered goat, *racka.* The farm even has a *puli* sheepdog, with its dreadlock-like coat.

Horse Show: The main event is a 40-minute presentation neatly designed to show off various aspects of Hungary's long equestrian tradition. While there may be commentary during the show, it might not be in English—here's what to watch for: First come the Magyar-style archers, who ride fast as they shoot arrows and throw spears with deadly accuracy at  a target (at first stationary, and then moving). Then Hungarian cowboys, clad in blue uniforms, crack their whips as they ride in. They'll show how the whips could be used to disarm an enemy, and to train horses not to be startled by gunshots. To demonstrate how well-trained the horses are, the cowboys get their horses to kneel, then lie down—all while the rider is still seated. (Nights spent out on the Great Hungarian Plain were far more comfortable when the cowboy could lie on top of his reclining horse.) Then the cowboys stage a competition to see who can spill the least amount of suds from a full mug of beer while galloping around the track. For comic relief, a rodeo-clown-type "shepherd boy" attempts to get his donkey to do some of the tricks he's seen the horses tackle. Then a carriage rumbles in, pulled by the gigantic gray longhorn cattle called *szürkemarha*—which, it's believed, accompanied those original Magyars on their initial trip here from Asia. A costumed "Sisi" rides out sidesaddle on a clever Lipizzaner stallion, who elegantly do-si-dos a brief routine. Then comes the stirring climax of the show: the famous "Puszta five," where a horseman stands with one foot on each of two horses, while leading three additional horses with reins—galloping at breakneck speed around the track as if waterskiing. Finally, the entire gang takes a victory lap.

Carriage Ride: After the show, you'll have the option to hop on an open carriage for a bumpy but fun 15-minute ride through the surrounding plain and forest.

Hollókő

Remote, minuscule Hollókő (HOH-loh-ker), nestled in the hills a 90-minute drive from Budapest, survives as a time capsule of Hungarian tradition. Proud Hollókő (worth ▲) is half living hamlet, half open-air folk museum—people actually reside in quite a few of the old buildings. To retain its "real village" status, Hollókő (pop. 300) has its own mayor, elementary school, general store, post office, and doctor (who visits twice a week). Your  visit focuses on the Old Village, with all the protected old houses, shops, and museums, and about 35 residents.

If you appreciate folk history or traditional handicrafts, or you're traveling with kids who would enjoy seeing a living artifact of the past, consider detouring to Hollókő for a few hours on your way between Budapest and Eger, or combine it with Gödöllő Palace and Lázár Lovaspark as a day trip from the capital. The village is particularly worthwhile on festival days (listed at www.holloko.hu) and busiest on summer weekends. It's least engaging on Mondays or off-season (Nov-Easter), when the village is quiet and many sights are closed or on a limited schedule.

GETTING THERE

Hollókő fills a little off-the-grid valley about 60 miles northeast of Budapest. By **car,** it's about a 90-minute drive: Take the M-3 expressway east, exit at Hatvan (exit 55), and follow road #21 north toward Salgótarján. Keep an eye out for the turnoff for Hollókő and Szécsény, then carefully track *Hollókő* signs. Once in town, follow *P* signs to the large pay parking lot just above the village (300 Ft/hour, 2-hour maximum payment covers you all day long).

It's possible (but more time-consuming) to reach Hollókő by public transit: A **bus** leaves from Budapest's Stadionok bus station daily year-round at 15:15; in summer (mid-June-Aug), and on weekends year-round, an additional bus departs at 8:30—allowing you to go and come back the same day. Buses return to Budapest on a similar schedule: A bus departs early each morning year-round (weekdays at 5:00 or on weekends at 7:30); then there's an afternoon bus on weekends year-round at 16:00, and on summer weekdays at 15:00—but there's no afternoon bus on off-season weekdays. The trip takes about two hours.

ORIENTATION TO HOLLÓKŐ

Cost and Hours: It's free to enter the Old Village itself, but each sight inside charges its own modest entry fee (most are 200-600 Ft). Most sights here are open Easter-Oct daily 10:00-17:00, though some of them are closed on Monday. There are also several shops (keeping similar hours) that are free to enter. Off-season, only a few main sights remain open—others are closed, but may open for good-weather weekends in the shoulder seasons (spring and fall).

It's possible to buy a combo-ticket (Falusétajegy) for 3,500 Ft that covers about half of the paid-admission sights. While this is convenient, it's more cost-effective to pick and choose only what you're interested in, and pay à la carte.

Information: There's no real TI, but there is a little info point (marked *Küszöb*, "Threshold") at the parking lot at the top of town, and there's a town website: www.holloko.hu.

Language Barrier: Assume that no English is spoken, but at most places, you can ask to borrow English translations. Or hire your own guide/translator (see below).

Local Guide: Because Hollókő is frequented mostly by Hungarian tourists, visitors may encounter a substantial language barrier. Fortunately, the village has an excellent local guide who's very affordable to hire and can explain and translate your choice of activities. This is virtually a must, to give your experience more meaning. **Ádám Kiss** is a city slicker who fell in love with Hollókő and moved here with his wife and kids to become part of the community. Ádám, who lived in Montana and speaks great English, brings enthusiasm and insight to your visit (around 10,000 Ft/2-hour tour, including entrance fees). Ádám also works as a driver/guide for nearby destinations, including Gödöllő Palace and Eger (see page 37 for contact info).

HOLLÓKŐ'S OLD VILLAGE WALK

Visitors enjoy strolling through the heart of Hollókő's Old Village. You'll begin at the start of town, near the bus stop and downhill from the parking lot. This area is marked by the Fehér Holló pub (drinks only) and the Hollóköves Infocafé (a reception desk for a network of rooms in the historic village). An ATM hides just uphill from here, near the grocery store.

Enter the **Old Village**—a perfectly preserved enclave of the folk architecture, dress, and traditions of the local Palóc culture. Because it's in a dead-end valley, Hollókő's folk traditions survived here well into the 20th century. (Only when villagers began commuting to other towns for work in the 1950s did they realize how "backward" they seemed to other Hungarians.)

Head down Hollókő's cobbled main drag, ogling the **traditional homes.** The exteriors cannot be changed without permission, but interiors are modern (with plumbing, electricity, Wi-Fi, and so on). They once had thatched roofs with no chimneys (to evade a chimney tax), but a devastating fire in 1909 compelled residents to replace the thatch with tiles and add little chimneys. The thick walls are made of a whitewashed, adobe-type mix of mud and dung (which keeps things cool in summer and warm in winter). Thick walls, small doors, small windows...small people back then. The big, overhanging roof (nicknamed the house's "skirt") prevents rain from damaging this fragile composition. Most of these homesteads began as one simple house along the road; as children grew and needed homes of their own, a family compound evolved around a central courtyard.

I'll narrate a little loop through town, pointing out each possible stop. These descriptions are designed to help you pick and choose. Also, as this is a living village rather than a true open-air museum, shops and exhibits tend to open and close all the time—so don't be surprised if some of these aren't there (or are in new locations).

On the right is the **Palóc Playhouse,** where you can play with traditional village toys (and kids can pay a small fee to play with the larger toys in the yard). Upstairs is a small Hollókő model made of Legos. Next, on the right, is a small shop selling **minerals,** followed by the main sit-down restaurant in the village, **Muskátli** (described later). Next up are several shops: **wood-carver** (Ajándékbolt Kézművesműhely), ceramics and pottery, and handwoven items **(Kosaras).**

On the left, **Kalácsos Pékség** is a charming bakery where

you can grab a snack—strudel *(rétes)* or *pogácsa,* little balls of fried dough.

Just before the village church, on the right, is the **Schoolmaster's House** (Oskolamester Háza), a schoolhouse displaying a traditional student desk, works from the wood-carver who lived next door, and touchscreens with fairy tales in English.

Pause at the fork in the road, in front of Hollókő's **church.** A traveling priest says Mass here twice weekly. This is a popular wedding spot for Budapest urbanites charmed by its simplicity.

Take the fork to the right (Petőfi út) and wander past a few more shops: the **grocery store** (Szatócsbolt), selling wine, candy, preserves, and gifty edibles, and the Pottery House (Fazekasház).

After the public WC is the **Dance House** (Tánchá, on the right). The owner here shows a film about traditional costumes and dances, and—if you like—can teach you some dance moves.

Next, the roads rejoin near the **People and Landscape Museum,** which displays photos of Hollókő in the olden days, with thatched roofs and dirt roads...but otherwise looking much the same as now. A couple of doors past that is a high-end pottery shop. Beyond this point is where most residents of the Old Village actually reside.

Now's the logical time to detour to the castle, about a 10-minute steep hike uphill (trailhead across the street from the People and Landscape Museum)—unless you want to save it for before or after your town visit; it's a slightly easier hike from the village parking lot.

Hollókő's **castle** *(vár),* built upon a foundation of natural rock, dates from the 13th century. By the 16th century, it was on the frontier between Habsburg-held Hungary and the Ottoman invaders (who eventually conquered the castle). After the Habsburgs had retaken Hungary, Emperor Leopold I destroyed the castle as a precaution (in 1711, just after the failed War of

Independence) to ensure that his Hungarian subjects wouldn't use it against him. It was restored beginning in the 1960s, and now holds humble exhibits and grand views. Work your way up through the castle's many levels, enjoying the various exhibits. You'll see mannequins in period dress, a model of the castle in the 13th century, a reconstructed kitchen and bedroom with replica furniture and a WC dangling out over the cliff, and a giant rainwater cistern.

From the top, you can see all the way to Slovakia (900 Ft, daily 10:00-17:30, shorter hours off-season).

Back in the main part of the village, turn back the way you came, but this time take the *other* road (Kossuth út). On the right is the **Doll Museum** (Palóc Babamúzeum), with some 200 dolls dressed in traditional costumes of the area. Each is labeled with the specific place of origin and a basic English description, allowing you to see the subtle changes from village to village.

Soon after, also on the right, is a **wine cellar** (Borkóstolás), where you can sample some locally produced wines; upstairs is a **textile museum** (Guzsalyas), with videos showing how they traditionally made linen, silk, and so on.

After that, on the left is a **leather workshop** (Bőrműves Műhely); on the right is a traditional, fully functional **printing press** (Kézműves Nyomdaműhely); and on the left is a **cheese shop** (Sajtbolt), selling cheeses made just across the courtyard—buy a sample.

Next up, on the right, is the town's most important sight, the **Village Museum**—worth ▲. You enter into the **kitchen,** where most of the family (including piles of kids) would sleep on the floor, near the warmth of the stove. The doors on the back wall (behind the stove) lead to a smoker. This very efficient design allowed them to heat the house, cook, bake, and smoke foods all at the same time.

Then head into the **main room** (to the left). Even today, many older Hungarians have a "show room" where they keep their most prized possessions and decora-

tions. They let visitors peek in to see their treasures...then make them sit in the kitchen to socialize. The pillows and linens— typically from the dowry of the lady of the house—were piled on the bed during the day, as most family members bunked on the floor. The matching furniture is delicately painted. The dresser is well-built and intricate, indicating that a carpenter was paid to make it (other furniture would have been more roughly built by the head of the household). The glass in the windows is not authentic; back then, they would have stretched pig bladders over the windows instead. The rafters are painted blue to ward off flies (the blue hue contains copper sulfate, a natural insecticide). People would hang their boots (their most expensive item of clothing) up high to prevent mice from ruining them.

Now cross back over to the **storage room,** housing tools and food. The matriarch of the house slept in here (on the uncomfortable-looking rope bed) and kept the key for this room, doling out the family's ration of food—so in many ways, Grandma was the head of the household. When Granny wasn't watching, and while the rest of the family slept elsewhere in the house, a young woman of courting age could come here to meet up with a suitor, who'd sneak in through the window. (The Hungarians even have a verb for these premarital interactions—roughly, "storaging.") Find the crude crib, used to bring a baby along with adults working the fields (it could be covered like a teepee to protect from the sun's rays). In other parts of Hungary, peasants were known to partially bury their babies in the ground to prevent them from moving around while they worked. (These days, we use mesmerizing YouTube videos—is that really so much more humane?) Look up to find the bread rack suspended from the ceiling—again, to rescue the bread from those troublesome mice.

Farther along, on the right, is the **Postal Museum** (Postamúzeum), an endearing old collection of dusty memorabilia.

From here, just continue up the main drag—you'll wind up where you started.

SLEEPING AND EATING IN HOLLÓKŐ

DAY TRIPS

This is a very sleepy place to spend the night, but those who really want to delve into village Hungary might enjoy it. **$$ Hollóköves Infocafé** rents out rooms in rustic buildings within the Old Village, from a central reception desk at the start of town (mobile +3620-626-2844, www.holloko.hu). **$$ Castellum Hotel Hollókő** is the only real hotel in town, and it's a doozy—a big, modern, four-star complex with a swimming pool perched at the very top of town, about a 5-minute downhill (or 10-minute uphill) hike from the Old Village. It's big and impersonal, with 69 rooms and a good restaurant (Sport út 14, tel. 21/300-0500, www.hotelholloko.hu).

Eating: The **$ bakery** and **$ cheese shop** mentioned earlier are good places to get a bite. If you want a full, sit-down meal, there's just one real restaurant in the Old Village: **$$ Muskátli Restaurant,** near the start of town on the right. Be warned that it closes early (by 17:00, just after the day-trippers go home), so don't wait too long for dinner. (A second restaurant in the village closed for renovation, but may reopen—keep an eye out). High above town, there's also a (pricey) restaurant at **$$$ Castellum Hotel Hollókő** (described above), which is open until 21:00. The pub at the start of the village sells only drinks, no food; just above that, you'll find a grocery store that keeps unpredictable hours (likely closed weekend afternoons).

The Danube Bend

The Danube, which begins as a trickle in Germany's Black Forest, becomes the Mississippi River of Eastern Europe—connecting 10 countries and four capitals (Vienna, Bratislava, Budapest, Belgrade) as it flows southeast through the Balkan Peninsula toward the Black Sea. Just south
of Bratislava, the river squeezes
between mountain ranges,
which force it to loop back on itself—creating the scenic "Danube Bend" (Dunakanyar). Here
Hungarians stroll and sunbathe
along the banks of the Danube,
or hike in the rugged hills that
rise up from the river. Hungar-

ian history hides around every turn of the Bend: For centuries, Hungarian kings ruled not from Buda or Pest, but from Visegrád and Esztergom. And during the Ottoman occupation of Hungary, this area was a buffer zone between Christian and Muslim Europe.

Today, three river towns north of Budapest on the Danube Bend offer a convenient day trip getaway. Closest to Budapest is Szentendre, whose colorful, storybook-cute Baroque center is packed with tourists. The ruins of a once-mighty castle high on a hill watch over the town of Visegrád. Esztergom, birthplace of Hungary's first Christian king, has the country's biggest and most important church. All of this is within a one-hour drive of the capital, and also reachable (up to a point) by public transportation.

PLANNING YOUR TIME

Remember, Szentendre is the easiest Danube Bend destination—just a quick suburban-train (HÉV) ride away, it can be done in a few hours. Visegrád and Esztergom are more difficult to reach by public transportation; either one can require a substantial walk or taxi ride from the train or bus stop to the town's major sight.

With a **car,** you can fit everything into one ambitious day: Leave Budapest by 9:00, wander lazy Szentendre in the morning and have an early lunch there, hike up to the Citadel in Visegrád, get to Esztergom Basilica by late afternoon, then head back to Budapest before dinner. The Danube Bend towns are also a fine way to break up the journey from Budapest to points west (Sopron, Bratislava, or Vienna), but seeing all three en route makes for a very long day—get an early start, or skip one.

By **public transportation,** don't try to see all three towns in one day; focus on one or two. (I'd skip Visegrád, whose castle is a

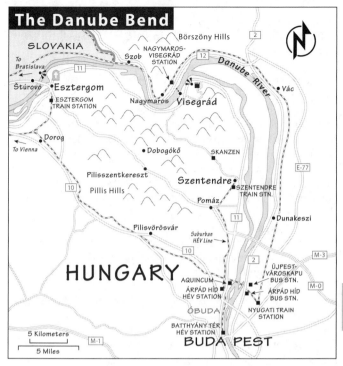

The Danube Bend

SLOVAKIA

To Bratislava

Štúrovo • Esztergom

ESZTERGOM TRAIN STATION

To Vienna

• Dorog

Szob

Nagymaros

NAGYMAROS-VISEGRÁD STATION

Börzsöny Hills

Danube River

• Vác

Visegrád

Pilisszentkereszt

Pillis Hills

• Dobogókő

SKANZEN

Szentendre •

SZENTENDRE TRAIN STN.

Pomáz

E-77

• Dunakeszi

• Pilisvörösvár

Suburban HÉV Line

HUNGARY

AQUINCUM

ÁRPÁD HÍD HÉV STATION

ÓBUDA

BATTHYÁNY TÉR HÉV STATION

ÚJPEST-VÁROSKAPU BUS STN.

ÁRPÁD HÍD BUS STN.

NYUGATI TRAIN STATION

BUDA PEST

5 Kilometers

5 Miles

M-1

M-3

M-0

DAY TRIPS

headache to reach without a car.) To do the whole shebang, take a tour, rent a car, or hire a driver (see page 27) or local guide (page 34).

GETTING AROUND THE DANUBE BEND

Going north from Budapest, the three towns line up along the same road on the west side of the Danube—Szentendre, Visegrád, Esztergom—each spaced about 15 miles apart.

By Car: Get on road #11 going north out of Buda, which will take you through each of the three towns—the road bends with the Danube. As you approach Szentendre, branch off to the right, toward the old center and the river promenade. To return from Esztergom to Budapest, see "Route Tips for Drivers" at the end of this chapter.

By Boat: In the summer, Mahart runs boats from Budapest up the Danube Bend, including slower riverboats (1.5 hours to Szentendre, 3 hours to Visegrád, and 5 hours to Esztergom) and much faster hydrofoils (none to Szentendre, 1 hour to Visegrád, 1.5 hours to Esztergom). While this sounds romantic, this is a slow way to go and the scenery isn't that spectacular. The boats typically run only in summer (daily except Mon), and stop running off-season. Check schedules and buy tickets at the Mahart office in Budapest (dock near Vigadó tér in Pest, tel. 1/484-4010, www. mahartpassnave.hu).

By Train: The three towns are on three separate train lines. Szentendre is easy by train, while Visegrád and Esztergom are less convenient.

Getting to **Szentendre** is a breeze on the HÉV, Budapest's suburban rail (catch train on H5/purple line at Batthyány tér in Buda's Víziváros neighborhood, 2-7/hour, 45 minutes each way, last train returns from Szentendre around 23:00).

The nearest train station to **Visegrád** is actually across the river in Nagymaros (this station is called "Nagymaros-Visegrád"; don't get off at the station called simply "Nagymaros"). From the station, you'll walk five minutes to the river and take a ferry across to Visegrád (hourly, usually in sync with the train). Trains run hourly between Nagymaros-Visegrád and Nyugati/Western Station in Budapest (trip takes about 45 minutes).

To **Esztergom,** trains run hourly from Budapest's Nyugati/ Western Station (1 hour), but the Esztergom train station is a 45-minute walk from the basilica—I'd take a bus or boat instead.

By Bus: Without a car, buses are the best way to hop between the three towns. They're as quick as the train if you're coming from Budapest, but can be standing room only. There are two main routes.

The **river route** runs hourly from Budapest's Újpest-Városkapu bus station (at the M3/blue line Metró station of the same name) and goes along the Danube through Szentendre (30 minutes) and Visegrád (75 minutes, makes several stops in this town—see "Orientation to Visegrád," later), then past Esztergom Basilica (2 hours, Iskola Utca stop) to the Esztergom bus station (more frequent during weekday rush hours). Note: On weekends in May-Sept, a few public buses go all the way up to Visegrád's Citadel; otherwise, you'll have to get off in town and take the "City Bus" shuttle up.

A different bus takes the **overland shortcut** (skipping Szentendre and Visegrád) to directly connect Budapest and Esztergom (1-2/hour, 75 minutes, departs from Budapest's Árpád híd station on the M3/blue Metró line). Buses make many stops en route, so you'll need to pay attention for your stop (ask driver or other passengers for help).

Szentendre

Worth ▲, Szentendre (SEHN-tehn-dreh, "St. Andrew" in English) rises gently from the Danube—a postcard-pretty village with a twisty Mediterranean street plan filled with Habsburg Baroque houses. This "Balkans in Miniature" village—settled by a diverse community of Serbs, Croats, and Greeks (see sidebar)—provides

a taste of Hungarian village life without having to stray far from Budapest...though it sometimes feels like too many other people have the same idea. Szentendre is where Budapesters bring their significant others for that special weekend lunch. The town has a long tradition as an artists' colony, and it still has more than its share of museums and galleries. Venture off the souvenir-choked, tourist-clogged main streets...and you'll soon have the quiet back lanes under colorful Baroque steeples all to yourself.

Orientation to Szentendre

Little Szentendre (pop. 23,000) is easy to navigate. It clusters along a mild incline rising from the Danube, culminating at the main square (Fő tér) at the foot of Church Hill (Templomdomb).

Tourist Information: The TI sits at the southern end of the old center, near the blocky modern tower of the Evangelical Church (daily 10:00-18:00, shorter hours off-season, Dumtsa Jenő utca 22, tel. 26/317-965, https://iranyszentendre.hu).

ARRIVAL IN SZENTENDRE

By Train or Bus: The combined **train/HÉV and bus station** is at the southern edge of town. It's a pleasant 10-minute walk into the town center: At the head of the train tracks, go through the pedestrian underpass, which funnels you onto Kossuth Lajos utca. Follow this through town and across a bridge, where you'll see the TI on your right. From here, the Old Town center and main square are straight ahead.

By Boat: Most boats arrive near Lázár Cár tér, just a short walk from the main square: Turn left along the embankment, then go up any of the little lanes on your right. All of these run up to the main drag, touristy Bogdányi út, which runs right into the square.

By Car: Approaching on road #11 from Budapest, turn right at the traffic light just after several signs directing you to hotels. Park anywhere along the embankment road (pay and display); from here, it's an easy uphill walk into town (see above).

A Taste of the Balkans: Szentendre's History

Szentendre feels more Balkan than Hungarian. That's because it was built as a melting pot of Serbs, Greeks, and Dalmatians.

The Habsburgs forced the Ottomans out of Hungary in the late 17th century, pushing them farther south in the Balkan Peninsula. Especially after the Ottomans' successful 1690 siege of Belgrade, a flood of 40,000 families—Serbs, Dalmatians (from today's Croatia), and Greeks—sought shelter up the Danube. Many settled here in Szentendre.

At first, these refugees built temporary houses and shops, following the narrow street plan of their homeland. They mainly settled in four neighborhoods representing regions of Serbia, plus Greeks and Dalmatians. Each neighborhood had its own church, plus the original, medieval Catholic church.

While they were waiting to return home, the Balkan refugees supported the Habsburgs (who were facing down the Hungarians in the War of Independence). This loyalty earned the favor of the emperor, who rewarded Szentendre with trade privileges.

By the time the Ottomans were forced out of the Balkans, the onetime refugees in Szentendre had decided to stay. They benefited from the increased trade flowing up the Danube (from lands recently liberated from the Ottomans) and replaced temporary buildings with permanent ones—mostly in the snazzy Baroque and Rococo styles popular in Habsburg lands. That's why many Szentendre churches are Baroque Catholic on the outside with strikingly Orthodox interiors.

Fortunes began to change in the 1770s, when the reformist Emperor Josef II revoked Szentendre's special rights. Commerce shifted to Buda and Pest. And then, a phylloxera pest infestation in the 1880s devastated the town's vineyards.

By the late 19th century, Szentendre was a partial ghost town. Artists began to discover the village, and were inspired by its colorful cultural pastiche, atmospheric stair-step lanes, low rents, and closeness to nature—all within close proximity to the bustling metropolis of Budapest. A "Szentendre School" of artists emerged, putting the town on the map of art history. Today Szentendre has six museums dedicated to local artists (the best showcases Margit Kovács), with many more starving art students who toil away, hoping to fill their own gallery someday. Szentendre is also a bedroom community for wealthy Budapesters—near the big city, but in a tranquil and beautiful setting.

Sights in Szentendre

Sightseeing in Szentendre is low-impact. While there are ample museums and churches to visit, I've highlighted the most worth-while. It's perhaps most satisfying simply to stroll and people-watch through town and along the elevated Danube riverbank.

▲Main Square (Fő Tér)

Szentendre's top sight is the town itself. Start at the main square (Fő tér). Take a close look at the **cross,** erected in 1763 to give thanks for surviving the plague. Notice the Cyrillic lettering at the monument's base. This is a reminder that in many ways, Szentendre is more of a Serbian town than a Hungarian one (see sidebar).

Face the cross from the downhill side and get oriented: Behind the cross, the square narrows as it curls around Church Hill, with

its hilltop Catholic church; just behind that is the Orthodox Ca-thedral. On the left, attached to the Korona restaurant, is the fun Micro Art Museum. The street to the left (Dumtsa Jenő utca) leads to the Marzipan Museum, TI, and train station. To the right, the church fronting the square is Orthodox (called Bla-govestenszka); Szentendre's top art collection, the Margit Kovács Museum, is down the lane to the right of the church. All of these sights are described below.

Margit Kovács Museum (Kovács Margit Múzeum)

The best of Szentendre's small art museums celebrates the local artist Margit Kovács, highly regarded for her whimsical, primi-tive-looking, wide-eyed pottery sculptures. Kovács (1902-1977) was the first female Hungarian artist to be accepted as a major tal-ent by critics and by her fellow artists. She came from a close-knit family and had a religious upbringing—both themes that would appear frequently in her work. The down-to-earth Kovács, who never married, lived with her mother—her best friend and most constructive critic.

Cost and Hours: 1,200 Ft, daily 10:00-18:00, www.pmmi. hu. From Fő tér, head down the lane to the right of the yellow church steeple, then watch for the museum entrance on your right (at Vastagh György utca 1).

Visiting the Museum: This collection of Kovács' beautiful and evocative ceramic sculptures is displayed on several floors and ex-plained in English. You'll see Christian, mythological, and folk-loric subjects depicted side by side; even in many biblical scenes, the subjects wear traditional Hungarian clothing. Notice that many statues feature women in pairs or groups—suggesting the close bond Kovács felt with her mother. And in her later works—after her mother's death—you'll begin to notice a more somber tone. On the top floor, in the replica of Kovács' study, find the gnarled tree stump. This tree, which once stood on Budapest's Margaret Island, had been struck by lightning, and its twisted forms inspired Kovács.

Micro Art Museum (Mikro Csodák Múzueuma)

This charming "Micro Miracles" collection, while a bit of a tourist trap, is well worth a squint. Ukrainian artist Mykola "Howdedoodat" Syadristy has crafted an array of 15 literally microscopic pieces of art—a detailed chessboard on the head of a pin, a pyramid panorama in the eye of a needle, a swallow's nest in half a poppy seed, a golden lock on a single strand of hair, and even a minuscule portrait of Abe Lincoln. You'll go from microscope to microscope, peering at these remarkably detailed sculptures (with English descriptions).

Cost and Hours: 800 Ft, daily 9:00-18:00, next to Korona restaurant at Fő tér 6, tel. 26/313-651, www.microart.hu.

Marzipan Museum

This collection (attached to a popular candy and ice-cream store) features two floors of sculptures made of marzipan. Feast your eyes on Mickey Mouse, Muppets, over-the-top wedding cakes, a life-size Michael Jackson, Princess Di, and, of course, portraits of Hungarian VIPs and patriotic national symbols (the Parliament, the Turul bird, and so on). Note that Eger also has a marzipan museum (see page 343)—visiting more than one is redundant.

Cost and Hours: Free to enter shop, small fee to enter museum, daily 9:00-19:00, between the main square and the train station at Dumtsa Jenő utca 12, enter from Batthyány utca, tel. 26/311-931, www.szamosmarcipan.hu.

Church Hill Loop

For a representative look at Szentendre's seven churches, visit the best two, connected by this loop walk.

• *Begin on the main square (Fő tér). Go a few steps up the street at the top of the square (behind the cross).*

Just before the white Town Hall (Városháza), climb the stairs on your right, and work your way up to the hilltop park, called...

Church Hill (Templomdomb)

This hill-capping perch offers some of the best views over the jumbled,   Mediterranean-style rooftops of old Szentendre. (See how many steeples you can count in this church-packed town.) Looking down on Fő tér (find the cross poking just above the roofline), you can see how the town's market square evolved at the place where its three trade roads converged.

• *The hill's centerpiece is...*

St. John Catholic Church (Keresztelő Szent János)

This was the first house of worship in Szentendre, around which the Balkan settlers later built their own Orthodox churches. If it's

open, step into the humble interior (free, sporadic hours). Pay special attention to the apse, which was colorfully painted by starving artists in the early 20th century.

• *Exiting the church, loop around its far side and take the downhill lane toward the red-and-yellow steeple.*
Turn right and find the gate in the wall (along Alkotmány street) to enter the yard around this church. Pay a visit to the...

▲Belgrade Serbian Orthodox Cathedral (Belgrádi Székesegyház)

This offers perhaps Szentendre's best opportunity to dip into an Orthodox church.

Cost and Hours: 700 Ft, also includes museum, Tue-Sun 10:00-18:00, closed Mon, shorter hours off-season; during winter, go to the museum first, then they'll let you into the church.

Visiting the Church: Standing in the gorgeous **church interior,** ponder the Orthodox faith that dominates in most of the Balkan Peninsula (starting just south and east of the Hungarian border). Notice the lack of pews—worshippers stand through the service, with men separate from women, as a sign of respect before God. The Serbian Orthodox Church uses essentially the same Bible as Catholics, but it's written in the Cyrillic alphabet (which you'll see displayed around Orthodox churches). Following Old Testament Judeo-Christian tradition, the Bible is kept on the altar behind the iconostasis—the big wall in the middle of the room covered with

icons (golden paintings of saints), which separates the material world from the spiritual one.

Orthodox icons are typically not intended to be lifelike. Packed with intricate symbolism, and cast against a shimmering golden background, they're meant to remind viewers of the metaphysical nature of Jesus and the saints rather than their physical form. However, this church, which blends pure Orthodoxy with Catholic traditions of Hungary, features some Baroque-style statues that are unusually fluid and lifelike.

Orthodox services generally involve chanting (a dialogue that goes back and forth between the priest and the congregation), and the church is filled with the evocative aroma of incense. The incense, chanting, icons, and standing up are all intended to heighten the experience of worship. While many Catholic and Protestant services tend to be more theoretical and rote, Orthodox services are about creating an actual religious experience.

Don't miss the adjacent **museum,** covered by the same ticket. You'll see religious objects, paintings, vestments, and—upstairs—icons, with good English descriptions.

• *For a scenic backstreets stroll before returning to the tourist crush, explore the zone on the far side of this church. Wander through what was the Dalmatian neighborhood to charming Rab-Ráby tér. The lanes between here and the waterfront are among the most appealing and least crowded in Szentendre.*

Hungarian Open-Air Folk Museum (Szabadtéri Néprajzi Múzeum, aka Skanzen)

Three miles northwest of Szentendre is Skanzen, a sprawling open-air museum featuring examples of traditional Hungarian architecture from all over the country. As with similar museums throughout Europe, these aren't replicas—each building was taken apart at its original location, transported piece by piece, and reassembled here. The admission price includes a map in English, and the museum shop sells a good English guidebook. While interesting, it's time-consuming to visit—I'd skip it unless you're captivated by folk architecture.

Cost and Hours: 2,000 Ft, Tue-Sun 9:00-17:00, closed Mon, closed off-season except for some weekends in March and Nov, Sztaravodai út, tel. 26/502-537, www.skanzen.hu.

Getting There: It takes about five minutes to **drive** from Szentendre to Skanzen (pay parking). **Bus** #7 heads from Szentendre to Skanzen when the museum's open (runs sporadically—see Skanzen website for specific schedule). A **taxi** from Szentendre to the museum should cost no more than 2,000 Ft; the TI can call one for you (mobile +3630-663-3333 or +3626-314-314).

Visegrád

Visegrád (VEE-sheh-grahd, Slavic for "High Castle," pop. 1,600) is a small village next to the remains of two major-league castles: a

hilltop citadel and a royal riverside palace. While the town itself disappoints many visitors, others enjoy the chance to be close to these two chapters of history.

The Romans were the first to fortify the steep hill overlooking the river. Later, Károly Róbert (Charles Robert), from the French/Neapolitan Anjou dynasty, became Hungary's first non-Magyar king in 1323. He was so unpopular with the nobles in Buda that he had to set up court in Visegrád, where he built a new residential palace down closer to the Danube. (For more on this king, see page 197.) Later, King Mátyás (Matthias) Corvinus—notorious for his penchant for Renaissance excess—ruled from Buda but made Visegrád his summer home, and turned the riverside palace into what some called a "paradise on earth." Matthias knew how to party; during his time here, red-marble fountains flowed with wine. (To commemorate these grand times, the town hosts a kitschy Renaissance restaurant, with period cookware, food, costumed waitstaff, and live lute music.)

Today, both citadel and palace are but a shadow of their former splendor. The citadel was left to crumble after the Habsburg reoccupation of Hungary in 1686, while the palace was covered by a mudslide during the Ottoman occupation and is still being excavated. Frankly, Visegrád's sights are skippable, especially for those relying on public transportation—but if you're driving through the town anyway, it's worth a 10-minute detour up to the citadel for the views.

Orientation to Visegrád

The town of Visegrád is basically a wide spot in the riverside road, squeezed between the hills and the riverbank. Coming from Budapest, first you'll pass the hokey Renaissance Restaurant; farther along, near the Királyi Palota bus stop, are the Info Visegrád office and the Royal palace; and finally, at the main intersection in the village (by the Nagymarosi Rév bus stop), you can turn left and twist about 10 minutes up through the wooded hills to the Citadel (watch for pay parking lot just below the fortress entrance).

Public Transportation to the Citadel: Arriving in Visegrád by bus, train/ferry, or boat (see "Getting Around the Danube Bend," earlier), you have two options for visiting the citadel: Either hike about 45 minutes steeply up, or take the misnamed "City Bus," which is actually a minivan taxi that runs on demand (2,500 Ft one-way, no matter how many people ride along, www.city-bus. hu). You can call to request it yourself (tel. 26/397-372), or you can ask pretty much anyone in town to call for you—try the Info Visegrád shop, or any big hotel or restaurant.

Tourist Information: Visegrád lacks an official TI, but the handy, privately run **Info Visegrád** shop along the main road answers questions (daily 10:00-16:00, closed Mon in winter, tel. 26/397-188, www.visitvisegrad.hu).

Sights in Visegrád

Visegrád Citadel (Fellegvár)

The remains of Visegrád's hilltop citadel have paltry exhibits, with limited English, but it can be fun to scramble around the ramparts. Best of all, the upper levels of the citadel offer commanding views over the Danube Bend.

Cost and Hours: 1,700 Ft, daily 9:00-17:00, May-Sept until 18:00, may have shorter hours in off-season, closed in icy winter weather, tel. 26/398-101, www.parkerdo.hu/visegradi_var.

Visiting the Castle: From the parking lot, hike up the stairs and through the first turret to buy your ticket. From there, follow the path toward the castle entry. On the way up, you can pay extra to try your hand at a bow and arrow.

Belly up to the viewpoint for sweeping **Danube Bend views.** From here, you can see that the Danube actually does a double-bend—a smaller one (upstream), then a bigger one (downstream)—creating an S-shaped path before settling into its southward groove. It's easy to understand why the Danube, constricted between mountains, is forced to bend here. The river narrows as it passes through this gorge, then widens again below the castle, depositing sediment that becomes the islands just down-

stream. Just upstream from Visegrád, the strange half-lake on the riverbank is all that's left of an aborted communist-era dam project to tame the river.

Now climb the steep stairs and enter the first part of the exhibition, where you'll see a replica of the Hungarian crown. The real one (now safely stored under the Parliament dome in Budapest) was actually kept here, off and on, for some 200 years, when this was Hungary's main castle.

Deeper into the complex, you reach the **waxworks** *(panoptikum)*, illustrating a scene from an important medieval banquet: In 1335, as Habsburg Austria was rising to the west, the kings of Hungary, Poland, and Bohemia converged here to strategize against this new threat. Centuries later, history repeated itself: In February 1991, after the fall of the Iron Curtain, the heads of state of basically the same nations—Hungary, Poland, and Czechoslovakia— once again came together here, this time to compare notes about Westernization. To this day, Hungary, Poland, the Czech Republic, and Slovakia are still sometimes referred to collectively as the "Visegrád countries." The adjoining room features a scene of medieval merriment: music, dancing, and flirting.

Continue up to the top of the complex, the **inner castle.** Here you'll find a hunting exhibit (dioramas with piles of stuffed animals) and the armory (with a few weapons, and coats of arms of knights). To conquer the castle, climb up to the very top tower, where you can explore the ramparts.

Royal Palace (Király Palota)

Under King Matthias Corvinus, this riverside ruin was one of Europe's most elaborate Renaissance palaces. During the Ottoman occupation, it was deserted and eventually buried by a mudslide. For generations, the palace's existence faded into legend, so its rediscovery in 1934 was a surprise. Today, the partially excavated remains are tourable, with sparse English descriptions. The palace courtyard, decorated with a red-marble fountain, evokes its Renaissance glory days. Upstairs, look for the giant green ceramic stoves, and at the top level, find the famous canopied fountain with lions. This "Hercules Fountain"—pictured on the back of the 1,000-Ft note—once

had wine spouting from the lions' mouths, with which Matthias used to ply visiting dignitaries to get the best results.

Cost and Hours: 1,300 Ft, Tue-Sun 9:00-17:00, closed Mon, tel. 26/398-026.

Esztergom

Esztergom (EHS-tehr-gohm, pop. 29,000) is an unassuming town with a big Suzuki factory. You'd never guess it was the first capital of Hungary—until you see the towering 19th-century Esztergom Basilica, built on the site where István (Stephen) I, Hungary's first Christian king, was crowned in AD 1000. Today, that basilica is the most important church in the country—you

can think of it as the Hungarian Canterbury (the Archbishop of Esztergom is the head of the Hungarian Catholic Church). The basilica's vast interior and evocative crypt are worth a visit and can be seen quickly.

ARRIVAL IN ESZTERGOM

Drivers have it easy: You'll virtually run right into the looming basilica as you pass through town on the main road; turn off on the right and use the pay parking lot directly in front of the church's esplanade.

Esztergom's **boat dock** is more convenient to the basilica than the bus or train stations (can't miss the basilica as you disembark—hike on up). If arriving on the **riverside bus** from Visegrád, get off by the basilica (Iskola Utca stop)—not at the bus station. If you're coming by **train,** or on the **overland bus** from Budapest, it's a long 45-minute walk to the basilica; it's better to take a taxi.

Sights in Esztergom

▲▲Esztergom Basilica (Esztergomi Bazilika)

This basilica, on the site of a cathedral founded by Hungary's beloved St. István, commemorates Hungary's entry into the fold of

Western Christendom. St. István was born in Esztergom on Christmas Day in the year 1000. Shortly after marrying the daughter of the king of Bavaria and accepting Christianity, he was crowned here by a representative of the

pope (for more on St. István, see page 203). Centuries later, after Esztergom had been retaken from the retreating Ottomans, the Hungarians wanted to build a "small Vatican" complex to celebrate the Hungarian Catholic Church and their triumphant return to the region. The Habsburgs who controlled the area at the time (and were also good Catholics) agreed, but did not want to be upstaged, so progress was sluggish. The Neoclassical basilica was erected slowly between 1820 and 1869, on top of the remains of a ruined hilltop castle. With a 330-foot-tall dome, this is the tallest building in Hungary.

Cost and Hours: Basilica—free, daily 8:00-18:00, May-Aug until 19:00, Nov-March until 16:00. Tower climb—700 Ft or "panorama hall"—300 Ft, both daily 9:00-18:00, May-Aug until 19:00, closed Nov-March and in bad weather. Crypt—300 Ft, daily 9:00-17:00, May-Aug until 18:00, Nov-Feb until 16:00. Treasury—900 Ft, same hours as crypt. Tel. 33/402-354, www. bazilika-esztergom.hu.

Visiting the Basilica: Approaching the church is like walking toward a mountain—it gets bigger and bigger, yet you never quite reach it. In front of the church is a **statue of Mary,** the "Head, Mother, and Patron" of the Hungarian Church. She's wearing the regalia of Hungarian royalty—the crown, orb, and scepter that currently reside under the Parliament dome in Budapest (you just saw the replicas, if you visited Visegrád).

Head to the big arch on the left side of the basilica. Directly under this arch, on the left, is the ticket office (for optional sights within the basilica—the crypt and treasury are most worthwhile); the basilica entrance is directly opposite.

Enter the basilica. In the foyer, the stairway leading down to the right goes to the **crypt.** Pick up the self-guided tour brochure as you enter. This frigid space, with tree-trunk columns, culminates at the tomb of Cardinal József Mindszenty, revered and persecuted for standing up to the communist government (see sidebar). Notice how his tomb is still bedecked with memorial wreaths; there's also a photo of Pope John Paul II paying his respects here. In another side chapel is the ornate tomb of János Csernoch (1913-1927), a popular cardinal. Back in the main chamber, look for original red-tinted tombstones of 15th-century archbishops.

Return upstairs and proceed into the cavernous **nave.** Take in the enormity of the third-biggest church in Europe (by square footage). The lack of supporting pillars in the center of the church further exaggerates its vastness. This space was consecrated in 1856—before the entire building was finished—at a Mass with music composed by Franz Liszt.

As you face the altar, find the chapel on the left before the transept. This Renaissance **Bakócz Chapel,** part of an earlier

Cardinal József Mindszenty
(1892-1975)

József Mindszenty was a Hungarian priest who rose through the ranks to become Archbishop of Esztergom, cardinal, and head of the Hungarian Catholic Church. This outspoken cleric was arrested several times, by very different regimes: in 1919 for defying the early Hungarian communist leader Béla Kun; during World War II, for criticizing the Arrow Cross's deportation of Jews; and again in 1948, for speaking out against the communist regime.

Upon his arrest in 1948, Mindszenty was relentlessly tortured to extract a confession. He became the subject of a high-profile "show trial," and was convicted to life in prison. (An enraged Pope Pius XII excommunicated those who had tried and convicted Mindszenty.) The cleric's plight was dramatized in the 1955 film *The Prisoner,* starring Alec Guinness as the cardinal.

During the 1956 Uprising, Mindszenty was freed for a brief time. But when the uprising was put down with violence, he sought refuge in the US Embassy on Budapest's Szabadság tér—where he stayed for 15 years, unable to leave for fear of being recaptured. Many American Catholics who grew up during this time remember praying for Cardinal Mindszenty every day when they were kids. In 1971, he agreed to step down from his position, then fled to Austria.

On his deathbed in 1975, Mindszenty said that he did not want his body returned to Hungary as long as there was a single Russian soldier still stationed there. As the Iron Curtain was falling in 1989, Mindszenty emerged as an important hero to Hungarian democrats, who wanted to bring his remains back to his homeland. But Mindszenty's secretary, in accordance with the cardinal's final wishes, literally locked himself to the coffin—refusing to let the body be transported as long as any Soviet soldier remained in Hungary. In May of 1991, as Russian troops withdrew from Hungary, Mindszenty's remains were finally brought to the crypt in the Esztergom Basilica.

church that stood here, predates the basilica by 350 years. It was commissioned by the archbishop during King Matthias Corvinus' reign. The archbishop imported Italian marble-workers to create a fitting space to house his remains. Note the typically Renaissance red marble—the same marble that decorates Matthias' palace at Visegrád. When the basilica was built, the chapel was disassembled into 1,600 pieces and rebuilt inside the new structure. The heads carved on the chapel's altar were defaced by the Ottomans, who, as Muslims, believed that only God—not sculptors—can create man.

Continue to the **transept.** On the right transept wall, St. István offers the Hungarian crown to Mary—seemingly via an angelic DHL courier. There's a depiction of this very church towering on the horizon. Mary is particularly important to Hungarians, because István—the first Christian king of Hungary—had no surviving male heir, so he appealed to Mary for help. (Eventually one of István's cousins, András I, took the crown and managed to keep his kingdom in the fold of Christianity.)

And one more tour-guide factoid: Above the **altar** is what's reputed to be the biggest single-canvas oil painting in the world. (It's of the Assumption, by Michelangelo Grigoletti.)

To the right of the main altar, you have the opportunity to go higher to get some views—you can either climb 120 steps to the **"panorama hall"** (a large-windowed space at the top of the main building), or 430 steps all the way up to the **dome.**

Also in this area, you have the opportunity to tour the **treasury** (do this last, as you'll exit outside the building). Head up the spiral staircase to view the impressive collection. After a display of vestments, you'll wander a long hall tracing the evolution of ecclesiastical art styles: Gothic, Renaissance, Baroque, Rococo, and Modern. In the first (Gothic) section, find the giant drinking horns, used by kings at royal feasts. The second (Renaissance) section shows off some intricately decorated chalices. A close look at the vestments here shows that they're embroidered with 3-D scenes and slathered with gold and pearls. In the case on the wall, find the collection's prized possession: an incredibly ornate example of Christ on the cross—but Jesus here bears an unmistakable likeness to King Matthias Corvinus. In the third (Baroque) and fourth (Rococo) sections, notice things getting frilly—and bigger and bigger, as the church got more money. The fifth (Modern) section displays an array of kissable bishop rings.

The exit takes you out to a **Danube-view terrace.** For the best river-bend view, walk a hundred yards or so downstream (right,

past the café) to the modern statue of St. István. It shows Hungary's favorite saint being crowned by the local bishop after converting to Christianity; St. István symbolically holds up the arches of the Hungarian Church. (Until this statue was built in 2003, this was *the* choice spot for Esztergom teens to kiss.) Directly below, between the statue and the river, you can see the ruins of an Ottoman bath and the evocative stub of a ruined minaret, with its spiral staircase exposed and going nowhere.

That's **Štúrovo, Slovakia** across the river, connected to Hungary by the Mária Valéria Bridge—destroyed in World War II and rebuilt only in 2001. Before its reconstruction, no bridges spanned the Danube between Budapest and Bratislava. You can walk or drive across the bridge to Slovakia for the best views back to this basilica (no passport checks).

Near the Basilica: This hilltop was once heavily fortified, and some ruins of its castle survive—now part of the **Castle Museum** next to the basilica (opposite side from the István statue). In 2007, restorers discovered a fresco of the four virtues, likely by Sandro Botticelli (but it's under restoration and not currently viewable). The complex also includes the chapel where St. István was supposedly born, as well as lots of dusty old exhibits about arcane Hungarian history, from the Stone Age through the Ottoman period (1,600 Ft, Tue-Sun 10:00-18:00, off-season until 16:00, closed Mon year-round, www.mnmvarmuzeuma.hu).

Esztergom Connections

DAY TRIPS

BY BUS

For connections, see "Getting Around the Danube Bend," earlier in this chapter. When choosing between the riverside bus and the direct overland bus, note that the overland bus—while faster and offering different scenery—departs much farther from the basilica than the riverside bus.

ROUTE TIPS FOR DRIVERS

To return from Esztergom to Budapest, the easiest choice is to retrace your route on road #11 around the Bend to Budapest. But to save substantial time and see different scenery, I prefer "cutting the Bend" and taking a shortcut through the Pilis hills (takes just over an hour total, depending on traffic).

To Cut the Bend: From the basilica in Esztergom, continue along the main road #11 (away from Budapest) to the roundabout with the round, yellow, Neoclassical church (built as a sort of practice before they started on the basilica). Here you can choose your exit: If you exit toward **Budapest/Dorog,** it'll take you back on road #11 for a while, then route you onto the busier road #10 (which can have heavy traffic—especially trucks—on weekdays). Better yet, if you head for **Dobogókő,** you'll follow a twistier but faster route—through remote-feeling, wooded hills—via the town of Pilisszentkereszt to Budapest. After about 30 minutes on this road, in the town of Pomáz (south of Szentendre), you'll rejoin the Budapest-bound road #11.

More Hungarian Destinations

The destinations I've covered in depth in this book will keep you busy for at least two weeks in Hungary. But if you have more time or a special interest, there's much more of Hungary to experience. Here are some ideas to get you started on planning a visit to other parts of the country.

SOUTH OF BUDAPEST: THE GREAT HUNGARIAN PLAIN

More than half of Hungary (essentially everything southeast of the Danube) constitutes the Great Hungarian Plain, or Puszta. Broad, flat, desolate, and parched in the late summer and autumn, the Great Hungarian Plain is the Magyar version of Big Sky Country. Most of the sights listed here (except Hortobágy National Park) line up along the M-5 expressway south of Budapest; a train line also connects them (trains depart Budapest hourly, 1.5 hours to Kecskemét, 2.5 hours to Szeged).

▲▲Traditional Horse Shows

If the idea of a traditional Hungarian horse show (described earlier, under "Lázár Lovaspark Horse Show") intrigues you, consider experiencing a similar performance in its original setting, on the Great Hungarian Plain. Various farms around the Puszta put on these shows frequently in summer, and by request off-season. The various options all hew pretty close to the same format: performance, tour of stables and farm, carriage ride, and sometimes a traditional goulash lunch from a copper pot over an open fire. One popular choice is in the village of **Bugac,** deep in the countryside roughly halfway between Kecskemét and Szeged (about 45 minutes from either town; www.bugacpuszta.hu). Another option is in **Hortobágy National Park,** two hours' drive due east of Budapest (www.hnp.hu). It's important to call or email them in advance to confirm the schedule and let them know you're coming.

Kecskemét

This low-impact, charming city (pop. 115,000, www.kecskemet.hu) is handy for a stretch-your-legs break on your drive south (about an hour south of Budapest on M-5; follow *Centrum* signs and park in the garage for the big Malom shopping mall adjacent to the main square).

Kecskemét (KETCH-keh-mayt) has a downtown core made up of a series of wide, interlocking squares with a mix of beautiful Art Nouveau and Secessionist architecture (as well as some unfortunate communist-era drabness). Sometimes called the "garden city," Kecskemét is ringed by inviting parks and greenbelts.

DAY TRIPS

The city is also known for producing wine as well as apricot brandy *(barackpálinka).* While there aren't many "sights" to enter, Kecskemét gives you a taste of a largely untouristy midsize city.

If taking a lunch break in Kecskemét, do it at **$$ Kecskeméti Csárda,** a traditional, almost folksy, borderline-kitschy restaurant that hides just a few blocks off of the main drag. The service is warm, and the Hungarian specialties are executed as well here as anywhere (daily for lunch and dinner, Kölcsey utca 7, tel. 76/488-686, www.kecskemeticsarda.hu).

Near Kecskemét: Just off of M-5 between Kecskemét and Szeged, **Ópusztaszer Heritage Park** celebrates those original Hungarians who arrived on the Great Plain more than 11 centuries ago: the Magyars. This complex has an open-air museum of traditional village architecture, a wrap-around panorama painting of the arrival of the Magyars, a cluster of "Csete-yurts" in the distinctive Organic architecture style, and frequent special events that include equestrian shows (www.opusztaszer.hu).

▲Szeged

Szeged (SEH-gehd; pop. 160,000, including 23,000 university students) is the leading city of the Great Hungarian Plain. It boasts a livable town center with gorgeous Art Nouveau architecture, some impressive sights and baths, and a fascinating multiethnic collage.

Historically and culturally, Szeged is southern Hungary's main crossroads. It sits along the Tisza River, at the intersection of three countries: From here, Serbia and Romania are each within a 15-minute drive. Remember that well into the 20th century, Hungary was triple the size it is now, and back then, Szeged was quite central rather than a southern outpost. The neighboring regions of Vojvodina (now in Serbia) and Transylvania (now in Romania) still have substantial Hungarian populations.

Weighty history aside, Szeged is simply enjoyable. It's a purely late-19th-century city. After a devastating 1879 flood (known locally as "The Great Catastrophe"), Szeged was swiftly rebuilt in the eye-pleasing Art Nouveau and Secessionist styles that were so popular during that age. Today, Szeged's wealth of Hungarian Art Nouveau masterpieces is second only to Budapest's. And, as Szeged enjoys a particularly sun-drenched climate, it's also synonymous with both paprika (Szeged is one of Hungary's two main paprika production centers) and with spicy salami (the Pick brand, made here, is sold at grocery stores nationwide).

While Szeged's outer sprawl is disheartening—especially the heavily industrialized Új-szeged ("New Szeged") district, purpose-built by the communists to increase the city's output—its central core is a delight. The very center of town is a grid of **pedestrianized**

streets with finely restored old buildings, abundant outdoor cafés, and whimsical statues. Stroll the perpendicular main drags, Kölcsey utca and Kárász utca, and linger over an al fresco coffee or strudel.

This pedestrian zone is flanked by pretty squares: At the north end, the café-ringed Klauzál tér is just across the street from Szeged's "main square": **Széchenyi tér.** This vast space feels more like a park than a square, with a broad, traffic-free boulevard flanked by stately, towering plane trees; civic buildings (including the City Hall); and a smattering of dynamic monuments celebrating great Hungarians.

At the southern edge of the pedestrian zone is **Dugonics tér**—a leafy square wrapped around a large, communist-style fountain built in 1979 for the centennial of Szeged's big flood. This lively people zone is also home to the main branch of the **TI** (www.szegedtourism.hu). Just north from here along the ring road, facing its own little square, is the **Reök Palace,** a decadent high-water mark (no pun intended) of Szeged's post-flood Art Nouveau flourishing.

Just to the south of the traffic-free core, **Cathedral Square** (Dóm tér)—which, locals are eager to point out, has identical di-

mensions to St. Mark's Square in Venice—is home to the soaring twin spires of the cathedral. Officially called the **Votive Church** (Fogadalmi Templom), it was built as a "thank the Lord anyway" gesture after the devastating 1879 flood (www. fogadalmitemplom.hu). Although relatively new (completed in 1930), it feels ancient inside: Its interior is a riot of lavish, gilded, Neo-Byzantine mosaics that trumpet the greatness of Hungarian culture. The Orthodox-looking icons also evoke the cultural connection to Szeged's Balkan neighbors, the Romanians and Serbs. The Virgin Mary who floats ethereally on the dome above the altar wears a pair of Szeged's unique red-velvet slippers. Outside, the square is ringed by a brick arcade with more than a hundred small plaques and monuments honoring local and national big shots.

The inner ring road that hems in the town center (Tisza Lajos körút) links several other fine sights. A block west of the ring road, on Gutenberg utca, is Szeged's most impressive sight, its lavish **New Synagogue**—which takes a backseat to Budapest's in size (it's still among the biggest in Europe), but not in opulence. Designed in Moorish Art Nouveau style in 1903, its unassuming exterior hides a stunning blue-hued interior with Zsolnay tile decorations, glittering chandeliers, stained-glass windows illustrating the Jewish faith, and menorahs that were modeled after engravings of Jerusalem on Rome's Arch of Titus. Typical of the Historicist style of the day, the synagogue mashes up a variety of historical features: Gothic windows, Romanesque columns, a Renaissance Greek-cross floor plan, a Baroque exterior, and Byzantine decorations.

Along the northwestern edge of the ring road are the **Anna Thermal Baths,** a beautifully restored late-19th-century palace that nearly approaches the elegance of Budapest's baths (www.szegedsport.hu). Roughly across the ring road and a block up Vidra utca, **Szent István tér** is an inviting urban park with a gorgeous circa-1904 water tower as its centerpiece.

Sleeping and Eating in Szeged: For both class and hipster modernity, **$$ Tiszavirág** ("Tisza Flower") has 12 rooms that are stylish and upscale, but still affordable; the public areas—from the hangout café to the cozy lounge to the well-respected restaurant—make this a delightful home base (near the synagogue at Hajnóczy utca 1B, just across the ring road from the pedestrian core, restaurant closed Sun, www.tiszaviragszeged.hu).

The riverfront is sleepy, but gives a chance to sample the local specialty, *halászlé* ("fishermen's soup")—a paprika-flavored fish goulash. While several places around town sell this, the best option is **$$ Halászcsárda** ("Fishermen's Inn"), on Roosevelt tér facing the town's main bridge (at #12—look for the big terrace on the corner closest to the river, www.sotarto-halaszcsarda.hu).

Local Guide: A knowledgeable guide to Szeged, **István Koteczki** has a passion for his hometown and shares it well (mobile +3630-400-8898, koteczki@hotmail.com).

▲Makó

A small town of less than 30,000 people, Makó (MAH-koh) sits just east of Szeged—it's practically a suburb. (It's a 30-minute drive; if you make a wrong turn, you'll wind up in Romania.) Makó has two big claims to fame: It was the birthplace of Joseph Pulitzer (the New York publisher and politician who emigrated stateside as a teenager) and has the highest concentration anywhere of buildings

by Hungary's foremost postcommunist architect, Imre Makovecz, whose Organic style defines Hungarian architecture over the past 20 years (for more on Makovecz and Organic style, see page 347). The most stunning Makovecz work in Makó—and perhaps in

Hungary—is the **Makó Hagymatikum Thermal Baths.** Typical of Organic works, the bath complex looks like it's rising up out of the ground—a bulbous, bulging mushroom hiding an array of hot-water fun. While the otherworldly architecture is reason enough for a visit, the bath's modern facilities—with indoor and outdoor sections, both relaxing and fun zones, and everything from massages to water slides—also make it one of the best options outside of Budapest for just splashing around (www.hagymatikum. hu). The **TI** inside the bath complex's main entry can tell you more about the nine Makovecz buildings scattered around town; architecture pilgrims enjoy going on a scavenger hunt.

Subotica, Serbia (Суботица/Szabadka)

If you appreciate Szeged's Art Nouveau architecture, go to Serbia. Before 1920, Subotica (SOO-boh-teet-seh, pop. 98,000) was a Hungarian burg, and fully participated in the architectural boom of the late 19th century. Many of Szeged's top architects designed equally stunning works in Subotica. Today part of Serbia, Subotica is worth a visit for adventurous travelers who'd enjoy seeing a different facet of Hungarian culture (as the city still has a large Hungarian population)—and getting another stamp for their passport. You can side-trip from Szeged to Subotica, or use it as a scenic international detour on the ride between Szeged and Pécs (to avoid needless delays or disappointment at the border, make sure you have the car-rental company's permission to cross into Serbia). For more on Subotica, see the town's excellent website: www. visitsubotica.rs. The lakeside resort of **Palić** (Палић in Cyrillic, Palics in Hungarian)—which sits along the road from Szeged to Subotica—also has some fine Art Nouveau buildings, and is worth a quick stop (www.palic.rs).

WEST OF BUDAPEST: LAKE BALATON AND NEARBY

Landlocked Hungary doesn't have a seafront, but it does have the next best thing: Lake Balaton, the "Hungarian Riviera." Balaton—bigger than Switzerland's Lake Geneva—is one of Europe's largest freshwater lakes. The long, skinny lake—48 miles long and never wider than about 9 miles across—begins an hour's drive west of Budapest, then stretches to the southwest. Its long shoreline and shallow waters harbor a variety of tourist attractions, almost all of them catering to vacationing Hungarians. Many Budapest urbanites have humble summer cottages on or near Balaton, and in July and August, the capital empties out as people hit the beach.

Beloved as it is among Hungarians, Balaton has less to offer international tourists. (It'd be a bit like a Hungarian traveling all the way to the US just to see Fort Lauderdale.) But if you're driving in western Hungary, you might consider a quick stopover at one or more of the attractions near Lake Balaton. I've listed a few good options below.

Balaton's North Bank

Balaton's scenic north bank offers several worthwhile stops. Rolling hills rise up from the lakeshore, forming the Balaton-Felvidéki ("Highland") National Park as well as a thriving wine-growing region. The lakeside road is punctuated with several resorty towns, the biggest being Balatonfüred. The attractions noted below are the most worthwhile.

▲Tihany

Near Balatonfüred, the bulbous peninsula called Tihany (TEE-hayn) juts out into the lake. At the crest of the peninsula's hill, overlooking virtually the entire lake, is the extremely tidy, scenic village of Tihany (which boasts the highest property values in the country). Tihany village is capped by a Benedictine abbey and church, with the 11th-century tomb of King András I (one of only two Hungarian royal tombs that were not desecrated by Ottoman invaders) and finely carved 18th-century decorations. The surrounding terrace offers sweeping views over the waters of Balaton. Count the sailboats in the marina, and ponder a Hungarian seaside holiday. From the tip of the peninsula, ferries make the quick crossing to the south bank (less than a mile away).

▲Hévíz Thermal Lake

The town of Keszthely (with its fine, Baroque Festetics Palace) anchors the western tip of Lake Balaton. Nearby is the thermal lake and spa of Hévíz (HAY-veez), which fills a volcanic crater. The world's second-largest thermal lake (*gyógy-tó*, about 500,000 square feet), Hévíz is continually fed by thermal waters that bubble up from springs a hundred feet below. All of this constant, natural flushing ensures that the lake's waters refresh completely every two days, and the temperature never drops below about 70°F (and stays closer to 95°F in summer). Extremely popular with aging Russians and Germans, the lake's unique mineral composition is supposedly excellent for easing arthritis, joint pain, and other ailments. Some credit the lightly (and naturally) radioactive water; it's recommended that bathers be in the water for only about 30 minutes at a time, punctuated by 30-minute breaks. For a somewhat surreal spa experience, stop by Hévíz to take a dip (www.spaheviz.hu).

DAY TRIPS

You'll change in the locker room, then follow the walkways to the pavilion in the middle of the lake, where you can ease into the waters. Rent a pool noodle so you can slowly float and paddle your way around the lake. Weave between the lily pad lotuses as you glide in slow motion across the lake's tranquil surface. All around you, portly, aching, aging bodies bob in the steamy surf. If you want a break, stroll partway around the shoreline, and surrender to the allure of a sunbathing perch.

Herend Porcelain Factory

Set back from the north bank of Balaton, but an easy detour (about 20 miles/30 minutes' drive inland from the lakefront), is the Herend Porcelain Factory. Herend has been Hungary's main producer of fine porcelain since 1826, and supplied the Habsburg emperors as well as other royal families across Europe. Today they welcome guests to their "Porcelanium" visitors center to explore their museum and tour the "minimanufactory," a small-scale factory designed to educate curious porcelain lovers about the manufacturing process (www.herend.com).

Lake Balaton's South Bank

With the highest concentration of summer-fun tourist attractions (beaches, campgrounds, nightclubs), Balaton's largely flat south bank is less interesting for visitors. The M-7 expressway, which connects Budapest to Zagreb, Croatia, runs roughly parallel to Balaton's south bank, offering a peek. Siófok is the main town here, and the resort hub for all of Balaton. But unless you're truly on vacation Hungarian-style, I'd skip the south bank.

DAY TRIPS

EGER

Eger (EH-gehr) is a county-seat town in northern Hungary, with about 60,000 people and a thriving teacher-training college. While you've probably never heard of Eger, among Hungarians, the town has various claims to fame. Its powerful bishops have graced it with gorgeous churches. It has some of the best and most beloved spas in this hot-water-crazy country (including some worth-a-detour options in the nearby countryside). And, perhaps most of all, Eger makes Hungarians proud as the town that, against all odds, successfully held off the Ottoman advance into Europe in 1552. This stirring history makes Eger a field trip mecca for Hungarian schoolkids. If the town is known internationally for anything, it's for the surrounding wine region (its best-known red wine is Bull's Blood, or Egri Bikavér).

And yet, refreshingly, enchanting Eger remains mostly off the tourist trail. Egerites go about their daily routines amidst lovely Baroque buildings, watched over by one of Hungary's most important castles. Everything in Eger is painted with vibrant colors, and even the communist apartment blocks seem quaint. The sights are few but fun, the ambience is great, and strolling is a must. It all comes together to make Eger an ideal taste of small-town Hungary.

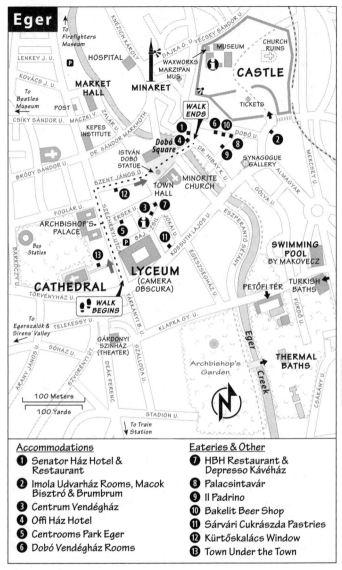

Eger

↑ To Firefighters Museum

LENKEY J. U.

KOVÁCS J. U.

To Beatles Museum

KNEZICH KÁROLY

DAJKA G.–VÉCSEY SÁNDOR U.

MUSEUM

CHURCH RUINS

HOSPITAL

WAXWORKS MARZIPAN MUS.

CASTLE

MARKET HALL

MINARET

POST

KEPES INSTITUTE

CSÍKY SÁNDOR U.   MACZKY V.   ZALÁR U.

DR. SÁNDOR MARKHOTH

BRÓDY SÁNDOR U.

WALK ENDS

Dobó Square

TICKETS

❶ ❹   ⓾ ❻

István Dobó Statue

DR. HIBAY K. U.

❽ DOBÓ U. ❷

❾

SYNAGOGUE GALLERY

SZENT JÁNOS U.

MINORITE CHURCH

ALMAGYAR

MÉKCSEY U.

SZÉCHENYI UTCA

ÉRSEK U.

❸

TOWN HALL

❼

GÓLYA U.

ESZPERANTÓ SÉTÁNY

FOGLÁR U.

ARCHBISHOP'S PALACE

Bus Station

❺ ❻ BAJ. ZSIG. U.

JÓKAI U.

❶❶

KOSSUTH LAJOS U.

SWIMMING POOL BY MAKOVECZ

BARKÓCZY U.

⓬

⓭

LYCEUM (CAMERA OBSCURA)

EGÉSZSÉGHÁZ U.

PETŐFI TÉR

TURKISH BATHS

FÜRDŐ U.

CATHEDRAL

TÖRVÉNYHÁZ U.

WALK BEGINS

TÁRKÁNYI B. U.

KLAPKA GY. U.

To Egerszalók & Sirens' Valley

TELEKESSY U.

GÁRDONYI SZÍNHÁZ (THEATER)

SÓHÁZ U.   DEÁK FERENC   SZÁLLODA U.

Archbishop's Garden

THERMAL BATHS

Eger Creek

CSÁKÁNY U.

ARANY JÁNOS U.   SZVORÉNYI U.

100 Meters

100 Yards

STADION U.

↓ To Train Station

N

Accommodations

❶ Senator Ház Hotel & Restaurant
❷ Imola Udvarház Rooms, Macok Bisztró & Brumbrum
❸ Centrum Vendégház
❹ Offi Ház Hotel
❺ Centrooms Park Eger
❻ Dobó Vendégház Rooms

Eateries & Other

❼ HBH Restaurant & Depresso Kávéház
❽ Palacsintavár
❾ Il Padrino
⓾ Bakelit Beer Shop
❶❶ Sárvári Cukrászda Pastries
⓬ Kürtőskalács Window
⓭ Town Under the Town

PLANNING YOUR TIME

Mellow Eger is a fine side trip from Budapest. It's a doable round-trip in a single day (about two hours by train, car, or bus each way), but it's much more satisfying and relaxing to spend the night.

Get oriented with my self-guided town walk, including visits to the cathedral and the Lyceum's fine old library and thrillingly low-tech camera obscura. Have a memorable lunch on the square, and—if you enjoy organ music—take in the midday concert in the cathedral (May-Oct only). Then hike up to the castle for views over town. In the late afternoon, unwind at a thermal bath—either in Eger or in the countryside. Round out your day with dinner on the square or a visit to Eger's touristy wine caves in the Sirens' Valley.

In July and August (when Hungarians prefer to go to Lake Balaton), Eger is busy with international visitors; in September and October, around the wine harvest, most of the tourists are Hungarians.

Orientation to Eger

Eger Castle sits at the top of the town, hovering over Dobó Square (Dobó István tér). Two blocks west of Dobó Square—away from the castle—is the main pedestrian drag, Széchenyi utca, where you'll find the Lyceum and the cathedral. A few blocks south from the castle (along the small creek) is Eger's thermal baths complex.

TOURIST INFORMATION

Staff at Eger's TI (TourInform) are eager to answer your questions (Mon-Fri 9:00-18:00, Sat-Sun until 13:00; off-season Mon-Fri 9:00-17:00, Sat until 13:00, closed Sun; Bajcsy-Zsilinszky utca 9, tel. 36/517-715, http://www.visiteger.com).

ARRIVAL IN EGER

By Train: Eger's tiny train station is a 20-minute walk south of the center. The baggage-deposit desk is out along the platform by track 1, between the WCs (daily 7:00-19:00; if you can't find attendant, ask at ticket desk). An ATM is at the Spar grocery store just up the street (turn left out of station, walk about 100 yards, and look for red-and-white supermarket on your right; the ATM is next to the main door, around front).

Taxis generally wait out front to take new arrivals into town (1,000-1,200 Ft). Try to take a taxi marked with a company name and number.

To catch the **bus** toward the center, go a block straight out of the station. Buses #11, #12, and #14 cut about 10 minutes off the walk into town (tickets are 350 Ft from driver or 255 Ft at train station newsstand facing track 1—ask for *helyijárat buszjegy*). Get off the bus when you reach the big yellow cathedral.

To **walk** all the way, leave the station straight ahead, walk one block, take the hard right turn with the road, and then continue straight (along busy Deák Ferenc utca) about 10 minutes until you run into the cathedral.

By Car: In this small town, most hotels will provide parking or help you find a lot. For a short visit, head for the pay parking garage near the market hall (just north of the main square), or park in the pay lot near the thermal bath complex and swimming pool on Petőfi Sándor tér (a 10-minute walk south of the main square).

GETTING AROUND EGER

Everything of interest in Eger is within walking distance. But a taxi can be helpful to reach outlying sights, including the Sirens' Valley wine caves and the thermal baths in the countryside (taxi meter starts at 450 Ft, then around 380 Ft/km; try City Taxi, tel. 36/555-555, toll-free tel. 0680-622-622).

HELPFUL HINTS

Blue Monday: Note that the castle museums, the Lyceum's library, and the Kepes Institute are closed on Mondays. But you can still visit the cathedral (and enjoy its organ concert), swim in the thermal bath, explore the market, see the castle grounds, and enjoy the local wine.

Market: Eger has a humble, old-fashioned Market Hall (Piaccsarnok), which offers a taste of local life. This ramshackle hall is a totally untouristy scene, with rough plastic tubs piled high with an abundance of fresh local produce (opens daily at 6:00; while open weekday afternoons, it's best in the mornings).

Nightlife: Things quiet down pretty early in this sedate town. Youthful student bars and hangouts cluster along the main "walking street," Széchenyi utca (especially Fri and Sat nights). Older travelers feel more at home on Little Dobó Square, with schmaltzy live music until 21:00 or 22:00 in summer; wine bars nearby may stay open later.

Eger Town Walk

Charming Eger is a delight to stroll. This walk begins near two of the city's main landmarks—in an area more local than touristy—then heads to its delightful main square, before winding up to its castle. It includes pretty much anything you'd want to see in town and takes less than an hour, not including sightseeing stops (at the Lyceum and castle).

• *We'll begin on the parklike square called Eszterházy tér, at the southern edge of the town center—between the cathedral (with two yellow rectangular towers and a dome) and the Lyceum (with a tall tower capped by an oxidized copper bulb). To get here from the main square, angle up Bajcsy–Zsilinszky utca, passing a fine Art Nouveau facade and the TI.*

Eszterházy Tér

This square is named for Bishop Károly Eszterházy (1725-1799), who helped put Eger on the map during his 40 years in power. Eszterházy had serious clout, which he wielded to transform Eger from a provincial town into a beautiful small city—with lovely architecture that far exceeded its lowly position.

Face the blocky building at the bottom of the square—the **Lyceum,** or teacher-training college. Eszterházy wanted a university in Eger, but Habsburg empress Maria Theresa refused to allow it. And so, instead, Eszterházy built the most impressive teacher-training college on the planet—and stocked it with the best books and astronomical equipment that money could buy. The Lyceum still trains local teachers (enrollment: about 2,000). Tourists also roam the halls of the Lyceum; they come to visit its classic old library and its astronomy museum (which has a fascinating camera obscura), both tucked away in the big, confusing building. For details, see "Sights in Eger," later.

Now turn 180 degrees and face the cathedral, up the grand staircase at the opposite end of the square. (We'll go inside soon.) The palace that sprawls to the right is the residence of the archbishop. And on the right side of the steps is the entrance to the **Town Under the Town** (Város a Város Alatt), a 45-minute guided tour of the archbishop's former wine cellar network (1,500 Ft, generally departs at the top of each hour—schedule posted at door, 5-person minimum, you'll get a little English sprinkled in with the Hungarian; daily 9:00-18:00, Oct-March until 17:00—these are last tour times, tel. 20/961-4019, www.varosavarosalatt.hu).

Head up the grand staircase. You'll pass saints István and László—Hungary's first two Christian kings—and then the apostles Peter and Paul.

• *At the top of the stairs, gape up at...*

Eger Cathedral

The second-biggest church in Hungary (after Esztergom's—see the Day Trips from Budapest chapter) is worth ▲▲. The cathedral was built in the 1830s by an Austrian archbishop who had previously served in Venice and who thought Eger could use a little more class. The colonnaded Neoclassical facade, painted a pretty Habsburg yellow, boasts some fine Italian sculpture.

Cost and Hours: 300-Ft donation requested, Mon-Sat 9:00-11:00 & 12:00-18:00, Sun 13:30-18:00, Pyrker János tér 1.

Organ Concerts: The cathedral organ booms out a glorious 30-minute concert daily in summer—800 Ft, May-Oct Mon-Sat at 11:30, Sun at 12:45.

Visiting the Cathedral: As you head inside, look near the back-left corner for the statue of **Szent Rita,** a local favorite (that's the 15th-century saint Rita of Cascia, from Italy). The votive plaques that say *köszönöm* and *hálából* are offering "thanks" and "gratitude" for prayers answered.

Across from Rita is a statue honoring St. Maksymilian Kolbe (1894-1941), a Polish priest who was executed at Auschwitz; around the corner from him (in the corridor) is another 20th-century martyr, the Hungarian cardinal József Mindszenty (1892-1975), who ran afoul of the communist authorities and lived in the US embassy in Budapest until he escaped to the US (for more on him, see page 320).

Now walk down the nave, to the first collection box. Then, turning back to face the door, look up at the ornate **ceiling fresco:** On the left, it shows Hungarians in traditional dress; and on the right, the country's most important historical figures. At the bottom, you see this cathedral, celestially connected with St. Peter's in Rome (opposite). This symbol of devotion to the Vatican was a brave statement when it was

painted in 1950. The communists were closing churches in other small Hungarian towns, but the Eger archbishop had enough clout to keep this one open.

Continue to the transept, stopping directly underneath the main dome. The **stained-glass windows** decorating the north and south transepts were donated to the cathedral by a rich Austrian couple to commemorate the 1,000th anniversary of Hungary's conversion to Christianity—notice the dates: 1000 (when St. István converted the Magyars to Christianity), and 2000.

Turning to leave, notice the enormous **organ**—Hungary's second-largest—above the door (try to catch an organ concert—see details earlier).

• *Head back out of the church and down the stairs. When you reach the Lyceum, turn left and walk down...*

Széchenyi Utca

This is Eger's main walking street, lined with colorful townhouses,

EGER

cafés, and eateries. You'll find that the businesses are mostly oriented to locals (especially students), with a few touristy spots mixed in.

One block down the street, on the left, step through the gate into the grand garden courtyard of the **Archbishop's Palace.** In the peaceful garden, observe the statue on the left, honoring St. István (see page 203), and on the right, a statue for St. Erzsébet (Elisabeth, see page 162)—notice the roses in her apron, a nod to the most famous story about her. You can pay to enter the palace itself, with fine old halls described by the dryly informative audioguide (included in the entry fee). As you walk through the bishop's apartments, you'll see vestments, a model of the cathedral, chalices, rare books, a picture gallery, and a balcony looking down into the bishop's private chapel. However, it's pretty dull, and other sights in Eger are more interesting (1,800 Ft, Tue-Sun 10:00-18:00, cheaper and open until 16:00 Oct-March, closed Mon year-round).

Back out on Széchenyi utca, continue one more block, then turn right down Szent János utca (at the McDonald's). Enjoy Eger's pedestrianized core for one long block—noticing that these streets, too, are populated almost entirely by Egerites, despite being just a few steps off the main square. Near the end of the street, on the right at #10, look for the *kürtőskalács* window, selling that heavenly scented Hungarian sweet street food.

• *You'll pop out at...*

Dobó Square (Dobó István Tér)

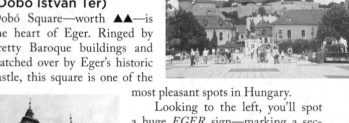

Dobó Square—worth ▲▲—is the heart of Eger. Ringed by pretty Baroque buildings and watched over by Eger's historic castle, this square is one of the

most pleasant spots in Hungary.

Looking to the left, you'll spot a huge *EGER* sign—marking a second, adjoining square along the town creek. If you walk past the sign and keep going just a couple of minutes, you'll run into the rustic town market (described earlier, under "Helpful Hints"). Between here and the *EGER* sign is a handy Spar supermarket, with an ATM by the door.

Dominating the main square are the twin towers of the exquisitely photogenic **Minorite Church**—often said

István Dobó and the Siege of Eger

In the 16th century, Ottoman invaders swept into Hungary. They easily defeated a Hungarian army—in just two hours—at the Battle of Mohács in 1526.

When Buda and Pest fell to the Ottomans in 1541, Eger became the last line of defense. István Dobó and his second-in-command, István Mekcsey, were put in charge of Eger's forces. They prepared the castle for a siege and waited.

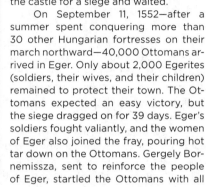

On September 11, 1552—after a summer spent conquering more than 30 other Hungarian fortresses on their march northward—40,000 Ottomans arrived in Eger. Only about 2,000 Egerites (soldiers, their wives, and their children) remained to protect their town. The Ottomans expected an easy victory, but the siege dragged on for 39 days. Eger's soldiers fought valiantly, and the women of Eger also joined the fray, pouring hot tar down on the Ottomans. Gergely Bornemissza, sent to reinforce the people of Eger, startled the Ottomans with all manner of clever and deadly explosives. His "fire wheel"—a barrel of gunpowder studded with smaller jars of explosives—would be lit and rolled downhill to wreak havoc until the final, deadly explosion. Ultimately, the Ottomans left in shame, Eger was saved, and Dobó was a national hero.

The unfortunate epilogue: The Ottomans came back in 1596 and succeeded in conquering an Eger Castle guarded by unmotivated mercenaries. The Ottomans controlled the region for close to a century.

In 1897, a castle archaeologist named Géza Gárdonyi moved from Budapest to Eger, where tales of the siege captured his imagination. Gárdonyi wrote a book about István Dobó and the 1552 Siege of Eger called *Egri Csillagok* ("Stars of Eger," translated into English as *Eclipse of the Crescent Moon,* available at local bookstores and souvenir stands). The book—a favorite of many Hungarians—is taught in schools, keeping the legend of Eger's heroes alive today.

EGER

to be the most beautiful Baroque church in Hungary. The shabby interior is less interesting but has some appealing details. Go inside (free, daily 9:30-17:30). Notice that each of the hand-carved wooden pews has a different motif. Pay close attention to the side altars that flank the nave: The first set (left and right) are 3-D illustrations, painted to replicate the wood altars that burned in a fire; the next set are real. And looking up at the faded ceiling frescoes, you'll see (in the second one from the entrance) the church's patron: St. Anthony of Padua, who's preaching God's word to the fishes after the townspeople refused to hear him.

The green, arcaded building to the right of the Minorite Church is the **Town Hall,** next to an old-fashioned **pharmacy.**

Walk to the dynamic statue in the middle of the square, which depicts **István Dobó** (EESHT-vahn DOH-boh). The square's namesake and Eger's greatest hero, Dobó defended the city—and all of Hungary—from an Ottoman invasion in 1552 (see his story in the sidebar). Next to Dobó is his co-commander, István Mekcsey. And right at their side is one of the brave women of Eger—depicted here throwing a pot down onto the attackers.

Behind the statue of Dobó is a bridge over the stream that bisects the city. Just before you reach that bridge, look to the left and you'll see the northernmost Ottoman **minaret** in Europe— once part of a mosque, it's now a tourist attraction (described later, under "Sights in Eger").

At the bridge, pause and look down at the little **creek** below street level. Notice the finely manicured trail that runs along the creek, beckoning to strollers and cyclists. If you follow this creek to the right, in less than 10 minutes you'll reach Eger's excellent thermal-bathing complex (described later, under "Experiences in Eger"). Like much of Hungary, this part of Eger sits on deposits of natural thermal water...can you detect a faint whiff of sulfur?

Across the bridge is the charming **Little Dobó Square** (Kis-Dobó tér), the most atmospheric place in Eger for an al fresco drink or meal. The wine bar on the square offers tastings, and you'll find more options just up the street.

• *Our brief orientation walk is over. The town's most prominent sight— the castle—is just overhead, hovering over Little Dobó Square. To reach it, bear right at the top of the square, then turn right on Dobó utca. Follow this pleasant street—lined with an ever-changing array of gift shops, wine bars and wine shops, eateries, and other tourist-oriented businesses—a few short blocks. Soon you'll reach a little park (with a lute-playing figure on a bench); the ramp up to the castle is just beyond this, on the left.*

Sights in Eger

▲EGER CASTLE (EGRI VÁR)

The great St. István—Hungary's first Christian king—founded a church on this hill a thousand years ago. The church was destroyed by Tatars in the 13th century, and this fortress was built to repel another attack. Most importantly, this castle is Hungary's Alamo, where István Dobó defended Eger from the Ottomans in 1552—as depicted in the relief just outside the entry gate. These days, it's usually crawling with field-tripping schoolchildren from all over the country. (Every Hungarian sixth grader reads *Eclipse of the Crescent Moon,* which thrillingly recounts the heroic siege of Eger.) For those of us who didn't grow up hearing the legend of István Dobó, the complex is hard to appreciate, and English information is sparse. Most visitors find that the most rewarding plan is simply to stroll up, wander the grounds, play "king of the castle" along the ramparts, and enjoy the

sweeping views over Eger's rooftops. I'd skip the "casements tour," which costs extra and is in Hungarian only.

Cost and Hours: 1,700 Ft, 850-Ft "walking ticket" gets you into the castle grounds after the museums have closed—a good option; waxworks costs 500 Ft extra; castle grounds open daily 8:00-22:00, Nov-March until 21:00; exhibits open Tue-Sun 10:00-18:00, off-season until 16:00, closed Mon year-round; tel. 36/312-744, www.egrivar.hu. The entrance ramp to the castle is at the end of Dobó István utca, a short walk from Little Dobó Square.

Visiting the Castle: Buy your ticket at the lower gate, then hike up the entry ramp and through the inner gate into the main courtyard—with grassy fields, souvenir stands, and easy access to the ramparts.

Get your bearings by walking up to the round turret with the tall Hungarian flag, to the left as you enter, and take a visual tour over the rooftops of Eger. (If you've completed my Eger Town Walk, this is a fun recap.)

Looking left, spot what looks like a church tower with the feathers of an arrow vertically embedded in the top, next to a big, wooden, bulbous building. This is the Aladár Bitskey Pool, designed by the great Organic architect Imre Makovecz. It anchors Eger's delightful thermal bath area—well worth considering for a break from sightseeing.

Panning 90 degrees to the right, look down over Eger's charming main square, with the twin towers of the Minorite Church. Just beyond, see the round dome and two rectangular towers of the cathedral, and the boxy Baroque tower with a copper bulb on top—that's the Lyceum, with its prized camera obscura. Széchenyi utca—the main walking street—stretches from these two buildings to the right, to the twin yellow church spires.

Looking farther right, try to spot Eger's minaret (which may be hidden behind the turret)—the northernmost Ottoman minaret still standing in Europe. And all around you are the wooded Bükk Hills, which hide an important wine-growing region.

Now head into the castle proper. Face straight ahead from where you entered. The **round tower** on your left usually holds good temporary exhibitions, down deep inside. And off on the right, just inside the wall, you may see an **archery** exhibit where you can pay to test your skill shooting old-fashioned bows and crossbows.

Now walk straight ahead, through the corridor with the little information window, and emerge into a pink, Gothic-style courtyard. Immediately to your left, notice the entrance to the **dungeon.** While the "casements" you may see advertised are not worth paying extra (or spending 45 minutes listening to Hungarian commentary), hiking down into this dungeon—covered by your castle ticket—is a similar experience. The long building on the left, next to the dungeon entrance, has the **$$$ 1552 Restaurant,** serving up big plates of hearty traditional food; upstairs are temporary exhibits.

Straight ahead, upstairs in the building with the Gothic arches, is the castle's **museum** (with English descriptions). You'll see some architectural decorations, swords and suits of armor, and models of the castle through history—including one illustrating the Ottoman siege of Eger. Also inside are some paintings and a screen showing a classic movie that dramatized the siege, adding to its legend. The most interesting exhibit is a small side room with objects the Ottomans left behind: weapons, everyday items (pots, bowls), a carpet, and some turban-shaped gravestones.

Head through the little gap between the two buildings of the courtyard to find the **waxworks,** or "Panoptikum." Run separately from the castle sights, this costs 500 Ft extra. And, while it's kind of silly, it's fun for kids or kids at heart. Think of it as a very low-tech, walk-through *Ottomans of the Caribbean.* You'll see a handful of eerily realistic heroes and villains from the siege of Eger (including István Dobó himself, and the leader of the Ottomans sitting in his colorful tent). Notice the exaggerated Central Asian features of the Egerites—a reminder that the Magyars were more Asian than

European. A visit to the waxworks also lets you scramble through a segment of the tunnels that run inside the castle walls (a plus, since it's not really worth it to wait around through the similar, Hungarian-language casements tour).

From here, you can explore the **grounds,** including the remains

of a once-grand cathedral and a smaller rotunda dating from the days of St. István (10th or 11th century; at the far-right corner as you enter).

SIGHTS IN THE LYCEUM (LÍCEUM)

Eger's teacher-training college fills a historic old building that—among all the students, classrooms, and professors' offices—houses

two sights worth a look: a glorious Baroque library, with shelves of historic books and a frescoed ceiling; and the "Magic Tower," with some scientific exhibits and a working camera obscura (Eszterházy tér 1). While both are inside the same building, they are treated as separate sights. For more on the history of this building, see my Eger Town Walk, earlier.

Cost and Hours: Library and Magic Tower cost 1,000 Ft each. Library open Tue-Sun 9:30-15:30, closed Mon and generally closed off-season (since there's no heating). Magic Tower open daily 9:30-17:30; closed Mon in spring and fall; shorter hours (likely weekend mornings only) or closed altogether in winter; www.varazstorony.hu.

▲▲Baroque Library

First, visit the Lyceum's old-fashioned Baroque library one floor up: From the main entry hall, cut through the middle of the courtyard, go up the stairs to the next floor, and look for Room 223, marked *Biblioteca Eszterhazyana* (it's on the right side of the

complex as you face it from the entrance). This library houses 60,000 books (here and in the two adjoining rooms, with several stacked two deep), all cataloged carefully. This is no easy task, since they're in over 30 languages—from Thai to Tagalog—and are shelved according to size, rather than topic. Only one percent of the books are in Hungarian—but half of them are in Latin. The shelves are adorned with golden seals depicting some of the great minds of science, philosophy, and religion. Marvel at the gorgeous ceiling fresco, dating from 1778. To thank the patron of this museum, say *köszönöm* to the guy in the second row up, to the right of the podium (above the entry door, second from left, not wearing a hat)—that's Bishop Károly Eszterházy, who founded the Lyceum and for whom the library is named. A portrait of him often stands on an easel at ground level. And the display cases ringing the room show off treasures from the collection—they are changed every year, to avoid exposing any books to sunlight for too long.

▲Magic Tower (Varázstorony)

Turn right as you leave the library to find the staircase that leads up the misnamed "Magic Tower," which is really all about science (*Varázstorony,* follow signs several flights up). First you'll reach the **Astronomical Museum.** Some dusty old stargazing instruments occupy one room, as well as a meridian line in the floor (a dot of sunlight dances along this line each day around noon). Across the hall is a fun, interactive **magic room,** where you can try out scientific experiments—such as using air pressure to make a ball levitate or sending a mini "hot-air balloon" up to the ceiling.

A few more flights up is the Lyceum's treasured **camera obscura**—one of just two originals surviving in Europe (the other is in Edinburgh). You'll enter a dark room and gather around a big, bowl-like canvas, where the guide will fly you around the streets of Eger (presentations about 2/hour, maybe more when busy). Fun as it is today, this camera must have astonished viewers when it was built in 1776—well before anyone had seen "moving pictures." It's a bit of a huff to get up here (nine flights of stairs, 302 steps)—but the camera obscura, and the actual view of Eger from the outdoor terrace just outside, are worth it.

OTHER SIGHTS IN EGER

Minaret

Once part of a mosque, this slender, 130-foot-tall minaret represents the century of Ottoman rule that left its mark on Eger and all of Hungary. The little cross at the top symbolizes the eventual Christian victory over Hungary's Ottoman invaders. You can climb the minaret's 97 steps for fine views of Eger, but it's not for those scared of heights or enclosed spaces. Because the staircase was designed for one man to climb to call the community to prayer, it's very tight. To avoid human traffic jams, they allow groups of visitors in about twice an hour.

Cost and Hours: 400 Ft, daily 10:00-18:00, April

and Oct until 17:00, closed Nov-March; if it's locked, ask around for the key.

▲Kopcsik Marzipan Museum (Kopcsik Marcipánia)

Lajos Kopcsik is a master sculptor who has found his medium: marzipan. Kopcsik can make this delicate mixture of sugar dough, ground almonds, egg whites, and tempera paints take virtually any form. Pass through the entryway, filled with awards, to enter this surprisingly engaging little museum. You'll see several remarkable, colorful examples of Kopcsik's skill: sword, minaret, gigantic wine bottle, suitcase, Russian stacking dolls, old-timey phonograph, grandfather clock, giant bell...and paintings galore (including Van Gogh's sunflowers and Picasso's musicians). Who'd have thought you could do so much with candy? Don't miss the "Baroque room"—furnished and decorated entirely in marzipan.

Cost and Hours: 800 Ft, no English information, daily 10:00-18:00, shorter hours off-season, near the minaret at Harangöntő utca 4, tel. 36/412-626, www.kopcsikmarcipania.hu.

▲Kepes Institute (Kepes Intézet)

This beautifully renovated, minimalist building—sitting proudly on Eger's main walking street, Széchenyi utca—has a permanent collection of György Kepes' works upstairs and fills several other halls with good temporary exhibits of contemporary artwork. Hungarian-born György Kepes (1906-2001) later moved to the US, where he was a university professor in Chicago and at MIT. A painter and photographer, Kepes followed the very Hungarian, left-brained artistic tradition of Op Artist Viktor Vasarely, drawing inspiration from geometry—except that Kepes ventured deeper into abstraction (producing canvases reminiscent of fuzzy Abstract Expressionism). In typical Hungarian fashion, Kepes combined art with practical purpose as he helped design effective camouflage for the US military.

Cost and Hours: 1,200 Ft, Tue-Sat 10:00-18:00, closed Sun-Mon, Széchenyi utca 16, tel. 36/440-044, www.kepeskozpont.hu.

Honorable Mentions

Eger has several other small museums that may be worthwhile for those with a special interest. Though Eger's Jewish population was wiped out during the Holocaust, one of its synagogues has been converted into the **Synagogue Gallery** (Zsinagóga Galéria), allowing you to see the roughly restored interior and peruse temporary exhibits on various topics (exhibits are generally not Jewish focused; entry price changes based on exhibit, Tue-Sun 10:00-18:00, closed Mon, two short blocks straight ahead from castle ramp at Kossuth Lajos utca 17).

The offbeat **"Egri Road" Beatles Museum** is surprisingly

good, heavily promoted, and unaccountably popular—though Eger has no connection to the Fab Four (other than, one must assume, at least one very avid fan). Loaded with Beatlemania memorabilia and arranged around a timeline of the band's rise and fall, it's endearing to nostalgic baby boomers and worth considering on a rainy day... but is *this* why you came all the way to Eger? (2,500 Ft; Tue-Sun 10:00-18:00 except Wed until 14:00, closed Mon; a five-minute gently uphill walk from Széchenyi utca at Csiky Sándor utca 30, www.beatlesmuzeum.hu).

The TI can give you information about the **Firefighters Museum** (Egri Tűzoltó Múzeum, a long walk north of downtown on Széchenyi utca, www.tuzoltomuzeum.hu), the **Sport Museum,** and more.

Experiences in Eger

AQUA EGER

Swimming and water sports are as important to Egerites as good wine. They're proud that many of Hungary's Olympic medalists in aquatic events have come from the surrounding county. The men's water polo team took the gold for Hungary at three Olympiads in a row (2000-2008), Katinka Hosszú shattered records at the Rio games in 2016, and speed swimmer László Cseh spent much of his career winning silver medals just behind Michael Phelps. The town's Aladár Bitskey swimming pool—arguably the most striking building in this part of Hungary—is practically a temple to water sports.

Eger also has several appealing thermal bath complexes: one right in town, and two more a few miles away (near the village of Egerszalók). Budapest offers classier bath experiences, but the Eger options are modern, fully accessible, and far less crowded with American tourists—making them, for some travelers, an all-around better experience. Before you go, be sure to read the Thermal Baths chapter.

Baths and Pools in Eger

All of these are managed by the same organization (www.egertermal.hu). Bring your swimsuit and (if you have them) flip-flops; you can rent a towel if you need to.

Getting There: Eger's bathing complex is a pleasant walk (less than 10 minutes) from the center of town. From the bridge on Dobó Square, follow the creek four blocks south (look for signs to *Strand*). When you reach Petőfi tér, you're in the aquatic area. The swimming pool is on your left (look for the unique steeple), and the thermal bathing complex is straight ahead; to reach the main entrance, continue straight into the park, then look for the entrance on your left, over a bridge, marked by a big dome. The Turkish bath entrance is around the other side of the complex.

Aladár Bitskey Swimming Pool (Bitskey Aladár Uszoda)

This striking swimming pool was designed by Imre Makovecz, the father of Hungary's Or-

ganic architectural style (see sidebar). Some Eger taxpayers resented the pool's big price tag, but it left the city with an iconic building befitting its love of water sports. The building is worth a peek—and you can swim in it, too.

Cost and Hours: 1,050 Ft, Mon-Fri 6:00-21:00, Sat-Sun 7:30-18:00, Frank Tivadar utca, tel. 36/511-810.

▲Eger Thermal Bath (Eger Termálfürdő)

For a refreshing break from the sightseeing grind, consider a splash at the spa. This is a wonderful opportunity to try a Hungarian bath: fun, accessible, and frequented mostly by locals. Note that there are two adjoining sections: the sprawling indoor/outdoor thermal bath section and the smaller Turkish bath. Each has its own ticket, but it's possible to move between them. If you're going to be at the bath complex for less than 2.5 hours, it's cheaper to enter through the Turkish bath section (see details later).

Cost and Hours: 1,900 Ft (cheaper Mon-Fri after 16:00); if you want to add on Turkish bath after buying the thermal bath ticket, it's an additional 1,300 Ft; complex open June-Aug daily 8:00-20:00, Sept-May daily 9:00-19:00, these are closing times—must be out of the pool 30 minutes earlier; Petőfi tér 2, main entrance is through Archbishop's Garden (Érsekkert), tel. 36/510-558.

Taking the Waters: Eger's bath complex uses a similar wristband system to the one in Budapest (see Thermal Baths chapter for details). After paying, you

are issued a wristband that you'll use to access your locker. Change, stow your stuff, then head out and have fun. The complex is huge, with a wide array of different pools, each one labeled with its depth and temperature. The best part is the double-domed, indoor-outdoor adventure bath, right at the main entrance (a very comfortable 34°C/93°F). Its cascades, jets, bubbles, geysers, and powerful current pool will make you feel like a kid again. The adjoining pool is warmer (36-38°C/97-100°F) and the most popular area to hang out—Egerites sit peacefully, ignore the slight stink, and feel their arthritis ebb away. Sprawling in both directions are additional pools—for kids, for swimming laps, and for hanging out. The waterslides at the right end (with your back to the main dome) are open only in summer, while the Turkish bath is in a smaller domed building at the opposite end, to the left.

▲Turkish Bath (Török Fürdő)

Eger recently refurbished its Turkish-style bath, tucked in one corner of the thermal bath complex. The Turkish bath is small but elegant. The underside of the central dome—over a 30°C/86°F pool—glitters with golden tile. Surrounding that are hotter mineral pools (34-36°C/93-97°F), as well as a sauna, steam bath, and aroma bath. This area connects to the thermal bath complex through a turnstile, and uses the same wristband system (Turkish bath entrance is around the left side, as you approach the bath complex from the center).

Cost and Hours: The 2,200-Ft Turkish bath is a great deal—it covers you for up to 2.5 hours in both the Turkish bath and the thermal bath area. (If you buy your bath ticket at the main entrance, then want to enter the Turkish bath, you'll be charged an extra entry fee—a poor value.) The Turkish bath is also open later: daily until 21:00 (Mon-Tue from 16:30, Wed-Thu from 15:00, Fri from 13:00, Sat-Sun from 9:00; exit the pools 30 minutes before closing; tel. 36/510-522). If you visit late in the day, a good strategy is to enter and change at the Turkish bath (entrance at Fürdő utca 3), head over to the thermal complex first, then move back into the Turkish bath when the rest is closed.

Baths near Eger, in Egerszalók

Two more thermal baths—Salt Hill and Demjén Cascade—sit in the countryside outside Eger, flanking a rocky hill between the villages of Egerszalók and Demjén. While these baths lack the old-fashioned class of the Budapest options, they more than compensate with soggy fun. Here's a fun and very hedonistic afternoon plan: Take the bus or taxi to the spa, taxi back to Eger's Sirens' Valley for some wine-cave hopping, then taxi back to your Eger hotel.

Getting There: Both baths are about a mile outside the vil-

Hungary's Organic Architecture

Hungary's postcommunist generation has embraced a unique, eye-catching style of architecture, called Organic, which was developed and championed by Imre Makovecz (1935-2011).

In his youth, Makovecz pursued a flowing style that was intentionally at odds with the rigid right angles of communist architecture. He was inspired by the Art Nouveau of a "decadent" Golden Age, and by pioneering architects from other countries (including American Frank Lloyd Wright, who employed a more angular style but a similar aesthetic of fitting his works to their surroundings).

After being blacklisted by the regime for his adherence to his architectural vision—and for his nationalistic politics—Makovecz ramped up his pursuit of something new. Makovecz made do with sticks, rocks, and other foraged building materials. He was also inspired by Transylvanian village architecture: whitewashed walls with large, overhanging mansard roofs (resembling a big mushroom).

After the fall of the regime, Makovecz swiftly became Hungary's premier architect. He believed that a building should be a product of its environment, rather than a cookie-cutter copy. Organic buildings use indigenous materials (especially wood) and take on unusual forms—often inspired by animals or plants—that blend in with the landscape. These buildings look like they're rising up out of the ground, rather than plopped down on top of it. Makovecz preferred to work in small communities such as Eger (see photo on page 345) instead of working for large corporations. Makovecz wanted his creations—from churches, thermal baths, and campgrounds to cultural centers, restaurants, and bus stations—to represent the civic pride of the local community. For more on Makovecz, visit www.makovecz.hu.

EGER

lage of Egerszalók, which is itself about three miles from Eger. **Drivers** leave Eger to the south, toward *Kerecsend*/Route 25; at the roundabout on the outskirts of town, turn right toward *Egerszalók* and *Demjén*. A few minutes later, watch (on the left) for the easy-to-miss turnoff to Saliris Resort (park along the road for 450 Ft)—or, for Demjén Cascade, carry on past this, turn left at the T intersection, and head into Demjén village.

Without a car, you can take a public **bus** from Eger's bus station to the baths (take bus going toward Demjén; for Salt Hill, get off at the *Egerszalók Gyógyfürdő* stop—tell the bus driver "EH-gehr-saw-lohk FEWR-dur"—just after leaving the town of Egerszalók; for Demjén Cascade, get off at the entrance to Demjén village; bus runs 9/day Mon-Sat, fewer on Sun, 20-minute trip, 500 Ft). Check the return bus information carefully (especially on weekends, when frequency plummets). Or you can take a **taxi** from Eger (about 4,000 Ft; tel. 36/555-555 for a return taxi from Egerszalók).

Nearby Wineries: The village of Egerszalók has several fine wineries, including the excellent **St. Andrea**—fun to combine with your bath visit (for details, see the "Wineries near the Baths in Egerszalók" section, later).

▲▲Salt Hill Thermal Spa (at the Saliris Resort)

For decades, Egerites would come to this "salt hill" (a natural terraced formation caused by mineral-rich spring water running

down the hillside) in the middle of nowhere and cram together to baste in pools of hot water. Then the developers arrived. Today, the gigantic Saliris Resort hotel and spa complex, built near those original formations, offers a world of hot-water fun tucked into a scenic valley. With 12 indoor pools and five outdoor ones—many cleverly overlapping one another on several levels—these baths are worth the trip outside Eger.

Cost and Hours: 5,800 Ft all day, 3,400 Ft for up to 3 hours, 2,200 Ft if you enter after 17:00, all ticket prices are 1,000 Ft extra on busy "special days"; 2,000 Ft extra for sauna world; towel rental, massage, and other treatments are also available; open June-Aug daily 10:00-20:00, pools close at 19:00, tel. 36/688-500, http://salirisresort.hu/en.

Visiting the Bath: This complex uses the same system as at Eger's thermal baths: Press your wristband against a computer screen to be assigned a locker, change in the private cabin, then have fun.

From the locker room, a blue carpet leads you out to the pools. Take some time to explore the sprawling complex. The two main pools—warm (32-34°C/90-93°F) and hot (35-39°C/95-102°F)—extend both inside and outside and cascade over several levels. Outside, down on the lower level, is a vast kiddie pool.

Tucked around the right side of the building (as you face the complex) is the "sauna world," with five different types of saunas, some quieter soaking pools, and a clothing-optional outdoor area with wood cabin-type huts that contain Finnish and Russian saunas (touch your wristband to the turnstile to pay extra for access to this area).

▲Demjén Cascade Thermal Spa

Just over the hill from Salt Hill Thermal Spa, Demjén Baths was recently converted into a high-end resort. The original "thermal valley" *(termál völgy)* part of the complex—pretty but unpretentious, with nicely rustic wooden buildings and pools—is reasonably priced and open extremely long hours, making it popular with locals. Jets, fountains, and other "adventure bath"-type features are rare, and the goal here is simply stewing in pools of warm water. A separate "aquapark" section adds waterslides and a diving pool, for an extra charge. But the big draw for thermal-bathing enthusiasts is the newer "cave bath" *(barlangfürdő)*—a subterranean complex of pools, channels, waterslides, hidden grottoes, eerie mood lighting, and a sci-fi/fantasy theme. While the Salt Hill spa described above is still a more enjoyable all-around experience, those intrigued by the novelty of an underground thermal playland might prefer to check out Demjén.

Cost and Hours: Thermal spa—1,900 Ft, daily 9:00-2:00 in the morning; aquapark—1,900 Ft extra, open in good weather only, closes at 20:00; cave bath—5,000 Ft, 500 Ft more on weekends, 500 Ft less if you stay 3 hours or less, ticket also includes thermal spa, Mon-Thu 10:00-21:00, Fri 10:00-22:00, Sat 9:00-22:00, Sun 9:00-21:00; mobile +3630-853-7419, www.demjencascade.hu.

EGER WINE

Eger is at the heart of one of Hungary's best-known wine regions, internationally famous for its **Bull's Blood** (Egri Bikavér). You'll likely hear various stories as to how Bull's Blood got its name during the Ottoman siege of Eger. My favorite version: The Ottomans were amazed at the ferocity displayed by the Egerites and wondered what they were drinking that boiled their blood and stained their beards so red...it must be potent stuff. Local merchants, knowing that the Ottomans were Muslim and couldn't drink alcohol, told them it was bull's blood. The merchants made a buck, and the name stuck.

Creative as these stories are, they're all bunk—the term dates only from 1851. Egri Bikavér is a blend (everyone has their own recipe), so you generally won't find it at small producers. Cabernet sauvignon, merlot, *kékfránkos*, and *kékoportó* are the most commonly used grapes.

But Bull's Blood is just the beginning of what the Eger wine region offers. Although Eger is better known for its reds, 42 of the 62 regional varieties are white. (For details, see the "Eating" section of the Practicalities chapter.)

Tasting Local Wine: While it would be enjoyable to drive around the Hungarian countryside visiting a few wineries (and I've recommended one great choice, St. Andrea), the most accessible way to get a quick taste of local wine is at a wine shop in town. Several cluster on Little Dobó Square (Kis-Dobó tér) and just uphill, along Dobó István utca. As specific shops tend to come and go, I'd simply stroll this area looking for signs advertising tastings or small glasses of wine, and find a clerk who speaks enough English to help you navigate your choices.

Sirens' Valley (Szépasszony-völgy)

When the Ottoman invaders first occupied Eger, some residents moved into the valley next door, living in caves dug into the hillside. Eventually the Ottomans were driven out, the Egerites moved back to town, and the caves became wine cellars. (Most Eger families who can afford it have at least a modest vineyard in the countryside.) There are more than 300 such caves in the valley to the southwest of Eger, several of which are open for visitors.

The best selection of these caves (about 50) is in the Sirens' Valley (sometimes also translated as "Valley of the Beautiful Women"—or, on local directional signs, the less poetic "Nice Woman Valley"). While the valley can feel vacant and dead (even sometimes in the summer), if you visit when it's busy it can be a fun scene—locals showing off their latest vintage, with picnic tables and tipsy tourists spilling out into the street. At some places, you'll be offered free samples; others have a menu for tastes or glasses of wine. While you're not expected to buy a bottle, it's a nice gesture to buy one if you've spent a while at one cave (and it's usually very cheap). Most caves offer something light to eat with the wine, and the area also has full-service restaurants. Some of the caves are fancy and finished, staffed by multilingual waiters in period costume. Others feel like a dank basement, with grandpa leaning on his moped out front and a monolingual granny pouring the wine inside.

This experience is a strange mix of touristy and local, but not entirely accessible to non-Hungarian-speakers—it works best with a bunch of friends and an easygoing, sociable attitude. Hopping from cave to musky cave can make for an enjoyable evening, but be sure to wander around a bit to survey the options before you dive in (cellars generally open 10:00-21:00 in summer, best June-Aug in the late afternoon and early evening, plus good-weather weekends in the shoulder season; it's sleepy and not worth a visit off-season, when only a handful of cellars remain open for shorter hours).

Getting to the Sirens' Valley: The valley is on the southwest outskirts of Eger. Figure no more than 1,300 Ft for a **taxi** between your hotel and the caves.

Wineries near the Baths in Egerszalók

The village of Egerszalók, near the Salt Hill and Demjén Cascade thermal baths, has a variety of fun wineries. The most interesting, and well worth a visit for wine lovers, is **St. Andrea.** This slick, modern, Napa Valley-esque facility offers cellar tours and tastings of their excellent wines, which show up on fine restaurant menus across Hungary. They're evangelical both about their spirituality (hence the name) and their wine, and enjoy explaining everything in English. They focus on blends that highlight the unique properties of this region, and produce some good, pungent whites with volcanic qualities. While it may be possible to simply drop in for a tasting, it's better to call ahead and let them know you're coming (3,900 Ft/person for 6 tastings, or 8,000 Ft/person for premium wines, bottles from 2,500 Ft, Mon-Sat 10:00-18:00, closed Sun, Ady Endre út 88 in Egerszalók, tel. 36/474-018, www.standrea.hu, kostolas@standrea.hu). They also have a top-end wine bar in Budapest (see page 274). It's most practical with a car (or by taxi), but you can also walk there from the bus stop in Egerszalók's town center (about a half-mile; head down Ady Endre út, toward the baths).

EGER

Sleeping in Eger

Eger is a good overnight stop. I've focused my listings on quaint, well-located hotels. There's no real "luxury" in this town—just bigger, tour-oriented places on the outskirts. Elevators are rare—expect to climb one or two flights of stairs to reach your room. Most of these hotels are in pedestrian zones, so get detailed driving and parking instructions from your hotel; many offer free or cheap parking, but it's often a block or two away. Most hotels quote their rates in euros but prefer to be paid in forints.

$ Senator Ház Hotel is one of my favorite small, family-run hotels in Eastern Europe. Though the 11 rooms are a bit worn, this place is cozy and well run by András and Csöpi Cseh and their right-hand man, Peter. It feels trapped in a nostalgic time warp, with oodles of character, all the right quirks, and a picture-perfect location just under the castle on Little Dobó Square (RS%, air-con, free parking a block away, Dobó István tér 11, tel. 36/411-711, www.senatorhaz.hu, info@senatorhaz.hu). The Cseh family also runs **$ Pátria Vendégház**—with two doubles and two luxurious apartments around a courtyard nearby.

$ Imola Udvarház rents 15 rooms and apartments—some with kitchen, living room, bedroom, and bathroom—all decorated in modern Ikea style. They're roomy, tastefully decorated, and well maintained, with a great location near the castle entrance, and the free on-site parking garage makes this a good choice for drivers (air-con, Tírodi Sebestyén tér 4, tel. 36/516-180, www.imolaudvarhaz. hu, info@imolaudvarhaz.hu).

$ Centrum Vendégház, at the bottom of the main square, has eight simple rooms and apartments around a courtyard. It's basic but comfortable, with parquet floors and traditional furnishings, and well run by László and Timea. Check in at the little grocery store on the ground floor (breakfast extra, Bajcsy-Zsilinszky 17, mobile +3630-591-3131, www.cve.hu, info@centrum-vendeghaz-eger.hu).

$ Offi Ház Hotel shares Little Dobó Square with Senator Ház (listed above). Its five rooms are classy and romantic but dated and a bit tight, with slanted ceilings. Communication can be tricky (German helps), but the location is superb (air-con, Dobó István tér 5, tel. 36/518-210, www.offihaz.hu, offihaz@upcmail.hu, Offenbächer family).

$ Centrooms Park Eger, an annex for the larger Hotel Park at the edge of town, is impersonal but indeed central, with 21 spartan but sleepable rooms right in the middle of town (breakfast extra and served at main hotel—better to just eat at a café on the square, air-con, Érsek utca 4, tel. 36/522-255, www.centroomseger.hu, info@centroomseger.hu).

¢ Dobó Vendégház, run by warm Marianna Kleszo, has seven basic but colorful rooms just off Dobó Square. Marianna speaks nothing but Hungarian but gets simple reservation emails translated by a friend (cash only, air-con in some upstairs rooms, free parking, Dobó utca 19, tel. 36/421-407, www.dobovendeghaz. hu, info@dobovendeghaz.hu).

Eating in Eger

$$ HBH Restaurant (named for the Hofbräuhaus beer on tap) offers traditional Hungarian dishes, either in a brick-and-wood dining room or—better—at fine outdoor tables at the bottom of the main square (on weekends, reserve a view table in advance). While the service can be curt, the lengthy, well-described menu and good wine list make this a fine choice for a classic Hungarian meal (daily 11:30-23:00, at the bottom of Dobó Square at Bajcsy-Zsilinszky utca 19, tel. 36/515-516, www.hbh-eger.hu).

$$$ Macok Bisztró, near the base of the ramp up to the castle, is the best choice in town for modern, upscale cuisine (and a more sophisticated dining experience). It has a classy interior, inviting tables filling a patio, a mix of Hungarian and international dishes, and an extensive wine list (Mon-Sat 10:00-22:00, Sun until 15:00, Tinódi Sebestyén tér 4, tel. 36/516-180, www.imolaudvarhaz.hu).

$$ Brumbrum is the cheaper, more casual side-restaurant of Macok. They offer tasty, unpretentious, street food-inspired plates of Hungarian and international fare, a variety of wines, and craft beer, all in an industrial-mod setting with subway tile and raw plywood (Tue-Sun 10:00-23:00, closed Mon, same contact information as above).

$$ Palacsintavár ("Pancake Castle"), near the ramp leading up to the castle, isn't your hometown IHOP. They serve up inventive, artfully presented crêpe-wrapped main courses to a mostly student clientele. The spacious interior is decorated with old cigarette boxes, rock music plays on the soundtrack, and the outdoor tables are appealing (Tue-Sun 12:00-23:00, closed Mon, Dobó utca 9, tel. 36/413-980, www.palacsintavar.hu).

$$ Restaurant Senator Ház, on Little Dobó Square, offers the best setting for al fresco dining in town, with good Hungarian and international food. Sure, you're paying a bit extra for the setting—but it's worth it for the postcard-perfect outdoor seating, from which you can survey the Little Dobó Square action (open daily 10:00-22:00, cheesy live music on summer evenings). Neighboring restaurants (such as Offi Ház) offer the same ambience.

$$ Depresso Kávéház brings a touch of modern hipness to Eger's stately main square. Despite its downer name, this young, fresh café features a wide variety of coffee drinks, wine, breakfasts, and a short menu of light meals (sandwiches, quiches, etc.). It owns a great location on the square—with fine outdoor tables facing the castle—and also has a bright, open interior (Mon-Thu 9:00-20:00, Fri-Sat until 21:00, Sun until 18:00, Érsek utca 14, mobile +3630-886-6742, www.depresso.hu).

$ Il Padrino is a popular place for simple, cheap, tasty pizzas. It's tucked down a non-touristy street a block over from the main square, with a kitschy interior and breezy outdoor tables (daily 11:00-22:00, Fazola Henrik utca 1, mobile +3620-547-9959, www.padrinopizza.hu).

Wine and Beer: To sample either of these, begin on Little Dobó Square and head up Dobó István utca. You'll pass a few **wine bars** featuring local wines, plus **Bakelit,** a craft beer shop selling a dizzying array of local and international craft beers (daily 10:00-22:00, Dobó utca 17, www.bakelitbeer.com).

Student Eats on Széchenyi Utca: To browse for an affordable, forgettable meal, go for a walk on Eger's main walking street, which begins at the cathedral. You'll find a row of lowbrow student eateries serving a variety of pizza, gyros, and burgers, plus lots of bakeries and bars with food. A few tourist-oriented places are mixed in. Don't come here for high cuisine—but it's handy and cheap, and most places have fine outdoor seating; on weekends, the street is enlivened with dueling live music.

Dessert: *Cukrászdák* (pastry shops) line the streets of Eger. For a more local scene, find the tiny **Sárvári Cukrászda,** a block behind the Lyceum. Their pastries are good, but Egerites line up here for homemade gelato (Mon-Fri 7:00-18:00, Sat-Sun from 18:00, Kossuth utca 1, between Jókai utca and Fellner utca). You'll spot several ice cream parlors in this town, where every other pedestrian seems to be licking a cone. Another good option is the *kürtőskalács* **window** on Szent János utca, where you can step up and grab a piping-hot chimney cake that's slow-cooked on a rotisserie, then rolled in toppings (daily 9:00-19:30, Szent János utca 10).

Eger Connections

BY TRAIN

The only major destination you'll get to directly from Eger's train station is **Budapest** (every 2 hours direct to Budapest's Keleti/Eastern Station, 2 hours; more frequent and faster with a change in Füzesabony—see below). For other destinations, you'll connect through Füzesabony or Budapest.

Eger is connected to the nearby junction town of **Füzesabony** (FEW-zesh-aw-bone) by frequent trains (13/day, 17 minutes). In Füzesabony, you can transfer to Budapest on either a slower milk run train or a speedier InterCity train (a little pricier, as it requires a supplement, but gets you to Budapest in just under 2 hours total).

BY BUS

Eger's bus station is right in town, a five-minute uphill walk behind Eger's cathedral and the Archbishop's Palace: Go behind the cathedral and through the park, and look for the modern, green, circular building. Blue electronic boards in the center of the station show upcoming departures.

From Eger to Budapest: The direct Eger-Budapest bus service is about the same price as the train and can be a bit faster (2/hour, tickets generally available just before departure). Express buses depart Eger at :15 after each hour and make the trip in one hour and 50 minutes; slower regular buses leave at :45 after each hour and take 20 minutes longer. While Eger's bus station is closer to the town center than its train station, this bus takes you to a less central point in Budapest (near Budapest's Stadionok bus station, on the M2/red Metró line).

To the Thermal Baths near Egerszalók: Buses from the same station also connect Eger to the thermal baths near Egerszalók (Salt Hill and Demjén Cascade; see "Getting There" on page 346). However, buses marked for *Egerszalók* do not actually go to the spa; instead, you need a bus going *beyond* Egerszalók, marked for *Demjén*.

PÉCS

An established settlement for nearly 2,000 years, Pécs (pronounced "paych") is a historic, museum-packed, and oh-so-pretty city near Hungary's southern frontier. Cheerful, inviting Pécs—with colorful buildings dripping with lavish Zsolnay porcelain decoration—feels unusually proud and prosperous. Pécs offers a strikingly diverse and satisfying day of sightseeing for a city its size. And you'll hardly see another tourist, as this place is rarely visited by Americans.

Pécs' position as the major city of southern Hungary often placed it at the crossroads of cultures. Owing to the city's illustrious history, museum-going is fun and enlightening here. You'll gradually peel back the many layers of Pécs' past: Walk in the footsteps of Romans through ancient crypts, stroll the medieval trade-town street plan, explore some rare surviving artifacts of the Ottoman occupation, ogle colorful Baroque and Art Nouveau buildings, get to know an eclectic array of beloved Hungarian artists with ties to the town (Zsolnay, Vasarely, Csontváry)...and enjoy the energetic bustle of one of Hungary's leading cities. The city's symbol—a mosque-turned-church—says it all.

The Mecsek Hills gently cradle the city, blocking out the colder weather from the north to give Pécs a mild Mediterranean climate closer to Croatia's than to Budapest's. It's no surprise that this bright and invigorating city has earned a reputation as a leading art colony. Students love it, too. Hungary's first university was founded here in 1367, and today's U. of Pécs rivals Budapest's ELTE as the country's biggest university. More than 30,000 students give the city a youthful buzz and a certain worldliness—the people of Pécs are smart, cosmopolitan, and tend to speak English more than in smaller towns (like Eger). Museums and restaurants are often staffed by eager young students, making it easy to connect with the people of Pécs.

PLANNING YOUR TIME

One full day is plenty to get your fill of Pécs. It's barely doable as a long day trip from Budapest (three hours each way by train)—so it's worth spending the night. With the better part of a day in Pécs, go for a walk through town following my self-guided commentary (under "Sights in Pécs"), dipping into the museums that appeal to you. Nearly everything is within a few minutes' walk of the main square. The one exception—the Zsolnay Cultural Quarter, a short bus or taxi ride or long walk east—is interesting but skippable, or can be squeezed into any remaining time you have on a busy day (or the next morning).

Orientation to Pécs

With about 170,000 people, Pécs is Hungary's fifth-largest city. But the tourist's Pécs feels like a small town, right down to the convivial strolling atmosphere that combusts along its pedestrian zone. The Belváros, or Inner Town, is hemmed in by a ring road (the site of the former town wall, some of which still stands). You can walk from one end of this city core to the other in about 15 minutes. All roads lead to the main square, Széchenyi tér, marked by the palatial yellow Town Hall and giant mosque/church. Because Pécs is nestled up against a gentle hillside, you'll go gradually uphill as you head north.

TOURIST INFORMATION

The helpful main TI—Pécs Infopoint—is right on the main square, in the big, yellow Town Hall building, sharing a space with a delightful café (Mon-Fri 8:00-18:00, Sat-Sun from 10:00, Széchenyi tér 1, tel. 72/213-315, www.iranypecs.hu).

ARRIVAL IN PÉCS

By Train: The Pécs train station is three-quarters of a mile due south of the city center's Széchenyi tér. Inside, the station is long but straightforward (lockers are in the waiting room).

Taxis wait to the right as you exit the station; the ride into town is a bargain at about 1,000 Ft (similar in cost to two bus tickets).

You can **walk** from the train station to the town center in about 15 minutes: Exit straight ahead from the station and walk up the tree-lined, slightly angled Jókai út, which funnels you directly to Széchenyi tér. It's gently uphill the entire way.

Various **bus** lines fan out from the station. If you exit to the right, bus #44 gets you closest to the center—dropping you off just above the mosque/church on the main square. For greater frequency, you can head left instead—to the stop marked *VI*—and

Pécs

To Mecsek Hills & TV Tower

MIKLÓS U.

NYIL. U.

VILMOS U.

MECSEK U.

JUHASZ GY. U.

HUNYADI U.

DAMJANICH U.

ARADI VÉRTANÚK ÚTJA

ZSOLNAY MUSEUM

KODÁLY Z. U.

CITY WALLS

MEDIEVAL UNIV.

LAPIDARIUM

MODERN HUNGARIAN ART MUSEUM

WALK ENDS

CATHEDRAL

Bus #35 (Barbakán) B

BRONZE GATE

MARTYN MUSEUM

KÁPTALAN U.

NEMES MUSEUM

BARBICAN

BISHOP'S PALACE

Dóm tér

CELLA SEPTICHORA

WC VISITOR CENTER

CAFÉ KIOSK

VASARELY MUSEUM

EORBÁT A. U.

KLIMÓ GYÖRGY U.

SANC U.

MAUSOLEUM

JANUS PANNONIUS U.

István tér

NEMES MUSEUM

Várkert

SZT. ISTVÁN TÉR

CSONTVÁRY MUSEUM

VÖRÖSMARTY U.

APÁCA U.

ALKOTMÁNY U.

CISZT

SARACEN PHARMACY

❼

FERENCESEK UTCÁJA

HUNGÁRIA U.

Kórház Tér

GARAY U.

MÁTYÁS KIRÁLY U.

ZRÍNYI MIKLÓS U.

VÁRADY ANTAL

DISCHKA GYŐZŐ

POST

EÖTVÖS U.

RÁKÓCZI B ÚT

Zsolnay-Sobor

JÓKAI U.

SZABADSÁG U.

RÉT U.

JÓZSEF ATTILA UTCA

To Train Station

PÉCS

Accommodations
1. Adele Boutique Hotel
2. Hotel Arkadia
3. Hotel König
4. Hotel Palatinus
5. Diána Hotel
6. STM3 Apartments

Eateries
7. Balkán Bisztró
8. Blöff Bisztró
9. Elefántos Ház
10. I Love Pécs Café
11. Oázis
12. Cooltour Café
13. Nappali

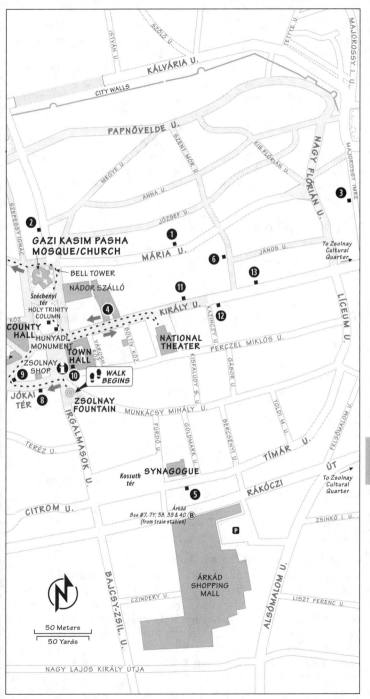

ISTVÁN U.
SZÓLÓ U.
KÁLVÁRIA U.
CITY WALLS
PAPNÖVELDE U.
TETTYE U.
MAJOROSSY I. U.
MEGYE U.
SZENT MÓR U.
KIS-FLÓRIÁN U.
NAGY FLÓRIÁN U.
MAJOROSSY IMRE U.
ANNA U.
JÓZSEF U.
❸
SZEPESSY IGNÁC U.
❷
MÁRIA U.
❶
JÁNOS U.
To Zsolnay Cultural Quarter
GAZI KASIM PASHA MOSQUE/CHURCH
❻
❽
LICEUM U.
BELL TOWER
Széchenyi tér
NÁDOR SZÁLLÓ
❹
KIRÁLY U.
❶❶
KAZINCZY U.
❶❷
HOLY TRINITY COLUMN
KÖZ
COUNTY HALL
HUNYADI MONUMENT
BOLTIV KÖZ
NATIONAL THEATER
PERCZEL MIKLÓS U.
KISFALUDY S. U.
GÁBOR U.
FELSŐMALOM U.
TOWN HALL
VÁROSH...
❶❶
❾
ZSOLNAY SHOP
❶❶
❿
WALK BEGINS
JÓKAI TÉR
❽
ZSOLNAY FOUNTAIN
MUNKÁCSY MIHÁLY U.
FÜRDŐ U.
GOLDMARK U.
BERCSÉNYI U.
TOLDI M. U.
TÍMÁR U.
PÉCS
TERÉZ U.
IRGALMASOK U.
Kossuth tér
SYNAGOGUE
RÁKÓCZI U.
ÚT
To Zsolnay Cultural Quarter
CITROM U.
❺
Árkád
Bus #7, 7Y, 38, 39 & 40 (from train station) Ⓑ
ZSINKÓ I. U.
Ⓟ
BAJCSY-ZSIL. U.
CZINDERY U.
ÁRKÁD SHOPPING MALL
ALSÓMALOM U.
LISZT FERENC U.

N

50 Meters
50 Yards

NAGY LAJOS KIRÁLY ÚTJA

hop on #7, #7Y, #38, #39, or #40, which go to the Árkád shopping center just south of the pedestrianized old center—a five-minute, gently uphill walk to the main square (head uphill on Irgalmasok utcája). For any bus, you can buy a ticket from the driver (see below).

GETTING AROUND PÉCS

In compact Pécs, you could easily get by without using local buses—but they may come in handy for getting into the town center from the train station, reaching the Zsolnay Cultural Quarter, or heading up into the hills. A single ticket is 350 Ft when purchased in advance at a kiosk, or 500 Ft when bought on the bus (www. tukebusz.hu). Once on the bus, validate your ticket by sticking it in the slot, then pulling the slot toward you.

HELPFUL HINTS

Shopping: The big **Árkád** shopping mall—with a supermarket, food court, and lots more—is just a block beyond the synagogue and Kossuth tér, at the southern edge of the Inner Town (shops open Mon-Sat 7:00-21:00, Sun 8:00-19:00, Bajcsy-Zsilinszky utca 11, www.arkadpecs.hu).

Tourist Train: A hokey tourist train does a 40-minute loop through the city center, and heads out to the Zsolnay Cultural Quarter (1,500 Ft, departs from in front of the mosque on Széchenyi tér, runs May-Sept, season extended in good weather, train cancelled in bad weather).

Local Guide: Knowledgeable **Brigitta Gombos** leads good tours of her hometown (20,000 Ft/3 hours, mobile +3670-505-3531, gombos.gerluc@gmail.com).

Sights in Pécs

I've listed these sights roughly in the order of a handy self-guided orientation walk through town.

ZSOLNAY FOUNTAIN TO THE CATHEDRAL

• *Begin in front of the little church next to the Town Hall, at the...*

▲Zsolnay Fountain (Zsolnay-kút)

This fountain, an icon of Pécs, was a gift from the beloved local Zsolnay (ZHOL-nay) family. The family invented an innovative material called pyrogranite that allowed colorful, delicate-seeming porcelain to be made frost-proof and hard as steel—ideal for external building decoration. The ox heads—modeled after an ancient drinking vessel found in Pécs—are specially glazed with another Zsolnay invention, eosin. Notice how the iridescent eosin glaze glimmers with a unique range of colors. (Since this glaze

compromises the pyrogranite, the
fountain must be covered in winter.)
Above the oxen heads are traditional
symbols of Pécs. One is the shield
with five tall churches, dating from
the Middle Ages. (Germans still call
the town Fünfkirchen.) This seal was
appropriated by the Zsolnay family as
a symbol of their porcelain. The other
seal is Pécs' coat of arms: a walled city
under vineyard-strewn hills.   .

This is the first of many gorgeous
Zsolnay decorations we'll see all over
town. But Pécs is just the beginning. In
the late 19th and early 20th centuries, Budapest and cities all over
Europe covered their finest buildings with decorations from this
city's Zsolnay Porcelain Manufacture. (For more, see the "Zsolnay
Porcelain" sidebar, later in this chapter.)

• *Across the pedestrian street from the fountain, and 20 yards uphill, is
the entrance to an enjoyable zone called...*

Jókai Tér

At the start of the street, notice the **game boards** on top of the
little pillars. When this street was renovated in 2000—with funky
benches and other playful elements—the designers wanted to
remind locals to take time to relax.

On the right (a few doors down, at #2), notice the **Zsolnay
porcelain shop.** Although the company was reduced to an
industrial supplier under the communists, today Zsolnay is proudly
reclaiming its role as a maker of fine art. Dipping into the shop,
you'll see that some of the decorative items use the same distinctive
eosin glaze as the fountain's oxen heads...and are priced accordingly
(Mon-Fri 10:00-18:00, Sat from 12:00, closed Sun).

Continuing to the corner, you enter a fine little square with
a kid-pleasing fountain. At the far end of the square, look left
down the street called **Ferencesek utcája.** When Pécs was a walled
market town, this street—and Király utca to the east, also now
pedestrianized—made up the main east-west road.

Now turn 180 degrees and look for the elephant high on the
corner. This used to be a grocery store, which likely imported exotic
Eastern goods, symbolized by the then-mysterious pachyderm.
Today it's a recommended pizzeria, still named for that landmark
elephant.

Walk up the street next to the elephant house, noticing the
former tram tracks preserved in the street. The yellow bricks
were pretty standard in 20th-century Hungary. Imagine how

unappealing this drag was when it was choked with tram and car traffic.

At the corner (on the left), look for the old-time **Saracen Pharmacy** (marked with the words *Sipöcz István* and an African prince over the door). Its interior—now a small museum—features gorgeous woodwork, little porcelain medicine pots, and a Zsolnay fountain (Tue-Sat 10:00-17:00, closed Sun-Mon).

• *Continuing up the street, you'll emerge into the main square...*

▲▲Széchenyi Tér

In the Middle Ages, Pécs was a major trading crossroads, located at the intersection of two Byzantine trade routes. Széchenyi tér was a natural meeting point and market zone. Today the market is gone, but this square remains the bustling city center, where both political demonstrations and the annual New Year's Eve festivities percolate.

Let's get oriented. Stand at the base of the square. Face the green-domed **Gazi Kasim Pasha Mosque** at the top of the square (described in detail later). On the right, the giant yellow-and-white building with the tower is the **Town Hall** (Városház, 1908), strategically located here since the olden days to watch over the

market activities. The Town Hall's tower plays laid-back organ ditties throughout the day. The **TI** is inside the Town Hall (on the lower level, attached to the recommended I Love Pécs Café). Across the square is the gorgeous, red-roofed **County Hall** (Megyháza, 1898), frosted like a wedding cake with sumptuous Zsolnay decorations. Because the building was originally a bank, it's adorned with beehives (one at the very peak of the building, and two more between the top-floor windows). Industrious bees, who carefully collect and store away their golden deposits, are a common symbol for banking.

Farther up the square on the right is the pink **Nádor Szálló**. In the early 20th century, this hotel was a popular gathering place for artists and intellectuals; today, the gutted interior is an industrial-mod gallery space where the arts faculty of the local university

PÉCS

showcases works by students and visiting artists. Peek inside to see what's on during your visit.

The square has two monuments. On the right is an equestrian statue of **János Hunyadi,** the war hero who fended off the Ottoman invaders at the 1456 Battle of Belgrade. Later those Ottomans took Pécs and built the mosque at the top of the square. But Hunyadi gets the last laugh: If you position yourself just right, Hunyadi's club smashes the crescent at the top of the mosque. (Try it.) This statue is a popular meeting point: Locals say, "I'll meet you under the horse's...tail." With perhaps unintended irony, Hunyadi—who died of the plague soon after that battle—shares the square with the **Holy Trinity Plague Column,** which townspeople built to give thanks to God after surviving a nasty bout of the plague in the late 17th century. Around its base are three saints known for protecting against disease or injury: Sebastian, who was killed by arrows (on left); Rocco, with his trusty dog and trademark leg wound (on right); and Anthony of Padua, who offers help recovering that which is lost—including health (behind the pillar).

• *We'll visit the mosque/church soon. But first, head down the street branching off to the right, next to the Town Hall.*

▲Walking Street: Király Utca

This vibrant Technicolor people zone—combined with Jókai tér and Ferencesek utcája, across the square—bisects the city center. Király utca ("Royal Street") is a delight to stroll. Walk its entire length, simply enjoying street musicians and people-watching, and noting its personality-filled architecture.

This street is lined with plenty of (largely interchangeable) **restaurants.** The lineup shifts constantly, but I've mentioned a few specifics under "Eating in Pécs," later. As you stroll, peruse the posted menus and scope out a place for a meal later.

About a block down (on the left, at #5), keep an eye out for the gorgeous, horseshoe-shaped **Hotel Palatinus;** step into its lobby for a taste of genteel (if faded) Secession architecture. The hotel's second wing is filled with a hoity-toity wine bar (Le Gourmet) in a nicely atmospheric, vintage setting. (One of Hungary's top wine-growing regions, Villány, is about 40 minutes' drive south of Pécs—and explained later in this chapter.) While the prices in this wine bar are high, it's a nice chance to peruse vintages produced by local wineries (as well as from other parts of Hungary).

PÉCS

Soon you'll reach the square in front of the **National Theater,** built (along with most of the other houses on this square) for the Hungarian millennial celebrations of 1896 (see page 27). The decorations on the theater—including the stone-like statues—are all made of Zsolnay pyrogranite. This is a popular venue in this city of culture, and hosts the local philharmonic (their season runs

Sept-May). Duck into the box office here (to the right of the big building) any time of year to see what's on, either here or elsewhere in town.

Farther along, you'll find a good ice-cream parlor (at #15, on the left); a very cool ruin pub (the recommended **Cooltour**—the name is a wordplay on *kultur* or "culture"—with an inviting garden out back; at #26, on the right); and, finally, a contemporary Hungarian painting gallery (at #31, on the left). If you kept following this street, eventually you'd leave the historical center, enter a more residential zone, and wind up at the Zsolnay Cultural Quarter.

While this part of Pécs appears wealthy and manicured, the region is struggling. In the early 1950s, Pécs had only about 50,000 residents. Coal and uranium mines kick-started the economy, causing the population to more than triple over the last 50 years. However, both mines are now closed, and while Pécs' university and business center continue to thrive, outlying communities are grappling with 30 percent unemployment. Tourism helps keep things afloat.

• *Head back to Széchenyi tér to visit the...*

▲▲Gazi Kasim Pasha Mosque
(Gázi Kászim Pasa Dzsámija)/Inner Town Parish Church

It's rare to find such a well-preserved Ottoman structure in Hungary. The Ottomans—who began their 150-year stay in Pécs in 1543—lived here in the Inner Town, while the dwindling Hungarian population moved to the outskirts. The Ottomans tore down the church that stood on this spot and used the stones to build the structure you see today. After the Ottomans were forced out, the Catholic Church

reclaimed this building and turned it into a church—which is why it's still intact today. Despite renovations over the years, it remains an offbeat hybrid of the Islamic and Christian faiths.

Cost and Hours: 1,800 Ft, Mon-Sat 9:00-17:00, Sun from 13:00.

Visiting the Mosque/Church: From the **outside,** notice the crescent moon of Islam capping the dome—but it's topped by the victorious Christian cross. The only decorations on the austere facade are the striped ogee arches over the windows. Before entering, notice the fig trees; locals are proud that their mild climate can support these heat-seekers.

Enter the modern ticket office on the lower level. From here, you'll walk through the crypt, which includes an exhibit with

interactive touchscreens that explain the three phases of this building's tumultuous history: church, mosque, church.

Follow *church* signs and head upstairs into the **interior.** Circle around to the main part of the church and look around. Are you in a church, or a mosque... or both? The striped arches over

the windows and the altar area are even more apparent inside. Notice the colorful Islamic-style stalactite decorations at the tops of the corners. The painting on the underside of the dome seems to combine Christian figures with the geometric designs of Islam. To the right of the main altar is a verse from the Quran translated into Hungarian and used for Christian worship (a reminder that Islam and Christianity are founded on many of the same principles).

Turning 180 degrees, scan the back wall for gray patches with faint Arabic script peeking through—most were whitewashed over

during the church-ification. In the middle of the wall, between the two doors, is a large **prayer niche** (mihrab). This niche, which faces Mecca (southeast from here), indicated to Muslim worshippers the direction they had to face to pray. The holy water basin in the niche and the crucifix suspended above it make it clear who's in charge now.

Mentally erase these and other Christian elements, and imagine worshipping here during the Ottoman period. There were no pews, and carpets covered the floor. Worshippers—men in front, women in back—stood and knelt as they prayed toward the mihrab. A step-stair pulpit, called a *mimber,* likely stood off to one side of the mihrab.

When the Christians reclaimed this building, they flipped it around, creating an entrance near the mihrab, and an altar at the former entrance. Much later, in 1940, they added the giant **apse** (semicircular area behind the altar, with the organ up top). Explore this area, with its striking 1930s-style murals. The modern paintings depict Bible scenes and events in Hungary's Christian history. And the giant organ is an Angster (made by a local Hungarian organ-maker). Next to the two side doors, look for small, rough-stone basins. These once stood outside the building, where the Ottoman worshippers performed their ablution, or ritual washing before prayer. For another view down on this area, follow *choir* signs upstairs to the choir loft.

To exit, go back down into the crypt, then head out the way you came in. Once outside, circle around the right side of the building to find the latest addition to this constantly evolving structure: the modern **bell tower** and a concrete footprint that recalls the original church that preceded the mosque. The statue is St. Bartholomew, the patron of this church. Depicted (as he always is) with his skin peeling away, he steps on a serpent, representing victory over evil (Islam?). Every day at 12:00 and 19:00, the bell tower mechanically rises 40 feet into the air to play a tune. Viewing the church from back here, you can also appreciate how jarringly ugly the 1940 concrete addition is.

• *While interesting, this is not Pécs' main church. To see that (and a lot more), go down the street at the upper-left corner of the square: From the bell tower, walk with the church/mosque on your left, and continue straight ahead along Janus Pannonius Utca. Passing a few grates heavy with padlocks (put there by lovers to commemorate their undying passion), continue along the street until you emerge into the little square. In the pretty, white, gray-roofed building on the left, you'll find Pécs' best art museum.*

▲▲Csontváry Museum (Csontváry Múzeum)

This small but delightful collection showcases the works of beloved Hungarian painter Tivadar Csontváry Kosztka. Csontváry produced only 100 paintings and 20 drawings, and about half are collected here. For a crash course on this enigmatic painter, read the sidebar before visiting; the paintings are described in English.

Cost and Hours: 1,500 Ft, Tue-Sun 10:00-18:00, closed Mon, Janus Pannonius utca 11, mobile +3630-313-8442.

Visiting the Museum: The museum is divided into five rooms. In Room 1 are Csontváry's art-school sketches, which capture people at unguarded moments and show the work of a budding

Tivadar Csontváry Kosztka (1853-1919)

Adored by Hungarians, but virtually unknown outside his homeland, the artist Tivadar Csontváry Kosztka had a life as fascinating as his paintings. Because of the time in which he lived and his struggles with mental illness, Csontváry (CHONT-vah-ree) is often compared to Van Gogh. While that's a stretch,

viewing Csontváry's works gives you a glimpse into the Hungarian psyche, and into his own fractured mind.

Tivadar Kosztka was born to an upper-class family, seemingly bound for a humdrum life. He didn't pick up a paintbrush until his 27th year. Idly sketching sleeping oxen while recovering from an illness, he had a revelation (or, perhaps, a psychotic episode): A voice told him that he was destined to become "the world's greatest *plein air* painter."

He adopted the pseudonym "Csontváry" and became driven by an almost pathological compulsion to prepare for his destiny. He worked as a pharmacist to finance his quest, and by age 41, he had saved enough to attend art school (in Munich and Paris). Seeking ideal subjects for his outdoor style, he traveled extensively in southeastern Europe and the Middle East: Italy, Croatia, Bosnia, Greece, Egypt, Lebanon, Jerusalem, and the Tatra Mountains. By the time he began painting in earnest, he had only six productive years (1903-1909).

Csontváry's rough, mostly self-taught style reveals his untrained origins, but contains a depth that exceeded his technical skill. While classified as a Post-Impressionist, Csontváry forged a style all his own. Like his contemporary Marc Chagall, he worked in almost childlike bright colors with big, bold themes. His most common subjects were the destinations to which he traveled.

After exhibitions in 1909 and 1910 failed to win him the praise he so desperately sought, he became consumed by schizophrenia and created only bizarre, surrealistic works. He died in obscurity in 1919. After Csontváry's death, his family nearly sold his works to wagon-makers, who wanted the valuable canvas (not the paintings themselves). Fortunately, a Budapest art collector bought them instead.

Csontváry remained largely unappreciated until the 1960s, when art lovers began to take notice. But one discerning eye for talent knew greatness when he saw it: Pablo Picasso reportedly discovered Csontváry's canvases at a 1949 exhibition and proceeded to lock himself in the room with them for an hour. Finally emerging, he told his friend Marc Chagall that Chagall could never produce a work half as good as Csontváry's.

genius. Rooms 2, 3, and 4 are mostly dedicated to Csontváry's many travel canvases. Room 2 has "postcards" from his trips to Sicily (Castellammare, Taormina) and Bosnia-Herzegovina (Mostar, Jajce), but the best canvas in here is from Hungary: *Storm over the Great Hortobágy* is a dynamic snapshot of life on the Great Hungarian Plain, where cowherds tend longhorn cattle. A storm brews on the horizon as a horseman races across the bridge. Notice the balance between movement and stillness, and between the yellow sky and the purple clouds. Room 3 features much larger canvases of Baalbek, the High Tatras (where Csontváry first had the epiphany that drove him to paint—and to madness), and a historical scene of Mary's well in Nazareth. In Room 4 is Csontváry's most acclaimed work, *Solitary Cedar:* a windblown tree on a ridge above the sea. The tree seems boldly independent even as it longs for companionship. Also in this room are scenes from Athens, Jerusalem's Wailing Wall, and other images from the Holy Land. The last room (5) displays Csontváry's final major painting, *Riders on the Seashore* (1909). This haunting valedictory canvas, with an equestrian party pausing by an eerily deep-blue cove, hints at the troubled depths of Csontváry's own psyche. Other works in this room date from Csontváry's final days, when—in his worsening mental state—he sketched large-scale, absurdist scenes.

• *Leaving the museum, cross the street and continue left down the tree-lined, pedestrian-only path. Soon you'll see a beautiful yellow kiosk (on the right)—an inviting place for a coffee break. A few steps beyond that, look for the modern entrance to the...*

▲Cella Septichora Visitor Center (Roman Crypts)

This unique, modern, well-presented museum allows visitors to take a peek inside some remarkably preserved Roman crypts. (Note: If you skip this museum, sneak a free look at some of the ruins through the glass behind the yellow kiosk.)

Cost and Hours: 1,900 Ft, Tue-Sun 10:00-18:00, Nov-March until 17:00, closed Mon year-round, Dóm tér, tel. 72/224-755, www.pecsorokseg. hu.

Background: There was a Roman settlement in today's Pécs from the year AD 30, and by the second century it was a provincial capital called Sopinae. During that time, this part of town was a vast cemetery, which included the graves of early Christian martyrs. Later, after Christianity became the state religion in the early fourth century, these tombs

PÉCS

attracted pilgrims from afar. Wealthy Christian families were now free to build a double-decker structure to hold the remains of their relatives: a sealed crypt below ground (painted with Bible scenes and floral motifs), with a chapel directly above for remembering and praying for the dead. About a century later, Rome fell. Nomadic invaders lived in the chapels and raided the crypts (then carefully covered them again). Today the remains of some of these crypt-chapels have been discovered, excavated, and opened to visitors.

Visiting the Crypts: Buy your ticket and head into the first area. Follow a passage until you emerge into the big, open space under the glass roof—the foundation of a **giant chapel with seven apses.** (The exhibit is named for this—Cella Septichora means "seven-apsed chapel.") Experts believe that the crypt of a different martyr would have been placed in each apse, and pilgrims would come here to worship. However, the structure was never finished.

From here, you'll climb up and down through the subterranean exhibit to the highlights. Unlike Rome's famous catacombs, these crypts were not originally connected underground; modern archaeologists built the tunnels you'll pass through to allow visitors easier access to all the tombs.

Follow signs down some long passageways to reach the **Wine Pitcher Burial Chamber.** Peer through the window to see the

paintings that decorate the crypt. Its nickname comes from the wine jug and glass painted in the niche above the body. Romans used wine to toast to the memory of the departed (the Roman version of "pour one out for the homies who ain't here"). Climb up the stairs to what was ground level, where you can view the foundation of the chapel and look down into the crypt. From here, you'll see other paintings (representing paradise), as well as the drain at the bottom of the sarcophagus. The Romans, ever the clever engineers,

provided drainage so that accumulating groundwater would not defile the body.

Retrace your steps back up the long hallway, then follow signs to the Peter and Paul Burial Chamber. Along the way, you'll pass through an area with remnants of the medieval wall and several **smaller crypts.** Notice that these didn't have large chapels up top; rather, worshippers would kneel and look inside a small decorative chapel. In one, a hole in the floor of the chapel indicates where tomb raiders broke in to search for valuables.

Just before Peter and Paul, watch for the glass gangplank that lets you walk out over the **Octagonal Burial Chamber,** which—like the seven-apsed chapel—was likely designed to be a pilgrim church. After this, you'll pass another small crypt that's more intact, showing the barrel vaulting that once covered all of these.

Take the spiral stairs all the way down to the bottom to enter the **Peter and Paul Burial Chamber.** Standing under the painted tomb, you'll see faded Sts. Peter and Paul flanking the Christogram (an ancient Christian symbol). The side walls are painted with biblical scenes, while the ceiling features another Christogram, four portraits (possibly the Four Evangelists), and more nature motifs—plants and birds. (An artist's rendering of the original version is nearby.) Notice the little window above the body. Experts believe that a ribbon tied to the sarcophagus led through this window up into the chapel, so the faithful could have a tangible connection to the dead. A video screen (English subtitles) tells the whole story. Finally, retrace your steps through the exhibit to exit. Before you go, you can ask about...

Related Sights Nearby: The same organization manages two other nearby excavations—both skippable unless you're an archaeology nut. The early-Christian **mausoleum,** displayed in the lower park in front of the bishop statue described next, is covered by the main Cella Septichora ticket. The **"Medieval University"**—the excavation of a 14th-century building behind the cathedral, which may or may not have been an early home to the city's historic university—costs 1,000 Ft (combo-ticket also available).

• *Exiting the exhibit, turn right and continue down Janus Pannonius utca, which deposits you at...*

István Tér and Dóm Tér

These two squares—the lower István Square, which belonged to the people, and the upper Cathedral Square, which was the bishop's—used to be separated by a wall and moat. But later, the enlightened **Bishop Szepesy** turned them into one big park. In the statue that dominates the square, the bishop is stepping down from the pulpit clutching a Bible—a reminder that he's believed to have been the first priest to use Hungarian.

Walk up the stairs and into Cathedral Square. The brown, Neo-Renaissance building on the left is the **Bishop's Palace**—recently restored and opened to the public. It's possible to tour the interior, including the so-called "Texas passage" that leads to a hidden garden. But it's pricey, and you can only visit the facility on a guided tour (tours depart 3/day, get details at cathedral ticket office).

At the corner of the Bishop's Palace that faces the park, notice the engaging statue of **Franz Liszt** by popular 20th-century sculptor Imre Varga. Liszt was a friend of the bishop, and Liszt's visit here in 1846 is still the stuff of legend.

• *Now turn your attention to the massive, four-towered...*

▲▲Cathedral

With an imposing exterior and an elaborately decorated interior, Pécs' cathedral is one of Hungary's finest churches. St. István established a bishopric in Pécs in the year 1009, and this church building grew in fits and starts from then on. By the 14th century, it had roughly the same floor plan as today, and gradually morphed with the styles of the day: Romanesque, Gothic, Renaissance. The Ottomans preserved the

building, using it first as a mosque and later as a stable, a grain store, and a library. Later, when it became the cathedral again, it got a Baroque makeover. Finally, in the 1880s, a bishop (likely hoping to be remembered as a visionary) grew tired of the architectural hodgepodge, gutted the place, and turned it into the Neo-Romanesque fortress of God you see today. The 12 apostles stand along the roofline, and the four distinctive corner towers anchor and fortify the massive structure. Meanwhile, the interior is a riot of finely executed and pristinely preserved golden decorations.

Cost and Hours: 1,800 Ft, Mon-Sat 9:00-17:00, Sun from 11:30, also open May-Sept Fri-Sat 19:30-22:00, can close for weddings Sat afternoons—especially in summer, tel. 72/513-057, https://pecsiegyhazmegye.hu/turisztika.

Visiting the Cathedral: Outside, study the symbolic **bronze gate** from 2000. The vines, grapes, and branches are all connected, symbolizing our connection to God. If you look closely, you'll find animals representing good (birds) and evil (snake, scorpion, frog). On the left, St. István gives Pécs to the first bishop; on the right, Jesus offers his hand to St. Peter.

PÉCS

Now circle around the left side of the cathedral to find the entrance and ticket office. **Inside,** you're struck by the rich Neo-Romanesque, 19th-century decor. It's clear that the renovating bishop did not subscribe to the "less is more" school of church decoration. Like the Matthias Church in Budapest—renovated at about the same time—every square inch is covered by a thick and colorful layer of paint.

Along the upper walls of the **nave** are paintings depicting the lives of the church's patrons, Sts. Peter and Paul. Above the arches are biblical scenes. The coffered ceiling of the nave depicts the 12 apostles and (near the organ) John the Baptist.

The **altar,** with its highly decorated canopy, is a replica of the 13th-century original. The mosaic on the apse dome (behind the altar, not entirely visible from here) features Jesus flanked by Peter and Paul (on the right) and, on the left, Mary and István (the patron saint of Hungary). For a better look, walk up the stairs to the right of the altar. Also in this area, your ticket lets you climb 133 steps to the top of one of the cathedral's four **towers,** with sweeping views over Pécs.

Back in the main church, stairs flanking the altar lead down to the **crypt.** This 11th-century forest of columns (redecorated like the rest of the church) is part of the original church building on this site. The bust at the front depicts the bishop who decided to renovate the church.

Related Sights Nearby: In addition to the Bishop's Palace (described earlier), the cathedral office runs two more skippable sights nearby: a **lapidarium** (collection of old stone sculptures and fragments) and a **treasury.** Details and tickets are at the cathedral ticket office.

• From in front of the cathedral, if you want to take a look at part of the old *city wall,* go down the stairs and turn right at the wide path, which will take you to a barbican (round tower) that helped fortify the walls. (For more on these walls, see "Elsewhere in Pécs," later in this chapter.) If you decide to visit the wall, on your way there—but just before the barbican and busy street—watch on the left for the gateway at #5 (marked Eoz!n Grillterasz Kultúrpark), which leads to a pleasant series of sleepy parks along the inside of the town wall, some modest views of the four cathedral steeples, and a rustic terrace serving drinks and grilled foods with views over the suburbs.

Otherwise, after you exit the cathedral, walk about halfway down

*the square, turn left before the steps, pass through the archway, walk over
the glassed-in Roman ruins, and head straight along...*

KÁPTALAN UTCA: "MUSEUM ROW"

A cluster of museums line tranquil Káptalan utca ("Chapterhouse
Street," where priests once lived). A few of the smaller museums are
skippable, but the Zsolnay and Vasarely museums are worthwhile
(www.jpm.hu). Nearby are museums that showcase the work of yet
two more local artists—Ferenc Martyn and Endre Nemes—and
the Modern Hungarian Art Museum.

▲Viktor Vasarely Museum (Vasarely Múzeum)

You might not know Viktor Vasarely (1908-1997), but you know
his work. Think optical illusions, and the dizzying Op Art that

inspired the psychedelic
1960s. Here in his
hometown, you can see
a museum of Vasarely's
eye-popping creations.
Inspired by nature,
Vasarely discovered that
the repetition and slight
variation of lines and
forms can play with the
viewer's brain to create
illusions of depth and movement. In other words, black-and-white
lines undulating across a canvas are trippy, baby. It's easy to get lost
in Vasarely's mind-bending designs—which make you go cross-
eyed before you stumble up the stairs to see him add more color to
the mix. You'll also see works by Vasarely's son, Jean-Pierre Yvaral
(1934-2002), who took his dad's designs and added his own spin.

Cost: 1,500 Ft, Tue-Sun 10:00-18:00, closed Mon, Káptalan
utca 3, mobile +3630-539-8069.

▲Zsolnay Porcelain Museum (Zsolnay Múzeum)

This museum, situated in the
former mansion of the porcelain-
making Zsolnay family, is as
much a shrine to the family as
a showcase of their work. (For
more on the family and their legacy, see the "Zsolnay Porcelain"
sidebar.) This exhibit provides
a concise, satisfying look at the
Zsolnay family and their gorgeous creations, and is well worth

Zsolnay Porcelain

Thanks to the pioneering Zsolnay (ZHOL-nay) family of Pécs, buildings all over Hungary are slathered with gorgeously colorful porcelain.

Miklós Zsolnay (1800-1880) opened a porcelain factory in Pécs in 1853. His innovative son, Vilmos Zsolnay (1828-1900), experimented with glazes and additives, and revolutionized the use of porcelain in building materials. He invented pyrogranite—a weatherproof ceramic as resilient as steel, but which could be delicately sculpted and vividly painted. Zsolnay pyrogranite made a splash at Vienna's 1873 World Exhibition, winning an avalanche of orders from all over Europe. The twists and curves that Zsolnay porcelain artists

could achieve were a perfect fit for the Art Nouveau style of the day.

In 1893, Vilmos Zsolnay unveiled his latest innovation: eosin, a shimmering, almost metallic iridescent glaze that has the effect of light striking the glistening surface of a soap bubble. This eosin technique is exemplified by Pécs' Zsolnay Fountain (described under "Sights in Pécs," earlier).

Boom time for the Zsolnays coincided with the 1896 millennial celebrations in Budapest. The city's architects, who had ample resources and imagination, were striving to create a unique Hungarian national style, and many adopted colorful pyrogranite tiles and decorations. In Budapest, the Great Market Hall, Matthias Church and National Archives on Castle Hill, and Ödön Lechner's Postal Savings Bank and Museum of Applied Arts are all roofed with Zsolnay pyrogranite tiles. Zsolnay decorative elements also adorn the Hungarian Parliament and Gellért Baths. To this day, Zsolnay tiles are a hallmark of Hungarian architecture.

All of that porcelain generated a lot of work for the Pécs factory. By the time World War I broke out, the Zsolnay family business was the Austro-Hungarian Empire's biggest company. But the stripped-down modern styles that emerged in the 20th century had little use for the fanciful Zsolnay decorations. The factory was nationalized by the communists, the Zsolnay name was abandoned, and quality plummeted.

Since the 1990s, private investors have made great strides toward rehabilitating the Zsolnay name. All over Hungary, you'll see shops selling beautiful, innovative Zsolnay tableware, and the company even makes (less elegant) dishes for Ikea.

PÉCS

a visit for those who lack the time or interest to visit the Zsolnay Cultural Quarter, described later.

Cost: 1,500 Ft, Tue-Sun 10:00-18:00, closed Mon, Káptalan utca 4, tel. 72/514-045.

Visiting the Museum: The collection is divided into two parts: architectural elements and decorative ware. Each room is well-described in English. In the architectural elements section (on the ground floor), you'll see impressively detailed and colorful decorations for the many buildings the Zsolnays were involved in renovating (including Budapest's Matthias Church and Parliament). You'll also see a playful duck fountain, with its colorful eosin glaze, and some beautiful pieces of the destroyed István Stove that once warmed Budapest's Royal Palace. Upstairs, the "memorial room" is furnished as it would have been during the Zsolnays' day. The decorative-ware collection displays vases, sculptures, and other objects that demonstrate the evolution of porcelain style. Notice how trends came and went over time.

• *From Káptalan utca, you're just a block above the main square and our starting point. If you have more time, consider some of the following sights.*

ELSEWHERE IN PÉCS
City Walls

Several segments of the city walls around the northern part of Pécs are still standing; a path leads around the outside of the wall that still hems in the top of town. Built after the Tatar invasions of the 13th century, and beefed up in the 15th century, the walls were no match for the Ottoman invaders who took the town in 1543. Still standing just west of the cathedral area is the

round, stout barbican defensive gate, which you can actually climb.

▲Synagogue (Zsinagóga)

Just south of the old center, overlooking the modern, beautifully renovated Kossuth tér, is Pécs' colorful synagogue. Dating from the 1860s but recently restored, this building is a powerful reminder of Pécs' Jewish heritage. The city had a thriving population of 4,000 Jews; only a few hundred survived the Holocaust.

Cost and Hours: 600 Ft, Sun-Fri 10:00-12:00 & 13:00-17:00, Nov-March 10:30-12:30, closed Sat year-round, Kossuth tér, tel. 72/315-881, synagoguepecs.wordpress.com.

PÉCS

Visiting the Synagogue:
The building feels like a humbler
little sibling to Budapest's Great
Synagogue, with wood-carved
pews and a double-decker arcade
(where women worshipped,
while the men gathered on the
main floor). Its finest feature is
the delicate ceiling decoration. The congregation here was Neolog
(similar to today's "reformed"); the organ at the front of the building
is a clear sign that this was not an Orthodox house of worship.

Like other Hungarian synagogues of this era, this building
seems to be trying hard to feel like a church—at a time when local
Jews were eager to feel integrated into the larger community. You
can head upstairs, into the galleries (enter from outside—it's the
door to the left of the main entrance) to find an exhibit about the
history of local Jews, with good English descriptions and several
actual artifacts (scrolls, postcards, personal effects) that characterize
Pécs' Jewish community.

Mecsek Hills

Pécs is picturesquely nestled in the Mecsek (MEH-chek) Hills, a
popular place to go for a hike. To get an aerial view of Pécs, ride
bus #35 or #35Y about 30 minutes up to the Misinatető stop, near
the TV tower that overlooks the city (catch this bus at the train
station, or at the northern entrance to the city center). Ascend the
580-foot-tall TV tower for views over the town and surrounding
region (1,100 Ft, daily 9:00-21:00, www.tvtoronypecs.hu).

ZSOLNAY CULTURAL QUARTER
(ZSOLNAY KULTURÁLIS NEGYED)

The first and last name in Pécs industry, the Zsolnay porcelain-
making family operated their major factory on the eastern edge of
town. Tucked in the middle of the sprawling brick industrial center
were some fine villas and houses and a leafy park. Now this facility has been thoroughly restored and converted into a community
cultural center with indoor and outdoor events venues, cafés, children's play zones, and—of course—a collection of small museums
celebrating the Zsolnay clan and their works. While it's out on the
edge of things—a dull 20-minute walk or quick bus or taxi ride
from downtown—the center is worth the trip if you've exhausted
your in-town sightseeing interests and are curious to see another
side of Pécs. And those taken with Zsolnay tiles will enjoy a pilgrimage to where they were created. (For more on the family and
their legacy, see the "Zsolnay Porcelain" sidebar, earlier.)

Cost: It's free to enter the complex and explore the grounds.

Each museum has its own admission price (listed later). It's worth buying all of your tickets at one ticket desk, as the more sights you visit, the bigger discount you get.

Hours: While the grounds are open daily 6:00-24:00, the individual sights are open substantially shorter hours: Tue-Sun 10:00-18:00, Nov-March until 17:00, most closed Mon year-round. A few exceptions are noted in the individual listings.

Information: Tel. 72/500-350, www.zsn.hu.

Getting There: It's due east of the town center. You can **walk** there in about 20 minutes: Follow Király utca (the main walking street) to its end, then continue straight (as the road becomes Felsővámház utca) through residential neighborhoods about 10 minutes farther to the complex. Just head for the many tall smokestacks.

Multiple **buses** run to the complex. From in front of Árkád shopping center, catch bus #2, #2A, #4, #13, #14, #15, #20, or #21, and get off at the Zsolnay Negyed stop, at the lower entrance to the complex. Or, from the train station, take bus #4 or #4Y to Zsolnay Negyed, or bus #40 to Bóbita Bábszínház, at the upper part of the complex.

You could also hop on the **tourist train** from Széchenyi tér, but it's pricey (see "Helpful Hints," earlier). A **taxi** costs about 1,500 Ft.

Orientation: There are two main gates to the complex: the lower gate (just up from Zsolnay Vilmos út) and the upper Ledina Gate (near the Puppet Theater, on Felsővámház utca). Once inside, you'll find a lower complex of buildings surrounding a small

park with a short, colorful chimney. The modern building just uphill houses the **Visitors Center** (with ticket office, open daily 9:00-18:00, Nov-March until 17:00), a planetarium, a kids' play zone with hands-on scientific exhibits, and the Pécsi Galéria (contemporary art installations). At the lower end of the complex is the E78 Pyrogranite Courtyard (a modern indoor theater and outdoor live music venue, plus a tall smokestack with colorful Zsolnay tiles embedded in the base).

Directly opposite the visitors center is the **Gyugyi Collection,** and the **1861 Gloves Manufacture** is also nearby. More sights cluster up the small hill, in a long, sprawling mansion—here you'll find (in the right half of the building) the **Pink Zsolnay Exhibition** and the **Zsolnay Live Manufactory,** and (in the left half) the **Zsolnay Family and Factory History Exhibition.** The building also contains various eateries and, tucked back in a little courtyard (follow the signs), the **American Corner**—a service of the US Embassy that strives to educate Hungarians about American culture with an English lending library, special events on American holidays, English conversation clubs, and other resources.

Finally, up a few more steps along the top of the hill is the upper gate, another ticket office, and the **"street of shops"**—basically a row of candy, chocolate, wine, and handicraft shops (generally open Tue-Sun 10:00-12:30 & 13:00-18:00, closed Mon). Leaving the gate by the ticket office, you'll turn right on Felsővámház utca and walk 200 yards to find the long staircase up to the **Zsolnay Mausoleum.** If you turn left on Felsővámház utca, you'll find the **Bóbita Puppet Theater** (Bóbita Bábszínház), which offers periodic performances for kids.

And, of course, the grounds are studded with pretty Zsolnay decorations—fountains, pillars, and statues. Posted maps and directional signs help you find your way.

Planning Your Time: While it sounds like a lot—and Zsolnay enthusiasts could spend hours here—for the casual visitor, it's enough to simply stroll the colorful grounds; the only sights I'd pay to enter are the Gyugyi Collection (if you didn't get your fill at the Zsolnay Museum downtown), the mausoleum, and possibly the Live Manufactory. Below are brief descriptions of each sight to help you decide.

▲Gyugyi Collection (Gyugyi-gyűjtemény)

Dr. László Gyugyi fled Hungary after the 1956 Uprising and set-tled in the US, where he gradually amassed a breathtaking col-lection of sumptuous decorative Zsolnay objects. Now he has do-nated them to their hometown of Pécs, where they are displayed at the heart of the complex. Also called "The Golden Age of Zsolnay," the exhibit includes a remarkable collection of His-toricist and Art Nouveau vases, platters, and other items, all beautifully displayed and well-

described in English on two floors. This is a better collection of decorative works than the Zsolnay Museum downtown—though unless you're a connoisseur, it may feel like a rerun, and it lacks the Zsolnay Museum's impressive collection of architectural features.

Cost and Hours: 1,600 Ft, see hours earlier—but also open Mon in April-Oct.

1861 Gloves Manufacture (1861 Kesztyűmanufaktúra)

This exhibit lets you watch artisans making Hamerli gloves (a well-respected brand that originated in Pécs) the way they have for more than 150 years.

Cost and Hours: 1,500 Ft, daily 9:00-16:00.

Pink Zsolnay Exhibition (Rózsaszín Zsolnay Kiállítás)

Early on, the Zsolnay factory focused on producing everyday items in the then-in-vogue hue of pink. This modest collection shows off more pink porcelain in one place than you'll see anywhere else. Unlike the finely detailed showpieces of the Gyugyi Collection, these are practical, unglamorous objects that were handmade, making them a bit rougher and with subtle imperfections. If it's fancy vases and plates you're hoping to see, skip it.

Cost and Hours: 1,300 Ft, see hours earlier—but also open Mon in April-Oct.

Zsolnay Live Manufactory (Látványmanufaktúra)

This lets you peer through windows at Zsolnay potters hard at work. Posted English information briefly outlines the manufacture process. You'll see two areas: The busy workshop where pieces are molded before being fired, and a more sedate room where artisans hand-paint the final decorations.

Cost and Hours: 1,000 Ft, see hours earlier, busiest Mon-Sat 10:00-16:00, at other times you won't see much action.

Zsolnay Family and Factory History Exhibition (Család-és Gyártörténeti Kiállítás)

Displayed on two floors (factory downstairs, family upstairs), this exhibit traces—with dry English descriptions—the history of this complex and the people who built it. The museum doesn't add much to your visit here, and the few pieces on display are less striking than those in the Gyugyi Collection or the Zsolnay Museum downtown. For me, the offbeat highlight was the Zsolnay porcelain bust of Lenin dating from 1960—after the factory was nationalized by the communists. There's also a fine old tiled cigar room on the ground floor.

Cost and Hours: 1,400 Ft, see hours earlier.

PÉCS

▲Zsolnay Mausoleum (Zsolnay Mauzóleum)

A short walk from the rest of the complex, this hilltop perch is the final resting place of Vilmos Zsolnay, who founded the factory

and enjoyed sitting on this hill to survey the family business. After his death in 1900, Vilmos' son Miklós commissioned this fine mausoleum—entirely decorated in Zsolnay tiles, of course (Miklós and his mother Terézia are also buried here). Everything is now carefully restored and gleaming. From the road, you'll climb a long ramp lined with 42 resting lions to reach the mausoleum itself. The entry doors (with eosin-glazed plaques depicting the 12 apostles) lead into a structure beautiful in its simplicity: a cylinder turned on end. Inside are an eosin altar and chandelier above an opening in the floor where you can peer down at Vilmos' monumental tomb. Back outside, you can circle around back to find stairs down for a better look (through a grate).

Cost and Hours: 1,300 Ft, see hours earlier, possibly closed in bad weather.

NEAR PÉCS: THE VILLÁNY WINE REGION

The golden hillsides south of Pécs, draped with cornfields and vineyards, produce some of Hungary's best-regarded wines. Most of the production is centered near the village called Villány (VEE-layn), which sits just below the neatly cone-shaped Mount Szársomlyó. The area produces a variety of reds, whites, and rosés, using a range of grapes: merlot, cabernet sauvignon, pinot noir, Riesling, and *kékfrankos* ("blue Frankish"). For more on Hungarian wines, see the "Eating" section of the Practicalities chapter.

Drivers find Villány and the surrounding countryside easy to visit from Pécs—it's just a 40-minute drive south. (But remember that Hungary has a zero blood-alcohol limit, so you're not supposed to drive even if you've had just a few tastes. Bring a designated driver.) You can also take a train from Pécs to Villány, then explore on foot from there (every 2 hours, 45 minutes).

In Villány and surrounding villages, cute little wine cellars line the main road, with picnic tables out front trying to lure in passersby for a taste. (*Pince* means "wine cellar.") This is a touristy scene, where the emphasis is not on top-quality wine but on the fun, folksy experience. Many of these places are endearingly humble, family-run affairs; they may offer you a few small tastes, hoping you'll buy a bottle, or give you a sample of their wine jelly—a tasty (and lightly alcoholic) addition to your cheese tray.

If you're more serious about wine, seek out one of the larger, more prestigious producers (Bock is perhaps the best-regarded, but also look for Gere, Sauska, Vylyan, Wunderlich, and Tiffán); some of these have tasting rooms in town, while others have big factories on the outskirts of town. For more information on Villány wines and wineries, see www.villanyiborvidek.hu.

The road leading from Villány west to Siklós is a popular wine road, which runs along the base of Mount Szársomlyó. You'll enjoy views of vines scampering up the hills and pass a few vineyards where you can pull over for a taste.

Just past Siklós, where the wine road ends, is the larger town of **Harkány**—famous for its huge outdoor thermal spa (www.harkanyfurdo.hu). From here, highway 58 zips right back up to Pécs.

Sleeping in Pécs

Most of Pécs' city-center accommodations are affordable pensions with simple but sleepable rooms. Lower your expectations here; the city simply doesn't have any truly high-end accommodations. In this college town, nighttime noise can be an issue, especially on weekends—ask for a quiet room. Most hotels quote their rates in euros but prefer to be paid in forints.

$$ Adele Boutique Hotel, a long block off the top of the main square, has 24 rooms and all the amenities. It's the nicest hotel in this otherwise quite lowbrow town. As the standard rooms are more basic, it's worth paying a little extra for the fine "superior" rooms (air-con, elevator, fitness room, sauna, Mária utca 15, tel. 72/510-226, www.adelehotel.hu, info@adelehotel.hu).

$ Hotel Arkadia is a minimalist, concrete place with 32 tight, modern rooms, conveniently located just a few steps above the mosque/church on the main square (air-con, elevator, pay parking on-site, Hunyadi út 1, tel. 72/512-550, www.hotelarkadiapecs.hu, info@hotelarkadiapecs.hu).

$ Hotel König is a practical choice a bit farther out (about an eight-minute walk to the main square, but still within the historical center). Simple and tidy, it has 17 rooms on a quiet back street (air-con, pay parking on-site, Dr. Majorossy Imre utca 3, tel. 72/510-850, www.konighotel.com, info@konighotel.com).

$ Hotel Palatinus epitomizes "faded elegance," with 94 rooms filling a grand old facade right on the main walking street. The showpiece 1915 building—and its lobby and breakfast room—have been restored to their turn-of-the-20th-century glory. However, the rooms fall far short of the historic facade; they have different categories, but even the best "superior" ones are well-worn, the service can be impersonal, and it's a popular venue for noisy late-night wedding receptions on weekends. Still, the location puts you right in the heart of the city (air-con in some rooms, elevator, sauna, pay parking garage, Király utca 5, tel. 72/889-400, www.danubiushotels.com/palatinus, palatinus.reservation@danubiushotels.com).

$ Diána Hotel has 22 woody, simple, but comfortable-enough rooms on a side street facing the synagogue, between the town center and the Árkád shopping mall (air-con, some street noise—request a room on the peaceful atrium, limited free parking or pay at nearby garage, Tímár utca 4a, tel. 72/333-373, www.hoteldiana.hu, info@hoteldiana.hu).

¢ STM3 Apartments is a solid budget choice, with two bright, fresh, spacious, well-equipped apartments in a big building just a block off the main walking street. Carefully communicate your arrival time (no breakfast but each unit has a kitchen, Szent Mór utca 3, tel. +3630-331-5066, www.stm3.hu, info@stm3.hu).

Eating in Pécs

As a student town with its share of tourism, Pécs has eateries playing to those two audiences: cheap student grub and tourist-pleasing (but not necessarily high-quality) meals. I've suggested the best of both types, focusing on the very center of the city. Note that Pécs tends to have unusually high restaurant turnover—don't be surprised if some of these are closed by the time you visit.

DINING ON JÓKAI TÉR AND NEARBY

This pedestrian strip, just off the main square, is home to some of the city's most reliable options for a sit-down meal. The first option is a five-minute walk down the pedestrianized Ferencesek utcája—and worth the extra effort.

$$ Balkán Bisztró—youthful and casual, with a fun energy and a loyal local following—is a reminder that Pécs is geographically (and culturally) close to the Balkans: Serbia, Bosnia, Croatia. It serves up a short but enticing menu of Balkan dishes, focusing on grilled meats (such as *ćevapi*—little minced-meat sausages, grilled on an open fire). If you need a geography lesson, peruse the map of the Balkans in the main dining room. But in good weather, I prefer to sit out on the long, skinny courtyard terrace (daily 12:00-22:00, Ferencesek utcája 32, mobile +3620-350-8919).

$$ Blöff Bisztró is popular for hearty portions of stick-to-your-ribs, beer hall-type food, ranging from basic (flatbread sandwiches) to higher-end (steaks and fish). It has a cozy, pubby, convivial interior and fine outdoor tables on the Jókai tér pedestrian zone (daily 11:00-24:00, Jókai utca 4, tel. 72/497-469).

$$ Elefántos Ház ("House at the Elephant")—named for the historic sign at the corner of the building—is a local favorite for good Italian fare. The pizzas from a wood-fired oven are a great choice, while the main courses tend to be overpriced. The terrace tables are more inviting than the white-arched interior (daily 11:30-23:30, Jókai tér 6, tel. 72/216-055).

Drinks and Light Food on the Main Square: Sharing a space with the TI in the landmark town hall building, the **$ I Love Pécs Café** is bright, cheery, and inviting. It's a good spot for a light meal, coffee, fresh-pressed juice, or cocktail (Mon-Fri 7:30-19:30, Sat-Sun 9:00-18:00, Széchenyi tér 1, tel. +0670-671-0642).

DRINKS AND LIGHT MEALS ON KIRÁLY UTCA

The walking streets branching off from the main square are lined with restaurants and cafés that feature outdoor tables with ideal people-watching. Király utca is lined with tourist-oriented cafés and student-oriented bars, many of which are convenient for a meal with a view. The specific lineup here tends to change from year to year—it's a good plan to simply stroll and comparison-shop, noticing which places are popular right now. Here are a few simple places worth tuning into (listed in the order you'll pass them):

$ Oázis is the place for a simple, cheap, fast, and good gyro or falafel. Grab one to go, or enjoy it at their outdoor tables (daily 10:00-23:00, Fri-Sat until late, Király utca 17).

$ Cooltour Café is a ruin pub with a bohemian vibe and rickety tables strewn around its hidden garden, draped with twinkling Christmas lights. The front room feels like a slightly shabby, old-school Hungarian sitting room. This is a fine place for a toasted sandwich, pastry, coffee, or drink; consider dropping by after dinner for a cocktail or beer (open nightly until the wee hours, Király utca 26).

$ Nappali, a bar on the ground floor of a gorgeously restored townhouse, is a student hangout, with light food (basic sandwiches) and good drinks. Their bohemian interior displays works by local artists, and their outdoor seating is delightful (daily 9:00-late, Király utca 23).

Pécs Connections

From Pécs by Train: For destinations in this book (including **Eger, Sopron,** and **Bratislava**), you'll generally change trains in Budapest. Direct trains connect Pécs and **Budapest** (every 2 hours direct, 3 hours). Note that some Pécs connections (and transfers) use Budapest's suburban **Kelenföld** station, which is fully integrated into the city's Metró system (it's the end station for line 4, a few stops from the center—just as easy to reach from downtown Budapest as any other station). Don't overlook Kelenföld connections, which may open up more options (you may have to search for "Kelenföld" rather than "Budapest").

One handy train each afternoon (departing at 14:15) follows a different route, near the Croatian border, connecting Pécs directly to **Sopron** (5.5 hours). Otherwise, you can make a slightly longer trip with a change in Budapest or Kelenföld (every 1-2 hours, 6 hours).

PÉCS

SOPRON

Sopron (SHOH-prohn), nestled in the foothills of the Alps a stone's throw from Austria, is a picture-perfect little Baroque town jam-packed with historic buildings. Its square—watched over by the town's symbol, the Fire Tower—may be Hungary's most romantic. Because Austrians flock over the border to sightsee, sample the local wine, and get dental work done (at a fraction of the cost they'd pay back home), the town's streets are lined with modest museums and dentist's offices.

Sopron, populated since Roman times, was a stop on the Amber Route of trade between the Adriatic and Baltic Seas. As a Hungarian backwater of Austria's Vienna, the town has long been a unique bilingual mix of Hungarian and Germanic culture. But it's always remained true to Hungary, most famously after World War I, when residents voted to stick with the Magyars rather than becoming part of Austria—earning it the nickname "the most loyal town." Even so, its proximity to Austria keeps Sopron in touch with its Germanic heritage. Today Sopron caters almost entirely to its German-speaking tourists (while English is in short supply).

Sopron is sleepy...sometimes *too* sleepy. After dark, the Main Square is magical—but deserted. Museum attendants react to your visit as though they've never seen a tourist before. With a little more vitality, Sopron could become a major draw. For now, this not-quite-ready-for-prime-time Hungarian burg is a delightful hidden gem.

PLANNING YOUR TIME

Sopron deserves a half-day. A few hours is more than enough time to exhaust its sightseeing options, and you'll find yourself doing laps up and down the same pretty streets. Sopron fits perfectly on a trip between Budapest and Vienna (adding about an hour to your total train time between those cities); it's a small-town alternative to seeing Bratislava en route. It could also work as a side trip from Vienna, for a little taste of Hungary (1.5-hour direct train). Consider arriving at midday and spend the afternoon here, then either take a late train out, or stay the night and leave the next morning.

On a brief visit, lock up your bag at the station and do a spin through the Old Town. With a little more time, explore the Ikva neighborhood northeast of town. If you're here for a while, head into the Lővér Hills for some hiking.

Skip Sopron on a Monday, when virtually all of its sights are closed.

Orientation to Sopron

Sopron, with about 60,000 inhabitants, is a manageable small city. The compact tourist zone of the Old Town (Belváros) contains

most of Sopron's attractions, and you can walk from one end to the other in less than 10 minutes. The retail district along the ring road (Várkerület) that follows the former outer walls surrounding the Old Town is livelier, and the gently rolling Lővér Hills embrace the entire city.

TOURIST INFORMATION

Sopron's TI (called TourInform) is a few steps off the Main Square, sharing a space with some excavated Roman ruins (daily 10:00-18:00, Szent György utca 2, tel. 99/951-975, www.turizmus. sopron.hu).

ARRIVAL IN SOPRON

By Train: Sopron's compact little train station is situated an easy half-mile walk south of the Old Town. Stepping into the main lobby with your back to the tracks, baggage lockers and an ATM are to your right; domestic ticket windows are ahead on the right; and international tickets are sold in the glassed-in office on the left (look for *Utascentrum* sign).

Outside on the left is a **taxi** stand (should cost no more than 1,500 Ft to hotels at the far end of town, taxi tel. 99/333-333).

You can also hop a **bus** heading into town (#1, #2, #10, #10Y, #12, #12A); all go directly to the base of the Old Town, then loop around the east side of the Várkerület ring road, with several stops

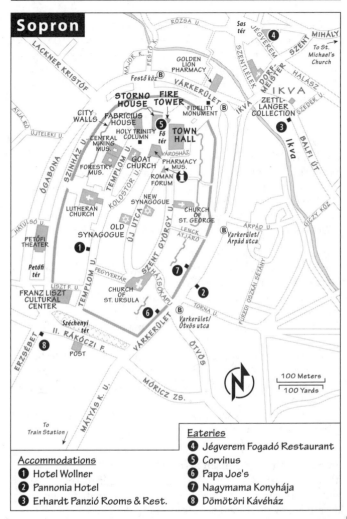

Sopron

RÓZSA U.

Sas tér

To St. Michael's Church

LACKNER KRISTÓF

MAJOR. K.

FESTŐ

GOLDEN LION PHARMACY

Festő köz ®

VÁRKERÜLET

SZENTLÉLEK

JÉGVEREM

SZENT MIHÁLY

DORF-MEISTER

HALÁSZ

IKVA

SZEDER

STORNO HOUSE

FIRE TOWER

ZETTL-LANGER COLLECTION

BALFI ÚT

IKVA

FIDELITY MONUMENT ®

CITY WALLS

FABRICIUS HOUSE

ATJÁRÓ

ÚJTELEKI U.

CENTRAL MINING MUS.

HOLY TRINITY COLUMN

Fő tér

TOWN HALL

GIGZY KÖZ

GOAT CHURCH

VÁROSHÁZ

PHARMACY MUS.

ÓGABONA

SZÍNHÁZ U.

TEMPLOM U.

FORESTRY MUS.

ROMAN FORUM

KOLOSTOR U.

NEW SYNAGOGUE

CHURCH OF ST. GEORGE

ÁRPÁD U.

Várkerület/ Árpád utca ®

LUTHERAN CHURCH

ÚJ UTCA

OLD SYNAGOGUE

LENCK ATJÁRÓ

HATULSÓ U.

PETŐFI THEATER

Petőfi tér

FEGYVERTÁR

SZENT GYÖRGY U.

SZÉLHÁSOKAPU

FÜREDI OSZKÁR SÉTÁNY

LISZT F. U.

CHURCH OF ST. URSULA

TORNA U.

FRANZ LISZT CULTURAL CENTER

Várkerület/ Ötvös utca ®

Széchenyi tér

II. RÁKÓCZI F.

VÁRKERÜLET

ERZSÉBET

POST

ÖTVÖS

MÓRICZ ZS.

N

100 Meters

100 Yards

To Train Station

MÁTYÁS K. U.

Eateries
4 Jégverem Fogadó Restaurant
5 Corvinus
6 Papa Joe's
7 Nagymama Konyhája
8 Dömötöri Kávéház

Accommodations
1 Hotel Wollner
2 Pannonia Hotel
3 Erhardt Panzió Rooms & Rest.

close to the Old Town (see the map). To see the sights in the order I've outlined below, get off at the Várkerület/Ötvös utca stop and walk a few minutes back around the base of the Old Town, to Széchenyi tér. Note: As you exit the station, the bus stop directly to your left is for buses going *away from* town; for buses *into* town, walk a half-block straight ahead and look for the stop on the right side of the street. You can buy a ticket for 320 Ft from a kiosk, or pay 390 Ft to the driver.

It's a 10-minute **walk** into the Old Town—just go straight out of the station and head four blocks up Mátyás király utca toward the big yellow building in the distance (halfway there, you'll cross the long, skinny park called Deák tér). When you reach the park-like Széchenyi tér, the Old Town is straight ahead. To connect Sopron's sights in the order I've outlined below, cross the square, turn left at the flagpole (commemorating Hungarian uprisings throughout history), and look for the big yellow building on the right (the Franz Liszt Cultural Center).

Sights in Sopron

OLD TOWN (BELVÁROS)

Sopron's Old Town is peppered with museums, but only a few are worthwhile (if tight on time or money, visit the Storno House and climb the Fire Tower, but skip the rest). I've organized these sights in the order of a handy orientation walk.

• *Begin exploring the town in front of the TI and the yellow...*

Franz Liszt Cultural Center

The huge building holds Sopron's main concert hall and central box office—step inside to see what's on during your visit. The side facing Széchenyi tér is boldly marked with the words *Magyar Művelődés Háza* ("House of Hungarian Culture") to show up their Germanic rivals. Its current name honors the composer who was born in Sopron county (back when it was part of Austria) and performed his first-ever public concert here in Sopron in 1820, when he was only nine years old. Notice the bust (to the right of the entrance) honoring this favorite son. You'll see "Liszt played here" signs all over town.

For coffee or cake, duck into the classic, recommended **Dömötöri Kávéház** across Széchenyi tér.

• *Now head into the Old Town on...*

Templom Utca ("Church Street")

This was where important local bigwigs lived: mayors, lawyers, and intelligentsia. The town's sturdy wall spared it from being devastated by the Tatar and Ottoman invaders who reshaped much of Hungary. However, a fire, quickly spread by the strong winds that blow through this valley, consumed the town in 1676. Sopron was rebuilt in Baroque style (often over earlier Gothic cellars), which has left it colorful and tidy-looking. You'll notice that every other building has a *MŰEMLÉK* ("historical monument") plaque. Although lots of locally important people and events have graced Sopron, very little of this history is meaningful to visitors. Don't worry about the nitty-gritty of the town's past—just enjoy its ambience.

Notice the many fine passages leading to noble courtyards. For example, near the end of the first, very long block, at #12 (on the left), go into the Gothic passage (lined with pointy arches), which leads into a little courtyard with a Renaissance porch (with rounded arches)—demonstrating the evolution of the local architecture.

Back on the main street and a few steps down, the big church on the left is Lutheran. Because the local mayor protected the rights of religious minorities, Sopron was unusually tolerant, attracting groups who were persecuted elsewhere (such as Lutherans at the time of the Reformation). The first Lutheran congregation here was established in 1565, and the current building dates from 1782. Notice the "Luther rose" in the middle of the cobbled square. Inside the church, the fine 1884 pipe organ and stately pulpit highlight the Lutheran emphasis on preaching the word of God. The white-marble 1946 monument just outside the door memorializes the boarded-up windows of Sopron's ethnic German population, who were forcibly evicted in the population shifts following World War II.

• *When the road forks at the green building, stay left. In the next block on the left are two very modest museums, dedicated to Sopron's major industries. First, at #4, is the...*

Forestry Museum (Erdészeti Gyűjtemény)

While most of Hungary's geography consists of rolling plains and farmland, the area around Sopron is heavily wooded. This museum, part of the local Forestry College, celebrates that heritage, but has virtually no English information and is worthwhile only if you have a special interest. One exhibit, upstairs, features the big- and small-game hunting trophies of Béla Hidvégi, a Hungarian sportsman who has traveled the world.

After the 1956 Uprising, there was an exodus of teachers and students from Sopron's Forestry College to Vancouver, British Columbia. To this day, Hungarians play a major role in the Canadian timber industry.

Cost and Hours: 800 Ft, Mon-Fri 10:00-16:00, Sat-Sun until 17:00, Templom utca 4, tel. 99/338-870.

• *Next door at #2 is the slightly more interesting...*

Central Mining Museum (Központi Bányászati Múzeum)

Displayed on two floors around a courtyard in the beautiful townhouse of a powerful local family, this surprisingly extensive and well-presented museum explains the lives of miners, and the history of Hungarian mining and coinage (with just enough English information). It's worth ▲▲ for those with an interest in industry. On the upper floor, collections include decorative items made of metal, and rock and mineral samples. Look for the little dioramas-in-bottles, which were created by miners. Down on the main floor is a life-size replica of a mineshaft and real-life mining equipment. One room features working models that trace the evolution of mine-digging technology over time—from basic

SOPRON

treadmills and watermills, to modern boring machines. The cellar is full of interactive exhibits for kids, including a mine slide and a mining car they can ride in.

Cost and Hours: 900 Ft, Tue-Sun 10:00-18:00, closed Mon, Templom utca 2, tel. 99/312-667, www.kbm.hu.

• *At the end of the block, the street opens into the main square. Before exploring the square, visit the Gothic church on the right.*

Goat Church (Kecske Templom)

So nicknamed for the goat on the coat of arms over its door, this prominent Benedictine church is a Sopron landmark. While much of the rest of Hungary was occupied by the Ottomans, this region remained in Hungarian hands—and this church was even used for a few royal coronations and parliament sessions.

Cost and Hours: Church only—500 Ft, all sights—900 Ft, daily 8:00-18:00, church open but sights closed Mon-Tue, may have shorter hours off-season, www.bencessopron.hu.

Visiting the Church: Step into the old, atmospheric interior, adorned with wood-carved Baroque altars and a Rococo pulpit. Notice how the once-clean Gothic apse has been obliterated by the retrofitted Baroque altar— illustrating how little regard each era had for the previous one's art. On the right, find the plaque listing the ancestors of István Széchenyi who are buried here. (Széchenyi was a powerful 18th-century aristocrat who championed the rights of the poor and built, among other things, Budapest's Chain Bridge.)

Other parts of the church require an additional admission fee (not worth it): the crypt, where various old graves and tombs have been consolidated into a tasteful modern mausoleum; a series of touchscreen terminals that offer additional information about specific church features; and the little cloister and chapter hall, where the carvings that top the columns represent human sins.

• *Leaving the church, you're in the middle of Sopron's...*

▲▲Main Square (Fő Tér)

One of the most appealing Old World squares in Hungary, this area is dominated by the giant **Holy Trinity Column,** erected in 1701 to commemorate the 1695 plague. Circle around to the far side of the column for a better look. The wealthy local couple who survived the plague and commissioned the column kneel in thanksgiving at its base. Above them, the column corkscrews up to heaven, marked by Jesus, God the Father, and a dove representing the Holy Spirit.

Gleeful cherubs, as if celebrating life after the plague, ride back down the column like kids on a waterslide.

Grand buildings surround the column. Do a quick spin tour to get oriented, starting with the tall **Fire Tower**—the town's main

landmark, which can be climbed for a great view (described later). To the right of that is the vast, off-white 19th-century **Town Hall,** in the eye-pleasing Historicist style of the day. (Those interested in ancient history can walk behind the Town Hall to see fragments of Roman-era Sopron, with posted English information.)

To the right of the Town Hall, the little yellow building sticking out into the square houses a small **Pharmacy Museum** (Patika-Ház), which was a working pharmacy from 1642 to 1967 (you can see most everything from the door with a sweep of your head,

or pay 500 Ft to examine the exhibits up close; Tue-Sun 10:00-14:00, closed Mon and Jan-March). In the early 16th century, local officials wanted to tear down this house to enlarge the square. But the king, who had visited Sopron earlier and enjoyed the square the way it was, decreed that it not be touched...making it Hungary's first government-protected building.

Circling farther to the right, you'll see the Goat Church's steeple, then the big, white, Neoclassical **County Hall.** To the right of it are three historic houses, two of which contain **museums**—described next.

• *If you're ready for some museum-going, consider the two collections in the pretty Baroque house with the corner turret overlooking the square.*

▲▲Storno House (Storno-Ház)

This prime real estate is marked with plaques celebrating visits by two big-league Hungarians: King Má-

tyás (Matthias) Corvinus and Franz Liszt. Today the building houses two exhibits: the Storno Collection—Sopron's best museum—and the "Boundless Story" historical exhibition.

Cost and Hours: Storno Collection—1,000 Ft, history exhibit—700 Ft, both open Tue-Sun 10:00-18:00, closed Mon, Fő tér 8, tel. 99/311-327, www.muzeum.sopron.hu.

Visiting the Storno Collection (Storno-Gyűjtemény): Franz Storno, the son of a poor 19th-century Swiss family of chimney sweeps, showed prodigious talent as an artist at a young age and ultimately became quite a Renaissance man. He moved here to Sopron, married a chimney-sweep master's widow, and became a restorer of buildings for the Habsburg Empire.

Today, in his creaky old house, charming attendants direct visitors through a series of jam-packed rooms to look at a random but fun grab-bag of paintings, decorative items, and other bric-a-brac that Franz collected in his renovation work. Borrow the English leaflet for a room-by-room description, and take time to look around at the wonderful little details.

In the entrance hall, check out the panorama painting of 18th-century Sopron (high up on the wall). Then head left and loop through the old apartments. A few rooms in, the corner room boasts a gorgeously painted, light-filled alcove with table and chairs (as well as more paintings of old Sopron). The old iron box in the middle of this room has a complicated secret-locking system. Passing through the painted door into the bedroom, look for the Biedermeier paintings on the ceilings. The antler chandelier shows a 3-D version of the family seal: chimney-sweeping brush in one hand, compass (for restoration work) in the other.

In the final room (the salon), you'll see square tables with hinged edges that can be brought up to make them circular. These were practical but also superstitious: It was considered bad luck for a young woman to sit at the corner of a table (either she'd never marry or have a difficult mother-in-law, depending on the legend), so this design ensured that would never happen.

"Boundless Story" Exhibit (Határtalan Történet): Downstairs, this well-presented exhibit ("History without Borders" might be a better translation) traces the history of Sopron, with good English information posted and a few touchscreens. You'll learn about the Reformation, guilds and craftsmen, and walls and warfare. Examine the delicate clothing from the 18th and 19th centuries, and the details of the intricate 19th-century manger scene (from the village of Donnerskirchen, just over the border in Austria), which unfolds on several levels. Also displayed are implements of torture, an old-timey bicycle with a big wheel, a piano played by Liszt, and items from the age of weights and measures standardization after Napoleon.

In the final room, find the exhibit about the post-World War I referendum in which Sopron elected to remain part of Hungary instead of Austria. The referendum, which took place in December 1921, asked citizens to vote with color-coded ballots whether they would join Austria or Hungary. Hungary won 15,334 votes to Austria's 8,227. This cemented Sopron's already-established reputation as being the "most loyal town." (Maybe it was because other Austrians would never let them live down the town's German name, Ödenburg, which roughly means "Dullsville.") Overhead, you'll see propaganda trying to convince locals to vote one way or another—such as the unsettling poster of the skeleton, clad in traditional Hungarian folk costume, menacingly serenading the town on his violin. Other 20th-century items in this room include an armband from the Arrow Cross (Hungary's Nazi puppet government) and a prisoner's uniform from Auschwitz.

• *Two buildings to the left of the Storno House is the...*

Fabricius House (Fabricius-Ház)

This historic mansion, once belonging to Sopron's most beloved mayor, is home to a pair of dull, skippable museums. The 17th- and 18th-century **Civic Apartments** (Polgári Lakások), basically a collection of old furniture, will appeal only to antique lovers. The **Archaeological Exhibit** (Régészet-Kőtár) is a very dry overview of the history of Sopron, especially relating to the Amber Road trade route that put the town on the map. The best part is the Roman Lapidarium in the cellar (same ticket)—a collection of Roman tombstones unearthed here, as well as the shattered fragments of three larger-than-life Roman statues.

Cost and Hours: Apartments—800 Ft, archaeological exhibit—700 Ft, both open Tue-Sun 10:00-18:00, closed Mon, Fő tér 6.

• *Dominating the Main Square is Sopron's symbol, the...*

▲Fire Tower (Tűztorony)

A Roman watchtower once stood here, but the current version was gradually expanded from the 13th to the 18th century. Fire watchmen would survey the town from the top of the tower, then mark the direction of a fire with colorful flags (by day) or a bright light (at night) to warn townspeople. Today you can climb its 119 steps for grand views over the Old Town's rooftops.

Cost and Hours: 1,150 Ft, daily 10:00-20:00, Oct-April until 18:00, can be closed in bad weather, Fő tér 1, www. tuztorony.sopron.hu.

Visiting the Tower: Just above the gate's passageway is a stone carving depicting **Hungária,** the female embodiment of Hungary—given to the city to thank them for choosing Hungary during the 1921 referendum. Once through the gate, the ticket office is on your left. Next to its door, look for the giant **key monument,** commemorating a "key" event in this loyal town's history. After presenting the Hungarian king with the key to their city when his rival was planning an invasion, Sopron was rewarded with free "royal town" status, which came with special privileges (in 1277).

Head inside, buy your ticket, and climb the tight spiral steps to the top. On the way up, pause at the landings to check out the exhibits. There are historic photos and drawings of the tower, and the original double-headed Habsburg eagle—with an "L" for the Emperor Leopold—that topped the tower's spire.

At the top, do a clockwise spin: First is a great view over the rooftops of the Old Town; beyond that, you can see the Lővér Hills,

Sopron's playground. (While the name sounds romantic, *lővér* refers to master archers who defended the border from Tatar invasions in the 13th century.) Continuing around the tower and looking down, you'll see remains of the city wall defining the Old Town; an outer wall was once located on the outside of today's ring road. Beyond the stadium lights is Austria (and its modern wind turbines). A bit farther to the right, the big steeple with the crown is St. Michael's, one of Sopron's historic churches. Farther to the right, the oddly shaped bulbous tower on the hill is a windmill missing its blades. This was used to garrison Habsburg troops after the 1848 Revolution.

From here, 30 more steps lead higher up to the former clockkeeper's room, where you can see the historic clockworks—still ticking after all these centuries.

Back down at the bottom, you can poke around the excavated cellars at the base of the tower, where you'll find a town model of Sopron.

• *Exiting the tower, turn left and head...*

Outside the Walls

Just beyond the ticket office for the tower, on the left, is the entrance to the **City Wall Walk** (Várfalsétány), where you can walk along part of the course of the surviving wall (not particularly scenic since it's outside the wall rather than on top of it; free, Mon-Fri 9:00-21:00, Sat-Sun until 18:00).

Just outside the Old Town, you reach the ring road and a livelier zone. Look (on your left) for a modern **sculpture** with three figures, each one representing a time when Sopron demonstrated its fidelity: 1277, when the town sided with the Hungarian king (described earlier); 1921, when they voted to remain part of Hungary; and 1989, when the Iron Curtain fell (symbolized by the woman breaking the barbed wire). In August of that fateful year—before the communists had officially given up the ghost—the "Pan-European Picnic" took place in the hills near Sopron. Residents of various Central European countries—East Germany, Austria, and Hungary—came together for the first time in decades, offering a tantalizing taste of freedom.

Across the busy ring road from this sculpture, look for the **Golden Lion Pharmacy** (*Gyógyszertár Apotheke* sign), which has beautiful Art Nouveau Zsolnay porcelain decorations.

Looking back toward the Old Town, notice the **colorful little shops** that cling like baby animals to the protective town walls.

• *From here, you can back-track to the Main Square and head down New Street to more sights, or keep going beyond the walls into the Ikva neighborhood (both options described below).*

*To see more of the **Old Town**, head back to the Main Square and take the street to the left of the Pharmacy Museum (as you face it). This is...*

New Street (Új Utca): Sopron's Jewish Quarter

This misnamed street is actually one of the oldest in town. Near the start of the street (a few steps down from the Main Square), the building at the fork houses the town **TI**. In the cellar are the remains of the original **forum** of Sopron's Roman settlement (ask the TI to show you the stairs down—free but donations gladly accepted).

Continue to the right, up New Street—which used to be called **"Jewish Street"** (*Zsidó utca*) until the Jews were kicked out in 1526. After the 1848 Revolution, they finally returned...but for less than a century. When the Nazis took control of Hungary, they walled off both ends of this street and turned it into a ghetto. Some 1,840 Sopron Jews were eventually sent to concentration camps... where 1,650 of them died.

Along the street, about one block down, are two synagogues. The first is the **New Synagogue** (*Új Zsinagóga*), in a dark passageway on the left at #11. Step inside to see the "Forgotten Sopron" exhibit, with photos and thumbnail biographies of some

Jewish Sopron citizens who were killed in the Holocaust (free but not a word of English, Tue-Sun 10:00-18:00, closed Mon).

A few steps down, on the right at #22, is the **Old Synagogue** (Ó Zsinagóga), dating from the early 14th century (800 Ft, Tue-Sun 10:00-18:00, closed Mon, Új utca 22, tel. 99/311-327). Rediscovered in 1968, it has been renovated but still retains a few of its original elements (such as the Torah holder). From inside the main hall—where men worshipped—notice the narrow, slit-like windows connecting to a second room, where women worshipped (and religious items are now on display).

• *New Street ends at Ursula Square (Orsolya tér), watched over by the Church of St. Ursula and a statue of Mary. If you double back to the left, you can head up the third of old Sopron's three parallel streets...*

St. George's Street (Szent György Utca)

A short walk down the street, on the right at #11, notice the big doorway leading to **Lenck átjáró** street—a passage running through several connected courtyards, lined with businesses, leading out to the ring road.

Farther along, on the right, is the red-and-white namesake for this street, **Church of St. George** (free, daily 8:00-18:00). The beautiful, stuccoed Baroque interior hosted Lutheran services for a time, but the Lutherans were evicted during the Counter-Reformation.

Head across the street and into the fine Renaissance **courtyard** at #12, where the Lutherans were forced to worship al fresco. Notice the stone pulpit carved into the upper balcony, and the metal rings used to secure a tarp that covered the service in bad weather. Today this courtyard hosts Sopron's good, modern children's museum, called **Macskakő** ("Cobblestones").

• *St. George's Street will take you right back up to the Main Square, where—if you haven't already—you can head into the...*

IKVA NEIGHBORHOOD, NORTHEAST OF THE OLD TOWN

With a little more time, venture into the workaday streets northeast of the Old Town—beyond the ring road and the Ikva brook (hidden here beneath the road). While lacking the storybook charm of the Old Town, this area is also historic. Back when wealthy aristocrats populated the Old Town, farmers and craftsmen lived here—giving it a rustic, lived-in ambience that's fun to explore. (It's also home

to several recommended accommodations, and the good Jégverem restaurant—all listed later in this chapter.)

The main drag changes names as it twists through this neighborhood (first called Ikva híd, then Dorfmeister utca, then Szent Mihály utca). Eventually it leads up a hill to **St. Michael's Church** (Szent Mihály Templom) and the adjacent little Romanesque chapel. The church complex is surrounded by a cemetery.

• *Closer to the Belváros, but still in the Ikva neighborhood, is one final Sopron sight, the...*

▲Zettl-Langer Collection (Zettl-Langer Gyűjtemény)

A Bavarian art lover named Gustav Zettl came to Sopron in the late 19th century, set up a distillery, and became a pillar of the community. Today his descendants (usually his great-granddaughter, Ágnes Langer, who speaks English) lead tours of this fine old townhouse that's jammed with Gustav's eclectic private collection of furniture, porcelain, paintings, knickknacks, and more. Ágnes will show you everything from a collection of ancient Roman vessels to fine inlaid furniture (find out why a "money changer's table" has a marble top) to delicately decorated windows to all manner of clever cupboards with hidden panels and  drawers. It's similar in many ways to the excellent Storno Collection on the Main Square, but because the family still resides here, this is a unique opportunity to see a very lived-in home that feels like a museum (or vice versa). Each item on display has been in the family for generations, and Ágnes relishes telling their stories in as much detail as you'd like to hear. Near the end is Gustav's death announcement, in a frame that also holds a stack of dozens more. It must be both sobering and comforting for Gustav's descendants to know that their death notices will be added to the family stack someday. The public can only visit with a tour (generally about 40 minutes); it's smart to call ahead to let Ágnes know you're coming.

Cost and Hours: 1,200 Ft per person to enter, plus 2,000 Ft for the group for the mandatory tour; Tue-Sun 10:00-12:00, closed Mon, Nov-March open Fri-Sun only; Balfi utca 11, tel. 99/311-136.

SOPRON

HIKING

With its forested hillsides and fresh air, Sopron is popular with hikers. To get to the best trailhead, take bus #1 or #2 from the Old Town to Lővér Szálló, and get off at the giant-domed bath complex. From here, several trails lead through the hills. Before setting out, get advice from the TI (they can give you a free map, or sell you a better one).

Sleeping in Sopron

While Sopron works best as a side trip or an on-the-way destination, it has a few fine, central accommodations for those wanting to settle in. Most hotels quote their rates in euros but prefer to be paid in forints.

$$ Hotel Wollner, a top option in Sopron, has real class. This 600-year-old Baroque townhouse on the Old Town's main street rents 18 tastefully appointed rooms. An inviting terraced garden in the rear rounds out its appeal (Templom utca 20, tel. 99/524-400, www.wollner.hu, wollner@wollner.hu).

$$ Pannonia Hotel sits on the ring road just across from the Old Town. The large public areas recall Sopron's faded elegance, while the 79 rooms are straightforward. It comes with big-hotel extras, such as a grand atrium breakfast room and a wonderful, small swimming pool and wellness center (some rooms have air-con, elevator, street noise—ask for quieter room, Várkerület 75, tel. 99/312-180, www.pannoniahotel.com, sopron@pannoniahotel.com).

$ Erhardt Panzió rents 12 rooms above their upscale-feeling restaurant, in a nicely restored house on an urban-feeling street just outside of the Old Town, at the base of the Ikva neighborhood (air-con, Balfi utca 10, tel. 99/506-711, www.erhardts.hu, info@erhardts.hu).

Eating in Sopron

You might notice lots of bean dishes on the menu in Sopron. The thrifty Germans—who were responsible for most of the winemaking in the surrounding hills—would plant beans in the earth between their rows of vines. In fact, in local dialect, German residents are called "bean farmers." Sopron is also known for its local beer (called Soproni) and for its local wines.

$$ Jégverem Fogadó ("Ice House Inn") is my reliable standby for heaping plates of tasty Hungarian food from a clever, descriptive menu ("this is why they invented Activia"). If you're seeking a traditional dining experience, it's worth the 5-minute walk outside the Old Town to the Ikva neighborhood. The circular table in the middle of the cozy dining room peers down into a pit where ice was stored, to be sold through the hot summer months. In good weather, sit out on the inviting terrace. As portions are huge, consider sharing or ordering a smaller dish (daily 11:00-23:00, Jégverem utca 1, tel. 99/510-113).

$$$ Erhardt Restaurant, also in the Ikva neighborhood, serves Hungarian and international fare in a sophisticated-feeling, white-tablecloth, mellow dining room. They also have a wine shop and a lengthy wine list (daily 11:30-22:00, Balfi utca 10, tel. 99/506-711).

On the Main Square: A few interchangeable eateries ring the Main Square. If any of these has an edge, it's **$$ Corvinus**—a no-brainer for a romantic al fresco dinner. With a traditional menu of good Hungarian classics and a few international dishes, the place sprawls into a wine cellar and its sister restaurant next door, the Generális café (Tue-Sun 11:30-22:00, closed Mon—but may be open in high season, Fő tér 7, tel. 99/505-035).

$$$ Papa Joe's, an American-style steakhouse, had my travel sensibilities crying, "No!"—but my stomach saying, "Hmmmm... maybe." Here's your chance to experience the Old West through Hungarian eyes. Done up to the nines like a cowboy saloon (including six-shooter-handle doorknobs and saddle barstools), this theme restaurant grills up steaks and other Tex-Mex dishes (such as baked beans). When locals want a break from Hungarian food, they come here (daily 11:00-24:00, Várkerület 108, tel. 99/340-933).

Fast and Cheap: Your best option for a quick, no-frills meal is **$ Nagymama Konyhája** ("Grandma's Kitchen"). This small self-service cafeteria, filled with locals, specializes in savory and sweet crêpes *(palacsinta)*, but also offers other traditional Hungarian dishes. Just point to what you want, or ask to see the clear English menu (Mon-Sat 10:00-21:00, Sun from 12:00, Várkerület 104, mobile +3620-315-8730).

Coffee and Cake: Locals satisfy their sweet tooth at **Dömötöri Kávéház,** a pastry and coffee shop slinging a wide array of cakes and fancy ice-cream dishes—with seating in a classy interior, in an aristocratic upstairs, and out on a pretty square across from the Franz Liszt Center (Mon-Thu 7:00-20:00, Fri until 21:00, Sat-Sun 8:00-21:00, Széchenyi tér 13, tel. 99/506-623).

Sopron Connections

From Sopron by Train to: Budapest (every 2 hours direct, 2.5 hours, more with transfer at Budapest-Kelenföld), **Eger** (about every 2 hours, 6 hours, transfer in Budapest and sometimes also in Füzesabony), **Pécs** (1/day direct in the morning, 5.5 hours;

otherwise about every 1-2 hours, 6 hours, most transfer at
Budapest's suburban Kelenföld station), **Bratislava,** Slovakia (about
every 2 hours direct, 2.5 hours on RegionalExpress/REX; more
with transfers at stations in downtown and/or suburban Vienna),
Vienna, Austria (about every 2 hours direct on RegionalExpress/
REX, 1.5 hours; more options with transfer in Weiner Neustadt).

SOPRON

BRATISLAVA, SLOVAKIA

The Slovak capital, Bratislava, is an unexpected charmer. Its old town bursts with colorfully restored facades, lively outdoor cafés, and swanky boutiques. The ramshackle industrial quarter to the east is rapidly being redeveloped into a forest of skyscrapers. The hilltop castle gleams from a recent facelift. And even the glum communist-era suburb of Petržalka has undergone a Technicolor makeover. Bratislava and Vienna have forged a new twin-city alliance for trade and commerce, making this truly the nexus of Central Europe.

It's easy to get the feeling that workaday Bratislavans—who strike some visitors as gruff—are being pulled to the cutting edge of the 21st century kicking and screaming. But many Slovaks embrace the changes and fancy themselves as the yang to Vienna's yin: If Vienna is a staid, elderly aristocrat sipping coffee, then Bratislava is a vivacious young professional jet-setting around Europe. Bratislava at night is a lively place; thanks in part to tens of thousands of university students, its youthful center thrives.

Bratislava's location—on the Danube (and the tourist circuit) smack-dab between Budapest and Vienna—makes it a convenient "on the way" destination. I admit that Bratislava used to leave me cold. But changes over the last 10-15 years have transformed it into a delightful destination. And its energy is inspiring.

PLANNING YOUR TIME

A few hours are plenty to get the gist of Bratislava. Head straight to the old town and follow my self-guided walk, finishing with one or more of the city's fine viewpoints: Ascend to the "UFO" observation deck atop the funky bridge, ride the elevator up to the Sky Bar for a peek (and maybe a drink), or hike up to the castle for the views. With more time, stroll along the Danube riverbank

Welcome to Slovakia

Sitting quietly in the very center of Central Europe, wedged between bigger and stronger nations (Hungary, Austria, the Czech Republic, and Poland), Slovakia was brutally disfigured by the communists, then overshadowed by the Czechs. But in recent years, this fledgling republic has found its wings. While the east of Slovakia is still catching up, locals brag that the region around Bratislava has the hottest economy and highest income per capita of any region in the former communist region of Europe.

With about 5.5 million people in a country of 19,000 square miles (similar to Massachusetts and New Hampshire combined), Slovakia is one of Europe's smallest nations. Recent economic reforms have caused two very different Slovakias to emerge: the modern, industrialized, flat, affluent west, centered on the capital of Bratislava; and the remote, poorer, mountainous, "backward" east, with high unemployment and traditional lifestyles.

Slovakia is ethnically diverse: In addition to the Slavic Slovaks, there are Hungarians (about 10 percent of the population, "stranded" here when Hungary lost this land after World War I) and Roma (called Gypsies in the past, also about 10 percent). Slovakia has struggled to incorporate both of these large and often-mistreated minority groups.

Slovakia has spent most of its history as someone else's backyard. For centuries, it was ruled from Budapest and known as "Upper Hungary." At other times, it was an important chunk

to the thriving, modern Eurovea development. If you spend the evening in Bratislava, you'll find it lively with students, busy cafés, and nightlife.

Note that museums and galleries are closed on Monday.

Day-Tripping Tip: Bratislava can be done as a long side-trip from Budapest (or a short one from Vienna), but it's most convenient as a stopover to break up the journey between Budapest and Vienna. Pay careful attention to train schedules, as connections alternate between Bratislava's two train stations: Hlavná Stanica (serving all trains to/from Prague and Budapest and half of all trains to/from Vienna) and Petržalka (remaining trains to/from Vienna). If checking your bag at the station, be sure that your return or onward connection will depart from there.

of the Habsburg Empire, ruled from neighboring Vienna. But most outsiders think first of another era: the 75 years that Slovakia was joined with the Czech Republic as the country of "Czechoslovakia." From its start in the aftermath of World War I, this union of Czechs and Slovaks was troubled; some Slovaks chafed at being ruled from Prague, while many Czechs resented the financial burden of their poorer neighbors to the east.

After gaining their freedom during 1989's peaceful Velvet Revolution, the Czechs and Slovaks began to think of the future. The Slovaks wanted to rename the country Czecho-Slovakia (with that all-important hyphen signifying an equal partnership), and to give themselves more autonomy. The Czechs balked, relations gradually deteriorated, and Slovak nationalist candidate Vladimír Mečiar fared surprisingly well in the 1992 elections. Taking it as a sign that the two peoples wanted to part ways, politicians pushed through (in just three months) the peaceful separation of the now-independent Czech and Slovak Republics. The "Velvet Divorce" became official on January 1, 1993.

At first the Slovaks struggled. Communist rule had been particularly unkind to them, and their economy was in shambles. Visionary leaders set forth bold solutions, including a flat tax (19 percent), followed by EU membership in 2004 and adoption of the euro currency in 2009. Before long, major international corporations began to notice the same thing the Soviets had: This is a great place to build stuff, thanks to its strategic location (300 million consumers live within a day's drive), low labor costs, and a well-trained workforce. Today multiple foreign automakers have plants here, and Slovakia produces one million cars a year, making it the world's biggest car producer per capita.

Bratislava's success story is impressive. The capital region enjoys almost full employment, and seems poised to lead Slovakia into a bright future.

Orientation to Bratislava

Bratislava, with 430,000 residents, is Slovakia's capital and biggest city. It has a compact, colorful old town *(staré mesto),* with the castle on the hill above. Most of the old town is traffic-free. This small area is surrounded by a vast construction zone, rotting residential districts desperately in need of beautification, and a sprawling communist-built suburb that is seeing new life (Petržalka, across the river).

TOURIST INFORMATION
The helpful TI is at Klobučnícka 2, on Primate's Square behind the Old Town Hall (daily 9:00-19:00, Nov-April until 18:00, tel.

02/16186, www.visitbratislava.com). They also have a branch at the main train station (Hlavná Stanica; daily 9:30-18:00).

Bratislava City Card: The TI sells this card (€15/1 day, €18/2 days), which includes free transit and free or discounted admission to local sights. It's worthwhile only if you're doing the included old town walking tour (€14 without the card—see "Tours in Bratislava," later).

ARRIVAL IN BRATISLAVA

For information on Bratislava's trains, buses, riverboats, and airport, see "Bratislava Connections" at the end of this chapter.

HELPFUL HINTS

Money: Slovakia uses the euro. You'll find ATMs all around town, including at the train stations and airport.

Language: Many Bratislavans speak English quite well (especially young people). The Slovak language is closely related to Czech and Polish. The local word used informally for both "hi" and "bye" is easy to remember: *ahoj* (pronounced "AH-hoy," like a pirate). "Please" is *prosím* (PROH-seem), "thank you" is *dakujem* (DYAH-koo-yehm), "good" is *dobrý* (DOH-bree), and "Cheers!" is *Na zdravie!* (nah ZDRAH-vyeh; think "nice driving").

Phone Tips: To call locally within Bratislava, dial the number without the area code. To make a long-distance call within Slovakia, start with the area code (which begins with 0). To call from Hungary to Slovakia or vice versa, use the country code (421 for Slovakia, 36 for Hungary) and follow the dialing instructions in the Practicalities chapter.

Taxis: Taxis come in handy here, but are poorly regulated—they can charge whatever rates they want. Any ride in the city center *should* be around €5. However, cabbies waiting at the train station and tourist spots (such as the castle) are accustomed to quoting an inflated, flat price—usually more like €10 or €15. To improve your odds, look for a taxi with a logo and telephone number prominently on the door, and insist that they use the meter. Locals call taxis rather than hailing them on the street—you can ask a hotelier or restaurant staffer to call one for you.

Supermarket: Centrally located, **Billa** is big and handy. Find it across from the Philharmonic, on Mostová street (Mon-Sat 7:00-21:00, Sun from 8:00).

Local Guidebook: For in-depth suggestions on Bratislava sightseeing, dining, and more, look for the eye-pleasing *Bratislava Active* guidebook (around €10, sold at every postcard rack).

Tours in Bratislava

Walking Tours

The TI offers a one-hour old town walking tour in English every day in summer at 14:00 (€14, free with Bratislava City Card). For €28, two people can book the same hour-long tour with the same guides as a private tour at whatever time is convenient. The TI can arrange this for you with a few hours' notice (see "Tourist Information," earlier in this chapter). This can be a great way to become friends with the city.

Local Guide

MS Agency, run by **Martin Sloboda,** offers quality guides (€130/3 hours, €160/4 hours, mobile 0905-627-265, www.bratislava-guide.sk, sloboda@

msagency.sk). Martin, a can-do entrepreneur and tireless Bratislava booster (and author of the great *Bratislava Active* guidebook described above) helped me put this chapter together. He's part of the ambitious young generation that came of age as communism fell—and whose energy and leadership are reshaping the city.

Bratislava Old Town Walk

This self-guided orientation walk circles delightfully traffic-free old Bratislava (figure 1.5 hours, not including sightseeing stops).
• *Start on the bridge about 50 yards uphill from the green copper spire of the watchtower, St. Michael's Gate (it looks like a church spire, at the top of the old town)—with the tram tracks of the ring road just beyond.*

St. Michael's Bridge

You're standing below a watchtower marking St. Michael's Gate (Michalská Brána), part of the town's medieval wall. It's capped with the Archangel Michael, busily killing a dragon.

The Hungarian king gave Pressburg (as Bratislava was called back then) city status in 1291. This meant the city had permission to fortify, offer protection, and tax trade. Bratislava was at the crossroads of two medieval trade routes (the north-south "Amber Route" from the Baltics to the Mediterranean, and the east-west "Oriental Route" along the Danube). You're standing over the

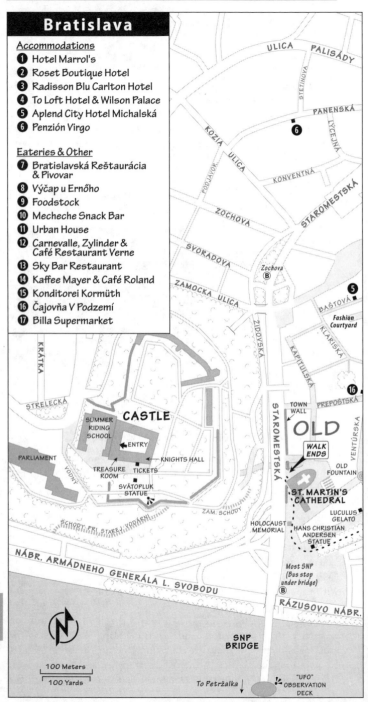

Bratislava

Accommodations
1. Hotel Marrol's
2. Roset Boutique Hotel
3. Radisson Blu Carlton Hotel
4. To Loft Hotel & Wilson Palace
5. Aplend City Hotel Michalská
6. Penzión Virgo

Eateries & Other
7. Bratislavská Reštaurácia & Pivovar
8. Výčap u Ernőho
9. Foodstock
10. Mecheche Snack Bar
11. Urban House
12. Carnevalle, Zylinder & Café Restaurant Verne
13. Sky Bar Restaurant
14. Kaffee Mayer & Café Roland
15. Konditorei Kormúth
16. Čajovňa V Podzemí
17. Billa Supermarket

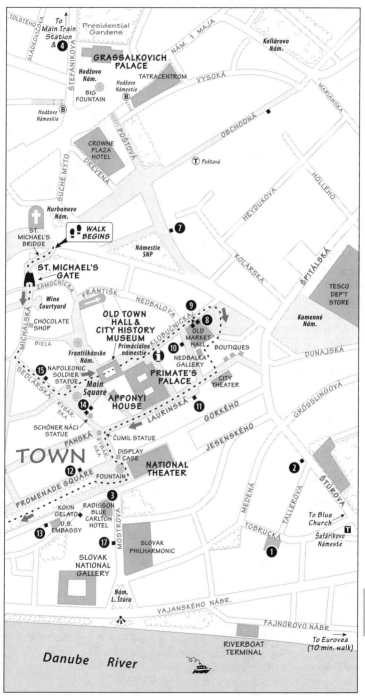

former dry moat, now a garden of the city library and an outdoor concert venue.

Before heading into the old town, look away from the tower. Notice the sleek-in-the-1920s Art Deco building on the right. Now a bar, when it was built in 1929 it was a supermodern department store designed to show off Bata shoes (a Czechoslovakian company that was once the largest shoe company in the world).

• *Stroll over the bridge and enter the old center. You're outside the wall, walking through a barbican—shaped like an "L" for better defense. Pause just after passing under the gate.*

St. Michael's Gate (Michalská Brána)

This is the last surviving tower of the city wall. Just below the gate, notice the "kilometer zero" plaque in the ground, marking the point from which distances in Slovakia are measured. But I wouldn't trust the distances...unless we're somehow on the equator: According to this, the North and South Poles are both 4,667 kilometers away.

• *Before you stretches...*

Michalská Street

Pretty as it is now, Bratislava's old center was a decrepit ghost town during the communist era. The communist regime believed that Bratislavans of the future would live in large, efficient apartment buildings. They saw the old town as a useless relic of the bad old days of poor plumbing, cramped living spaces, social injustice, and German domination—a view that left no room to respect, or maintain, the town's physical heritage.

For example, notice the uniform cobbles underfoot. In the 1950s, the communists sold Bratislava's original medieval cobbles to cute German towns that were rebuilding themselves in a way that preserved their elegant Old World character. Locals avoided this stripped-down, desolate corner of the city, preferring to spend time in the Petržalka suburb across the river.

With the fall of communism in 1989, the new government began sorting out who had the rights to the old town's buildings, and returning them to their original owners. During this time, little repair or development took place (since there was no point investing in a building until ownership was clearly established). By 1998, most of the property issues were resolved. The city made the old town traffic-free, spruced up the public buildings, and encouraged private owners to restore their buildings as well.

Two decades later, the result is this delightful street, lined with inviting cafés and restaurants. Poke around to experience Bratislava's charm. Courtyards and passageways—most of them open to the public—burrow through the city's buildings. Half a block down on the left, the courtyard at #12 was once home to vintners; their former cellars are now coffee shops, massage parlors, crafts boutiques, and cigar shops. More dead-end passages with characteristic shops are across the street, at #7 and #5.

The **Cukráreň na Korze** chocolate shop (on the left, at #6) is highly regarded among locals for its delicious hot chocolate and creamy truffles. Above the shop's entrance, the **cannonball** embedded in the wall recalls Napoleon's two sieges of Bratislava (the 1809 siege was 42 days long), which caused massive suffering—even worse than during World War II (the French consumed all of the wine stocks). This is just one of several cannonballs around town. Keep an eye out for more of these reminders of one of Bratislava's darkest times.

• *Two blocks down from St. Michael's Gate, where the street changes to Ventúrska (at the signpost and big rock in the street), turn left along Sedlárska street.*

*Peek into **Konditorei Kormüth** (a few doors down on the right, at #8). Mr. Kormüth dedicated many years and lots of money to creating a 17th-century setting for his café. For €10, you can enjoy a coffee and slice of cake in this unforgettable setting while reading his story on the menu.*

Farther on, you reach the historic...

Main Square (Hlavné Námestie)

This modest square, the centerpiece of Bratislava's old town, feels too petite for a national capital. Its style is a mishmash—every building around it seems to date from a different architectural period.

The **fountain,** the most beautiful and historic in town, is a history lesson just waiting to happen. It celebrates the 1563 coronation of Maximillian II—the first Habsburg emperor to also be crowned "King of Hungary." Back then, Slovakia was part of Hungary, which was ruled from Austria. (Got that?) As a mark of respect to the locals, Austrian emperors were crowned a second time, as Hungarian kings. (The German phrase for this arrangement—*König und Kaiser,* "king and emperor," often abbreviated *"K+K"*—remains a mark of quality to this day.) I suppose if your choice as a Hungarian was to be ruled by the Ottomans or by an Austrian Habsburg, the answer was easy.

This arrangement also helps explain why Vienna and Bratislava—the present-day capitals of Austria and Slovakia—are the closest of any two capitals in Europe (you can actually see the lights of one from the other). This closeness wasn't an accident—it was for security. Long before "Slovakia" existed, Bratislava (then called Pozsony) was the capital of "rump" Hungary—what was left of Hungary after most of its territory, including the capital Buda, was conquered by the Ottomans. Bratislava was as far from the Ottoman Turks as possible, while still being in Hungary, and very well fortified. The castle crowning the hill high above the old town was the royal residence and protector of the crown jewels during this time. (For more on the complicated tricultural mix of the city—Austrian/German, Hungarian, and Slavic/Slovak—see the "City of Three Cultures" sidebar, later in this chapter.)

Standing in the middle of the main square, do a quick clockwise spin tour. (You'll need to circle around the fountain to see everything.) Begin with the bold yellow tower of the **Old Town Hall** (Stará Radnica), which dominates the square. It's Gothic at the core, but with a Baroque facade. Near the bottom of the tower, to the left of the pointed window, there's another Napoleonic cannonball embedded in the facade.

Down the street to the right of the Old Town Hall is the **Apponyi House,** the mansion of an 18th-century aristocrat that also holds the Slovak National Collection of Wine (described under "Sights in Bratislava").

Turn farther right and note the venerable cafés. The classic choice is **Kaffee Mayer,** with dark awnings and outdoor seating facing the fountain. They've been selling coffee and cakes to a genteel clientele since 1873. You can enjoy your pick-me-up in the swanky old interior or out on the square.

At the corner in front of Kaffee Mayer (you may have to walk closer to see it) is a beloved statue. The jovial chap doffing his top hat is **Schöner Náci,** who lived in Bratislava until the 1960s. This eccentric old man, a poor carpet cleaner, would dress up in his one black suit and top hat, and go strolling through the city, offering gifts to the women he fancied. (He'd often whisper *"schön"*—German for "pretty," which is how he got his nickname.) Schöner Náci now gets to spend eternity greeting visitors outside his favorite café.

Across the street, the Art Nouveau **Café Roland** is known for its 1904 Klimt-style mosaics and historic photos of the city known as Pressburg (Austrian times) or Pozsony (Hungarian times). The building was once a bank. Step inside. These days the barista stands where a different kind of bean counter once did, guarding a vault that now holds coffee.

Now walk toward the Old Town Hall. Up the little side-square to the left is a jumble of cute **mini kiosks**—sporting old-time cityscape engravings on their roofs—selling local handicrafts and knickknacks. In December, the square transforms into the city's popular and atmospheric Christmas market.

Step through the passageway leading to the Old Town Hall's gorgeously restored courtyard, with its Renaissance arcades. (The entrance to the excellent **City History Museum**—described later—is inside the courtyard.)

Continue all the way through the courtyard into **Primate's Square** (Primaciálne Námestie). The pink mansion on the right is the **Primate's Palace**—the new town hall in the old archbishop's residence—with a fine interior decorated with English tapestries (described later). At the far end of this square is the **TI.**

Continue straight ahead (with the TI on your right) down the street called Klobučnícka—**"Hatters Street."** In the Middle Ages, craftsmen gathered according to their trade, and streets were named for the craft found there. If you needed a hat, you knew where to find one.

• *Continue two blocks straight ahead to a square on your right, fronted by a fine two-story Neoclassical market hall.*

Old Market Hall (Stará Tržnica)

Built in 1910, this busy community center today hosts concerts and a Saturday market. The market hall square is a lively gathering place, too; see details on its monthly food-truck festivals under "Eating in Bratislava," later.

On the right side of the square is a stark 12-story building—the tallest in town before WWII. If it looks barren, that was the point. It's from the Bauhaus school—the rage among German architects between the world wars. The battle cry for these harbingers of modernity: "form follows function," "less is more," and "luxury does not require ornamentation." Today its ground floor is home to a dingy bingo parlor (visitors welcome).

The bombs of World War II mostly spared the old town but pulverized a nearby oil refinery and dynamite plant—targeted by Allies because they were a key part of the occupying Nazi war economy. But a few bombs went awry and hit the area just uphill from here, which accounts for all the post-1945 buildings. The concrete jungle beyond the tram tracks is modernist architecture of the 1960s communist era.

• *Find a door just to the left of the Old Market Hall facade marked* Centrál Pasáž *(press buzzer if closed). It leads through a 1920s Art*

Deco shopping gallery (cutting edge a century ago) to a busy pedestrian boulevard.

Laurinská Street—Bratislava's Fashion Drag

This street is lined with fun-to-browse boutiques. In the little nook where the street bends (just to the left) are three popular, very Slovak shops: **Slowatch,** with casual clothes and bags; **Slávica,** a high-end design shop with jewelry and accessories; and **Kompot,** selling a fun variety of unique, Slovak-themed T-shirts. This is a good spot to browse for a quality, non-kitschy souvenir.

Across the street from where you entered Laurinská is the chillingly blocky facade of the communist-era **City Theater** (Mestské Divadlo). On the upper floor are Socialist Realist stained-glass windows—hard to see during the day, but illuminated at night, like a communist night light. We'll see the much fancier National Theater in a moment.

Turn right on Laurinská and stroll like a local for three long blocks—people-watching and window-shopping at more high-end shops. Soon you reach the Bratislava city seal in the cobbles (a three-towered castle with a gate half-open).

• *Just beyond that, on the left, look out or you might stumble over a bronze fellow peeking out of a manhole.*

Čumil ("the Peeper")

Čumil was the first—and is still the favorite—of the many whimsical statues that dot Bratislava's old town (such as Schöner Náci, whom we met earlier). Most date from the late 1990s, when city leaders wanted to entice locals back into the newly prettied-up and fun-loving center. There's no story behind this one—the artist simply wanted to create a playful icon and let the townspeople make up their own tales. Čumil has survived being driven over by a truck—twice—and he's still grinning.

• *Turn left at the man in the manhole and follow Rybárska to reach the long, skinny square called...*

Promenade Square (Hviezdoslavovo Námestie)

At the near end of this square is Bratislava's impressive opera house, the silver-topped **Slovak National Theater** (Slovenské Národné Divadlo). When the theater opened in the 1880s, half the shows were in German and half in Hungarian. Today, the official

language is Slovak. Across the way, the opulent, beige, Neo-Baroque building is home to the Slovak Philharmonic (Slovenská Filharmónia).

Right in front of the opera house, look down into the round, glass **display case** to see the foundation of the one-time Fishermen's Gate into the city. Water surrounds the base of the gate: This entire square was once a tributary of the Danube, and the Raddison Blu Carlton Hotel (long the VIP hotel in town) across the way was once a series of inns on different islands. The buildings along the old town side of the square mark where the city wall once stood. Now the square is a lively zone on balmy evenings, with several fine restaurants offering al fresco tables jammed with happy diners.

Turn right and stroll down the long square. Underfoot is a gigantic, cobbled version of Bratislava's city seal. After passing a statue of the square's namesake (Pavol Országh Hviezdoslav, a beloved Slovak poet), look for an ugly fence and barriers on the left. As usual, the US Embassy is the most heavily fortified building in the capital.

Just past the embassy is the low-profile entrance to the **Sky Bar,** an affordable rooftop restaurant with excellent views (ride the elevator to the seventh floor). The glass-roofed pavilion in the center of the square is a popular venue for summer concerts. Behind it, on the old town side of the square, is **Luculus,** where people are likely lined up outside for ice cream. (For ice cream without a line-up, you can backtrack to **Koun Gelato**—just before the US Embassy and immediately to the right of the Carlton Hotel.) On the right near the end of the park, a statue of Hans Christian Andersen is a reminder that the Danish storyteller enjoyed his visit to Bratislava, too.

• *Reaching the end of the square, you run into the barrier for a busy highway. Turn right and walk one block to find the big, black marble slab facing a modern monument.*

Holocaust Memorial

This was the site of Bratislava's original synagogue. You can see an etching of the building in the big slab. At the base of the memorial sculpture, look for the word "Remember" carved into the granite in Hebrew and Slovak, commemorating the 90,000 Slovak Jews who were deported to Nazi death camps. The fact that the town's main synagogue and main church (described next) were located side by

City of Three Cultures:
Pressburg, Pozsony, Bratislava

Historically more of an Austrian and Hungarian city than a Slovak one, Bratislava has always been a Central European melting pot. Over the years, notable visitors from Hans Christian Andersen to Casanova have sung the praises of this bustling burg on the Danube.

For most of its history, Bratislava was part of the Austrian Empire and known as Press-

burg, with a primarily German-speaking population. (Only the surrounding rural areas were Slovak.) The Hungarians used Pozsony (as they called it) as their capital during the century-and-a-half that Buda and Pest were occupied by Ottoman invaders.

By its turn-of-the-20th-century glory days, the city was a rich intersection of cultures—about 40 percent German, 40 percent Hungarian, and 20 percent Slovak. Shop clerks greeted customers in all three languages. It was said that the mornings belonged to the Slovaks (farmers who came into the city to sell their wares at market), the afternoons to the Hungarians (diplomats and office workers filling the cafés), and the evenings to the Austrians (wine producers who ran convivial neighborhood wine pubs where all three groups would gather). In those wine pubs, the vintner would listen to which language his customers used, then bring them a glass with the serving size expected in their home country: 0.3 liters for Hungarians, 0.25 liters for Austrians, and 0.2 liters for Slovaks (a distinction that still exists today). Jews (one-tenth of the population), and Roma (then called Gypsies) rounded out the city's ethnic brew.

side illustrates the tolerance that characterized Bratislava before Hitler. Ponder the modern statue: The open doors of an evacuated home with shadows of people who once lived there, all crowned with bullet holes and the Star of David. It evokes the fate of the more than 80,000 Slovak Jews who died in the Holocaust.

Hike up the stairs to the adjacent church. At the top of the stairs, pause to appreciate the view. Looking toward the river, you can't miss the huge **SNP**

When the new nation of Czechoslovakia was formed from the rubble of World War I, the city shed its German and Hungarian names, and took the newly created Slavic name of Bratislava. The Slovak population was on the rise, but the city remained tricultural.

World War II changed all of that. With the dissolution of Czechoslovakia, Slovakia became an "independent" country under the thumb of the Nazis—who all but wiped out the Jewish population. At the end of the war, Czechoslovakia reunited under the USSR, and expelled the city's ethnic Germans and Hungarians in retribution for the misdeeds of Hitler and Horthy (Hungary's wartime leader).

Bratislava's urban heritage suffered terribly under the communists. The historic city's multilayered charm and delicate cultural fabric were ripped apart, then shrouded in gray. The communists were prouder of their ultramodern SNP Bridge than of the city's historic Jewish quarter—which they razed to make way for the bridge. Now the bridge and its highway slice through the center of the old town, and heavy traffic rattles the stained-glass windows of St. Martin's Cathedral. The city's Germanic heritage was also deliberately obscured.

But Bratislava's most recent chapter is one of great success. Since the fall of communism, the city has gone from gloomy victim to thriving economic center and social hub. With a healthy free market economy, it now has the chance to re-create itself as Slovakia's national capital. And its advantageous position on the Danube, a short commute from Vienna, is prompting its redevelopment as one of Europe's up-and-coming cities. Once again, the streets of Bratislava are filled with German- and Hungarian-speakers...tourists and business travelers from nearby Vienna and Budapest.

Bridge (Most SNP), the communists' pride and joy. The "SNP" is shorthand for the 1944 Slovak National Uprising against the Nazis, a common focus of communist remembrance. As with most Soviet-era landmarks in former communist countries, locals aren't crazy about this structure—not only for the questionable Starship Enterprise design, but also because of the oppressive regime it represented. However, the restaurant and observation deck up top have been renovated into a posh eatery called (appropriately enough) "UFO." You can visit it for the views, a drink, or a full meal. (For details, see the listing, later.)

While the bridge was a groundbreaking design in 1972, the freeway that runs across it messed up the city. If the highway thundering a few feet in front of this historic church's door were any closer, the off-ramp would go through the nave. In the next decade, the plan is to move the highway into a tunnel that will emerge at the bridge—returning peace to this corner of Bratislava.

• *Now turn your attention to the church towering overhead.*

St. Martin's Cathedral (Dóm Sv. Martina)

Nineteen Hungarian kings and queens were crowned in this church—more than anywhere else in Hungary. A replica of the Hungarian crown still tops the steeple. There's relatively little to see inside the cathedral—but if it's open, duck in (Mon-Sat 9:00-11:30 & 13:00-18:00, Sun 13:30-16:30). In the fairly gloomy interior you'll find some fine carved-wood altarpieces (a Slovak specialty).

Just beyond the church is a stretch of the 15th-century **town wall.** The church was actually built into the wall, which explains its unusual north-side entry. In fact, look up to notice the fortified watchtower (with a WC drop on its left—and a security camera hanging out its hole) built into the corner of the church just above you.

• *Our walk is over. From here, you could either hike up to the **castle** (backtracking to the Holocaust Memorial, take the underpass beneath the highway, go up the stairs on the right marked by the* Hrad/Castle *sign, then turn left up the stepped lane marked* Zámocké Schody*), hike over the SNP Bridge (pedestrian walkway on lower level) to ride the elevator up the **UFO viewing platform**, or head for the river and stroll downstream to the thriving and futuristic new Bratislava—**Eurovea** (all these are described under "Sights in Bratislava," later).*

Or, you could carry on as described below to end up back where you started...

Back To St. Michael's Gate

Continue the rest of the way around the church and take the grand stony staircase back down to busy Panská street. Turn left and follow Panská to the corner with Ventúrska. The **old fountain** here marks the actual cross point of the two great medieval trade routes (north-south from the Baltics to the Mediterranean, and east-west along the Danube). Head left, uphill (or north toward the Baltics, if you're an amber merchant) toward St. Michael's Gate.

Over the next few blocks, you may see the names of great **composers** on plaques marking historical buildings. Franz Liszt performed in Bratislava at age nine for local aristocrats and was discovered and sent to Vienna. Beethoven composed his *Moonlight Sonata* here. Mozart performed here at age six. Haydn conducted the orchestra here, and in the 20th century Béla Bartók called Bratislava home.

If you feel like a cup of tea along the way—or you're nervous about a nuclear attack—at #9 on the left (a long block after the fountain), climb through the thick iron door and down into **Čajovňa V Podzemí** ("The Underground Tea Room," daily 14:00-22:00 except Tue and Thu from 11:00), which fills an old bomb shelter with pillows, incense, and herby frills. A couple more blocks takes you back to where you started this walk.

Sights in Bratislava

Although Bratislava's museums are underwhelming—and you could easily have a great day here without visiting any—a few right in the old town are worth considering.

ON OR NEAR THE OLD TOWN'S MAIN SQUARE
▲Primate's Palace (Primaciálny Palác)

This tastefully restored French-Neoclassical mansion (formerly the residence of the archbishop, or "primate") dates from 1781.

The religious counterpart of the castle, it filled in for Esztergom—the Hungarian religious capital—after that city was taken by the Ottomans in 1543. Even after the Ottoman defeat in the 1680s, this remained the winter residence of Hungary's archbishops. In the courtyard gurgles a fountain with St. George slaying a three-headed dragon; the exhibits are upstairs.

Cost and Hours: €3, Tue-Sun 10:00-17:00, closed Mon, Primaciálne Námestie 1, tel. 02/5935-6394, www.bratislava.sk.

Visiting the Museum: The palace, which now serves as the town hall, offers one fine floor of exhibits. Follow signs up the grand staircase to the ticket counter, then proceed up one more flight to the entrance lobby. From here, the Hall of Mirrors is on your left; straight ahead leads to a series of state apartments decorated with precious tapestries (on the right); and at the far end is a long picture gallery leading to the chapel.

Portraits hang in the lobby of the German-speaking royals who ruled Hungary, which ruled the Slovaks, who lived in this part of the vast Habsburg empire...history here is like a set of Russian stacking dolls. You'll see not one, but two portraits of Habsburg Empress Maria Theresa—young and old—as well as her father, Charles VI, and her son, Josef II. While Hungary was under Ottoman occupation, these Habsburg emperors came to Bratislava to also be crowned "kings of Hungary."

Hall of Mirrors: This is perhaps the most historic room in the city. In 1805, the "Peace of Pressburg" treaty was signed here—sorting out logistics after Napoleon beat the Austrians and Russians at the Battle of Austerlitz. This victory marked the peak of Napoleon's power. Today, the hall is used for concerts, city council meetings, and other important events. On the wall in the antechamber is a list of Bratislava's mayors since the 1280s.

State Rooms and Tapestries: This series of large public rooms, originally designed to impress, is now an art gallery. Distributed through several of these rooms is the museum's pride, and for many its highlight: a series of six English tapestries, illustrating the ancient Greek myth of the tragic love between Hero and Leander.

The tapestries were woven in England by Flemish weavers for the court of King Charles I (in the 1630s). They were kept in London's Hampton Court Palace until Charles was deposed and beheaded in 1649. Cromwell sold them to France to help fund his civil war, but after 1650, they disappeared...for centuries. In 1903, restorers broke through a false wall in this mansion and discovered the six tapestries, neatly folded and perfectly preserved. Nobody knows how they got here (perhaps they were squirreled away during the Napoleonic invasion, and whoever hid them didn't survive). The archbishop—who had just sold the palace to the city—cried foul and tried to claim the tapestries (valued at triple the sales price of the entire palace)...but the city said, "A deal's a deal."

Picture Gallery and Chapel: After traipsing through the grand rooms, go to the end of the main corridor and turn left down the hallway. This leads through the smaller rooms of the archbishop's private quarters, which are now a picture gallery decorated with minor Dutch, Flemish, German, and Italian paintings. At the end of this hall, a bay window looks down into the archbishop's own private chapel. When the archbishop became too ill to walk down to Mass, this window was built so he could take part in the service in his pajamas.

▲City History Museum (Mestské Múzeum)

Delving thoughtfully into Bratislava's past, this museum is rich in artifacts and well described in English and by the included audioguide. The core of the museum offers a sprawling, chronological look at local history through the 1920s, on two floors. The first floor features ecclesiastical art, including wood-carved statues. Upstairs, you'll have a chance to climb up into the Old Town Hall's tower, offering so-so views over the square, cathedral, and castle. Then you'll see more exhibits in rooms once used by the town council—courthouse, council hall, chapel, and so on. This is a fascinating look at Habsburg rule and slice-of-life Bratislava in the early 20th century. Look for the model of "Pressburg" during the age of Maria Theresa. Farther along, trilingual street signs are a reminder that historically, this was a city of three cultures and three languages (Slovak, German, Hungarian). The finale is down in the cellar: a graphic torture exhibit in the "law and order" zone, with replicas of torture equipment from the 16th through 18th centuries. At the far end of the exhibit, crouch down the passage to see three dreary and depressing cells...enough to make anybody behave.

Cost and Hours: €5, includes excellent audioguide, €6 combo-ticket with Apponyi House; open Tue-Fri 10:00-17:00, Sat-Sun 11:00-18:00, closed Mon; in the Old Town Hall—enter through courtyard, tel. 02/259-100-811, www.muzeum.bratislava.sk.

Apponyi House (Apponyiho Palác)

This nicely restored mansion of a Hungarian aristocrat is meaningless without the included audioguide (dull but informative). The museum has two parts. The cellar and ground floor feature an interesting exhibit on the vineyards of the nearby "Small Carpathian" hills, with historic presses and barrels, and a replica of an old-time wine-pub table. (If this exhibit interests you, consider a stop at the Slovak National Collection of Wine, also at Apponyi House and listed next). Upstairs are two floors of urban apartments from old Bratislava, called the Museum of Period Rooms. The first floor up shows off the 18th-century Rococo-style rooms of the nobility—fine but not ostentatious, with ceramic stoves. The second floor up (with lower ceilings and simpler decor) illustrates 19th-century bourgeois/middle-class lifestyles, including period clothing and some Empire-style furniture.

Cost and Hours: €4, includes audioguide, €6 combo-ticket with City History Museum, Tue-Fri 10:00-17:00, Sat-Sun 11:00-18:00, closed Mon, Radničná 1, tel. 02/5920-5135, www.muzeum.bratislava.sk.

Slovak National Collection of Wine

Run by the union of Slovak vintners, this room at the Apponyi House showcases the region's wines, 80 percent of which are white. Filling a 16th-century, brick-vaulted wine cellar, it features 100 Slovak wines that are open and eager to be tasted. Pick up the degustation list and track down what you like. An English-speaking sommelier is at your service.

Cost and Hours: Small tastings with explanations are an option, but for €23 you can taste up to 72 wines in 100 minutes... do this at the end of your sightseeing day (Tue-Fri 10:00-18:00,

BRATISLAVA

Sat from 11:00, closed Sun-Mon, Radničná 1, tel. 02/4552-9967, www.salonvin.sk).

▲Nedbalka Gallery of Slovak Modern Art

This sleek and modern gallery is owned by a local tech millionaire and run as a private nonprofit. Ride the elevator to the top floor and work chronologically through the permanent collection of 20th-century Slovak art on four delightful floors. The ground floor is dedicated to temporary exhibits. You'll notice glass is big in Slovakia (Chihuly is a Czech name, and Dale is well known and celebrated here). Admission includes a tablet multimedia guide and a nice coffee in the café.

Cost and Hours: €5, Tue-Sun 13:00-19:00, closed Mon, next to the Old Market Hall at Nedbalova 17, tel. 02/5441-0287, www.nedbalka.sk.

BEYOND THE OLD TOWN
Bratislava Castle and Museum
(Bratislavský Hrad a Múzeum)

The imposing Bratislava Castle, crowning Bratislava's hill, is the city's most prominent landmark. Big and iconic as it is, it's frankly dull up close—and the exhibits inside are not too exciting. Still, it's almost obligatory to head up here simply for the grand views over Bratislava and the Danube... though, if the weather's bad, you'd be forgiven for skipping it.

Cost and Hours: Castle grounds—free, museum—€10; Tue-Sun 10:00-18:00, Nov-March 9:00-17:00, closed Mon year-round, last entry one hour before closing; tel. 02/2048-3110, www.snm.sk.

Getting There: For the best walking route to the castle, see the end of the "Bratislava Old Town Walk," earlier in this chapter.

Background: When Habsburg Empress Maria Theresa took a liking to Bratislava in the 18th century, she transformed the castle from a military fortress to a royal residence suitable for holding court. She added a summer riding school (the U-shaped complex next to the castle), an enclosed winter riding school out back, and lots more. Maria Theresa's favorite daughter, Maria Christina, lived here with her husband, Albert, when they were newlyweds. Locals nicknamed the place "little Schönbrunn," in reference to the Habsburgs' summer palace on the outskirts of Vienna.

The palace became a fortress-garrison during the Napoleonic

Wars, then burned to the ground in an 1811 fire started by careless soldiers, and was left as a ruin for 150 years. An extensive rebuild, based on the original plans discovered in the Habsburg archives in 2008, has breathed new life into the castle (which is surrounded by a delightful public park).

Visiting the Castle: The best part of a visit here is the **grand view balcony** in front, overlooking the Danube, the Petržalka suburb across the river (marked by the SNP Bridge—described next), and—just below and upstream—the nondescript, boxy, white office building that houses the Slovak parliament. The castle is surrounded by gardens that are enjoyable on a nice day.

The dynamic statue in front of the castle's main entrance—with a knight waving his sword, rearing up on horseback—honors **Svätopluk** (846-894), the warrior-king who ruled over Great Moravia. His reign was the Slovaks' historical high-water mark, when its territory included parts of the present-day Czech Republic, Austria, Germany, Poland, Bulgaria, Romania, Serbia, Croatia, and Slovenia. Unfortunately, this dominance was short-lived; in the early 10th century, soon after Svätopluk's death, his kingdom was invaded by Magyars and folded into what became the Kingdom of Hungary—which Slovak lands would remain a part of for a thousand years. "Slovakia" has existed as a sovereign nation only since 1993; before that, you have to go all the way back to Svätopluk.

The castle **interior** features some modest exhibits and an opportunity to climb its tallest tower. It's overpriced and skippable, though the exhibits are gradually expanding—those with an interest in Slovak history might find it interesting. Inside, you'll pass through a modest exhibit about the restoration of the castle, then make your way up the grand, red-carpeted staircase to several floors of exhibits. On the third floor is a café (tucked amid a fun exhibit of nostalgic advertisements) and the "History of Slovakia" exhibit, which begins with the prehistoric Celts, tracks the arrival of the Slavs, and ends with the fall of Great Moravia after Svätopluk's time. Also on this floor, you can climb 87 steep, vertigo-inducing stairs to the top of the Crown Tower—the tallest part of the castle—for views over the city and the Danube basin (though the views from up top are not that much better than from down below).

BRATISLAVA

▲▲SNP Bridge and UFO

Bratislava's flying-saucer-capped bridge, completed in 1972 in heavy-handed communist style, has been reclaimed by capitalists.

The saucer-shaped structure called the UFO (at the Petržalka end of the bridge) is now a spruced-up café/restaurant and observation deck, allowing sweeping 360-degree views of Bratislava from about 300 feet above the Danube.

Cost and Hours: €7.50, for €2.50 more you can return for the view after dark, open daily 10:00-23:00, elevator free if you have a meal reservation or order food at the pricey restaurant, restaurant opens at 12:00, tel. 02/6252-0300, www.redmonkeygroup.com.

Getting There: Walk across the bridge from the old town (walkways cross the bridge on a level below the road; the elevator entrance is a few steps down from the downstream-side walkway).

Visiting the UFO: The **"elevator"** that takes you up is actually a funicular—you may notice you're moving at an angle. At the top, walk up the stairs to the observation deck, passing photos of the bridge's construction.

Begin by viewing the **castle** and **old town.** The area to the right of the old town, between and beyond the skyscrapers, is a massive construction zone where the new Bratislava is taking shape.

The huge TV tower caps a forested hill beyond the old town. Below and to the left of it, the pointy monument is **Slavín,** where more than 6,800 Soviet soldiers who fought to liberate Bratislava from the Nazis are buried. Under communist rule, a nearby church was forced to take down its steeple so as not to draw attention away from the huge Soviet soldier on top of the monument.

Now turn 180 degrees and cross the platform to face **Petržalka,** a planned communist suburb that sprouted here in the 1970s. The site was once occupied by a village, and the various districts of modern Petržalka still carry their original names (which now seem ironic): "Meadows" *(Háje),* "Woods" *(Lúky),* and "Courtyards" *(Dvory).* The ambitious communist planners envisioned a city laced with Venetian-style canals to help drain the marshy land, but the plans were abandoned after the harsh crackdown on the

1968 Prague Spring uprising. Without the incentives of private ownership, all they succeeded in creating was a grim and decaying sea of miserable concrete apartment *paneláky* ("panel buildings," so-called because they're made of huge prefab panels).

Today, one in six Bratislavans lives in Petržalka, and things are looking better. Like Dorothy opening the door to Oz, the formerly drab buildings have been splashed with bright new colors, and the interiors have been modernized. Far from being a slum, Petržalka is now a popular neighborhood for Bratislavan yuppies who can't yet afford to build their dream houses.

Petržalka is also a big suburban-style shopping zone (note the supermall down below). But there's still some history here. The **park** called Sad Janka Kráľa (originally, in German, Aupark)—just downriver from the bridge—was technically the first public park in Europe in the 1770s and is still a popular place for locals to relax and court.

Scanning the **horizon** beyond Petržalka, two things stick out: on the left, the old communist oil refinery (which has been fully updated and is now state-of-the-art); and on the right, a forest of modern windmills. These are just over the border, in Austria...and Bratislava is sure to grow in that direction quickly. Austria is about three miles that way, and Hungary is about six miles farther to the left.

Before you leave, consider a drink at the café. If nothing else, be sure to use the memorable WCs.

Blue Church of St. Elisabeth (Kostol Svätej Alžbety)

Just east of the old town—through a nicely manicured new park— is a fine little neighborhood of cheery, colorful Art Nouveau buildings. The main landmark here is the gentle-blue, fancifully decorated Church of St. Elisabeth—also called simply the "Little Blue Church." It's straight out of a fairy tale, with rounded edges, pretty flourishes, and vivid colors. Designed by the great Hungarian Secessionist architect Ödön Lechner, and completed in 1913, it's worth the short walk from the old town for architecture

BRATISLAVA

fans. While the interior is open limited hours to the public, you can often peek through the glass doors to see the similarly soft and pretty interior (Bezručova 2).

▲Eurovea and the New Bratislava

Just downstream from the old town is the modern Eurovea complex, with four layers, each a quarter-mile long: a riverside park, luxury condos, a thriving modern shopping mall, and an office park. While it's essentially a big riverfront shopping mall, those looking for a peek at the "new Bratislava" find it worth the lovely, short riverfront stroll from the old town...which is also a chance to check out all of the moored riverboats.

Eurovea's central public space is a fountain- and statue-filled people zone between the Danube and Bratislava's new National Theater. Directly in front of the theater, the pavement is pulled back to show original Roman paving stones that were excavated here (a reminder of the city's long history as a trade crossroads). At the river end of the square, under the lion-topped pillar, a statue features General Milan Rastislav Štefánik, who represented Slovakia in a 1918 meeting in Pittsburgh and signed the "Pittsburgh Agreement"—creating the combined state of Česko-Slovensko. He's holding a bronze copy of the document as he looks out at the Danube.

The riverfront strip of Eurovea is the embryo of a huge vision for a new Bratislava. Dozens of skyscrapers are being built at once, as the city's old industrial zone (destroyed in World War II, and now destined to be the city's future tech-industry home) is one big construction site.

Exploring the old town gives you a taste of where this country has been. But wandering this riverside park, enjoying a drink in one of its chic outdoor lounges, and then browsing the thriving mall, you'll enjoy a glimpse of where Slovakia is heading.

Sleeping in Bratislava

Because Bratislava is more business city than tourist city, you'll find weekends are a little less expensive. For locations, see the "Bratislava" map, earlier.

$$$ Hotel Marrol's, on a quiet urban street, is the town's most enticing splurge. Although the immediate neighborhood isn't interesting, it's just a five-minute walk from the old town, the public spaces are plush and generous, and its 53 rooms are luxurious and tastefully appointed Old World country-style. While pricey, rates drop on weekends (air-con, elevator, gorgeous lounge, Tobrucká 4, tel. 02/5778-4600, www.hotelmarrols.sk, rec@hotelmarrols.sk).

$$$ Roset Boutique Hotel, facing the ring road's tram tracks at the eastern edge of the old town (with some street noise), feels classy and upmarket. Its 28 rooms are spacious and plush (air-con, elevator, Štúrova 10, tel. 02/3217-1819, www.rosethotel.sk, reservations@rosethotel.sk).

$$$ Radisson Blu Carlton Hotel has been hosting VIPs for decades, with 170 rooms and all the big corporate trappings and expected services. It's beautifully located, facing the National Theater and Promenade Square (air-con, elevator, Hviezdoslavovo Námestie 3, tel. 02/5939-0000, www.radissonblu.com/hotel-bratislava, reservation.bratislava@radissonblu.com).

$$ Loft Hotel is an appealing midrange choice, tucked along the highway between the main train station and the old town (ask for a quieter back room facing the garden). It's professional, stylish, and trendy—with comfy leather couches in the lobby, an on-site brewpub, and a staff that prides itself on its service. Of the 121 rooms, the "standard" rooms are fine but forgettable; consider paying a bit more for a cushier, retro-industrial "superior" room (air-con, elevator, pay parking garage, Štefánikova 4, tel. 02/5751-1000, www.lofthotel.sk, reservation@lofthotel.sk). They also have 10 more expensive, high-end rooms in the attached **Wilson Palace,** in the original building facing the main road.

$ Aplend City Hotel Michalská is a tight little hotel with a peaceful back garden tucked just inside St. Michael's Gate in the old town. The 14 rooms are comfortable, and the location—on a picturesque lane—is ideal (air-con, elevator, Baštová 4, tel. 903/998-111, www.aplendcity.com/en/hotel-michalska, michalska@aplendcity.com).

$ Penzión Virgo, on a quiet residential street an eight-minute walk from the old town, rents 12 boutique-ish rooms (breakfast extra, reserve ahead for inexpensive parking, Panenská 14, tel. 02/2092-1400, mobile 0948-350-878, www.penzionvirgo.sk, reception@penzionvirgo.sk).

Eating in Bratislava

Slovak cooking involves some Hungarian and Austrian influences, but it's closer to Czech cuisine—lots of starches and gravy, and plenty of pork, cabbage, potatoes, and dumplings. Keep an eye out for Slovakia's intensely filling national dish, *bryndzové halušky* (small potato dumplings with sheep's cheese and bits of bacon). For a fun drink and snack that locals love, try a Vinea grape soda and a sweet, crescent-shaped *Pressburger* bagel in any bar or café.

Like the Czechs, the Slovaks produce excellent beer (*pivo,* PEE-voh). The dominant brand is Zlatý Bažant ("Golden Pheasant"). Bratislava's beer halls are good places to sample Slovak beers—whether macrobrews or microbrews—and to get a hearty, affordable meal of stick-to-your-ribs pub grub. The Bratislava region also produces wines, similar to the ones that Vienna is known for. But, as nearly all is consumed locally, most outsiders don't think of Slovakia as wine country.

Bratislava is packed with inviting new eateries. In addition to heavy Slovak staples, you'll find trendy new bars and bistros, and a smattering of non-European offerings. The best plan may be to stroll the old town and keep your eyes open for the setting and cuisine that appeals to you most. Or consider the areas listed below. All are within a short walk and offer a better, more interesting dining experience than the grotesquely touristy eateries that line Michalská street and other busy streets in the old town. For locations, see the "Bratislava" map, earlier.

Traditional Beer Hall on Námestie SNP

A couple of blocks north of the old town (and named for the Slovak National Uprising), the right side of this square is dominated by the following operation.

$$ Bratislavská is a sprawling complex of eateries. The main location (door on the right) is the Bratislavská Reštaurácia. Walk through a maze of old-timey rooms, then up a flight of stairs to a huge dining hall that smells hoppy and feels happy (with the waitstaff sporting "Bar-tislava" and "Bra-tislava" T-shirts). The menu features classic Slovak dishes, and the portions are hearty and cheap. For a more intimate setting, the door to the left leads to the tight, woody Kláštorný Pivovar ("Monastery Brewery"), with a cozier ambience and the same menu. They also have tables outside on the square (daily 12:00-23:00, Námestie SNP 8, mobile 0917-927-673).

Near the Old Market Hall

While there's often nothing actually inside the Old Market Hall (which fills a city block, at the eastern edge of the old town—a 5-minute walk from the main square), it's surrounded by intriguing and trendy options. Once a month, the square in front features a "Street Food Park" with a wide variety of food trucks (worth planning around—check schedule at www.staratrznica.sk). At other times, walk around the block to survey your options (listed in order, from the front door).

$ Výčap u Ernőho is a popular, no-frills beer hall, with a row of taps up front featuring a changing selection of quality beers. If you'd like to enjoy Slovak beers with local hipsters instead of the sloppy beer-hall tourist crowd, do it here (no food, Tue-Sat 12:00-24:00, Sun from 16:00, Mon from 15:00, Námestie SNP 25, mobile 0948-360-153).

$ Foodstock is an enticing, hip, and healthy vegetarian place that advertises "good mood food." It got its start as a food truck, and now serves up a brief menu of delicious, Asian-inspired dishes and all-you-can-drink homemade iced teas in a patchouli-scented space (daily 10:00-22:00, Klobučnícka 6, mobile 0905-456-654).

$$ Mecheche Snack Bar serves tiny, fancy sandwiches as if channeling a Barcelona tapas bar (Tue-Sat 17:00-24:00, closed Sun-Mon, Nedbalova 12, mobile 0948-853-444).

$$ Urban House, behind the Old Market Hall on fashionable Laurinská street, is California-trendy with a sprawling, industrial-mod, woody-bookstore ambience, great outdoor tables, and an appealing menu. The food (burgers, pizza, and so on) is nothing special, but the scene is fun (daily 9:00-24:00, Laurinská 14, mobile 0904-001-021).

Restaurants on Promenade Square (Hviezdoslavovo Námestie)

This square is lined with restaurants, nearly all with open-feeling interior seating and mellow tables out on the square under the trees—ideal for enjoying the promenade of strollers. There's no traffic, just the sound of fountains and the breeze. A strip of three places, side-by-side, makes for easy comparison-shopping; for a view, head up to Sky Bar.

$$$ Carnevalle is a hit for its steak. Their greeting? "Nice to meat you!" Their indoors feels outdoors—a spacious, glassed-in dining hall—and their tables on the square are inviting. The tasty dishes are nicely presented by a professional waitstaff (daily 11:00-24:00, at #20, mobile 0903-123-164).

$$ Zylinder ("Top Hat") recreates a circa-1900 atmosphere to serve classy bourgeoise cuisine that leans closer to Austrian than traditional Slovak—think sausages and schnitzels (daily 11:00-22:00, at #19, mobile 0903-123-134).

$ Café Restaurant Verne, university-owned and unburdened by the high rent of its neighbors, feels like the dive bar of the strip—with mismatched antique tables spilling out onto the cobbles. It has a cozy, lowbrow, and mellow student vibe with stick-to-your-rib plates (pasta, goulash, salads) and drinks. You get what you pay for, but the price is right (Mon-Fri 8:00-24:00, Sat-Sun from 10:00, at #18).

Rooftop View: $$$ Sky Bar Restaurant, just past the fenced-in US Embassy, features a Thai-meets-Mediterranean menu on its seventh-floor open-roof terrace. It's a pretentious place, with local big shots dropping by and stuffy service. But the food's good and so are the views. It's smart to reserve a view table in advance to dine here—or just drop by for a pricey vodka cocktail (daily 12:00-late, Hviezdoslavovo Námestie 7, mobile 0948-109-400, www.skybar. sk).

Eurovea

This modern development facing the Danube River (a short walk downstream from the old town) has huge outdoor terraces rollicking with happy eaters. A variety of upscale and high-energy **$$$ restaurants** lines the swanky riverfront residential and shopping-mall complex. Options include international—French, Italian, Brazilian—as well as branches of the Czech beer-hall chain **Kolkovna** and the British pan-Asian restaurant **Wagamama.** Or you can head to the **$ food court** in the shopping mall, where you'll eat cheap. While the restaurants here are nothing special, it's a fun excuse for a stroll along the Danube promenade, and to get a peek at the emerging "new Bratislava" zone beyond the old town cobbles.

Bratislava Connections

BY TRAIN

Bratislava has two major train stations: the main station, walkable to some accommodations and the old town (Hlavná Stanica, abbreviated "Bratislava hl. st." on schedules); and Petržalka station, in a suburb across the river and linked to town by bus. When checking schedules, pay attention to which station your train uses. Frequent bus #93 connects the two stations in about 10 minutes. For public transit info and maps, see http://imhd.sk.

Hlavná Stanica (Main Train Station)

This decrepit station is about a half-mile north of the old town. A left-luggage desk is to your right as you exit the tracks (*úschovňa batožín;* confirm open hours for pick-up). There are also a few lockers along track 1; more are to the left from the main hall (after the vending machines and through the door). The station also has a TI window, and there's an ATM in the main hall. A nicer, more modern waiting area is down the hallway to the left (with the tracks at your back).

Getting Downtown: It's a short bus ride or a boring 15-minute walk to the town center. (**Taxis** stand by, but with rip-off prices—they'll try to charge €15 rather than the legitimate €5 drop charge for the short ride. You can try insisting on the meter, but since they're basically unregulated, it likely won't help.)

Bus #93 leaves every five minutes from the right-hand curb 50 yards in front of the station; it stops at Grassalkovich Palace, Zochova (nearest the old town), and Most SNP (the bus station under the SNP Bridge, by the river). Buy a 15-minute *základný lístok/basic* ticket from the machine for €0.70, and stamp it as you get on the bus.

To **walk** downtown, exit out the station's front door and follow the covered walkway past the bus stops. After the road bends right, take the pedestrian overpass, then head straight downhill on the busy main drag, Štefánikova. You'll pass the presidential gardens, then Grassalkovich Palace, Slovakia's "White House". The old town—marked by the green steeple of St. Michael's Gate (the start of my self-guided walk)—is a long block ahead of you.

Petržalka Train Station (ŽST Petržalka)

Half of the trains from Vienna arrive at this quiet, modern little train station, across the river in the modernized suburb of Petržalka. The main hall has an ATM and luggage lockers (by the door to the tracks).

Getting Downtown: Two different buses head to the old town, from opposite sides of the station. For either bus, buy a 15-minute *základný lístok/basic* ticket from the machine for €0.70, and stamp it as you board. The stop closest to the old town is Zochova. **Bus #80** stops closest to the station but makes more stops on the way to town: From the main hall, exit, cross the street, and turn left to find the stop (direction: Kollárova nám). **Bus #93** is more direct but a longer walk from the station: Take the long tunnel under the tracks, exit on the other side, and follow the crosswalk straight across the busy highway to find the stop (direction: Hlavná Stanica).

From Bratislava by Train to: Budapest (7/day direct, 3 hours), **Vienna** (€12, 2/hour, 1 hour; departures alternate between the two stations—half from main station usually leaving hourly at :38, half from Petržalka usually leaving hourly at :15), **Sopron** (nearly hourly direct from Petržalka, 2.5 hours on RegionalExpress/REX), **Prague** (5/day direct, 4 hours). To reach other Hungarian destinations (including **Eger** and **Pécs**), it's generally easiest to change in Budapest.

BY BUS

Two companies run handy buses that connect Bratislava, **Vienna,** and the **airports** in each city: Flixbus (www.flixbus.com) and Slovak Lines/Postbus (tel. 0810-222-3336, www.slovaklines.sk) get you to Vienna for just €5-8. You can book ahead online, or (if arriving at the airport) just take whichever connection is leaving first.

BY BOAT

Riverboats connect Bratislava to Vienna. Conveniently, these boats dock right along the Danube in front of Bratislava's old town. While they are more expensive, less frequent, and slower than the train, some travelers enjoy getting out on the Danube. (Sail with your passport, as you'll be crossing a border.)

The **Twin City Liner** runs modern catamarans between a dock at the edge of Bratislava's old town, along Fajnorovo nábrežie, and Vienna's Schwedenplatz (where Vienna's town center hits the canal; €30-35 each way, 3-5/day, late March-Oct only, 1.5 hours; reservations smart, Austrian tel. 00-43-1-904-8880, www.twincityliner.com).

The competing Slovak **LOD** line connects the cities a little more cheaply (on older Russian hydrofoils), but runs just twice a day and uses Vienna's less-convenient Reichsbrücke dock on the main river, farther from the city center (€25 one-way, €44 round-trip, 1.5 hours, tel. 02/5293-2226, www.lod.sk).

BY PLANE

While Bratislava has a small airport (used mostly by discount airlines), the Vienna Airport is so close it's considered the local airport.

Bratislava Airport (Letisko Bratislava)

This airport (airport code: BTS, www.bts.aero) is six miles northeast of downtown Bratislava. Budget airline Ryanair has many flights here. Some airlines market it as "Vienna-Bratislava," thanks to its proximity to both capitals. It's compact and manageable, with all the usual amenities.

From the Airport to Downtown Bratislava: The airport has easy **public bus** connections to Bratislava's main train station (Hlavná Stanica, €1.20 one-hour ticket, bus #61, 3-4/hour, 30 minutes). A **taxi** from the airport into central Bratislava should cost about €20.

To Budapest: Take the bus or taxi to Bratislava's main train station, then hop a train to Budapest.

To Vienna: You can take the **Flixbus** to the Erdberg stop on Vienna's U-3 subway line (€8, runs every 1-2 hours, 1 hour, www.flixbus.com) or the **Slovak Lines/Postbus** bus to Vienna's Hauptbahnhof (€10, 1-2/hour, 2 hours, www.slovaklines.sk). A **taxi** from Bratislava Airport directly to Vienna costs €60-90 (depending on whether you use a cheaper Slovak or more expensive Austrian cab).

Vienna International Airport

This airport, 12 miles from downtown Vienna and 30 miles from downtown Bratislava, is well connected to both capitals (airport code: VIE, airport tel. 01/700-722-233, www.viennaairport.com). If you're heading straight to Bratislava, there's no need to go into Vienna from here. The easiest option is to take the Flixbus or Slovak Lines/Postbus bus described above. Check schedules on the airport website (under "Arrival & Parking") or ask the airport TI which bus is leaving first, then head straight out the door and hop on. After about 45 minutes, the bus stops in downtown Bratislava, then heads to the Bratislava airport.

HUNGARY: PAST & PRESENT

When describing the story of Budapest, it's tempting to fall back on the trusty onion metaphor: The city, which has been adored and destroyed by many different groups across the centuries, is layered with history...sometimes stinky, sometimes sweet. This chapter will help you peel back those layers, step-by-step.

The Hungarian story—essentially the tale of a people finding their home—is as epic as any in Europe. Over the course of a millennium, a troublesome nomadic tribe that was the scourge of Europe gradually assimilated with its neighbors and—through a combination of tenacity and diplomacy—found itself controlling a vast swath of Central and Eastern Europe. Since arriving in Europe in 896, the Hungarians adopted Christianity; fended off Tatars and Turks; lost, regained, then lost again two-thirds of their land; and built one of the world's great 19th-century cities.

Today, despite their mysterious origins and idiosyncrasies, the Hungarians have carved out a unique and vital niche in European life. Locals toss around the names of great historical figures such as Kossuth, Széchenyi, and Nagy as if they're talking about old friends. Take this crash course so you can keep up.

The story begins long, long ago and far, far away...

WELCOME TO EUROPE

The land we call Hungary has long been considered the place—culturally and geographically—where the West (Europe) meets the East (Asia). The Roman province of Pannonia once extended to the final foothills of the Alps that constitute the Buda Hills, on the west side of the Danube. Across the river, Rome ended and the barbarian wilds began. From here, the Great Hungarian Plain stretches in a long, flat expanse all the way to Asia—hemmed in to the north by the Carpathian Mountains. (Geologists consider this prairie-like plain to be the westernmost steppe in Europe—resembling the terrain that covers much of Central Asia.) After Rome collapsed and Europe fell into the Dark Ages, Hungary became the territory of Celts, Vandals, Huns, and Avars...until some out-of-towners moved into the neighborhood.

The seven nomadic Magyar tribes, led by the mighty Árpád (and, according to legend, guided by the mythical Turul bird),

thundered into the Carpathian Basin in AD 896. (For more on this rough-and-tumble clan, see the "Who Were the Magyars?" sidebar.) But after their long and winding westward odyssey, the Great Hungarian Plain felt comfortingly like home to the Magyars—reminiscent of the Asian steppes of their ancestors.

The Magyars would camp out in today's Hungary in the winters, and in the summers, they'd go on raids throughout Europe. They were notorious as incredibly swift horsemen, whose use of stirrups (an eastern innovation largely unknown in Europe at the time) allowed them to easily outmaneuver foes and victims. From Italy, France, Germany's Rhine, the Spanish Pyrenees, all the way to Constantinople (modern-day Istanbul)—the Magyars had the run of the Continent.

For half a century, the Magyars ranked with the Vikings as the most feared people in Europe. To Europeans, this must have struck a chord of queasy familiarity: a mysterious and dangerous eastern tribe running roughshod over Europe, speaking a gibberish language, and employing strange, terrifying, relentless battle techniques. No wonder they called the new arrivals "Hungarians."

Planted in the center of Europe, the Magyars effectively drove a wedge in the middle of the sprawling Slavic populations of the Great Moravian Kingdom (basically today's "Eastern Europe"). The Slavs were split into north and south—a division that persists today: Czechs, Slovaks, and Poles to the north; and Croats, Slovenes, Serbs, Bosniaks, and Bulgarians to the south. (You can still hear the division caused by the Magyars in the language: While Czechs and Russians call a castle *hrad*, Croats and Serbs call it *grad*.)

After decades of terrorizing Europe, the Magyars were finally defeated by a German and Czech army at the Battle of Augsburg in 955. Géza, Grand Prince of the Hungarians—realizing that if they were to survive, his people had to put down roots and get along with their neighbors—made a fateful decision that would forever

Who Were the Magyars?

The ancestors of today's Hungarians, the Magyars, are a mysterious lot. Of all the Asian invaders of Europe, they were arguably the most successful—integrating more or less smoothly with the Europeans, and thriving well into the 21st century. Centuries after the Huns, Tatars, and Ottomans retreated east (leaving behind only fragments of their culture), the Hungarians remain a fixture in contemporary Europe.

The history of the Magyars before they arrived in Europe in AD 896 is hotly contested. Because their language is related only to Finnish and Estonian, it's presumed that these three peoples were once a single group, which likely originated east of the Ural Mountains (in the steppes of present-day Asian Russia, near Mongolia).

After the Magyars' ancestors spent some time in Siberia, climatic change pushed them south and west, eventually (likely around the fifth century AD) crossing the Ural Mountains and officially entering Europe. They settled near the Don River (in today's southwestern Russia) before local warfare pushed them farther and farther west. The tribes went first north, to Scandinavia, where some stayed (the ancestors of today's Finns and Estonians). But others continued south, seeking the sun, and finally arrived in the Carpathian Basin—today's Hungary—around AD 896.

For a time, the Magyars ran raids into neighboring European lands. But eventually they settled down and began to intermarry with Germans, Slavs, and other European peoples. Gradually, their Asian features and customs mostly faded away. But the Hungarians compelled their European subjects to adopt the Hungarian language and some elements of the culture ("Magyarization"). Hungary became Central Europe's melting pot. After all these centuries, most Hungarians have lost track of the many tangled strains of their personal family histories. Many people who consider themselves "fully Hungarian" have last names that are obviously Polish, Jewish, German, Serbian, and so on—likely dating back generations.

But even though certain aspects of their Magyar heritage have been lost to time, the Hungarians have done a remarkable job of clinging to their Asian roots. They still do things their own way, making Hungary unmistakably different from its neighboring countries. And people of German-Hungarian, Slavic-Hungarian, and Jewish-Hungarian descent still speak a language that's not too far removed from the Asian tongue of those original Magyars.

shape Hungary's future: He adopted Christianity; baptized his son, Vajk; and married him to a Bavarian princess at a young age.

On Christmas Day in the year 1000, Vajk changed his name to István (Stephen) and was symbolically crowned by the pope (for

more on István, see page 161). At István's request, a Venetian missionary, Gerardo di Sagredo, came to Buda to help convert the Hungarians. But he was martyred for his efforts, becoming known to Hungarians as St. Gellért. The domestication of the nomadic Magyars was difficult—due largely to the resistance of István's uncles—but was ultimately successful. Hungary became a legitimate Christian kingdom, welcomed by its neighbors. Under kings such as László I, Kálmán "the Book Lover," and András II, Hungary entered a period of prosperity. (For more on these three kings, see pages 161-162.) Medieval Hungary ruled a vast empire—including large parts of today's Slovakia, Romania (Transylvania), Serbia (Vojvodina), and Croatia.

THE TATARS, THE OTTOMANS, AND OTHER OUTSIDERS (AD 1000-1686)

One of Hungary's earliest challenges came at the hands of fellow invaders from Central Asia. Through the first half of the 13th century, the Tatars—initially led by Genghis Khan—swept into Eastern Europe from Mongolia. In the summer of 1241, Genghis Khan's son and successor, Ögedei Khan, broke into Hungarian territory. The Tatars sacked and plundered Hungarian towns, laying waste to the kingdom. It was only Ögedei Khan's death in early 1242—and the ensuing dispute about succession—that saved the Hungarians, as Tatar armies rushed home and the Mongolian Empire contracted. The Hungarian king, Béla IV, was left to rebuild his ruined kingdom—creating some of the first stout hilltop castles that still line the Danube. (For more on Béla IV, see page 163.)

Each of Béla's successors left his own mark on Hungary, as the Magyar kingdom flourished. When the original Árpád dynasty died out in 1301, they imported French kings (from the Naples-based Anjou, or Angevin, dynasty) to continue building their young realm. King Károly Róbert (Charles Robert) won over the Magyars, and his son Nagy Lajos (Louis the Great) expanded Hungarian holdings (for more on these two, see pages 163-164).

This was a period of flux for all of Central and Eastern Europe, as the nearby Czech and Polish kingdoms also saw their long-standing dynasties expire. For a time, royal intermarriages juggled the crowns of the region between various ruling families. Most notably, for 50 years (1387-1437) Hungary was ruled by Holy Roman Emperor Sigismund of Luxembourg, whose holdings also included the Czech lands, parts of Italy, much of Croatia, and more.

For more than 150 years, Hungary did not have a Hungarian-blooded king. This changed in the late 15th century, when a

shortage of foreign kings led the enlightened King Mátyás (Matthias) Corvinus to ascend to the throne. The son of popular military hero János Hunyadi, King Matthias fostered the arts, sparked a mini-Renaissance, and successfully balanced foreign threats to Hungarian sovereignty (the Habsburgs to the north and west, and the Ottomans to the south and east). Under Matthias, Hungarian culture and political power reached a peak. (For more on this great Hungarian king, see page 197.)

But even before the reign of "good king Mátyás," the Ottomans (from today's Turkey) had already begun slicing their way through the Balkan Peninsula toward Central Europe. (It's ironic that the two greatest threats to the Magyar kingdom came in the form of fellow Asian invaders: Tatars and Turks. Or maybe it's not surprising, as these groups all found the steppes of Hungary so familiar and inviting.) In 1526, the Ottomans entered Hungary when Sultan Süleyman the Magnificent killed Hungary's King Lajos II at the Battle of Mohács. By 1541, they took Buda. The Ottomans would dominate Hungarian life (and history) until the 1680s—nearly a century and a half.

The Ottoman invasion divided Hungary into thirds: Ottoman-occupied "Lower Hungary" (more or less today's Hungary); rump "Upper Hungary" (basically today's Slovakia), with its capital at Bratislava (which they called "Pozsony"); and the loosely independent territories of Transylvania, ruled by Hungarian dukes. During this era, the Ottomans built some of the thermal baths that you'll still find throughout Hungary.

Ottoman-occupied Hungary became severely depopulated, and many of its towns and cities fell into ruins. While it was advantageous for a Hungarian subject to adopt Islam (for lower taxes and other privileges), the Ottomans rarely forced conversions—unlike the arguably more oppressive Catholics who controlled other parts of Europe at the time (such as the monarchs of Spain, who expelled the Jews and conducted the Spanish Inquisition). Ottoman rule meant that Hungary took a different course than other parts of Europe during this time. The nation fully enjoyed the Renaissance, but missed out on other major European historical events—both good (the Age of Discovery and Age of Reason) and bad (the devastating Catholic-versus-Protestant wars that plagued much of the rest of Europe).

Crippled by the Ottomans and lacking power and options, desperate Hungarian nobles offered their crown to the Austrian Habsburg Empire, in exchange for salvation from the invasion. The Habsburgs instead used Hungary as a kind of "buffer zone" between the Ottoman advance and Vienna. And that was only the beginning of a very troubled relationship between the Hungarians and the Austrians.

HABSBURG RULE, HUNGARIAN NATIONAL REVIVAL, AND REVOLUTION (1686-1867)

In the late 17th century, the Habsburg army, starting from Vienna, began a sustained campaign to push the Ottomans out of Hungary in about 15 years. They finally wrested Buda and Pest from the Ottomans in 1686. The Habsburgs repopulated Buda and Pest with Germans, while Magyars reclaimed the countryside. Even 25 years after the Ottomans were kicked out, the combined population of Buda and Pest was less than 20,000—and most of them were Germans from other parts of the Habsburg Empire.

As recently as the early 19th century, Hungary was considered practically beyond Europe; Vienna marked the end of the "civilized" European world. But that would soon change. The population of Buda and Pest grew nearly tenfold from the beginning to the end of the 19th century. The new Austrian rulers rebuilt Hungary in their favored colorful, frilly Baroque style. Even today, it seems every Hungarian town has a cheerfully painted church with a Habsburg-style steeple.

The Habsburgs governed the country as an outpost of Austria. The Hungarians—who'd had enough of foreign rule—fought them tooth and nail. Countless streets, squares, and buildings throughout the country are named Rákóczi, Széchenyi, or Kossuth—the "big three" Hungarian patriots who resisted the Habsburgs during this time.

Transylvanian prince Ferenc Rákóczi led Hungarians in the first major rebellion against the Habsburgs, the War of Independence (1703-1711). While Rákóczi initially enjoyed great territorial gains, his war ultimately failed, he went into exile in the Ottoman

Empire, and Habsburg rule continued. (For more on Rákóczi, see page 166.)

The early 19th century saw a thawing of Habsburg oppression. Here as throughout Europe, "backward" country traditions began to trickle into the cities, gaining more respect and prominence. It was during this time of reforms that Hungarian (rather than German) became the official language. It also coincided with a Romantic Age of poets and writers (such as Mihály Vörösmarty and Sándor Petőfi) who began using Hungarian to create literature for the first time. By around 1825, the Hungarian National Revival was underway, as the people began to embrace the culture and traditions of their Magyar ancestors. Like people across Europe—from Ireland to Italy, and from Prague to Scandinavia—the Hungarians were rediscovering what made them unique.

In Hungary, the movement was spearheaded by Count István Széchenyi, who had a compelling vision of a resurgent Hungarian nation, and the wealth and influence to make it happen. Széchenyi funded grand structures in Budapest (such as the iconic Chain Bridge) to give his Magyar countrymen something to take pride in. But even as Széchenyi spurred Hungarian patriotism, he was savvy enough not to push for total Hungarian independence—knowing that the volatile combination of strong Habsburg rule and a complicated ethnic mix would make an independent Hungarian state untenable. Rather, he sought some degree of autonomy within the empire. And it began to work, as the Habsburgs gave in to some Hungarian demands.

And yet, despite the "Reform Age" that was already brewing, the gradual progress was too little, too late for many Hungarians. In March of 1848, a wave of Enlightenment-fueled nationalism that began in Paris ignited a revolutionary spirit in cities such as Vienna, Milan...and Budapest.

In Hungary, it inspired a revolt against the Habsburgs. Széchenyi's slowly-but-surely patriotism was eclipsed by the militarism of popular orator Lajos Kossuth (pictured) and patriotic poet Sándor Petőfi.

Top 10 Dates That Changed Hungary

AD 896: The nomadic Magyars (a tribe from Central Asia) arrive in the Carpathian Basin and begin to terrorize Europe.

1000: King István (Stephen) accepts Christianity, marking the domestication of the Magyars.

1541: Invading Ottomans take Buda and Pest...and build thermal baths.

1686: The Austrian Habsburgs drive out the Ottomans, making Hungary part of their extensive empire (despite occasional rebellions from nationalistic Hungarians).

1867: A Golden Age begins, as Hungary gains semiautonomy from Austria; Budapest, the new co-capital of a vast empire, booms.

1920: A loser in World War I, Hungary is stripped of two-thirds of its territory and half its population in the Treaty of Trianon.

1945: Hungary allies with Germany for most of World War II. After the war, the Soviet Union "liberates" the country and establishes a communist state.

1956: Inspired by Imre Nagy, Hungarians bravely revolt. A massive invasion of Soviet tanks and soldiers brutally suppresses the rebellion, killing 2,500 (and executing Nagy).

1989: Hungary is the first Soviet satellite to open its borders to the West, sparking similar reforms throughout the Eastern Bloc.

2004: Hungary joins the European Union.

On March 15, the Revolution of 1848 began with Petőfi reading a rabble-rousing poem on the steps of the National Museum in Pest (see page 47).

For several tense months, the uprising led to little more than diplomatic wrangling (as the Habsburgs were distracted elsewhere). Meanwhile, minority groups inside Hungarian territory—most notably the Croats, led by Josip Jelačić—began to rise up, in turn, against the Hungarians. That winter, Habsburg Emperor Ferdinand I abdicated, replaced by his young nephew, Franz Josef. One of his first acts was to officially condemn Hungarian independence.

In the spring of 1849, the Hungarians mounted a bloody but successful offensive to take over a wide swath of territory, including Buda and Pest. But in June, Franz Josef enlisted the aid of his fellow divine monarch, the Russian czar, who did not want the Magyars to provide an example for his own independence-minded subjects. Some 200,000 Russian reinforcements flooded into Hungary, crushing the revolution by August. After the final battle, the Habsburgs executed 13 Hungarian generals, then celebrated by clinking mugs of beer. To this very day, clinking beer mugs is, for many traditional Hungarians, just bad style.

For a while, the Habsburgs cracked down on their unruly Hungarian subjects. It was a time of shame for Hungary. Lajos Kossuth, now in exile, traveled the world to convince foreign leaders to take an interest in Hungary's plight (for more on him, see page 166). The now-forgotten Count Széchenyi spent his final years in a mental hospital, before committing suicide in 1860. The poet Sándor Petőfi—Hungary's answer to Lord Byron—disappeared while participating in an 1849 battle, and is presumed to have been killed in the fighting.

In the 1860s, a clever elder statesman named Ferenc Deák—in an attempt to seize on the spirit of reform and the liberalization of the time—began to advocate for a power-sharing arrangement with the Habsburgs. Deák believed that diplomacy could be more effective than military action. His often-repeated motto: "Quiet persistence can succeed where violence fails." (In some ways, this could be the slogan for the whole of Hungarian history.)

After an important military loss to Bismarck's Prussia in 1866, Austria understood that it couldn't control its rebellious Slavic holdings all by itself. The Habsburgs found themselves governing a sprawling empire in which their own ethnic/linguistic group— Germans—was a tiny minority. In order to balance out the huge Slav population, they took Deák's advice and teamed up with the Hungarians.

And so, just 18 years after crushing the Hungarians in a war, the Habsburgs handed them the reins. With the Compromise *(Ausgleich)* of 1867, Austria granted Budapest the authority over the eastern half of their lands, creating the so-called Dual Monarchy of the Austro-Hungarian Empire. Hungary was granted their much-prized "home rule," where most matters (except finance, foreign policy, and the military) were administered from Budapest rather than Vienna. The Habsburg emperor, Franz Josef, agreed to a unique "king and emperor" *(König und Kaiser)* arrangement, where he was emperor of Austria, but only king of Hungary. In 1867, he was crowned Hungarian king in both Buda (at Matthias Church) and Pest (on today's March 15 Square). The insignia "K+K" *(König und Kaiser)*—which you'll still see everywhere—evokes these grand days. (For more on Franz Josef and his wife Sisi, see page 292.)

BUDAPEST'S GOLDEN AGE (1867-1918)

The *Ausgleich* marked a precipitous turning point for the Hungarians, who once again governed their traditional holdings: large parts of today's Slovakia, Serbia, and Transylvania, and smaller parts of today's Croatia, Slovenia, Ukraine, and Austria. To better govern their sprawling realm, in 1873, the cities of Buda, Pest, and Óbuda merged into one mega-metropolis: Budapest. But each part still retains its unique character. Buda, which was more Germanic, Catholic, and pro-Habsburg, remains the traditional, conservative part of town. And Pest, which was a hotbed of Magyar pride and the crucible of the uprisings of the mid-19th century, remains the more liberal, youthful, forward-looking part of town (with three times Buda's population).

Serendipitously, Budapest's new prominence coincided with the 1,000th anniversary of the Hungarians' ancestors, the Magyars, arriving in Europe...one more excuse to dress things up. Budapest's long-standing rivalry with Vienna only spurred them to build bigger and better. The year 1896 saw an over-the-top millennial celebration, for which many of today's greatest structures were created (see page 27).

No European city grew faster in the second half of the 19th century than Budapest; in the last quarter of the 19th century alone, Budapest doubled in size, building on the foundation laid by Széchenyi and other patriots. By 1900, the city was larger than Rome, Madrid, or Amsterdam. During this time, among other claims to fame, Budapest was the world's biggest mill city—grinding grains from across Hungary and throughout the Balkans. The speedy expansion of the city garnered comparisons with Chicago, another boomtown of that era.

Budapest's most characteristic and impressive architecture dates from this era. Today's palatial mansions and administra-

tive buildings—whether sooty and crumbling, or newly restored and gleaming—hint at this age of unbridled prosperity. Compelled to adopt the trends of the Habsburgs, but eager to distinguish their uniquely Hungarian style, local architects made  creative use of Historicism—borrowing bits and pieces of past styles, injecting a healthy dose of bigger-is-better modernity, and finishing it all off with striking, unique flourishes. Miklós Ybl and Ödön Lechner were two of the most prominent architects of this era, designing banks, museums, churches, and municipal buildings around Budapest. It was during this time that many buildings were first decorated with the colorful Zsolnay tiles—pretty as porcelain but hard as stone—invented in the city of Pécs (see page 374). To this day, these colorful adornments are a defining characteristic of Hungarian architecture.

It was also a period of great artistic and creative achievement.

Composers Franz Liszt and, later, Béla Bartók and Zoltán Kodály incorporated the folk and Roma (Gypsy) songs of the Hungarian and Transylvanian countryside into their music. As Magyar culture thrived, the traditions of the countryside flowed into the music salons of Budapest. (For more on these great musicians, see "Hungarian Music" on page 264.)

Observers at the time saw Hungarians as characterized by a strange combination of pessimism and optimism: pessimistic about their future, especially relating to the Habsburgs; and optimistic (or maybe even chauvinistic) about the influence of their culture—which, while thriving, remained something of an underdog, on the fringe of mainstream Europe. Hungarian historians proposed outrageous boasts about Magyar heritage (including suggesting that Adam and Eve must have been Magyars, and "proving" connections between the Magyars and the Huns and ancient Greeks).

During its time of plenty, Hungary—long-oppressed under the Habsburgs—became known for trampling its own minorities' rights. (More than half of the people in Hungarian territory were not ethnic Hungarians.) Most signs were in Hungarian only, and the Magyar tongue was taught in every school in the realm. Minorities—who were given virtually no say in government—staged uprisings and revolts, and in 1868 Croatia was even granted semiautonomy. (It wasn't enough—as early as 1890, Croats began grumbling with Serbs and other South Slavs to create their own Yugo-Slavia.)

However, this did have the intended effect of "Magyarization": People from all ethnic backgrounds adopted the Hungarian language and culture, giving it an uncanny persistence for something so very foreign and so very old. Germans and Jews adapted their names to Hungarian. For example, the Hungarian communist leader Béla Kun was born Aaron Kohn.

Before long, the optimist in every Hungarian would be proven very wrong indeed—as the Golden Age came crashing to an end, and Hungary plunged into its darkest period.

THE CRISIS OF TRIANON (1918-1939)

World War I marked the end of the age of divine monarchs, as the Romanovs of Russia, the Ottomans of Asia Minor, and, yes, the Habsburgs of Austria-Hungary saw their empires break apart. Hungary, which had been riding the Habsburgs' coattails for the past half-century, now paid the price. As retribution for their role on the losing side of World War I, the 1920 Treaty of Trianon (named for the palace on the grounds of Versailles where it was signed) reassigned two-thirds of Hungary's former territory and

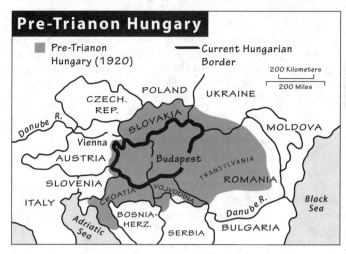

Pre-Trianon Hungary

Pre-Trianon Hungary (1920)

Current Hungarian Border

200 Kilometers
200 Miles

POLAND
UKRAINE
CZECH. REP.
Danube R.
SLOVAKIA
MOLDOVA
Vienna
AUSTRIA
Budapest
TRANSYLVANIA
SLOVENIA
VOJVODINA
ROMANIA
ITALY
CROATIA
Danube R.
Black Sea
Adriatic Sea
BOSNIA-HERZ.
SERBIA
BULGARIA

half of its population to Romania, Ukraine, Czechoslovakia, and Yugoslavia.

It is impossible to overstate the impact of the Treaty of Trianon on the Hungarian psyche—and on Hungarian history. Not unlike the overnight construction of the Berlin Wall, towns along the new Hungarian borders were suddenly divided down the middle. Many Hungarians found themselves unable to visit relatives or commute to jobs that were in the same country the day before. This sent hundreds of thousands of Hungarian refugees—now "foreigners" in their own towns—into Budapest, sparking a bittersweet boom in the capital.

To this day, the Treaty of Trianon is regarded as one of the greatest tragedies of Hungarian history. Like the Basques and the Serbs, the Hungarians feel separated from each other by circumstances outside their control. Today, more than two million ethnic Hungarians live outside Hungary (mostly in Romania)—and many Hungarians claim that these lands still belong to the Magyars. The sizeable Magyar minorities in neighboring countries have often been mistreated—particularly in Romania (under Ceauşescu), Yugoslavia (under Milošević), and Slovakia (under Mečiar). You'll see maps, posters, and bumper stickers with the distinctive shape of a much larger, pre-WWI Hungary...patriotically displayed by Magyars who feel as strongly about Trianon as if it happened yesterday. Some Hungarians see the enlargement of the European Union as a happy ending in the big-picture sense: They have finally been reunited with Slovakia, Romania, and Croatia.

After Trianon, the newly shrunken Kingdom of Hungary had to reinvent itself. The Hungarian crown sat unworn in the Royal Palace, as if waiting for someone worthy to claim it. The

WWI hero Admiral Miklós Horthy had won many battles with the Austro-Hungarian navy. Though the new Hungary had no sea and no navy, Horthy retained his rank and ruled the country as a regent. A popular joke points out that during this time, Hungary was a "kingdom without a king" and a landlocked country ruled by a sea admiral. This sense of compounded deficiency pretty much sums up the morose attitude Hungarians have about those gloomy post-Trianon days.

Adding insult to injury, in the mid-1940s Hungary's currency (the *pengő*) underwent the worst inflation spike in the history of money. At the lowest point of the crisis, the government issued a 100,000,000,000,000,000,000-*pengő* note. Their plan for a 1,000,000,000,000,000,000,000-*pengő* bill fell through when the note became worthless after they printed it, but before they had a chance to circulate it.

The mounting financial crisis, and lingering resentment about the strict post-WWI reparations, made Hungary fertile ground for some bold new fascist ideas.

WORLD WAR II AND THE ARROW CROSS (1939-1945)

As Adolf Hitler rose to power in Germany, some other countries that had felt mistreated in the aftermath of World War I—including Hungary—saw Nazi Germany as a vehicle to greater independence. Admiral Horthy joined forces with the Nazis with the hope that they might help Hungary regain the crippling territorial losses of Trianon. In 1941, Hungary (somewhat reluctantly) declared war on the Soviet Union in June—and against the US and Britain in December.

Being an ally to the Nazis, rather than an occupied state, also allowed Hungary a certain degree of self-determination through the war. And, although Hungary had its own set of anti-Semitic laws and was complicit in the mass murder of Jews lacking citizenship and living within their borders, the vast majority of its sizeable Jewish population was spared from immediate deportation to Nazi concentration camps. Winning back chunks of Slovakia, Transylvania, and Croatia in the early days of World War II also bolstered the Nazis' acceptance in Hungary.

As Nazism took hold in Germany, the Hungarian fascist movement—spearheaded by the Arrow Cross Party (Nyilas-keresztes Párt)—gained popularity within Hungary. As Germany increased its demands for Hungarian soldiers and food, Admiral Horthy resisted...until Hitler's patience wore thin. In March of 1944, the Nazis invaded and installed the Arrow Cross in power. The Arrow Cross made up for lost time, immediately beginning a savage campaign to execute Hungary's Jews—not only sending them to death camps, but butchering them in the streets. Almost 600,000 Hungarian Jews were murdered. (For more on this dark era of Hungarian history, see the Great Synagogue and Jewish Quarter Tour chapter.)

The Soviet Army eventually "liberated" Hungary, but at the expense of Budapest: A months-long siege, from Christmas of 1944 to mid-February of 1945, reduced the proud city to rubble. One out of every ten Hungarian citizens perished in the war.

COMMUNISM...WITH A PINCH OF PAPRIKA (1945-1989)

After World War II, Hungary was gradually compelled to adopt Moscow's system of government. The Soviet-puppet hardliner premier, Mátyás Rákosi, ruled Hungary with an iron fist. Everyday people were terrorized by the KGB-style secret police (called the ÁVO, later ÁVH) and intimidated into accepting the new regime. Non-Hungarians were deported, potential and actual dissidents disappeared into the horrifying gulag system of Siberia (and similar forced-work camps in Hungary), food shortages were epidemic, people were compelled to spy on their friends and families, and countless lives were ruined. Coming on the heels of Trianon and two devastating world wars, communist rule was a blow that Hungary is still recovering from. (For much more on life in Soviet-controlled Hungary, see the House of Terror Tour chapter.)

Beginning on October 23, 1956, the Hungarians courageously staged a monumental uprising, led by Communist Party reformer Imre Nagy. Initially, it appeared that one of the cells on the Soviet Bloc might win itself the right to semiautonomy. But Moscow couldn't let that happen. In a Tiananmen Square-style crackdown, the Soviets sent in tanks to brutally put down the uprising and occupy the city. When the dust settled, 2,500 Hungarians were dead, and 200,000 fled to the West. (If you know any Hungarian Americans, their families more than likely fled in 1956.) Nagy was arrested, given a sham trial, and executed in 1958. For more on these events, see the "1956" sidebar on page 96.

The Hungarians were devastated. They were frustrated that the Suez Canal crisis distracted the world from their uprising.

Many felt betrayed that the US—which spoke so boldly against the Soviet Union—did not offer them military support (contrary to the promises of the American-operated Radio Free Europe). While the US and its Western allies understandably did not want to turn the Cold War hot, the Hungarians (also understandably) felt abandoned.

Weeks after the uprising came the now-legendary "Blood in the Water" match at the Melbourne Olympics. Soviet satellite states were often ordered to "throw" matches to allow the USSR's athletes to prevail. On December 6, 1956, Moscow issued such a decree to the Hungarian men's water polo team in their semifinal against the Soviet Union. The Hungarians refused and played their hearts out, much to the delight of their fans (and the rest of the world). The game turned violent, and in one indelible image, a Hungarian athlete emerged from the pool with blood pouring from a gash above his right eye. The Hungarians won, 4-0, and went on to take the gold.

After the uprising, the USSR installed János Kádár—a colleague of Nagy's who was loyal to Moscow—to lead Hungary. For a few years, things were bleak, as the secret police ratcheted up their efforts against potential dissidents. But in the 1960s, Kádár's reformist tendencies began to cautiously emerge. Seeking to gain the support of his subjects (and avoid further uprisings), Kádár adopted the optimistic motto, "If you are not against us, you are with us." While still mostly cooperating with Moscow, Kádár gradually allowed the people of Hungary more freedom than citizens of neighboring countries had—a system dubbed "goulash communism." The "New Economic Mechanism" of 1968 partly opened Hungary to foreign trade. People from other Warsaw Pact countries—Czechs, Slovaks, and Poles—flocked to Budapest's Váci utca to experience "Western evils" unavailable to them back home, such as Adidas sneakers and Big Macs. People half-joked that Hungary was the happiest barrack in the communist camp.

In the late 1980s, the Eastern Bloc began to thaw. And Hungary—which was always skeptical of the Soviets (or any foreign rule)—was one of the first satellite states that implemented real change. In February of 1989, the Hungarian communist parliament, with little fanfare, essentially voted to put an expiration date on their own regime. There were three benchmarks in that fateful year: May 2, when Hungary was the first Soviet Bloc country to effectively open its borders to the West (by removing its border fence with Austria); June 16, when communist reformer Imre Nagy and his comrades were given a proper, ceremonial reburial on Heroes' Square; and August 19, when, in the first tentative steps toward the reunification of Europe, Hungarians and Austrians came together in a field near the town of Sopron for the so-called "Pan-European

PAST & PRESENT

Picnic." (Some 900 East Germans seized this opportunity to make a run for the border...and slipped into the West when Hungarian border guards refused orders to shoot defectors.) On October 23—the anniversary of the 1956 Uprising—the truly democratic Republic of Hungary triumphantly replaced the People's Republic of Hungary.

Hungary's first postcommunist president, Árpád Göncz, was a protester from the 1950s who was famous for learning English while in prison...a skill that later came in handy when he translated *The Lord of the Rings* into Hungarian. Fantasy was becoming a reality in Hungary. Change was in the air.

HUNGARY TODAY: CAPITALISM, GYURCSÁNY, AND ORBÁN (1989-Present)

The transition from communism to capitalism was not easy. While many Hungarians were eager for the freedom to travel and pursue the interests that democracy allowed them, many others struggled to cope with the sudden reduction of government-provided services. Postcommunist governments have attempted to preserve as many social services as possible while stepping down taxation— leaving Hungary with rampant inflation unmatched in Europe (and bringing back unpleasant memories of the *pengő* debacle of the 1940s).

The process of privatization (returning property once seized by the communist government to its original owners) has been messy. When possible, the government attempted to find the original owners of the property, and allow them to purchase it at a low price. But this was often difficult, or impossible. And so, in many cases, people were simply given the opportunity to purchase the apartment or house where they happened to be living on the day of the transition. If you had a nice apartment, this was good news; if not, you were out of luck.

In 2004, Hungary joined the European Union. And in recent years, Hungary has often been in the international news, as its fitful transition to democracy has taken some attention-grabbing turns.

The Hungarian Socialist Party (MSzP), which took control of parliament in 2002, stubbornly maintained and even extended some social programs, despite worries that mounting public debt would bankrupt the country. After they won re-election in April of 2006, Prime Minister Ferenc Gyurcsány gave a shockingly frank "wake-

Viktor Orbán and Fidesz: Reshaping Hungary in the 21st Century

Prime Minister Viktor Orbán came of age during Hungary's transition from communism to democracy. Today he leads his party (Fidesz) and his nation with a populist authoritarianism that pleases his traditional supporters even as it outrages both Hungarian and international critics.

Born in the town of Székesfehérvár in 1963, Orbán had a varied career before entering the political realm: He earned a law degree, played professional soccer, and studied political philosophy at England's Oxford University. In 1989, when he was just 25, an unkempt, rabble-rousing Orbán entered public life when he delivered a stirring speech at Imre Nagy's ceremonial reburial on Heroes' Square. By that time, he had already co-founded the Fidesz party (the Federation of Young Democrats, later renamed the Hungarian Civic Alliance). Through the 1990s, this youthful, anticommunist party evolved into Hungary's dominant right-wing political institution, and in 1998, Orbán became prime minister of Hungary at age 35. He quickly moved to consolidate his power, tweaking the still-fledgling system of government to his advantage—a practice that his critics say has been typical of his entire political career.

In 2002, Fidesz lost power to a left-wing coalition. But Orbán continued to agitate in opposition, and watched as the Hungarian left imploded under Ferenc Gyurcsány. Fidesz won the 2010 elections in a landslide—returning Orbán to the prime ministership.

The plainspoken Orbán is famous for wearing a children's soccer backpack as a symbol of his down-to-earth populism. He also considers himself the standard bearer of Hungary's Christian historical tradition. He takes advantage both of his faith and of hot-button Hungarian issues (such as lingering resentment over the loss of territory after World War I) to curry favor with his base.

Most Hungarians you'll likely meet (i.e., progressive urbanites in the tourist trade) have nothing good to say about Orbán or Fidesz. You may wonder: Who's voting for these people? But Fidesz's base is similar to Donald Trump's in the United States, or Vladimir Putin's in Russia: traditional, proudly nationalistic, somewhat insular voters in small towns and the countryside who appreciate their leader's willingness to take a stand for their deeply held values.

With their re-elections in 2018, it seems that Orbán and Fidesz are here to stay. Will Orbán's reign soon run its natural course? Or will his reforms prove successful enough to keep Fidesz enshrined in power in the long term, potentially threatening the fabric of Hungary's democracy? Stay tuned.

up call" speech in a private session for his party's leaders...which was secretly recorded. A few months later, Hungarians turned on their TVs to hear their prime minister detailing the ways he and his party had driven their country to the brink of ruin: "We have screwed up. Not a little but a lot. No country in Europe has screwed up as much as we have... We did not actually do anything for four years. Nothing... We lied morning, noon, and night." The release of the tape sparked protests—which occasionally turned violent— as furious demonstrators demanded Gyurcsány's resignation. He refused.

Rampant inflation continued to wrack the country. In late 2008, with Gyurcsány warning of "state bankruptcy" and a currency collapse, Hungary received a $25 billion bailout package from the EU, International Monetary Fund, and World Bank. Gyurcsány finally resigned in early 2009, acknowledging that he was getting in the way of Hungary's economic recovery.

Viktor Orbán, of the nationalistic, right-wing Fidesz Party, became prime minister in a landslide in May of 2010. Fidesz—a strange hybrid of populist and authoritarian—stands for traditional Christian and Hungarian values, economic interventionism, and severe skepticism about immigration and European Union membership. (For more on Orbán and Fidesz, see the sidebar.)

Orbán seized on his two-thirds coalition majority to adopt a new, Fidesz-favorable constitution that stripped away checks and balances and entrenched party leaders in institutions that had previously been considered apolitical. Almost immediately, international observers—including the EU and US—grew concerned.

In early 2011, Orbán's party created a new FCC-like media authority with broad latitude for suppressing material that it considers inappropriate. Fidesz also extended Hungarian citizenship to people of Hungarian descent living in neighboring countries. This stoked century-old Hungarian resentment about the territorial losses from the Treaty of Trianon. Orbán also insists on flying the flag of Transylvania (a part of Hungary that was lost in Trianon)—rather than the EU flag—from the Hungarian Parliament.

Fidesz has a penchant for reinterpreting Hungarian history— rehabilitating some figures (such as Miklós Horthy, who forged an alliance with Hitler's Nazi Germany), while brushing other, less Fidesz-friendly figures under the rug. The party went on a renaming binge—rechristening more than two dozen streets, squares, and other features of Budapest—and has been aggressive about tearing down old monuments and erecting new ones. (For more on this, see the Leopold Town Walk chapter.)

On a positive note, Fidesz has also been proactive about

funneling European Union funds into public-works projects, and Budapest has made stunning progress in renovating formerly dreary streets and squares. But this always seems to come with a Fidesz-approved aesthetic that evokes the party's values. Some critics have described these new spaces—vast and bombastic, as if designed to trumpet historical greatness and host military parades—as "fascistic."

Other Orbán and Fidesz policies have also been controversial—from nationalizing the school system (the same Fidesz-approved textbooks are now used in every school in Hungary) to proposing a per-use Internet tax. (That last one resulted in enormous public protests in the fall of 2014, and Orbán quickly backpedaled.)

Outrageous as Fidesz seems to younger, EU-supporting, highly educated Hungarians, the party pleased its base enough to easily retain its power in the 2014 parliamentary elections. (Fidesz's control of the media didn't hurt its chances either.) Many international observers worry that Fidesz's success could be the death knell for true democracy in Hungary.

In the fall of 2015, Fidesz was in the international news once more, as Orbán took a particularly hard line against Syrian immigrants flooding through Eastern Europe on their way to a better life in wealthy Western European nations. The government erected barbed wire fences and dispatched an intimidating border defense squad to make it clear that refugees weren't welcome. While humanitarians condemned Orbán's actions—which violated the European Union's open-borders agreements, and left many desperate people with nowhere to go—his supporters touted his success in preventing unwanted refugees from flooding the country.

In the 2018 elections, Fidesz retained control of parliament, keeping Orbán firmly in position as prime minister. But in the months following that, it appeared that Hungarians had finally reached a breaking point. In December 2018, Fidesz announced a new law to roll back overtime protections for workers. (Because of their restrictive immigration stance, and because young Hungarian workers have left the country in droves to escape restrictive Fidesz policies, Hungary suffers from a labor shortage.) The policy—nicknamed the "Slave Law"—spurred widespread protests against Fidesz. Even many Fidesz supporters criticized the irony of a party ostensibly dedicated to "family values" essentially requiring people to work longer hours. It could be that the "Slave Law" represents a sea change that will eventually sweep Fidesz from power.

With the rise of Donald Trump in the United States, Orbán is seen as a harbinger of sorts for a new, pan-national movement of traditionalism and nativism. While most Americans have never heard of Orbán, they're very familiar with his political playbook.

PRACTICALITIES

This chapter covers the practical skills of European travel: how to get tourist information, pay for things, sightsee efficiently, find good-value accommodations, eat affordably but well, use technology wisely, and get between destinations smoothly. For more information on these topics, see www.ricksteves.com/travel-tips.

Tourist Information

The Hungarian National Tourist Office **in the US** is a wealth of information. Before your trip, contact their office to request brochures on topics or regions that interest you. Call 212/695-1221 or visit https://hellohungary.com/en.

In Hungary, a good first stop is generally the tourist information office (abbreviated **TI** in this book). TIs are in business to help you enjoy spending money in their town, but even so, I still make a point to swing by to confirm sightseeing plans, pick up a city map, and get information on public transit, walking tours, special events, and nightlife. Anticipating a harried front-line staffer, prepare a list of questions and a proposed plan to double-check.

Budapest has its own tourism organization, called Budapest Info (www.budapestinfo.hu), with several branches in the city (for details, see page 24). Other towns have their own local tourist information offices, which all belong to a large government agency called "TourInform"; these are marked by a white *i* in a green rectangle (www.tourinform.hu). Tourist offices vary in quality; those in some of the smaller towns (including Eger's) can be excellent, while Budapest's are hit-or-miss.

Travel Tips

Emergency and Medical Help: For any emergency service—ambulance, police, or fire—call **112** from a mobile phone or landline. Operators, who in most countries speak English, will deal with your request or route you to the right emergency service.

If you get sick, do as the locals do and go to a pharmacy (*gyógyszertár* or *patika*) for advice. Or ask at your hotel for help—they'll know the nearest medical and emergency services. Budapest also has a private, English-speaking medical center (see page 25).

Theft or Loss: To replace a passport, you'll need to go in person to an embassy or consulate (see next). If your credit and debit cards disappear, cancel and replace them (see "Damage Control for Lost Cards," later). File a police report, either on the spot or within a day or two; you'll need it to submit an insurance claim for lost or stolen rail passes or travel gear, and it can help with replacing your passport or credit and debit cards. For more information, see www.ricksteves.com/help.

Embassies and Consulates: The US Embassy is on Liberty Square, in the center of town (Mon-Fri 8:00-12:00 & 13:00-16:00, closed Sat-Sun, Szabadság tér 12, district V, tel. 1/475-4400, emergency tel. 1/475-4400, https://hu.usembassy.gov). The **Canadian Embassy** is on the Buda side, north of Castle Hill (Mon-Thu 8:00-16:30, Fri 8:00-13:30, closed Sat-Sun, Ganz utca 12, district II, tel. 1/392-3360, www.hungary.gc.ca); for after-hours emergencies, call collect to Canadian tel. 613/996-8885.

In Bratislava, Slovakia, the US Embassy is at Hviezdoslavovo Námestie 4 (Mon-Fri 8:00-11:45 & 14:00-15:15, closed Sat-Sun, tel. 02/5443-0861 http://slovakia.usembassy.gov). The Canadian Embassy is at Mostová 2 (Mon-Fri 8:30-12:30 & 13:30-16:30, closed Sat-Sun, tel. 02/5920-4031, www.austria.gc.ca). For after-hours emergencies, call collect to Canadian tel. 613/996-8885.

Borders: Hungary officially has open borders with the 25 other Schengen Agreement countries (including neighbors Slovakia, Austria, and Slovenia; Croatia may also join in 2020). However, with the flow of refugees into Hungary in the fall of 2015, the government began restricting its borders once again. Depending on current events, you may breeze right through these borders without stopping—or you may have to go through an old-fashioned checkpoint. (Hungary's southern and eastern neighbors—Croatia, Serbia, Romania, and Ukraine—have not yet joined Schengen, so you'll definitely need to show your passport when entering any of those places.)

Time Zones: Hungary, like most of continental Europe, is generally six/nine hours ahead of the East/West Coasts of the US. The exceptions are the beginning and end of Daylight Saving Time: Europe "springs forward" the last Sunday in March (two weeks after most of North America), and "falls back" the last Sunday in October (one week before North America). For a handy time converter, use the world clock app on your mobile phone or download one (see www.timeanddate.com).

Business Hours: Most stores are open Monday through Friday (roughly 10:00-18:00), often with a late night on Thursday (until 20:00 or 21:00). On Saturday, shops are usually open only from 10:00 to 13:00 or 14:00. On Sundays, sightseeing attractions are generally open (except churches, which are closed to tourists until early afternoon), but shops are closed.

Watt's Up? Europe's electrical system is 220 volts, instead of North America's 110 volts. Most newer electronics (such as laptops, battery chargers, and hair dryers) convert automatically, so you won't need a converter, but you will need an adapter plug with two round prongs, sold inexpensively at travel stores in the US. Avoid bringing older appliances that don't automatically convert voltage; instead, buy a cheap replacement in Europe.

Discounts: Discounts for sights are generally not listed in this book. However, seniors (age 60 and over), youths under 18, and students and teachers with proper identification cards (www.isic.org) can get discounts at many sights—always ask. Some discounts are available only to European citizens.

Online Translation Tips: Google's Chrome browser instantly translates websites; Translate.google.com is also handy. The Google Translate app converts spoken or typed English into most European languages (and vice versa), and can also translate text it "reads" with your phone's camera.

Money

Here's my basic strategy for using money in Europe:
- Upon arrival, head for a cash machine (ATM) at the airport and withdraw some local currency, using a debit card with low international transaction fees.

- Pay for most purchases with your choice of cash or a credit card. You'll save money by minimizing your credit and debit card exchange fees. The trend is for bigger expenses to be paid by credit card, but cash is still the standby for small purchases and tips.
- Keep your cards and cash safe in a money belt.

PLASTIC VERSUS CASH

Although credit cards are widely accepted in Europe, cash is sometimes the only way to pay for cheap food, taxis, tips, and local guides. Some businesses (especially smaller ones, such as B&Bs and mom-and-pop cafés and shops) may charge you extra for using a credit card—or might not accept credit cards at all. Having cash on hand helps you out of a jam if your card randomly doesn't work.

I use my credit card to book and pay for hotel reservations, to buy advance tickets for events or sights, and to cover most other expenses. It can also be smart to use plastic near the end of your trip, to avoid another visit to the ATM.

WHAT TO BRING

I pack the following and keep it all safe in my money belt.

Debit Card: Use this at ATMs to withdraw local cash.

Credit Card: Handy for bigger purchases (at hotels, shops, restaurants, travel agencies, car-rental agencies, and so on), payment machines, and ordering online.

Backup Card: Some travelers carry a third card (debit or credit; ideally from a different bank), in case one gets lost, demagnetized, eaten by a temperamental machine, or simply doesn't work.

A Stash of Cash: I always carry $100-200 as a cash backup. A stash of cash comes in handy for emergencies, such as if your ATM card stops working.

What NOT to Bring: Resist the urge to buy **forints or euros** before your trip or you'll pay the price in bad stateside exchange rates. Wait until you arrive to withdraw money. I've yet to see a European airport that didn't have plenty of ATMs.

BEFORE YOU GO

Use this pre-trip checklist.

Know your cards. Debit cards from any major US bank will work in any standard European bank's ATM (ideally, use a debit card with a Visa or MasterCard logo). As for credit cards, Visa and MasterCard are universal, American Express is less common, and Discover is unknown in Europe.

Know your PIN. Make sure you know the numeric, four-digit PIN for all of your cards, both debit and credit. Request it if you don't have one and allow time to receive the information by mail.

PRACTICALITIES

Exchange Rates

Hungary still uses its traditional currency, the **forint** (abbreviated Ft, or sometimes HUF). Check www.oanda.com for the latest exchange rates.

275 Ft = about $1

To very roughly convert prices in forints to dollars, divide by three and drop the last two digits. For example, 1,000 Ft = about $3 (actually $3.60), 5,000 Ft = about $17 (actually $18), and 10,000 Ft = about $30 (actually $36). The exchange rate has fluctuated wildly in recent years—these are just rough estimates.

While Hungary is on track to adopt the Europe-wide **euro** currency, it likely won't happen for several years. However, you might already see some prices (especially hotel rates in Budapest) listed in euros for the convenience of international visitors. Even when you see prices listed in euros, locals gladly accept (and sometimes prefer) payment in forints. Hungary's neighbors Slovakia (whose capital, Bratislava, is included in this book), Austria, and Slovenia all use the euro.

1 euro (€) = about $1.20

To roughly convert prices in euros to dollars, add 20 percent: €20 is about $24, €50 is about $60, and so on.

So, that 1,500-Ft canister of paprika costs about $5, that €25 meal in Bratislava is about $30, and that 25,000-Ft taxi ride through Budapest is...uh-oh.

All credit and debit cards now have chips that authenticate and secure transactions. Europeans insert their chip cards into the payment machine slot, then enter a PIN. American cards should work in most transactions without a PIN—but may not work at self-service machines at train stations, toll booths, gas pumps, or parking lots. I've been inconvenienced a few times by self-service payment machines in Europe that wouldn't accept my card, but it's never caused me serious trouble.

If you're concerned, a few banks offer a chip-and-PIN card that works in almost all payment machines, including those from Andrews Federal Credit Union (www.andrewsfcu.org) and the State Department Federal Credit Union (www.sdfcu.org).

Report your travel dates. Let your bank know that you'll be using your debit and credit cards in Europe, and when and where you're headed.

Adjust your ATM withdrawal limit. Find out how much you can take out daily and ask for a higher daily withdrawal limit if you want to get more cash at once. Note that European ATMs will withdraw funds only from checking accounts; you're unlikely to have access to your savings account.

Ask about fees. For any purchase or withdrawal made with a card, you may be charged a currency conversion fee (1-3 percent) and/or a Visa or MasterCard international transaction fee (1 percent). If you're getting a bad deal, consider getting a new debit or credit card. Reputable no-fee cards include those from Capital One, as well as Charles Schwab debit cards. Most credit unions and some airline loyalty cards have low-to-no international transaction fees.

IN EUROPE
Using Cash Machines

European cash machines have English-language instructions and work just like they do at home—except they spit out local currency instead of dollars, calculated at the day's standard bank-to-bank rate.

In most places, ATMs are easy to locate—in Hungary ask for a *bankjegy-automata* (BONK-yedge OW-toh-maw-taw). Most Hungarians also recognize the international term *Bankomat.* When possible, withdraw cash from a bank-run ATM located just outside that bank. Ideally use it during the bank's opening hours so if your card is munched by the machine, you can go inside for help.

If your debit card doesn't work, try a lower amount—your request may have exceeded your withdrawal limit or the ATM's limit. If you still have a problem, try a different ATM or come back later—your bank's network may be temporarily down.

Avoid "independent" ATMs, such as Travelex, Euronet, Moneybox, Cardpoint, and Cashzone. Common in Budapest (especially at the airport and train stations), these have high fees, can be less secure than a bank ATM, and may try to trick users with "dynamic currency conversion" (see below).

Exchanging Cash

Avoid exchanging money in Europe; it's a big rip-off. In a pinch you can always find exchange desks at major train stations or airports—convenient but with crummy rates. Anything over 5 percent for a transaction is piracy. Banks generally do not exchange money unless you have an account with them.

Using Credit Cards

US cards no longer require a signature for verification, but don't be surprised if a European card reader generates a receipt for you to sign. Some card readers will accept your card as is; others may prompt you to enter your PIN (so it's important to know the code for each of your cards). If a cashier is present, you should have no problems.

At self-service payment machines (transit-ticket kiosks,

parking, etc.), results are mixed, as US cards may not work in unattended transactions. If your card won't work, look for a cashier who can process your card manually—or pay in cash.

Drivers Beware: Be aware of potential problems using a US credit card to fill up at an unattended gas station, enter a parking garage, or exit a toll road. Carry cash and be prepared to move on to the next gas station if necessary. When approaching a toll plaza, use the "cash" lane.

Dynamic Currency Conversion

If merchants offer to convert your purchase price into dollars (called dynamic currency conversion, or DCC), refuse this "service." You'll pay extra for the expensive convenience of seeing your charge in dollars. If an ATM offers to "lock in" or "guarantee" your conversion rate, choose "proceed without conversion." Other prompts might state, "You can be charged in dollars: Press YES for dollars, NO for forints." Always choose the local currency.

Security Tips

Pickpockets target tourists. Keep your cash, credit cards, and passport secure in your money belt, and carry only a day's spending money in your front pocket or wallet.

Before inserting your card into an ATM, inspect the front. If anything looks crooked, loose, or damaged, it could be a sign of a card-skimming device. When entering your PIN, carefully block other people's view of the keypad.

Don't use a debit card for purchases. Because a debit card pulls funds directly from your bank account, potential charges incurred by a thief will stay on your account while the fraudulent use is investigated by your bank.

While traveling, to access your accounts online, be sure to use a secure connection (see the "Tips on Internet Security" sidebar, later).

Damage Control for Lost Cards

If you lose your credit or debit card, report the loss immediately to the respective global customer-assistance centers. Call these 24-hour US numbers collect: Visa (tel. 303/967-1096), MasterCard (tel. 636/722-7111), and American Express (tel. 336/393-1111). In Hungary, to make a collect call to the US, dial 06-800-011-11. Press zero or stay on the line for an English-speaking operator. European toll-free numbers can be found at the websites for Visa and MasterCard.

You'll need to provide the primary cardholder's identification-verification details (such as birth date, mother's maiden name, or Social Security number). You can generally receive a temporary card within two or three business days in Europe (see www.ricksteves.com/help for more).

If you report your loss within two days, you typically won't be responsible for any unauthorized transactions on your account, although many banks charge a liability fee of $50.

TIPPING

Tipping in Hungary isn't as automatic or as generous as in the US. For special service, tips are appreciated, but not expected. As in the US, the proper amount depends on your resources, tipping philosophy, and the circumstances, but some general guidelines apply.

Restaurants: Tipping is an issue only at restaurants that have table service. If you order your food at a counter, don't tip. Note that in Budapest, many restaurants automatically levy a 10-12 percent service charge; if this appears on your bill, no additional tip is expected. For more on tipping at restaurants, see the "Eating" section, later.

Taxis: For a typical ride, round up your fare a bit (for instance, if the fare is 1,350 Ft, pay 1,500 Ft). If the cabbie hauls your bags and zips you to the airport to help you catch your flight, you might want to toss in a little more. But if you feel like you're being driven in circles or otherwise ripped off, skip the tip.

Services: In general, if someone in the service industry does a super job for you, a small tip (100-300 Ft) is appropriate...but not required. If you're not sure whether (or how much) to tip, ask a local for advice.

GETTING A VAT REFUND

Wrapped into the purchase price of your Hungarian souvenirs is a Value-Added Tax (VAT) of about 27 percent. You're entitled to get most of that tax back if you purchase more than 54,001 Ft (about $195) worth of goods at a store that participates in the VAT-refund scheme. Typically, you must ring up the minimum at a single retailer—you can't add up your purchases from various shops to reach the required amount. (If the store ships the goods to your US home, VAT is not assessed on your purchase.)

Getting your refund is straightforward...and worthwhile if you spend a significant amount on souvenirs.

Get the paperwork. Have the merchant completely fill out the necessary refund document. You'll have to present your passport. Get the paperwork done before you leave the store to ensure you'll have everything you need (including your original sales receipt).

Get your stamp at the border or airport. Process your VAT document at your last stop in the European Union (such as at the airport) with the customs agent who deals with VAT refunds.

Arrive an additional hour before you need to check in to allow time to find the local customs office—and wait. Some customs desks are positioned before airport security; confirm the location before going through security.

It's best to keep your purchases in your carry-on. If they're not allowed as carry-on (such as knives), pack them in your checked bags and alert the check-in agent. You'll be sent (with your tagged bag) to a customs desk outside security; someone will examine your bag, stamp your paperwork, and put your bag on the belt. You're not supposed to use your purchased goods before you leave. If you show up at customs wearing your new communist-kitsch T-shirt, officials might look the other way—or deny you a refund.

Collect your refund. You can claim your VAT refund from refund companies, such as Global Blue or Premier Tax Free, with offices at major airports, ports, or border crossings (either before or after security, probably strategically located near a duty-free shop). These services (which extract a 4 percent fee) can refund your money in cash immediately or credit your card (within two billing cycles). Otherwise you'll need to mail the stamped refund documents to the address given by the shop where you made your purchase.

CUSTOMS FOR AMERICAN SHOPPERS

You can take home $800 worth of items per person duty-free, once every 31 days. Many processed and packaged foods are allowed, including vacuum-packed cheeses, dried herbs, jams, baked goods, candy, chocolate, oil, vinegar, mustard, and honey. Fresh fruits and vegetables and most meats are not allowed, with exceptions for some canned items. As for alcohol, you can bring in one liter duty-free (it can be packed securely in your checked luggage, along with any other liquid-containing items).

To bring alcohol (or liquid-packed foods) in your carry-on bag on your flight home, buy it at a duty-free shop at the airport. You'll increase your odds of getting it onto a connecting flight if it's packaged in a "STEB"—a secure, tamper-evident bag. But stay away from liquids in opaque, ceramic, or metallic containers, which usually cannot be successfully screened (STEB or no STEB).

For details on allowable goods, customs rules, and duty rates, visit http://help.cbp.gov.

Sightseeing

Many of Budapest's museums are dusty and a bit old-fashioned. But with patience and imagination, and a solid background in the topic (provided by this book's descriptions, self-guided tours, in-depth sidebars, and the Hungary: Past & Present chapter), Budapest's sights come to life and become genuinely enthralling.

Sightseeing can be hard work. Use these tips to make your visits to Budapest's finest sights meaningful, fun, efficient, and painless.

MAPS AND NAVIGATION TOOLS

A good map is essential for efficient navigation while sightseeing. The maps in this book are concise and simple, designed to help you locate recommended destinations, sights, and local TIs, where you can pick up more in-depth maps.

You can also use a mapping app on your mobile device. Be aware that pulling up maps or looking up turn-by-turn walking directions on the fly requires an internet connection: To use this feature, it's smart to get an international data plan. With Google Maps or City Maps 2Go, it's possible to download a map while online, then go offline and navigate without incurring data-roaming charges, though you can't search for an address or get real-time walking directions. A handful of other apps—including Apple Maps, OffMaps, and Navfree—also allow you to use maps offline.

PLAN AHEAD

Set up an itinerary that allows you to fit in all your must-see sights. For a one-stop look at opening hours, see "Budapest at a Glance" (page 40; also see the "Daily Reminder" on page 22). Most sights keep stable hours, but you can easily confirm the latest by checking with the TI or visiting museum websites.

Don't put off visiting a must-see sight—you never know when a place will close unexpectedly for a holiday, strike, or restoration. Many museums are closed or have reduced hours at least a few days a year, especially on holidays such as Christmas, New Year's, and Labor Day (May 1). A list of holidays is in the appendix; check online for possible museum closures during your trip. In summer, some sights may stay open late; in the off-season, hours may be shorter.

Going at the right time helps avoid crowds. This book offers tips on the best times to see specific sights. Try visiting popular sights very early or very late. Evening visits (when possible) are usually peaceful, with fewer crowds.

If you plan to hire a local guide, reserve ahead by email. Popular guides can get booked up.

Study up. To get the most out of the self-guided tours and sight descriptions in this book, read them the night before your visit. A walk through the communist relics at Memento Park, for instance, is more meaningful if you've read up on the Soviet era the night before. When you arrive at the sight, use the overview map to get the lay of the land and the basic tour route.

AT SIGHTS

Here's what you can typically expect:

Entering: Be warned that you may not be allowed to enter if you arrive less than 30 to 60 minutes before closing time. And guards start ushering people out well before the actual closing time, so don't save the best for last.

Many sights (including the Parliament, Great Synagogue, and Holocaust Memorial Center) have a security check. Allow extra time for these lines. Some sights require you to check daypacks and coats. (If you'd rather not check your daypack, try carrying it tucked under your arm like a purse as you enter.)

Photography: If the museum's photo policy isn't clearly posted, ask a guard. Generally, taking photos without a flash or tripod is allowed. Some sights ban selfie sticks; others ban photos altogether.

Temporary Exhibits: Museums may show special exhibits in addition to their permanent collection. Some exhibits are included in the entry price, while others come at an extra cost (which you may have to pay even if you don't want to see the exhibit).

Once inside, you'll generally follow a confusing one-way tour route through a maze of rooms with squeaky parquet floors, monitored by attendants who listlessly point you in the right direction.

While most museums label exhibits in English, most don't post full descriptions; you'll have to buy a book, rent an audioguide, or borrow laminated translations. In a few cases, none of these is available.

Expect Changes: Items can be on tour, on loan, out sick, or shifted at the whim of the curator. Pick up a floor plan as you enter, and ask museum staff if you can't find a particular item.

Audioguides and Apps: Many sights rent audioguides, which generally offer dry recorded descriptions in English. Many audioguides have a standard output jack, so if you bring your own earbuds, you can often enjoy better sound. To save money, bring a Y-jack and share one audioguide with your travel partner. Museums and sights often offer free apps that you can download to your mobile device (check their websites).

Services: Important sights usually have a reasonably priced on-site café or cafeteria (handy places to rejuvenate during a long visit). The WCs at sights are free and generally clean.

Before Leaving: At the gift shop, scan the postcard rack or thumb through a guidebook to be sure that you haven't overlooked something that you'd like to see. Every sight and museum offers more than what is covered in this book. Use the information in this book as an introduction—not the final word.

Sleeping

Extensive and opinionated listings of good-value rooms are a major feature of this book's Sleeping sections. Rather than list accommodations scattered throughout a town, I choose hotels in my favorite neighborhoods that are convenient to your sightseeing.

My recommendations run the gamut, from dorm beds to fancy rooms with all the comforts. I like places that are clean, central, relatively quiet at night, reasonably priced, friendly, small enough to have a hands-on owner or manager, and run with a respect for Hungarian traditions. I'm more impressed by a handy location and fun-loving philosophy than room service and a fancy gym. Most of my recommendations fall short of perfection. But if I can find a place with most of these features, it's a keeper.

Book your accommodations as soon as your itinerary is set, especially if you want to stay at one of my top listings or if you'll be traveling during busy times. September is extremely tight (because of conventions), with October close behind. The Formula 1 races (one weekend in late July or early Aug) send rates through the roof. See the appendix for a list of major holidays and festivals in Hungary.

RATES AND DEALS

I've categorized my recommended accommodations based on price, indicated with a dollar-sign rating (see sidebar). The price ranges suggest an estimated cost for a one-night stay in a standard double room with a private toilet and shower in high season, include breakfast, and assume you're booking directly with the hotel (not through a booking site, which extracts a commission). Room prices can fluctuate significantly with demand and amenities (size, views, room class, and so on), but relative price categories remain constant.

Remember, in Budapest, most hotels quote their rates in euros. But outside of the capital, the prices are more often in forints. When you check out, most places will charge you in forints (figured at the exchange rate on the day of payment). Unless I note otherwise in the listing, you can assume the hotel accepts credit cards—though smaller places always prefer cash. If they offer different currencies when you pay with a credit card, always choose forints. Most hotels don't include the 4 percent tourist tax in their rates.

Room rates are especially volatile at larger hotels that use "dynamic pricing" to set rates. Prices can skyrocket during festivals and conventions, while business hotels can have deep discounts on weekends when demand plummets. Of the many hotels I recom-

Sleep Code

Hotels in this book are categorized according to the average price of a standard double room with breakfast in high season.

$$$$	**Splurge:**	Most rooms over €170 (53,000 Ft)
$$$	**Pricier:**	€130-170 (40,500-53,000 Ft)
$$	**Moderate:**	€90-130 (28,000-40,500 Ft)
$	**Budget:**	€50-90 (15,500-28,000 Ft)
¢	**Backpacker:**	Under €50 (15,500 Ft)
RS%	**Rick Steves discount**	

Unless otherwise noted, credit cards are accepted, English is spoken, and free Wi-Fi is available. Comparison-shop by checking prices at several hotels (on each hotel's own website, on a booking site, or by email). For the best deal, *book directly with the hotel.* Ask for a discount if paying in cash; if the listing includes **RS%,** request a Rick Steves discount.

mend, it's difficult to say which will be the best value on a given day—until you do your homework.

Booking Direct: Once your dates are set, compare prices at several hotels. You can do this by checking Hotels.com, Booking. com, and hotel websites. To get the best deal, contact family-run hotels directly by phone or email. When you go direct, the owner avoids the commission paid to booking sites, thereby leaving enough wiggle room to offer you a discount, a nicer room, or a free breakfast (if it's not already included). If you prefer to book online or are considering a hotel chain, it's to your advantage to use the hotel's website.

Getting a Discount: Some hotels extend a discount to those who pay cash or stay longer than three nights. And some accommodations offer a special discount for Rick Steves readers, indicated in this guidebook by the abbreviation **"RS%."** Discounts vary: Ask for details when you reserve. Generally, to qualify for this discount, you must book direct (not through a booking site), mention this book when you reserve, show this book upon arrival, and sometimes pay cash or stay a certain number of nights. In some cases, you may need to enter a discount code (which I've provided in the listing) in the booking form on the hotel's website. Rick Steves discounts apply to readers with either print or digital books. Understandably, discounts do not apply to promotional rates.

TYPES OF ACCOMMODATIONS
Hotels

My Budapest hotel options range from €20 bunks to €500-plus splurges. Rooms outside the capital—such as in Eger, Pécs, and

Using Online Services to Your Advantage

From booking services to user reviews, online businesses are playing a greater role in travelers' planning than ever before. Take advantage of their pluses—and be wise to their downsides.

Booking Sites

Hotel booking websites, including Priceline's Booking.com and Expedia's Hotels.com, offer one-stop shopping for hotels. While convenient for travelers, they present a real problem for small, independent, family-run hotels. Without a presence on these sites, these hotels become almost invisible. But to be listed, a hotel must pay a sizeable commission...and promise that its own website won't undercut the price on the booking-service site.

Here's the work-around: Use the big sites to research what's out there, then book directly with the hotel by email or phone, in which case hotel owners are free to give you whatever price they like. Ask for a room without the commission markup (or ask for a free breakfast if not included, or a free upgrade). If you do book online, be sure to use the hotel's website. The price will likely be the same as via a booking site, but your money goes to the hotel, not agency commissions.

As a savvy consumer, remember: When you book with an online booking service, you're adding a middleman who takes roughly 20 percent. To support small, family-run hotels whose world is more difficult than ever, book direct.

Short-Term Rental Sites

Rental juggernaut Airbnb (along with other short-term rental sites) allows travelers to rent rooms and apartments directly from locals, often providing more value than a cookie-cutter hotel. Airbnb fans appreciate feeling part of a real neighborhood and getting into a daily routine as "temporary Europeans." Depending on the host, Airbnb can provide an opportunity to get to know a local person, while keeping the money spent on your

Sopron—are much cheaper. Hoteliers know what their beds are worth, so generally you get what you pay for.

Some hotels can add an extra bed (for a small charge) to turn a double into a triple; some offer larger rooms for four or more people (I call these "family rooms" in the listings). If there's space for an extra cot, they'll cram it in for you. In general, a triple room is cheaper than the cost of a double and a single. Three or four people can economize by requesting one big room.

Arrival and Check-In: Hotels and B&Bs are sometimes located on the higher floors of a multipurpose building with a secured door. In that case, look for your hotel's name on the buttons by the main entrance. When you ring the bell, you'll be buzzed in.

Hotel elevators are becoming more common, though some

accommodations in the community.

Critics view Airbnb as a threat to "traditional Europe," saying it creates unfair, unqualified competition for established guesthouse owners. In some places, the lucrative Airbnb market has forced traditional guesthouses out of business and is driving property values out of range for locals. Some cities have cracked down, requiring owners to occupy rental properties part of the year (and staging disruptive "inspections" that inconvenience guests).

As a lover of Europe, I share the worry of those who see residents nudged aside by tourists. But as an advocate for travelers, I appreciate the value and cultural intimacy Airbnb provides.

User Reviews

User-generated review sites and apps such as Yelp and TripAdvisor can give you a consensus of opinions about everything from hotels and restaurants to sights and nightlife. If you scan reviews of a restaurant or hotel and see several complaints about noise or a rotten location, you've gained insight that can help in your decision-making.

But as a guidebook writer, my sense is that there is a big difference between the uncurated information on a review site and the vetted listings in a guidebook. A user-generated review is based on the limited experience of one person, who stayed at just one hotel in a given city and ate at a few restaurants there. A guidebook is the work of a trained researcher who forms a well-developed basis for comparison by visiting many restaurants and hotels year after year.

Both types of information have their place, and in many ways, they're complementary. If something is well reviewed in a guidebook and it also gets good online reviews, it's likely a winner.

older buildings still lack them. You may have to climb a flight of stairs to reach the elevator (if so, you can ask the front desk for help carrying your bags up). Elevators are typically very small—pack light, or you may need to send your bags up without you.

The EU requires that hotels collect your name, nationality, and ID number. When you check in, the receptionist will normally ask for your passport and may keep it for anywhere from a couple of minutes to a couple of hours. (If not comfortable leaving your passport at the desk for a long time, ask when you can pick it up.)

If you're arriving in the morning, your room probably won't be ready. Check your bag safely at the hotel and dive right into sightseeing.

In Your Room: Most hotel rooms have a TV, telephone, and

Making Hotel Reservations

Reserve your rooms as soon as you've pinned down your travel dates. For busy national holidays, it's wise to reserve far in advance (see page 495).

Requesting a Reservation: For family-run hotels, it's generally cheaper to book your room directly via email or a phone call. For business-class hotels, or if you'd rather book online, reserve directly through the hotel's official website (not a booking website). For complicated requests, send an email. Almost all of my recommended hotels take reservations in English.

The hotelier wants to know:
- Type(s) of rooms you want and size of your party
- Number of nights you'll stay
- Your arrival and departure dates, written European-style as day/month/ year (for example, 18/06/20 or 18 June 2020)
- Special requests (en suite bathroom, cheapest room, twin beds vs. double bed, quiet room)
- Applicable discounts (such as a Rick Steves reader discount, cash discount, or promotional rate)

Confirming Reservation: Most places will request a credit-card number to hold your room. If you're using an online reservation form, look for the *https* or a lock icon at the top of your browser. If you book direct, you can email, call, or fax this information.

Canceling a Reservation: If you must cancel, it's courteous—and smart—to do so with as much notice as possible, especially for smaller family-run places. Cancellation policies can be strict;

free Wi-Fi (although in old buildings with thick walls, the Wi-Fi signal might be available only in the lobby). Simpler places rarely have a room phone.

More pillows and blankets are usually in the closet or available on request. Towels and linens aren't always replaced every day, so hang your towel up to dry. You might be tempted to borrow your hotel towel for your visit to the thermal baths (saving the towel-rental cost). Some hotels frown on this, others forbid it, and a few will loan you a special towel for this purpose.

Breakfast and Meals: Most hotels listed here include a buffet breakfast. Some smaller budget places serve no breakfast at all, while larger chain hotels charge (too much) extra for it; in these cases, I've noted it in the listing. Consider having breakfast instead at one of two good cafés I've recommended in the Eating in Budapest chapter: Gerlóczy Café or Callas.

Checking Out: While it's customary to pay for your room upon departure, it can be a good idea to settle your bill the day before, when you're not in a hurry and while the manager's in.

Hotelier Help: Hoteliers can be a good source of advice. Most

From:	rick@ricksteves.com
Sent:	Today
To:	info@hotelcentral.com
Subject:	Reservation request for 19-22 July

Dear Hotel Central,

I would like to stay at your hotel. Please let me know if you have a room available and the price for:
• 2 people
• Double bed and en suite bathroom in a quiet room
• Arriving 19 July, departing 22 July (3 nights)

Thank you!
Rick Steves

read the fine print before you book. Many discount deals require prepayment, with no cancellation refunds.

Reconfirming Your Reservation: Always call to reconfirm your room reservation a few days in advance. For B&Bs or very small hotels, I call again on my day of arrival to tell my host what time to expect me (especially important if arriving late—after 17:00).

Phoning: For tips on how to call hotels overseas, see page 480.

know their city well, and can assist you with everything from public transit and airport connections to finding a good restaurant, the nearest launderette, or a late-night pharmacy. Of my recommended hotels, all of the places in Budapest (and virtually all those outside of Budapest) have English-speaking staff. In the rare instance where they do not, you'll find a note in my listing.

Hotel Hassles: Even at the best places, mechanical breakdowns occur: Sinks leak, hot water turns cold, toilets may gurgle or smell, the Wi-Fi goes out, or the air-conditioning dies when you need it most. Report your concerns clearly and calmly at the front desk.

If you find that night noise is a problem (if, for instance, your room is over a nightclub), ask for a quieter room in the back or on an upper floor. To guard against theft in your room, keep valuables out of sight. Some rooms come with a safe, and other hotels have safes at the front desk. I've never bothered using one and in a lifetime of travel, I've never had anything stolen from my room.

For more complicated problems, don't expect instant results. Above all, keep a positive attitude. Remember, you're on vacation.

If your hotel is a disappointment, spend more time out enjoying the place you came to see.

Short-Term Rentals

A short-term rental—whether an apartment, house, or room in a local's home—is an increasingly popular alternative, especially if you plan to settle in one location for several nights. For stays longer than a few days, you can usually find a rental that's comparable to—and cheaper than—a hotel room with similar amenities. Plus, you'll get a behind-the-scenes peek into how locals live.

Many places require a minimum stay and have strict cancellation policies. And you're generally on your own: There's no hotel reception desk, breakfast, or daily cleaning service.

Finding Accommodations: Aggregator websites such as Airbnb, FlipKey, Booking.com, and the HomeAway family of sites (HomeAway, VRBO, and VacationRentals) let you browse properties and correspond directly with European property owners or managers. If you prefer to work from a curated list of accommodations, consider using a rental agency such as InterhomeUSA.com or RentaVilla.com. Agency-represented apartments typically cost more, but this method often offers more help and safeguards than booking direct.

Before you commit, be clear on the location. I like to virtually "explore" the neighborhood using the Street View feature on Google Maps. Also consider the proximity to public transportation and how well-connected it is with the rest of the city. Ask about amenities (elevator, air-conditioning, laundry, Wi-Fi, parking, etc.). Reviews from previous guests can help identify trouble spots.

Think about the kind of experience you want: Just a key and an affordable bed...or a chance to get to know a local? There are typically two kinds of hosts: those who want minimal interaction with their guests, and hosts who are friendly and may want to interact with you. Read the promotional text and online reviews to help shape your decision.

Confirming and Paying: Many places require you to pay the entire balance before your trip. It's easiest and safest to pay through the site where you found the listing. Be wary of owners who want to take your transaction offline; this gives you no recourse if things go awry. Never agree to wire money (a key indicator of a fraudulent transaction).

Apartments or Houses: If you're staying somewhere for four or more nights, it's worth considering an apartment or rental house (shorter stays aren't worth the hassle of arranging key pickup, buying groceries, etc.). Apartment or house rentals can be especially cost-effective for groups and families. European apartments, like hotel rooms, tend to be small by US standards. But they often come with

Keep Cool

If you're visiting Hungary in the summer, you'll want an air-conditioned room. Most hotel air-conditioners come with a control stick (like a TV remote; the hotel may require a deposit) that generally has similar symbols and features: fan icon (click to toggle through wind power, from light to gale); louver icon (choose steady airflow or waves); snowflake and sunshine icons (cold air or heat, depending on season); clock ("O" setting: run X hours before turning off; "I" setting: wait X hours to start); and the temperature control (20 degrees Celsius is comfortable). When you leave your room for the day, turning off the air-conditioning is good form.

laundry machines and small, equipped kitchens, making it easier and cheaper to dine in.

Rooms in Private Homes: Renting a room in someone's home is a good option for those traveling alone, as you're more likely to find true single rooms—with just one single bed, and a price to match. These can range from air-mattress-in-living-room basic to plush-B&B-suite posh. Some places allow you to book for a single night; if staying for several nights, you can buy groceries just as you would in a rental house. While you can't expect your host to also be your tour guide—or even to provide you with much info—some may be interested in getting to know the travelers who come through their home.

Other Options: Swapping homes with a local works for people with an appealing place to offer (don't assume where you live is not interesting to Europeans). A good place to start is HomeExchange. To sleep for free, Couchsurfing.com is a vagabond's alternative to Airbnb. It lists millions of outgoing members who host fellow "surfers" in their homes.

Hostels

A hostel provides cheap beds in dorms where you sleep alongside strangers for about €20 per night. Travelers of any age are welcome if they don't mind dorm-style accommodations and meeting other travelers. Most hostels offer kitchen facilities, guest computers, Wi-Fi, and a self-service laundry. Hostels almost always provide bedding, but the towel's up to you (though you can usually rent one for a small fee). Family and private rooms are often available.

Independent hostels tend to be easygoing, colorful, and informal (no membership required; www.hostelworld.com). You may pay slightly less by booking directly with the hostel. **Official hostels** are part of Hostelling International (HI) and share an online booking site (www.hihostels.com). HI hostels typically require that you be a member or else pay a bit more per night.

Eating

For listings in this guidebook, I look for restaurants that are convenient to your hotel and sightseeing. When restaurant-hunting, choose a spot filled with locals, not the place with the big neon signs boasting, "We Speak English and Accept Credit Cards." Venturing even a block or two off the main drag leads to higher-quality food for a better price.

While you'll find the standard Hungarian fare, most big-city restaurants like to dabble in international cuisine. Many of my listings feature an international menu with some Hungarian flourishes. (If you want truly traditional Hungarian fare, you'll do better in smaller towns.) But Hungarian chefs are so skilled that any cuisine is done well here.

Most restaurants have an English menu posted (or you can ask to see one). Virtually any restaurant specializing in purely "traditional Hungarian food" is catering almost entirely to tourists. Locals prefer "modern Hungarian" places—melding traditional ingredients with Mediterranean and other international influences—which is what I've emphasized in my listings.

If the place isn't full, you can usually just seat yourself (get a server's attention to be sure your preferred table is OK)—the American-style "hostess," with a carefully managed waiting list, isn't common here.

Once seated, feel free to take your time. In fact, it might be difficult to dine in a hurry. Only a rude waiter will rush you. Hungarian service is polite, but formal; don't expect "Hi, I'm László and I'll be your server—how you folks doin' tonight?" chumminess. At traditional places, your tuxedoed server might bring your food to the table, bow with a formal click of the heels...then go back to the kitchen to apply more wax to his moustache. At any eatery, good service is deliberate (slow to an American).

An *étterem* ("eatery") is a nice sit-down restaurant, while a *vendéglő* is usually more casual (similar to a tavern or an inn), and a *bisztró* is a trendy eatery with a concise but well-executed menu. A *söröző* ("beer place") is a pub that sells beer and pub grub. A *kávéház* ("coffeehouse"), or café, is where Budapesters gather to meet friends, get a caffeine fix...and sometimes to

have a great meal. (I've listed my favorite cafés—including a few that serve great food—in the Eating in Budapest chapter.) Other cafés serve only light food, or sometimes only desserts. But if you want a wide choice of cakes, look for a *cukrászda* (pastry shop—*cukr* means "sugar").

Menus usually list drink prices by the tenth of a liter, or deciliter (dl), not by the glass; this is an honest and common practice, but can trip up visitors.

When the server comes to take your order, he might say *"Tessék"* (TEHSH-shayk), or maybe the more formal *"Tessék parancsolni"* (TEHSH-shayk PAW-rawn-chohl-nee)—"Please command, sir." When they bring the food, they will probably say, *"Jó étvágyat!"* (yoh AYT-vah-yawt)—"Bon appétit." When you're ready for the bill, you can simply say, *"Fizetek"* (FEE-zeh-tehk)—"I'll pay."

At any restaurant, it's smart to check the bill and count your change carefully. While most Hungarian restaurateurs are honest, there are a few rip-off joints in downtown Budapest's tourist zone—especially along the main walking street, Váci utca. (Frankly, I'd never eat on Váci utca, which practically guarantees bad food and service for high prices.) Avoid any place with a menu that doesn't list prices, and tune in to the fine print (such as the service charge—explained next).

TIPPING

Hungarians tip less than Americans do. Most restaurants in Budapest automatically add a 10 percent service charge to

the bill. (A few of the more tourist-oriented eateries have nudged this up to 12 or even 15 percent, which Hungarian diners consider excessive.) The extra charge should be noted on the menu and appears as a line item after the subtotal on the bill (look for "service," "tip," *felszolgálási díj,* or *szervízdíj*). In these cases, an additional tip is not necessary for adequate service.

If the service fee is not included, waiters expect a tip of about 10 percent (or a little less; more than 10 percent is reserved for exceptional service). For example, for a 3,650-Ft bill with no service charge, I'd hand over 4,000 Ft (that's a 350-Ft tip, or a bit more than 9 percent—perfectly acceptable). If you're not sure whether your bill includes the tip, just ask. In smaller cities and towns outside Budapest, it's very rare for the service charge to be tacked on—rounding the bill up 10 percent is more than enough.

Restaurant Code

Eateries in this book are categorized according to the average cost of a typical main course. Drinks, desserts, and splurge items can raise the price considerably.

$$$$ **Splurge:** Most main courses over 4,500 Ft
$$$ **Pricier:** 3,000-4,500 Ft
$$ **Moderate:** 2,000-3,000 Ft
$ **Budget:** Under 2,000 Ft

In Hungary, takeout food or a cafeteria-type place is $; an unpretentious sit-down eatery is $$; an upmarket but still casual restaurant is $$$; and a swanky splurge is $$$$.

RESTAURANT PRICING

I've categorized my recommended eateries based on the average price of a typical main course, indicated with a dollar-sign rating (see sidebar). Obviously, expensive specialties, fine wine, appetizers, and dessert can significantly increase your final bill.

The categories also indicate the personality of a place:

Budget eateries include street food, takeaway, order-at-the-counter shops, basic cafeterias, and bakeries selling sandwiches.

Moderate eateries are nice (but not fancy) sit-down restaurants, ideal for a straightforward, fill-the-tank meal. Most of my listings fall in this category—great for getting a good taste of the local cuisine on a budget.

Pricier eateries are a notch up, with more attention paid to the setting, presentation, and (often inventive) cuisine.

Splurge eateries are dress-up-for-a-special-occasion swanky—typically with an elegant setting, polished service, intricate cuisine, and an expansive (and expensive) wine list.

HUNGARIAN CUISINE

Most Eastern Europeans dine on a starchy meat-and-potatoes cuisine to maximize calories and carbs through a harsh winter. But, as with many things, Hungary is different. Hungarians don't just eat to live—they live to eat. This makes Hungarian cuisine the undisputed best in Central Europe. It delicately blends Magyar peasant cooking (with rich spices), refined by the elegance of French preparation, with a delightful smattering of flavors from the vast, multiethnic Austro-Hungarian Empire (including Germanic, Balkan, Jewish, and Carpathian). Everything is heavily seasoned: with paprika, tomatoes, and peppers of every shape, color, size, and flavor.

When foreigners think of Hungarian cuisine, what comes to mind is goulash. But tourists are often disappointed when

"real Hungarian goulash" isn't the thick stew that they were expecting. The word "goulash" comes from the Hungarian *gulyás leves,* or "shepherd's soup"—a tasty, rustic, nourishing dish originally eaten by cowboys and shepherds on the Great Hungarian Plain. Here in its homeland, it's a clear, spicy broth with chunks of meat, potatoes, and other vegetables. Elsewhere (such as in neighboring Germanic and Slavic countries), the word "goulash" does describe a thick stew. The hearty Hungarian stew called *pörkölt* is probably closer to what most people think of as goulash.

Aside from the obligatory *gulyás,* make a point of trying another unusual Hungarian specialty: cold fruit soup *(hideg gyümölcs leves).* This sweet, cream-based treat—generally eaten before the meal, even though it tastes more like a dessert—is usually made with *meggy* (sour cherries), but you'll also see versions with *alma* (apples), *körte* (pears), and other fruits. Other Hungarian soups *(levesek)* include *bableves* (bean soup), *zöldségleves* (vegetable soup), *gombaleves* (mushroom soup), *halászlé* (fish broth with paprika), and *húsleves* (meat or chicken soup).

Hungarians adore all kinds of meat. *Hús* or *marhahús* is beef, *csirke* is chicken, *borjú* is veal, *kacsa* is duck, *liba* is goose, *sertés* is

pork, *sonka* is ham, *kolbász* is sausage, *szelet* is schnitzel (*Bécsi szelet* means Wiener schnitzel)—and the list goes on. One trendy ingredient you'll see on menus is *mangalica.* This uniquely Hungarian, free-range woolly pig (basically a domesticated boar) is high in unsaturated fat—which fits perfectly with the current foodie culture that elevates the mighty pig. *Libamáj* is goose liver, which shows up everywhere (anything prepared "Budapest style" is topped with goose liver). Lard is used extensively in cooking, making Hungarian cuisine very rich and filling.

Meat is often covered with delicious sauces or garnishes, from rich cream sauces to spicy pastes to fruit jam. For classic Hungarian flavors, you can't beat chicken or veal *paprikás* (described in the "Paprika Primer" sidebar).

Vegetarians have a tricky time in traditional Hungarian

Paprika Primer

The quintessential ingredient in Hungarian cuisine is paprika. In Hungarian, the word *paprika* can mean both peppers (red or green) and the spice that's made from them. Peppers can be stewed, stuffed, sautéed, baked, grilled, or pickled. For seasoning, red shakers of dried paprika join the salt and pepper on tables.

Locals say paprika is best from the sunny south of Hungary. There are more than 40 varieties of paprika spice, with two main types: hot (*csípős* or *erős*) and sweet (*édesnemes* or simply *édes*, often comes in a white can; sometimes also called *csemege*—"delicate"). Hungarians typically cook with sweet paprika to add flavor and color. Then, at the table, they put out hot paprika so each diner can adjust the heat to his or her preferred taste. A can or bag of paprika is a handy and tasty souvenir of your trip (see the Shopping in Budapest chapter).

On menus, anything cooked *paprikás* (PAW-pree-kash) comes smothered in a spicy red paprika gravy, thickened with sour cream. Most often you'll see this option with *csirke* (chick-en) or *borjú* (veal), and it's generally served with dump-ling-like boiled egg noodles called *nokedli* (similar to German *Spätzle*). This dish is *the* Hungarian staple—if you sample just one dish in Hungary, make it chicken or veal *pa-prikás*.

To add even more kick to your food, ask for a jar of the bright-red, sambal-like paste called *Erős Pista* (EH-rewsh PEESH-taw). Literally "Spicy Steve," this Hungarian answer to Tabasco is best used spar-ingly. Or try *Édes Anna* (AY-desh AW-naw, "Sweet Anna"), a variation that's more sweet than spicy. You'll also see tubes of *Gulyáskrém* (a bright-orange, sweet-but-not-hot paste for jazzing up soups) and *Piros Arany* ("Red Gold," a deep-red, intensely flavorful, spicy paste).

restaurants, many of which offer only a plate of deep-fried vegetables. A traditional Hungarian "salad" is composed mostly or entirely of pickled vegetables (cucumbers, cabbage, peppers, and others); even many modern restaurants haven't quite figured out how to do a good, healthy, leafy salad. Fortunately, the more modern, trendy eateries in the capital often offer excellent vegetarian options.

Starches *(köretek)* can include *nokedli* (small, boiled "drop noodles," a.k.a. *Spätzle*), *galuska* (noodles), *burgonya* (potatoes), *sült krumpli* (French fries), *krokett* (croquettes), or *rizs* (rice). *Kenyér* (bread) often comes with the meal. A popular snack—especially to accompany a wine tasting—is a *pogácsa,* a little ball of cheesy fried dough (like a savory doughnut).

Sometimes your main dish will come with steamed, grilled, or deep-fried vegetables. A common side dish is *káposzta* (cabbage, often prepared like sauerkraut). You may also see *töltött káposzta* (cabbage stuffed with meat) or *töltött paprika* (stuffed peppers). *Lecsó* (LEH-chew) is the Hungarian answer to ratatouille: a richly flavorful stew of tomatoes, peppers, and other vegetables.

Thin, crêpe-like pancakes *(palacsinta)* are usually a starter, but sometimes served as a main dish. A delicious traditional Hungarian dish is *Hortobágyi palacsinta* (Hortobágy pancakes, named for the Great Hungarian Plain where the dish originates). This is a savory crêpe wrapped around a tasty meat filling and drenched with creamy paprika sauce.

Pancakes also appear as desserts, stuffed and/or covered with fruit, jam, chocolate sauce, walnuts, poppy seeds, or whipped cream. Most famous is the *Gundel palacsinta,* named for *the* top-of-the-line Budapest restaurant—stuffed with walnuts and raisins in a rum sauce, topped with chocolate sauce, and flambéed.

Pastries are a big deal in Hungary. In the late 19th century, pastry-making caught on here in an attempt to keep up with the renowned desserts of rival Vienna. Today Hungary's streets are still lined with *cukrászda* (pastry shops) where you can simply point to whichever treat you'd like. Try the *Dobos torta* (a many-layered chocolate-and-vanilla cream cake), *flódni* (layer cake of Jewish origin, with apples, walnuts, and poppy seeds), *Rákóczi turós* (sweet cheese curd cake with jam), *somlói galuska* (rum-soaked sponge cake), *krémes* (delicate custard wafer cake), anything with *gesztenye* (chestnuts), and *rétes* (strudel with various fillings, including *túrós,* curds). And many *cukrászda* also serve *fagylalt* (ice cream, *fagyi* for short), sold by the *gomboc* (ball).

DRINKS

Kávé (KAH-vay) and *tea* (TEH-aw) are coffee and tea. (Confusingly, *tej* is not tea—it's milk.) As for water (*víz,* pronounced "veez"), it comes as *szódavíz* (soda water, sometimes just carbonated tap water) or *ásványvíz* (spring water, more expensive).

Hungary is first and foremost a wine country. For the complete rundown on Hungarian wines, see the next section. In summer, consider a refreshing wine spritzer, called a *fröccs*—all the rage in Budapest these days.

Hungary isn't particularly well-known for its beer (*sör,* pronounced "shewr"), but Dreher and Borsodi are two of the better brands. *Világos* is lager; if you prefer something darker, look for *barna* (brown). And, like everywhere, craft breweries are opening up all over the country. I've recommended some places to try Hungarian microbrews in Budapest (see the Entertainment in Budapest chapter) and in Eger.

Hungary is almost as proud of its spirits as its wines. The local firewater, *pálinka,* is a powerful schnapps made from various fruits (most often plum, *szilva;* or apricots, *barack*). Also look for the pear-flavored Vilmos brandy.

Unicum is a unique and beloved Hungarian bitter liquor made of 40 different herbs and aged in oak casks. Look for the round bottle with the red cross on the label. The flavor is powerfully unforgettable—like Jägermeister, but harsher. Unicum started out as a medicine and remains a popular digestif for easing an upset stomach (especially if you've eaten too much rich food—not an uncommon problem in Hungary). Purists claim it's better to drink it at room temperature (so you can fully appreciate its bouquet), but novices find it easier to slug back when chilled. If the original Unicum overwhelms your palate, try one of the newer variations: Unicum Next, with more of a citrus flavor, and Unicum Szilva (with a golden plum on the label), which is aged in plums that cut some of the bitterness with a rich sweetness (www.zwack.hu). For more on the epic story behind Unicum, see page 56.

If you're drinking with some new Magyar friends, impress them with the standard toast: *Egészségedre* (EH-gehs-shay-geh-dreh; "to your health").

HUNGARIAN WINES

Wine *(bor)* is an essential part of Hungarian cuisine. Grapes have been cultivated here since Roman times, and Hungarian wines had

an excellent reputation (winning raves from the likes of France's King Louis XIV and Ludwig von Beethoven) up until World War II. Under communism, most vineyards were collectivized, and the quality suffered terribly. But since the end of that era, many wine-growing families have reclaimed their property and gone back to their roots

(literally). Today they're resuscitating the reputation of Hungarian wines, and once again, vintages from this corner of Europe are earning international raves.

Hungary boasts 22 designated wine-growing regions. The area around Eger is the most famous, but that's only the beginning. The Villány Hills south of Pécs—with a semi-Mediterranean climate at the same latitude as Bordeaux, France—produce full-bodied, tannic reds. The Sopron region near the Austrian border produces both reds and whites. (Northern reds like these tend to be fruity and light.) The hillsides above Lake Balaton (west of Budapest) and the Szekszárd area (along the Danube in southern Hungary) also produce well-respected wines.

Whites *(fehér)* can be sweet *(édes)*, half-dry *(félszáraz)*, or dry *(száraz)*. Whites include the standards (riesling, chardonnay), as well as some wines made from more typically Hungarian grapes: *leányka* ("little girl"), a half-dry, fairly heavy, white table wine; *cserszegi fűszeres*, a spicy, light white that can be fruity; the half-dry, full-bodied *hárslevélű* ("linden leaf"); and the dry *furmint* and *kéknyelű* ("blue stalk").

Reds *(vörös)* include the familiar varieties (cabernet sauvignon, cabernet franc, merlot, pinot noir), and some that are less familiar. *Kekporto* is better known as *blauer Portugieser* in German-speaking countries. In Eger, don't miss **Bull's Blood,** a.k.a. Egri Bikavér, a distinctive blend of reds that comes with a fun local legend (described on page 349). The spicy, medium-body *kékfrankos* ("blue Frankish") supposedly got its name because when Napoleonic soldiers  were here, they could pay either with valuable blue-colored bank notes or unstable white ones...and local vintners wanted the blue francs. (Like most wine origin legends, this story is untrue—*kékfrankos* wasn't cultivated here until after Napoleon's time.)

The most famous Hungarian wine is **Tokaji Aszú,** a sweet, late-harvest, honey-colored dessert wine made primarily from *furmint* grapes. Known as the "wine of kings, and the king of wines," Tokaji Aszú is a D.O.C. product, meaning that to have that name, it must be grown in a particular region. Tokaj is a town in northeastern Hungary, while *aszú* is a "noble rot" grape. The wine's unique, concentrated flavor is made possible by a fungus *(Botrytis cinerea)* that thrives on the grapes in the late fall. The grapes are left

Hurdling the Language Barrier

The language barrier in Hungary is no bigger than elsewhere in Europe. As a monolingual visitor, I find that it's actually easier to communicate in Hungary than in Italy or France. Since Hungary is small and not politically powerful, its people realize that it's unreasonable to expect visitors to learn Hungarian (which has only 12 million speakers worldwide). So they learn English early and well. You'll find that most people in the tourist industry—and virtually all young people—speak fine English.

Of course, not *everyone* speaks English. You'll run into the most substantial language barriers in situations with a less highly educated clerk or service person (train station and post-office counters, housekeepers, museum guards, bakers, and so on)—especially outside of Budapest. Be reasonable in your expectations. Museum ticket-sellers in Hungary are every bit as friendly and multilingual as they are in the US.

Luckily, it's relatively easy to get your point across in these places. I've often bought a train ticket simply by writing out the name of my destination; the time I want to travel (using the 24-hour clock); and the date I want to leave (year first, then month, then day). Here's an example of what I'd show a ticket-seller at a train station: "Eger, 10:30, 2020.08.18."

Hungarians, realizing that their language intimidates Americans, often invent easier nicknames for themselves—so András becomes "Andrew," Erzsébet goes by "Elisabeth," and István tells you, "Call me Steve."

There are certain universal English words all Hungarians know: "hello," "please," "thank you," "super," "pardon," "stop," "menu," "problem," and "no problem." While Hungarians don't expect you to be fluent in their tongue, they appreciate it when you make an effort to pronounce Hungarian words correctly or to use the local pleasantries. For pronunciation tips, see page 10. For survival phrases in Hungarian, see the appendix.

Don't be afraid to interact with locals. Hungarians might initially seem shy, overly formal, or even brusque (a holdover from the closed communist society)—but usually a simple smile is the only icebreaker you need to make a new friend. You'll find that doors open a little more quickly when you know a few words of the language. Give it your best shot. The locals will appreciate your efforts.

on the vine, where they burst and wither like raisins before they are harvested in late October and November. This sucks the water out of the grape, leaving behind very high sugar content and a deep golden color. Tokaji Aszú wines are numbered, from three to six, indicating how many eight-gallon tubs *(puttony)* of these "noble rot" grapes were added to the base wine—the higher the number, the sweeter the wine. Other variations on Tokaji can be less sweet.

(This might sound like another bizarre Hungarian custom, but the French Sauterne and German Beerenauslese wines are also made from "noble rot" grapes. The similarly named French Tokay wine—which derives from the same word—is a different story altogether.)

Finally, note that, except for Bull's Blood and Tokaji Aszú, Hungarian wines are not widely available in the US. A bottle or two (transported in your checked luggage) is a unique souvenir.

Staying Connected

One of the most common questions I hear from travelers is, "How can I stay connected in Europe?" The short answer is: more easily and cheaply than you might think.

The simplest solution is to bring your own device—mobile phone, tablet, or laptop—and use it just as you would at home (following the tips below, such as getting an international plan or connecting to free Wi-Fi whenever possible). Another option is to buy a European SIM card for your US mobile phone. Or you can use European landlines and computers to connect. Each of these options is described below, and more details are at www.ricksteves.com/phoning. For a very practical one-hour lecture covering tech issues for travelers, see www.ricksteves.com/mobile-travel-skills.

Because calling a Hungarian mobile phone can be confusing, be sure to read the instructions in the "How to Dial" chart.

USING A MOBILE PHONE IN EUROPE

Here are some budget tips and options.

Sign up for an international plan. To stay connected at a lower cost, sign up for an international service plan through your carrier. Most providers offer a simple bundle that includes calling, messaging, and data. Your normal plan may already include international coverage (T-Mobile's does).

Before your trip, call your provider or check online to confirm that your phone will work in Europe, and research your provider's international rates. Activate the plan a day or two before you leave, then remember to cancel it when your trip's over.

Use free Wi-Fi whenever possible. Unless you have an unlimited-data plan, you're best off saving most of your online tasks for Wi-Fi. You can access the internet, send texts, and even make voice calls over Wi-Fi.

Most accommodations in Europe offer free Wi-Fi, but some—especially expensive hotels—charge a fee. Many cafés (including Starbucks and McDonald's) have free hotspots for customers; look for signs offering it and ask for the Wi-Fi password when you buy something. You'll also often find Wi-Fi at TIs, city squares, major

How to Dial

International Calls

Whether phoning from a US landline or mobile phone, or from a number in another European country, here's how to make an international call. I've used one of my recommended Eger hotels as an example (tel. 36/411-711).

Initial Zero: Drop the initial zero from international phone numbers—except when calling Italy.

Mobile Tip: If using a mobile phone, the "+" sign can replace the international access code (for a "+" sign, press and hold "0").

US/Canada to Europe

Dial 011 (US/Canada international access code), country code (36 for Hungary), area code (36 for Eger), and phone number.

▸ To call the Eger hotel from home, dial 011-36-36/411-711.

Country to Country Within Europe

Dial 00 (Europe international access code), country code, area code and phone number.

▸ To call the Eger hotel from Germany, dial 00-36-36/411-711.

Europe to the US/Canada

Dial 00, country code (1 for US/Canada), and phone number.

▸ To call from Europe to my office in Edmonds, Washington, dial 00-1-425-771-8303.

Domestic Calls

To dial a landline within the same Hungarian city, simply dial direct, with no area code.

▸ To call the Eger hotel from within Eger, dial 411-711.

To call long-distance to a landline within Hungary, add the prefix 06, followed by the area code (36 for Eger).

▸ To call the Eger hotel from Budapest, dial 06-36/411-711.

Hungarian Mobile Phones: Hungarian mobile phone numbers begin with +3620, +3630, +3631, or +3670. Use this prefix when calling from a mobile phone to another mobile phone. If you call these numbers from a landline within Hungary (such as from your hotel room phone), you'll need to replace the +36 with 06.

---

museums, public-transit hubs, airports, and aboard trains and buses.

Minimize the use of your cellular network. Even with an international data plan, wait until you're on Wi-Fi to Skype, download apps, stream videos, or do other megabyte-greedy tasks. Using a navigation app such as Google Maps over a cellular network can take lots of data, so do this sparingly or use it offline.

▶ To call a local guide with the number +3620-926-0557, dial exactly that from your US phone or Hungarian mobile phone—but from a Hungarian land line, dial 06-20-926-0557.

More Dialing Tips

Toll and Toll-Free Calls: Mobile phones (see prefixes in "Hungarian Mobile Phones") cost substantially more to dial; numbers beginning with 0680 are toll-free; and 0681 and 0690 are expensive toll lines. International rates apply to US toll-free numbers dialed from Hungary—they're not free.

More Phoning Help: See www.howtocallabroad.com.

European Country Codes		Ireland & N. Ireland	353 / 44
Austria	43	Italy	39
Belgium	32	Latvia	371
Bosnia-Herzegovina	387	Montenegro	382
Croatia	385	Morocco	212
Czech Republic	420	Netherlands	31
Denmark	45	Norway	47
Estonia	372	Poland	48
Finland	358	Portugal	351
France	33	Russia	7
Germany	49	Slovakia	421
Gibraltar	350	Slovenia	386
Great Britain	44	Spain	34
Greece	30	Sweden	46
Hungary	36	Switzerland	41
Iceland	354	Turkey	90

Limit automatic updates. By default, your device constantly checks for a data connection and updates apps. It's smart to disable these features so your apps will only update when you're on Wi-Fi. Also, change your device's email settings from "auto-retrieve" to "manual" (or from "push" to "fetch").

When you need to get online but can't find Wi-Fi, simply turn on your cellular network just long enough for the task at hand.

Tips on Internet Security

Make sure that your device is running the latest version of its operating system, security software, and apps. Next, ensure that your device is password- or passcode-protected.

On the road, use only secure, password-protected Wi-Fi hotspots. Ask the hotel or café staff for the specific name of their Wi-Fi network, and make sure you log on to that exact one.

If you must access your financial info online, use a banking app rather than accessing your account via a browser. A cellular connection is more secure than Wi-Fi. Avoid logging onto personal finance sites on a public computer.

Never share your credit-card number (or any other sensitive information) online unless you know that the site is secure. A secure site displays a little padlock icon, and the URL begins with *https* (instead of the usual *http*).

When you're done, avoid further charges by manually switching off data roaming or cellular data (either works) in your device's settings. Another way to make sure you're not accidentally using data roaming is to put your device in "airplane" mode (which also disables phone calls and texts), and then turn your Wi-Fi back on as needed.

Use Wi-Fi calling and messaging apps. Skype, WhatsApp, FaceTime, and Google+ Hangouts are great for making free or low-cost calls or sending texts over Wi-Fi. With an app installed on your phone, tablet, or laptop, you can log on to a Wi-Fi network and contact friends or family members who use the same service. If you buy credit in advance, with some of these services you can call or send a text anywhere for just pennies per minute.

Some apps, such as Apple's iMessage, will use the cellular network if Wi-Fi isn't available: To avoid this possibility, turn off the "Send as SMS" feature.

USING A EUROPEAN SIM CARD

With a European SIM card, you get a European mobile number and access to cheaper rates than you'll get through your US carrier. This option works best for those who want to make a lot of local calls, need a local phone number, or want faster connection speeds than their US carrier provides. It's simple: You buy a SIM card in Europe to replace the SIM card in your "unlocked" US phone or tablet (check with your carrier about unlocking it) or buy a basic cell phone in Europe.

SIM cards are sold at department-store electronics counters, some newsstands, and vending machines. If you need help setting it up, buy one at a mobile-phone shop (you will need to register the SIM card with your passport). Costing about $5-10, SIM cards usually include prepaid calling credit, with no contract and no commitment. Expect to pay $20-40 more for a SIM card with a gigabyte of data.

There are no roaming charges for EU citizens using a domestic SIM card in other EU countries. Theoretically, providers don't have to offer Americans this "roam-like-at-home" pricing, but most do. To be sure, buy your SIM card at a mobile-phone shop and ask if non-EU citizens also have roam-like-at-home pricing.

When you run out of credit, you can top up your SIM card at newsstands, tobacco shops, mobile-phone stores, or many other businesses (look for your SIM card's logo in the window), or possibly online.

WITHOUT A MOBILE PHONE

It's possible to travel in Europe without a mobile device. You can make calls from your hotel and check email or browse websites using public computers.

Most **hotels** charge a fee for placing calls—ask for the rates before you dial. You can use a prepaid international phone card (usually available at newsstands, tobacco shops, and train stations) to call out from your hotel. Dial the toll-free access number, enter the card's PIN code, then dial the number.

You'll only see **public pay phones** in a few post offices and train stations. Most don't take coins but instead require insertable phone cards, which you can buy at a newsstand, convenience store, or post office. Except for emergencies, they're not worth the hassle.

Some hotels have **public computers** in their lobbies for guests to use; otherwise you may find them at public libraries (ask your hotelier or the TI for the nearest location). On a European keyboard, use the "Alt Gr" key to the right of the space bar to insert the extra symbol that appears on some keys. If you can't locate a special character (such as @), simply copy it from a Web page.

MAIL

You can mail one package per day to yourself worth up to $200 duty-free from Europe to the US (mark it "personal purchases"). If you're sending a gift to someone, mark it "unsolicited gift." For details, visit www.cbp.gov, select "Travel," and search for "Know Before You Go." The Hungarian postal service works fine, but for quick transatlantic delivery (in either direction), consider services such as DHL (www.dhl.com).

Transportation

If you're focusing on Budapest, you definitely don't want a car. Virtually all of the attractions listed in this book (with the possible exception of some minor day trips from Budapest) are easily reachable by public transit. Even so, some areas—such as the Danube Bend and Hollókő—can be done more efficiently by car. Instead of hassling with a car of your own, consider splurging by hiring a local guide or a driver (see listings for both in the Orientation to Budapest chapter).

If your trip will cover more of Hungary than just Budapest, you may need to take a long-distance train, rent a car, or fly. I give some specifics on trains, driving, buses, and flights here. For more detailed information on transportation throughout Europe, see www.ricksteves.com/transportation.

TRAINS

Hungary's train network is run by MÁV (Magyar Államvasutak). From centrally located Budapest, train lines branch out across Hungary, like spokes on a wheel. Most connections between outlying cities aren't direct—you often end up having to go back through Budapest. While Hungary's trains are generally good, some are old and fairly slow; major routes use faster, newer, and slightly more expensive InterCity trains (marked with an "IC" or a boxed

"R" on schedules). To ride an InterCity train, you must pay extra for a required reservation (which is printed on a separate ticket).

If traveling to international destinations such as Bratislava or Vienna, other trains are faster and more direct than the InterCity. Between Budapest and Bratislava, EuroCity (EC) trains are fastest and most direct. If traveling from Budapest to Vienna, Austrian RailJet (RJ) trains are fastest and direct, and don't require seat assignments (but advance-purchase discounts lock you into a specific departure).

Warning: Trains can be very crowded on weekends, when it's smart to book a reservation for any train trip.

For timetables, the first place to check is Germany's excellent all-Europe site, www.bahn.com. You can also check Hungary's own timetable website at http://elvira.mav-start.hu. For general rail information in Hungary, call 0640-494-949 (from outside Hungary, dial +36-1-444-4499).

It's easiest to book domestic train tickets online, at www. mavcsoport.hu. The site is a bit clunky, but it's in English and you'll be emailed an eticket to show to the conductor. International train tickets must be purchased at a train station; try using the ticket machines rather than waiting in long lines. For more on buying tickets, see page 277.

Rail Passes: Hungary is covered by a Eurail Hungary pass, a Central Europe Triangle Pass (Vienna-Budapest-Prague), a four-country European East pass (together with Austria, the Czech Republic, and Slovakia), and the more expensive Eurail Global Pass. If your train travel will be limited to a handful of rides and/or short distances (for example, within Hungary), you're probably better off without a pass—tickets are cheap to buy as you go. But if you're combining Hungary with farther-flung international destinations, a rail pass could save you money. For more detailed advice on figuring out the smartest rail pass options for your train trip, visit RickSteves.com/rail.

TAXIS AND RIDE-BOOKING SERVICES

Most European taxis are reliable and cheap. In many cities, two people can travel short distances by cab for little more than the cost of bus or subway tickets. Uber does not operate in Hungary.

RENTING A CAR

It's cheaper to arrange most car rentals from the US, so research and compare rates before you go. Most of the major US rental agencies (including Avis, Budget, Enterprise, Hertz, and Thrifty) have offices throughout Europe. Also consider the two major Europe-based agencies, Europcar and Sixt. Consolidators such as Auto Europe/Kemwel (www.autoeurope. com, or the sometimes cheaper www.autoeurope.eu) compare rates at several companies to get you the best deal.

Wherever you book, always read the fine print. Ask about add-on charges—such as one-way drop-off fees, airport surcharges, or mandatory insurance policies—that aren't included in the "total price."

Rental Costs and Considerations

Figure on paying roughly $250 for a one-week rental for a basic

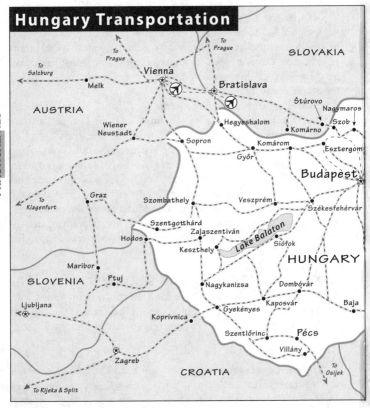

Hungary Transportation

compact car. Allow extra for supplemental insurance, fuel, tolls, and parking. To save money on fuel, request a diesel car.

Manual vs. Automatic: Almost all rental cars in Europe are manual by default—and cars with a stick shift are generally cheaper. If you need an automatic, request one in advance. When selecting a car, don't be tempted by a larger model, as it won't be as maneuverable on narrow, winding roads or when squeezing into tight parking lots.

Age Restrictions: Some rental companies impose minimum and maximum age limits. Young drivers (25 and under) and seniors (69 and up) should check the rental policies and rules section of car rental websites. If you're considered too young or too old, look into leasing (covered later), which has less stringent age restrictions.

Choosing Pick-up/Drop-off Locations: Always check the hours of the locations you choose: Many rental offices close from midday Saturday until Monday morning and, in smaller towns, at lunchtime. When selecting an office, plug the address into a mapping website to confirm the location. A downtown site is generally cheaper—and might seem more convenient than

the airport. But pedestrianized and one-way streets can make navigation tricky when returning a car at a big-city office or urban train station. Wherever you select, get precise details on the location and allow ample time to find it.

Have the Right License: If you're renting a car in Hungary, bring your driver's license. You're also technically required to have an International Driving Permit—an official translation of your license (sold at AAA offices for about $20 plus the cost of two passport-type photos; see www.aaa.com). While that's the letter of the law, I generally rent cars without having this permit. How this is enforced varies from country to country: Get advice from your car rental company.

Crossing Borders in a Rental Car: Be aware that international trips—say, picking up in Budapest and dropping off in Bratislava—can be very expensive; most rental companies assess a very high international drop-off fee. It may be cheaper to drop your car off at a point within Hungary, near the border, then hop on a train to the next country.

Always tell your car-rental company exactly which count⌐

you'll be entering. Some companies levy extra insurance fees for trips taken in certain countries with certain cars (such as BMWs, Mercedes, and convertibles). Double-check with your rental agent that you have all the documentation you need before you drive off (especially if you're crossing borders into non-Schengen countries, such as Croatia, where you might need to present proof of insurance).

Picking Up Your Car: Before driving off in your rental car, check it thoroughly and make sure any damage is noted on your rental agreement. Rental agencies in Europe are very strict when it comes to charging for even minor damage, so be sure to mark everything. Find out how your car's gearshift, lights, turn signals, wipers, radio, and fuel cap function, and know what kind of fuel the car takes (diesel vs. unleaded). When you return the car, make sure the agent verifies its condition with you. Some drivers take pictures of the returned vehicle as proof of its condition.

Car Insurance Options

When you rent a car in Europe, the price typically includes liability insurance, which covers harm to other cars or motorists—but not the rental car itself. To limit your financial risk in case of damage to the rental, choose one of these options: Buy a Collision Damage Waiver (CDW) with a low or zero deductible from the car-rental company (roughly 30-40 percent extra), get coverage through your credit card (free, but more complicated), or get collision insurance as part of a larger travel-insurance policy.

Basic **CDW** costs $15–30 a day and typically comes with a $1,000-2,000 deductible, reducing but not eliminating your financial responsibility. When you reserve or pick up the car, you'll be offered the chance to "buy down" the deductible to zero (for an additional $10-30/day; this is sometimes called "super CDW" or "zero-deductible coverage").

If you opt for **credit-card coverage,** you must decline all coverage offered by the car-rental company—which means they can place a hold on your card for up to the full value of the car. In case of damage, it can be time-consuming to resolve the charges. Before relying on this option, quiz your card company about how it works.

If you're already purchasing a **travel-insurance policy** for your trip, adding collision coverage can be an economical option. For example, Travel Guard (www.travelguard.com) sells affordable renter's collision insurance as an add-on to its other policies; it's valid everywhere in Europe except the Republic of Ireland, and some Italian car-rental companies refuse to honor it, as it doesn't cover you in case of theft.

For more on car-rental insurance, see www.ricksteves.com/cdw.

Leasing

For trips of three weeks or more, consider leasing (which automatically includes zero-deductible collision and theft insurance). By technically buying and then selling back the car, you save money on taxes and insurance. Leasing provides you a brand-new car with unlimited mileage and a 24-hour emergency assistance program. You can lease for as little as 21 days to as long as five and a half months. Car leases must be arranged from the US. One of several companies offering affordable lease packages is Auto Europe.

Navigation Options

If you'll be navigating using your phone or a GPS unit from home, remember to bring a car charger and device mount.

Your Mobile Phone: The mapping app on your phone works fine for navigation in Europe, but for real-time turn-by-turn directions and traffic updates, you'll need mobile data access. And driving all day can burn through a lot of very expensive data. The economical work-around is to use map apps that work offline. By downloading in advance from Google Maps, Apple Maps, Here WeGo, or Navmii, you can still have turn-by-turn voice directions and maps that recalibrate even though they're offline. (However, offline maps don't include real-time traffic information—which can help you avoid traffic jams and other delays.)

You must download your maps before you go offline—and it's smart to select large regions. Then turn off your data connection so you're not charged for roaming. Call up the map, enter your destination, and you're on your way. Even if you don't have to pay extra for data roaming, this option is great for navigating in areas with poor connectivity.

GPS Devices: If you want the convenience of a dedicated GPS unit, consider renting one with your car ($10-30/day). These units offer real-time turn-by-turn directions and traffic without the data requirements of an app. The unit may come loaded only with maps for its home country; if you need additional maps, ask. Also make sure your device's language is set to English before you drive off.

A less-expensive option is to bring a GPS device from home. Be sure to buy and install the European maps you'll need before your trip.

Maps and Atlases: Even when navigating primarily with a mobile app or GPS, I always make it a point to have a paper map. It's invaluable for getting the big picture, understanding alternate routes, and filling in when my phone runs out of juice. The free maps you get from your car-rental company usually don't have enough detail. It's smart to buy a better map before you go, or pick one up at a European gas station, bookshop, newsstand, or tourist shop.

DRIVING

Road Rules: Be aware of typical European road rules; for example, many countries require headlights to be turned on at all times, and nearly all forbid handheld mobile-phone use. Seatbelts are mandatory in Hungary, children under age 3 must ride in a child seat, and it's illegal to drink any alcohol at all before driving. In Europe, you're not allowed to turn right on a red light, unless there is a sign or signal specifically authorizing it, and on expressways it's illegal to pass drivers on the right. In roundabouts, cars to the left have the right of way. Ask your car-rental company about these rules, or check the "International Travel" section of the US State Department website (www. travel.state.gov, search for your country in the "Country Information" box, then click "Travel and Transportation").

Toll Stickers: Hungary has a fine network of expressways, which always begin with "M" (e.g., the M-3 expressway runs east of Budapest toward Eger). To drive on Hungarian expressways, you'll need a toll sticker, called an *autópálya matrica* (also called a "vignette"; 3,500 Ft/10 days, 4,780 Ft/month, www.motorway.hu). Ask about this when you rent your car (if it's not already included, you'll have to buy one). It's not uncommon to be pulled over at an on- or off-ramp to be checked for a toll sticker; those caught without one are subject to a hefty fine. If you drive into Slovakia or Austria, you'll also need to buy a toll sticker to use their highways (Slovakia—*úhrada*, €10/10 days; Austria—*Vignette*, €9.50/10 days, €26/2 months). You don't need a

toll sticker if you'll be dipping into the country on minor roads—
only for major highways.

FLIGHTS

To compare flight costs and times, begin with a travel search engine: Kayak.com is the top site for flights to and within Europe, easy-to-use Google Flights has price alerts, and Skyscanner.com includes many inexpensive flights within Europe.

Flights to Europe: Start looking for international flights about four to six months before your trip, especially for peak-season travel. Depending on your itinerary, it can be efficient and no more expensive to fly into one city and out of another. If your flight requires a connection in Europe, see my hints on navigating Europe's top hub airports at www.ricksteves.com/hub-airports.

Flights Within Europe: Flying between European cities has become surprisingly affordable. Before buying a long-distance train or bus ticket, first check the cost of a flight on one of Europe's air-

lines, whether a major carrier or a no-frills outfit like EasyJet and Ryanair.

Malév Hungarian Airlines went bust in 2012—leaving Hungary without an official national airline. But many major international lines (such as LOT, Lufthansa, and Austrian Airlines) still serve Budapest, and the void has been capably filled by various low-cost airlines. The most prominent of these is Budapest-based **Wizz Air** (www.wizzair.com)—which also has hubs in the Polish cities of Warsaw, Gdańsk, and Katowice (near Kraków).

If you're not finding the flight you want out of Budapest, consider flying out of **Bratislava**, Slovakia, instead—it's less than a three-hour train ride away. Bratislava is well-served by the budget carrier Ryanair. **Vienna**, Austria—just three hours from Budapest by train—is the hub for Austrian Airlines, and has cheap flights on Eurowings and others.

Be aware of the potential drawbacks of flying with a discount airline: nonrefundable and nonchangeable tickets, minimal customer service, time-consuming treks to secondary airports, and stingy baggage allowances (also an issue on major airlines). To avoid unpleasant surprises, read the small print about the costs for "extras" such as reserving a seat, checking a bag, or checking in and printing a boarding pass.

Flying to the US and Canada: Because security is extra tight for flights to the US, be sure to give yourself plenty of time at the airport. It's also important to charge your electronic devices before you board because security checks may require you to turn them on (see www.tsa.gov for the latest rules).

Resources from Rick Steves

Begin Your Trip at RickSteves.com

My mobile-friendly **website** is *the* place to explore Europe in preparation for your trip. You'll find thousands of fun articles, videos, and radio interviews; a wealth of money-saving tips for planning your dream trip; travel news dispatches; a video library of my travel talks; my travel blog; my latest guidebook updates (www.ricksteves.com/update); and my free Rick Steves Audio Europe app. You can also follow me on Facebook and Twitter.

Our **Travel Forum** is a well-groomed collection of message boards where our travel-savvy community answers questions and shares their personal travel experiences—and our well-traveled staff chimes in when they can be helpful (www.ricksteves.com/forums).

Our **online Travel Store** offers bags and accessories that I've designed to help you travel smarter and lighter. These include my popular carry-on bags (which I live out of four months a year), money belts, totes, toiletries kits, adapters, guidebooks, and planning maps (www.ricksteves.com/shop).

Our website can also help you find the perfect **rail pass** for your itinerary and your budget, with easy, one-stop shopping for rail passes, seat reservations, and point-to-point tickets (www.ricksteves.com/rail).

Rick Steves' Tours, Guidebooks, TV Shows, and More

Small Group Tours: Want to travel with greater efficiency and less stress? We offer more than 40 itineraries reaching the best destinations in this book...and beyond. Each year about 30,000 travelers join us on about 1,000 Rick Steves bus tours. You'll enjoy great guides and a fun bunch of travel partners (with small groups of 24 to 28 travelers). You'll find European adventures to fit every vacation length. For all the details, and to get our tour catalog, visit www.ricksteves.com or call us at 425/608-4217.

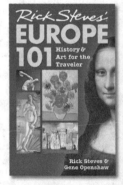

Books: *Rick Steves Budapest* is just one of many books in my series on European travel, which includes country and city guidebooks, Snapshots (excerpted chapters from bigger guides), Pocket guides (full-color little books on big cities), "Best Of" guidebooks (condensed, full-color country guides), and my budget-travel skills handbook, *Rick Steves Europe Through the Back Door*. A more complete list of my titles—including phrase books, cruising guides, and more—appears near the end of this book.

TV Shows and Travel Talks: My public television series, *Rick Steves' Europe*, covers Europe from top to bottom with over 100 half-hour episodes—and we're working on new shows every year (watch full episodes at my website for free). Or, to raise your travel I.Q. check out the video versions of our popular classes (covering most European countries as well as travel skills, packing smart, cruising, tech for travelers, European art, and travel as a political act www.ricksteves.com/travel-talks).

Radio: My weekly public radio show, *Travel with Rick Steves*, features interviews with travel experts from around the world. It airs on 400 public radio stations across the US, or you can hear it as a podcast. A complete archive of programs is available at www.ricksteves.com/radio.

Audio Tours on My Free App: I've produced dozens of free, self-guided audio tours of the top sights in Europe. For those tours and other audio content, get my free **Rick Steves Audio Europe app,** an extensive online library organized by destination. For more on my app, see page 4.

PRACTICALITIES

APPENDIX

Holidays and Festivals

This list includes selected festivals in Budapest, plus national holidays observed throughout Hungary. While nominally a Catholic country, most Hungarians are not very devout. Catholic holidays (such as Epiphany, Ascension, Corpus Christi, and the Assumption of Mary) are observed, but with less impact than in some other countries. Many sights and banks close on national holidays—keep this in mind when planning your itinerary. Before planning a trip around a festival, verify the dates with the festival website, the Budapest tourist office, or my "Upcoming Holidays and Festivals in Hungary" web page (www.ricksteves.com/europe/hungary/festivals). Many of Budapest's top festivals share a website (www.fesztivalvaros.hu).

Jan 1	New Year's Day
March 15	National Day (celebrates 1848 Revolution, closures)
April	Easter weekend (Good Friday-Easter Monday): April 19-22, 2019; April 10-13, 2020
April	Budapest Spring Festival (2 weeks; opera, ballet, classical music; www.btf.hu)

April	Szentendre Spring Festival (art festival with theater, concerts, film, activities; www.szentendreprogram.hu)
May 1	Labor Day (closures)
May	Ascension: May 30, 2019; May 21, 2020
May/June	Pentecost and Whitmonday: June 9-10, 2019; May 31-June 1, 2020
Late May-mid-June	Jewish Art Days, Budapest (2 weeks, www.zsidomuveszetinapok.hu)
Early July	Early Music Days, Sopron (1 week, http://regizeneinapok.hu)
Late July	Formula 1 races, Budapest (www.hungaroinfo.com/formel1)
Aug	Sziget Festival, Budapest (1 week, rock and pop music, www.sziget.hu)
Aug 15	Assumption of Mary
Aug 20	St. István's Day (also known as Constitution Day; fireworks, celebrations)
Oct 23	Republic Day (remembrances of 1956 Uprising)
Mid-Oct	Café Budapest Contemporary Arts Festival (www.cafebudapestfest.hu)
Nov 1	All Saints' Day/Remembrance Day (religious festival, some closures)
Dec 24-25	Christmas Eve and Christmas Day
Dec 26	Boxing Day

Books and Films

To learn more about Hungary past and present, check out a few of these books and films.

Nonfiction

Lonnie Johnson's *Central Europe: Enemies, Neighbors, Friends* is the best historical overview of Hungary and the surrounding nations.

John Lukacs' *Budapest 1900* is a scholarly but readable cultural study that captures Budapest at its turn-of-the-20th-century zenith.

Patrick Leigh Fermor's *Between the Woods and the Water* is the vividly recounted memoir of a young man who traveled by foot and on horseback across the Balkan Peninsula (including Hungary) in 1933.

András Török's irreverent *Budapest: A Critical Guide*, while technically a guidebook, offers more local insight (and wit) than any other source.

Timothy Garton Ash has written several good "eyewitness account" books analyzing the transition in Central and Eastern Europe from the late 1980s through the 1990s, including *History of the Present* and *The Magic Lantern*.

Anne Applebaum's *Iron Curtain: The Crushing of Eastern Europe 1944-1956* is an accessible account of how the Soviets exerted their influence on the nations they liberated from the Nazis; her *Gulag: A History* delves into one particularly odious mechanism they used to intimidate their subjects.

Tina Rosenberg's dense but thought-provoking *The Haunted Land* asks how individuals who actively supported communist regimes should be treated in the postcommunist age.

James Michener's *The Bridge at Andau* tells the story of the 1956 Uprising, and the Hungarians who fled following its crushing defeat.

Benjamin Curtis' *The Habsburgs: The History of a Dynasty* is an illuminating portrait of the Austrian imperial family that shaped so much of Eastern European history (and ruled Hungary for many centuries).

For information on Eastern European Roma (Gypsies), consider the textbook-style *We Are the Romani People* by Ian Hancock, and the more literary *Bury Me Standing* by Isabel Fonseca.

For a look at life during communist times—albeit not in Hungary—Croatian journalist Slavenka Drakulić has written a pair of insightful essay collections from a woman's perspective: *Café Europa: Life After Communism* and *How We Survived Communism and Even Laughed*.

If you're going to Eger, consider reading Géza Gárdonyi's *Eclipse of the Crescent Moon*, an epic about the Siege of Eger that's read and beloved by every Hungarian grade-schooler.

Fiction

Imre Kertész, a Hungarian-Jewish Auschwitz survivor who won the Nobel Prize for Literature in 2002, is best known for his semiautobiographical novel *Fatelessness (Sorstalanság)*, which chronicles the experience of a young concentration-camp prisoner.

Arthur Phillips' confusingly titled novel *Prague* tells the story of American expats negotiating young-adult life in postcommunist Budapest, where they often feel one-upped by their compatriots doing the same in the Czech capital (hence the title).

Joseph Roth's *The Radetzky March* details the decline of an aristocratic family in the Austro-Hungarian Empire.

The Newbery Honor book *Zlateh the Goat* (Isaac Bashevis Singer) includes seven folktales of Jewish Eastern Europe.

Films

One of the more accessible English-language films for an introduction to Budapest is *Sunshine* (1999, starring Ralph Fiennes, directed by István Szabó; not to be confused with Danny Boyle's very different 2007 film of the same name). Tracing three generations of an aristocratic Jewish family in Budapest—from the Golden Age, through the Holocaust, to the Cold War—*Sunshine* is an enlightening if melodramatic look at recent Hungarian history. Also in English, the 1998 Oscar-winning documentary *The Last Days* chronicles the fate of Jews when the Nazis took over Hungary in 1944.

For Hungarian-language films, *Fateless*, the 2005 adaptation of Imre Kertész's Nobel Prize-winning novel about a young man in a concentration camp, was scripted by Kertész himself. Another Holocaust-themed film, László Nemes' *Son of Saul* (*Saul Fia*, 2015)—telling the story of a Hungarian inmate at Auschwitz concentration camp—won the Grand Prix at Cannes, an Oscar, and a Golden Globe. The surreal dark comedy *Kontroll* (2003) is about ticket inspectors on the Budapest Metró whose lives are turned upside down by a serial killer lurking in the shadows. *The Witness* (*A Tanú*, a.k.a. *Without a Trace*, 1969), a cult classic about a simple man who mysteriously wins the favor of communist bigwigs, is a biting satire of the darkest days of Soviet rule. *Time Stands Still (Megáll Az Idö)*, a hit at the 1982 Cannes Film Festival, tells the story of young Hungarians in the 1960s. *Children of Glory* (*Szabadság, Szerelem*, 2006) dramatizes the true story of the Hungarian water polo team that defiantly trounced the Soviets at the Olympics just after the 1956 Uprising.

Many American studios have taken advantage of Hungary's low prices to film would-be blockbusters in Budapest (such as the 2015 Melissa McCarthy film *Spy,* and the similarly named 2002 Eddie Murphy/Owen Wilson action-comedy *I Spy*). More often, Budapest stands in for other cities—for example, as Buenos Aires in Madonna's 1996 film *Evita,* and as various European locales in Stephen Spielberg's 2005 film *Munich.*

Two German movies—while not about Hungary—are still excellent for their insight into the surreal and paranoid days of the Soviet Bloc. The Oscar-winning *Lives of Others* (2006) chronicles the constant surveillance that the communist regime employed to keep potential dissidents in line. For a funny and nostalgic look at postcommunist Europe's fitful transition to capitalism, *Good Bye Lenin!* (2003) can't be beat.

Conversions and Climate

Numbers and Stumblers

- Europeans write a few of their numbers differently than we do. 1 = $\it{1}$, 4 = $\it{4}$, 7 = $\it{7}$.
- In Hungary, dates appear as year/month/day, so Christmas 2020 is 2020/12/25 (or dots can be used instead: 2020.12.25).
- Commas are decimal points and decimals commas. A dollar and a half is $1,50, and there are 5.280 feet in a mile.
- Hungarians usually list their surname first (for example, Bartók Béla instead of Béla Bartók).
- When counting with fingers, start with your thumb. If you hold up your first finger to request one item, you'll probably get two.
- What Americans call the second floor of a building is the first floor in Europe.
- On escalators and moving sidewalks, Europeans keep the left "lane" open for passing. Keep to the right.

APPENDIX

Metric Conversions

A **kilogram** equals 1,000 grams (about 2.2 pounds). One hundred **grams** (a common unit at markets) is about a quarter-pound. One **liter** is about a quart, or almost four to a gallon.

A **kilometer** is six-tenths of a mile. To convert kilometers to miles, cut the kilometers in half and add back 10 percent of the original (120 km: 60 + 12 = 72 miles). One meter is 39 inches—just over a yard.

1 foot = 0.3 meter	1 square yard = 0.8 square meter
1 yard = 0.9 meter	1 square mile = 2.6 square kilometers
1 mile = 1.6 kilometers	1 ounce = 28 grams
1 centimeter = 0.4 inch	1 quart = 0.95 liter
1 meter = 39.4 inches	1 kilogram = 2.2 pounds
1 kilometer = 0.62 mile	32°F = 0°C

Clothing Sizes

When shopping for clothing, use these US-to-European comparisons as general guidelines (but note that no conversion is perfect).

Women: For pants and dresses, add 30 in Hungary (US 10 = Hungarian 40). For blouses and sweaters, add 8 for most of Europe (US 32 = European 40). For shoes, add 30-31 (US 7 = European 37/38).

Men: For shirts, multiply by 2 and add about 8 (US 15 = European 38). For jackets and suits, add 10. For shoes, add 32-34.

Children: For clothing, subtract 1-2 sizes for small children and subtract 4 for juniors. For shoes up to size 13, add 16-18, and for sizes 1 and up, add 30-32.

Hungary's Climate

First line, average daily high; second line, average daily low; third line, average days with some rain. For more detailed weather statistics for destinations in this book (as well as the rest of the world), check www.wunderground.com.

J	F	M	A	M	J	J	A	S	O	N	D
34°	39°	50°	62°	71°	78°	82°	81°	74°	61°	47°	39°
25°	28°	35°	44°	52°	58°	62°	60°	53°	44°	38°	30°
13	12	11	11	13	13	10	9	7	10	14	13

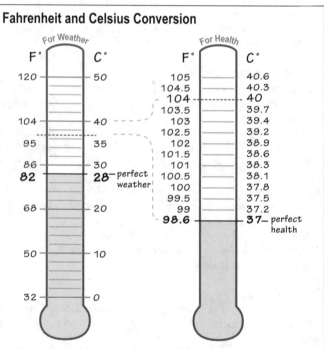

Fahrenheit and Celsius Conversion

Europe takes its temperature using the Celsius scale, while we opt for Fahrenheit. For a rough conversion from Celsius to Fahrenheit, double the number and add 30. For weather, remember that 28°C is 82°F—perfect. For health, 37°C is just right. At a launderette, 30°C is cold, 40°C is warm (usually the default setting), 60°C is hot, and 95°C is boiling. Your air-conditioner should be set at about 20°C.

Packing Checklist

Whether you're traveling for five days or five weeks, you won't need more than this. Pack light to enjoy the sweet freedom of true mobility.

Clothing

- ❑ 5 shirts: long- & short-sleeve
- ❑ 2 pairs pants (or skirts/capris)
- ❑ 1 pair shorts
- ❑ 5 pairs underwear & socks
- ❑ 1 pair walking shoes
- ❑ Sweater or warm layer
- ❑ Rainproof jacket with hood
- ❑ Tie, scarf, belt, and/or hat
- ❑ Swimsuit
- ❑ Sleepwear/loungewear

Money

- ❑ Debit card(s)
- ❑ Credit card(s)
- ❑ Hard cash (US $100-200)
- ❑ Money belt

Documents

- ❑ Passport
- ❑ Tickets & confirmations: flights, hotels, trains, rail pass, car rental, sight entries
- ❑ Driver's license
- ❑ Student ID, hostel card, etc.
- ❑ Photocopies of important documents
- ❑ Insurance details
- ❑ Guidebooks & maps

Toiletries Kit

- ❑ Basics: soap, shampoo, toothbrush, toothpaste, floss, deodorant, sunscreen, brush/comb, etc.
- ❑ Medicines & vitamins
- ❑ First-aid kit
- ❑ Glasses/contacts/sunglasses
- ❑ Sewing kit
- ❑ Packet of tissues (for WC)
- ❑ Earplugs

Electronics

- ❑ Mobile phone
- ❑ Camera & related gear
- ❑ Tablet/ebook reader/laptop
- ❑ Headphones/earbuds
- ❑ Chargers & batteries
- ❑ Phone car charger & mount (or GPS device)
- ❑ Plug adapters

Miscellaneous

- ❑ Daypack
- ❑ Sealable plastic baggies
- ❑ Laundry supplies: soap, laundry bag, clothesline, spot remover
- ❑ Small umbrella
- ❑ Travel alarm/watch
- ❑ Notepad & pen
- ❑ Journal

Optional Extras

- ❑ Second pair of shoes (flip-flops, sandals, tennis shoes, boots)
- ❑ Travel hairdryer
- ❑ Picnic supplies
- ❑ Water bottle
- ❑ Fold-up tote bag
- ❑ Small flashlight
- ❑ Mini binoculars
- ❑ Small towel or washcloth
- ❑ Inflatable pillow/neck rest
- ❑ Tiny lock
- ❑ Address list (to mail postcards)
- ❑ Extra passport photos

APPENDIX

Hungarian Survival Phrases

Remember, the letter *a* is pronounced "aw," while *á* is a brighter "ah." In the phonetics, *dj* is pronounced like the *j* in "jeans."

English	Hungarian	Pronunciation
Hello. (formal)	Jó napot kívánok.	yoh **nah**-poht **kee**-vah-nohk
Hi. / Bye. (informal)	Szia. / Hello.	**see**-yaw / "Hello"
Do you speak English?	Beszél angolul?	beh-sayl **awn**-goh-lool
Yes. / No.	Igen. / Nem.	**ee**-gehn / nehm
I (don't) understand.	(Nem) értem.	(nehm) **ayr**-tehm
Please.	Kérem.	**kay**-rehm
You're welcome.	Szívesen.	**see**-veh-shehn
Thank you (very much).	Köszönöm (szépen).	**kur**-sur-nurm (**say**-pehn)
Excuse me. / I'm sorry.	Bocsánat.	**boh**-chah-nawt
No problem.	Semmi gond.	**sheh**-mee gohnd
Good.	Jól.	yohl
Goodbye.	Viszontlátásra.	**vee**-sohnt-lah-tahsh-raw
one / two / three	egy / kettő / három	edj / **keh**-tur / **hah**-rohm
four / five / six / seven	négy / öt / hat / hét	naydj / urt / hawt / hayt
eight / nine / ten	nyolc / kilenc / tíz	nyolts / **kee**-lehnts / teez
hundred / thousand	száz / ezer	sahz / **eh**-zehr
How much?	Mennyi?	**mehn**-yee
forint (local currency)	forint (Ft)	**foh**-reent
Where is it?	Hol van?	hohl vawn
Is it free (no charge)?	Ingyen van?	een-**jehn** vawn
Where can I find / buy...?	Hol találok / vehetek...?	hohl **taw**-lah-lohk / **veh**-heh-tehk
I'd like / We'd like...	Kérnék / Kérnénk...	**kayr**-nayk / **kayr**-naynk
...a room.	...egy szobát.	edj **soh**-baht
...a ticket (to ___).	...egy jegyet (___-ig).	edj **yehdj**-eht (___-ig)
Is it possible?	Lehet?	leh-**heht**
Where is the ___?	Hol van a ___?	hohl vawn aw ___
big train station (in Budapest)	pályaudvar	**pah**-yood-vawr
small train station (elsewhere)	vasútállomás	**vaw**-shoot-ah-loh-mahsh
bus station	buszpályaudvar	**boos**-pah-yood-vawr
tourist information office	turista információ	**too**-reesh-taw **een**-for-maht-see-yoh
toilet	toalet / WC	**toh**-aw-leht / **vayt**-say
men / women	férfi / női	**fayr**-fee / **nur**-ee
left / right	bal / jobb	bawl / yohb
straight	egyenesen	**edj**-eh-neh-shehn
At what time...?	Mikor...?	**mee**-kor
...does this open / close	...nyit / zár	nyit / zahr
Just a moment.	Egy pillanat.	edj **pee**-law-nawt
now / soon / later	most / hamarosan / később	mohsht / **haw**-maw-roh-shawn / **kay**-shurb
today / tomorrow	ma / holnap	maw / **hohl**-nawp

In a Hungarian Restaurant

English	Hungarian	Pronunciation
I'd like to reserve a table for one / two people.	Szeretnék foglalni egy asztalt egy / két fő részére.	**seh**-reht-nayk **fog**-lawl-nee edj **aws**-tawlt edj / kayt few **ray**-say-reh
Is this table free?	Ez az asztal szabad?	ehz oz **aws**-tawl saw-**bawd**
Can I help you?	Tessék?	**tehsh**-shayk
The menu (in English), please.	Kérem az (angol), étlapot.	**kay**-rehm oz (**awn**-gohl) **ayt**-law-poht
service (not) included	a számla a felszolgálási díjat (nem) tartalmazza	aw **sahm**-law aw **fehl**-sohl-gah-lah-shee **dee**-yawt (nehm) **tawr**-tawl-maw-zaw
"to go"	elvitelre	**ehl**-vee-tehl-reh
with / without	___-val / nélkül	___-vawl / **nayl**-kewl
and / or	és / vagy	aysh / vawdj
fixed-price meal (of the day)	(napi) menü	(**naw**-pee) **meh**-new
daily special	napi ajánlat	**naw**-pee **aw**-yahn-lawt
main courses	főételek	**fur**-ay-teh-lehk
appetizers	előételek	**eh**-lur-ay-teh-lehk
bread / cheese	kenyér / sajt	**kehn**-yayr / shayt
sandwich	szendvics	**send**-veech
soup / salad	leves / saláta	**leh**-vehsh / **shaw**-lah-taw
meat / poultry	hús / szárnyasok	hoosh / **sahr**-nyaw-shohk
fish	halak	**haw**-lawk
seafood	tengeri halak	**tehn**-geh-ree **haw**-lawk
fruit / vegetables	gyümölcs / zöldség	**jewm**-urlch / **zulrd**-shayg
dessert	desszert	**deh**-sehrt
vegetarian	vegetáriánus	**veh**-geh-tah-ree-ah-noosh
(tap) water	(csap) víz	(chawp) veez
mineral water	ásványvíz	**ash**-vawn-veez
milk / (orange) juice	tej / (narancs) lé	**tay**ee / (**naw**-rawnch) lay
coffee / tea	kávé / tea	**kah**-vay / **teh**-aw
beer / wine	sör / bor	shohr / bohr
red / white	vörös / fehér	**vur**-rursh / **feh**-hayr
sweet / dry / semi-dry	édes / száraz / félszáraz	**ay**-dehsh / **sah**-rawz / **fayl**-sah-rawz
glass / bottle	pohár / üveg	**poh**-hahr / **ew**-vehg
Cheers!	Egészségedre!	**eh**-gehs-sheh-geh-dreh
More. / Another.	Még. / Máskikat.	mayg / **mah**-shee-kawt
The same.	Ugyanazt.	**oodj**-aw-nawst
Bill, please. (literally, "I'll pay.")	Fizetek.	**fee**-zeh-tehk
tip	borravaló	**boh**-raw-vaw-loh
Bon appétit!	Jó étvágyat!	yoh **ayt**-vah-yawt
Delicious!	Finom!	**fee**-nohm

INDEX

INDEX

INDEX

INDEX

INDEX

MAP INDEX

Explore Europe

At ricksteves.com you can browse through thousands of articles, videos, photos and radio interviews, plus find a wealth of money-saving travel tips for planning your dream trip. And with our mobile-friendly website, you can easily access all this great travel information anywhere you go.

TV Shows

Preview the places you'll visit by watching entire half-hour episodes of Rick Steves' Europe (choose from all 100 shows) on-demand, for free.

your travel dreams into affordable reality

Radio Interviews

Enjoy ready access to Rick's vast library of radio interviews covering travel

tips and cultural insights that relate specifically to your Europe travel plans.

Travel Forums

Learn, ask, share! Our online community of savvy travelers is a great resource

for first-time travelers to Europe, as well as seasoned pros. You'll find forums on each country, plus travel tips and restaurant/hotel reviews. You can even ask one of our well-traveled staff to chime in with an opinion.

Travel News

Subscribe to our free Travel News e-newsletter, and get monthly updates from Rick on what's happening in Europe.

Rick Steves has

Experience maximum Europe

Save time and energy

This guidebook is your independent-travel toolkit. But for all it delivers, it's still up to you to devote the time and energy it takes to manage the preparation and logistics that are essential for a happy trip. If that's a hassle, there's a solution.

Rick Steves Tours

A Rick Steves tour takes you to Europe's most interesting places with great

guides and small groups of 28 or less. We follow Rick's favorite itineraries, ride in comfy buses, stay in family-run hotels, and bring you intimately

close to the Europe you've traveled so far to see. Most importantly, we take away the logistical headaches so you can focus on the fun.

Join the fun
This year we'll take thousands of free-spirited

travelers—nearly half of them repeat customers— along with us on four dozen different itineraries, from Ireland to Italy to Athens. Is a Rick Steves tour the right fit for your travel dreams? Find out at ricksteves.com, where you can also request Rick's latest tour catalog. Europe is best experienced with happy travel partners. We hope you can join us.

A Guide for Every Trip

BEST OF GUIDES

Full-color guides in an easy-to-scan format. Focused on top sights and experiences in the most popular European destinations

Best of England
Best of Europe
Best of France
Best of Germany
Best of Ireland
Best of Italy
Best of Scotland
Best of Spain

COMPREHENSIVE GUIDES

City, country, and regional guides printed on Bible-thin paper. Packed with detailed coverage for a multi-week trip exploring iconic sights and venturing off the beaten path

Amsterdam & the Netherlands
Barcelona
Belgium: Bruges, Brussels, Antwerp & Ghent
Berlin
Budapest
Croatia & Slovenia
Eastern Europe
England
Florence & Tuscany
France
Germany
Great Britain
Greece: Athens & the Peloponnese
Iceland
Ireland
Istanbul
Italy
London
Paris
Portugal
Prague & the Czech Republic
Provence & the French Riviera
Rome
Scandinavia
Scotland
Sicily
Spain
Switzerland
Venice
Vienna, Salzburg & Tirol

E BEST OF ROME

aly's capital, is studded with emnants and floodlit-fountain from the Vatican to the Colos- crazy traffic in between, Rome ul, huge, and exhausting. The heat, and the weighty history

of the Eternal City where Caesars walked can make tourists wilt. Recharge by taking siestas, gelato breaks, and after-dark walks, strolling from one atmospheric square to another in the refreshing evening air.

ntheon—which e until the 00 years old r 1,500).

ens in the *Vat-* *e humanistic*

tors fought r, entertaining

e ristorante.

POCKET GUIDES

Compact color guides for shorter trips

Amsterdam	Paris
Athens	Prague
Barcelona	Rome
Florence	Venice
Italy's Cinque Terre	Vienna
London	
Munich & Salzburg	

SNAPSHOT GUIDES

Focused single-destination coverage

Basque Country: Spain & France
Copenhagen & the Best of Denmark
Dublin
Dubrovnik
Edinburgh
Hill Towns of Central Italy
Krakow, Warsaw & Gdansk
Lisbon
Loire Valley
Madrid & Toledo
Milan & the Italian Lakes District
Naples & the Amalfi Coast
Nice & the French Riviera
Normandy
Northern Ireland
Norway
Reykjavík
Rothenburg & the Rhine
Sevilla, Granada & Southern Spain
St. Petersburg, Helsinki & Tallinn
Stockholm

CRUISE PORTS GUIDES

Reference for cruise ports of call

Mediterranean Cruise Ports
Scandinavian & Northern European
 Cruise Ports

Complete your library with...

TRAVEL SKILLS & CULTURE

*Study up on travel skills and gain
insight on history and culture*

Europe 101
Europe Through the Back Door
European Christmas
European Easter
European Festivals
Postcards from Europe
Travel as a Political Act

PHRASE BOOKS & DICTIONARIES

French
French, Italian & German
German
Italian
Portuguese
Spanish

PLANNING MAPS

Britain, Ireland & London
Europe
France & Paris
Germany, Austria & Switzerland
Iceland
Ireland
Italy
Spain & Portugal

Credits

CONTRIBUTOR
Gene Openshaw

 Gene has co-authored a dozen *Rick Steves* books, specializing in writing walks and tours of Europe's cities, museums, and cultural sights. He also contributes to Rick's public television series, produces tours for Rick Steves Audio Europe, and is a regular guest on Rick's public radio show. Outside of the travel world, Gene has co-authored *The Seattle Joke Book.* As a composer, Gene has written a full-length opera called *Matter*, a violin sonata, and dozens of songs. He lives near Seattle with his daughter, enjoys giving presentations on art and history, and roots for the Mariners in good times and bad.

ACKNOWLEDGMENTS

Many thanks to Ian Watson, and to our Hungarian friends for sharing their invaluable insights: Péter Pölczman, Andrea Makkay, Elemér Boreczky, George Farkas, Etelka Parine Berecz, Eszter Bokros, and István Koteczki. *Köszönjük szépen!*

PHOTO CREDITS

Front Cover: Danube River and Parliament in Budapest © Jean-Pierre Lescourret/Getty Images

Title Page: Castle Hill © Dominic Arizona Bonuccelli

Public Domain via Wikimedia Commons: 414 (top)

Additional Photography: Dominic Arizona Bonuccelli, Cameron Hewitt, Gene Openshaw, Rick Steves, Gretchen Strauch. Photos are used by permission and are the property of the original copyright owners.

Avalon Travel
Hachette Book Group
1700 Fourth Street
Berkeley, CA 94710

Printed in Canada by Friesens.
First printing June 2019.

ISBN 978-1-64171-089-3

For the latest on Rick's talks, guidebooks, tours, public television series, and public radio show, contact Rick Steves' Europe, 130 Fourth Avenue North, Edmonds, WA 98020, tel. 425/771-8303, www.ricksteves.com, rick@ricksteves.com.

Rick Steves' Europe

Managing Editor: Jennifer Madison Davis
Assistant Managing Editor: Cathy Lu
Special Publications Manager: Risa Laib
Editors: Glenn Eriksen, Julie Fanselow, Tom Griffin, Suzanne Kotz, Rosie Leutzinger, Teresa Nemeth, Jessica Shaw, Carrie Shepherd
Editorial & Production Assistant: Megan Simms
Editorial Intern: Christina Ausley
Graphic Content Director: Sandra Hundacker
Maps & Graphics: David C. Hoerlein, Lauren Mills, Mary Rostad
Digital Asset Coordinator: Orin Dubrow

Avalon Travel

Senior Editor and Series Manager: Madhu Prasher
Editors: Jamie Andrade, Sierra Machado
Copy Editor: Maggie Ryan
Proofreader: Patrick Collins
Indexer: Stephen Callahan
Production: Kit Anderson, Lisi Baldwin, Ravina Schneider
Cover Design: Kimberly Glyder Design
Maps & Graphics: Kat Bennett, Mike Morgenfeld

Let's Keep on Travelin'

Your trip doesn't need to end.

Follow Rick on social media!